UNITED STATES

DEPARTMENT OF HOMELAND SECURITY
HANDBOOK

International Business Publications, USA
Washington, DC, USA

UNITED STATES
DEPARTMENT OF HOMELAND SECURITY HANDBOOK

Editorial content: International Business Publications, USA

Editor-in-Chief: Dr. Igor S. Oleynik
Editor: Natasha Alexander
Managing Editor: Karl Cherepanya

Published by: International Business Publications, USA
P.O.Box 15343, Washington, DC 20003
Phone: (202) 546-2103, Fax: (202) 546-3275.
E-mail: rusric@erols.com

UPDATED ANNUALLY

We express our sincere appreciation to all government agencies and international organizations which provided information and other materials for this guide

Databases & Information: International Business Publications, USA
Cover Design: International Business Publications, USA

2003 International Business Publications, USA
ISBN 0-7397-9272-5

For customer service and information, please contact:
in the USA: **International Business Publications, USA**
             P.O.Box 15343, Washington, DC 20003
             Phone: (202) 546-2103, Fax: (202) 546-3275.
             E-mail: rusric@erols.com

Printed in the USA

UNITES STATES

DEPARTMENT OF HOMELAND SECURITY HANDBOOK

TABLE OF CONTENTS

DEPARTMENT ORGANIZATION **6**

New Department Components 7

LEADERSHIP 10

Secretary: Governor Tom Ridge 10

Deputy Secretary: Gordon England 11

Under Secretary for Management: Janet Hale 13

Under Secretary for Emergency Preparedness & Response: Michael Brown 13

Under Secretary for Information Analysis and Infrastructure Protection: Frank Libutti 14

Chief Information Officer: Steven I. Cooper 14

Acting Director of the Bureau of Citizenship and Immigration Services: Eduardo Aguirre, Jr. 15

Under Secretary for Science and Technology: Dr. Charles E. McQueary 17

Inspector General: Clark Kent Ervin 18

Commissioner of Customs and Border Protection: Robert C. Bonner 18

Assistant Secretary, Bureau of Immigration and Customs Enforcement: Michael J. Garcia 19

General Counsel of the Department of Homeland Security: Joe D. Whitley 20

Assistant Secretary for Public Affairs: Susan K. Neely 21

Chief Financial Officer: Bruce Marshall Carnes 22

Assistant Secretary for Information Analysis: Paul J. Redmond .. 23

Assistant Secretary: C. Stewart Verdery 23

Director of National Capital Region Coordination for Emergency Response: Michael F. Byrne 24

Commandant, U.S. Coast Guard: Admiral Thomas H. Collins 25

MAIN OBJECTIVES 26

Building A Secure Homeland 26

DEPARTMENT COMPONENTS 26

MAJOR DIRECTORATES 27

Border & Transportation Security 27

    Bureau of Immigration and Customs Enforcement 29

Emergency Preparedness & Response 29

Science & Technology 30

Information Analysis & Infrastructure Protection 31

Management 33

Coast Guard 33

Secret Service 35

Citizenship & Immigration Services 36

For additional analytical, business and investment opportunities information, please contact Global Investment & Business Center, USA at (202) 546-2103. Fax: (202) 546-3275. E-mail: rusric@erols.com

DHS FUNCTIONS AND THIR IMPLEMENTATION 37

EMERGENCIES AND DISASTERS PREVENTION AND RESOLUTION........ 37

Planning & Prevention... 37
   Hazard Mitigation... 37
   Natural Resource Protection... 40
   Marine Safety 42
Response & Recovery.. 43
   First Responders 43
   Maritime Search & Rescue.. 47
   U.S. Coast Guard Search & Rescue Programs 47
Declared Disasters & Assistance 48
   Public Assistance... 50
   Individual Assistance... 50
Weapons of Mass Destruction.. 55
Grants... 56

TRAVEL AND TRANSPORTATION 56
Customs & Inspections.. 57
   Enforcement Initiatives 57
Airport Security.. 59
Maritime Mobility.. 61

IMMIGRATION 61

RESEARCH & TECHNOLOGY 62
   Weapons of Mass Destruction.. 63
   Chem-Bio Defense 63
   Radiological & Nuclear Weapons 63
Fact Sheet on Dirty Bombs... 64
   Background 64
   Impact of a Dirty Bomb.. 64
   Sources of Radioactive Material 65
   Control of Radioactive Material.. 65
   What People Should Do Following an Explosion 65
   Risk of Cancer 65

THREATS AND PROTECTION... 66
Synthesizing and Disseminating Information....................................... 66
   Homeland Security Advisory System.. 66
   Protecting Our Communities.. 68
   Safeguarding America's Mail 69
   Transportation 70
   Banking & Finance.. 70
   Health & Safety 72
   Law Enforcement 75
   Federal Protective Service 76

IMPORTANT OFFICIAL ATATEMENTS... 77

PRESIDENT INCREASES FUNDING FOR BIOTERRORISM BY 319 PERCENT 77
PRESIDENT PROMOTES FUNDING FOR EMERGENCY FIRST RESPONDER 82

BASIC EXECUTIVE ORDERS, LEGISLATION AND REGULATIONS AND OFFICIAL STATEMENTS... 87

**For additional analytical, business and investment opportunities information,
please contact Global Investment & Business Center, USA
at (202) 546-2103. Fax: (202) 546-3275. E-mail: rusric@erols.com**

MESSAGE TO THE CONGRESS OF THE UNITED STATES 87
EXECUTIVE ORDER, FEBRUARY 28, 2003 92
HOMELAND SECURITY PRESIDENTIAL DIRECTIVE/HSPD-5 114
OFICIAL STATEMENTS AND TESTIMONIES 122
    *The Nomination of The Honorable Tom Ridge to be Secretary of the Department of
    Homeland Security* *122*
    *Remarks by Governor Tom Ridge, Homeland Security - Designate in a Town Hall Meeting
    for Future Employees of the Department of Homeland Security* *131*
    *Secretary Tom Ridge testifies before the Senate Committee on Commerce, Science and
    Transportation* *150*
    Statement of Secretary Tom Ridge before the Senate Appropriations Committee *152*
    Testimony of Secretary Ridge before the Senate Judiciary Committee *154*
    *The Nomination of the Honorable Gordon England to be Deputy Secretary of the
    Department of Homeland Security* *157*
    Remarks by Secretary Ridge to Los Angeles County First Responders *160*
    Statement by Secretary Ridge before the House Subcommittee on Appropriations *165*
    Remarks by Secretary Tom Ridge to National League of Cities *167*
    Remarks by Secretary Tom Ridge to the NEMA Conference *175*
SELECTED PERSS RELEASES 185
    BCIS Takes First Step to Offer Online Filing *185*
    U.S.-Mexico Border Partnership Joint Statement on Progress Achieved *186*
    Homeland Security and DOE Deliver Refurbished Radiological Detection Equipment *189*
    Department of Homeland Security FY '03 Supplemental Funding Fact Sheet *190*
    Joint Press Conference with Secretary Tom Ridge and British Home Secretary Blunkett . *194*

SUPPLEMENTS **201**

STATE HOMELAND SECURITY CONTACTS 201
MAJOR DISASTER DECLARATIONS 210
    Emergency Declarations *210*
PERMITTED AND PROHIBITED ITEMS 211
SMALLPOX FREQUENTLY ASKED QUESTIONS 217

For additional analytical, business and investment opportunities information,
please contact Global Investment & Business Center, USA
at (202) 546-2103. Fax: (202) 546-3275. E-mail: rusric@erols.com

DEPARTMENT ORGANIZATION

Where will DHS be located?

Effective Monday, January 27, the Department of Homeland Security headquarters will be located at the Nebraska Avenue Center (NAC) in Northwest Washington, D.C. The selection of this site coincides with the establishment of the new Department, which officially stands up on Friday, January 24. The NAC is a United States Navy facility which provides the secure connectivity needed to begin operations immediately. Headquarters for the new Department will remain at the NAC for at least a period of several months. The vast majority of incoming DHS employees based in the Washington, D.C. area will continue to work at their current locations.

How does the mission of the Department of Homeland Security differ from those of other agencies?
The new Department of Homeland Security (DHS) has three primary missions: Prevent terrorist attacks within the United States, reduce America's vulnerability to terrorism, and minimize the damage from potential attacks and natural disasters.

Working with DHS

My associates and I provide services that we think DHS could use. We would like to know more about business partnership opportunities. What is or will be available, and who should we contact?
As you know, uniting 22 agencies is a complicated reorganization process. Each agency brings its own set of skills and services, and our primary goal is to utilize the services our agencies will provide. The best way to bring a new idea to the table at this time is to contact the agency that needs it most. The Department of Homeland Security as a whole cannot accept other solicitations at this time.

Will DHS have an office in my state? Can I get a job there?

An essential part of homeland security is working with the local stakeholders around the country. As Secretary Designate Ridge has said, "When our hometowns are secure, our nation will be secure." As we finalize the structure of the Department of Homeland Security, we will establish regional offices to which our citizens can turn. It is a critical function of homeland security to ensure that our state and local governments, police, fire departments, paramedics, and concerned citizens are able to connect with local people representing the department. Where and how these regions will be drawn is an issue upon which we are still working. When positions do become available on the regional level, they will be posted on the OPM website at www.USAJOBS.opm.gov.

I would like to volunteer at the new Department. What qualifications do I need? Can I volunteer at locations across the country? How do I apply?

The successful prevention of terrorist attacks will rest partly on the active participation of all American citizens. Please check the "Citizens" link on our home page to read about some of the many ways you can be prepared to help as DHS continues to grow. At this time, we do not have a volunteer program established at DHS headquarters. We do want your help, so please continue to check our web site for updates on new opportunities.

How can I get a job at the new Department of Homeland Security?

We realize that there is a lot of excitement and interest in DHS, and we believe that the success of DHS will rest largely on the enthusiasm and dedication of its employees. The transition office is in the process of determining what jobs will be available, but we are committed to hiring the best and the brightest for this historic new Department. Beginning on January 24, 2003, vacancies at DHS headquarters will be listed on the federal government's Employment Information System, at www.USAJOBS.opm.gov. If you are interested in a position with any of our incoming agencies, you should submit an application using the instructions provided in the vacancy announcement on the USAJOBS site. If you do not have access to the internet, you can also access USAJOBS by calling (478) 757-3000 or TDD (478) 744-2299.

NEW DEPARTMENT COMPONENTS

The agencies slated to become part of the Department of Homeland Security will be housed in one of four major directorates: Border and Transportation Security, Emergency Preparedness and Response, Science and Technology, and Information Analysis and Infrastructure Protection.

The Border and Transportation Security directorate will bring the major border security and transportation operations under one roof, including:

- The U.S. Customs Service (Treasury)
- The Immigration and Naturalization Service (part) (Justice)
- The Federal Protective Service (GSA)
- The Transportation Security Administration (Transportation)
- Federal Law Enforcement Training Center (Treasury)
- Animal and Plant Health Inspection Service (part)(Agriculture)
- Office for Domestic Preparedness (Justice)

For additional analytical, business and investment opportunities information,
please contact Global Investment & Business Center, USA
at (202) 546-2103. Fax: (202) 546-3275. E-mail: rusric@erols.com

The Emergency Preparedness and Response directorate will oversee domestic disaster preparedness training and coordinate government disaster response. It will bring together:

- The Federal Emergency Management Agency (FEMA)
- Strategic National Stockpile and the National Disaster Medical System (HHS)
- Nuclear Incident Response Team (Energy)
- Domestic Emergency Support Teams (Justice)
- National Domestic Preparedness Office (FBI)

The Science and Technology directorate will seek to utilize all scientific and technological advantages when securing the homeland. The following assets will be part of this effort:

- CBRN Countermeasures Programs (Energy)
- Environmental Measurements Laboratory (Energy)
- National BW Defense Analysis Center (Defense)
- Plum Island Animal Disease Center (Agriculture)

The Information Analysis and Infrastructure Protection directorate will analyze intelligence and information from other agencies (including the CIA, FBI, DIA and NSA) involving threats to homeland security and evaluate vulnerabilities in the nation's infrastructure. It will bring together:

- Critical Infrastructure Assurance Office (Commerce)
- Federal Computer Incident Response Center (GSA)
- National Communications System (Defense)
- National Infrastructure Protection Center (FBI)
- Energy Security and Assurance Program (Energy)

The Secret Service and the Coast Guard will also be located in the Department of Homeland Security, remaining intact and reporting directly to the Secretary. In addition, the INS adjudications and benefits programs will report directly to the Deputy Secretary as the Bureau of Citizenship and Immigration Services.

Department of Homeland Security

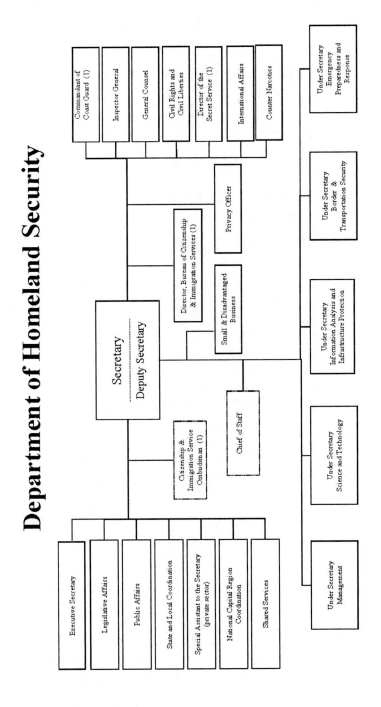

Note (1): Effective March 1st, 2003

LEADERSHIP

SECRETARY: GOVERNOR TOM RIDGE

On January 24, 2003, Tom Ridge became the first Secretary of the Department of Homeland Security. Ridge will work with more than 180,000 employees from combined agencies to strengthen our borders, provide for intelligence analysis and infrastructure protection, improve the use of science and technology to counter weapons of mass destruction, and to create a comprehensive response and recovery division.

Tom Ridge was sworn in as the first Director of the Office of Homeland Security in October 2001, following the tragic events of September 11. The charge to the nation's new director of homeland defense was to develop and coordinate a comprehensive national strategy to strengthen the United States against terrorist threats or attacks. In the words of President George W. Bush, he had the strength, experience, personal commitment and authority to accomplish this critical mission.

Ridge was twice elected Governor of Pennsylvania, serving from 1995 to 2001. He kept his promise to make Pennsylvania "a leader among states and a competitor among nations." Governor Ridge's aggressive technology strategy helped fuel the state's advances in the priority areas of economic development, education, health and the environment.

Governor Ridge cut taxes every year he was in office. To ensure Pennsylvania was home to the jobs of the future, the Governor created industry-led Greenhouse initiatives in advanced computing technologies and the life sciences.

He signed into law the Education Empowerment Act, to help more than a quarter-million children in Pennsylvania's lowest-performing schools. His education technology initiatives brought anytime, anywhere learning to Pennsylvanians from pre-school to adult education.

During his years in the Governor's office the number of children receiving free or low-cost health care through Pennsylvania's nationally recognized Children's Health Insurance Program increased by 145 percent increase.

For additional analytical, business and investment opportunities information, please contact Global Investment & Business Center, USA at (202) 546-2103. Fax: (202) 546-3275. E-mail: rusric@erols.com

ASSISTANT SECRETARY FOR PUBLIC AFFAIRS: SUSAN K. NEELY

Susan has almost 25-years experience in senior communications and management positions in the public and private sector. She currently serves as the Assistant Secretary for Public Affairs of the new U.S. Department of Homeland Security. She oversees both external and internal communications for the Department, its 22 component agencies and nearly 180,000 employees. Prior to this position, Susan helped establish the nation's first Office of Homeland Security in the White House, where she served as Special Assistant to the President and Senior Director of Communications for Homeland Security.

Her other experience in the political and government arena includes senior positions on the staffs of Governor Terry Branstad (IA), Congressman Sid Morrison (WA) and Congressman Jim Leach (IA).

In the private sector, Susan served as Senior Vice President for Communications at the Association of American Medical Colleges, a trade association representing all 125 medical schools and over 400 teaching hospitals. She also was Senior Vice President of the Health Insurance Association of America, a trade association of commercial health insurance companies, made famous for the creation of the "Harry and Louise" television commercials and campaign. Susan founded a Washington, D.C. office for the advertising and public relations firm of CMF&Z, a subsidiary of Young & Rubicam, and built it to the fastest growing group in the company.

A graduate of the University of Iowa in journalism and French civilization, Susan also has a Master of Public Administration from Drake University. She was elected the first woman president of the 90-year-old Washington Rotary Club, serving in 1996-97. She is a past president of the Washington Rotary's $6 million foundation. She is Vice President of the University Club of Washington, D.C., where she was the first woman to be named Member of the Year in 1996. She served three terms as a director of the Board of the Greater Washington Boys and Girls Clubs. She also served as Chair-elect of the Public Affairs Council. Susan received the 2002 Trailblazer Award from Dialogue on Diversity, and the 2003 Alumni Achievement Award from Drake University.

Susan and her husband, Joe, an attorney, have two children, Eve (age 5 ½) and Ben (age 2 ½).

CHIEF FINANCIAL OFFICER: BRUCE MARSHALL CARNES

President Bush announced on March 3 his intention to appoint Bruce Marshall Carnes to be the Chief Financial Officer (CFO) for the Department of Homeland Security. He currently serves as CFO at the Department of Energy.

Mr. Carnes entered federal service in 1976. Initially, he served as a program analyst for the Office of Postsecondary Education in the U.S. Office of Education, Washington, D.C., but was soon appointed a program specialist for graduate training, responsible for administration of graduate fellowship and legal training programs.

In 1979, he joined the National Endowment for the Humanities as Assistant Director, Office of Planning and Policy Analysis. He later assumed the post of Director, Office of Planning and Budget, managing the development of overall agency program policy, budget, legislative proposals, congressional testimony and agency management issues.

In 1985, Mr. Carnes was nominated by President Reagan and confirmed by the Senate to Deputy Under Secretary of Education for Planning, Budget, and Evaluation, in charge of developing policy proposals in education, departmental program budget and legislative proposals, oversight of program operations and manpower resources, and congressional testimony as principal and supporting witness. During his tenure in that position, he also served as the Education Department's Acting Deputy Under Secretary for Management, responsible for overall department policy and operations in personnel, contracts and grants, finance and accounting, ADP, and administrative resources.

Mr. Carnes became Director for the Office of Planning, Budget and Administration, Office of National Drug Control Policy, Executive Office of the President, in 1989. In this capacity, he developed program budget processes and the government-wide national drug control budget; coordinated the development of the national drug control strategy; conducted research and analyses on drug control issues; and represented the office before other federal agencies, Congress and the public. From February to June 1993, he also served as the Office of Drug Control Policy's Acting Director.

In 1993, Mr. Carnes became Assistant Deputy Director for Plans and Management for the Defense Finance and Accounting Service, a nearly 20,000-employee Defense Agency responsible for the Defense Department's worldwide financial operations. He served briefly as Acting Principal Deputy Director of the DFAS Columbus Center, and in 1996 became the agency's Deputy Director for Resource Management.

As Director of Resource Management, Mr. Carnes served as the agency's Chief Financial Officer, advising the Director and staff on all matters pertaining to resource management, including programming, budget formulation, presentation and execution, and work force management. In addition to managing all funds provided to DFAS, Mr. Carnes conducted economic and cost-benefit studies and analyses on proposals and initiatives involving accounting and finance activities, and oversaw the agency's plans, congressional liaison, public affairs, customer service, internal audit and administrative functions as well as Operations Mongoose program and the Acquisition Support Organization. He was also responsible for measuring the cost savings associated with the standardization and consolidation of accounting and finance policies, procedures and operations – the primary goal of DFAS.

In 1999, Mr. Carnes became the Deputy Director of DFAS, where he functioned as the Agency's Chief Operating Officer, overseeing DFAS's budget, human resources, acquisition, and planning activities and the finance and accounting operations of the Department of Defense.

In the spring of 2001, Mr. Carnes was nominated by President Bush and confirmed by the Senate as Chief Financial Officer for the Department of Energy. In addition, he served as Director of the Office of Management, Budget and Evaluation, in charge of the Department's budget, finance and accounting operations, human resources, acquisition, and program and project evaluation.

Mr. Carnes has a B.A. from the University of Colorado and an M.A. and Ph.D. from Indiana University. Prior to joining the government, Mr. Carnes was an assistant professor of English at James Madison University in Harrisonburg, VA. He and his wife live in Springfield, VA.

ASSISTANT SECRETARY FOR INFORMATION ANALYSIS: PAUL J. REDMOND

The President intends to appoint Paul J. Redmond of Massachusetts, to be Assistant Secretary for Information Analysis, Department of Homeland Security. Mr. Redmond currently serves as a consultant to the Director of the Central Intelligence Agency (CIA). Mr. Redmond has spent over 30 years of service with the CIA, both overseas and domestically. Most recently, he served as Associate Deputy Director for Operations for Counterintelligence, Special Assistant to the Director for Counterintelligence and Security, and Deputy Chief of the D.C.I. Counterintelligence Center. Mr. Redmond is a recipient of the Federal Order of Merit and the Distinguished Intelligence Medal for his service. He received his bachelor's degree from Harvard University.

ASSISTANT SECRETARY: C. STEWART VERDERY

The President intends to nominate C. Stewart Verdery, Jr. of Virginia, to be Assistant Secretary of Homeland Security (Border and Transportation Security Policy). Mr. Verdery is currently the Senior Legislative Counsel at Vivendi Universal Entertainment. Previously, he served as General Counsel for the U.S. Senate Assistant Republican Leader, Don Nickels. Earlier in his career, he served as Counsel for the Senate Committees on the Judiciary and on Rules and Administration. Mr. Verdery is a graduate of Williams College and earned his law degree from the University of Virginia School of Law.

For additional analytical, business and investment opportunities information, please contact Global Investment & Business Center, USA at (202) 546-2103. Fax: (202) 546-3275. E-mail: rusric@erols.com

DIRECTOR OF NATIONAL CAPITAL REGION COORDINATION FOR EMERGENCY RESPONSE: MICHAEL F. BYRNE

On March 9, 2003, Michael Byrne, a former New York City firefighter who helped direct the Federal government's response at the World Trade Center in 2001, became the first Director of National Capital Region Coordination for Emergency Response for the Department of Homeland Security. Byrne will oversee and coordinate Federal programs for and relationships with State, local, and regional authorities in the National Capital Region.

Mr. Byrne joined the Office of Homeland Security as the Senior Director for Response and Recovery in October of 2001 where he was instrumental in shaping the national vision and policy for emergency preparedness and response. He contributed substantially to the development of the President's First Responder Initiative, and to the development of a formal process for National Security Special Event designation. In addition, Mr. Byrne contributed significantly in the development of the National Strategy for Homeland Security which provides the vision of a national incident management system and single national response plan that will lay the foundation for emergency preparedness and response in the United States.

Mr. Byrne began his career in public service in 1979 with the New York City Fire Department (FDNY) where he served as a firefighter and company officer for 20 years. During his time with FDNY, he led Ladder Company 12 in their response to the 1993 World Trade Center Bombing. He also served with the Office of the Fire Commissioner, working as the Director for Strategic Planning and the Chief Information Officer. As a part of the Commissioner's staff he was instrumental in implementing the integration of Emergency Medical Service operations with Fire operations, improvements to the Division of Training, and the development of the Fire Commissioner's Management Report.

Upon retiring from FDNY, Mr. Byrne joined the Federal Emergency Management Agency in 1999 as the Response and Recovery Division Director in FEMA Region II (covering New York, New Jersey, Puerto Rico, and the Virgin Islands) where he led the federal response operations for Hurricanes Lenny and Floyd and Tropical Storm Allison. In 2001 he served as the Deputy Federal Coordinating Officer for Operations at Ground Zero in New York, where he was responsible for all federal response assets and recovery program administration in New York City.

A native of New York City, Mr. Byrne has received many awards for his service over the years including the prestigious Federal Executive Board Award for Teamwork in 2000 and 2002 for exceptional organizational achievement while in the service of the United States Government and the International Association of Fire Chiefs President's Recognition Award in 2002 for his leadership and representation of the interests of the fire service in homeland security.

COMMANDANT, U.S. COAST GUARD: ADMIRAL THOMAS H. COLLINS

 Admiral Thomas H. Collins assumed the duties of Commandant of the U.S. Coast Guard on May 30th, 2002. His leadership priorities are readiness, people and stewardship. He is personally committed to making effective use of emerging technologies and developing innovative methods to improve Coast Guard mission perfo rmance.

Prior to becoming Commandant, he served as the Coast Guard's Vice Commandant from 2000 - 2002 where he created the Innovation Council, spearheaded service-wide process improvement initiatives and directed system enhancements as the Coast Guard Acquisition Executive. From 1998 - 2000 he served as Commander, Pacific Area and Eleventh Coast Guard District, where he developed the successful Coast Guard response to the increase in illegal drug and migrant smuggling traffic in the Eastern Pacific. His other flag assignments include serving as Commander, Fourteenth Coast Guard District in Honolulu, HI and Chief, Office of Acquisition at Coast Guard Headquarters where he managed the acquisition of twelve major systems worth nearly $3 billion and laid the foundation for the Integrated Deepwater System project, which will modernize the ships, aircraft and sensors that the Coast Guard uses to perform its many open ocean missions.

Prior to his promotion to Flag Officer in 1994, he served as the Chief, Programs Division at Coast Guard Headquarters, and then the Coast Guard's Deputy Chief of Staff.

Admiral Collins began his Coast Guard career as a deck watch officer and first lieutenant aboard the cutter VIGILANT. Following that assignment, he served a two-year tour as Commanding Officer of the cutter CAPE MORGAN, a patrol boat homeported in Charleston, SC. His shore operational assignments include Deputy Commander, Group St. Petersburg, FL, and Commander of Coast Guard Group and Captain of the Port, Long Island Sound, in New Haven, CT.

Admiral Collins graduated from the Coast Guard Academy in 1968 and later served as a faculty member within the Humanities Department. He earned a Master of Arts degree in Liberal Studies from Wesleyan University and a Master of Business Administration from the University of New Haven.

The Admiral is the recipient of the Coast Guard Distinguished Service Medal, the Legion of Merit (three awards), the Meritorious Service Medal (two awards), and the Coast Guard Commendation Medal (three awards).

A native of Stoughton, MA, Admiral Collins is married to the former Nancy Monahan of New London, CT. They have two daughters, Christine and Kathryn.

MAIN OBJECTIVES

BUILDING A SECURE HOMELAND

The creation of the Department of Homeland Security (DHS) is the most significant transformation of the U.S. government since 1947, when Harry S. Truman merged the various branches of the U.S. Armed Forces into the Department of Defense to better coordinate the nation's defense against military threats.

DHS represents a similar consolidation, both in style and substance. In the aftermath of the terrorist attacks against America on September 11th, 2001, President George W. Bush decided 22 previously disparate domestic agencies needed to be coordinated into one department to protect the nation against threats to the homeland.

The new department's first priority is to protect the nation against further terrorist attacks. Component agencies will analyze threats and intelligence, guard our borders and airports, protect our critical infrastructure, and coordinate the response of our nation for future emergencies.

Besides providing a better-coordinated defense of the homeland, DHS is also dedicated to protecting the rights of American citizens and enhancing public services, such as natural disaster assistance and citizenship services, by dedicating offices to these important missions.

DEPARTMENT COMPONENTS

DHS has Five Major Divisions, or "Directorates":

I. Border and Transportation Security (BTS): BTS will be led by Under Secretary Asa Hutchinson, and is responsible for maintaining the security of our nation's borders and transportation systems. The largest of the Directorates, it will become home to agencies such as the Transportation Security Administration, U.S. Customs Service, the border security functions of the Immigration and Naturalization Service, Animal & Plant Health Inspection Service, and the Federal Law Enforcement Training Center.

II. Emergency Preparedness and Response (EPR): This Directorate, which will be headed up by Under Secretary Mike Brown, ensures that our nation is prepared for, and able to recover from, terrorist attacks and natural disasters.

III. Science and Technology (S & T): Under the direction of Under Secretary Dr. Charles McQueary, this Directorate will coordinate the Department's efforts in research and development, including preparing for and responding to the full range of terrorist threats involving weapons of mass destruction.

IV. Information Analysis and Infrastructure Protection (IAIP): IAIP merges the capability to identify and assess a broad range of intelligence information concerning threats to the homeland under one roof, issue timely warnings, and take appropriate preventive and protective action.

V. Management: The Under Secretary of Management Designate, Janet Hale, will be responsible for budget, management and personnel issues in DHS.

Besides the five Directorates of DHS, several other critical agencies are folding into the new department or being newly created:

- **United States Coast Guard:** The Commandant of the Coast Guard will report directly to the Secretary of Homeland Security. However, the USCG will also work closely with the Under Secretary of Border and Transportation Security as well as maintain its existing independent identity as a military service. Upon declaration of war or when the President so directs, the Coast Guard would operate as an element of the Department of Defense, consistent with existing law.
- **United States Secret Service:** The primary mission of the Secret Service is the protection of the President and other government leaders, as well as security for designated national events. The Secret Service is also the primary agency responsible for protecting U.S. currency from counterfeiters and safeguarding Americans from credit card fraud.
- **Bureau of Citizenship and Immigration Services:** While BTS will be responsible for enforcement of our nation's immigration laws, the Bureau of Citizenship and Immigration Services will dedicate its full energies to providing efficient immigration services and easing the transition to American citizenship. The Director of Citizenship and Immigration Services will report directly to the Deputy Secretary of Homeland Security.
- Office of State and Local Government Coordination: A truly secure homeland requires close coordination between local, state and federal governments. This office will ensure that close coordination takes place with state and local first responders, emergency services and governments.
- **Office of Private Sector Liaison:** The Office of Private Sector Liaison will provide America's business community a direct line of communication to the Department of Homeland Security. The office will work directly with individual businesses and through trade associations and other non-governmental organizations to foster dialogue between the Private Sector and the Department of Homeland Security on the full range of issues and challenges faced by America's business sector in the post 9-11 world.
- **Office of Inspector General:** The Office of Inspector General serves as an independent and objective inspection, audit, and investigative body to promote effectiveness, efficiency, and economy in the Department of Homeland Security's programs and operations, and to prevent and detect fraud, abuse, mismanagement, and waste in such programs and operations. To contact Acting Inspector General Clark Kent Ervin, or his staff, call 202-927-5240. To report waste, fraud or abuse, call the Hotline at 1-800-323-8603.

MAJOR DIRECTORATES

BORDER & TRANSPORTATION SECURITY

Securing Our Borders

Securing our nation's air, land, and sea borders is a difficult yet critical task. The United States has 5,525 miles of border with Canada and 1,989 miles with Mexico. Our maritime border includes 95,000 miles of shoreline, and a 3.4 million square mile exclusive economic zone. Each year, more than 500 million people cross the borders into the United States, some 330 million of whom are non-citizens.

On March 1st, the Department of Homeland Security, through the Directorate of Border and Transportation Security, will assume responsibility for securing our nation's borders and transportation systems, which straddle 350 official ports of entry and connect our homeland to the rest of the world. BTS will also assume responsibility for enforcing the nation's immigration laws.

The Department's first priority will be to prevent the entry of terrorists and the instruments of terrorism while simultaneously ensuring the efficient flow of lawful traffic and commerce. BTS will manage and coordinate port of entry activities and lead efforts to create a border of the future that provides greater security through better intelligence, coordinated national efforts, and unprecedented international cooperation against terrorists, the instruments of terrorism, and other international threats.

To carry out its border security mission, BTS will incorporate the United States Customs Service (currently part of the Department of Treasury), the enforcement division of the Immigration and Naturalization Service (Department of Justice), the Animal and Plant Health Inspection Service (Department of Agriculture), the Federal Law Enforcement Training Center (Department of Treasury) and the Transportation Security Administration (Department of Transportation). BTS will also incorporate the Federal Protective Service (General Services Administration) to perform the additional function of protecting government buildings, a task closely related to the Department's infrastructure protection responsibilities.

The BTS Directorate will also be responsible for securing our nation's transportation systems, which move people from our borders to anywhere in the country within hours. The recently created Transportation Security Administration, which will become part of the BTS Directorate, has statutory responsibility for security of all of the airports. Tools it uses include intelligence, regulation, enforcement, inspection, and screening and education of carriers, passengers and shippers. The incorporation of TSA into the new Department will allow the Department of Transportation to remain focused on its core mandate of ensuring that the nation has a robust and efficient transportation infrastructure that keeps pace with modern technology and the nation's demographic and economic growth.

Another important function of BTS's border management mission will be enforcing the nation's immigration laws - both in deterring illegal immigration and pursuing investigations when laws are broken. On March 1st BTS will absorb the enforcement units of the Immigration and Naturalization Service, such as the Border Patrol and investigative agents of INS. Working together with agents from other agencies that will comprise the BTS Directorate, such as the U.S. Customs Service and Transportation Security personnel, these well-trained law enforcement professionals will provide a coordinated defense against unlawful entry into the United States.

In the war against terrorism, America's already existent science and technology base provides us with a key advantage. The Department will press this advantage with a national research and development enterprise for homeland security comparable in emphasis and scope to that which has supported the national security community for more than fifty years. This is appropriate, given the scale of the mission and the catastrophic potential of the threat. Many of the needed systems are potentially continental in scope, and thus the technologies must scale appropriately, in terms of complexity, operation, and sustainability.

This research and development emphasis will be driven by a constant examination of the nation's vulnerabilities, constant testing of our security systems, and a thorough evaluation of the threats and its weaknesses. The emphasis within this enterprise will be on catastrophic terrorism - threats to the security of our homeland that could result in large-scale loss of life and major economic impact. It will be aimed at both evolutionary improvements to current capabilities as well as the development of revolutionary new capabilities.

INFORMATION ANALYSIS & INFRASTRUCTURE PROTECTION

Synthesizing and Disseminating Information

The Department of Homeland Security, through the Directorate of Information Analysis and Infrastructure Protection (IAIP) will merge under one roof the capability to identify and assess current and future threats to the homeland, map those threats against our vulnerabilities, issue timely warnings and take preventive and protective action.

Intelligence Analysis and Alerts

Actionable intelligence - that is, information which can lead to stopping or apprehending terrorists--is essential to the primary mission of DHS. The timely and thorough analysis and dissemination of information about terrorists and their activities will improve the government's ability to disrupt and prevent terrorist acts and to provide useful warning to the private sector and our population. The Directorate will fuse and analyze information from multiple sources pertaining to terrorist threats. The Department will be a full partner and consumer of all intelligence-generating agencies, such as the National Security Agency, the CIA and the FBI.

The Department's threat analysis and warning functions will support the President and, as he directs, other national decision-makers responsible for securing the homeland from terrorism. It will coordinate and, as appropriate, consolidate the federal government's lines of communication with state and local public safety agencies and with the private sector, creating a coherent and efficient system for conveying actionable intelligence and other threat information. The IAIP Directorate will also administer the Homeland Security Advisory System.

As designed, IAIP fully reflects the President's commitment to safeguard our way of life, including the integrity of our democratic political system and the essential elements of our individual liberty. To further ensure such protections, DHS will establish an office for a chief Privacy Officer.

Critical Infrastructure Protection

The attacks of September 11 highlighted the fact that terrorists are capable of causing enormous damage to our country by attacking our critical infrastructure -food, water, agriculture, and health and emergency services; energy sources (electrical, nuclear, gas and oil, dams); transportation (air, road, rail, ports, waterways); information and telecommunications networks; banking and finance systems; postal and other assets and systems vital to our national security, public health and safety, economy and way of life.

Protecting America's critical infrastructure is the shared responsibility of federal, state, and local government, in active partnership with the private sector, which owns approximately 85 percent of our nation's critical infrastructure. IAIP will take the lead in coordinating the national effort to secure the nation's infrastructure. This will give state, local, and private entities one primary contact instead of many for coordinating protection activities within the federal government, including vulnerability assessments, strategic planning efforts, and exercises.

Cyber Security

Our nation's information and telecommunications systems are directly connected to many other critical infrastructure sectors, including banking and finance, energy, and transportation. The consequences of an attack on our cyber infrastructure can cascade across many sectors, causing widespread disruption of essential services, damaging our economy, and imperiling public safety. The speed, virulence, and maliciousness of cyber attacks have increased dramatically in recent years. Accordingly, the Directorate places an especially high priority on protecting our cyber infrastructure from terrorist attack by unifying and focusing the key cyber security activities performed by the Critical Infrastructure Assurance Office (currently part of the Department of Commerce) and the National Infrastructure Protection Center (FBI). The Directorate will augment those capabilities with the response functions of the Federal Computer Incident Response Center (General Services Administration). Because our information and telecommunications sectors are increasingly interconnected, DHS will also assume the functions and assets of the National Communications System (Department of Defense), which coordinates emergency preparedness for the telecommunications sector.

Indications and Warning Advisories. In advance of real-time crisis or attack, IAIP will provide:

- Threat warnings and advisories against the homeland including physical and cyber events.
- Processes to develop and issue national and sector-specific threat advisories through the Homeland Security Advisory System.
- Terrorist threat information for release to the public, private industry, or state and local government.

Partnerships. The IAIP team will establish:

- Partnerships with key government, public, private and international stakeholders to create an environment that enables them to better protect their infrastructures.

- Awareness programs, development of information sharing mechanisms, and sector focused best practices and guidelines.

National Communications System. The IAIP team will provide:

- Coordination of planning and provision of National Security and Emergency Preparedness (NS/EP) communications for the Federal government.

MANAGEMENT

Building a Team of Professionals

The Under Secretary for Management is responsible for budget, appropriations, expenditure of funds, accounting and finance; procurement; human resources and personnel; information technology systems; facilities, property, equipment, and other material resources; and identification and tracking of performance measurements relating to the responsibilities of the Department.

Key to the success of the Department overall is the success of its employees, and the Directorate for Management is responsible for ensuring that employees have clear responsibilities and means of communication with other personnel and management. An important resource for communications will be the office of the Chief Information Officer, who is responsible for maintaining the information technology necessary to keep the more than 170,000 employees of DHS connected to and fully a part of the goals and mission of the Department.

COAST GUARD

Guardian of the Seas

Since its founding as the Revenue Cutter Service in 1790, the United States Coast Guard has unfailingly provided vital services and benefits to America because of its distinctive blend of humanitarian, security and law enforcement, diplomatic and military capabilities. The nation's "Guardian of the Seas," the Coast Guard saves lives and property in peril on the water, protects critical infrastructures and resources, ensures homeland defense, safeguards U.S. maritime sovereignty, and defends American citizens, interests, and friends worldwide.

As the nation's "maritime first responder," the Coast Guard serves as a crucial and responsive element of the Department of Homeland Security. Its well-trained crews react to a wide variety of maritime disasters, such as plane crashes, groundings, bridge and waterway accidents, and other maritime calamities. The Coast Guard's specially trained National Strike Force teams around the nation provide a flexible and adaptive resource of the Department of Homeland Security, deploying swiftly to clean up oil spills and hazardous materials, provide assistance during natural disasters such as hurricanes and flooding, and works hand in hand with EPA, FEMA, state, local, and other key agencies to save lives and protect property.

After the 9-11 attacks in New York City, Coast Guard port officials immediately closed the port, coordinated the evacuation of hundreds of thousands of stranded citizens, and moved emergency supplies and teams to the stricken area. National Strike Force teams were some of the first homeland security responders at Ground Zero in New York - ensuring buildings were safe from dangerous gases for entry by disaster recovery teams.

For our homeland to be secure it must also be economically strong, as over 95% of U.S. trade comes by sea. The Coast Guard ensures that our maritime transportation system and its waterways are safe. Our waterways and maritime productivity depend on our nation's aids to navigation systems -- buoys and markers, lighthouses, and electronic navigations systems such as LORAN and Differential Global Positioning System (DGPS) along with Coast Guard Vessel Traffic Services in key ports - all combine to help keep our homeland waters safe, secure and productive.

As the Nation's lead agency for maritime law enforcement, Coast Guard vessels and aircraft constantly patrol both our offshore and coastal regions, "pushing our borders out" and extending our vigilance and awareness of potential approaching threats, enforcing US immigration policies, customs laws, stopping drug smugglers, all of which strengthen our nation's maritime homeland security. The Coast Guard interdicts thousands of illegal migrants each year, it stops tons of drugs from reaching our streets and arrests hundreds of smugglers, and works tirelessly in interagency teams with its homeland security partners such as U. S. Customs, Immigration, Department of Defense and state and local authorities to help identify threats far off our coasts and help secure our maritime borders and our homeland.

Specifically, the Coast Guard's mission includes:

- **Maritime Safety:** Eliminate deaths, injuries and property damage associated with maritime transportation, fishing, and recreational boating. The Coast Guard's motto is Semper Paratus - (Always Ready), and the service is always ready to respond to calls for help at sea.
- **National Defense:** Defend the nation as one of the five U.S. armed services. Enhance regional stability in support of the National Security Strategy, utilizing the Coast Guard's unique and relevant maritime capabilities.
- **Maritime Security:** Protect America's maritime borders from all intrusions by: (a) halting the flow of illegal drugs, aliens, and contraband into the United States through maritime routes; (b) preventing illegal fishing; and (c) suppressing violations of federal law in the maritime arena.
- **Mobility:** Facilitate maritime commerce and eliminate interruptions and impediments to the efficient and economical movement of goods and people, while maximizing recreational access to and enjoyment of the water.
- **Protection of Natural Resources:** Eliminate environmental damage and the degradation of natural resources associated with maritime transportation, fishing, and recreational boating.

For additional analytical, business and investment opportunities information, please contact Global Investment & Business Center, USA at (202) 546-2103. Fax: (202) 546-3275. E-mail: rusric@erols.com

General Defense Duties of the Coast Guard

For more than 210 years, the Coast Guard has served the nation as one of the five armed forces. Throughout its distinguished history, the Coast Guard has enjoyed a unique relationship with the Navy. By statute, the Coast Guard is an armed force, operating in the joint arena at any time and functioning as a specialized service under the Navy in time of war or when directed by the President. It also has command responsibilities for the U.S. Maritime Defense Zone, countering potential threats to American's coasts, ports, and inland waterways through numerous port-security, harbor-defense, and coastal-warfare operations and exercises. Today, U.S. national security interests can no longer be defined solely in terms of direct military threats to America and its allies. With the terrorist attacks on September 11, 2001, the U.S. has fully realized the threat faced on the home front from highly sophisticated and covert adversarial groups. The Coast Guard has assumed one of the lead roles in responding to these attacks upon our nation by providing homeland security in our nation's harbors, ports and along our coastlines. Commercial, tanker, passenger, and merchant vessels have all been subject to increased security measures enforced by the Coast Guard.

In the immediate days after the destruction of the World Trade Center and Pentagon, over 2,600 reservists were recalled to provide operational and administrative support. Reservists and active duty Coast Guard members worked in unison to provide additional manpower to clean-up efforts in New York City and heightened port security in the ports of Seattle, Los Angeles, New York and Boston to include the implementation of "sea marshals." As the nation re-defines national security and government leaders organize the Homeland Security Council, the Coast Guard will continue its efforts to reduce the risk from terrorism to commercial and passenger vessels traversing U.S. waterways and designated waterfront facilities.

SECRET SERVICE

Guarding the President

As the nation's agency dedicated to the protection of the President and senior executive personnel, as well as the country's currency and financial infrastructure, the Secret Service will become a crucial component of the new Department of Homeland Security on March 1st, 2003.

The Secret Service will remain intact, and its primary mission will remain the protection of the President and other government leaders. The agency will also continue to provide security for designated national events, and preserve the integrity of the nation's financial and critical infrastructures. However, it will now do so with the added efficiency of access to DHS intelligence analysis and coordination with other key agencies.

Unquestionably, economic security is a key factor in homeland security overall. As technology and communication methods have evolved, so has the Secret Service investigative methods and mission. The Secret Service utilizes prevention-based training and methods to combat the cyber criminals and terrorists who attempt to use identity theft, telecommunications fraud and other technology-based crimes to defraud and undermine American consumers and industry.

CITIZENSHIP & IMMIGRATION SERVICES

Serving Visitors and New Citizens

The Department of Homeland Security (DHS) will administer the nation's immigration laws on March 1st when the Immigration and Naturalization Service becomes part of DHS. Through the Bureau for Citizenship and Immigration Services (BCIS), DHS will continue the tradition of welcoming immigrants into the country by administering services such as immigrant and nonimmigrant sponsorship; adjustment of status; work authorization and other permits; naturalization of qualified applicants for U.S. citizenship; and asylum or refugee processing. Immigration enforcement, which is the responsibility of the Directorate of Border and Transportation Security, includes preventing aliens from entering the country unlawfully, detecting and removing those who are living in the U.S. unlawfully, and preventing terrorists and other criminal aliens from entering or residing in the United States. The Department will make certain that America continues to welcome visitors and those who seek opportunity within our shores while excluding terrorists and their supporters.

DHS FUNCTIONS AND THIR IMPLEMENTATION

EMERGENCIES AND DISASTERS PREVENTION AND RESOLUTION

In the event of a terrorist attack, natural disaster or other large-scale emergency, the Department of Homeland Security will assume primary responsibility on March 1st for ensuring that emergency response professionals are prepared for any situation. This will entail providing a coordinated, comprehensive federal response to any large-scale crisis and mounting a swift and effective recovery effort. The new Department will also prioritize the important issue of citizen preparedness. Educating America's families on how best to prepare their homes for a disaster and tips for citizens on how to respond in a crisis will be given special attention at DHS.

PLANNING & PREVENTION

HAZARD MITIGATION

Planning Ahead in Case of Disaster

Hazard mitigation is sustained action to alleviate or eliminate risks to life and property from natural or man-made hazard events. Through such actions as sound land use planning and landscape design, adoption of building codes, property acquisition and relocation outside of floodplains, mitigation activities can protect critical community facilities to assure functionality following an event, reduce exposure to liabilities, and minimize disruptions to the community. A goal of mitigation is to decrease the need for a response as opposed to increasing the response capability. In-turn, hazard mitigation activities may reduce post-disaster expenditures across all levels of government and to property owners.

Mitigation can be best implemented through three stages of the disaster cycle: planning, response, and recovery. Some of the work in the planning stages before a disaster includes building public awareness of mitigation techniques, creating state and local hazard mitigation plans, integrating hazard mitigation criteria into comprehensive plans, and engineering public facilities to withstand the effects of an event. Immediately following an event, typical response phase activities include evacuation activities and location of emergency equipment and supplies out of high-risk areas. Through lessons learned, recovery activities following an event may include relocation or retrofitting.

Much as already been accomplished in the hazard mitigation arena at all levels of government and within the public and private sector. However, these accomplishments have been replaced by future challenges. Working with our state, local and private partners we hope to be contributing players in moving our communities towards meeting those challenges.

On the Horizon

How-To Manuals (Planning)

This series of manuals will walk you through processes involved in planning for the mitigation of natural hazards. Some of the subjects covered will be:

- An Overview of Mitigation Planning and How to Get Started (organizing to plan; involving the public; coordinating with other agencies)
- Setting Goals and Priorities (using the results of risk assessment to review mitigation options and drafting a strategy)
- Bringing the Plan to Life (adopting and implementing the strategy; evaluating and revising the plan)
- Using Benefit/Cost Analysis throughout the Mitigation Planning Process

Copies will be available through FEMA Publication Warehouse (1-800-480-2520).

Local Planning Review
A Planning Initiative: Documenting "Best Practices" in Local Communities

The initiative to document best practices of local mitigation planning is well underway. It has been quite an effort, however much has been accomplished in the recent weeks. The survey instrument is in the final stages of completion, a database to capture and retrieve survey information has been designed and demonstrated and nine pilot communities have been chosen to test run the project.

Our pilot communities are: Saltaire, NY, Tucker County, West Virginia, North Greeneville, Mississippi, Deerfield Beach, Florida, Dane County Wisconsin, St. Tammany, Louisiana, Los Angeles, California, Pierce County, Wisconsin, Hilo, Hawaii. These communities have already provided their most current plans and have identified local points of contact for further follow-up. Working with these plans and interviewing those responsible for them will enable us to test our survey instrument and our software system prior to launching the project this summer.

As the pilot goes on during the month of March our regional offices will be working with their state counterparts to obtain mitigation plans from the remaining selected communities and to identify local points of contact so that the interview portion of the survey can be easily completed.

Wondering how you are going to implement the Disaster Mitigation Act of 2000 that is now on the horizon? Wondering just what are the steps of the mitigation planning process and how do you get started? Wondering what other states are doing to encourage local mitigation planning?

To present the legislative changes and their impact on and connection to hazard mitigation funding and planning and to outline a successful process for creating state and local mitigation plans, we are designing a 30 minute video that would introduce the major ingredients of both for state and local officials. The video is intended to:

- highlight the expectations of the legislation,

- recommend how States and locals can work to create strong planning programs that meet these new Stafford Act requirements and
- demonstrate effective tools which are now available to help in the planning process.

Federal Insurance & Mitigation Administration (FIMA)

FIMA combines organizational activities to promote protection, prevention, and partnerships at the federal, state, local, and individual levels. FIMA is the cornerstone of emergency management. It's the ongoing effort to lessen the impact disasters have on peoples lives and property through damage prevention and flood insurance. Through measures such as, building safely within the floodplain or removing homes altogether; engineering buildings and infrastructures to withstand earthquakes: and creating and enforcing effective building codes to protect property from floods, hurricanes and other natural hazards, the impact on lives and communities is lessened.

Mitigation Activities

Building Performance Assessment Team (BPAT)

Increased damage resistance is achieved through improvements in construction codes and standards, designs, methods, and materials used for both new construction and post-disaster repair and recovery. The Building Performance Assessment Team (BPAT) Program is an integral part of this process.

Sustainability/Sustainable Re-development

The concept of sustainability brings a relatively new approach to environmental, economic, and social policy, and has the potential to enhance the achievement of mitigation goals in the post-disaster (as well as pre-disaster) environment. Sustainability enables a community, through specific development, to maintain or enhance economic opportunity and community well being while respecting, protecting and restoring the natural environment upon which people and economies depend.

Mitigation Assistance Program

The Mitigation Assistance Program (MAP) provides financial assistance to States for the purpose of the development and maintenance of a comprehensive Statewide hazard mitigation capability for the purpose of implementing pre- and post-disaster mitigation.

Mitigation Assistance combines three categories of assistance: State Hazard Mitigation Program assistance (SHMP), for which all States and Territories are eligible; Hurricane Program (HP) hazard assistance, for which States and Territories subject to tropical storm hazards are eligible; and Earthquake Program (EP) hazard assistance for which States and Territories subject to seismic hazards are eligible. For more information on the Flood Mitigation Assistance program (FMA)...

Community Assistance Program - State Support Services Element

The Community Assistance Program (CAP) is a product-oriented financial assistance program directly related to the flood loss reduction objectives of the National Flood Insurance Program (NFIP). States and communities that are participating in the NFIP are eligible for this assistance. The CAP is intended to identify, prevent, and resolve floodplain management issues in participating communities before they develop into problems requiring enforcement action.

Planning Resource Center

Planning for Post-disaster Recovery and Reconstruction

This landmark report breaks new ground by introducing community planners to their pivotal roles in guiding rebuilding and recovery after disasters, and provides guidance on how to plan for post-disaster reconstruction side by side with all the other players involved. Prepared by the American Planning Association and FEMA in 1998, the key theme throughout this report, and one that should be equal in importance to community recovery, is the need to rebuild in such a way as to create a community that is more resistant to future disasters. The report is filled with checklists, worksheets, a model recovery ordinance, and references to technical resources that are available to assist in implementing planning and construction techniques that will minimize future risk to natural hazards in both the pre- and post-disaster timeframes. It also includes guidance on developing a natural hazards element as part of a local, general or comprehensive plan. This document thus equips planners and all others involved in post-disaster reconstruction issues at all levels of government with the tools needed to create (or re-create) communities that will withstand most natural disasters.

Copies available from FEMA Publication Warehouse (1-800-480-2520) (Request by title, no FEMA number)

Natural Hazards Element of a Local Comprehensive or General Plan

FEMA has worked with the American Planning Association to incorporate natural hazards considerations into their "Growing Smart" initiative. "Growing Smart" is a multi-year effort to help States modernize statutes affecting planning and the management of community growth and change. The principal product of this initiative is a Legislative Guidebook, which includes information on what should be included in a comprehensive plan in order to include natural hazards in ongoing community planning activities.

NATURAL RESOURCE PROTECTION

Historic Preservation & Cultural Resources

The goal of FEMA's Historic Preservation and Cultural Resources Program is to address the needs of communities in preventing, responding to and recovering from the devastating effects of disasters on historic properties and cultural resources. Our

began patrolling the area to warn mariners of ice dangers shortly after the tragic loss of Titanic and the International Ice Patrol was formalized by the first Safety of Life at Sea (SOLAS) convention in 1914. The Ice Patrol is funded by 17 signatory nations in proportion to their vessel tonnage transiting the area during the ice season. Since the establishment of the Ice Patrol there has been no loss of life or property for vessels that have heeded Ice Patrol's warnings. The status of the Ice Patrol during periods of national emergency has not yet been determined, but during the two World Wars, Ice Patrol operations were suspended.

The Grand Banks Operations Area is a hazardous and very dynamic environment characterized by poor visibility, (70 percent cloud or fog), due to the combination of the very cold Labrador current and the warm North Atlantic current. Therefore aerial reconnaissance focuses on RADAR detection and identification. The International Ice Patrol uses long-range aircraft equipped with Side-Looking Airborne Radar (SLAR) and Forward Looking Airborne Radar (FLAR) to detect icebergs and determine the limits of all known ice in the patrol region. A computer drift and deterioration model is used to predict future iceberg positions that are validated by later reconnaissance flights. The model requires data on current, winds, waves and sea surface temperatures from the Navy's Fleet Numerical Meteorological and Oceanography Center, the National Oceanic and Atmospheric Administration, and the Meteorological Service of Canada, and from satellite-tracked drift buoys.

RESPONSE & RECOVERY

The Office of Emergency Preparedness (OEP)

The OEP is responsible managing and coordinating Federal health, medical, and health related social services and recovery to major emergencies and Federally declared disasters including:

- Natural Disasters
- Technological Disasters
- Major Transportation Accidents
- Terrorism

FIRST RESPONDERS

Office for Domestic Preparedness

The Office of Domestic Preparedness (ODP) is responsible for enhancing the capacity of state and local jurisdictions to respond to, and mitigate the consequences of, incidents of domestic terrorism.

In the 1998 Appropriations Act (Public Law 105-119) and accompanying report, the Congress expressed its concern regarding the real and potentially catastrophic effects of a chemical or biological act of terrorism. Congress stated that while the Federal Government plays an important role in preventing and responding to these types of threats, state and local public safety personnel are typically first to respond to the scene when such incidents occur. As a result, Congress authorized the Attorney General to assist state and local public safety personnel in acquiring the specialized training and equipment necessary to safely respond to and manage terrorist incidents involving weapons of mass destruction (WMD). On April 30, 1998 the Attorney General delegated authority to the Office of Justice Programs (OJP) to develop and administer training and equipment assistance programs for state and local emergency response agencies to better prepare them against this threat. To execute this mission, the Office of Justice Programs established ODP to develop and administer a national Domestic Preparedness Program.

About First Responders

America's first line of defense in any terrorist attack is the "first responder" community - local police, firefighters, and emergency medical professionals. Properly trained and equipped first responders have the greatest potential to save lives and limit casualties after a terrorist attack. Currently, our capabilities for responding to a terrorist attack vary widely across the country. Many areas have little or no capability to respond to terrorist attack using weapons of mass destruction. Even the best prepared States and localities do not possess adequate resources to respond to the full range of terrorist threats we face.

Facts About First Responders

- There are over 1 million firefighters in the United States, of which approximately 750,000 are volunteers.
- Local police departments have an estimated 556,000 full-time employees including about 436,000 sworn enforcement personnel.
- Sheriffs' offices reported about 291,000 full-time employees, including about 186,000 sworn personnel.
- There are over 155,000 nationally registered emergency medical technicians(EMT)

First Responder Initiative

Facts about First Responders

- There are over 1 million firefighters in the United States, of which approximately 750,000 are volunteers.
- Local police departments have an estimated 556,000 full-time employees including about 436,000 sworn personnel.
- Sheriffs' offices reported about 291,000 full-time employees, including about 186,000 sworn personnel.
- There are over 155,000 nationally registered Emergency Medical Technicians (EMT).

The President's 2003 Budget proposes to spend $3.5 billion on enhancing the homeland security response capabilities of America's first responders -- a greater than 10-fold increase in Federal resources.

Strengthening America's first responder community will make our homeland safer. Nearly two million first responders regularly put their lives at risk to save lives and make our country safer.

Hundreds of firefighters, police officers and emergency medical workers gave their lives on September 11 as they worked to save others.

The First Responder Initiative will help these brave Americans do their jobs better. Building on existing capabilities at the Federal, State, and local level, the First Responder Initiative provides an incentive to develop mutually supportive programs that maximize effective response capability. Through joint planning, clear communication, comprehensive coordination, mutual aid at all levels and increased information sharing, America's first responders can be trained and equipped to save lives in the event of a terrorist attack.

The benefits of building first responder capability are immediate and widespread -- making the nation safer from terrorist attacks while also bolstering everyday response capabilities. Hundreds of firefighters, police officers and emergency medical workers gave their lives on September 11 as they worked to save others.

The First Responder Initiative will help these brave Americans do their jobs better. Building on existing capabilities at the Federal, State, and local level, the First Responder Initiative provides an incentive to develop mutually supportive programs that maximize effective response capability. Through joint planning, clear communication, comprehensive coordination, mutual aid at all levels and increased information sharing, America's first responders can be trained and equipped to save lives in the event of a terrorist attack.

The benefits of building first responder capability are immediate and widespread -- making the nation safer from terrorist attacks while also bolstering everyday response capabilities.

Mutual Aid Agreements: Support for First Responders outside Major Metropolitan Areas

Terrorists can strike anytime, anywhere. Crop dusters, power generating plants, dams and reservoirs, crops, livestock, trains and highways are among the resources that could be targets. Homeland security in the heartland is just as important as homeland security in America's largest cities.

First responders from communities outside major metropolitan areas who must protect large geographic areas with small populations face many response challenges. In fact, over half of our firefighters protect small or rural communities of fewer than 5,000 people. Many of these communities rely upon volunteer departments with scarce resources. Fewer than 10% of counties surveyed by the National Association of Counties said they are prepared to respond to a bioterrorist attack.

For additional analytical, business and investment opportunities information, please contact Global Investment & Business Center, USA at (202) 546-2103. Fax: (202) 546-3275. E-mail: rusric@erols.com

One of the best strategies to build capability in communities outside major metropolitan areas is to develop mutual aid agreements to share resources. First responders from smaller communities need assistance in organizing and developing the unified command and control procedures and protocols necessary for operationally sound mutual aid. These agreements will enable neighboring jurisdictions to share specialized resources, rather than duplicate them in every jurisdiction.

President Bush's 2003 budget provides $140 million to assist these communities in planning and establishing mutual aid agreements. While mutual cooperation and mutual aid agreements have existed over the years in support of civil defense, fire, and National Guard activities, this is the first time that the federal government has directly supported the establishment of mutual aid agreements with federal resources.

As an established mechanism for sharing or pooling limited resources to augment existing capabilities and supplementing jurisdictions that have exhausted existing resources due to disaster, mutual aid processes will help ensure that jurisdictions across the United States can benefit from each other's efforts to enhance their first response capabilities. Jurisdictions can use the funding provided under this initiative to create or improve their response capabilities, without duplicating their efforts. Many areas have little or no capability to respond to terrorist attack using weapons of mass destruction. Even the best prepared States and localities do not possess adequate resources to respond to the full range of terrorist threats we face.

Citizen Corps: Supporting the Community and our First Responders

In the wake of the terrorist attacks of September 11, 2001, Americans have looked for and found many opportunities to help in their communities. President Bush created the USA Freedom Corps in an effort to capture those opportunities and foster an American culture of service, citizenship and responsibility. These volunteers are especially important in smaller communities where resources may be limited.

Citizen Corps is the arm of USA Freedom Corps that provides opportunities for citizens that want to help make their communities more secure. Since the President made his call to two years of volunteer service during his State of the Union address, there have been more than 1.6 million hits to the new www.citizencorps.gov web site. Almost 24,000 Americans from all 50 states and U.S. territories have volunteered to work with one or more of the Citizen Corps programs. These include:

- More than 15,000 volunteers are looking to be trained in emergency response skills through FEMA's Community Emergency Response Team program;
- Almost 7,000 volunteers have signed up to get involved in Neighborhood Watch activities in their communities
- More than 15,000 potential volunteers have expressed interest in the new Volunteers in Police Service and Operation TIPS programs being developed by the Department of Justice presently; and,
- More than 5,000 potential volunteers have expressed an interest in joining a Medical Reserve Corps in their community as part of a program being developed

by the Department of Health and Human Services to tap the skills of doctors, nurses and other health care professionals in times of community crisis.

MARITIME SEARCH & RESCUE

About Search & Rescue

Search and Rescue (SAR) is one of the Coast Guard's oldest missions. Minimizing the loss of life, injury, property damage or loss by rendering aid to persons in distress and property in the maritime environment has always been a Coast Guard priority. Coast Guard SAR response involves multi-mission stations, cutters, aircraft and boats linked by communications networks. The National SAR Plan divides the U.S. area of SAR responsibility into internationally recognized aeronautical and maritime SAR regions. The Coast Guard is the SAR Coordinator for U.S. aeronautical and maritime search and rescue regions that are near America's oceans, including Alaska and Hawaii. To meet this responsibility, the Coast Guard maintains SAR facilities on the East, West and Gulf coasts; in Alaska, Hawaii, Guam, and Puerto Rico, as well as on the Great Lakes and inland U.S. waterways. The Coast Guard is recognized worldwide as a leader in the field of search and rescue.

U.S. COAST GUARD SEARCH & RESCUE PROGRAMS

U.S. Coast Guard Search & Rescue Programs

Rescue 21
The Coast Guard currently uses the National Distress and Response System to monitor for maritime distress calls and coordinate response operations. The system consists of a network of VHF-FM antennae high sites and with analog transceivers that are remotely controlled by regional communications centers and rescue boat stations providing coverage out to approximately 20 nautical miles from the shore in most areas.

Salvage Assistance & Technical Support
The Marine Safety Center Salvage Assistance and Response Team provide on-scene technical support at maritime catastrophes in order to predict events and mitigate their impact.

Operational Command, Control and Communications
The NSFCC provides oversight and strategic direction to the Strike Teams, ensuring enhanced inter-operability through a program of standardized operating procedures for response, equipment, training, and qualifications. The NSFCC conducts at least six major government-led spill response exercises each year under the National Preparedness for Response Exercise Program; maintains a national logistics network, using the Response Resource Inventory; implements the Coast Guard Oil Spill Removal Organization program; and administers the National Maintenance Contract for the Coast Guard's thirty million dollar inventory of pre-positioned spill response equipment.

Amver
Amver is a ship reporting system for search and rescue. It is a global system that enables identification of other ships in the area of a ship in distress, which could then be

sent to its assistance. Amver information is used only for search and rescue and is made available to any rescue coordination center in the world responding to a search and rescue case. The Coast Guard actively seeks to increase participation in this voluntary reporting system. Each year, more vessels participate in the system and more lives are saved. Currently, ships from more than 143 nations participate.

Amver represents "free" safety insurance during a voyage by improving the chances for aid in an emergency. By regular reporting, someone knows where a ship is at all times on its voyage in the event of an emergency. Amver can reduce the time lost for vessels responding to calls for assistance by "orchestrating" a rescue response, utilizing ships in the best position or with the best capability to avoid unnecessary diversions in response to a MAYDAY or SOS call.

Pollution Control

The Response Operations Division develops and maintains policies for marine pollution response. They also coordinate activities with the international community, intelligence agencies and the Federal government in matters concerning threats or acts of terrorism in U. S. ports and territorial waters.

The National Strike Force (NSF)
The National Strike Force (NSF) was established in 1973 as a direct result of the Federal Water Pollution Control Act of 1972. The NSF's mission is to provide highly trained, experienced personnel and specialized equipment to Coast Guard and other federal agencies to facilitate preparedness and response to oil and hazardous substance pollution incidents in order to protect public health and the environment. The NSF's area of responsibility covers all Coast Guard Districts and Federal Response Regions.

The Strike Teams provide rapid response support in incident management, site safety, contractor performance monitoring, resource documentation, response strategies, hazard assessment, oil spill dispersant and operational effectiveness monitoring, and high capacity lightering and offshore skimming capabilities.

DECLARED DISASTERS & ASSISTANCE

Guide to the Disaster Declaration Process and Federal Disaster Assistance[1]

Local and State governments share the responsibility for protecting their citizens from disasters, and for helping them to recover when a disaster strikes. In some cases, a disaster is beyond the capabilities of the State and local government to respond.

The Robert T. Stafford *Disaster Relief and Emergency Assistance Act*, Public Law 93-288, as amended (the Stafford Act) was enacted to support State and local governments and their citizens when disasters overwhelm them. This law establishes a process for requesting and obtaining a Presidential disaster declaration, defines the type and scope of assistance available under the Stafford Act, and sets the conditions for obtaining that

---

[1] See supplement

assistance. This paper explains the declaration process and provides an overview of the assistance available.

The Declaration Process

The Stafford Act (§401 and 501) requires that: "All requests for a declaration by the President that a major disaster or emergency exists shall be made by the Governor [chief executive] of the affected State." A State also includes the District of Columbia, Puerto Rico, the Virgin Islands, Guam, American Samoa, the Commonwealth of the Northern Mariana Islands, Federated States of Micronesia and the Republic of the Marshall Islands. The Governor's request is made through the regional FEMA office. State, local, and Federal officials conduct a preliminary damage assessment (PDA) to estimate the extent of the disaster and its impact on individuals and public facilities. The information gathered during the PDA documents the severity and magnitude of the event and is included in the Governor's request. Normally, the PDA is completed prior to the submission of the Governor's request. However, when an obviously severe or catastrophic event occurs, the Governor's request may be submitted prior to the PDA. Nonetheless, the Governor must still make the request and damage assessments are still conducted.

As part of the request, the Governor must note that the State's emergency plan has been implemented and the situation is of such severity and magnitude that the response is beyond State and local capability and Stafford Act assistance is necessary. The Governor shall furnish information on the nature and amount of State and local resources that have been or will be committed to alleviating the results of the disaster, provide an estimate of the amount and severity of damage and the impact on the private and public sector, and provide an estimate of the type and amount of assistance needed under the Stafford Act. In addition, the Governor will need to certify that, for the current disaster, State and local government obligations and expenditures (of which State commitments must be a significant portion) will comply with all applicable cost-sharing requirements.

Based on the Governor's request, the President may declare that a major disaster or emergency exists, thus activating an array of Federal programs to assist in the response and recovery effort.

Assistance Available Under A Major Disaster Declaration

Not all programs, however, are activated for every disaster. The determination of which programs are activated is based on the needs found during the joint preliminary damage assessment and any subsequent information that may be discovered.

Federal disaster assistance available under a major disaster declaration falls into three general categories:

- Individual Assistance - aid to individuals, families and business owners;

- Public Assistance - aid to public (and certain private non-profit) entities for certain emergency services and the repair or replacement of disaster-damaged public facilities;
- Hazard Mitigation Assistance - funding for measures designed to reduce future losses to public and private property. In the event of a major disaster declaration, all counties within the declared State are eligible to apply for assistance under the Hazard Mitigation Grant Program.
- Some declarations will provide only individual assistance or only public assistance. Hazard mitigation opportunities are assessed in most situations.

PUBLIC ASSISTANCE

About FEMA's Public Assistance Progam

As much as we try to prepare for catastrophic disasters and to reduce our risk from their devastation, hurricanes, tornadoes, major earthquakes and other disasters still happen.

When they do, local and state officials are the first to respond. If the loss of life and property overwhelms this response, the federal government—including FEMA—is called upon to help.

FEMA's Public Assistance (PA) Grant Program is one way federal assistance gets to the state and local governments and to certain private nonprofit organizations. These grants allow them to respond to disasters, to recover from their impact and to mitigate impact from future disasters. While these grants are aimed at governments and organizations—their final goal is to help a community and all its citizens recover from devastating natural disasters.

The PA Program provides the basis for consistent training and credentialing of staff (people) who administer the program; more accessible and understandable guidance and policy for participating in the grant program; improved customer service throughout a ore efficient grant delivery process, applicant –centered management, and better information exchange; and continuing performance evaluations and program improvements.

INDIVIDUAL ASSISTANCE

About FEMA's Individual Assistance Program

The Individual Assistance mission of the Response and Recovery Division is to ensure that individuals and families that have been affected by disasters have access to the full range of Response and Recovery programs in a timely manner and that the best possible level of service is provided to applicants in the administration of these programs. This mission also includes developing partnerships with the States, voluntary organizations, the private sector and other Federal agencies that are delivering similar kinds of assistance to the same groups of individuals.

This mission is carried out by developing and maintaining programs, policies and partnerships to administer human services programs; making the option of applying for disaster assistance or obtaining other information over the telephone a convenient and effective option for those in need agencies, through the direct management of a national teleregistration and helpline capability; conducting timely, high quality inspections of disaster damaged dwellings as the basis for determining the kinds and amounts of Response and Recovery assistance to be provided to individuals and families; providing assistance to individuals as quickly as possible while ensuring proper stewardship primarily travel trailers and mobile homes, for disaster victims; and finally, continuously evaluating the effectiveness of our programs and systems, on the basis of feedback from our customers and designing enhancements to improve our services and reduce operating costs.

Helping Children Cope with Disaster

Earthquakes...Tornadoes...Fires... Floods...Hurricanes... Hazardous Materials Spills

Disaster may strike quickly and without warning. These events can be frightening for adults, but they are traumatic for children if they don't know what to do.

During a disaster, your family may have to leave your home and daily routine. Children may become anxious, confused or frightened. As an adult, you'll need to cope with the disaster in a way that will help children avoid developing a permanent sense of loss. It is important to give children guidance that will help them reduce their fears.

The Federal Emergency Management Agency (FEMA) and the American Red Cross have prepared this brochure to help you help your children cope. Ultimately, you should decide what's best for your children, but consider using these suggestions as guidelines.

Children and Their Response to Disaster

Children depend on daily routines: They wake up, eat breakfast, go to school, play with friends. When emergencies or disasters interrupt this routine, children may become anxious.

In a disaster, they'll look to you and other adults for help. How you react to an emergency gives them clues on how to act. If you react with alarm, a child may become more scared. They see our fear as proof that the danger is real. If you seem overcome with a sense of loss, a child may feel their losses more strongly.

Children's fears also may stem from their imagination, and you should take these feelings seriously. A child who feels afraid is afraid. Your words and actions can provide reassurance. When talking with your child, be sure to present a realistic picture that is both honest and manageable.

Feeling or fear are healthy and natural for adults and children. But as an adult, you need to keep control of the situation. When you're sure that danger has passed, concentrate on your child's emotional needs by asking the child what's uppermost in his or her mind. Having children participate in the family's recovery activities will help them feel that their life will return to "normal." Your response during this time may have a lasting impact.

For additional analytical, business and investment opportunities information, please contact Global Investment & Business Center, USA at (202) 546-2103. Fax: (202) 546-3275. E-mail: rusric@erols.com

Be aware that after a disaster, children are most afraid that--

- the event will happen again.
- someone will be injured or killed.
- they will be separated from the family.
- they will be left alone.

Advice to Parents: Prepare for Disaster

You can create a Family Disaster Plan by taking four simple steps. First, learn what hazards exist in your community and how to prepare for each. Then meet with your family to discuss what you would do, as a group, in each situation. Next, take steps to prepare your family for disaster such as: posting emergency phone numbers, selecting an out-of-state family contact, assembling disaster supplies kits for each member of your household and installing smoke detectors on each level of your home. Finally, practice your Family Disaster Plan so that everyone will remember what to do when a disaster does occur.

- Develop and practice a Family Disaster Plan. Contact your local emergency management or civil defense office, or your local Red Cross chapter for materials that describe how your family can create a disaster plan. Everyone in the household, including children, should play a part in the family's response and recovery efforts.
- Teach your child how to recognize danger signals. Make sure your child knows what smoke detectors, fire alarms and local community warning systems (horns, sirens) sound like.
- Explain how to call for help. Teach your child how and when to call for help. Check the telephone directory for local emergency phone numbers and post these phone numbers by all telephones. If you live in a 9-1-1-service area, tell your child to call 9-1-1.
- Help your child memorize important family information. Children should memorize their family name, address and phone number. They should also know where to meet in case of an emergency. Some children may not be old enough to memorize the information. They could carry a small index card that lists emergency information to give to an adult or babysitter.

AFTER THE DISASTER: TIME FOR RECOVERY

Immediately after the disaster, try to reduce your child's fear and anxiety.

- Keep the family together. While you look for housing and assistance, you may want to leave your children with relatives or friends. Instead, keep the family together as much as possible and make children a part of what you are doing to get the family back on its feet. Children get anxious, and they'll worry that their parents won't return.
- Calmly and firmly explain the situation. As best as you can, tell children what you know about the disaster. Explain what will happen next. For example, say,

For additional analytical, business and investment opportunities information, please contact Global Investment & Business Center, USA at (202) 546-2103. Fax: (202) 546-3275. E-mail: rusric@erols.com

"Tonight, we will all stay together in the shelter." Get down to the child's eye level and talk to them.

- Encourage children to talk. Let children talk about the disaster and ask questions as much as they want. Encourage children to describe what they're feeling. Listen to what they say. If possible, include the entire family in the discussion.
- Include children in recovery activities. Give children chores that are their responsibility. This will help children feel they are part of the recovery. Having a task will help them understand that everything will be all right.

You can help children cope by understanding what causes their anxieties and fears. Reassure them with firmness and love. Your children will realize that life will eventually return to normal. If a child does not respond to the above suggestions, seek help from a mental health specialist or a member of the clergy.

Am I Eligible for Disaster Assistance? How Do I Apply?

Individuals, families, farmers and businesses are eligible for federal assistance if they live or own a business in a county declared a Major Disaster Area, incur sufficient property damage or loss, and, depending on the type of assistance, do not have the insurance or resources to meet their needs.

To apply for Assistance to Individuals and Households, all you have to do is call the special tollfree telephone number, 1-800-621-FEMA (TTY: 1-800-462-7585) and register. Specially trained operators at one of FEMA's National Processing Service Centers will process your application. This assistance includes housing assistance (grants or services for home repairs, rental of another place to live temporarily, lodging expenses reimbursement, home replacement, and in special circumstances, permanent housing construction). It also includes grants for other needs, such as medical, dental, funeral, and transporation expenses. SBA and FSA applications may be made at locally-announced locations.

The Disaster Assistance Process for Individuals

Call to Apply for Assistance 1-800-621-FEMA (3362)

- For use ONLY by people in designated federal disaster areas.
- Be prepared to give your Social Security number, describe your losses, provide financial information, and give directions to the damaged property.
- What You Can Do If You're Having Trouble Getting Through

The information you provide is put into the computer

- You are now in the system
- The recovery process begins

Call us if you have Questions 1-800-621-FEMA (3362)

For additional analytical, business and investment opportunities information, please contact Global Investment & Business Center, USA at (202) 546-2103. Fax: (202) 546-3275. E-mail: rusric@erols.com

- Refer to the application number the registrars gave you when you applied.

Making an optional visit to a Disaster Recovery Center to receive more information after you have registered by phone

- Here you will find local, state, federal, and voluntary agencies that may be able to assist you

Inspector will call to schedule an appointment.

- There is NO FEE for the inspection.
- Inspectors will set up an appointment to visit your property within a few days of application.
- Inspectors are contractors; they are not FEMA employees, but they will have FEMA ID.

Inspector will visit damaged property.

- Be present for your scheduled appointment.
- They will inspect the damage, verify ownership and occupancy, and make a report. Inspectors do not determine eligibility.
- If eligible, you will receive a housing assistance check within 7-10 days.

If eligible, housing assistance check will arrive.

- Money may be spent for housing needs.

Packet will arrive in mail.

- There may be an SBA application enclosed.
- You MUST fill out and return this to be eligble for any further assistance.
- Refer to SBA home page for more information. (www.sba.gov/disaster/)

To reduce future loss, consider taking steps to rebuild safer and smarter.

- Take measures to reduce losses in the future.
- Encourage community to participate in National Flood Insurance Program (NFIP).
- Consider buying flood insurance.

Call the FEMA Fraud Hotline if you suspect someone is filing false damage claims

- **1-800-323-8603**
- Make sure disaster aid goes to those who deserve it.
- It is a violation of Federal law to file a false claim.

For additional analytical, business and investment opportunities information, please contact Global Investment & Business Center, USA at (202) 546-2103. Fax: (202) 546-3275. E-mail: rusric@erols.com

WEAPONS OF MASS DESTRUCTION

Nuclear Incident Response Team (Department Of Energy)

We provide expert personnel and specialized equipment to a number of federal emergency response entities that deal with nuclear emergencies, nuclear accidents, and nuclear terrorism. Our emergency response personnel are experts in such fields as device assessment, device disablement, intelligence analysis, credibility assessment, and health physics. They participate in exercised and drills to hone deployment readiness and technical capabilities and to perfect coordintation with other response groups.

Customs Role in Countering the Spread of Weapons of Mass Destruction

One of the most serious international threats facing the world today is the proliferation of weapons of mass destruction. The Customs Service, as the only federal agency authorized to perform inbound and outbound warrantless border searches, enforce broad economic sanctions, and investigate the smuggling and illegal exportation of munitions and critical technology, is uniquely qualified to help counter this threat.

National Nuclear Security Administration

The Office of the National Nuclear Security Administration provides support to the Administrator, and includes the functions of legislative affairs, public affairs and liaison with other Federal agencies, State, tribal and local governments and the public. It also provides support for resource management in the areas of budget formulation, guidance, and execution; personnel; and procurement management and the administration of contracts; as well as other activities as determined by the Administrator.

The Administrator has authority over, and is responsible for, all programs and activities of the Administration (except for the functions of the Deputy Administrator for Naval Reactors under Executive Order 12344).

National Disaster Medical System

The National Disaster Medical System (NDMS) is a cooperative asset-sharing program among Federal government agencies, state and local governments, and the private businesses and civilian volunteers to ensure resources are available to provide medical services following a disaster that overwhelms the local health care resources.

The NDMS is a Federally coordinated system that augments that Nation's emergency medical response capability. The overall purpose of the NDMS is to establish a single, integrated national medical response capability for assisting state and local authorities in dealing with the medical and health effects of major peacetime disasters and providing support to the military and Veterans Health Administration medical systems in caring for casualties evacuated back to the U.S. from overseas armed conflicts.

For additional analytical, business and investment opportunities information, please contact Global Investment & Business Center, USA at (202) 546-2103. Fax: (202) 546-3275. E-mail: rusric@erols.com

GRANTS

Mitigation Grants Programs

Mitigation is the cornerstone of emergency management. It's the ongoing effort to lessen the impact disasters have on people and property. Mitigation involves keeping homes away from floodplains, engineering bridges to withstand earthquakes, creating and enforcing effective building codes to protect property from hurricanes -- and more.

FEMA currently has three mitigation grant programs: the Hazards Mitigation Grant Program (HGMP), the Pre-Disaster Mitigation program (PDM), and the Flood Mitigation Assistance (FMA) program.

USFA Grants Programs

The purpose of the program is to award one-year grants directly to fire departments of a State to enhance their abilities with respect to fire and fire-related hazards. This program seeks to identify departments that lack the basic tools and resources necessary to protect the health and safety of the public and their firefighting personnel. Our primary goal is to provide assistance to meet these needs.

TRAVEL AND TRANSPORTATION

Protecting Travelers and Commerce

On March 1, DHS inherited the professional workforce, programs and infrastructure of the Coast Guard, Customs Service, Immigration and Naturalization Service, and the Transportation Security Administration. Collectively these public servants are responsible for protecting our nation's transportation systems and supervising the entry of people and goods into the United States. This is no easy task given that 730 million people travel on commercial aircraft each year and that there are now more than 700 million pieces of baggage being screened for explosives each year. Additionally, there are 11.2 million trucks and 2.2 million rail cars that cross into the US each year. Also, 7,500 foreign flagships make 51,000 calls in US ports annually.

DHS is responsible for protecting the movement of international trade across US borders, maximizing the security of the international supply chain, and for engaging foreign governments and trading partners in programs designed to identify and eliminate security threats before these arrive at US ports and borders.

Below are some popular links to help get you started in finding the information you need to expedite your travel plans and what your government is doing to ensure your travel is secure and that there is safe movement of goods into the US.

For additional analytical, business and investment opportunities information, please contact Global Investment & Business Center, USA at (202) 546-2103. Fax: (202) 546-3275. E-mail: rusric@erols.com

CUSTOMS & INSPECTIONS

ENFORCEMENT INITIATIVES

The Bureau of Immigration and Customs Enforcement
Beginning March 1, 2003, the enforcement and investigative arms of the Customs Service, the investigative and enforcement functions of the former Immigration and Naturalization Service, and the Federal Protective Service, come together to form the Bureau of Immigration and Customs Enforcement as part of the U.S. Department of Homeland Security.

Project Shield America

An integral part of U.S. Customs Service export control strategy, which depends upon the cooperation of the U.S. manufacturing and exporting community.

Mission and Necessity of Shield America

Mission
Project Shield America is an integral part of the U.S. Customs Service strategy of preventing illegal exporters, targeted foreign countries, terrorist groups, and international criminal organizations from trafficking in Weapons of Mass Destruction (WMD) and their components; obtaining and illegally exporting licensable commodities, technologies, conventional munitions, and firearms; exporting stolen property; and engaging in financial and other transactions which support these activities or which violate U.S. sanctions and embargoes.

Customs is the first line of defense at our Nation's borders to protect the American public from international terrorism. Our mission in combating international terrorism is two-fold:

- Protect the American public from the introduction of WMD and other instruments of terror into the U.S.
- Prevent international terrorists and criminal organizations from obtaining WMD materials and technologies, arms, funds, and other support from U.S. and foreign sources.

Necessity of Shield America

Adversaries of the U.S. have acquired U.S. and Western technology since the Second World War by various means, both legal and illegal. Such acquisitions have provided these countries with the fruits of Western research and strategic technology largely without cost, and have permitted these countries to channel their resources to other areas. U.S. munitions and technology have assisted our adversaries in jeopardizing our soldiers, citizens, and interests. The fact that nuclear, chemical, and biological weapons and their components are more widely available to terrorists and rogue Nations now than at any other time in our history, has necessitated the development, implementation, and success of Project Shield America.

Amount of Illegal Exports

As with any illegal trade, the exact volume is difficult to measure or even to estimate. The U.S. Customs Service criminal investigations and seizures indicate, however, that such trade can be valued in the tens of millions of dollars annually.

The monetary value of the illegal exports discovered by Customs is often secondary to the strategic and potential military value of these products. For example, in one investigation a sophisticated military aviation guidance system was seized by Customs prior to its exportation from the U.S. While the value of this system was only a few thousand dollars, its acquisition by our adversaries could have jeopardized the security of the U.S. and its allies.

Some of the strategic technology most urgently needed by certain proscribed countries includes:

- Modern manufacturing technology for the production of microelectronics, computers, digital electronic components, and signal processing systems.
- Technology necessary for the development of aircraft, missile, and other tactical weapon delivery systems.
- All types of advanced signal and weapons detection, tracking and monitoring systems.
- Technology and equipment used in the construction of nuclear weapons and materials.
- Biological, chemical warfare agents and precursors, and associated manufacturing equipment.

Implementation

The U.S. Customs Service has designed and implemented Project Shield America to work in concert with the three-pronged effort of its Export Enforcement Program:

- **Inspection/Interdiction**
  The inspection and interdiction effort utilizes specially trained Customs Inspectors stationed at high threat ports to selectively inspect suspect export shipments.
- **Investigations**
  The investigations effort involves Customs Special Agents deployed throughout the country, who initiate and pursue high quality cases which result in the arrest, prosecution, and conviction of offenders of the Export Administration Act, Arms Export Control Act, Trading with the Enemy Act, International Emergency Economics Powers Act, and other related statutes. Office of Investigations efforts are concentrated in the proactive mode utilizing various techniques to detect and disrupt illegal exports before they can cause damage to the national security interests of the United States.
- **International Cooperation**
  The international cooperation effort focuses on the use of Customs Attachés stationed in foreign countries, enlisting the support of their host governments.

For additional analytical, business and investment opportunities information, please contact Global Investment & Business Center, USA at (202) 546-2103. Fax: (202) 546-3275. E-mail: rusric@erols.com

This is done in an effort to initiate new investigative leads which are based on information provided by their foreign contacts, and to develop information in support of on-going domestic investigations.

Information developed by Customs as the result of Project Shield America industry contacts, is used to support and enhance these three interdependent efforts.

These efforts are all supported by the Exodus Command Center located in Washington, D.C. This Center maintains contacts with the U.S. Department of Commerce, State, Defense, and other agencies concerned with the export of critical U.S. technologies, munitions, and services.

AIRPORT SECURITY

What To Expect At Airport Security

Prepare for Takeoff: A comprehensive travel guide for you, the flying public. Here you will find everything you need to know about new airport security measures. You will discover a list of timesaving tips, information on assistance for special needs, the latest list of prohibited and permitted items, and other information that will help guide you smoothly through the security process. website.

What to Expect at Airport Security: The Transportation Security Administration (TSA) has developed standardized security screening procedures for all airports. TSA is committed to both excellent security and customer service. A primary goal of TSA is to treat all passengers with courtesy, dignity and respect during the security screening processes. For more information visit the "What to Expect at Airport Security" part of the Transportation Security Administration website.

It is Safe to Fly: The Transportation Safety Administration has established layers of security in our "system of systems" to ensure that we stay ahead of the terrorists that threaten our homeland. That "system of systems" includes:

- Thousands of federal air marshals flying on tens of thousands of flights each month.
- Tapping innovations in technology - such as a more robust passenger pre-screening system and 100% screening of checked baggage.
- Better perimeter security and hardened cockpit doors.
- Dedicated screeners - 56,000 of them, hired, trained and deployed to all 429 commercial airports. On average, they move some 2 million air travelers, and 2 million-plus pieces of luggage, safely through security every day.

Can I Take It With Me? - Permitted & Prohibited Items

Listing of items not allowed on an airplane such as weapons, explosives, and items that seem harmless, but can be used as a weapon.

For additional analytical, business and investment opportunities information, please contact Global Investment & Business Center, USA at (202) 546-2103. Fax: (202) 546-3275. E-mail: rusric@erols.com

Reminder: The two most common items surrendered at the security checkpoint are scissors and pen knives.

Permitted and Prohibited Items (See supplement)

Security for Other Modes of Transport

It is the responsibility of a number of government agencies - federal, state and local - to coordinate the security for the following transportation modes:

- **Trains**: Security is a critical part of railroad safety. The events of September 11 focused Federal Railroad Administration's (FRA) attention on the need to address whatever security vulnerabilities may exist in the railroad system. Under AAR leadership, the rail industry has conducted its own assessment of those risks. All new improvements will be coordinated with the Transportation Security Administration (TSA) which has overall responsibility for transportation security among all modes of transportation, including rail and transit lines. The increased awareness of security issues will cause us to bring such issues into sharper focus in our rulemaking projects. For example, threats to security that might prevent the proper functioning of a PTC system will need to be considered. Furthermore, FRA is working in partnership with the FTA to assess the security of commuter railroads and are jointly funding security risk assessments on the ten largest commuter railroad systems. FRA is also funding a similar security risk assessment for Amtrak. These security risk assessments are intend to identify potential security risks and appropriate security enhancements to mitigate those risks. For more information, please visit the Department of Transportation and Amtrak websites.

- **Trucks**: Ensuring that the security of the drivers and the cargo are not compromised. For more information visit the Federal Motor Carrier section of the Department of Transportation website.

- **Cruise Ships**: Security for passengers traveling on cruise ships is well at hand including screening of all baggage brought aboard a vessel. For more information visit the U.S. Coast Guard website.

- **Buses**: Intercity Bus Security Grants - $15 million - will enhance security for intercity bus operations by focusing on protecting the driver; monitoring and communicating with over-the-road buses; implementing and operating passenger and baggage screening programs; assessing critical security needs and vulnerabilities; and training transportation personnel to recognize and respond to criminal attacks and terrorist threats, as well as in evacuation procedures. For more information visit the Department of Transportation and House of Representatives websites.

- **Airplanes**: Security on our commercial airliners is the best it's ever been. The Transportation Security Administration has focused its first year on hiring, training and deploying 57,000 security screeners to help keep you and your baggage secure.

MARITIME MOBILITY

Port and Border Security

Ensuring that our maritime transportation system, the waterways upon which it navigates, and the ports into which the vessels travel are safe and secure.

Early Ship Identification: All cargo or passenger ships entering a U.S. Ports are required to provide advance detailed information (4 days in advance) about their crew, their cargo and their ship. Vessels are inspected for compliance with safety, pollution and immigration regulations. Passenger vessels - cruise ships or ferries - are closely watched to protect our citizens and maritime commerce. Additionally, we team with other federal, state, local and industry teams to provide comprehensive maritime homeland security contingency plans and threat responsiveness in our 361 major ports. There are $105 million dollars available for grant for ports across the county to improve security. For more information visit the Department of Transportation and U.S. Coast Guard websites.

Navigating our Waters: Our nation's economy is dependent upon the safe navigation of ships through our waterways; therefore, buoys, beacons, lighthouses, sound signals, and radar-reflecting devices mark navigable channels and hazards. For more information visit the "Navigating our Waters" section of the U.S. Coast Guard website.

Cargo Security: Initiatives underway through Operation Safe Commerce - a test bed project between TSA, DOT, Customs, USCG, DoD, INS, OHS, State, Justice and Commerce - to identify and fund business driven initiatives to enhance security for the movement of cargo throughout the entire supply chain. For more information visit the "Cargo Security Grants" section of the Department of Transportation website.

Border Security: Our borders are entryway for people and goods into our country. For more information visit the "Securing the U.S. Borders" section of this website.

IMMIGRATION

On March 1 the Department of Homeland Security became responsible for securing our nation's borders and managing the immigration process. In the past, these two important missions were bundled together within one agency - the Immigration and Naturalization Service. Under DHS, however, immigration services and border enforcement functions will be divided into separate agencies, allowing both missions to receive the full attention they deserve.

Under DHS the newly created Bureau of Citizenship and Immigration Services will focus exclusively on providing services such as efficiently processing applications for U.S.

For additional analytical, business and investment opportunities information,
please contact Global Investment & Business Center, USA
at (202) 546-2103. Fax: (202) 546-3275. E-mail: rusric@erols.com

citizenship, administering the Visa program, administering work authorizations and other permits, and providing services for new residents and citizens.

Border security and the enforcement of immigration laws, however, will be handled by the Directorate of Border and Transportation Security. BTS will absorb the INS's Border Patrol agents and investigators who will join with agents from the U.S. Customs Service, Transportation Security Administration and other enforcement personnel to protect the nation's borders. This mission includes not only managing illegal immigration, but also securing the borders against illicit drugs, unlawful commerce and - as the Department's main priority - the entry of terrorists and the instruments of terrorism.

By making use of cutting-edge technologies, enhancing the flow of information, coordinating with state and local governments, and improving efficiency within the federal government, DHS is uniquely qualified to meet the challenge of safeguarding our borders while facilitating commerce and economic movement and improving the efficiency of our immigration and naturalization process.

Securing the U.S. Borders

DHS is responsible for:

- Managing the nation's borders and ports-of-entry
- Preventing the passage of individuals or goods from entering the United States unlawfully
- Working overseas to strengthen U.S. defenses against illegal smuggling and immigration

Providing Benefits & Information

On March 1st DHS will be responsible for:

- Providing immigration benefits to those individuals who are entitled to stay in the U.S. on a temporary or permanent basis
- These benefits include the granting of U.S. citizenship to those who are eligible to naturalize, authorizing individuals to reside in the U.S. on a permanent basis, and providing aliens with the eligibility to work in the United States
- DHS will meet this responsibility through the creation of the Bureau of Citizenship and Immigration Services

RESEARCH & TECHNOLOGY

Cutting Edge Technology to Protect America

The Department of Homeland Security is committed to using cutting edge technologies and scientific talent in our quest to make America safer. DHS's Science & Technology directorate is tasked with researching and organizing the scientific, engineering and technological resources of the United States and leveraging these existing resources into technological tools to help protect the homeland. Universities, the private sector, and

For additional analytical, business and investment opportunities information, please contact Global Investment & Business Center, USA at (202) 546-2103. Fax: (202) 546-3275. E-mail: rusric@erols.com

the federal laboratories will be important DHS partners in this endeavor. Another DHS priority is the creation of the Advanced Research Projects Agency to jumpstart and facilitate early research and development efforts to help address critical needs in homeland defense on the scientific and technological front. The Homeland Security Act also mandates the creation of a 20-member Science & Technology advisory committee.

WEAPONS OF MASS DESTRUCTION

DHS's Science & Technology Directorate will tap into scientific and technological capabilities in the United States to provide the means to detect and deter attacks using weapons of mass destruction. S&T will guide and organize research efforts to meet emerging and predicted needs and will work closely with universities, the private sector, and national and federal laboratories.

Chemical & Biological Weapons

The S&T Directorate will promote research and technology to develop sensors to detect chemical and biological weapons from production to employment.

CHEM-BIO DEFENSE

Chemical and biological weapons, sometimes referred to as the "poor man's nuclear weapons," pose a significant threat in the post-Cold War environment. The relative low cost and simplicity of their design and technology, in comparison to nuclear weapons, make them the weapons of mass destruction choice for a variety of rogue states and terrorist, non-state organizations. This threat has been made all the more tangible by the use of chemical agent in a Tokyo subway, and allegations over Iraq's development of chemical and biological weapons and its actual use of CW in combat operations.

In order to counter these threats more effectively and develop better means of responding, DTRA draws upon the disparate chemical and biological weapons defense expertise in the Department of Defense in acting as the focal point for DOD technical expertise in these areas. In doing so, the Agency directs and manages Chem-Bio defense efforts. Only by centralizing and focusing DOD efforts in Chem-Bio defense can the United States confidently pursue proper preparation and response in the event of a chemical or biological weapons attack against U.S. forces or territory, or those of our allies.

RADIOLOGICAL & NUCLEAR WEAPONS

The S&T Directorate will promote research and technology to develop sensors which detect nuclear and radiological weapons from production to employment.

For additional analytical, business and investment opportunities information, please contact Global Investment & Business Center, USA at (202) 546-2103. Fax: (202) 546-3275. E-mail: rusric@erols.com

Dirty Bombs

Dirty bombs are weapons which combine an explosive with some form of radioactive material to create a specific type of bomb.

FACT SHEET ON DIRTY BOMBS

BACKGROUND

In order to better inform the public on what a dirty bomb is and what terrorists might intend to try to accomplish in setting off such a weapon, the following information is provided. Given the scores of exercises–federal, state and local–being staged to assure that all emergency response organizations are properly equipped, trained and exercised to respond to terrorist chemical, biological or radiological attack, we believe members of the public, as well as news organizations, will value some concise, straightforward information.

Basically, the principal type of dirty bomb, or Radiological Dispersal Device (RDD), combines a conventional explosive, such as dynamite, with radioactive material. In most instances, the conventional explosive itself would have more immediate lethality than the radioactive material. At the levels created by most probable sources, not enough radiation would be present in a dirty bomb to kill people or cause severe illness. For example, most radioactive material employed in hospitals for diagnosis or treatment of cancer is sufficiently benign that about 100,000 patients a day are released with this material in their bodies.

However, certain other radioactive materials, dispersed in the air, could contaminate up to several city blocks, creating fear and possibly panic and requiring potentially costly cleanup. Prompt, accurate, non-emotional public information might prevent the panic sought by terrorists.

A second type of RDD might involve a powerful radioactive source hidden in a public place, such as a trash receptacle in a busy train or subway station, where people passing close to the source might get a significant dose of radiation.

A dirty bomb is in no way similar to a nuclear weapon. The presumed purpose of its use would be therefore not as a Weapon of Mass Destruction but rather as a Weapon of Mass Disruption.

IMPACT OF A DIRTY BOMB

The extent of local contamination would depend on a number of factors, including the size of the explosive, the amount and type of radioactive material used, and weather conditions. Prompt detectability of the kind of radioactive material employed would greatly assist local authorities in advising the community on protective measures, such as quickly leaving the immediate area, or going inside until being further advised. Subsequent decontamination of the affected area could involve considerable time and expense.

Sources of Radioactive Material

Radioactive materials are widely used at hospitals, research facilities, industrial and construction sites. These radioactive materials are used for such purposes as in diagnosing and treating illnesses, sterilizing equipment, and inspecting welding seams. For example, the Nuclear Regulatory Commission, together with 32 states which regulate radioactive material, have over 21,000 organizations licensed to use such materials. The vast majority of these sources are not useful for constructing an RDD.

Control of Radioactive Material

NRC and state regulations require licensees to secure radioactive material from theft and unauthorized access. These measures have been stiffened since the attacks of September 11, 2001. Licensees must promptly report lost or stolen material. Local authorities make a determined effort to find and retrieve such sources. Most reports of lost or stolen material involve small or short-lived radioactive sources not useful for an RDD.

Past experience suggests there has not been a pattern of collecting such sources for the purpose of assembling a dirty bomb. Only one high-risk radioactive source has not been recovered in the last five years in the United States. However, this source (Iridium-192) would no longer be considered a high-risk source because much of the radioactivity has decayed away since it was reported stolen in 1999. In fact, the combined total of all unrecovered sources over a 5-year time span would barely reach the threshold for one high-risk radioactive source. Unfortunately, the same cannot be said world-wide. The U.S. Government is working to strengthen controls on high-risk radioactive sources both at home and abroad.

What People Should Do Following an Explosion

- Move away from the immediate area--at least several blocks from the explosion-- and go inside. This will reduce exposure to any radioactive airborne dust.
- Turn on local radio or TV channels for advisories from emergency response and health authorities.
- If facilities are available, remove clothes and place them in a sealed plastic bag. Saving contaminated clothing will allow testing for radiation exposure.
- Take a shower to wash off dust and dirt. This will reduce total radiation exposure, if the explosive device contained radioactive material.
- If radioactive material was released, local news broadcasts will advise people where to report for radiation monitoring and blood and other tests to determine whether they were in fact exposed and what steps to take to protect their health.

Risk of Cancer

Just because a person is near a radioactive source for a short time or gets a small amount of radioactive dust on himself or herself does not mean he or she will get cancer. The additional risk will likely be very small. Doctors will be able to assess the risks and suggest mitigating measures once the radioactive source and exposure level have been determined.

It should be noted that Potassium Iodide (KI) would not be protective except in the very unlikely event that the dirty bomb contained radioactive iodine isotopes in large quantities. Radioactive iodine isotopes are not particularly attractive for use in an RDD for a variety of technical reasons. KI only protects the thyroid from radioactive iodine, but offers no protection to other parts of the body or against other radioactive isotopes.

THREATS AND PROTECTION

SYNTHESIZING AND DISSEMINATING INFORMATION

The Department of Homeland Security merges under one roof the capability to anticipate, preempt and deter threats to the homeland whenever possible, and the ability to respond quickly when such threats do materialize. DHS will serve as a central hub of intelligence analysis and dissemination, working with agencies throughout the federal government such as the FBI, CIA, NSA, DEA, the Department of Defense and other key intelligence sources.

Equally important to collecting and analyzing information is the ability to act on it quickly and decisively. DHS will coordinate the federal government's lines of communication with state and local public safety agencies and the general public, including monitoring the nation's threat level and keeping the nation alert via the Homeland Security Advisory System and a system of public alerts.

DHS is also responsible for assessing the vulnerabilities of the nation's critical infrastructure, such as energy and transportation sources; information, computer and telecommunications networks; banking and finance systems; health and emergency services; and systems vital to our national security, public health and safety, economy and way of life. DHS will take the lead in evaluating these vulnerabilities and coordinating with other federal, state, local, and private entities to ensure the most effective response.

HOMELAND SECURITY ADVISORY SYSTEM

Following a review of intelligence and an assessment of threats by the intelligence community, the Department of Homeland Security, in consultation with the Homeland Security Council, has made the decision to lower the threat advisory level to an elevated risk of terrorist attack, or "yellow level."

While we continue to be at risk to the threat of terrorism at an elevated level, extensive protective measures remain in place throughout our nation. As Secretary Rumsfeld has noted, hostilities from Operation Iraqi Freedom still continue and there is, "a lot of work left to do." We must be vigilant and alert to the possibility that al-Qaida and those sympathetic to their cause, as

For additional analytical, business and investment opportunities information, please contact Global Investment & Business Center, USA at (202) 546-2103. Fax: (202) 546-3275. E-mail: rusric@erols.com

well as former Iraqi-regime state agents and affiliated organizations, may attempt to conduct attacks against the U. S. or our interests abroad.

Understanding the Homeland Security Advisory System

The world has changed since September 11, 2001. We remain a nation at risk to terrorist attacks and will remain at risk for the foreseeable future. At all Threat Conditions, we must remain vigilant, prepared, and ready to deter terrorist attacks. The following Threat Conditions each represent an increasing risk of terrorist attacks. Beneath each Threat Condition are some suggested Protective Measures, recognizing that the heads of Federal departments and agencies are responsible for developing and implementing appropriate agency-specific Protective Measures:

1. Low Condition (Green). This condition is declared when there is a low risk of terrorist attacks. Federal departments and agencies should consider the following general measures in addition to the agency-specific Protective Measures they develop and implement:

- Refining and exercising as appropriate preplanned Protective Measures;
- Ensuring personnel receive proper training on the Homeland Security Advisory System and specific preplanned department or agency Protective Measures; and
- Institutionalizing a process to assure that all facilities and regulated sectors are regularly assessed for vulnerabilities to terrorist attacks, and all reasonable measures are taken to mitigate these vulnerabilities.

2. Guarded Condition (Blue). This condition is declared when there is a general risk of terrorist attacks. In addition to the Protective Measures taken in the previous Threat Condition, Federal departments and agencies should consider the following general measures in addition to the agency-specific Protective Measures that they will develop and implement:

- Checking communications with designated emergency response or command locations;
- Reviewing and updating emergency response procedures; and
- Providing the public with any information that would strengthen its ability to act appropriately.

3. Elevated Condition (Yellow). An Elevated Condition is declared when there is a significant risk of terrorist attacks. In addition to the Protective Measures taken in the previous Threat Conditions, Federal departments and agencies should consider the following general measures in addition to the Protective Measures that they will develop and implement:

- Increasing surveillance of critical locations;
- Coordinating emergency plans as appropriate with nearby jurisdictions;
- Assessing whether the precise characteristics of the threat require the further refinement of preplanned Protective Measures; and

- Implementing, as appropriate, contingency and emergency response plans.

4. High Condition (Orange). A High Condition is declared when there is a high risk of terrorist attacks. In addition to the Protective Measures taken in the previous Threat Conditions, Federal departments and agencies should consider the following general measures in addition to the agency-specific Protective Measures that they will develop and implement:

- Coordinating necessary security efforts with Federal, State, and local law enforcement agencies or any National Guard or other appropriate armed forces organizations;
- Taking additional precautions at public events and possibly considering alternative venues or even cancellation;
- Preparing to execute contingency procedures, such as moving to an alternate site or dispersing their workforce; and
- Restricting threatened facility access to essential personnel only.

5. Severe Condition (Red). A Severe Condition reflects a severe risk of terrorist attacks. Under most circumstances, the Protective Measures for a Severe Condition are not intended to be sustained for substantial periods of time. In addition to the Protective Measures in the previous Threat Conditions, Federal departments and agencies also should consider the following general measures in addition to the agency-specific Protective Measures that they will develop and implement:

- Increasing or redirecting personnel to address critical emergency needs;
- Assigning emergency response personnel and pre-positioning and mobilizing specially trained teams or resources;
- Monitoring, redirecting, or constraining transportation systems; and
- Closing public and government facilities.

PROTECTING OUR COMMUNITIES

Protecting our communities is a top priority of the Department of Homeland Security. Whether it is protecting our children in their schools, our computers from hackers and viruses, or our mail, DHS realizes our communities are on the front-line.

Safe School Initiative

As part of its mission to provide leadership and guidance in the prevention of instances of targeted violence, the United States Secret Service National Threat Assessment Center (NTAC) initiated a data-based research project to examine the incidents of school-based attacks. Since September 1999 NTAC staff has been conducting the Safe School Initiative, an operational study of 37 U.S. school shootings involving 41 perpetrators, that have occurred over the past 25 years.

Using methodology similar to that employed in the Exceptional Case Study Project, NTAC researchers are examining school shootings, starting from the incident and working backward to development of the original idea. Through this incident-focused, behavior-based analysis, NTAC researchers hope to increase understanding of the patterns of communication, planning and preparation that precede these attacks. The goal of the Safe School Initiative is to provide accurate and useful information to school administrators, educators, law enforcement professionals and others who have protective and safety responsibilities in schools, to help prevent incidents of school-based targeted violence.

USSS Partnership with the Boys and Girls Clubs of America

At the annual Congressional breakfast on September 20, 2000, the U.S. Secret Service signed a partnership agreement with the Boys and Girls Clubs of America to recognize these clubs and the work they do. The Boys and Girls Clubs of America is a non-profit youth organization with almost 2,400 clubs that help 3.3 million young people in our country. New clubs are being formed every day, and the number of youth who belong is expected to reach 5 million by 2006.

By entering into this partnership, the U.S. Secret Services has pledged its support in assisting with programs that discourage violence and drug abuse, while encouraging good citizenship and educational accomplishments.

SAFEGUARDING AMERICA'S MAIL

America's mail is vitally important to its people and its economy. We depend on the Postal Service to keep the mail moving safely and securely and to keep customers and employees safe and secure. The information below describes how to identify a suspicious mail piece and the procedures to follow:

What constitutes a suspicious letter or parcel?

Some typical characteristics which ought to trigger suspicion include letters or parcels that:

- Have any powdery substance on the outside.
- Are unexpected or from someone unfamiliar to you.
- Have excessive postage, handwritten or poorly typed address, incorrect titles or titles with no name, or misspellings of common words.
- Are addressed to someone no longer with your organization or are otherwise outdated.
- Have no return address, or have one that can't be verified as legitimate.
- Are of unusual weight, given their size, or are lopsided or oddly shaped.
- Have an unusual amount of tape.
- Are marked with restrictive endorsements, such as "Personal" or "Confidential."
- Have strange odors or stains.

What Should I do if I Receive an Anthrax Threat by Mail?

- Do not handle the mail piece or package suspected of contamination.
- Make sure that damaged or suspicious packages are isolated and the immediate area cordoned off.
- Ensure that all persons who have touched the mail piece wash their hands with soap and water.
- Notify your local law enforcement authorities.
- List all persons who have touched the letter and/or envelope. Include contact information and have this information available for the authorities.
- Place all items worn when in contact with the suspected mail piece in plastic bags and have them available for law enforcement agents.
- As soon as practical, shower with soap and water.
- Notify the Center for Disease Control Emergency Response at 770-488-7100 for answers to any questions.

The simple act of paying attention to incoming mail will go a long way in keeping it safe and viable. Everyone, in the mailing community, as well as the American public, should exercise common sense.

TRANSPORTATION

Freedom of Movement

11.2 million trucks and 2.2 million rail cars cross into the United States annually, and 7,500 foreign-flag ships make 51,000 calls in U.S. ports annually, providing us with goods and services.

The Transportation Security Administration protects the Nation's transportation systems to ensure freedom of movement for people and commerce.

BANKING & FINANCE

Securing Our Financial Institutions

Identity theft and crimes associated with financial institutions pose an everyday threat to our community. These crimes include: bank fraud, debit and credit card fraud, telecommunications and computer crimes, fraudulent identification, fraudulent government securities, and electronic fund transfer fraud.

Credit Card Fraud/Identity Theft

Financial industry sources estimate that losses associated with credit card fraud are in the billions of dollars annually. The Secret Service is the primary federal agency tasked with investigating access device fraud and its related activities under Title 18, United States Code, Section 1029. Although it is commonly called the credit card statute, this law also applies to other crimes involving access device numbers including debit cards, automated teller machine (ATM) cards, computer passwords, personal identification numbers (PINs) used to activate ATMs, credit card or debit card account numbers, long-distance access codes, and the computer chips in cellular phones that assign billing.

During fiscal year 1996, the Secret Service opened 2,467 cases, closed 2,963 cases, and arrested 2,429 individuals for access device fraud. Industry sources estimate that losses associated with credit card fraud are in the billions of dollars annually.

Advance Fee Fraud

The perpetrators of Advance Fee Fraud are often very creative and innovative. This fraud is called "4-1-9" fraud after the section of the Nigerian penal code that addresses fraud schemes. Nigerian nationals, purporting to be officials of their government or banking institutions, will fax or mail letters to individuals and businesses in the United States and other countries. The correspondence will inform the recipient that a reputable foreign company or individual is needed for the deposit of an overpayment on a procurement contract. The letter will claim that the Nigerian government overpaid anywhere from $10 to $60 million on these contracts. There is the perception that no one would enter such an obviously suspicious relationship; however, many victims have been enticed into believing they can share in such windfall profits.

On July 2, 1996, officials of the Federal Investigation and Intelligence Bureau (FIIB) of the Nigerian National Police, accompanied by Secret Service agents in an observer/advisor role, executed search warrants on 16 location in Lagos that resulted in the arrests of 43 Nigerian nationals. Evidence seized included telephones and facsimile machines, government and Central Bank of Nigeria letterhead, international business directories, scam letters, and addressed envelopes, and files containing correspondence from victims throughout the world.

Counterfeit Currency & the Creation of the Secret Service

On July 5, 1865, the Secret Service was created with the sole mission of suppressing counterfeit currency. The Secret Service has exclusive jurisdiction for investigations involving the counterfeiting of United States obligations and securities. Some of the counterfeited United States obligations and securities commonly dealt with by the Secret Service include U.S. currency and coins; U.S. Treasury checks; Department of Agriculture food coupons and U.S. postage stamps. The Secret Service remains committed to the mission of combating counterfeiting by working closely with state and local law enforcement agencies, as well as foreign law enforcement agencies, to aggressively pursue counterfeiters. To perform at the highest level, the Secret Service constantly reviews the latest reprographic/lithographic technologies to keep a step ahead of the counterfeiters. The Secret Service maintains a working relationship with the Bureau of Engraving and Printing and the Federal Reserve System to ensure the integrity of our currency.

History of Counterfeiting

The counterfeiting of money is one of the oldest crimes in history. At some periods in early history, it was considered treasonous and was punishable by death.

For additional analytical, business and investment opportunities information, please contact Global Investment & Business Center, USA at (202) 546-2103. Fax: (202) 546-3275. E-mail: rusric@erols.com

During the American Revolution, the British counterfeited U.S. currency in such large amounts that the Continental currency soon became worthless. "Not worth a Continental" became a popular expression that is still heard today.

During the Civil War, one-third to one-half of the currency in circulation was counterfeit. At that time, approximately 1,600 state banks designed and printed their own bills. Each bill carried a different design, making it difficult to detect counterfeit bills from the 7,000 varieties of real bills.

HEALTH & SAFETY

Defending Against Biological Terrorism

For Immediate Release
Office of the Press Secretary
February 5, 2002

"Disease has long been the deadliest enemy of mankind. Infectious diseases make no distinctions among people and recognize no borders. We have fought the causes and consequences of disease throughout history and must continue to do so with every available means. All civilized nations reject as intolerable the use of disease and biological weapons as instruments of war and terror."
- President George W. Bush
November 1, 2001

One of the most important missions we have as a Nation is to be prepared for the threat of biological terrorism - the deliberate use of disease as a weapon. An effective biodefense will require a long-term strategy and significant new investment in the U.S. health care system. The President is taking steps now that will significantly improve the Nation's ability to protect its citizens against the threat of bioterrorism. The President's Budget for 2003 proposes $5.9 billion to defending against biological terrorism, an increase of $4.5 billion -- or 319 percent -- from the 2002 level. This new funding will focus on:

1. **Infrastructure**. Strengthen the State and local health systems, including by enhancing medical communications and disease surveillance capabilities, to maximize their contribution to the overall biodefense of the Nation.

2. **Response.** Improve specialized Federal capabilities to respond in coordination with State and local governments, and private capabilities in the event of a bioterrorist incident and build up the National Pharmaceutical Stockpile.

3. **Science**. Meet the medical needs of our bioterrorism response plans by developing specific new vaccines, medicines, and diagnostic tests through an aggressive research and development program.

Responsibility for detecting and managing a bioterrorist attack needs to be shared among a wide range of Federal, State, local, and private entities. The resources made available in the President's Budget for 2003 will help the Nation develop an effective

For additional analytical, business and investment opportunities information, please contact Global Investment & Business Center, USA at (202) 546-2103. Fax: (202) 546-3275. E-mail: rusric@erols.com

"early warning" system against a possible bioterrorist attack, and mount an effective operational response to manage its medical consequences. These enhanced capabilities, once in place, will also enhance the Nation's ability to respond to outbreaks of naturally occurring diseases.

Infrastructure: Strengthening America's Public Health System

The President is committed to improving the ability of State and local public health care systems to deal with bioterrorism. State and local medical personnel are a principal line of defense against bioterrorism, and will often be the first to recognize that we are under a biological attack. Ensuring that State and local health care providers have the appropriate tools and the training is critical as our health care community works to carry out this mission.

Many of our health care systems are not adequately prepared for a large-scale attack:

- The health care system lacks the surge capabilities needed to handle quickly large numbers of victims and have insufficient isolation facilities for contagious patients.
- The information system that knits together hospital emergency rooms and public health officials is antiquated and inadequate.
- Little has been done to promote regional mutual aid compacts among health care institutions for bioterrorism attacks.
- Training for health care providers in the handling of bioterrorism victims has been infrequent.

In his 2003 Budget, the President has proposed $1.6 billion to assist State and local health care systems in improving their ability to manage both contagious and non-contagious biological attacks, to expand health care surge capabilities, to upgrade public health laboratory capabilities, and to provide training for medical personnel. The Budget also makes available funding to support the development of regional medical mutual aid compacts. In the event of an emergency, these compacts will enable State and local emergency managers to augment local medical care providers quickly and efficiently. Finally, the communications network that links the acute care providers of our communities with their public health counterparts will be modernized and improved so that vital information on the detection and treatment of disease can flow swiftly.

Response: Enhancing Specialized Federal Capabilities

A major act of biological terrorism would almost certainly overwhelm existing State, local, and privately owned health care capabilities. For this reason, the Federal government maintains a number of specialized response capabilities for a bioterrorist attack. The President's Budget invests $1.8 billion to ensure that these specialized Federal resources are adequate for the threat we face.

The President and the Congress have already taken steps to acquire a national supply of smallpox vaccine and ensure that by the end of fiscal year 2002, the National

Pharmaceutical Stockpile will contain sufficient antibiotics to treat 20 million people against diseases such as anthrax, plague and tularemia. The President's Budget for 2003 provides $650 million to carry the process of enhancing the National Pharmaceutical Stockpile even further through:

- The acquisition of the next-generation anthrax vaccine, and the maintenance of and improvements to the national supply of smallpox vaccine. The budget will also provide resources to acquire sufficient amounts of vaccinia immunoglobulin (VIG) to treat those that might experience adverse reactions to inoculations.
- Continued maintenance of and improvements to the "push packs" that can be used in the case of both biological and conventional attacks. These pre-assembled packages contain life-saving antidotes, pharmaceuticals, and other medical supplies, and are deployed to the disaster site within 12 hours of a request. The first emergency use of the "push packs" came on September 11 in New York City. In fiscal year 2002, the national supply of these "push packs" was increased from 8 to 12.
- An enhanced vendor managed inventory program so that the Federal government can quickly obtain the additional antibiotics, antidotes, and medical equipment and supplies if an incident requires a larger or multi-phased response.
- Funding support for the States and localities to plan for the receipt and distribution of medicines from the National Pharmaceutical Stockpile.
- The streamlining and integration the Federal bioterrorism response efforts into a unified plan.

Recognizing the potentially global nature of bioterrorism, the Budget for 2003 devotes $10 million to create a team of epidemiological scientists who are committed to working with their counterparts in foreign countries to provide information, research, awareness, and early warning of potential health threats from abroad. Finally, the President's Budget for 2003 provides $20 million to strengthen the Epidemiological Intelligence Service (EIS) at the Centers for Disease Control in Atlanta. Established in 1951 following the start of the Korean War as an early-warning system against biological warfare, the EIS today has expanded into a surveillance and response unit for all types of epidemics.

Science: A New Medical Toolkit for Fighting Bioterrorism

Whether we succeed or fail in our response to an act of bioterrorism depends in large measure on the quality and effectiveness of our diagnostic tests, vaccines, and therapeutic drugs. Our experience responding to the anthrax letter attacks of October 2001 has revealed major inadequacies in our existing medical "toolkit" for fighting bioterrorism. Some of the diagnostics, vaccines, and therapeutics available to us today were developed during the Cold War and hence do not harness the full power of modern biomedical science.

The President's Budget for 2003 devotes $2.4 billion to jump-starting the research and development process needed to provide America with the medical tools needed to support an effective response to bioterrorism. These resources will be focused in the following areas:

- $1.75 billion will be provided to the National Institutes of Health to conduct basic and applied research needed to provide solutions to a range of specific operational problems in our bioterrorism response plans. To do this, NIH will lead a partnership with industry, academia, and government agencies dedicated to understanding the pathogenesis of potential bioterrorism agents and to translating this knowledge into required medical products.
- Over $600 million will be allocated to the Department of Defense, of which $420 million will be used to accelerate efforts to develop better detection, identification, collection, and monitoring technology. Additionally, the scientists working under Defense auspices will support the law enforcement, national security, and medical communities by improving our understanding of how potential bioterrorism pathogens may be weaponized, transported, and disseminated.
- $75 million will go to the Environmental Protection Agency to develop better methods for decontaminating buildings where bioterrorism agents have been released.

LAW ENFORCEMENT

Enforcing the Nation's Laws

The Department of Homeland Security will absorb many different law enforcement resources and organizations on March 1 to help make the Nation safer.

ENFORCEMENT INITIATIVES

The Bureau of Immigration and Customs Enforcement
Beginning March 1, 2003, the enforcement and investigative arms of the Customs Service, the investigative and enforcement functions of the former Immigration and Naturalization Service, and the Federal Protective Service, come together to form the Bureau of Immigration and Customs Enforcement as part of the U.S. Department of Homeland Security.

Project Shield America
An integral part of U.S. Customs Service export control strategy, which depends upon the cooperation of the U.S. manufacturing and exporting community.

Green Quest - Finding the Missing Piece of the Terrorist Puzzle
The Treasury Department established Operation Green Quest in October 2001 as an essential part of America's response to the events of September 11.

Most Wanted
Check out U.S. Customs Service top fugitives, keep your eyes peeled and report any sightings to **1-800-BE-ALERT** as soon as possible! To view detailed profiles of each suspect select the photo or name of the fugitive.

Child Exploitation Unit - Customs CyberSmuggling Center (C3)
The presence of child pornography on the Internet is a disturbing and growing phenomenon. The U.S. Customs Service is the country's front line of defense to combat the importation and proliferation of this illegal material.

Seizures and Penalties
U.S. Customs Service has full authority to assess penalties and liquidated damages claims

FEDERAL PROTECTIVE SERVICE

Effective March 1, 2003, the Federal Protective Service has been transferred to the Border and Transportation Security Directorate of the Department of Homeland Security. Until further notice, all phone numbers and points of contact contained in this www.gsa.gov website for FPS personnel nationwide and emergency and non-emergency numbers remain unchanged.

At FPS, our goal is to become a premier facility security organization that provides a safe environment in which Federal agencies can conduct their business.

To accomplish this, we will reduce threats posed against Federal facilities which range from terrorism to workplace violence to larcenies. FPS is committed to ensuring the appropriate level of security is in place at each GSA managed facility, regardless of its location throughout the country.

IMPORTANT OFFICIAL ATATEMENTS

PRESIDENT INCREASES FUNDING FOR BIOTERRORISM BY 319 PERCENT

1:55 P.M. EST

THE PRESIDENT: Thank you very much. Thanks for that warm welcome. It's great to be back in Pittsburgh. Never did I think I'd come back and say, America is under attack. Never did I dream I'd come back to this beautiful city and say, we've got to be on alert. But here I am and that's what I'm saying.

I walk into the Oval Office every morning. And, by the way, walking into the Oval Office is a fabulous experience. (Laughter.) It's -- I can't tell you what an honor it is. It is -- it's great. It is a beautiful office. I get there early in the morning. Spot, the dog, goes with me. (Laughter.) I don't let Barney go. Got a brand new rug, so he doesn't get to go. (Laughter.)

But I sit at this magnificent desk. It's a desk that was used by President Roosevelt and President Kennedy and President Reagan. And I read threats to the United States of America. Every morning, I'm reminded that my most important job is to make our country secure; is to protect the homeland of the United States of America. And that's what I want to talk to you all about today -- how best to protect the homeland.

The best way to start to do so is to pick a good general, somebody who knows how to organize, somebody who's tough, somebody who's smart, and somebody who can articulate the issues we face. And I found a good one right here in Pennsylvania in your former governor. (Applause.)

I've also got a great team, a wonderful team of Americans who are there to serve something greater than their own self-interests. Not only do I have a great foreign policy team, I've got a wonderful domestic policy team. And one of the key members of that team is a former governor, friend of mine, who is doing a fabulous job, and that's Tommy Thompson of Health and Human Services. (Applause.)

I'm sorry your current governor couldn't be here, but he's giving his budget address. I completely understand why he's not here. But I also want to thank him publicly for his work in coordinating the anti-terrorist activities of the state of Pennsylvania -- the Commonwealth of Pennsylvania -- with the federal government. He's doing a fine job, and you need to be proud of his efforts and his desire to make Pennsylvania as safe a place as possible. (Applause.)

I also want to thank two members of the United States Congress who are here, one Democrat, Mike Doyle; one Republican, Melissa Hart. The reason I bring them up with their party affiliations is there is no difference, as far as I can tell, in Washington, D.C. about love for country. You don't have to be a Republican to love the country, or a

For additional analytical, business and investment opportunities information, please contact Global Investment & Business Center, USA at (202) 546-2103. Fax: (202) 546-3275. E-mail: rusric@erols.com

Democrat to love the country; we all love our country. And one of the healthy things that I think is beginning to happen in Washington, D.C. is we're beginning to recognize that it's time to put aside partisan differences and focus on what's best for America and do what's right for our citizens. (Applause.) So I want to welcome you both here. Thank you.

I also want to thank those who have briefed us on some of the innovative work that is going on here at the University of Pittsburgh, as well as with Carnegie Mellon -- Mike Wagner and Andrew Moore. They gave us a fascinating program I'm going to explain briefly in a second. I appreciate D.A. Henderson, the Director of the Office of Public Health Preparedness, who has traveled from Washington with us. D.A., where are you? Thank you for coming, D.A.

D.A.'s got a big job. His job is to take some of the interesting things that have been developed in places such as Pittsburgh and make sure they're duplicated around the country, make sure others go to school on what you've done at this school, so that America is safe as it can possibly be.

I also want to welcome Tony Fauci here of the NIH. Tony, thank you for coming. Tony does a fabulous job at the NIH. He represents a very important part of the research and develop arm of the United States. We've significantly boosted the NIH budget, not only to help fight the war against terror, but also to help fight the war against disease. And I'm proud of the efforts of our NIH folks. And thanks for coming, Tony. (Applause.)

I want to thank Mark Nordenberg for letting us come. It kind of strains the resources when the President shows up. I fully understand. But thanks, Mark, for letting us use your beautiful campus, and Jared Cohon, as well, from Carnegie Mellon. Thank you for greeting us and briefing us today. And Arthur Levine, I want to thank you, as well. You did a fine job of explaining what's going on. And I look forward to kind of sharing some of that with the American people.

Homeland defense takes many forms. One, of course, is to secure our borders, to make sure we understand who's coming in and out of our country. Part of making sure America's safe is to have as good information as possible about what takes place in our ports of entry. That's why I spent a little time in Maine the other day, talking about how we're going to boost the presence of the Coast Guard, for example, to make sure our border and our homeland is as secure as possible.

Part of having a secure homeland is to have a good airport system, that's safe for people to travel; an airport system that is inspecting bags by inspectors who are qualified to inspect bags. Part of a homeland defense is to have good intelligence sharing between the federal, the state and the local level. Part of homeland security is to have a first responders mechanism that's modern and current. And part of homeland security is to be prepared to fight any kind of war against bio-terror.

And that's what I want to spend some time talking about today. Some of us remember that back in the '50s we had what was called the DEW line on the Arctic Circle, to warn us if enemy bombers were coming over the North Pole to attack America. Well, here in Pittsburgh, I had the honor of seeing a demonstration of the modern DEW line, a Real-time Outbreak and Disease Surveillance system, developed right here, which is one of the country's leading centers on monitoring biological threats.

What we saw was how to take real -- data on a real-time basis to determine if there was an outbreak of any kind, including a terrorist attack. The best way to protect the homeland is to understand what's taking place on the homeland so we can respond. And so the modern-day DEW line to me was fascinating. And I appreciate those who have worked so hard to come up with an incredibly useful tool for America, a useful tool to protect ourselves.

I also appreciate the fact that the University of Pittsburgh and Carnegie Mellon Institute launched what's called a biomedical security institute to help protect the nation in all ways from the insidious biological attack.

You know, I've come to realize -- having spent some time in Pittsburgh and particularly hearing the briefings today, that while Pittsburgh used to be called "Steel Town," you need to call it "Knowledge Town." (Applause.) There's a lot of smart people in this town. And I'm proud to report to my fellow citizens, they're working in a way to make America safe. A lot of money, obviously, comes from the state government for that. We are grateful. But the federal government has a role to play, as well.

I'm proud to say the Department of Defense, the Centers for Disease Control and Prevention, the Department of Health and Human Services all provide financial support to the Biomedical Security Institute. But, as you can tell from reading the papers and tell from my -- hopefully, if you listened to my State of the Union address, I have made the homeland security a top budget priority and I asked Congress to respond in a positive way to this request.

For example, we're asking for $1.6 billion. This is additional money for state and local governments to help hospitals and others improve their ability to cope with any bio-terror attack. One, it's important to be able to recognize what's happening; and, secondly, we've got to respond, respond in a modern way, a way that will help the American people survive any attack if it were to come.

I want to make sure that each region around the country has the proper equipment and the right amount of medicine for the victims of any attack, should it occur. We've got to upgrade our communications, not only between the federal government and the state government, but between state governments and local communities, and between counties and local jurisdictions. We've got to be able to talk to each other better, so that there's real time communications, so that we can share information in a crisis. Information-sharing will help save lives. And so part of the money is to bring our systems up to speed, to make them more modern and more responsive.

The budget also adds $2.4 billion to develop new test protocols and new treatments for bio-terror weapons. We were able to save lives during the anthrax outbreak, but some infections were identified too late, and some people were too badly infected to save. We must do everything in our power, everything to protect our fellow Americans. We need

For additional analytical, business and investment opportunities information, please contact Global Investment & Business Center, USA at (202) 546-2103. Fax: (202) 546-3275. E-mail: rusric@erols.com

better testing, better vaccines, and better drugs if America is going to be as safe as it can possibly be.

And there's some hopeful news. Scientists tell us that research we do to fight bioterrorism is likely to deliver great new advances in the treatment of many other diseases, such as tuberculosis, pneumonia, malaria and HIV/AIDS. The monies we spend to protect America today are likely to yield long-term benefits, are likely to provide some incredible cures to diseases that many years ago never thought would be cured. It's an investment that will pay off not only for better security, but for better health. And I ask Congress to support me on spending this money.

We're also going to expand our nation's stockpile of antibiotics and vaccines. We're going to have more of these important antibiotics and vaccines readily available. By the end of the current fiscal year, we'll have enough antibiotics on hand to treat up to 20 million people for anthrax, plague and other bio-terrorist diseases. We're preparing for the worst.

We'll provide funds to states to make sure they can distribute medicines swiftly. And we're also going to expand our bio-terror intelligence service. During the Korean War, we created what was called an Epidemic Intelligence Service to help defend America if any of our Cold War enemies tried to use bio-weapons against us. Now we need to adapt the EIS to a new era and to a new mission. We'll make the commitment to expand and modernize the service, and to work with scientists in this country and friendly nations around the world.

All in all, my budget will commit almost $6 billion to defend ourselves against bioterrorism -- as Tom mentioned, an increase of over 300 percent. It's money that we've got to spend. It's money that will have good impact on the country. It's money that will enable me to say that we're doing everything we can to protect America at home.

But I want to remind you all, the surest way to protect America at home is to find the enemy where it hides and bring them to justice. The surest way to protect America is to unleash the mighty arm of our United States military, and find the killers, wherever they hide, and rout them out, and bring them to justice. (Applause.)

History has called us into action, here at home and internationally. We've been given a chance to lead, and we're going to seize the moment in this country. As we've mentioned more than once, what we do here at home is going to have lasting impact for a long time. And I want to tell you what we're doing abroad is going to have lasting impact, as well.

I view this as an opportunity to secure the peace for a long time coming. I view this as a struggle of tyranny versus freedom, of evil versus good. And there's no in between, as far as I'm concerned. Either you're with us, or you're against us. Either you stand for a peaceful world for our children and our grandchildren, either you're willing to defend freedom to its core, or you're going to be against the mighty United States of America.

I truly believe that by leading the world, by rallying a vast coalition, by holding people accountable for murderous deeds, the world will be a more peaceful place for our children and our grandchildren. (Applause.)

And I'm proud to report this country understands what I just said. We are patient; we're deliberate. Oh, I know the news media likes to say, where's Osama bin Laden? He's not the issue. The issue is international terror. I like our chances against bin Laden, however. (Laughter.) There's no cave deep enough for him to hide. He can run, and he thinks he can hide, but we're not going to give up until he and every other potential killer, and every other body who hates freedom will be brought to justice.

You know, the enemy hit us, and they said, oh, this great country is going to wilt. They're not great, they're weak. I like to needle them by saying, they must have been watching too much daytime TV. (Laughter.) They got the wrong impression of America, because quite the opposite is happening. We're unified; we're focused; we are deliberate; we're patient. We're certain of our values, and sure of the need to defend freedom. And for that, the enemy is going to pay a serious price.

You know, I'm asked all the time here at home, what can I do to help. Well, when I look out and see the docs, every day you show up for work, you're helping, by helping develop some antibiotic, or perhaps helping some poor person who can't afford health care.

The reason I bring that up is because I think the way to fight off evil is to do some acts of goodness. See, the great strength of the country is the hearts and souls of our fellow Americans. And the best way to declare our position, the best way to make our position known to the world, is through what I like to call the gathering momentum of millions of acts of kindness and compassion and decency; acts of compassion and decency which take place on a daily basis, in all kinds of ways.

People say, how can I help? Well, just walk across the street and tell a shut-in you love her, and what can you do to visit to make her day complete? Or how about mentoring a child in a school, and teaching that child how to read? Maybe if you're interested in helping fight the war on terror you should become a mentor to a child whose mother or dad may be in prison, so that child can have somebody put their arm around them, and say, I love you. In America, it belongs just as much to you, as it does to me.

Now, there's all kinds of ways to join this war against terror. And it starts by Americans leading with their heart. There's no doubt in my mind we'll make the right decisions here at home. There is no doubt in my mind that the United States will prevail in the war of terror. And there's no doubt in my mind that out of the incredible evil that was done, great goodness will come, and America will be better off for it.

May God bless you all. (Applause.)

For additional analytical, business and investment opportunities information, please contact Global Investment & Business Center, USA at (202) 546-2103. Fax: (202) 546-3275. E-mail: rusric@erols.com

PRESIDENT PROMOTES FUNDING FOR EMERGENCY FIRST RESPONDER

Remarks by the President to South Carolina First Responders
Wyche Pavilion
Greenville, South Carolina
10:25 A.M. EST

THE PRESIDENT: Thank you very much. It is great to be back in South Carolina. I didn't realize I was going to be giving an address on my old jogging path. (Laughter.)

Mr. Mayor, I have fond memories of your beautiful city. And thank you very much for your leadership and your hospitality and thank you all for coming.

One of the things that I'm not surprised about is how the good folks of South Carolina responded on September the 11th in the aftermath. The good people here hurt for the people of New York, because they realized an attack on one part of America was an attack on all of America.

And I want to thank you all for donating a brand new fire truck to New York City. I want to thank you for sending men and women to New York City in response to the emergency. I know that fire fighters and casualty experts, emergency management director headed up north to provide help. And I'm here to thank you for that. And I'm here also to thank you for what you do every single day.

You know, the evil ones hit us, but out of that evil has come some good. I'm going to talk to you about some of that good. And one of the good things that's come is a sincere appreciation and respect for the men and women who wear the uniform, the police and fire and emergency medical units all across the country. And I'm here to thank you as well for your dedication and your service to the people of your communities here in South Carolina.

I appreciate so very much Tom Ridge's service. You know, he was a governor there in Pennsylvania, just kind of cruising along. Life was pretty good. And then the President called him and said, I've got an assignment for you, to come and set a national strategy for our homeland security. The enemies hit us and we'd better be ready in case the enemy hits us again, and we need a strategy.

And I'm telling you, he's come to Washington, D.C., with a vision and a capacity and we're developing and have got a strategy, some of which I will share with you today. And, Tom, I want to thank you for your service. (Applause.)

And I want to thank the other fellow on the stage here, Jim DeMint. He is a strong congressman. (Applause.) He cares deeply about the people of this state. He is -- he is an ally of mine in the House because he is a man of integrity. He cares deeply about national issues and issues that affect the people here in his district. He understands the

For additional analytical, business and investment opportunities information, please contact Global Investment & Business Center, USA at (202) 546-2103. Fax: (202) 546-3275. E-mail: rusric@erols.com

need for us to be tough and diligent and forceful when it comes to fighting terrorists. He understands the need for us to be strong at home, as well.

And that's why he has led a discussion on a strategy to make sure that the textile industry here in South Carolina gets not only the attention of the administration, but a strategy to help people who work in the textile industry. This man is a leader, and he needs to go back to Washington, D.C. (Applause.)

And we've got some other people from the fine South Carolina delegation, Lindsey Graham is here, and a little later on, I'm going to try to give Lindsey a little boost. (Laughter.) And I appreciate Hank Brown for being here as well, thank you for coming. And I want to thank members of the State House who have come.

You've got a fine lieutenant governor and attorney general. Thank you both for coming. And, of course, your speaker, a home-grown boy, David Wilkins. I'm honored that you all have been here today. (Applause.)

I drove in and went by the BMW plant for about the hundredth time, and it was good that I was traveling by it with Carroll Campbell, who made sure that the BMW plant came here the first time around. Governor, it's good to see you. Thank you for coming. (Applause.)

I want to thank the High Sheriff of Greenville County, Sam Simmons -- I don't know if you call him the High Sheriff around here or not. But, play like you do, if you don't. (Laughter.) But I want to thank the Sheriff, I want to thank Willie Johnson, the Chief. I want to thank Tom McDowell, Chief of the Fire Department; John Zaragoza, as well. And, again, I want to thank you all for coming.

The interesting thing about September the 11th is that even though the attacks were on two major cities, it reminded us -- and in the aftermath reminded us that we're all vulnerable as well. I mean, after all, you might remember that some of the initial discussions after September the 11th about potential threat was about crop dusters. Now, they don't have a lot of crop dusters, you know, in Manhattan. They've got a lot of crop dusters in South Carolina or Texas.

In other words, some of the intelligence we were getting was that not only were the enemy willing to use airplanes, obviously, as weapons, but what we were concerned about was that they would use other methods -- like using a crop duster to spray a weapons of mass destruction, if possible. It's an indication that we had to be on alert to defend all sites and all locations in our country.

We knew they were evil. And we're beginning to learn how really evil their intentions were after September the 11th. And that's why Tom and I and many of you all and others around the country have got plans in place to defend power generating plants, dams and reservoirs, livestock and crops, all kinds of areas.

I mean, the truth of the matter is, homeland security in the heartland is just as important as homeland security in the big cities. And that's what we're here to talk about today; to

For additional analytical, business and investment opportunities information, please contact Global Investment & Business Center, USA at (202) 546-2103. Fax: (202) 546-3275. E-mail: rusric@erols.com

make sure that America is safe. See, that's my most important job. My most important job is to work with federal, state and local officials to prevent the enemy from hitting us again and taking innocent life.

I think about it every day. And even though they're still under threat and we are under threat, we're getting better prepared every day. I sent a budget up to Congress that reflects my priority. The first responders of America, all across America, must have the resources necessary to respond to emergencies and save lives. (Applause.)

In the budget we sent up, there is a thousand percent increase for first responders; $3.5 billion, to make your jobs easier. I've requested $327 million right away, right off the bat, to provide critical training and equipment to first responders; $327 million will come this year, hopefully, $3.5 billion is for next budget cycle.

In places like Pickens, South Carolina and Union and Greer -- and, by the way, I've been to all three, and enjoyed every minute of it. One of the bedrock principles of small-town life is you help a neighbor in need. A volunteer firefighter in Fort Mills, South Carolina put it this way: we may not be a big department like New York City, but we have the same goal, to help our neighbors in time of trouble.

That's how you all feel, too. That's how the Crawford, Texas volunteer fire department feels, as well. I'm a proud booster.

And one of the things we've got to do is to understand that we've got to strengthen security in small town America, as well, by helping smaller communities and smaller counties develop what we call mutual aid agreements. And in the budget that I've submitted to Congress, there's $140 million to do just that.

If one town has got them a good hospital facility, another may be able to lend fire trucks, a third may be a home to hazardous material experts -- but we've got to develop these mutual pacts so that we can coordinate efforts, pool resources, all aimed at helping a neighbor in need, if we need to.

So one of the things we're doing is focusing on the big cities, medium-sized cities like Greenville. But we understand we've got to have a strategy for rural South Carolina and rural America, as well. And I'm here to assure the good folks of South Carolina that the strategies that we're putting out, the strategies that we're going to outline and work with the states and local authorities on will also include rural South Carolina, to make sure that assets are pooled, personnel is coordinated. All aimed at buttoning-up the homeland of the United States and preparing our country.

But I want you to know that the best homeland security, the best way to secure the homeland and protect innocent life is to find the enemy wherever they hide and bring them to justice. And that's exactly what we're going to do. (Applause.)

We will hunt them down one-by-one. And after September the 11th, we started. And I said as plainly as I could speak, mustering up as much Midland, Texas as I could find -- I said either you are with us or you're against us. (Applause.) And I made it clear that if

For additional analytical, business and investment opportunities information, please contact Global Investment & Business Center, USA at (202) 546-2103. Fax: (202) 546-3275. E-mail: rusric@erols.com

anybody harbored a terrorist or they fed a terrorist or they hid a terrorist, they're just as guilty as the murderers who took innocent life on September the 11th.

And thanks to a mighty United States military, the Taliban found out exactly what I meant. (Applause.)

I'm proud of our military. And for those of you who have got a relative in the military, I want you to thank them on behalf of a grateful nation. But we've got to do more than thank them. We've got to make sure that they've got the best training, the best equipment, the best pay possible. And that's why the budget I submitted to the United States Congress not only includes a significant increase for first responders and homeland security issues, but it is the largest increase in military spending in two decades.

Because I understand that the price of freedom is high; but as far as I'm concerned, it is never too high when it comes to the defense of freedom. (Applause.)

And that's what we're defending. We don't seek revenge. We seek justice. But it's more than just justice. This nation will defend freedom. We defend the freedom to worship; we defend the freedom to speak; we defend the freedom for all Americans -- regardless of their background -- to enjoy a country that says if you work hard, you can realize your dreams. That's what we defend.

And this enemy of ours hates what we stand for. They can't stand us. They're ruthless murderers. And they must not have understood America when they attacked us. They thought we were weak. They thought we were so self-absorbed in our materialism that all we would probably do is just sue them. (Laughter.) Man, were they wrong.

We've thrown the Taliban out. And this past weekend, for the first time, many young women went to school. We went into Afghanistan not as conquerors, but as liberators; as people who are willing to sacrifice to defend our freedoms.

The first phase of the war is over, holding people accountable for harboring a terrorist. That message is now loud and clear. I think other governments have heard that message. And the next message is this: we're going to keep you on the run. If you're a killer, we're going to treat you for what you are, an international criminal with no place to hide, no place to sleep.

Oh, I know some of them think there's a cave deep enough. We're patient, we're determined, we're united. (Applause.) As proud and patriotic Americans, I can assure you that this distance between September the 11th is not going to cause me to weaken in my determination to defend our country and to fight for freedom.

I also want to explain right quickly what I meant when I was talking about the axis of evil. Let me put it to you this way: we cannot allow nations that have got a history of totalitarianism, dictatorship -- a nation, for example, like Iraq that poisoned her own people -- to develop a weapon of mass destruction and mate-up with terrorist organizations who hate freedom-loving countries. We can't afford to do that for the sake of our children and our children's children.

History has called this nation into action, and we're not going to let the world's worst leaders develop and maintain and deploy and aim at us or our friends the world's worst weapons.

My fellow Americans, we've got a lot at stake. We've got a lot at stake at home and a lot at stake around the world. We've been called, and I'm here to assure you this great country is prepared and willing and will answer the call to freedom. (Applause.)

And I believe there's another calling at home, as well. I believe that we have an opportunity to fight evil at home in a different kind of way than people would have imagined. I'm asked all the time by people, what can I do in a war against terror? You all are answering that call.

But there's something else I'd like for you and others in South Carolina and around America to do. You see, in order to fight evil, we can stand strongly in the face of evil with acts of kindness and compassion. We can better love our neighbor like we'd like to be loved ourself.

You see, the great strength of America is not necessarily our military might and it's certainly not our government, even though the system is great and the military is strong. The great strength of America are the hearts and soul -- the great strength is the heart and soul of our country, that's our strength. The strength of the country comes when somebody walks across the street to a neighbor in need and says, what can I do to help you? When somebody walks in to a shut-in and says, I care about you. Or somebody mentors a child, teaching that child how to read. Or a church or a synagogue or a mosque comes up with a program based upon faith of the Almighty to help a person whip alcohol or drugs. That's the great strength of America.

And I believe out of this evil will come incredible goodness. I know this country can stand squarely in the face of evil by loving a neighbor just like you'd like to be loved yourself.

And today we've got a high school student, Gus Samuel. Please stand up, Gus. Gus is here, because he is a living example of what I'm talking about. This guy goes to high school, and yet he is active in the Salvation Army and he finds time to work with youngsters in the Girls and Boys Club.

Our society can be changed one heart, one soul, one conscience at a time. And it's the gathering momentum of millions of acts of kindness, because of guys like Gus, that we will show the world the true heart of America. And we will stand squarely in the face of the evil ones who did not understand who they were attacking.

Out of the evil will come a more lasting peace if we're tough and firm. And out of the evil will come a new renewal of heart in the greatest land on the face of the earth.

May God bless you all, and may God bless America. Thank you all. (Applause.)

For additional analytical, business and investment opportunities information,
please contact Global Investment & Business Center, USA
at (202) 546-2103. Fax: (202) 546-3275. E-mail: rusric@erols.com

BASIC EXECUTIVE ORDERS, LEGISLATION AND REGULATIONS AND OFFICIAL STATEMENTS

MESSAGE TO THE CONGRESS OF THE UNITED STATES

TO THE CONGRESS OF THE UNITED STATES:

I hereby transmit to the Congress proposed legislation to create a new Cabinet Department of Homeland Security.

Our Nation faces a new and changing threat unlike any we have faced before -- the global threat of terrorism. No nation is immune, and all nations must act decisively to protect against this constantly evolving threat.

We must recognize that the threat of terrorism is a permanent condition, and we must take action to protect America against the terrorists that seek to kill the innocent.

Since September 11, 2001, all levels of government and leaders from across the political spectrum have cooperated like never before. We have strengthened our aviation security and tightened our borders. We have stockpiled medicines to defend against bioterrorism and improved our ability to combat weapons of mass destruction. We have dramatically improved information sharing among our intelligence agencies, and we have taken new steps to protect our critical infrastructure.

Our Nation is stronger and better prepared today than it was on September 11. Yet, we can do better. I propose the most extensive reorganization of the Federal Government since the 1940s by creating a new Department of Homeland Security. For the first time we would have a single Department whose primary mission is to secure our homeland. Soon after the Second World War, President Harry Truman recognized that our Nation's fragmented military defenses needed reorganization to help win the Cold War. President Truman proposed uniting our military forces under a single entity, now the Department of Defense, and creating the National Security Council to bring together defense, intelligence, and diplomacy. President Truman's reforms are still helping us to fight terror abroad, and today we need similar dramatic reforms to secure our people at home.

President Truman and Congress reorganized our Government to meet a very visible enemy in the Cold War. Today our Nation must once again reorganize our Government to protect against an often-invisible enemy, an enemy that hides in the shadows and an enemy that can strike with many different types of weapons. Our enemies seek to obtain the most dangerous and deadly weapons of mass destruction and use them against the innocent. While we are winning the war on terrorism, Al Qaeda and other terrorist organizations still have thousands of trained killers spread across the globe plotting attacks against America and the other nations of the civilized world.

Immediately after last fall's attack, I used my legal authority to establish the White House Office of Homeland Security and the Homeland Security Council to help ensure that our Federal response and protection efforts were coordinated and effective. I also directed Homeland Security Advisor Tom Ridge to study the Federal Government as a whole to determine if the current structure allows us to meet the threats of today while preparing for the unknown threats of tomorrow. After careful study of the current structure, coupled with the experience gained since September 11 and new have concluded that our Nation needs a more unified homeland security structure.

I propose to create a new Department of Homeland Security by substantially transforming the current confusing patchwork of government activities into a single department whose primary mission is to secure our homeland. My proposal builds on the strong bipartisan work on the issue of homeland security that has been conducted by Members of Congress. In designing the new Department, my Administration considered a number of homeland security organizational proposals that have emerged from outside studies, commissions, and Members of Congress.

The Need for a Department of Homeland Security

Today no Federal Government agency has homeland security as its primary mission. Responsibilities for homeland security are dispersed among more than 100 different entities of the Federal Government-. America needs a unified homeland security structure that will improve protection against today's threats and be flexible enough to help meet the unknown threats of the future.

The mission of the new Department would be to prevent terrorist attacks within the United States, to reduce America's vulnerability to terrorism, and to minimize the damage and recover from attacks that may occur. The Department of Homeland Security would mobilize and focus the resources of the Federal Government, State and local governments, the private sector, and the American people to accomplish its mission.

The Department of Homeland Security would make Americans safer because for the first time we would have one department dedicated to securing the homeland. One department would secure our borders, transportation sector, ports, and critical infrastructure. One department would analyze homeland security intelligence from multiple sources, synthesize it with a comprehensive assessment of America's vulnerabilities, and take action to secure our highest risk facilities and systems. One department would coordinate communications with State and local governments, private industry, and the American people about threats and preparedness. One department would coordinate our efforts to secure the American people against bioterrorism and other weapons of mass destruction. One department would help train and equip our first responders. One department would manage Federal emergency response activities.

Our goal is not to expand Government, but to create an agile organization that takes advantage of modern technology and management techniques to meet a new and constantly evolving threat. We can improve our homeland security by minimizing the duplication of efforts, improving coordination, and combining functions that are currently fragmented and inefficient. The new Department would allow us to have more security officers in the field working to stop terrorists and fewer resources in Washington managing duplicative activities that drain critical homeland security resources.

The Department of Homeland Security would have a clear and efficient organizational structure with four main divisions: Border and Transportation Security; Emergency Preparedness and Response; Chemical, Biological, Radiological and Nuclear Countermeasures; and Information Analysis and Infrastructure Protection.

Border and Transportation Security

Terrorism is a global threat and we must improve our border security to help keep out those who mean to do us harm. We must closely monitor who is coming into and out of our country to help prevent foreign terrorists from entering our country and bringing in their instruments of terror. At the same time, we must expedite the legal flow of people and goods on which our economy depends. Securing our borders and controlling entry to the United States has always been the responsibility of the Federal Government. Yet, this responsibility and the security of our transportation systems is now dispersed among several major Government organizations. Under my proposed legislation, the Department of Homeland Security would unify authority over major Federal security operations related to our borders, territorial waters, and transportation systems.

The Department would assume responsibility for the United States Coast Guard, the United States Customs Service, the Immigration and Naturalization Service (including the Border Patrol), the Animal and Plant Health Inspection Service, and the Transportation Security Administration. The Secretary of Homeland Security would have the authority to administer and enforce all immigration and nationality laws, including the visa issuance functions of consular officers. As a result, the Department would have sole responsibility for managing entry into the United States and protecting our transportation infrastructure. It would ensure that all aspects of border control, including the issuing of visas, are informed by a central information-sharing clearinghouse and compatible databases.

Emergency Preparedness and Response

Although our top priority is preventing future attacks, we must also prepare to minimize the damage and recover from attacks that may occur.

My legislative proposal requires the Department of Homeland Security to ensure the preparedness of our Nation's emergency response professionals, provide the Federal Government's response, and aid America's recovery from terrorist attacks and natural disasters. To fulfill these missions, the Department of Homeland Security would incorporate the Federal Emergency Management Agency (FEMA) as one of its key components. The Department would administer the domestic disaster preparedness grant programs for firefighters, police, and emergency personnel currently managed by FEMA, the Department of Justice, and the Department of Health and Human Services. In responding to an incident, the Department would manage such critical response assets as the Nuclear Emergency Search Team (from the Department of Energy) and the National Pharmaceutical Stockpile (from the Department of Health and Human Services). Finally, the Department of Homeland Security would integrate the Federal interagency emergency response plans into a single, comprehensive, Government-wide plan, and would work to ensure that all response personnel have the equipment and capability to communicate with each other as necessary.

Chemical, Biological, Radiological, and Nuclear Countermeasures

Our enemies today seek to acquire and use the most deadly weapons known to mankind -- chemical, biological, radiological, and nuclear weapons.

The new Department of Homeland Security would lead the Federal Government's efforts in preparing for and responding to the full range of terrorist threats involving weapons of mass destruction. The Department would set national policy and establish guidelines for State and local governments. The Department would direct exercises for Federal, State, and local chemical, biological, radiological, and nuclear attack response teams and plans. The Department would consolidate and synchronize the disparate efforts of multiple Federal agencies now scattered across several departments. This would create a single office whose primary mission is the critical task of securing the United States from catastrophic terrorism.

The Department would improve America's ability to develop diagnostics, vaccines, antibodies, antidotes, and other countermeasures against new weapons. It would consolidate and prioritize the disparate homeland security-related research and development programs currently scattered throughout the executive branch, and the Department would assist State and local public safety agencies by evaluating equipment and setting standards.

Information Analysis and Infrastructure Protection

For the first time the Government would have under one roof the capability to identify and assess threats to the homeland, map those threats against our vulnerabilities, issue timely warnings, and take action to help secure the homeland.

The Information Analysis and Infrastructure Protection division of the new Department of Homeland Security would complement the reforms on intelligence-gathering and information-sharing already underway at the FBI and the CIA. The Department would analyze information and intelligence from the FBI, CIA, and many other Federal agencies to better understand the terrorist threat to the American homeland.

The Department would comprehensively assess the vulnerability of America's key assets and critical infrastructures, including food and water systems, agriculture, health systems and emergency services, information and telecommunications, banking and finance, energy, transportation, the chemical and defense industries, postal and shipping entities, and national monuments and icons. The Department would integrate its own and others' threat analyses with its comprehensive vulnerability assessment to identify protective priorities and support protective steps to be taken by the Department, other Federal departments and agencies, State and local agencies, and the private sector. Working closely with State and local officials, other Federal agencies, and the private sector, the Department would help ensure that proper steps are taken to protect high-risk potential targets.

Other Components

In addition to these four core divisions, the submitted legislation would also transfer responsibility for the Secret Service to the Department of Homeland Security. The Secret Service, which would report directly to the Secretary of Homeland Security, would retain its primary mission to protect the President and other Government leaders. The Secret Service would, however, contribute its specialized protective expertise to the fulfillment of the Department's core mission.

Finally, under my legislation, the Department of Homeland Security would consolidate and streamline relations with the Federal Government for America's State and local governments.

The new Department would contain an intergovernmental affairs office to coordinate Federal homeland security programs with State and local officials. It would give State and local officials one primary contact instead of many when it comes to matters related to training, equipment, planning, and other critical needs such as emergency response.

The consolidation of the Government's homeland security efforts as outlined in my proposed legislation can achieve great efficiencies that further enhance our security. Yet, to achieve these efficiencies, the new Secretary of Homeland Security would require considerable flexibility in procurement, integration of information technology systems, and personnel issues. My proposed legislation provides the Secretary of Homeland Security with just such flexibility and managerial authorities. I call upon the Congress to implement these measures in order to ensure that we are maximizing our ability to secure our homeland.

Continued Interagency Coordination at the White House

Even with the creation of the new Department, there will remain a strong need for a White House Office of Homeland Security. Protecting America from terrorism will remain a multi-departmental issue and will continue to require interagency coordination. Presidents will continue to require the confidential advice of a Homeland Security Advisor, and I intend for the White House Office of Homeland Security and the Homeland Security Council to maintain a strong role in coordinating our government-wide efforts to secure the homeland.

The Lessons of History

History teaches us that new challenges require new organizational structures. History also teaches us that critical security challenges require clear lines of responsibility and the unified effort of the U.S. Government.

President Truman said, looking at the lessons of the Second World War: "It is now time to discard obsolete organizational forms, and to provide for the future the soundest, the most effective, and the most economical kind of structure for our armed forces." When skeptics told President Truman that this proposed reorganization was too ambitious to be enacted, he simply replied that it had to be. In the years to follow, the Congress acted upon President Truman's recommendation, eventually laying a sound organizational foundation that enabled the United States to win the Cold War. All Americans today enjoy the inheritance of this landmark organizational reform: a unified Department of Defense that has become the most powerful force for freedom the world has ever seen.

Today America faces a threat that is wholly different from the threat we faced during the Cold War. Our terrorist enemies hide in shadows and attack civilians with whatever means of destruction they can access. But as in the Cold War, meeting this threat requires clear lines of responsibility and the unified efforts of government at all levels -- Federal, State, local, and tribal -- the private sector, and all Americans. America needs a homeland security establishment that can help prevent catastrophic attacks and mobilize national resources for an enduring conflict while protecting our Nation's values and liberties.

Years from today, our world will still be fighting the threat of terrorism. It is my hope that future generations will be able to look back on the Homeland Security Act of 2002 -- as we now remember the National Security Act of 1947 -- as the solid organizational foundation for America's triumph in a long and difficult struggle against a formidable enemy.

History has given our Nation new challenges -- and important new assignments. Only the United States Congress can create a new department of Government. We face an urgent need, and I am pleased that Congress has responded to my call to act before the end of the current congressional session with the same bipartisan spirit that allowed us to act expeditiously on legislation after September 11.

These are times that demand bipartisan action and bipartisan solutions to meet the new and changing threats we face as a Nation. I urge the Congress to join me in creating a single, permanent department with an overriding and urgent mission -- securing the homeland of America and protecting the American people. Together we can meet this ambitious deadline and help ensure that the American homeland is secure against the terrorist threat.

GEORGE W. BUSH
THE WHITE HOUSE,
June 18, 2002.

EXECUTIVE ORDER, FEBRUARY 28, 2003

The White House
Office of the Press Secretary
February 28, 2003
For Immediate Release

For additional analytical, business and investment opportunities information, please contact Global Investment & Business Center, USA at (202) 546-2103. Fax: (202) 546-3275. E-mail: rusric@erols.com

Executive Order

By the authority vested in me as President by the Constitution and the laws of the United States of America, including the Homeland Security Act of 2002 (Public Law 107-296) and section 301 of title 3, United States Code, and in order to reflect the transfer of certain functions to, and other responsibilities vested in, the Secretary of Homeland Security, the transfer of certain agencies and agency components to the Department of Homeland Security, and the delegation of appropriate responsibilities to the Secretary of Homeland Security, it is hereby ordered as follows:

Section 1. Executive Order 13276 of November 15, 2002 ("Delegation of Responsibilities Concerning Undocumented Aliens Interdicted or Intercepted in the Caribbean Region"), is amended by:

(a) striking "The Attorney General" wherever it appears in section 1 and inserting "The Secretary of Homeland Security" in lieu thereof; and

(b) striking "the Attorney General" wherever it appears in section 1 and inserting "the Secretary of Homeland Security" in lieu thereof.

Sec. 2. Executive Order 13274 of September 18, 2002 ("Environmental Stewardship and Transportation Infrastructure Project Reviews"), is amended by inserting "Secretary of Homeland Security," after "Secretary of Defense," in section 3(b).

Sec. 3. Executive Order 13271 of July 9, 2002 ("Establishment of the Corporate Fraud Task Force"), is amended by:

(a) inserting "(b) the Secretary of Homeland Security;" after "(a) the Secretary of the Treasury;" in section 4; and

(b) relettering the subsequent subsections in section 4 appropriately.

Sec. 4. Executive Order 13260 of March 19, 2002 ("Establishing the President's Homeland Security Advisory Council and Senior Advisory Committees for Homeland Security"), is amended by:

(a) striking "the Assistant to the President for Homeland Security (Assistant)" in section 1(c) and inserting "the Secretary of Homeland Security (Secretary)" in lieu thereof;

(b) striking "the Assistant" wherever it appears in sections 2 and 3 and inserting "the Secretary" in lieu thereof;

(c) striking "the Office of Administration" in section 3(d) and inserting "the Department of Homeland Security" in lieu thereof;

(d) striking "the Administrator of General Services" in section 4(a) and inserting "the Secretary of Homeland Security" in lieu thereof; and

(e) inserting "of General Services" after "Administrator" in section 4(a).

Executive Order 13260 of March 19, 2002, is hereby revoked effective as of March 31, 2003.

Sec. 5. Executive Order 13257 of February 13, 2002 ("President's Interagency Task Force to Monitor and Combat Trafficking in Persons"), is amended by:

(a) inserting "(v) the Secretary of Homeland Security;" after "(iv) the Secretary of Health and Human Services;" in section 1(b); and

(b) renumbering the subsequent subsections in section 1(b) appropriately.

Sec. 6. Executive Order 13254 of January 29, 2002 ("Establishing the USA Freedom Corps"), is amended by striking "Director of the Federal Emergency Management Agency;" in section 3(b)(viii) and inserting "Secretary of Homeland Security;" in lieu thereof.

Sec. 7. Executive Order 13231 of October 16, 2001 ("Critical Infrastructure Protection in the Information Age"), as amended, is further amended to read in its entirety as follows:

"Critical Infrastructure Protection in the Information Age

By the authority vested in me as President by the Constitution and the laws of the United States of America, and in order to ensure protection of information systems for critical infrastructure, including emergency preparedness communications and the physical assets that support such systems, in the information age, it is hereby ordered as follows:

Section 1. Policy. The information technology revolution has changed the way business is transacted, government operates, and national defense is conducted. Those three functions now depend on an interdependent network of critical information infrastructures. It is the policy of the United States to protect against disruption of the operation of information systems for critical infrastructure and thereby help to protect the people, economy, essential human and government services, and national security of the United States, and to ensure that any disruptions that occur are infrequent, of minimal duration, and manageable, and cause the least damage possible. The implementation of this policy shall include a voluntary public-private partnership, involving corporate and nongovernmental organizations.

Sec. 2. Continuing Authorities. This order does not alter the existing authorities or roles of United States Government departments and agencies. Authorities set forth in 44 U.S.C. chapter 35, and other applicable law, provide senior officials with responsibility for the security of Federal Government information systems.

(a) Executive Branch Information Systems Security. The Director of the Office of Management and Budget (OMB) has the responsibility to develop and oversee the implementation of government-wide policies, principles,

standards, and guidelines for the security of information systems that support the executive branch departments and

agencies, except those noted in section 2(b) of this order. The Director of OMB shall advise the President and the appropriate department or agency head when there is a critical deficiency in the security practices within the purview of this section in an executive branch department or agency.

(b) National Security Information Systems. The Secretary of Defense and the Director of Central Intelligence (DCI) shall have responsibility to oversee, develop, and ensure implementation of policies, principles, standards, and guidelines for the security of information systems that support the operations under their respective control. In consultation with the Assistant to the President for National Security Affairs and the affected departments and agencies, the Secretary of Defense and the DCI shall develop policies, principles, standards, and guidelines for the security of national security information systems that support the operations of other executive branch departments and agencies with national security information.

(i) Policies, principles, standards, and guidelines developed under this subsection may require more stringent protection than those developed in accordance with section 2(a) of this order.

(ii) The Assistant to the President for National Security Affairs shall advise the President and the appropriate department or agency when there is a critical deficiency in the security practices of a department or agency within the purview of this section.

(iii) National Security Systems. The National Security Telecommunications and Information Systems Security Committee, as established by and consistent with NSD-42 and chaired by the Department of Defense, shall be designated as the "Committee on National Security Systems."

(c) Additional Responsibilities. The heads of executive branch departments and agencies are responsible and accountable for providing and maintaining adequate levels of security for information systems, including emergency preparedness communications systems, for programs under their control. Heads of such departments and agencies shall ensure the development and, within available appropriations, funding of programs that adequately address these mission systems, especially those critical systems that support the national security and other essential government programs. Additionally, security should enable, and not unnecessarily impede, department and agency business operations.

Sec. 3. The National Infrastructure Advisory Council. The National
Infrastructure Advisory Council (NIAC), established on October 16, 2001, shall provide the President through the Secretary of Homeland Security with advice on the security of

information systems for critical infrastructure supporting other sectors of the economy: banking and finance, transportation, energy, manufacturing, and emergency government services.

(a) Membership. The NIAC shall be composed of not more than 30 members appointed by the President. The members of the NIAC shall be selected from the private sector, academia, and State and local government. Members of the NIAC shall have expertise relevant to the functions of the NIAC and generally shall be selected from industry Chief Executive Officers (and equivalently ranked leaders of other organizations) with responsibilities for security of information infrastructure supporting the critical sectors of the economy, including banking and finance, transportation, energy, communications, and emergency government services. Members shall not be full-time officials or employees of the executive branch of the Federal Government. The President shall designate a Chair and Vice Chair from among the members of the NIAC.

(b) Functions of the NIAC. The NIAC will meet periodically to:

(i) enhance the partnership of the public and private sectors in protecting information systems for critical infrastructures and provide reports on this issue to the Secretary of Homeland Security, as appropriate;

(ii) propose and develop ways to encourage private industry to perform periodic risk assessments of critical information and telecommunications systems;

(iii) monitor the development of private sector Information Sharing and Analysis Centers (ISACs) and provide recommendations to the President through the Secretary of Homeland Security on how these organizations can best foster improved cooperation among the ISACs, the Department of Homeland Security, and other Federal Government entities;

(iv) report to the President through the Secretary of Homeland Security, who shall ensure appropriate coordination with the Assistant to the President for Homeland Security, the Assistant to the President for Economic Policy, and the Assistant to the President for National Security Affairs under the terms of this order; and

(v) advise lead agencies with critical infrastructure responsibilities, sector coordinators, the Department of Homeland Security, and the ISACs.

(c) Administration of the NIAC.

(i) The NIAC may hold hearings, conduct inquiries, and establish subcommittees, as appropriate.

(ii) Upon request of the Chair, and to the extent permitted by law, the heads of the executive departments and agencies shall provide the NIAC with information and advice relating to its functions.

(iii) Senior Federal Government officials may participate in the meetings of the NIAC, as appropriate.

(iv) Members shall serve without compensation for their work on the NIAC. However, members may be reimbursed for travel expenses, including per diem in lieu of subsistence, as authorized by law for persons serving intermittently in Federal Government service (5 U.S.C. 5701-5707).

(v) To the extent permitted by law and subject to the availability of appropriations, the Department of Homeland Security shall provide the NIAC with administrative services, staff, and other support services, and such funds as may be necessary for the performance of the NIAC's functions.

(d) General Provisions.

(i) Insofar as the Federal Advisory Committee Act, as amended (5 U.S.C. App.) (Act), may apply to the NIAC, the functions of the President under that Act, except that of reporting to the Congress, shall be performed by the Department of Homeland Security in accordance with the guidelines and procedures established by the Administrator of General Services.

(ii) The NIAC shall terminate on October 15, 2003, unless extended by the President.

(iii) Executive Order 13130 of July 14, 1999, was revoked on October 16, 2001.

(iv) Nothing in this order shall supersede any requirement made by or under law.

Sec. 4. Judicial Review. This order does not create any right or benefit, substantive or procedural, enforceable at law or in equity, against the United States, its departments, agencies, or other entities, its officers or employees, or any other person."

Sec. 8. Executive Order 13228 of October 8, 2001 ("Establishing the Office of Homeland Security and the Homeland Security Council"), as amended, is further amended by:

(a) amending section 3(g) to read "(g) **Incident Management.** Consistent with applicable law, including the statutory functions of the Secretary of Homeland Security, the Assistant to the President for Homeland Security shall be the official primarily responsible for advising and assisting the President in the coordination of domestic incident management activities of all departments and agencies in the event of a terrorist threat, and during and in the aftermath of terrorist attacks, major disasters, or other emergencies, within the United States. Generally, the Assistant to the President for Homeland Security shall serve as the principal point of contact for and to the President with respect to the coordination of such activities. The Assistant to the President for Homeland Security shall coordinate with the Assistant to the President for National Security Affairs, as appropriate."; and

(b) inserting ", including the Department of Homeland Security" after "Government departments and agencies" in section 7.

Sec. 9. Executive Order 13223 of September 14, 2001 ("Ordering the Ready Reserve of the Armed Forces to Active Duty and Delegating Certain Authorities to the Secretary of Defense and the Secretary of Transportation"), as amended, is further amended by:

(a) striking "the Secretary of Transportation" in the title and wherever it appears in sections 1, 5, 6, and 7, and inserting "the Secretary of Homeland Security" in lieu thereof; and

(b) striking "the Department of Transportation" in section 7 and inserting "the Department of Homeland Security" in lieu thereof.

Sec. 10. Executive Order 13212 of May 18, 2001 ("Actions to Expedite Energy-Related Projects"), is amended by inserting "Homeland Security," after "Veterans Affairs," in section 3.

Sec. 11. Executive Order 13165 of August 9, 2000 ("Creation of the White House Task Force on Drug Use in Sports and Authorization for the Director of the Office of National Drug Control Policy to Serve as the United States Government's Representative on the Board of the World Anti-Doping Agency"), is amended by inserting "the Department of Homeland Security," after "the Department of Transportation," in section 2.

Sec. 12. Executive Order 13154 of May 3, 2000 ("Establishing the Kosovo Campaign Medal"), is amended by striking "the Secretary of Transportation" in section 1 and inserting "the Secretary of Homeland Security" in lieu thereof.

Sec. 13. Executive Order 13133 of August 5, 1999 ("Working Group on Unlawful Conduct on the Internet"), is amended by:

(a) inserting "(6) The Secretary of Homeland Security." after "(5) The Secretary of Education." in section 3(a); and

(b) renumbering the subsequent subsections in section 3(a) appropriately.

Sec. 14. Executive Order 13120 of April 27, 1999 ("Ordering the Selected Reserve and Certain Individual Ready Reserve Members of the Armed Forces to Active Duty"), is amended by striking "the Secretary of Transportation" and inserting "the Secretary of Homeland Security" in lieu thereof.

Sec. 15. Executive Order 13112 of February 3, 1999 ("Invasive Species"), is amended by inserting "the Secretary of Homeland Security," after "Secretary of Transportation," in section 3(a).

Sec. 16. Executive Order 13100 of August 25, 1998 ("President's Council on Food Safety"), is amended by inserting "and Homeland Security," after "Health and Human Services," in section 1(a).

Sec. 17. Executive Order 13076 of February 24, 1998 ("Ordering the Selected Reserve of the Armed Forces to Active Duty"), is amended by striking "the Secretary of Transportation" and inserting "the Secretary of Homeland Security" in lieu thereof.

Sec. 18. Executive Order 13011 of July 16, 1996 ("Federal Information Technology"), as amended, is further amended by:

(a) striking "17. Federal Emergency Management Agency;" in section 3(b); and

(b) renumbering the subsequent subsections in section 3(b) appropriately.

Sec. 19. Executive Order 12989 of February 13, 1996 ("Economy and Efficiency in Government Procurement through Compliance with Certain Immigration and Naturalization Act Provisions"), is amended by:

(a) striking "Naturalization" in the title and inserting "Nationality" in lieu thereof;

(b) striking ", the Attorney General" in section 3;

(c) inserting "the Secretary of Homeland Security"

before "may" in section 3(a);

(d) inserting "the Secretary of Homeland Security" before "shall" in section 3(b);

(e) inserting "the Attorney General" before "shall" in section 3(c);

(f) inserting "Secretary of Homeland Security or the" before "Attorney General" wherever it appears in section 4;

(g) striking "The Attorney General's" in section 4(b) and inserting "Such" in lieu thereof;

(h) striking "the Attorney General" wherever it appears in the first two sentences of section 5(a) and inserting "the Secretary of Homeland Security and Attorney General" in lieu thereof;

(i) striking "the responsibilities of the Attorney General" in section 5(a) and inserting "their respective responsibilities" in lieu thereof;

(j) inserting "Secretary of Homeland Security or the" before "Attorney General" wherever in appears in the third sentence of section 5(a);

(k) inserting "Secretary of Homeland Security and the" before "Attorney General" in section 6;

(l) striking "the Attorney General's" in section 6 and inserting "their respective" in lieu thereof; and

(m) inserting "Secretary of Homeland Security, the" before "Attorney General" in section 7.

Sec. 20. Executive Order 12985 of January 11, 1996 ("Establishing the Armed Forces Service Medal"), is amended by striking "the Secretary of Transportation" in section 2 and inserting "the Secretary of Homeland Security" in lieu thereof.

Sec. 21. Executive Order 12982 of December 8, 1995 ("Ordering the Selected Reserve of the Armed Forces to Active Duty"), is amended by striking "the Secretary of Transportation" and inserting "the Secretary of Homeland Security" in lieu thereof.

Sec. 22. Executive Order 12978 of October 21, 1995 ("Blocking Assets and Prohibiting Transactions with Significant Narcotics Traffickers"), is amended by inserting ", the Secretary of Homeland Security," after "the Attorney General" wherever it appears in sections 1 and 4.

Sec. 23. Executive Order 12977 of October 19, 1995 ("Interagency Security Committee"), is amended by:

(a) striking "the Administrator of General Services ("Administrator")" in section 1(a) and inserting "the Secretary of Homeland Security ("Secretary")" in lieu thereof;

(b) striking "and" after "(16) Central Intelligence Agency;" in section 1(b);

(c) inserting "and (18) General Services Administration;" after "(17) Office of Management and Budget;" in section 1(b);

(d) striking section 1(c)(2) and redesignating sections 1(c)(3) and 1(c)(4) as sections 1(c)(2) and 1(c)(3), respectively;

(e) striking "Administrator" wherever it appears in sections 2, 5(a)(3)(E), 6(a), and 6(c), and inserting "Secretary" in lieu thereof; and

(f) striking ", acting by and through the Assistant Commissioner," in section 6(c).

Sec. 24. Executive Order 12919 of June 3, 1994 ("National Defense Industrial Resources Preparedness"), is amended by:

(a) striking "The Director, Federal Emergency Management Agency ("Director, FEMA")" in section 104(b) and inserting "The Secretary of Homeland Security ("the Secretary")" in lieu thereof;

(b) striking "The Director, FEMA," in sections 201(c) and 601(f) and inserting "The Secretary" in lieu thereof;

(c) striking "the Director, FEMA," wherever it appears in sections 201(e), 202(c), 305, 501, 701(e), and 802(e), and inserting "the Secretary" in lieu thereof; and

(d) inserting "the Department of Homeland Security," after "Attorney General," in section 801.

Sec. 25. Executive Order 12906 of April 11, 1994 ("Coordinating Geographic Data Acquisition and Access: The National Spatial Data Infrastructure"), is amended by:

(a) striking "and" in section 7(b)(ii);

(b) striking the period at the end of section 7(b)(iii) and inserting "; and" in lieu thereof; and

(c) inserting a new section 7(b)(iv) to read "(iv) the national security-related activities of the Department of Homeland Security as determined by the Secretary of Homeland Security.".

Sec. 26. Executive Order 12870 of September 30, 1993 ("Trade Promotion Coordinating Committee"), is amended by:

(a) inserting "(j) Department of Homeland Security;" after "(i) Department of the Interior;" in section 1; and

(b) relettering the subsequent subsections in section 1 appropriately.

Sec. 27. Executive Order 12835 of January 25, 1993 ("Establishment of the National Economic Council"), is amended by:

(a) inserting "(k) Secretary of Homeland Security;" after "(j) Secretary of Energy;" in section 2; and

(b) relettering the subsequent subsections in section 2 appropriately.

Sec. 28. Executive Order 12830 of January 9, 1993 ("Establishing the Military Outstanding Volunteer Service Medal"), is amended by striking "the Secretary of Transportation" wherever it appears and inserting "the Secretary of Homeland Security" in lieu thereof.

Sec. 29. Executive Order 12824 of December 7, 1992 ("Establishing the Transportation Distinguished Service Medal"), is amended by:

(a) striking "Transportation" in the title and inserting "Homeland Security" in lieu thereof; and

(b) striking "Transportation" wherever it appears and inserting "Homeland Security" in lieu thereof.

Sec. 30. Executive Order 12807 of May 24, 1992 ("Interdiction of Illegal Aliens"), is amended by striking "the Attorney General" in section 2(c)(3) and inserting "the Secretary of Homeland Security" in lieu thereof.

Sec. 31. Executive Order 12793 of March 20, 1992 ("Continuing the Presidential Service Certificate and Presidential Service Badge"), is amended by striking "the Secretary of Transportation" in section 1 and inserting "the Secretary of Homeland Security" in lieu thereof.

Sec. 32. Executive Order 12789 of February 10, 1992 ("Delegation of Reporting Functions Under the Immigration Reform and Control Act of 1986"), is amended by striking "The Attorney

General" in section 1 and inserting "The Secretary of Homeland Security" in lieu thereof.

Sec. 33. Executive Order 12788 of January 15, 1992 ("Defense Economic Adjustment Program"), is amended by:

(a) inserting "(15) Secretary of Homeland Security;" after "(14) Secretary of Veterans Affairs;" in section 4(a); and

(b) renumbering the subsequent subsections in section 4(a) appropriately.

Sec. 34. Executive Order 12777 of October 18, 1991 ("Implementation of Section 311 of the Federal Water Pollution Control Act of October 18, 1972, as Amended, and the Oil Pollution Act of 1990"), is amended by:

(a) inserting "and the Secretary of the Department in which the Coast Guard is operating" after "the Secretary of Transportation" in sections 2(b)(2) and 2(d)(2);

(b) striking "the Secretary of Transportation" in section 2(e)(2) and wherever it appears in sections 5 and 8 and inserting "the Secretary of the Department in which the Coast Guard is operating" in lieu thereof; and

(c) inserting "the Secretary of the Department in which the Coast Guard is operating," after "Agriculture," in section 10(c).

Sec. 35. Executive Order 12743 of January 18, 1991 ("Ordering the Ready Reserve of the Armed Forces to Active Duty"), is amended by:

(a) striking "the Department of Transportation" in section 1 and inserting "the Department of Homeland Security" in lieu thereof; and

For additional analytical, business and investment opportunities information, please contact Global Investment & Business Center, USA at (202) 546-2103. Fax: (202) 546-3275. E-mail: rusric@erols.com

(b) striking "the Secretary of Transportation" in section 1 and inserting "the Secretary of Homeland Security" in lieu thereof.

Sec. 36. Executive Order 12742 of January 8, 1991

("National Security Industrial Responsiveness"), is amended by:

(a) inserting "Homeland Security," after "Transportation," in section 104(a); and

(b) striking "the Director of the Federal Emergency Management Agency" in section 104(d) and inserting "the Secretary of Homeland Security" in lieu thereof.

Sec. 37. Executive Order 12733 of November 13, 1990 ("Authorizing the Extension of the Period of Active Duty of Personnel of the Selected Reserve of the Armed Forces"), is amended by striking "the Secretary of Transportation" and inserting "the Secretary of Homeland Security" in lieu thereof.

Sec. 38. Executive Order 12728 of August 22, 1990 ("Delegating the President's Authority to Suspend any Provision of Law Relating to the Promotion, Retirement, or Separation of Members of the Armed Forces"), is amended by striking "the Secretary of Transportation" in sections 1 and 2 and inserting "the Secretary of Homeland Security" in lieu thereof.

Sec. 39. Executive Order 12727 of August 27, 1990 ("Ordering the Selected Reserve of the Armed Forces to Active Duty"), is amended by striking "the Secretary of Transportation" in section 1 and inserting "the Secretary of Homeland Security" in lieu thereof.

Sec. 40. Executive Order 12699 ("Seismic Safety of Federal and Federally Assisted or Regulated New Building Construction"), is amended by:

(a) striking "Federal Emergency Management Agency (FEMA)" in section 3(d) and inserting "Department of Homeland Security" in lieu thereof;

(b) striking "The Director of the Federal Emergency Management Agency" in section 4(a) and inserting "The Secretary of Homeland Security" in lieu thereof; and

(c) striking "The Federal Emergency Management Agency" and "The FEMA" in section 5 and inserting "The Department of Homeland Security" in lieu thereof (in both places).

Sec. 41. Executive Order 12657 of November 18, 1988 ("Federal Emergency Management Agency Assistance in Emergency Preparedness Planning at Commercial Nuclear Power Plants"), is amended by:

(a) striking "Federal Emergency Management Agency" in the title and inserting "Department of Homeland Security" in lieu thereof;

(b) striking "Federal Emergency Management Agency ("FEMA")" in section 1(b) and inserting "Department of Homeland Security ("DHS")" in lieu thereof;

(c) striking "FEMA" wherever it appears in sections 1(b), 2(b), 2(c), 3, 4, 5, and 6, and inserting "DHS" in lieu thereof; and

(d) striking "the Director of FEMA" in section 2(a) and inserting "the Secretary of Homeland Security" in lieu thereof.

Sec. 42. Executive Order 12656 of November 18, 1988 ("Assignment of Emergency Preparedness Responsibilities"), as amended, is further amended by:

(a) striking "The Director of the Federal Emergency Management Agency" wherever it appears in sections 104(c) and 1702 and inserting "The Secretary of Homeland Security" in lieu thereof;

(b) striking "the Director of the Federal Emergency Management Agency" wherever it appears in sections 104(c), 201(15), 301(9), 401(10), 501(4), 501(7), 502(7), 601(3), 701(5), 801(9), 1302(4), 1401(4), 1701, and 1801(b), and inserting "the Secretary of Homeland Security" in lieu thereof;

(c) striking "consistent with current National Security Council guidelines and policies" in section 201(15) and inserting "consistent with current Presidential guidelines and policies" in lieu thereof;

(d) striking "Secretary" in section 501(9) and inserting "Secretaries" in lieu thereof;

(e) inserting "and Homeland Security" after "Labor" in section 501(9);

(f) striking "and" after "State" in section 701(6) and inserting a comma in lieu thereof;

(g) inserting ", and Homeland Security" after "Defense" in section 701(6);

(h) striking "the Director of the Federal Emergency Management Agency," in section 701(6); and

(i) striking "Federal Emergency Management Agency" in the title of Part 17 and inserting "Department of Homeland Security" in lieu thereof.

Without prejudice to subsections (a) through (i) of this section, all responsibilities assigned to specific Federal officials pursuant to Executive Order 12656 that are substantially the same as any responsibility assigned to, or function transferred to, the Secretary of Homeland Security pursuant to the Homeland Security Act of 2002 (regardless of whether such responsibility or function is expressly required to be carried out through another official of the Department of Homeland Security or not pursuant to such Act), or intended or required to be carried out by an agency or an agency component transferred to the Department of Homeland Security pursuant to such Act, are hereby reassigned to the Secretary of Homeland Security.

Sec. 43. Executive Order 12580 of January 23, 1987 ("Superfund Implementation"), as amended, is further amended by:

(a) inserting "Department of Homeland Security," after Department of Energy," in section 1(a)(2); and

(b) striking "Federal Emergency Management Agency" in section 1(a)(2).

Sec. 44. Executive Order 12555 of November 15, 1985 ("Protection of Cultural Property"), as amended, is further amended by:

(a) striking "the Secretary of the Treasury" in sections 1, 2, and 3, and inserting "the Secretary of Homeland Security" in lieu thereof; and

(b) striking "The Department of the Treasury" in the heading of section 3 and inserting "The Department of Homeland Security" in lieu thereof.

Sec. 45. Executive Order 12501 of January 28, 1985 ("Arctic Research"), is amended by:

(a) inserting "(i) Department of Homeland Security;" after "(h) Department of Health and Human Services;" in section 8; and

(b) relettering the subsequent subsections in section 8 appropriately.

Sec. 46. Executive Order 12472 of April 3, 1984 ("Assignment of National Security and Emergency Preparedness Telecommunications Functions"), is amended by:

(a) inserting "the Homeland Security Council," after "National Security Council," in sections 1(b), 1(e)(4), 1(f)(3), and 2(c)(4);

(b) striking "The Secretary of Defense" in section 1(e) and inserting "The Secretary of Homeland Security" in lieu thereof;

(c) striking "Federal Emergency Management Agency" in sections 1(e)(3) and 3(j) and inserting "Department of Homeland Security" in lieu thereof;

(d) inserting ", in consultation with the Homeland Security Council," after "National Security Council" in section 2(b)(1);

(e) inserting ", the Homeland Security Council," after "National Security Council" in sections 2(d) and 2(e);

(f) striking "the Director of the Federal Emergency Management Agency" in section 2(d)(1) and inserting "the Secretary of Homeland Security" in lieu thereof;

(g) striking "Federal Emergency Management Agency. The Director of the Federal Emergency Management Agency shall:" in section 3(b) and inserting "Department of Homeland Security. The Secretary of Homeland Security shall:" in lieu thereof; and

(h) adding at the end of section 3(d) the following new paragraph: "(3) Nothing in this order shall be construed to impair or otherwise affect the authority of the Secretary of Defense with respect to the Department of Defense, including the chain of command for the armed forces of the United States under

section 162(b) of title 10, United States Code, and the authority of the Secretary of Defense with respect to the Department of Defense under section 113(b) of that title.".

Sec. 47. Executive Order 12382 of September 13, 1982 ("President's National Security Telecommunications Advisory Committee"), as amended, is further amended by:

(a) inserting "through the Secretary of Homeland Security," after "the President," in sections 2(a) and 2(b);

(b) striking "and to the Secretary of Defense" in section 2(e) and inserting ", through the Secretary of Homeland Security," in lieu thereof; and

(c) striking "the Secretary of Defense" in sections 3(c) and 4(a) and inserting "the Secretary of Homeland Security" in lieu thereof.

Sec. 48. Executive Order 12341 of January 21, 1982 ("Cuban and Haitian Entrants"), is amended by:

(a) striking "The Attorney General" in section 2 and inserting "The Secretary of Homeland Security" in lieu thereof; and

(b) striking "the Attorney General" in section 2 and inserting "the Secretary of Homeland Security" in lieu thereof.

Sec. 49. Executive Order 12208 of April 15, 1980 ("Consultations on the Admission of Refugees"), as amended, is further amended by:

(a) striking "the following functions: (a) To" in section 1?101 and inserting "to" in lieu thereof;

(b) striking "the Attorney General" in section 1-101(a) and inserting "the Secretary of Homeland Security" in lieu thereof;

(c) striking sections 1-101(b) and 1-102; and

(d) redesignating sections 1-103 and 1-104 as sections 1-102 and 1-103, respectively.

Sec. 50. Executive Order 12188 of January 2, 1980 ("International Trade Functions"), as amended, is further amended by:

(a) inserting "(12) The Secretary of Homeland Security" after "(11) The Secretary of Energy" in section 1-102(b); and

(b) renumbering the subsequent subsections in section 1?102(b) appropriately.

Sec. 51. Executive Order 12160 of September 26, 1979 ("Providing for Enhancement and Coordination of Federal Consumer Programs"), as amended, is further amended by:

(a) inserting "(m) Department of Homeland Security." after "(l) Department of the Treasury." in section 1-102;

(b) striking "(s) Federal Emergency Management Agency." in section 1-102; and

(c) relettering the subsequent subsections in section 1-102 appropriately.

Sec. 52. Executive Order 12148 of July 20, 1979 ("Federal Emergency Management"), as amended, is further amended by:

(a) striking "the Federal Emergency Management Agency" whenever it appears and inserting "the Department of Homeland Security" in lieu thereof; and

(b) striking "the Director of the Federal Emergency Management Agency" wherever it appears and inserting "the Secretary of Homeland Security" in lieu thereof.

Sec. 53. Executive Order 12146 of July 18, 1979 ("Management of Federal Legal Resources"), as amended, is further amended by:

(a) striking "15" in section 1-101 and inserting "16" in lieu thereof;

(b) inserting "(n) The Department of Homeland Security." after "(m) The Department of the Treasury." in section 1-102; and

(c) relettering the subsequent subsections in section 1-102 appropriately.

Sec. 54. Executive Order 12002 of July 7, 1977 ("Administration of Export Controls"), as amended, is further amended by inserting ", the Secretary of Homeland Security," after "The Secretary of Energy" in section 3.

Sec. 55. Executive Order 11965 of January 19, 1977 ("Establishing the Humanitarian Service Medal"), is amended by striking "the Secretary of Transportation" wherever it appears in sections 1, 2, and 4, and inserting "the Secretary of Homeland Security" in lieu thereof.

Sec. 56. Executive Order 11926 of July 19, 1976 ("The Vice Presidential Service Badge"), is amended by striking "the Secretary of Transportation" in section 2 and inserting "the Secretary of Homeland Security" in lieu thereof.

Sec. 57. Executive Order 11858 of May 7, 1975 ("Foreign Investment in the United States"), as amended, is further amended by:

(a) inserting "(8) The Secretary of Homeland Security." after "(7) The Attorney General." in section 1(a); and

(b) redesignating subsection (8) as subsection (9) in section 1(a).

Sec. 58. Executive Order 11800 of August 17, 1974 ("Delegating Certain Authority Vested in the President by the Aviation Career Incentive Act of 1974"), as amended, is further amended by striking "the Secretary of Transportation" in section 1 and inserting "the Secretary of Homeland Security" in lieu thereof.

Sec. 59. Executive Order 11645 of February 8, 1972 ("Authority of the Secretary of Transportation to Prescribe Certain Regulations Relating to Coast Guard Housing"), is amended by striking "the Secretary of Transportation" in the title and in sections 1 and 2 and inserting "the Secretary of Homeland Security" in lieu thereof.

Sec. 60. Executive Order 11623 of October 12, 1971 ("Delegating to the Director of Selective Service Authority to Issue Rules and Regulations under the Military Selective Service Act"), as amended, is further amended by:

(a) striking "the Secretary of Transportation" in section 2(a) and inserting "the Secretary of Homeland Security" in lieu thereof; and

(b) striking "the Department of Transportation" in section 2(a) and inserting "the Department of Homeland Security" in lieu thereof.

Sec. 61. Executive Order 11448 of January 16, 1969 ("Establishing the Meritorious Service Medal"), as amended, is further amended by striking "the Secretary of Transportation" in section 1 and inserting "the Secretary of Homeland Security" in lieu thereof.

Sec. 62. Executive Order 11446 of January 16, 1969 ("Authorizing the Acceptance of Service Medals and Ribbons from Multilateral Organizations Other Than the United Nations"), is amended by striking "the Secretary of Transportation" and inserting "the Secretary of Homeland Security" in lieu thereof.

Sec. 63. Executive Order 11438 of December 3, 1968 ("Prescribing Procedures Governing Interdepartmental Cash Awards to the Members of the Armed Forces"), as amended, is further amended by:

(a) striking "the Secretary of Transportation" in sections 1 and 2 and inserting "the Secretary of Homeland Security" in lieu thereof; and

(b) striking "the Department of Transportation" wherever it appears in sections 2 and 4 and inserting "the Department of Homeland Security" in lieu thereof.

Sec. 64. Executive Order 11366 of August 4, 1967 ("Assigning Authority to Order Certain Persons in the Ready Reserve to Active Duty"), is amended by striking "The Secretary of Transportation" in sections 2 and 3(b) and inserting "The Secretary of Homeland Security" in lieu thereof.

Sec. 65. Executive Order 11239 of July 31, 1965 ("Enforcement of the Convention for Safety of Life at Sea, 1960"), as amended, is further amended, without prejudice to section 1-106 of Executive Order 12234 of September 3, 1980 ("Enforcement of the Convention for the Safety of Life at Sea"), by:

(a) striking "the Secretary of Transportation" in sections 1, 3, and 4, and inserting "the Secretary of Homeland Security" in lieu thereof; and

(b) striking "The Secretary of Transportation" in sections 2 and 3 and inserting "The Secretary of Homeland Security" in lieu thereof.

Sec. 66. Executive Order 11231 of July 8, 1965 ("Establishing the Vietnam Service Medal"), as amended, is further amended by striking "the Secretary of Transportation" in section 1 and inserting "the Secretary of Homeland Security" in lieu thereof.

Sec. 67. Executive Order 11190 of December 29, 1964 ("Providing for the Screening of the Ready Reserve of the Armed Forces"), as amended, is further amended by striking "the Secretary of Transportation" in section 1 and inserting "the Secretary of Homeland Security" in lieu thereof.

Sec. 68. Executive Order 11139 of January 7, 1964 ("Authorizing Acceptance of the United Nations Medal and Service Ribbon"), is amended by striking "the Secretary of the Treasury" and inserting "the Secretary of Homeland Security" in lieu thereof.

Sec. 69. Executive Order 11079 of January 25, 1963 ("Providing for the Prescribing of Regulations under which Members of the Armed Forces and Others May Accept Fellowships, Scholarships or Grants"), as amended, is further amended by striking "the Secretary of Transportation" and inserting "the Secretary of Homeland Security" in lieu thereof.

Sec. 70. Executive Order 11046 of August 24, 1962 ("Authorizing Award of the Bronze Star Medal"), as amended, is further amended by striking "the Secretary of Transportation" in section 1 and inserting "the Secretary of Homeland Security" in lieu thereof.

Sec. 71. Executive Order 11016 of April 25, 1962 ("Authorizing Award of the Purple Heart"), as amended, is further amended by striking "the Secretary of Transportation"

in sections 1 and 2 and inserting "the Secretary of Homeland Security" in lieu thereof.

Sec. 72. Executive Order 10977 of December 4, 1961 ("Establishing the Armed Forces Expeditionary Medal"), as amended, is further amended by striking "the Secretary of Transportation" in section 2 and inserting "the Secretary of Homeland Security" in lieu thereof.

Sec. 73. Executive Order 10789 of November 14, 1958 ("Authorizing Agencies of the Government To Exercise Certain Contracting Authority in Connection With National-Defense Functions and Prescribing Regulations Governing the Exercise of Such Authority"), as amended, is further amended by:

(a) striking "The Federal Emergency Management Agency" in paragraph 21 and inserting "Department of Homeland Security" in lieu thereof; and

(b) inserting at the end thereof the following new Part:

"Part III -- Coordination with Other Authorities

25. After March 1, 2003, no executive department or agency shall exercise authority granted under paragraph 1A of this order with respect to any matter that has been, or could be, designated by the Secretary of Homeland Security as a qualified anti-terrorism technology as defined in section 865 of the Homeland Security Act of 2002, unless--

(a) in the case of the Department of Defense, the Secretary of Defense has, after consideration of the authority provided under subtitle G of title VIII of the Homeland Security Act of

2002, determined that the exercise of authority under this order is necessary for the timely and effective conduct of United States military or intelligence activities;

and

(b) in the case of any other executive department or agency that has authority under this order, (i) the Secretary of Homeland Security has advised whether the use of the authority provided under subtitle G of title VIII of the Homeland Security

Act of 2002 would be appropriate, and (ii) the Director of the Office and Management and Budget has approved the exercise of authority under this order.".

Sec. 74. Executive Order 10694 of January 10, 1957 ("Authorizing the Secretaries of the Army, Navy, and Air Force to Issue Citations in the Name of the President of the United States to Military and Naval Units for Outstanding Performance in Action"), is amended by adding at the end thereof the following new section: "5. The Secretary of the Department in which the Coast Guard is operating may exercise the same authority with respect to the Coast Guard under this order as the Secretary of the Navy may exercise with respect to the Navy and the Marine Corps under this order.".

Sec. 75. Executive Order 10637 of September 16, 1955 ("Delegating to the Secretary of the Treasury Certain Functions of the President Relating to the United States Coast Guard"), is amended by:

(a) striking "The Secretary of the Treasury" in sections 1 and 2 and inserting "The Secretary of Homeland Security" in lieu thereof;

(b) striking "the Secretary of the Treasury" in the title and in subsections 1(j), 1(k), and 5, and inserting "the Secretary of Homeland Security" in lieu thereof; and

(c) striking subsection 1(r) and redesignating subsection 1(s) as subsection 1(r).

Sec. 76. Executive Order 10631 of August 17, 1955 ("Code of Conduct for Members of the Armed Forces of the United States"), as amended, is further amended by: striking "the Secretary of Transportation" and inserting "the Secretary of Homeland Security" in lieu thereof.

Sec. 77. Executive Order 10554 of August 18, 1954 ("Delegating the Authority of the President to Prescribe Regulations Authorizing Occasions Upon Which the Uniform May Be Worn by Persons Who Have Served Honorably in the Armed Forces in Time of War"), is amended by striking "the Secretary of the Treasury" and inserting "the Secretary of Homeland Security" in lieu thereof.

Sec. 78. Executive Order 10499 of November 4, 1953 ("Delegating Functions Conferred Upon the President by Section 8 of the Uniformed Services Contingency Option Act of 1953"), as amended, is further amended by striking "the Treasury" in sections 1 and 2 and inserting "Homeland Security" in lieu thereof.

Sec. 79. Executive Order 10448 of April 22, 1953 ("Authorizing the National Defense Medal"), as amended, is further amended by striking "the Secretary of Transportation" in sections 1 and 2 and inserting "the Secretary of Homeland Security" in lieu thereof.

Sec. 80. Executive Order 10271 of July 7, 1951 ("Delegating the Authority of the President to Order Members and Units of Reserve Components of the Armed Forces into Active Federal service"), is amended by striking "the Secretary of the Treasury" and inserting "the Secretary of Homeland Security" in lieu thereof.

Sec. 81. Executive Order 10179 of November 8, 1950 ("Establishing the Korean Service Medal"), as amended, is further amended by striking "the Secretary of the Treasury" in sections 1 and 2 and inserting "the Secretary of Homeland Security" in lieu thereof.

Sec. 82. Executive Order 10163 of September 25, 1950 ("The Armed Forces Reserve Medal"), as amended, is further amended by striking "the Secretary of the Treasury" in sections 2 and 7 and inserting "the Secretary of Homeland Security" in lieu thereof.

Sec. 83. Executive Order 10113 of February 24, 1950 ("Delegating the Authority of the President to Prescribe Clothing Allowances, and Cash Allowances in lieu thereof, for Enlisted Men in the Armed Forces"), as amended, is further amended by striking "the Secretary of the Treasury" in sections 1 and 2 and inserting "the Secretary of Homeland Security" in lieu thereof.

Sec. 84. Executive Order 4601 of March 1, 1927 ("Distinguished Flying Cross"), as amended, is further amended by:

(a) striking "The Secretary of War, the Secretary of the Navy," in sections 2 and 12 and inserting "The Secretary of Defense" in lieu thereof; and

(b) striking "the Secretary of the Treasury" in sections 2 and 12 and inserting "the Secretary of Homeland Security" in lieu thereof.

Sec. 85. Designation as a Defense Agency of the United States.

I hereby designate the Department of Homeland Security as a defense agency of the United States for the purposes of chapter 17 of title 35 of the United States Code.

Sec. 86. Exception from the Provisions of the Government Employees Training Act.

Those elements of the Department of Homeland Security that are supervised by the Under Secretary of Homeland Security for

Information Analysis and Infrastructure Protection through the Department's Assistant Secretary for Information Analysis are, pursuant to section 4102(b)(1) of title 5, United States Code, and in the public interest, excepted from the following provisions of the Government Employees Training Act as codified in title 5: sections 4103(a)(1), 4108, 4115, 4117, and 4118, and that part of 4109(a) that provides "under the regulations prescribed under section 4118(a)(8) of this title and".

Sec. 87. Functions of Certain Officials in the Coast Guard.

The Commandant and the Assistant Commandant for Intelligence of the Coast Guard each shall be considered a "Senior Official of the Intelligence Community" for purposes of Executive Order 12333 of December 4, 1981, and all other relevant authorities.

Sec. 88. Order of Succession.

Subject to the provisions of subsection (b) of this section, the officers named in subsection (a) of this section, in the order listed, shall act as, and perform the functions and duties of, the office of Secretary of Homeland Security ("Secretary")

during any period in which the Secretary has died, resigned, or otherwise become unable to perform the functions and duties of the office of Secretary.

(a) Order of Succession.

(i) Deputy Secretary of Homeland Security;

(ii) Under Secretary for Border and Transportation Security;

(iii) Under Secretary for Emergency Preparedness and Response;

(iv) Under Secretary for Information Analysis and Infrastructure Protection;

(v) Under Secretary for Management;

(vi) Under Secretary for Science and Technology;

(vii) General Counsel; and

(viii) Assistant Secretaries in the Department in the order of their date of appointment as such.

(b) Exceptions.

(i) No individual who is serving in an office listed in subsection (a) in an acting capacity shall act as Secretary pursuant to this section.

(ii) Notwithstanding the provisions of this section, the President retains discretion, to the extent permitted by the Federal Vacancies Reform Act of 1998, 5 U.S.C. 3345 et seq., to depart from this order in designating an acting Secretary.

Sec. 89. Savings Provision.

Except as otherwise specifically provided above or in Executive Order 13284 of January 23, 2003 ("Amendment of Executive Orders, and Other Actions, in Connection With the Establishment of the Department of Homeland Security"), references in any prior Executive Order relating to an agency or an agency component that is transferred to the Department of Homeland Security ("the Department"), or relating to a function that is transferred to the Secretary of Homeland

Security, shall be deemed to refer, as appropriate, to the Department or its officers, employees, agents, organizational units, or functions.

Sec. 90. Nothing in this order shall be construed to impair or otherwise affect the authority of the Secretary of Defense with respect to the Department of Defense, including the chain of command for the armed forces of the United States under section 162(b) of title 10, United States Code, and the authority of the Secretary of Defense with respect to the Department of Defense under section 113(b) of that title.

Sec. 91. Nothing in this order shall be construed to limit or restrict the authorities of the Central Intelligence Agency and the Director of Central Intelligence pursuant to the National Security Act of 1947 and the CIA Act of 1949.

Sec. 92. This order shall become effective on March 1, 2003.

Sec. 93. This order does not create any right or benefit, substantive or procedural, enforceable at law or in equity, against the United States, its departments, agencies, or other entities, its officers or employees, or any other person.

GEORGE W. BUSH
THE WHITE HOUSE,
February 28, 2003.

HOMELAND SECURITY PRESIDENTIAL DIRECTIVE/HSPD-5

The White House
Office of the Press Secretary
February 28, 2003
For Immediate Release

Subject: Management of Domestic Incidents

Purpose

(1) To enhance the ability of the United States to manage domestic incidents by establishing a single, comprehensive national incident management system.

Definitions

(2) In this directive:

(a) the term "Secretary" means the Secretary of Homeland Security.

(b) the term "Federal departments and agencies" means those executive departments enumerated in 5 U.S.C. 101, together with the Department of Homeland Security; independent establishments as defined by 5 U.S.C. 104(1); government corporations as defined by 5 U.S.C. 103(1); and the United States Postal Service.

(c) the terms "State," "local," and the "United States" when it is used in a geographical sense, have the same meanings as used in the Homeland Security Act of 2002, Public Law 107 296.

Policy

(3) To prevent, prepare for, respond to, and recover from terrorist attacks, major disasters, and other emergencies, the United States Government shall establish a single, comprehensive approach to domestic incident management. The objective of the United States Government is to ensure that all levels of government across the Nation have the capability to work efficiently and effectively together, using a national approach to domestic incident management. In these efforts, with regard to domestic incidents, the United States Government treats crisis management and consequence management as a single, integrated function, rather than as two separate functions.

(4) The Secretary of Homeland Security is the principal Federal official for domestic incident management. Pursuant to the Homeland Security Act of 2002, the Secretary is responsible for coordinating Federal operations within the United States to prepare for, respond to, and recover from terrorist attacks, major disasters, and other emergencies. The Secretary shall coordinate the Federal Government's resources utilized in response to or recovery from terrorist attacks, major disasters, or other emergencies if and when any one of the following four conditions applies: (1) a Federal department or agency acting under its own authority has requested the assistance of the Secretary; (2) the resources of State and local authorities are overwhelmed and Federal assistance has been requested by the appropriate State and local authorities; (3) more than one Federal department or agency has become substantially involved in responding to the incident; or (4) the Secretary has been directed to assume responsibility for managing the domestic incident by the President.

(5) Nothing in this directive alters, or impedes the ability to carry out, the authorities of Federal departments and agencies to perform their responsibilities under law. All Federal departments and agencies shall cooperate with the Secretary in the Secretary's domestic incident management role.

(6) The Federal Government recognizes the roles and responsibilities of State and local authorities in domestic incident management. Initial responsibility for managing domestic incidents generally falls on State and local authorities. The Federal Government will assist State and local authorities when their resources are overwhelmed, or when Federal interests are involved. The Secretary will coordinate with State and local governments to ensure adequate planning, equipment, training, and exercise activities. The Secretary will also provide assistance to State and local governments to develop all hazards plans and capabilities, including those of greatest importance to the security of the United States, and will ensure that State, local, and Federal plans are compatible.

(7) The Federal Government recognizes the role that the private and nongovernmental sectors play in preventing, preparing for, responding to, and recovering from terrorist attacks, major disasters, and other emergencies. The Secretary will coordinate with the

private and nongovernmental sectors to ensure adequate planning, equipment, training, and exercise activities and to promote partnerships to address incident management capabilities.

(8) The Attorney General has lead responsibility for criminal investigations of terrorist acts or terrorist threats by individuals or groups inside the United States, or directed at United States citizens or institutions abroad, where such acts are within the Federal criminal jurisdiction of the United States, as well as for related intelligence collection activities within the United States, subject to the National Security Act of 1947 and other applicable law, Executive Order 12333, and Attorney General-approved procedures pursuant to that Executive Order. Generally acting through the Federal Bureau of Investigation, the Attorney General, in cooperation with other Federal departments and agencies engaged in activities to protect our national security, shall also coordinate the activities of the other members of the law enforcement community to detect, prevent, preempt, and disrupt terrorist attacks against the United States. Following a terrorist threat or an actual incident that falls within the criminal jurisdiction of the United States, the full capabilities of the United States shall be dedicated, consistent with United States law and with activities of other Federal departments and agencies to protect our national security, to assisting the Attorney General to identify the perpetrators and bring them to justice. The Attorney General and the Secretary shall establish appropriate relationships and mechanisms for cooperation and coordination between their two departments.

(9) Nothing in this directive impairs or otherwise affects the authority of the Secretary of Defense over the Department of Defense, including the chain of command for military forces from the President as Commander in Chief, to the Secretary of Defense, to the commander of military forces, or military command and control procedures. The Secretary of Defense shall provide military support to civil authorities for domestic incidents as directed by the President or when consistent with military readiness and appropriate under the circumstances and the law. The Secretary of Defense shall retain command of military forces providing civil support. The Secretary of Defense and the Secretary shall establish appropriate relationships and mechanisms for cooperation and coordination between their two departments.

(10) The Secretary of State has the responsibility, consistent with other United States Government activities to protect our national security, to coordinate international activities related to the prevention, preparation, response, and recovery from a domestic incident, and for the protection of United States citizens and United States interests overseas. The Secretary of State and the Secretary shall establish appropriate relationships and mechanisms for cooperation and coordination between their two departments.

(11) The Assistant to the President for Homeland Security and the Assistant to the President for National Security Affairs shall be responsible for interagency policy coordination on domestic and international incident management, respectively, as directed by the President. The Assistant to the President for Homeland Security and the Assistant to the President for National Security Affairs shall work together to ensure that the United States domestic and international incident management efforts are seamlessly united.

(12) The Secretary shall ensure that, as appropriate, information related to domestic incidents is gathered and provided to the public, the private sector, State and local authorities, Federal departments and agencies, and, generally through the Assistant to the President for Homeland Security, to the President. The Secretary shall provide standardized, quantitative reports to the Assistant to the President for Homeland Security on the readiness and preparedness of the Nation at all levels of government to prevent, prepare for, respond to, and recover from domestic incidents.

(13) Nothing in this directive shall be construed to grant to any Assistant to the President any authority to issue orders to Federal departments and agencies, their officers, or their employees.

Tasking

(14) The heads of all Federal departments and agencies are directed to provide their full and prompt cooperation, resources, and support, as appropriate and consistent with their own responsibilities for protecting our national security, to the Secretary, the Attorney General, the Secretary of Defense, and the Secretary of State in the exercise of the individual leadership responsibilities and missions assigned in paragraphs (4), (8), (9), and (10), respectively, above.

(15) The Secretary shall develop, submit for review to the Homeland Security Council, and administer a National Incident Management System (NIMS). This system will provide a consistent nationwide approach for Federal, State, and local governments to work effectively and efficiently together to prepare for, respond to, and recover from domestic incidents, regardless of cause, size, or complexity. To provide for interoperability and compatibility among Federal, State, and local capabilities, the NIMS will include a core set of concepts, principles, terminology, and technologies covering the incident command system; multi-agency coordination systems; unified command; training; identification and management of resources (including systems for classifying types of resources); qualifications and certification; and the collection, tracking, and reporting of incident information and incident resources.

(16) The Secretary shall develop, submit for review to the Homeland Security Council, and administer a National Response Plan (NRP). The Secretary shall consult with appropriate Assistants to the President (including the Assistant to the President for Economic Policy) and the Director of the Office of Science and Technology Policy, and other such Federal officials as may be appropriate, in developing and implementing the NRP. This plan shall integrate Federal Government domestic prevention, preparedness, response, and recovery plans into one all-discipline, all-hazards plan. The NRP shall be unclassified. If certain operational aspects require classification, they shall be included in classified annexes to the NRP.

(a) The NRP, using the NIMS, shall, with regard to response to domestic incidents, provide the structure and mechanisms for national level policy and operational direction for Federal support to State and local incident managers and for exercising direct Federal authorities and responsibilities, as appropriate.

For additional analytical, business and investment opportunities information,
please contact Global Investment & Business Center, USA
at (202) 546-2103. Fax: (202) 546-3275. E-mail: rusric@erols.com

(b) The NRP will include protocols for operating under different threats or threat levels; incorporation of existing Federal emergency and incident management plans (with appropriate modifications and revisions) as either integrated components of the NRP or as supporting operational plans; and additional operational plans or annexes, as appropriate, including public affairs and intergovernmental communications.

(c) The NRP will include a consistent approach to reporting incidents, providing assessments, and making recommendations to the President, the Secretary, and the Homeland Security Council.

(d) The NRP will include rigorous requirements for continuous improvements from testing, exercising, experience with incidents, and new information and technologies.

(17) The Secretary shall:

(a) By April 1, 2003, (1) develop and publish an initial version of the NRP, in consultation with other Federal departments and agencies; and (2) provide the Assistant to the President for Homeland Security with a plan for full development and implementation of the NRP.

(b) By June 1, 2003, (1) in consultation with Federal departments and agencies and with State and local governments, develop a national system of standards, guidelines, and protocols to implement the NIMS; and (2) establish a mechanism for ensuring ongoing management and maintenance of the NIMS, including regular consultation with other Federal departments and agencies and with State and local governments.

(c) By September 1, 2003, in consultation with Federal departments and agencies and the Assistant to the President for Homeland Security, review existing authorities and regulations and prepare recommendations for the President on revisions necessary to implement fully the NRP.

(18) The heads of Federal departments and agencies shall adopt the NIMS within their departments and agencies and shall provide support and assistance to the Secretary in the development and maintenance of the NIMS. All Federal departments and agencies will use the NIMS in their domestic incident management and emergency prevention, preparedness, response, recovery, and mitigation activities, as well as those actions taken in support of State or local entities. The heads of Federal departments and agencies shall participate in the NRP, shall assist and support the Secretary in the development and maintenance of the NRP, and shall participate in and use domestic incident reporting systems and protocols established by the Secretary.

(19) The head of each Federal department and agency shall:

(a) By June 1, 2003, make initial revisions to existing plans in accordance with the initial version of the NRP.

(b) By August 1, 2003, submit a plan to adopt and implement the NIMS to the Secretary and the Assistant to the President for Homeland Security. The Assistant to the

President for Homeland Security shall advise the President on whether such plans effectively implement the NIMS.

(20) Beginning in Fiscal Year 2005, Federal departments and agencies shall make adoption of the NIMS a requirement, to the extent permitted by law, for providing Federal preparedness assistance through grants, contracts, or other activities. The Secretary shall develop standards and guidelines for determining whether a State or local entity has adopted the NIMS.

Technical and Conforming Amendments to National Security Presidential Directive 1 (NSPD 1)

(21) NSPD 1 ("Organization of the National Security Council System") is amended by replacing the fifth sentence of the third paragraph on the first page with the following: "The Attorney General, the Secretary of Homeland Security, and the Director of the Office of Management and Budget shall be invited to attend meetings pertaining to their responsibilities.".

Technical and Conforming Amendments to National Security Presidential Directive 8 (NSPD 8)

(22) NSPD 8 ("National Director and Deputy National Security Advisor for Combating Terrorism") is amended by striking "and the Office of Homeland Security," on page 4, and inserting "the Department of Homeland Security, and the Homeland Security Council" in lieu thereof.

Technical and Conforming Amendments to Homeland Security Presidential Directive-2 (HSPD-2)

(23) HSPD-2 ("Combating Terrorism Through Immigration Policies") is amended as follows:

(a) striking "the Commissioner of the Immigration and Naturalization Service (INS)" in the second sentence of the second paragraph in section 1, and inserting "the Secretary of Homeland Security" in lieu thereof ;

(b) striking "the INS," in the third paragraph in section 1, and inserting "the Department of Homeland Security" in lieu thereof;

(c) inserting ", the Secretary of Homeland Security," after "The Attorney General" in the fourth paragraph in section 1;

(d) inserting ", the Secretary of Homeland Security," after "the Attorney General" in the fifth paragraph in section 1;

(e) striking "the INS and the Customs Service" in the first sentence of the first paragraph of section 2, and inserting "the Department of Homeland Security" in lieu thereof;

(f) striking "Customs and INS" in the first sentence of the second paragraph of section 2, and inserting "the Department of Homeland Security" in lieu thereof;

(g) striking "the two agencies" in the second sentence of the second paragraph of section 2, and inserting "the Department of Homeland Security" in lieu thereof;

(h) striking "the Secretary of the Treasury" wherever it appears in section 2, and inserting "the Secretary of Homeland Security" in lieu thereof;

(i) inserting ", the Secretary of Homeland Security," after "The Secretary of State" wherever the latter appears in section 3;

(j) inserting ", the Department of Homeland Security," after "the Department of State," in the second sentence in the third paragraph in section 3;

(k) inserting "the Secretary of Homeland Security," after "the Secretary of State," in the first sentence of the fifth paragraph of section 3;

(l) striking "INS" in the first sentence of the sixth paragraph of section 3, and inserting "Department of Homeland Security" in lieu thereof;

(m) striking "the Treasury" wherever it appears in section 4 and inserting "Homeland Security" in lieu thereof;

(n) inserting ", the Secretary of Homeland Security," after "the Attorney General" in the first sentence in section 5; and

(o) inserting ", Homeland Security" after "State" in the first sentence of section 6.

Technical and Conforming Amendments to Homeland Security Presidential Directive-3 (HSPD-3)

(24) The Homeland Security Act of 2002 assigned the responsibility for administering the Homeland Security Advisory System to the Secretary of Homeland Security. Accordingly, HSPD 3 of March 11, 2002 ("Homeland Security Advisory System") is amended as follows:

(a) replacing the third sentence of the second paragraph entitled "Homeland Security Advisory System" with "Except in exigent circumstances, the Secretary of Homeland Security shall seek the views of the Attorney General, and any other federal agency heads the Secretary deems appropriate, including other members of the Homeland Security Council, on the Threat Condition to be assigned."

(b) inserting "At the request of the Secretary of Homeland Security, the Department of Justice shall permit and facilitate the use of delivery systems administered or managed by the Department of Justice for the purposes of delivering threat information pursuant to

For additional analytical, business and investment opportunities information,
please contact Global Investment & Business Center, USA
at (202) 546-2103. Fax: (202) 546-3275. E-mail: rusric@erols.com

the Homeland Security Advisory System." as a new paragraph after the fifth paragraph of the section entitled "Homeland Security Advisory System."

(c) inserting ", the Secretary of Homeland Security" after "The Director of Central Intelligence" in the first sentence of the seventh paragraph of the section entitled "Homeland Security Advisory System".

(d) striking "Attorney General" wherever it appears (except in the sentences referred to in subsections (a) and (c) above), and inserting "the Secretary of Homeland Security" in lieu thereof; and

(e) striking the section entitled "Comment and Review Periods."

GEORGE W. BUSH

OFICIAL STATEMENTS AND TESTIMONIES

THE NOMINATION OF THE HONORABLE TOM RIDGE TO BE SECRETARY OF THE DEPARTMENT OF HOMELAND SECURITY

I would like to first thank you, Senator Collins and Senator Lieberman, and all the members of the Committee for moving expeditiously to conduct today's hearing.

As I have said many times before my nomination was announced, and as I have said many times since, to me there is no more serious job in all the land than stopping future terrorist incidents from occurring on American soil. I can imagine no mission more imperative than protecting the American people; and should another terrorist attack occur, I can think of nothing more crucial than working to ensure that every single echelon of society is as prepared as possible to respond.

I wish to commend the Congress again for pressing forward and taking bold and historic steps to establish this new Department of Homeland Security. Together, the Congress and the Executive Branch realized the current structure of our government limited our ability to protect America. Now, for the first time, we will have a Federal Department whose primary mission is the protection of the American people.

America is undoubtedly safer and better prepared today than on September 10th, 2001. We have taken key steps to protect America - from pushing our maritime borders farther from shore and professionalizing airport screening to developing vaccination plans and tightening our borders. Public servants at all levels of government, private sector employees, and citizens all across the United States have changed the way in which they live and work in a unified effort to improve our security since the September 11th attacks.

For the first time in our Nation's history, the President has created a *National Strategy for Homeland Security*, a strategy which provides the framework to mobilize and organize the nation - the federal government, state and local governments, the private sector, and the American people - in the complex mission to protect our homeland. We have begun the very first steps of critical work in the initiative by identifying and assessing our vulnerabilities to see where we are exposed to an unpredictable enemy.

That said, we are only at the beginning of what will be a long struggle to protect our Nation from terrorism. While much has been accomplished, there is much more work to do. We are a country that is built from ingenuity and hard work and we will not rest on our laurels. We must stay focused. We must stay vigilant.

We have no higher purpose than to ensure the security of our people to protect and preserve our democratic way of life. Terrorism directly threatens the foundations of our Nation, our people, our freedom, and our economic prosperity. We face a hate-filled, remorseless enemy that takes many forms, has many places to hide, and is often invisible.

For additional analytical, business and investment opportunities information,
please contact Global Investment & Business Center, USA
at (202) 546-2103. Fax: (202) 546-3275. E-mail: rusric@erols.com

The role of the Secretary of Homeland Security will be, first and foremost, the protection of the American people. Since being sworn in by the President as the first Homeland Security Advisor on October 8th, 2001, I have been focused solely on this mission.

Shortly after the President made his speech to the nation announcing his intention to propose the creation of the Department of Homeland Security, he also appointed me as Director of the Transition Planning Office. It was in that capacity that I testified in front of Congressional committees in both the House and Senate about the vision we were undertaking that began the critical partnership of working with Congress to ensure the success of this venture.

In the time since, I have helped to guide the men and women in the Transition Planning Office, who are detailed from all of the agencies affected by the legislation. They have been working undeterred and with a strong sense of urgency. In the nearly 60 days since the President signed the Homeland Security Act of 2002 into law, our Transition staff has laid the framework for an organizational structure that will best accomplish our goals and create a professional workforce focused first and foremost on the mission of protecting our homeland.

The Secretary of Homeland Security, however, is only one person who, without the support of those who have dedicated and risked their lives to protecting America, will not succeed. Should I be confirmed as the Secretary of Homeland Security, I will go to work every single morning with the mission of protecting the American people from the threat of terrorist attack, knowing that the most valuable asset the new Department will have is not funding, or technology, or equipment, but the men and women who work there.

These are the true patriots in every sense of the term. They are vital to the mission.

The more than 170,000 future employees of the Department of Homeland Security will be doing the same job in the new Department that they are doing today: protecting our country from terrorist attack. That focus exists now, and it will exist long after the Department is created.

We will also not forget the breadth of the task at hand. This is the largest and most significant transformation of the U.S. government in over a half-century. We will not be naive to the challenge of merging 22 separate work cultures, operating procedures and management procedures into one cohesive organization. At the same time, we cannot lose sight of the individual missions of each of the agencies. But we must create a mindset in which everyone is thinking about how each of their missions fit into the larger mission of protecting our homeland. From day one, we will not allow for invisible barriers to lead to the breakdown of information. To be successful, we will need to foster teamwork and a strong sense of pride about working together to accomplish the mission.

However, unifying in one Department on the federal level will not in itself be able to stop all attempts to do harm to America. We must realize fully the value of cultivating partnerships and cooperating with our partners in other federal agencies, state and local governments, the private sector and with the American people.

As a former Governor, I am keenly aware of the shared responsibility that exists between the federal, state, and local governments for homeland security. In fact, over the past year I have often said that "when our hometowns are secure, our homeland will be secure." That is not merely rhetoric, but a fundamental principle of the nation's homeland security effort.

I'm pleased to report that all 50 states and the territories have appointed homeland security advisors and that they participate regularly in meetings at the White House and in bi-monthly conference calls with the Office of Homeland Security. We have, for the first time, created a single entry point to address many of the homeland security concerns of our Governors and Mayors.

We know, however, that much more needs to be done. We must recognize that communities and state and local governments face new and unprecedented threats. As such, the new Department should stand ready to work with them to obtain the tools, resources, and information they need to do their jobs. We also must develop new channels of communication with private sector organizations, and provide clear, concise, scientifically sound and easily accessible information so that Americans citizens can be prepared in the event their community is affected by a terrorist act.

If I should become the new Secretary, you have my pledge that I will focus on increased collaboration and coordination so that public and private resources are better aligned to secure the homeland and support each one of our critical missions.

Supporting the *National Strategy for Homeland Security*

I also wish to state my promise that I will do everything in my power to use the office of the secretary to keep the Department focused on all six of its critical missions outlined in the *National Strategy for Homeland Security*. They include:

- Intelligence and Warning,
- Border and Transportation Security,
- Domestic Counterterrorism,
- Protecting Critical Infrastructure and Key Assets,
- Defending Against Catastrophic Threats, and
- Emergency Preparedness and Response.

While each of these missions is unique, each is essential to our primary mission of protecting the security of the United States. Some, such as Emergency Preparedness and Response, have long played key roles in helping society overcome hardship and emergencies; while others are byproducts of the harsh reality that terrorism can strike on our soil.

As I said earlier, the future employees of the Department of Homeland Security will be doing the same job in the new Department that they are doing today. The difference is that the new structure of the Department will refocus, consolidate and reorganize the functions of each of the 22 agencies involved in protecting the homeland.

The Department will be structured into four Directorates, each responsible for implementing the applicable components of the six critical missions. They are:

- Border and Transportation Security,
- Information Analysis and Critical Infrastructure Protection,
- Emergency Response and Preparedness, and
- Science and Technology.

The United States Coast Guard and Secret Service will retain their independence and will play key roles in supporting all of the critical missions.

I would like to give you a sense of how I believe this unified homeland security structure will mobilize and focus the resources of the federal government, state and local governments, the private sector, and the American people to accomplish its mission; beginning first with one of the most sizable challenges, border and transportation security.

Border and Transportation Security

America has historically relied on two vast oceans and two friendly neighbors for border security. And our country has long cherished its identity as a nation of immigrants. Nearly 500 million people enter our country each year at our numerous border checkpoints, seaports and airports. The sheer volume of those wishing to visit our great country or move here permanently in search of the American dream, coupled with the burden of processing vast amounts of information from disparate federal agencies, has severely taxed our border security and immigration systems. Even before September 11th, it had become apparent that the system could no longer determine who exactly was in our country, for what reason, and whether they left when they said they were going to leave.

Since then, we have made substantial improvements to tighten security in areas like visa issuances and border patrol; but more importantly, we have laid the foundation for a comprehensive plan with tangible benchmarks to measure success through the *National Strategy for Homeland Security*.

The new Department will be organized to implement this plan efficiently and meet its two inherent strategic goals: to improve border security while at the same time, facilitate the unimpeded flow of legitimate commerce and people across our borders.

We will implement the President's plan to separate the Immigration and Naturalization Service into two functions: services and enforcement. This plan will allow the new Department to greatly improve the administration of benefits and services for applicants, while at the same time ensuring full enforcement of the laws that regulate the flow of aliens to the United States. I realize that this is no simple task. But if we are to remain the land of freedom and opportunity, we must retain complete control over who enters our country and maintain the integrity of our immigration system so that we always know who is in our country and for what purpose.

The integrity of our borders goes hand-in-hand with the security of our transportation systems. Today, Americans are more mobile than ever. We enjoy the freedom to go where we want, when we want, using the best transportation system in the world. This efficient system is also one of the engines that drives our economy. Shutting down that engine is not a viable option.

But the destructive potential of modern terrorism requires that we fundamentally rethink how we should protect this system. Virtually every community in America is connected to the global transportation network by seaports, airports, highways, railroads, and waterways.

One area in which we have shown significant progress is security at our nation's airports. The Transportation Security Administration, under the leadership of the Department of Transportation, has hired, trained and deployed a new federal screening workforce that is professional and focused on providing the highest levels of security without hindering our aviation system. We need to build on that success, but at the same time realize we have farther still to go. The new Department must work with its federal and private sector partners to assess and take the necessary steps to secure our means of transportation, including our railways, roadways, bridges, waterways and especially our seaports.

We must take immediate action to make sure our seaports are open to process the flow of goods and commercial traffic, but are closed to terrorists. A vast majority of container cargo remains unscreened. Port security remains the responsibility of a myriad of local port authorities, federal agencies and the Coast Guard. However, we are making changes. We must enhance risk management and implement practices that allow for higher efficiency screening of goods. Our fundamental goal is to make certain that heightened security does not obstruct legitimate trade.

Progress, however, is already underway. Programs like the Container Security Initiative are helping nations spot and screen the highest-risk containers. Operation Safe Commerce focuses on business-driven initiatives to enhance security for the movement of cargo throughout the entire supply chain. Most recently, Congress passed the Maritime Transportation Security Act, which gives authority to the Coast Guard and Customs Service to develop standards and procedures for conducting port vulnerability assessments.

United States Coast Guard

The men and women of the United States Coast Guard, who live under the guiding principle *Semper Paratus* or Always Ready, have been performing the mission of Homeland Security in a complex and dangerous maritime environment for more than 200 years. The Coast Guard's fundamental responsibilities -- preparedness, protection, response and recovery -- cut across all facets of the Department's mission.

Every day since the September 11th terrorist attacks, the Coast Guard pushes our maritime borders farther from shore. All ships bound for the U.S., regardless of registry, face a multi-layered, interagency security screening process in addition to traditional safety, environmental and operational standards enforcement, plus random boardings.

Vessels now must provide 96-hour advance notice of arrival to the Coast Guard National Vessel Movement Center, including detailed crew and passenger information, cargo details, and voyage history. The Coast Guard has also created highly trained and specially equipped Maritime Safety and Security Teams to add an extra layer of security and additional quick-response capabilities in key U.S. ports.

But let me make one thing clear. The new Department will not lose focus of the Coast Guard's other critical missions. From search and rescue, anti-drug and illegal migrant patrols to fisheries enforcement and aids to navigation, I will work personally to ensure that the Department continues to support the entirety of the Coast Guard mission.

No branch of the Armed Forces has as much history in protecting the homeland, and should I be confirmed as Secretary, I can think of no honor that would make me more proud than calling myself a Service Secretary of the Coast Guard.

United States Secret Service

The Secret Service represents another unique critical mission that aligns with the core competencies of the new Department and will remain independent. Through its two distinct missions, protection and criminal investigation, the Secret Service is responsible for the protection of the President, the Vice President and their families; heads of state; the security for designated National Special Security Events; and the investigation and enforcement of laws relating to counterfeiting, fraud and financial crimes.

The Secret Service is, and has been for decades, in the business of assessing vulnerabilities and designing ways to reduce them in advance of an attack. This expertise will greatly benefit the Department as we strive to create an overall culture of anticipation, vulnerability assessment, and threat reduction. Building on these institutional ideals will be of the utmost importance as it pertains to nearly all of the missions in the Department, but none more so than protecting our critical infrastructure.

Information Analysis and Critical Infrastructure Protection

On September 11th, we were dealt a grave, horrific blow, and today we face the real possibility of additional attacks of similar or even greater magnitude. Our enemy will choose their targets deliberately based upon weaknesses in our defenses and preparations. Thus, a fundamental priority in our mission must be to analyze the threat, while concurrently and continuously assessing our vulnerabilities. The Department is structured in such a way as to efficiently conduct this task.

The Information Analysis and Critical Infrastructure Directorate will bring together for the first time under one roof the capability to identify and assess threats to the homeland, map those threats against our vulnerabilities, issue warnings, and provide the basis from which to organize protective measures to secure the homeland.

For this Directorate to play an effective role in the mission of securing our homeland, I believe a top priority will be to work with the CIA, the FBI and other intelligence-gathering agencies to define the procedures from which to obtain the appropriate intelligence. This means that the Department will be a full participant, at all levels, in the mechanisms for setting foreign intelligence requirements, including the prioritization for terrorism, weapons of mass destruction, and other relevant foreign intelligence collection activities. We also must continue to work with the FBI as they reorganize to most effectively collect domestic intelligence.

More than just countering each identified threat, the Department will design and implement a long-term comprehensive and nationwide plan for protecting America's critical infrastructure and key assets. A key mission of the Information Analysis and Critical Infrastructure Protection division will be to catalogue and reduce the Nation's domestic vulnerability.

America's critical infrastructure encompasses a large number of sectors ranging from energy and chemical to banking and agriculture. Each has unique vulnerabilities, and each requires different kinds of protection. This, coupled with the fact that nearly 85 percent of critical infrastructure is owned by the private sector - and that 12 separate federal agencies have oversight authority -- creates an enormous challenge.

Realizing the breadth of this task, the Office of Homeland Security began working with the federal lead departments and agencies for each of the 14 critical infrastructure sectors designated in the President's *National Strategy for Homeland Security*. This cooperation has included the identification of infrastructures and assets of national-level criticality within each sector; facilitating the sharing of risk and vulnerability assessment methodologies and best practices; and enabling cooperation between federal departments and agencies, state and local governments, and the private sector.

This process, however, is only the beginning. The Department of Homeland Security will provide greater uniformity to these efforts and further strengthen the relationships with the private sector and state and local governments so that we can integrate the threat and vulnerability analysis in a way that will help produce effective countermeasures. As this information is collected and mapped to critical infrastructure vulnerabilities, our top priority must be to get this information to those federal, state and local officials to whose mission the information is relevant. These individuals represent the first line of defense against and response to a terrorist attack, and we must make it a priority to keep them properly informed and aware.

Emergency Preparedness and Response

Our nation's three million firefighters, police officers, and EMTs are the first on the scene in a crisis and the last to leave. Their heroic efforts saved lives and speeded the recovery from the attacks of September 11th, and they will be called upon to do so in the event of future attacks against our hometowns. They're living proof that homeland security is a national, not a federal effort.

We must give these brave men and women all the assistance and support possible. Under the Emergency Preparedness and Response Directorate in the new Department, we will strengthen our relationship with first responders and partner with the states, cities and counties that manage and fund them. We will work with Congress to provide them with the resources they need, beginning with the President's First Responder Initiative, which offered a thousand-percent increase in funding to equip, train and drill first responders to meet a conventional attack or one involving a weapon of mass destruction.

We will build on the strong foundation already in place by the Federal Emergency Management Agency, which for decades has provided command and control support and funding support in disasters, whether caused by man or Mother Nature.

The new Department of Homeland Security will consolidate at least five different plans that currently govern federal response to disasters into one genuinely all-discipline, all-hazard plan - between "crisis management" and "consequence management." Moreover, it will consolidate grant programs for first responders and citizen volunteers that are now scattered across numerous federal agencies. This will prevent waste and duplication, and ultimately save lives, including the lives of first responders.

In a crisis, the Department will for the first time provide a direct line of authority from the President through the Secretary of Homeland Security to a single on-site federal response coordinator. All levels of government will have complete incident awareness and open communication.

The Department will also direct our federal crisis response assets, such as the National Pharmaceutical Stockpile and nuclear incident response teams - assets that work best when they work together. In doing all this, we believe we can build the capabilities for a proactive emergency management culture - one that is well-planned, well-organized and well-equipped to not just manage the risk, but reduce the risk of death and damage to property.

It is vitally important to remember that no matter what steps we take to preempt terrorists, we cannot guarantee that another attack will not occur. However, we must be prepared to respond. We must also take brave new steps, think creatively and invest in homeland security technologies that aim to stay one step ahead of the technologically proficient terrorists.

Science and Technology

As stated in the President's *National Strategy for Homeland Security*, our Nation enjoys a distinct advantage in science and technology. We must exploit that advantage. And just as technology has helped us to defeat enemies from afar, so too will it help us to protect our homeland.

Creating a Directorate in the new Department specifically devoted to Science and Technology for the homeland represents an exciting milestone. For the first time, the federal government will harness American ingenuity to develop new synergies and form robust partnerships with the private sector to research, develop and deploy homeland security technologies that will make America safer.

The science and technology organizational structure, while still being defined, is envisioned to be a streamlined, integrated team that will access the technical resources and assets of the private sector, academia, and federal government. It will be based on customer-focused portfolios for countering chemical, biological, radiological and nuclear attacks and for conducting and enhancing the normal operations of the Department. Research, development, test and evaluation programs will address the greatest threats and highest priorities based on assessments of threats, customer requirements and technological capabilities.

The technologies developed through this research and development should not only make us safer, but also make our daily lives better. These technologies fit well within our physical and economic structure and our national habits. And the Science and Technology Directorate will have a structure that ensures those who are the end users of all technologies provide their expertise throughout the entire lifecycle of research, development and acquisition of systems.

Before any new homeland security technologies are deployed, we will ensure that we are upholding the laws of the land. Any new data mining techniques or programs to enhance information sharing and collecting must and will respect the civil rights and civil liberties guaranteed to the American people under the Constitution. Furthermore, as we go about developing new technologies and programs to strengthen our homeland, treating citizens differently on the basis of religion or ethnicity will not be tolerated.

Before I close, I wish to again underscore an earlier point. No matter how this organization is structured it will not achieve its mission without the dedication of its employees. And the key to ensuring the Department's mission and focus throughout the transition will be the continuing support of those conducting the day-to-day work. This will be an all-inclusive effort. We will eagerly solicit and consider advice from employees, unions, professional associations and other stakeholders.

We will create a human resource model that will be collaborative, responsive to both its employees and the mission of the agency.

First, we will work to create some measure of stability for employees even as we undergo the transition. For the first year, employees can expect to receive at least the same pay and benefits, and probably in the same location. Some people will certainly be able to take advantage of new career opportunities.

Second, we will work hard to create a modern, flexible, fair, merit-based personnel system. Third, we will communicate to ensure that personnel know what to expect and when to expect it. Fourth, we will work hard to ensure that employees continue to receive the same civil service protections that they currently enjoy. Most importantly, we aim for the Department's employees to be better able to do their jobs with more support and more effective use of resources.

Finally, I will insist on measurable progress from all of the agencies and bureaus that will make up the Department of Homeland Security. Americans must and will know when improvements have been made.

In a town hall I hosted with future employees of the Department in December, I made all of these promises to them, as well as the pledge to keep them informed and aware of historic changes before them. Should I be confirmed, I make that same pledge to you.

In closing, during our darkest hour on September 11th, American spirit and pride rose above all else to unify our Nation. In the time since, we have fought a new kind of war - one that has a new enemy, new techniques, new strategies, new soldiers and is fought on a new battlefield -- our own homeland. Our response has been strong, measured and resolute. But nothing has been more profound as the creation of one Department whose primary mission is the protection of the American people.

The Department of Homeland Security will better enable every level of federal, state and local government; every private sector employee; and, ultimately, every citizen in our Nation to prevent terrorist attacks, reduce America's vulnerability and respond and recover when attacks do occur.

The road will be long, and the mission difficult. We will not have truly succeeded until the day when terrorists know the futility of attacking Americans and Americans know we have the ability to protect them. The bottom line is, we will secure the homeland - whether by the efforts of thousands of people working together, or by a single scientist working alone in a laboratory - whether from behind a desk in Washington, or at the far corners of the continent. We will accomplish our mission.

REMARKS BY GOVERNOR TOM RIDGE, HOMELAND SECURITY - DESIGNATE IN A TOWN HALL MEETING FOR FUTURE EMPLOYEES OF THE DEPARTMENT OF HOMELAND SECURITY

December 17, 2002

Ronald Reagan Building
Washington, D.C.
2:05 P.M. EST

MR. SESNO: (Welcoming remarks.)

GOVERNOR RIDGE: Thanks very much for accepting our invitation to host what I consider to be one of the most important events that I will undertake as -- hopefully -- an appointed Secretary of the Department of Homeland Security: and that is beginning the conversation with the men and women with whom I'll be working, men and women who will be getting up every morning, as I do, to go to work, whose mission will be to protect America -- protect their citizens, protect their neighborhoods, to protect our way of life. And so I want to thank you for accepting our invitation to join us this afternoon.

I know there's a lot of anxiety. I suspect there's an enormous amount of uncertainty. Hopefully, there's a little bit of excitement because we have the opportunity to do something that happens in this town every 50 or 60 years, and that's create a new department. And in this instance, perhaps, to create a legacy and preserve and protect a way of life that is unique to each and every one of us, that is so important to every one of us.

And I know that there are a lot of questions you're going to ask this afternoon. And hopefully, we can answer most. But I wanted to assure you that this is just the beginning of the dialogue that we have to have. Because at the end of the day, in order for us to fulfill our mission to protect America and our way of life, we have to fulfill that mission together. And we have to respond to the challenges together.

Now, in my 20 years of public service as a congressman and as a governor, and most recently in the job I presently hold as an assistant to the President, I have been privileged to actually see how you and your colleagues work and to see how well you work. Most recently I saw, not only Customs at the Ambassador Bridge in Detroit. But I saw how hard and how well you were working on the Cargo Security Initiative in Rotterdam. It's something we need to do. You're going to do it and you're going to do it very, very well.

I see INS down at El Paso working side by side with their colleagues in Customs. And you've got an enormous task ahead of you because we have to design the entry-exit system for this country so that we remain an open and welcoming and trusting country, we do a better job of identifying those who visit, identify why they are visiting and making sure when that opportunity to visit has expired, that they leave as promised. Huge undertaking. And I know you're up to it.

I've had the pleasure, way back when, in the '80s as congressman, to put my fingerprints and work on the Stafford Act that directs the good folks over at the Federal Emergency Management Agency, and have had the privilege to watch my great friend Joe Allbaugh and his extraordinary team respond to the tragedy and the horror of September 11th, 2001.

I travel commercially. I fly from time to time. And I've seen the great work that the Transportation Department and the Transportation Security Administration under Admiral Loy have done, getting people through those gates with the professionalism they demonstrated over the Thanksgiving holiday. There were a lot of people that said that couldn't be done within a year; you couldn't ramp up and find 40,000 or 45,000 people and get them in place, and bring the professionalism and the training to that enterprise.

So I've seen that and I've benefitted by the work at so many of the other agencies that will be pooled in and other units that will be pooled in from Commerce and Agriculture and Justice. So I know what you do, and I know how well you do it. And I really believe that all of us, in one department, finally a department whose primary mission is to protect our fellow citizens and our way of life, will have an opportunity to do it even better.

So this is a special time. It's an historic time. I believe we are up to the task, and I'm grateful to have the opportunity this afternoon to spend a little time with you and will

For additional analytical, business and investment opportunities information, please contact Global Investment & Business Center, USA at (202) 546-2103. Fax: (202) 546-3275. E-mail: rusric@erols.com

certainly look forward in the weeks and months and years ahead to take on the mission side by side with each and every one of you.

Thank you. (Applause.)

MR. SESNO: Well, Governor Ridge, as I listen to you, and as I think about people sitting at home, whether they're federal employees or not, it seems to me that this would be one of those appropriate places that, as you could see by the roadside, you know, your tax dollars at work.

GOVERNOR RIDGE: Works well.

MR. SESNO: You're creating a large, new, cobbled-together department to respond to issues of homeland security.

So, the question, really -- and maybe this is more for the general public than for the crowd here, at least to begin with -- as a practical matter, how will this make America safer?

GOVERNOR RIDGE: Let me count the ways. We will get people and cargo across our borders quicker, we will need and help drive some of the technological innovation that will make us safer, we will have the opportunity to not only fuse and analyze, but share information with law enforcement and first responders in an unprecedented way. We will truly have the opportunity to engage our partners at the state and local level. People will see that.

This unit, this department, will work with the private sector to identify vulnerabilities. Because one of the challenges we have in this country is that the terrorists don't have to bring weapons. They can take advantage of the diversity that we have in this country, the strong economic diversity we have and find both weapons and targets out there. And we will be working with the private sector and we'll see on a daily basis the interaction of this department with men and women in workplaces around the country.

So whether you're working with the private sector, whether we're working at the borders, whether we're monitoring those who come into this country more effectively, whether we're improving our security at the airports, and the list goes on and on, every single day there will be a way that we manifest that by working together we do a better job of protecting America.

MR. SESNO: It really is a merger -- 22 departments and agencies coming together. So as a practical matter, again, what starts happening on March 1st, when you start setting up shop? How quickly is this merger going to come together?

GOVERNOR RIDGE: Well, on March 1st, just about all of the departments and agencies move into the Department of Homeland Security. Shortly thereafter, we will begin the process of trying to rationalize and take 22 different management systems and personnel systems into one.

For additional analytical, business and investment opportunities information, please contact Global Investment & Business Center, USA at (202) 546-2103. Fax: (202) 546-3275. E-mail: rusric@erols.com

But on March 1st, by and large, every man and women in this office and 170,000 plus employees around this country will go to work doing the same thing they're doing now. But in time, we hope that we can empower them and enable them, through a variety of different means, to do an even better job than they're doing now. And I believe that's going to happen.

MR. SESNO: Also, as within any merger -- and I've heard stories from inside some offices in what will be DHS -- there's something of analysis paralysis that takes place as a merger looms. People start wondering where they're going to go to work, who is going to be their boss, what's going to happen to their boss, will they survive or not.

How do you counter analysis paralysis, and is it getting in the way of homeland security in the meantime?

GOVERNOR RIDGE: These men and women have been going to work, protecting the homeland before September 11th, 2001. They've been doing their job on a regular basis before we decided that we could do an even better job by merging these departments.

And all we ask of them is, continue to do that job as well as they've been doing it, and it's up to us to empower them in other ways to enable them to do an even better job. There will be some changes, clearly. But changes bring opportunities. And in my sense, in my judgement, that we have opportunities to work more closely together than we ever have before, we have an opportunity to get -- put together a contemporary personnel system that gives us the kind of merit-based, fairness-based program that we want to govern all 22 presently different departments and agencies.

We obviously have to create a personnel system around which the interaction between all of us is solid -- it's positive. So I'm very optimistic about our ability to work with the new units as we bring them together to create one agency for the first time ever whose primary mission -- you and I are going to talk probably a little bit about some of the other historical missions, and we've got to stay focused on that. But our primary mission every morning when we wake up to go to work is to protect America.

MR. SESNO: So this is not -- this department is fundamentally different from other departments?

GOVERNOR RIDGE: I think -- I know my colleagues in public service that are here with us this afternoon and are listening to the broadcast appreciate and admire what their other colleagues do throughout all levels of government. But this is the first time, because of the unique nature of the new enemy that we confront, where we've asked public servants on our own soil, outside the Department of Defense, to work together to defend America and protect our way of life.

MR. SESNO: Of course, there has been some suggestion and some discussion about the whole question of unions and collective bargaining and civil service and protections. Is there a reason that this department is or should be different from any other place in government?

For additional analytical, business and investment opportunities information,
please contact Global Investment & Business Center, USA
at (202) 546-2103. Fax: (202) 546-3275. E-mail: rusric@erols.com

GOVERNOR RIDGE: First of all, we don't envision any changes. If you're in a collective bargaining unit now, you're moving into a collective bargaining unit when you transfer into the new department. We tried to underscore publicly -- and this gives me an opportunity to say it again with a larger audience -- that all the civil service protections that are very appropriately associated with the men and women who wear the public service uniform, the Fair Labor Standards Act and the Hatch Act and the whistleblower protection and a variety of these other protections, they move right along in the department.

It would be our job to make sure that they understand those protections exist, because they need them, they deserve them, and they'll continue to be a part of the employment infrastructure of the new department.

MR. SESNO: Many of the aspects of the new department come with tasks. And many Americans -- I'm sure they realize it, but they may not realize the degree of it -- tasks that do not necessarily relate directly to homeland security. FEMA, for example, where you had, I think, 89 major natural disasters from -- what is it, from January 2001 to December of this year. That's hurricanes, floods, tornadoes --

GOVERNOR RIDGE: Right.

MR. SESNO: FEMA -- or what will be FEMA will be part of Homeland Security. Customs and other organizations, agencies, are also doing things that do not relate directly to homeland security. How do you prevent those other tasks from being lost or sublimated to the larger priority of homeland security?

GOVERNOR RIDGE: I think we begin with the notion that the historic mission that these agencies have been on remains an integral part of how they do business each and every day. Clearly, we've got Customs that does a variety of different things in support of this country -- been doing it for 200 plus year. You want a great lecture on that, get Rob Bonner. He'll tell you all about what Customs does.

But the fact of the matter is, in the process of doing the things that they normally do at our borders, for example, with additional support from us, be it in terms of personnel or technology, as they work more closely with the successor to INS focusing in on people and cargo, they'll be able to do an even better job of protecting America.

Joe Allbaugh in FEMA -- clearly, that mission has changed over the past 20 years. At one time, 20 plus years ago, it was really

-- in the middle of the Cold War, a defensive mechanism. What happens if there's a strike on this country? Then it evolved into a response agency in natural disasters. They continue to do that. But the skills and the training and the services they provide in response to a natural disaster -- very similar to the skills, training, and response we want them to provide after a terrorist event.

And if you talk to the people in New York and you talk to the people here in the Washington, D.C. area, I think they would say that FEMA's response after that terrorist

For additional analytical, business and investment opportunities information,
please contact Global Investment & Business Center, USA
at (202) 546-2103. Fax: (202) 546-3275. E-mail: rusric@erols.com

event was professional. It was compassionate. And it made a difference in their lives. All across the board.

So you've got the Coast Guard. They do fisheries and they rescue and they protect our borders. But we've got to have them focus on ports. And they've been doing that now; but, again, with some assistance from the new department, they can do an even better job.

So I guess I would say to each and every one of you, if your responsibilities in this particular department or agency are not directed toward homeland security, what you're doing -- some way, some manner, shape or form -- will be a part of the system we have to protect this country. And again, we think bringing these people together, they'll do an even better job. And they do a good job right now.

I mean, the best asset we have in this new department will not be the money, will not be the technology, will be the men and women who have been going to work every day trying to help their fellow countrymen. And we'll just build on that. And we think we can make even greater strides and provide even greater and deeper protection for the department.

MR. SESNO: When will people who are being pulled into this Department of Homeland Security know if they're changing their place of work, know if their supervisor is changing? Or very basic questions that you need to know --

GOVERNOR RIDGE: Fair question.

MR. SESNO -- to show up and go to work and do your best every day.

GOVERNOR RIDGE: Well, the fair question is that presently, we have not even begun -- we haven't really moved down that path very far. We're trying to assemble and are in the process of assembling a solid management team. I think everyone understands that for a year after their unit or department moves into the Department of Homeland Security, everything about them remains the same -- their pay, benefits. There is this great concern that there will be this massive dislocation of people. But by and large, people at the borders will stay at the borders. People at the ports are going to stay at the ports.

I mean, there's not going to be this -- well, there's anxiety about this huge dislocation. Clearly, we change -- there may also come some career opportunities that heretofore didn't exist. But by and large, we want people to be -- remain at their station. We're just going to give them a little bit more help in the process.

MR. SESNO: I want to start getting ready to turn to you for some of your questions out in the audience now. As I said, we have four microphones. For those of you who would be brave enough to start, please raise your hand. We'll get a microphone moving toward you. And I'm sure we've got many volunteers.

But while you do that -- and please raise your hand as I turn to the Governor with the next question. It's not just the merger of these 22 departments and agencies; it's also

For additional analytical, business and investment opportunities information,
please contact Global Investment & Business Center, USA
at (202) 546-2103. Fax: (202) 546-3275. E-mail: rusric@erols.com

working much more closely with state and local authorities. Now, how does the fundamental relationship to knit together Homeland Security unfold over the coming months?

GOVERNOR RIDGE: When the President created the Office for Homeland Security, he talked about the development of a national strategy to secure the homeland. One of the reasons we recommended to the President that we create this department and bring these people and their experiences together was we felt it was the best way to build and then sustain, permanently, relationships with state government, with local government, with the private sector and, for that matter, down the road with individual citizens.

And, again, the notion being that as well-intentioned as we are in Washington -- and we're going to have funding and resources from Washington and leadership from Washington, we'll set standards from Washington -- but we need to engage America, all of America, all levels of government -- the private sector, the academic sector, and even individual citizens, to resist and confront this new threat.

One of the best ways to do that is bringing these agencies together, and then as we reorganize these agencies, go do it in a way that facilitates the creation as well as our ability to sustain those relationships permanently. It's an enduring vulnerability.

MR. SESNO: Sure.

GOVERNOR RIDGE: We accept it as a permanent condition of life, so we have to make permanent changes in order to deal with it.

MR. SESNO: Right. Because you need to hear from some sheriff out there or someone who knows of the security of a rail yard.

GOVERNOR RIDGE: Well, we love those sheriffs out there. I mean, those sheriffs and that law enforcement community out there, they're about 650,000 to 700,000 strong. One of these days in the very distant future, in our infrastructure analysis -- information analysis and infrastructure unit, first of all, we become a customer of the CIA. We become a customer of the FBI. We get their reports. We generate our own internally. And working with the FBI, we want to engage state and local law enforcement. It's a great force multiplier. So that sheriff, that local constable, that state policeman down the road, we'll pull them in.

MR. SESNO: All right, let's turn to our first question from the audience. We'll come back to law enforcement, I hope, in a few minutes.

GOVERNOR RIDGE: Okay.

MR. SESNO: Go ahead, if you would introduce yourself and tell us your department or your agency.

Q TSA. Sir, we have the homeland to secure and take care of. But there's large impacts and relationships across the borders and international standards and rules. How do we play in that? How do we deal with the policy of foreign interaction?

GOVERNOR RIDGE: Well, your question with regard to the connection between the department and the international world is a very important one and a critical piece of the new department. We've already seen that there are several agencies who are moving into the new department who have begun to take a leadership role in that effort because the reach of these terrorists is global. We may be the primary target -- we are the primary target, make no mistake about it. But their reach and their impact has been global. It's a French tanker off of Yemen. It's vacationers from many countries in Bali. And the list goes on and on.

So we need -- if we are to worry about commercial aviation and set security standards -- to engage the community around the world. Again, it's something that -- FEMA has a representative that I spent some time with at the European Union in terms of coordinating preparedness and response. This cargo security initiative that Rob Bonner and his team came up with is an immediate response to the vulnerability we have at our ports, because we get about 6 million containers at our ports from around the world every year. About two-thirds of those come from about 20 ports.

Now, Rob and his team didn't wait for the new department. They went out, and Customs created a cargo security initiative. And we're going to put non-intrusive technology and some of Customs' best people in 20 of these ports so we can do the inspections before those containers even get on the ship. So whether it's shipping, commercial aviation, preparedness and response, best practices, information sharing, intelligence gathering, there's a huge, huge international dimension to this effort.

MR. SESNO: We have another question. The gentleman in the back.

Q GSA, Federal Protective Service.

GOVERNOR RIDGE: Yes, sir.

Q Sir, in our shop there has been discussions about job security and with the amount of people and the amount of agents and things. Because we are a small agency -- we weren't even mentioned today, the Federal Protective Service -- whether or not we will maintain our jobs and continue to do -- I heard you say we will be doing the things we were doing. But with all these other agents coming into Homeland Security, will we still be able to complete our mission, as we do right now?

GOVERNOR RIDGE: Yes, sir. You have a unique and specific mission. I didn't list all 22 departments or agencies and I apologize for excluding yours. You've got a unique and important mission and we're proud to have you.

And it's just -- there will be, I think, as we design the new personnel system that over-arches all the 22 departments and agencies in here, I think, we hope to design it in a way that we can recognize performance. We can actually enhance our recruiting efforts.

For additional analytical, business and investment opportunities information,
please contact Global Investment & Business Center, USA
at (202) 546-2103. Fax: (202) 546-3275. E-mail: rusric@erols.com

And obviously one of the areas that we want to focus on down the road is to take a look at the equipment and the training and the technology that we give to people who we've asked and we've empowered with these critical responsibilities. So we're glad to have you as part of the team and look forward to working with you again as part of that team.

MR. SESNO: Governor, before I take the next question, let me follow on the gentleman's question, if I may, for just a moment with something I heard you say before when you were talking about certain things. You said, nothing will change for a year.

GOVERNOR RIDGE: Yes.

MR. SESNO: What happens after a year?

GOVERNOR RIDGE: Yes. Well, that is the time that we hope -- first of all, Congress and the President and everybody has recognized that the most important asset in this entire effort are the men and women who work there.

In order to provide some stability, in order to hopefully alleviate, not eliminate, some of the anxiety, the Congress said, from a year after your unit moves into the new department, there is no change. Your job is secure, your pay is secure, your benefits are secure.

And then it's our responsibility to sit down with those who represent the unionized work force and the non-unionized work force to work out a personnel system. But we thought it was very, very important to try to reduce as much concern and anxiety as possible to say, this is going to take a while to do, we want to do it right, and so let's tell everybody: your job is secure, your pay is secure, your benefits are secure until we meet with your representatives and try to work out, we think, a contemporary system that will be much better than the existing one.

MR. SESNO: A question over here.

Q Good afternoon, Governor.

GOVERNOR RIDGE: Yes, sir.

Q I'm from the Department of Justice. A question about personnel. From what I understand, right now I am in the competitive civil service with 29 years service, and I can apply for vacancies in the competitive civil service. But when I am moved into the Department of Homeland Security, I will be thrown out of the competitive civil service and put into the accepted service.

And as a member of the accepted service, I will no longer be allowed to apply for vacancies in the competitive civil service. Is this correct?

GOVERNOR RIDGE: That sounds the way it existed under the old system. Hopefully, by the time we configure the new system, you may have the kind of options that we would like to create within the department for professional promotion and advancement.

I cannot answer specifically that question, but I've got your name and I'm going to get back to you with a specific answer. You might want to check it on the website. It's www.dhs.gov. That's one of the ways we're going to try and stay in touch with you over the next couple of weeks. I think after the first of the year, we're going to put in an 800-number that you can call.

We're going to start getting a newsletter out to you from time to time to answer fundamental questions like that. It's a legitimate concern someone with all your experience to have. You deserve the answer. We'll find ways to get it to you. All right?

MR. SESNO: Other question right in front of us here. Sir?

Q TSA. I'm interested in the Homeland Security Advanced Research Projects Agency that the law instituted.

GOVERNOR RIDGE: Yes.

Q But as far as I can tell, there's no one there yet. So how can we avail ourselves of opportunities such as that?

MR. SESNO: And, Governor, perhaps you would explain briefly what that is --

GOVERNOR RIDGE: Yes, right, right --

MR. SESNO: -- for people who are watching and may not be familiar with that.

GOVERNOR RIDGE: One of the units that the President proposed and the Congress really enthusiastically embraced within the new department is a unit that will deal with the science and technology that we think we need to deploy in this country to help us combat terrorism, the technology of detection. It goes across the board. There are literally hundreds, if not thousands of companies, that have already seen an area where they believe technology can enhance our ability to protect ourselves.

This unit will not only give strategic focus -- be used to give strategic focus to the hundreds of millions of dollars that are spent in other agencies on technology for security purposes, but this unit will also have some of its own money to work with the academic research community, the private sector.

As we assess needs in our country, based on the intelligence we receive, we will have the capacity to direct dollars for a technological application we believe will help us either prevent the attack, reduce our vulnerability to the attack, or give us the capacity to respond even more quickly to an event.

So we're in the process of setting up a personnel system. We're obviously going to need some people within the department to help provide that strategic focus. And that information will also be provided to you down the road if that's a career path you're interested in following.

MR. SESNO: Okay. Other question, in the back, sir.

Q Good afternoon, sir. I'm with the Federal Emergency Management Agency. The question I have is if you can give us an update on the location of the new department? (Laughter.)

GOVERNOR RIDGE: I was going to ask you that question.

MR. SESNO: And I'll have a follow-up.

GOVERNOR RIDGE: Well, good, good. Well, maybe you know. Here's what I know that a couple of days ago the requirements for a headquarters building went out. And I believe that there was a very short time frame, five to seven days, for people to get back with us, who have taken a look at the requirements. There's absolutely no decision that's been made as to its location. Obviously, it's going to be within the community -- D.C., Maryland, Virginia. That's all I can tell you.

We obviously are not going to have a headquarters -- and this may be comforting to you and depending on the kind of environment you work in, maybe you'll be disappointed. But you've got 15,000 to 17,000 men and women working in the new department as of March 1st here. This new headquarters is not going to accommodate 15,000-plus people. But as soon as we know, we'll let you know.

MR. SESNO: That leads to another question, if I may, and that is, for people who are working in departments, agencies that become part of DHS in Colorado or in Virginia or in Texas or wherever, will they still be working where they are now?

GOVERNOR RIDGE: Most of them will remain where they are. Depending on how we restructure some of those offices, again, there may be some change -- no, there will be change. I mean, change is inevitable. So I don't want to suggest to you that there will not be some changes out there. But, again, by and large, most of the people we have at critical venues -- airports, land ports, seaports -- most of them will remain pretty close to where they are.

MR. SESNO: Sir?

Q Yes, sir, United States Customs.

GOVERNOR RIDGE: Yes, sir.

Q I had a question. I know that it costs a lot to maintain our borders, to protect our borders. Is there going to be more allocations of money towards protection of our borders, helping us to do our job? Even if it means overtime? (Laughter.)

GOVERNOR RIDGE: I tell you what, that's the best response any question has received all day. (Applause.)

We are working on budget issues right now. As you know, the President in last year's budget asked for additional dollars for Customs and INS, for people and for payroll. Number one, we're hoping that when the Congress gets back, they can finish the appropriation cycle from last year's budget before getting to this year's budget.

We know we need to do more at the borders. A lot of people focus in on more bodies and more people. And, clearly, in the immediate response to 9/11 we were able to put in place hundreds, if not thousands, of National Guard personnel around the country. But I think one of the applications for some of the technology that has been used in the foreign war on terrorism may have -- does definitely have application on the borders as well.

So it will be people, technology -- and if you're working overtime, doggone it, you deserve to be paid for it. So that's just the way it ought to be, all right? (Laughter.)

MR. SESNO: Sir.

Q National Communications System. Over the past 15 months, the Office of Cyber Security and your Office of Homeland Security have done

some exceptional focus on issues and a lot of excellent work. Will those offices continue, or will they be merged into the new department?

GOVERNOR RIDGE: The Office of Homeland Security, as the President indicated during the -- our discussion on the Hill with regard to the creation of the new department, will remain in the White House. And how it relates to either the existing Office of Cyber Security, I really can't answer that question. I do not know.

I thank you for giving the kind of public tribute you did to Dick Clark and his Cyber Security folks and others. When people think of critical infrastructure, they have a tendency to think of bricks and mortar. But given the interdependency of just about every physical piece of critical infrastructure, energy, telecommunications, financial institutions and the like with the Internet and the cyber side of their business, we need to be focused on both, and will be.

But how those two will relate after the new department is hooked up, I cannot tell you. I don't know at this point.

MR. SESNO: Governor, I'm doing some work with George Mason University's critical infrastructure project, and 85 percent of the critical infrastructure of which you speak is owned by the private sector. How is this new department going to work in different ways, once you pull it together, with the private sector, whether it's a chemical plant someplace or an Internet service provider?

GOVERNOR RIDGE: We are close to completing a strategy to deal with -- well, strategy doesn't mean much to folks, so let me just distill it. We've got a way forward so that we can work with the private sector to assess how they're vulnerable, to share best practices, to reduce their vulnerability. And it will be one of the primary functions of this new department because we're going to get a lot of information in, a lot of threat information. We're going to have analysts working -- not only in Washington -- but elsewhere, whose responsibility will be to work with the private sector to shore up those vulnerabilities.

The notion behind the President's initiative -- the notion behind the President's initiative was, first of all we got to map the vulnerabilities in this country. And one of the provisions in the new -- the legislation that created the department was a freedom of information exemption. So that when we're working with the private sector and we're asking them -- and they work very closely with us -- but we need to know where you view yourselves as most vulnerable. That's not exactly information we want to share with the rest of the world. So we have that Freedom of Information Act exemption.

We need to do a national overview of our infrastructure, map vulnerabilities, then set priorities, and then work with the private sector to reduce the vulnerabilities based on our priorities. One of the challenges that I think we have -- if you don't mind, Frank, let me just digress here, just a for a minute -- all of us, and we have to fulfill our mission together, all of us -- there is no conceivable way that this country can harden every target, do everything humanly and technologically possible with regard to every person that comes across the border, every piece of cargo that comes across the border, every potential vulnerability in the private sector or the public sector. We can't possibly do that.

We're too open. We're too diverse. We're too large. It cannot be done. So the approach that we have to take -- all of us -- is manage the risk. Manage the risk based on vulnerabilities and consequence, manage the risk based on threat information that we receive -- either generated within this country or other sources that we have around the world. There will be a lot of very difficult and challenging decisions that we're going to have to make in this new department. But we have to manage the risk. And we'll do that using your judgment, using the best scientific analysis that we can get. We'll use it doing modeling.

One of the pieces of the new department provides for us to be able to set up some modeling at national labs or academic labs so we can make different assessments about different kinds of vulnerabilities and different kinds of consequences if one of those vulnerabilities is hit. So, again, we're going to manage the risk. We can do it. But I think we just have to remind ourselves that we are a large, open, diverse, trusting country, and we shouldn't kid ourselves as to our capacity of being able to be immune forever from everything. I think we all understand that.

One thing we do know about how the terrorists act, though, you start moving to protect a particular sector or building or target, they'll pull back. And we're going to have to start thinking internally like terrorists from time to time. But around this whole enterprise is the notion of all of us working together to manage the risk.

Q I'm a long-time employee for the U.S. Coast Guard. I'm under the old CSRS retirement system, and a lot of us are worried that we're going to get forced out before we're ready to retire or that you're going to change the retirement system on us.

GOVERNOR RIDGE: We don't want to force you out; we like experience and we're not going to change the retirement system.

MR. SESNO: Period?

Q Thank you. (Applause.)

MR. SESNO: There we go. Yes, ma'am.

Q I'm USDA. Governor, you're bringing together personnel with regulatory cultures, law enforcement culture and military. I'd like to know if you could share with us what is your vision for the culture in DHS and how we would get there?

GOVERNOR RIDGE: There are probably differences we can point to in culture and history of the organizations that you're talking about. But there's one great unifying theme, and that is that we are together in these -- we are together in this enterprise to protect America.

We know that if we -- we've done a pretty good job working separately protecting America. I think I can convince you we can do an even better job working together to protect America. We will be united around a common purpose and a common mission. And we want to do everything we can to respect the history of some of these organizations and their historic missions.

But the unifying element through this enterprise is we're going to wake up every single day going to do whatever we're asked to do in our individual jobs as best we possibly can because we can't afford any gaps in the system, that's where terrorists get through. And we're unified around the notion and the culture of protecting our friends and neighbors and our way of life.

I mean, I think that gets us there. I mean, you have been doing it instinctively. You haven't really thought about being part of a homeland security team until people, such as yours truly, recommended to the President we need a department to bring everybody together to be part of a homeland security enterprise.

I'm sure that those good people working in INS offices day after day after day, they're doing a good job, they're trying to monitor people coming in, monitor their conduct while they're here, seeing if they leave town. But you never thought of yourself as part of a homeland security operation. Certainly, the people at FEMA running out, trying to respond to tornadoes and hurricanes and the like, never saw themselves as part, necessarily, of a homeland security operation to defeat terrorists.

You know, I think the folks at the borders over the years have had an inkling that not only dealing with drugs and illegal -- other illegal contraband and illegal immigration, but there might be some terrorist that might filter through. But nobody, really, I think, on a day to day basis said, I'm wearing a uniform of public service. It's not the Department of Defense, but my mission is to help secure my country in my country. That's pretty heady stuff.

For additional analytical, business and investment opportunities information, please contact Global Investment & Business Center, USA at (202) 546-2103. Fax: (202) 546-3275. E-mail: rusric@erols.com

So it's not just about building a new department, it's about taking on this mission. And we calculated, I think, if you take a look at the number of people that come across the borders, cargos into the ports, ships into the ports, planes that land, there's an excess of a billion transactions that all of us have to monitor and watch annually. Think about that: a billion-plus, and we've got to be right every day. I think there is no greater unifying element that we are working together, we can fulfill this mission. (Applause.)

Q Good afternoon, sir. I'm from the Air and Marine Interdiction Division, U.S. Customs Service. Given how critically important the Department of Defense is to our national counterterrorism effort, has your policy team had time to think about the line that needs to be drawn between the military and domestic law enforcement agencies when jointly conducting security operations in the homeland?

GOVERNOR RIDGE: We have been doing more than thinking about it. We've begun discussions with our colleagues at the Department of Defense, because Secretary Rumsfeld, as you know, has created a northern command in the Department of Defense. And this gives us an opportunity because there is a focal point through the civilian chain of command where, Secretary to Secretary and our designees can sit down and work out in advance when we would need and when we could access the very unique capabilities that the Department of Defense would provide for us in either preventing or responding to an attack.

So what has happened, as we're creating this new department, the Secretary of Defense created a new command obviously dealing with Mexico and Canada as well. But because of the new structure over there, we have a single point of access -- again, not directly from me to the General, but from Secretary to Secretary and our designees to work out these very important questions that you raise.

We've got special assets. We want to be able to say in advance if such and such occurrence occurs, these things will follow. And rarely, but we know we mean to use them and we'd like to plan them in advance.

MR. SESNO: Let me follow that with something that's separate but related in a sense. And that is the whole question of intelligence-gathering information analysis.

You'll get information -- you'll get information from the likes of the CIA and the FBI, as you said. But you will also collect it through Customs, GSA conceivably, you name it. How is that going to be fashioned? Will this department set the priorities from the analysis of that information, or as some are suggesting, does that need to be done by an altogether different entity, still to be created?

GOVERNOR RIDGE: One of the features of the new department and one of the basic units -- and I referred to it earlier -- was the unit we call Information Analysis and Infrastructure Protection. This department, as I said before, will get the reports and the analysis from the CIA and the FBI. I can speak from personal experience that we will institutionalize it. If we have to go back to the CIA or to the FBI for additional information, we will get it. We meet every single day with the President of the United States, and I am personal witness to the collaboration not just between the FBI and the CIA, but there have been occasions when we received information, we needed greater detail about the information, we went back to either agency and we received it.

You add to that the information that is collected by and among the units that are coming into the new department. Customs collects information, INS collects information, Coast Guard collects information, TSA gets information, other entities get information that all come into that unit.

So we will actually be in a position from time to time to share, particularly with the FBI, some information that we had acquired and analyzed and ship it over for them, as they deal with the disruption of terrorist activity in this country. So we will have access to all the intelligence, all the information that relates to homeland security, domestic security, and then our primary responsibility is to take that and shore up or harden America. The primary responsibility of the FBI is to take all that information and go out and disrupt those who would -- those individuals who would be responsible for terrorist activity.

MR. SESNO: If your department says we need more of that information, they will do it?

GOVERNOR RIDGE: Yes. I mean, that -- again, that has been my experience to date, and on a personal level I think all of us are working together to make sure that it is an institutionalized within the framework of the a department. But, in fact, Congress placed in the language of the new bill, an affirmative obligation on those entities to share that information with us. But I want to divide.

The dividing line is that, they will share with us -- we're going to have an intelligence product that we're going to share with others, as well. Our use of this information is to go out and work with law enforcement and the private sector to make sure that if there's a threat and there's a vulnerability, we're prepared to respond to that vulnerability and maybe harden that target.

The FBI's responsibility in this is to go disrupt the actors, go out there and get those potential terrorists before they strike us.

MR. SESNO: Would you like to have a domestic intelligence function centralized?

GOVERNOR RIDGE: I think -- right now, it's centralized every day within the President's -- within the Oval Office. The President feels very, very strongly that -- and I think it's appropriate -- that when you have an intelligence-gathering, foreign intelligence-gathering entity, that person shouldn't be reporting to a Secretary of the Cabinet. That person should be reporting directly to the President of the United States.

Bob Mueller, under the FBI, at the direction of the President, has shifted. Again, they've had an historic mission. But like we're asking other agencies to do, shift resources and personnel into another mission and that is intelligence-gathering and disruption activity of these potential terrorists.

I think between or among the different responsibilities assigned to the different agencies, for the time being I'm quite satisfied with the arrangement because I know that as far as we are concerned in our department we will get the information we need from the relevant agencies.

Q I'm from the Immigration Service.

GOVERNOR RIDGE: Yes, ma'am.

Q I think the DHS provides an opportunity for us to do our mission much more effectively. And my question is, is there a means or a way for agency employees to present ideas for change and improvement to DHS and the people who will be involved in handling the reorganization? Thank you.

GOVERNOR RIDGE: Absolutely. One of the things I've discovered in public service, but also interacting with the private sector and others, is when you ask the men and women who are involved -- whether it's in government or in a factory or elsewhere, how they might be able to do more or better with the resources they have, or what recommendations they might have so that they can do a better job -- because people go to work every day, you want to go a good job.

Everybody goes to work trying to do a good job. I believe that. I believe everybody here, when you go into that office, wherever you go, you say, I'm going to do as best I can -- myself, my country, and my job and today. That's the mind set that you bring in. Along the way, you say to yourself, gee, I wish the superintendent or so and so would rethink about how we get this information, or rethink about this process, or how we do that.

I'll give you perfect example, when I was Governor of Pennsylvania, I went into the J. Edgar Thompson works -- steel mill in Pennsylvania. And in Pennsylvania, the labor and management in steel mills didn't always get along. The fact of the matter is, management sat down with these individuals and they changed a lot of the process on the floor, increased safety, improved productivity, enhanced profitability, didn't cost anybody a dime. They just listened to the employees.

We know that you bring a lot of experience and a lot of ideas to what you do when you go into that office every day trying to do a good job. Part of our job is, like I said, we're in this mission together. We will only fulfill this mission if we work closely together and listen to one another. That doesn't mean we're going to accept every recommendation. But I tell you, we are all ears.

INS -- you've got a real tough job. A very important job. And as you know, the legislation really takes INS -- it terminates the agency, as it presently exists, on January 24th. You're divided into three sections, the judicial, review, stays of justice. And there's a citizenship and immigration bureau, and then there's an enforcement bureau.

As we go about creating this new 21st century department, it will be very important for us to hear how you think you can do your job better. And I am sure you have the opportunity to do that.

MR. SESNO: We're going to take one more question from the floor. Sir.

Q Hello, Governor. I'm with the U.S. Customs Service. My question relates to how you plan to ramp-up the department headquarters. I know sitting where we sit, it's -- I think most of us are eager to, number one, find out what's going to happen. But, number two, to continue to move. And we'd like to have counterparts to work with up at the department level.

Obviously, some of the people over in your Office of Homeland Security have been trying to fulfill those roles, and there's a transition team.

GOVERNOR RIDGE: Right.

Q But the department, itself, has got to obviously have a headquarters. Do you have a schedule for that?

GOVERNOR RIDGE: ASAP, I guess, is the schedule. (Laughter.) We'd like to -- we'd like to be able to identify that as quickly as possible and begin the transition, but I can't give you a time certain. All I know is that we've put out -- I want to assure you that the beautiful offices that the Customs have are off limits. (Laughter.) Nice offices you've got here, Rob. That's okay, we're not going to touch them.

But we're going to try to move as quickly as possible. But I can't tell you when. I don't think it's going to be by the end of January. I would be very surprised -- hopefully by March 1st we'll have identified a place that the headquarters team can move into.

MR. SESNO: Governor, before we wrap and before I ask you if you have any final questions, I'd like to bring this conversation back down to earth in a sense, and to a very basic question. I don't know how much detail you'll be able to go into. But how would you characterize right now, today, the nature of the threat, the terrorist threat, confronting this country?

GOVERNOR RIDGE: We have the national threat system that has us at an elevated level of alert, which is a pretty significant level. And it's based upon the operations that we have seen conducted around the world. It will be the responsibility of the new department and the new Secretary to reassess that level of threat every single day.

We know -- ladies and gentlemen, we're dealing with an enemy without uniforms, that's not centrally located, that doesn't distinguish between civilians and combatants, and it sees the United States as its primary battleground. So it's a serious level, it's an elevated level.

And that is why we've asked, and the federal government has done it, but that is why we've asked states and companies, as we adjust to the new threat environment and as we tell you that the level of threat remains high, we see operations around the rest of the world -- we could only conclude that -- and we know there are people who are sympathetic or supportive or actually even potentially terrorists within this country, so we have an elevated level of risk. And we want down the road for companies and states and local governments to take a look at those five levels of threat and then come up with protective measures.

Depending on the level of threat, what does your department do. Now, the federal government has done that. They've all done that. But we want companies to do the same thing. We want -- most of the states are now developing their own plans. So I kind of segue into, it's not just the level of threat; what do we do as a country based on our assessment of the threat to protect ourselves.

Jay Leno said, in one of his monologues one night, he said, hey Governor Ridge, he said, this new, color-coded system, he says, it's got five colors. He says, Americans have trouble with the three colors in the traffic light. What makes you think they're going to deal with five? (Laughter.)

Well, we're going to deal with five, and for every level of threat, we will in time have a level of protective measures that we will undertake.

MR. SESNO: So we'll see more specificity with --

GOVERNOR RIDGE: We'll keep working on that. We've got to make sure -- the system has to mature.

MR. SESNO: We've got about a minute left or so. Any closing remarks? The floor is yours.

GOVERNOR RIDGE: Yes. For those who participated today and for those who have had a chance to observe, it's a little presumptuous for someone that's been designated as a Secretary to presume that the confirmation will get Senate support. I'm hopeful, and I guess I'm allowed to be a little optimistic, because I'm here. (Laughter.)

But the fact of the matter is that this is a unique and it's an historic opportunity. And there are a lot of people that we could point to who have risen to the occasion of dealing with the enormous change and powerful circumstances. And I was looking to try to find one in our history that you might relate to. Abraham Lincoln said at one time, at his second inaugural, when he told us that "the occasion was piled high with difficulty." But it was under those circumstances that he asked America to think and to act anew. "History will not escape us," said Lincoln.

Well, we've got a unique opportunity in our history right now to do it now, to do it right, and not only to build a department, but to make America a safer place. You know, I take a look at myself, my kids are 15 and 16, and I have a pretty good life. I'm 57 years of age and I've lived in this country where things are about as good as they've ever been any place, anywhere at any time. But now I take a look at my kids and your kids and your grandkids, and suddenly we've got this new threat. And it's incumbent on all of us who are given the opportunity to do something about it, to understand that together we can fulfill the mission.

And I'm absolutely convinced that we can. And I look forward to partnering with each and every one of you, with our colleagues of state government, everybody else to get this done.

One final word. I didn't answer all your questions today and you're going to have a lot more. We'll make sure that we, our communication is regular and honest and candid. And together, as I said before, we'll fulfill our mission.

Thank you very, very much. (Applause.)

MR. SESNO: Governor Ridge, thank you very much. I want to remind the audience here and those who may be watching at home or elsewhere, that if there's any part of this conversation that you'd like to see or to reference, you can go to www.dhs.gov -- that's Department of Homeland Security dot gov. to see the videostreamed version of this. So in the spirit of the 21st century, we are there.

GOVERNOR RIDGE: We're there.

MR. SESNO: Governor, thank you very much and good luck.

GOVERNOR RIDGE: Thanks, all. Thank you.

SECRETARY TOM RIDGE TESTIFIES BEFORE THE SENATE COMMITTEE ON COMMERCE, SCIENCE AND TRANSPORTATION

April 9, 2003

Good morning Chairman McCain, Senator Hollings and other distinguished members of the committee. It is a pleasure and a privilege to be here with you this morning to describe the efforts of the Department of Homeland Security to secure our nation's transportation systems, border and ports of entry.

Thank you for the opportunity to hear your concerns, and to discuss with you the substantial challenges that lie ahead. We at the Department of Homeland Security are committed to working closely with you, state and local governments, and private industry to address these challenges and ensure that America's future is prosperous and secure.

In protecting our systems of commerce and transportation, we face a two pronged challenge; safeguard our homeland, and at the same time, ensure that the free flow of people, goods and commerce is not disrupted. The Department of Homeland Security is leading the effort to reach this objective, but it will not be achieved strictly within the DHS.

It will require a sustained and coordinated effort by governmental and private partners. It will require investment by all parties, the development of new approaches, and the application of new technologies. It will require us to make difficult decisions, critical assessments, and work to find the elusive balance point between the substantial and measurable costs of security and even more substantial and immeasurable costs of insecurity.

Since the terrorist attacks on 9/11, we have made great strides to protect the national transportation system. Congress created the Transportation Security Administration and empowered it to manage transportation security in all modes of transportation. TSA will play a strategic role in developing the National Transportation System Security Plan, a key portion of the National Strategy for Homeland Security.

Two other key components within the Department include the U.S. Coast Guard as lead in the maritime domain and the Bureau of Customs and Border Protection in dealing directly with the movement of people, goods and cargo across our borders.

In February, Admiral Loy appeared before this Committee and provided you with a comprehensive overview of TSA's progress on aviation security. I would like to add several recent successes. Under the purview of the FAA, approximately 95 percent of 6,000 commercial airlines will have hardened cockpit doors as of today. On February 25, we initiated the Federal Flight Deck Officer program. The first training session will begin next Monday at the Federal Law Enforcement Training Center.

Additionally, we continue to make progress in deploying explosives detection systems at the few remaining airports where not all baggage is screened using this technology.

We continue to develop the next generation of the Computer-Assisted Passenger Prescreening System. CAPPS II will be a critical element in TSA's "system of systems" and will effectively enhance the screening of airline passengers moving the screening further from the gate while safeguarding their civil liberties.

Along our nation's coasts and in our seaports, the Coast Guard, TSA, BCBP, the Department of Transportation's Maritime Administration and Saint Lawrence Seaway Development Corporation, all play a role to provide increased security at our ports. These efforts were furthered with the passage of the Maritime Transportation Security Act last November. I am taking steps to ensure we implement the Act in an integrated, timely manner.

The Coast Guard and TSA continue their progress on conducting port security assessments in coordination with our Directorate of Information Analysis and Infrastructure Protection . TSA, in conjunction with the Coast Guard and MARAD, awarded an initial round of $92 Million in port security grants last summer to 51 different seaports and in January made available an additional $100 million for our nation's seaports.

In the cargo container security arena, the Department is providing security for the nearly 6 million containers that enter our ports each year by partnering with other countries and the private sector to push our zone of security outward. One program to implement this strategy includes the Container Security Initiative, or CSI, which identifies high-risk cargo containers and partners with other governments to pre-screen those containers at foreign ports, before they are shipped to America.

The Department has been working with and will continue to work closely with the Department of Transportation, and the many stakeholders in the railroad industry to enhance rail security. We will leverage the industry relationships and regulatory structure that FRA has long developed. As an example of this cooperation, TSA and FRA recently collaborated in reviewing Amtrak's security plan and advised this Committee of the results of that review.

DHS is following a similar approach for mass transit security including rail, inter-city buses, and ferries. Security in these modes presents a continuing challenge due to the lack of security in place at this point and the public's desire and need for the freedom to move through each mode.

Highway security is an additional challenge that we are beginning to address. Cooperation with the Federal Highway Administration and states is crucial. The enactment of the Critical Infrastructure Information Act of 2002, assists this effort by protecting information that is voluntarily submitted to the federal government.

The thousands of miles of pipelines throughout American represent another unique challenge. In order to secure such a vast network, the communications between our Federal, State and industry partners has been streamlined. TSA and DOT's Research and Special Programs Administration continue to focus on implementing coordinated, risk-based protocols to ensure operators are putting security practices into place at critical facilities.

Mr. Chairman, transportation security is a collaborative effort between the Department of Homeland Security, other federal agencies, state and local governments, the private sector, and individual Americans. Together we have made great advances in securing our transportation systems, while protecting civil liberties, and ensuring the free flow of people and commerce, but we recognize that more needs to be done.

The Department of Homeland Security is dedicated to accomplishing the objectives set forth in the President's National Strategy for Homeland Security. This strategy provides the framework to mobilize and organize the nation. We are proud of our efforts thus far and are eager to press forward with the mission of building a safer and more secure future for our country.

This concludes my prepared statement. I thank you for the opportunity to speak before you today. I would be happy to answer any questions you may have.

STATEMENT OF SECRETARY TOM RIDGE BEFORE THE SENATE APPROPRIATIONS COMMITTEE

Good morning. Chairman Stevens, Senator Byrd, and distinguished members of the Committee - I am privileged to be with you today to discuss the President's wartime Supplemental Budget Request for the Department of Homeland Security.

As I begin, I want to take a moment to acknowledge the men and women of our armed forces who are bravely serving our nation in defense of our freedoms and values. Their efforts on behalf of this Nation are truly noteworthy. In particular, I want to recognize the sacrifices that each of these men and women are making and thank their families on behalf of a grateful nation for their service. As we have already seen, freedom comes at a price and for some, the ultimate price has been paid as they laid down their lives in service to our country.

I also want to pause to reflect on the men and women who are providing security to our homeland. Our effort abroad would be incomplete without dedicated individuals at home who have accepted the call to safeguard our homeland - from First Responders to those who secure our borders, ports, waterways, and critical infrastructure - their efforts are crucial to preserving our way of life.

Collectively, our armed forces and our men and women securing the homeland exemplify the best of our National spirit and determination to defend liberty at home and abroad.

It is with gratitude for their sacrifice and service that we request this supplemental budget to the Congress to help support their efforts in this war on terrorism.

As America executes Operation Iraqi Freedom, the Department of Homeland Security requests an increase of $3.5 billion to support Operation Liberty Shield and other measures to enhance our security at home.

The resources provided through this supplemental budget request will allow the Department to assist our partners at the state and local level to prepare our nation's first responders and to protect our Nation from the threat of terrorism.

Specifically, the Department seeks $2.0 billion for state and local terrorism preparedness and prevention. These resources will support further enhancements to state and local terrorism preparedness efforts, including Federally-coordinated prevention and security enhancements. This request will help state and local First Responders with new equipment, training, and better emergency planning. As part of Operation Liberty Shield, the funding will also improve protection at critical infrastructure facilities and help secure high threat urban areas.

The supplemental budget request builds upon ongoing efforts of the Office for Domestic Preparedness which made available nearly $600 million to states earlier this month. It also enables states and localities to meet emerging and short-term homeland security measures.

Funding is requested for three activities:

- $1.5 billion of the supplemental request will go towards enhancing the capacity of state and local jurisdictions to prepare for incidents of terrorism on U.S. soil. Grant funds for state and local terrorism and preparedness activities may be used for the acquisition of equipment, training, exercises, and planning. Consistent with past practices, at least 80% of the total amount will be passed through to local governments for First Responders in the various cities. To the extent practicable, state and local spending plans should be consistent with the most recent state preparedness strategy.

For additional analytical, business and investment opportunities information,
please contact Global Investment & Business Center, USA
at (202) 546-2103. Fax: (202) 546-3275. E-mail: rusric@erols.com

- $450 million is requested for states to augment security at critical infrastructure facilities during the duration of Operation Liberty Shield. Grants will be allocated to states by formula, but no less than one-third of each grant must be allocated to local jurisdictions.
- $50 million is requested to enable the Secretary of Homeland Security to support additional protection or preparedness needs of selected urban areas facing a particular high threat.

The supplemental budget request also includes $1.5 billion for the Department of Homeland Security for the costs of providing support to prevent, counter, investigate and respond to unexpected threats or acts of terrorism - during this period of heightened threat.

This funding is intended to support:

- Increased operations tempo in the Border and Transportation Security directorate, including additional screening of visitors crossing the border, more secondary inspection of immigrants and visitors at ports-of-entry, increased inspection of high-risk goods and cargo at ports-of-entry, additional flight hours for airspace security, and increased security between ports-of-entry on the northern border.
- Pre-deployment of federal emergency response assets in preparation for potential terrorist attacks, and activation of government emergency response plans and activities as well as other urgent homeland security requirements based on threats that may emerge.
- Enhance Coast Guard protection of critical U.S. ports during the duration of the conflict. The funding will support the activation of over 6,000 reservists.
- Funding will also support Coast Guard forces already deployed or in the process of being deployed to the operational theater and the protection of the military out-loads in U.S. ports.

In summary, the supplemental budget request for the Department of Homeland Security supports the Administration's objectives to support our troops abroad and increase safety at home.

This supplemental budget will provide the Department with the resources to manage its responsibilities and continue its work of securing the homeland for the American people.

Mr. Chairman and Members of the Committee, this concludes my prepared statement. I would be happy to answer any questions you may have at this time.

TESTIMONY OF SECRETARY RIDGE BEFORE THE SENATE JUDICIARY COMMITTEE

Mr. Chairman, Senator Leahy, distinguished members of the committee. It is a distinct pleasure and privilege to appear before you today in what is my first opportunity to testify before the Congress as the Secretary of Homeland Security. I appreciate the opportunity to appear with my colleagues, the Attorney General and FBI Director Mueller, two distinguished public servants, and two of my closest allies in the ongoing campaign to enhance the safety and security of our American Homeland. Thank you for this opportunity to highlight the activities and accomplishments of the Department of Homeland Security over the brief 40 days since we came into being. I hope also to talk about ongoing efforts, and address future plans within the Department.

To say it has been a busy six weeks at DHS would be a profound understatement. The men and women of the Department have been, and still are, pressing forward with skill, tenacity and clear understanding of the importance of the work they do. As a result of their efforts, I am proud to say that what was little more than a bold idea and an ambitious legislative undertaking four months ago is now a real and functioning Department.

Last Saturday, the first of March, 2003, we integrated nearly two dozen agencies or entities into the Department of Homeland Security. With them came some 180,000 dedicated Federal workers who have all been serving their country with distinction from various departments within the government. This momentous milestone means that there is now real muscle on the skeleton of a department that was created back in January. With these agencies and these people come tremendous capabilities, as well as challenges. We are a Department that must now set about the business of melding this collection of capable but diverse organizations into a cohesive, effective and efficient team. And we must do it without losing focus, for even an instant, on the critical mission that is ours.

But we have not simply been waiting for March 1 to arrive. Since January we have undertaken a number of initiatives to enhance our Homeland Security today, and into the future.

In order to better protect our borders, Undersecretary Asa Hutchinson, with my strong support, has launched a well conceived and much needed plan to combine the forces of the Customs Service, the Immigration and Naturalization Service, the agricultural inspection functions of the Animal and Plant Health Inspection Service and the Federal Protective Service. His initiative, based on the vision articulated in the Homeland Security Act, combines the four entities into two, a Bureau of Customs and Border Protection, and a Bureau of Immigration and Customs Enforcement. This is an important step that will leverage the operational expertise of all those involved and move us toward a future where there will be one organizational face at our borders, instead of the current three. This realignment of resources has already demonstrated its benefit. Last week, customs, immigration and agriculture border inspectors reported to three separate port directors who in turn reported up separate chains of command to three separate cabinet secretaries. Today, these inspectors now report to one interim port director, who reports through a unified chain of command, to one cabinet Secretary.

Two weeks ago we rolled out the Department's Citizen Preparedness program. The public response has been overwhelming, with our ready.gov website receiving more than 2.5 million visits per day since becoming operational. This program provides immediate and practical guidance to the millions of Americans who, to their credit, know that preparing makes sense. I ask you to encourage your constituents to visit our web site www.Ready.gov or call 1-800-bereday as an important first step in ensuring they and their loved ones are prepared for an emergency, whether it's brought on by the forces of evil, or simply the forces of nature.

As of 1 March, we have entered into a number of Memoranda of Understanding that consolidate previously dispersed, national incident support functions into DHS. We have taken responsibility and control of Domestic Emergency Support Team, the Strategic National Stockpile, and America's National Disaster Medical System and Teams. Restructuring these authorities gives the Department the ability to manage major domestic incidents by establishing a single, comprehensive, and coherent national incident management system.

More important than the accomplishments that lie behind us though are the milestones and challenges that still lie ahead.

We are beginning the budgetary cycle for Fiscal Year 2004, another first for our new Department. The President's budget, requesting some $36.2 billion dollars clearly communicates this administration's commitment to investing in our Homeland Security. It contains a 7.4% increase over the funds our agencies received in FY 03, calls for $18 billion to secure our borders, $6 billion dollars for emergencies and first responders, $829 million for assessing and preventing threats, and $803 million for science and technology. In order to ensure those, and our current funds, are properly managed we have established policies and procedures for integrating financial management and accounting functions for all our incoming organizational elements.

Also ahead of us are other challenges as well as opportunities to work more efficiently and effectively. We are making good progress on a regional structure that will help to enhance overall accountability and efficiency, but the plan is still under development. When we have a better idea how the regions will be organized we look forward to presenting a final plan to the Congress. And we are working with the Office of Personnel Management to design a personnel management system that will maximize the productivity, morale and efficiency of our most precious resource -our workforce.

We continue to build and refine our partnerships with other Federal Departments, State and Local governments and the private sector. There is no Federal plan that will ensure our Homeland Security, it must be a National plan that involves all Americans. And, it must go beyond even this, working closely with our neighbors and allies overseas, to build an international plan and an international response. We are working to build just such a plan.

While this work goes on we must continue to carefully tend to all the critical missions of the Department of Homeland Security, especially those that are not directly security related. Please be assured that we will continue to provide the level of service we have all come to expect.

For additional analytical, business and investment opportunities information, please contact Global Investment & Business Center, USA at (202) 546-2103. Fax: (202) 546-3275. E-mail: rusric@erols.com

We have the support of our partners, like the gentlemen who join me here today, and we have the support of the Congress, which has been critical in bringing us to this point.

The challenges before us are substantial, but we will overcome them because we must. Our American homeland is safer today than it was a year ago, but we live in dangerous times and we cannot count on times to change. That is why the Department of Homeland Security was created, that is why we are moving forward.

I appreciate the opportunity to be here today to talk about the work we are doing to make America a safer home for us, for our children and for generations to come. Thank you for inviting me to appear before you today, and I look forward to answering your questions.

THE NOMINATION OF THE HONORABLE GORDON ENGLAND TO BE DEPUTY SECRETARY OF THE DEPARTMENT OF HOMELAND SECURITY

Thank you Senator Collins, Senator Lieberman and all the Members of the Committee for giving me the opportunity to testify today.

Before I begin, I want to first thank President Bush and Secretary Tom Ridge for their leadership and vision -- and for placing his confidence in me. Homeland security relies on partnerships and I am honored and humbled that they would make me a partner in this great national effort.

The Secretary has brought together an extraordinary team of patriots and public servants. I have met a great many of them. No matter what agency or bureau they may hail from, they are resolute and united behind the mission of homeland security: to protect the American people and our way of life from terrorism. For the first time, we now have a single Department whose primary mission is exactly that - and which will help them do their jobs even better.

The effort to secure the homeland can be summed up as follows: prevent terrorist acts; identify and reduce our vulnerabilities to terrorist threats; and ensure our preparedness to effectively respond and recover while saving as many lives as possible in the event of a future attack.

To achieve those goals, the President's National Strategy for Homeland Security - the nation's first -- identifies six critical mission areas the new Department will focus on: intelligence and warning; domestic counterterrorism; border and transportation security; the protection of critical infrastructure and key assets; defense against catastrophic threats; and emergency preparedness and response.

Significant progress has been, and continues to be made in each of those mission areas. As Secretary Ridge indicated before this committee, since 9-11 this nation has clearly improved its protective capabilities. Our maritime borders have been pushed farther from shore. Our land border security has been tightened, and walls torn down between the law enforcement and intelligence communities, so we better know who is in our country and why.

Tens of thousands of professional screeners have been deployed at every one of our commercial airports, and thousands of air marshals are on our planes. We've acquired a billion doses of antibiotics and instituted a major smallpox vaccination program. Working with Congress, billions of dollars has been allocated for bioterrorism training and food and water security -- and the President continues to work with Congress on his proposed thousand-percent increase in funding for first responders.

In short, as Secretary Ridge said, the homeland is indeed far safer and better prepared today than on 9-11 -- and will be safer still tomorrow as we develop new capabilities through the Department of Homeland Security.

As Deputy Secretary, I will do whatever the President and the Secretary ask of me in order to achieve those goals and accomplish our mission of protecting the American people from terrorism. They have placed their confidence in me -- and I will do my utmost to repay that confidence.

I believe my record and experience show I am qualified for this task.

As Secretary of the Navy, I managed a force of nearly 900,000 active and reserve troops and civilian employees, and a budget of more than a hundred billion dollars. In that role, I was charged by Secretary Rumsfeld with finding and eliminating waste and using the savings to improve our fighting capability. Such an effort, I believe, is critical in any large, complex organization. And as Deputy Secretary of the Department of Homeland Security, I will work with Secretary Ridge, the Under Secretaries and Congress to ensure that the resources allocated toward the protection of Americans from terrorism are actually used to protect Americans from terrorism.

Secretary Ridge said he would insist that measurable progress be made by the new Department and its component agencies. I could not agree more. At the Pentagon, a new initiative had to meet several criteria: does it benefit our troops and improve their ability to fight? Does it provide common good across the entire Department of Defense? And does it result in identifiable savings? Measuring our programs on how well they meet the criteria we assign to them must be a constant and consistent emphasis.

I believe the key test for homeland security is not inputs, but outcomes. Success must be measured by the capabilities we create with the resources we have. Capabilities to protect more people -- deter more terrorist acts -- and reduce and eliminate more vulnerabilities.

Our first and most immediate challenge, of course, is the merger. We must blend 22 separate work cultures and operating and management procedures into one cohesive organization, as seamlessly and expeditiously as possible to meet our deadlines. We must create a mindset in which each agency and the people within them calibrate their missions and responsibilities toward the primary mission of homeland security. At the same time, as Secretary Ridge has indicated, we cannot lose sight of the individual missions of each agency and our need to carry them out both during and after the merger.

For additional analytical, business and investment opportunities information, please contact Global Investment & Business Center, USA at (202) 546-2103. Fax: (202) 546-3275. E-mail: rusric@erols.com

I believe I offer some expertise on the matter. In addition to my public service, I have spent more than four decades working in the private sector. Part of that time I was a merger and acquisitions consultant. Later, at General Dynamics, I helped facilitate the merger of the Fort Worth Company with Lockheed.

I know from direct experience that merging large organizations takes great patience and open and constant communication. We must ensure that those affected are fully invested in the process and aware of its progress. After all, we are not moving chess pieces; we are moving people.

As Secretary Ridge has indicated, we must not allow invisible barriers to get in the way of our overall mission. As we build the Department, we will foster teamwork and a strong sense of pride behind our primary mission.

And we must act always with the understanding that homeland security is not just a federal effort, but a national one. We will continually cultivate partnerships with other agencies, state and local governments, the private sector and academia, and the American people themselves.

This is the largest reorganization of government in more than half a century. It is a great challenge. But the Transition Planning Office has laid the framework for a strong and sound organizational structure to accomplish these goals. I believe we are well on our way to creating a professional workforce focused on the protection of our homeland from terrorism.

Let me now talk about one of our greatest allies in this effort: technology. In fact, we have an entire directorate dedicated to Science and Technology. As a former member of the Defense Science Board, I especially look forward to "standing up" that Directorate.

Our ability to improve communication vertically and horizontally - to spot and capture terrorists and their deadly cargo - to quickly identify an outbreak of disease - and, of course, to merge 22 agencies into one Department -- all rely on technology.

As an Executive Vice President of General Dynamics, I was responsible for Information Systems throughout the company and I saw the transformative power of technology first-hand. I also learned the importance of ensuring that the technology was accessible and understandable by the entire company and those we worked with. We face the same challenge, on a much larger scale, with the creation of the Department of Homeland Security. As Deputy Secretary, I will work to ensure that challenge is met.

Science and technology are some of America's greatest weapons in this fight. They are a direct result of our innovative, entrepreneurial spirit. I believe that innovation and risk must be rewarded. In my experience, a good idea can come from anywhere. And that good idea must be able to travel up and down the chain of command, where it can be examined and acted upon for the good of the entire Department.

Finally, I want to echo the comments Secretary Ridge made on what he believes is the most valuable asset of the Department of Homeland Security: its people. I cannot say it

For additional analytical, business and investment opportunities information,
please contact Global Investment & Business Center, USA
at (202) 546-2103. Fax: (202) 546-3275. E-mail: rusric@erols.com

better than he did: "New funding, technology and equipment are important - but no more so than the people who willingly serve in the new Department."

Secretary Ridge has done a superb job of ensuring that the federal employees whose jobs and lives are affected by this merger are at all times informed and engaged in the process, and that their workplace rights are protected.

As for myself, my door will be open to all 170,000 employees. I believe in treating public servants with the dignity and respect they deserve. Their support can make the difference between success and failure. And so they have my support.

As Secretary of the Navy, I traveled 75,000 miles, visiting more than 50 bases and I heard the hopes and fears of our men and women in uniform. I also, on several occasions, had to write letters of condolence to their families. These patriots risked and sometimes gave their lives for our freedom. Unfortunately, many of the employees of the Department of Homeland Security may also face similar risks. You have my vow to do what it takes to make their jobs easier and safer. What they do for all of us will not be taken for granted.

Let me make one final point. One of the most promising aspects of homeland security, in my opinion, is something that President Bush and Secretary Ridge continually emphasize: its potential to make us not just a safer nation, but a better and stronger nation.

In creating new capabilities to protect the homeland, new spinoff benefits in science, technology, health and medicine, trade, and the economy may well emerge.

The terrorists who sought to make us weak with fear, will instead find that they have spurred us on to greater heights.

We face another defining moment in history. Our nation is at war with the third "ism" of my lifetime. It took a World War to defeat fascism and a Cold War to defeat communism. Now we are at war with terrorism.

History has not yet recorded how this war will be won. But we have an opportunity to begin writing that history today. And, with your approval, I look forward to being a part of it.

Thank you.

REMARKS BY SECRETARY RIDGE TO LOS ANGELES COUNTY FIRST RESPONDERS

April 24, 2003

First of all I want to thank Sheriff Lee Baca for hosting this great event. I am happy to be out in Los Angeles.

I am also pleased to share the stage with:

- Governor Gray Davis
- California State Attorney General Bill Lockyer
- Congressman Chris Cox
- Congresswoman Jane Harman
- L.A City Mayor Jim Hahn
- LAPD Chief Bratton

It is a privilege for me to share the stage with you and other distinguished guests who are working to secure the State of California. I am especially pleased that we are joined today by so many Police and Fire Chiefs. It is an honor to be with you here today.

If interest in homeland security can be gauged by the size of the audience then I'd say the interest is running pretty high!

I want to thank those of you who participated in the roundtable. I look forward to addressing your concerns.

In Southern California you can clearly see the entire homeland security panorama. Begin with the challenges at our border. This morning I began the day with Secretary Creel of Mexico at the California - Mexico border.

As you head north, you pass nuclear power plants, oil and gas refineries and other guarded, yet highly visible critical infrastructure. Farther northwest are the Ports of Los Angeles and Long Beach, the busiest and 2nd-busiest in the nation. Add several airports, including LAX, to the mix.

Finally, there's Los Angeles County itself, home to 10 million people, with 88 independent cities and 94 school districts; larger than 42 states.

It's an enormous -- and enormously complex -- challenge.

But let me begin by saying that whether you stand in Los Angeles or in Washington, D.C., you can see that America is meeting that challenge. America is far safer and more secure as a nation than we were on September 11th, 2001. We have traveled a long way, in a very short period of time.

Some of the credit belongs to the new structure we've put in place at the Department of Homeland Security.

Some of the credit belongs to our efforts to educate communities and citizens about the threat.

Some of the credit goes to new resources provided by Federal, state, and local governments to pay for equipment, training, and overtime. There are continuing needs and millions of additional federal dollars more are on the way.

Much of the credit goes to men and women such as you - people who go to work everyday to keep America safe - the law enforcement professionals and first responders.

Since 9-11 you've improved communication, cooperation and information-sharing -- three qualities essential to homeland security.

And you've integrated traditional functions in new ways, enabling you to "organize to mobilize" for any threat.

Now we must take the next step.

Homeland security affects everybody; and that's exactly who must be involved. We are all stakeholders.

Businesses, schools and communities are seamlessly integrated in peacetime. We cannot allow them to be isolated from one another in a crisis.

Our challenge is to ensure that stakeholders are committed to prevention before a crisis -- and that our response is seamless and well-coordinated during a crisis.

This isn't "civil defense" - this is civil offense. We want to take back the initiative from terrorists. And I believe we've made a great start. And together we can make this vision a reality.

Let's start with the Department itself - which is now a reality due in large part to the sustained support it received from people like you. Your collective voice was heard in Washington, and the President and I thank you for it.

Unifying 22 federal agencies into one Department, under one chain of command, was one reason Homeland Security was created. Another was the advantage of having a single point of contact to communicate with states and localities, and the private sector and to educate the public at large.

One of the ways that we communicate to homeland security professionals at the state and local level when there is a change in the threat level is through the Homeland Security Advisory System. This system is designed to help homeland security decision-makers at all levels determine the right protective measures for their critical targets and communities.

When we raised the threat level in March, with your help we launched Operation Liberty Shield - our first unified, national operation to protect Americans and our critical resources.

The State of California and Los Angeles city and County were ready to act - having put in place protocols for each threat level, protocols that were communicated to every city and jurisdiction.

Your officers and first responders worked longer days, increased your presence and visibility at airports and transportation hubs, conducted more random searches and educated the public.

Additional law enforcement and the National Guard were deployed at LAX and other critical sites around the state and nation.

The Coast Guard increased the number of security patrols and vessel escorts nationwide. We enhanced security in and around critical infrastructure sites and at key ports.

Together, we initiated these additional protections not only to increase national security, but to ensure that commerce, travel and our way of life would continue as always. For all of us engaged in Operation Liberty Shield, protecting our liberties was an essential part of the mission. After all, it's called Operation "Liberty Shield" - the "liberty" is just as important as the "shield".

We know that mobilizing at a high level of readiness presents a financial burden to communities. That's why the President signed an emergency supplemental appropriations bill that allocates more than $2.2 billion to help reimburse state and local governments.

This includes:

$1.3 billion in state formula grants

$200 million for critical infrastructure protection

and $700 million to be distributed to high threat areas for critical infrastructure protection.

In addition to the billions of dollars for state and local governments in the FY 03 supplemental, $45 million in grants for First Responders has already been made available to California.

Another $12.5 million will go to the City of Los Angeles as part of our Urban Area Security Initiative.

You told us that high-visibility, high-density urban areas may be at extra risk for terrorism, and therefore deserve extra protection. We listened, and we agreed.

This is just the start. Other funding is in the pipeline or awaits approval by Congress.

First, last week the Department of Homeland Security announced the availability of $165 million in Emergency Management Performance grants. These can be used by states to develop, maintain and improve state and local emergency management capabilities.

For additional analytical, business and investment opportunities information,
please contact Global Investment & Business Center, USA
at (202) 546-2103. Fax: (202) 546-3275. E-mail: rusric@erols.com

We've also made available $750 million in fire grants for direct use by fire departments. It is the largest amount ever for firefighters' grants, twice as much as the previous year's amount.

And the President's '04 Budget requests $3.5 billion for grants for first responders. I invite you to talk to Chris Cox and Jane Harman about this number!

The more resources we provide, the more important it is to make sure the money is spent to fight terrorism. Investments must always lead to outcomes that better protect our country.

That points to the importance of planning - seeing the big picture. We must train as we fight.

As Constance Perett of the LA County Office of Emergency Management puts it, "emergency management is the 'hub'" of the wheel.

Los Angeles County has long known the importance of comprehensive emergency planning and management. You operate under an "all-hazards" approach, based on lessons learned from mobilizing for natural disasters such as earthquakes, fires and floods. That's the right approach.

Sheriff Baca and Chief Freeman help lead the Standardized Emergency Management System, a statewide system that takes a regional approach, in which mutual aid is legally defined and routine.

Your cities get regular emergency management training and participate in countywide exercises.

Let me also say a word about your Terrorism Early Warning Group. It is a model for other cities and states. I am really looking forward to seeing the operation up close later today.

And you've involved the public through education and training campaigns for students as well as adults.

LAPD Chief Bill Bratton often speaks about "tipping point" leadership - meaning that once the minds and energies of a critical mass of people are engaged behind an idea, fundamental change will come swiftly. Our job is to engage this "critical mass" of people in their own protection.

It's still early. But based on the progress we've made together, I believe we're well on our way to finding that "tipping" point where we start going on offense instead of only playing defense. Ladies and gentlemen, thank you for helping us attain that level.

STATEMENT BY SECRETARY RIDGE BEFORE THE HOUSE SUBCOMMITTEE ON APPROPRIATIONS

March 20, 2003

Before I begin, I would like to say that my thoughts and prayers are with the men and women overseas fighting in the latest front in the global war on terrorism to protect all Americans and make the world a safer place.

The Department of Homeland Security and other federal agencies implemented Operation Liberty Shield earlier this week in order to prevent terrorist attacks and protect Americans here at home.

This comprehensive national plan has resulted in the deployment of more resources, more personnel and more assets throughout America. We are pleased that our partners in the state, cities and private sector have joined in this effort.

Good morning Chairman Rogers, Congressman Sabo, distinguished members of the subcommittee. It is a distinct pleasure to appear before you to discuss the President's FY 2004 budget request for the Department of Homeland Security. For historical purposes, I would like to note that this is the first budget request ever for a Department of Homeland Security. For practical purposes, I would add that we are a Department engaged in many firsts, with each of these new undertakings presenting both challenges and opportunity.

I would like to thank this subcommittee, and the committee that created it, for the supportive approach you have demonstrated in taking on the challenge of advancing the cause of homeland security.

I would also like to add my compliments and thanks to your staff for their professionalism, flexibility and patience as we work together through this most important "first ever" DHS budget. The President's Budget request for Fiscal Year 2004 lays a critical and solid foundation for the future of the Department of Homeland Security. It is a $ 36.2 billion commitment to advancing the safety and security of our America.

This request represents a 7.4% increase in funding for DHS programs over FY 03. It contains critical initiatives to advance the efficiency and effectiveness of our Department, supports ongoing efforts and programs, and sustains vital, non-security services and missions throughout the Department.

The President's budget contains $18.1 billion for Border and Transportation Security. This figure reflects organizational improvements, funds personnel enhancements, training, and improves the technologies needed to support two of the Department's strategic goals to improve border and transportation security while at the same time, facilitate the unimpeded flow of legitimate commerce and people across our borders and through our seaports and airports.

For additional analytical, business and investment opportunities information, please contact Global Investment & Business Center, USA at (202) 546-2103. Fax: (202) 546-3275. E-mail: rusric@erols.com

The budget request also calls for $3.5 billion to strengthen the readiness capabilities of state and local governments that play a critical role in the Nation's ability to prepare for and respond to acts of terrorism and supports a "one-stop" shop for state and local response funding and training needs within the Office of Domestic Preparedness.

Funding requested for Emergency Preparedness and Response totals $5.9 billion. These funds will be used to enhance nationwide readiness to manage and respond to disasters, whether caused by the forces of nature, or the forces of evil.

In addition to fully funding traditional FEMA programs, the President's budget includes needed investment in America's pharmaceutical and vaccine stockpiles. It also includes nearly a billion dollars for project BioShield, a critically needed incentive for the development and deployment of new and better drugs and vaccines to protect Americans from the threat of bioterrorism.

The request for Information Analysis and Infrastructure Protection is $829 million. The funds will support the directorate's efforts to analyze intelligence and other information to evaluate terrorist threats, assess the vulnerability of critical infrastructure, issue timely warnings to private sector industries, and work with Federal, state, local and private stakeholders to take appropriate protective action. The President's request provides the resources necessary for us to carry out these most important and unique DHS responsibilities.

$809 million is requested for the directorate of Science and Technology. In the quest to secure our Homeland, we face fanatical and sinister enemies. Their willingness to contemplate the most evil of means, and the possibility that others might help them to acquire those means, create an absolute imperative that we sustain a scientific and technological edge to stay ahead of our enemies.

The funds requested for Science and Technology will support the essential research, development, testing and evaluation needed to do just that, through existing programs and institutions as well as new entities like the Homeland Security Advanced Research Projects Agency.

The President requests $6.8 billion for the United States Coast Guard, a 10 percent increase over FY 03 for this vital component of the new Department of Homeland Security charged with pushing our maritime borders farther out to sea.

This request will support continued and enhanced operations of the service across its broad portfolio of indispensable missions. It enables the Coast Guard to grow to meet its ever-increasing security responsibilities, while at the same time sustaining operational excellence in non-security functions. The request provides for vital recapitalization of the Coast Guard's offshore, near shore, and communications assets.

The proposed budget also contains $1.3 billion for the United States Secret Service so they may perform their unique mission of protection and criminal investigation. The funds will support the Secret Service's protection of the President, the Vice President and their families; heads of state; the security for designated National Special Security Events;

and the investigation and enforcement of laws relating to counterfeiting, fraud and financial crimes.

$1.8 billion of the President's budget request will support the Bureau of Citizenship and Immigration Services, including $500 million aimed at reducing the backlog of applications and ensuring a six-month process standard for all applications.

In summary, this budget request for the Department of Homeland Security supports the President's National Strategy for Homeland Security. This strategy provides the Administration's basic framework to mobilize and organize the nation--federal, state and local governments, the private sector, and the American people--in the complex mission to protect our homeland.

We have begun the first steps of our critical work, but we are only at the beginning of what will be a long struggle to protect our nation from terrorism. While much has been accomplished, there is much more work to do. This budget will provide the resources to enable the Department to manage its responsibilities and lead the effort to make our country safer and more secure.

America's response to terrorism has been strong, measured and resolute. The Department of Homeland Security is committed to carrying that response forward by preventing terrorist attacks, reducing America's vulnerability, and effectively responding to attacks that might occur. By doing so, we will build a better future, a safer future, for ourselves, our children, and our country. I look forward to working with this committee and each of you individually in this challenging, critical and most noble of missions.

Mr. Chairman and Members of the Subcommittee, this concludes my prepared statement. I would be happy to answer any questions you may have at this time.

REMARKS BY SECRETARY TOM RIDGE TO NATIONAL LEAGUE OF CITIES

.S. Department of Homeland Security
Office of the Press Secretary
March 10, 2003
For Immediate Release

Washington Hilton Hotel
Washington, D.C.

SECRETARY RIDGE: Thank you, Mayor. Thank all of you for that warm greeting. Thank all of you for staying here and listening to the last speaker of the day. (Laughter.)

First of all, to my friend, Mayor Williams, as you know, the President asked me, when I served in the White House, to put together a Homeland Security Advisory Council. And part of our effort was to reach out to organizations such as yours and to ask members representing different levels of government and different groups whose perspective I thought--the President thought was needed on an advisory council to participate.

You should know that Mayor Williams of Washington, D.C. has represented your interest very, very well. He has worked tirelessly not only on the Homeland Security Advisory Council but many of you have asked for the Department of Homeland Security and the Advisory Council to develop a template to establish state wide, regional and urban security plans. You know, what are the foundation needs that we have, what are the questions we need to ask ourselves in order to get--make the right decisions.

And there have been about 40 people from around the people that have engaged in that, state and local officials, first responders and others. And I just want to thank him for his prodigious work with Governor Leavitt. And you both chair and co-chair that effort. And in the weeks ahead we hope to--not hope, we will be releasing that plan to your organization and to the mayors and the governors and homeland security advisors around the country.

So I thank him. And I also want to thank the National League of Cities for your support in creating the new department. Your advocacy was a huge help, and I thank you for that. I want to thank you for your support of the state and local unit that is becoming a formal part of the new Department of Homeland Security.

And I would be certainly remiss if I didn't not only thank you for the personal and professional support that the organization has given me, but I hope some of my friends from the cities from around Pennsylvania have remained, because I've got to thank them for the support they have sent my way, as well. Are my friends from Pennsylvania here? Once a governor, always a governor. You know that, ladies and gentlemen.

But I felt that perhaps one of the reasons that the President was so keen in getting state and local people involved in this Homeland Security Advisory Council and the President was keen in having a state and local unit within the new department, was he understood instinctively as a former governor himself that the partnership we need to build a national capacity to prevent terrorist attacks, to reduce our vulnerability and then to respond to an attack are partners with our governors and our mayors.

And so I thank you again for the opportunity to share with you some thoughts today.

It's been just over a week that the Homeland Security Department took responsibility for nearly 180,000 men and women who go to work every day to secure our homeland. We're putting the structure in place, we're reorganizing to build new and better and stronger capacities. Now we must provide the resources and the leadership, resources that go directly to protecting Americans from terrorism and leadership at all levels of government, not just from the federal level, but from the state and local level, as well.

And I'd like to take a moment to share with you what will be spent this year on homeland security. It's the fiscal '03 budget. We've submitted an '04 budget. I just want to share with you a couple thoughts about what you can expect in the next several months with regard to homeland security, all of it affecting you, some of it more directly than not.

We have nearly doubled federal spending, government wide, for homeland security from the year before. Now, many of you have heard me say this, and I believe it, we cannot secure the homeland, ultimately, from Washington, D.C. We have to have partners at the state and local level. And at the end of the day, the homeland is secure when the hometown is secure.

And so in the 2003 budget, the funds aren't for many new programs in Washington, but for security enhancements, new equipment and resources in our homelands, in our hometowns, in our states, at our borders and in our cities. This investment will create new capabilities to protect us against terrorism, and I frankly think we'll be able to integrate traditional security functions in a new and a much, much better way.

Much of it builds on the progress we've made over the past 18 months. The bottom line is that we believe these investments improve our ability to prevent a terrorist attack, not just prepare for one. And you need to understand that while there's a lot of public discussion and debate about first responders--and we know that's one of the critical roles of the Department of Homeland Security, to build a national capacity so that we can respond as quickly as possible to a terrorist event -- the number one priority must be to prevent an attack from occurring in the first place.

So the dollars that I'm talking about are for prevention, for reducing our vulnerability to attack, as well as preparing ourselves to respond to an event if it occurs.

With an emphasis on prevention--and these are some things that I think you need to know, and if you are a border state or a border mayor, you'll understand it more dramatically than most. The new investment in 2003 includes funding to hire more than 1,700 new inspectors at our ports of entry of land and sea and air, and an additional 600 border patrol agents. So again, we have this responsibility to put as many people to--at our borders and at our ports--land, air and sea--and the 2003 budget adds an additional 2,300 people for that purpose.

This budget will give us nearly $400 million toward the development-- continued development of an entry-exit visa system. And I don't know how many of you have had the privilege of go to Ellis Island, and appreciate the stories associated with the building of America there. We've got one side of our family-- actually could probably put two bricks there, but we've got a brick there that represents my mother's side of the family.

We are a nation of immigrants. We are open, we are welcoming, we are trusting, we are diverse. We don't want to change that in the future. But after 9/11, there are some changes we must make to the process of being open and trusting and diverse. And part of that is the development of an entry-exit visa system. We have to remain open to visitors. Our economy depends upon it, our country depends upon it.

But once the time has expired, once the time has elapsed, then we have to monitor and make sure those who have come in to this country leave the country, unless they have formally applied or there's another good reason to keep them here. So there's a substantial investment in that effort, as well.

Now, identifying and removing terrorists is only part of the battle. We must be equally adept at stopping their deadly cargo. Again, distinguishing between legitimate goods and people and illegitimate goods at people at our borders is one of the critical responsibilities of this new department.

By the way, it's an enormous challenge, since we have not only 500 plus million people come back and forth across our borders and to our land, sea and airports, but we have hundreds of billions of dollars worth of cargo that comes across our borders and through our sea, air and land ports as well.

I'll report to you that we've made great progress over the 18 months. For the border states, you should note that we have forged agreements with Canada and Mexico to create smarter, 21st century borders, to keep terrorists out while obviously facilitating the movement of legitimate people and goods across those borders.

One example is the NEXUS program, which we have with Canada, which reduces border delays for people known to both sides as non-terrorists, and which is now in operation at most of our major crossings along the northern border. And Congress gave us substantial dollars as we go about making infrastructure improvements at the border to facilitate the development of these 21st century border agreements.

We've got a Customs trade partnership agreement with over 2,000 companies. And here we set up a very rigorous protocol with these companies. They agree to a -- the acceptance of the protocol we design, that they have to follow all the way through their supply chain--all the way through their supply chain.

Again, as we're building national partnerships, we have to include the private sector, as well. So these companies agree on the protocol, they agree to be audited--very important expression, trust, but verify--you're going to sign up to, but we're going to audit you to do it, and from time to time, we're going to randomly inspect your trucks as they come across the border. And that's a very, very significant improvement and a significant change in how we deal with commerce coming across our borders, as well.

We've got a container security initiative that the Customs, leaning forward many, many months ago began. I perhaps mentioned this to you before, but we get about 65 percent of our containers from 20 countries around the world -- huge volume we call the megaports. Well, Customs has been out there negotiating with these countries, so we are going to put Customs officials in those ports, we're going to put non-intrusive technology in those ports, we're going to target many of those containers. There's a new requirement that we get the manifests to these Customs agents before they even load these containers on those ships, so we can inspect them there, in these megaports.

Obviously we want to apply that procedure to the rest of the ports around the world, but we needed to be focus--focused on those 20 megaports that generate about two-thirds of the commercial traffic.

We have to make smart choices and smart investments, and technology is one of them. We're investing in non-intrusive inspection systems. As I mentioned before, we have mobile machines for inspections. We can apply some of those at railroad yards, some of those at ports. We have portable radiation detectors.

Now with the consolidation of our border units -- because we felt that when you come across the border you shouldn't see three faces or four faces of America, you see one -- everybody at the borders will be equipped -- whether they formally worked at INS, they formally worked at APHIS, they formally worked at Customs -- they will all be equipped with portable radiation detectors.

I can't talk about securing our borders without talking about our Coast Guard, one of the most extraordinarily under-appreciated units of government this country has ever seen. (Applause.) I don't know if you've served on the Coast Guard, or you've got friends and neighbors or family. An extraordinary group of people. And they do a lot of things for us, with regard to protecting our sovereignty and our fisheries and rescue and those kind of things.

But they've really enhanced their responsibility and role in port and border security. Just in the past couple of years, they've conducted more than 35,000 port security patrols, 3,500 air patrols, and they've boarded more than 10,000 vessels.

Which leads me to another observation I'd like to make to, hopefully, bring you more assurance, rather than less. There's sometime, from time to time, when you get to see the talking heads on TV and they say, my god, they're only investigating two or three percent of the ships that come into the country. I want to assure you it's not random. They just don't wake up that morning and say, hmmm, I wonder how many ships are at sea; which ones should we board. There's a targeting system they use, based on information they receive from a variety of different sources. There are very specific reasons they have boarded those vessels.

And as we continue to improve our data collection system -- and Congress gave us a lot of money to do that -- get more and better technology, and the Coast Guard ramps up -- and the budget, the 2003 budget provides the largest increase for Coast Guard operating expenses since World War II -- more targeting, more boarding, greater security. Again, the Coast Guard at work, doing what it does so well and what it's been doing for 200-plus years, and that's protecting America.

As I said before, our first objective is to prevent terrorism. Our second is to reduce our vulnerability to an attack. Congress is going to invest nearly $200 million on a program and a new unit in our department that's called the Information Analysis and Infrastructure Protection Directorate. Isn't that a mouthful. All that means, ladies and gentlemen, is that we're going to have our own little intelligence unit. We're going to get information from Customs and from Transportation and from the Coast Guard and from a lot of other people. But we're also going to have access to information from every other intelligence-gathering agency in the government. Every one of them. Even to the point where if we need to, we can go back and get raw data, regardless of the source, if we request it.

For additional analytical, business and investment opportunities information, please contact Global Investment & Business Center, USA at (202) 546-2103. Fax: (202) 546-3275. E-mail: rusric@erols.com

And we're going to take that information and we're going to map it against different vulnerabilities that we might have, so that we can harden America; so that we can protect our infrastructure. Not just government infrastructure -- 85 percent of it is owned by the private sector. It's in your communities. You deal with these corporate executives, you deal with these companies on a day-to-day basis.

And so what the President has designed, and Congress has agreed is the creation of a unit whose primary responsibility is take that threat, map it against the vulnerabilities, see what kind of protective measures are out there. And then make sure we've done everything we can to secure either that location, that economic sector, whatever the venue might be.

And the Congress has leaned forward and given us some significant help. So we've begun to identify and assess the threats. We'll map those threats. And this is also going to be the agency that, as of March 1st, issues the warnings to the country, but will also issue guidance to mayors and to the private sectors, to the kinds of things we hope you do under certain circumstances to improve your ability to prevent a terrorist attack or to reduce your vulnerability. We have to be partners; we are partners, up and down the line.

Our third objective is response and recovery. And again I address you as partners in this effort. Your police, your fire departments, your emergency medical technicians -- we know you're the first ones. We know that if something happens in your community, they don't hit the phone and dial area code 202 -- they're not dialing Washington, D.C. They may or -- they like to -- they want to get information from the Visitor's Bureau. But they dial 911, they dial the folks at home. So we know we've got a responsibility to assist you in that effort, as well.

For the first time, again in the new Department of Homeland Security, what has been known as FEMA, the Federal Emergency Management Agency, will become the nation's all-hazard incident manager. If it's a terrorist incident, if it's a natural disaster, whatever it is, this new department, through FEMA will be on the scene and manage the response.

Now, we clearly know that there is a question of funding that has been discussed and will continue to be discussed, probably at this organization and quite a few others, not only today, but for the months and the years ahead. And it needs to be discussed, and we will continue to discuss it. Let me just tell you where we're coming from in 2003, and we need your help in 2004.

First of all, as of today -- we just got the appropriations measure a couple weeks ago -- we just set up the department on March 1 -- but as of today, there's nearly $1.3 billion the department will be making available in '03 funding to help better equip and train your dedicated first responders. (Applause.)

Now, on Friday, the department made available nearly $600 million in grants for first responders through the Office of Domestic Preparedness. You remember that program; it used to be in Justice. It comes over to us. And you know the money is used by state and locals, purchase new equipment, training, planning and exercises. Those aps went up on Friday.

Today we've announced that we will have $750 million available for the assistance to firefighters grant program, which is the largest increase in the history of the program. Last year it was $345 million. (Applause.)

Here I'm going to need to ask your help. There's a lot of money here -- three-quarters of a billion dollars. And we've had this discussion before, we've had this conversation before. Preserving the $345 million from last year was good; they added another $350 million plus on it to get you to the three-quarters of a billion. But we didn't quite get the flexibility that I thought we needed for local communities to use these dollars, not just for fire equipment, but for equipment that can be used to respond to a terrorist incident.

And so I'm going to ask you from your position of leadership -- and I might add, responsibility in your communities -- to take a look at not only what your communities are doing, but what the region is doing. Because, as you know, this program operates -- the fire department can only get one grant. So maybe, as you take a look around the region, you can develop mutual aid arrangements, so that one fire department picks up one kind of equipment; another picks up another kind of equipment; somebody else pays for some training and exercises with their money. So you can really add value by putting together and pooling some of these resources and taking a regional approach toward securing these dollars.

Mutual aid agreements with neighboring cities; developing new training programs; and buying equipment that perhaps have a dual use. You can use if fighting fire, but you can also use it in response to a terrorist attack. Now, that's the $1.3 billion.

You should also know that the 2003 budget provides us about a billion plus, with the kind of flexibility that we wanted. And we'll be working to get those applications out the door for your consideration as soon as possible. As you know, I served in Congress for 12 years; earmarking is something that they've been doing in Congress for 200 plus years. They're going to continue to do it forever. But as we go to combat terrorism, I'm hopeful that in the years ahead, we can get even more money where there's flexibility for the state and locals to purchase what they decide they need, rather than what somebody thinks they want. I figure you guys are in the better position -- (applause.) You're in a better position.

So you've been very supportive, you've been very supportive all along the line. You helped me when we were in the Office of the White House as an assistant to the President. You've been very supportive of the new department. So we'll work with you as we work with Congress. They ultimately appropriate the dollars; we respect that. But I'd sure like to see you get some more flexibility.

There's a long list of additional funding matters -- more money for urban search and rescue teams, for interoperable communications. The 2003 budget is good. We just didn't quite get the flexibility that we wanted, and we look forward to working with you to get improved and expanded flexibility in 2004.

We're going to get nearly a half a billion dollars transferred in the new department -- and this is something I know you'll be interested in -- into our science and technology unit. I'm convinced at the end of the day we have many, many advantages over those who would do us harm and bring death and destruction to us and to our enemies [sic.] Many, many advantages. One that we are going to focus on in our new department is the brilliance, the creativity, the ingenuity of the American mind, and how we can apply technology to prevention, reduction of vulnerability, and response to an attack.

So we're going to get about a half a billion dollars this year. We'll take a look at some on-the-shelf technology to see if it's as good as it says it is, to see if we can deploy it immediately -- the technology of detection, technology of protection, some new devises that are out there. So this funding I think will go a long way in helping us create a national capacity that is driven by the technology sector of this great country.

Finally, I would say to you that we've come a long way. Many of you have been very helpful and supportive of the ready.gov initiative that we began promoting about a week and a half ago. I must tell you that I've been the subject of quite a few duct tape jokes. (Laughter.) I'm starting to think it's pretty funny, too, I guess. (Laughter.) Actually, it is. Because I think that humor is a very good way of dealing with some very difficult subjects. And actually, if your local newspapers have any good political cartoons, send them into me. I'm keeping a collection. (Laughter.) There are some really good ones.

Somebody sent me one the other day with a duck that was taped to the wall, and said, "Now that my duck is taped, what else should I do?" (Laughter.) I had a couple ideas, but I couldn't -- (laughter.) But you know, that whole period of time when people were talking about duct tape got everybody interested in the website that we put up, the ready.gov. And you believe in your citizens like I believe in them -- if you inform them, give them information that they can deal with, then they can make choices and do things on their own.

We've had over 100 million hits, over 100 million hits on that website. Over 5 million people have stayed there for on the average of 15 minutes. So, obviously, they're either taking notes or printing it out. But, I mean, this is the kind of approach that we need to take. Working together. If you have a website up for your city or community, maybe you can make that connection, pull them into the ready.gov.

Secretary Paige and I announced a website that speaks to school districts and makes some recommendations as to what they can do to prepare. Because when we're armed with information, when we're armed with knowledge, we can act on that. And individual citizens can take some, I think, comfort and hopefully reduce some of the anxiety associated with the notion of what am I supposed to do.

And what we're saying to the rest of the country are, do these things; pay attention to what your school might have to do; if they don't have a contingency plan, help them with one; have your emergency kit, have your communication plan with your kids. And then get on the business of being America. Let your mayor worry about it. Let your police chief and fire chief worry about it. Let the Department of Homeland Security worry about it. But you do these things for yourself and your community, and then let the professionals take care of everything else.

So I report to you the past 10 days, great progress built on the progress of the previous year, much of which has been built upon the partnership we've established with the mayors in the cities across this country. And you should know, both on a personal level, as well as a professional level, I look forward to an even stronger and better partnership in the months and the years ahead.

So I thank you very much for inviting me today, and I wish you the very, very best. Thank you. (Applause.)

REMARKS BY SECRETARY TOM RIDGE TO THE NEMA CONFERENCE

U.S. Department of Homeland Security
Office of the Press Secretary
February 24, 2003
For Immediate Release

Grand Hyatt Hotel
Washington, D.C.

SECRETARY RIDGE: I could say thanks to each and every one to you, because you have already given the Department a tremendous amount of support since we started in the office of the White House, when I served the President as Assistant to the President for Homeland Security. So I want to thank you for the invitation to return to address your group.

I want to say hello to my Pennsylvania Emergency Management Director Dave Sanko. I saw my buddies Charlie, who used to serve in that capacity. Is Charlie here? Charlie. Good.

So it's a great pleasure to be back and I thank you for the opportunity to share a few thoughts with you this afternoon. First of all, I want to acknowledge a couple of colleagues of mine in this enterprise. The first is Mike Brown. Mike succeeds a great personal friend of mine and yours, a big guy with a big heart that did a big job as FEMA director, Joe Allbaugh. And Mike has been leading the transition planning and the effort, as we bring the Federal Emergency Management Agency into the new Department. He brings the same energy, tremendous commitment. We're well ahead on that transitioning process. And he reminds me every day, although I don't need a reminder, it is an all-hazards emergency management agency. Applause. Did I do okay? (Applause.)

And I've had the opportunity to interact with literally dozens of men and women in the administration over the past year to 15 months. But Jerry Hauer at HHS has been one that I have worked with on many, many issues. And his professionalism and his responsiveness and his dedication to getting the job done is -- ranks among the best in this town. So, Jerry, it's a pleasure to be in the same program with you as well.

One of the imperatives of homeland security is the need for partners to communicate constantly. I consider you an integral part of this effort to build a national capacity to prevent terrorist attack, reduce vulnerabilities, to respond to one. So, as a partner, you must be informed of your priorities and your concerns, and I must keep you informed of our vision and our way ahead, as well. Our shared effort to secure our country depends upon it.

It is a challenging time for the new Department of Homeland Security. It's a time of growth, it's a time of progress. On March 1st, just over three months since it was signed into law, the Department of Homeland Security will finally become one united force for securing the homeland. March 1st is the date when most of those 22 member agencies come on board.

It's been noted before that it's the largest and most significant transformation of American government since the Truman administration, and it will truly be an historic day for this country. But I would share with you that I think March 1st is less of a beginning than a continuation. I think it's important to remind ourselves of that and, from my perspective, it's important to remind the American public about. It's a continuation of the hard work of over 175,000 Americans who go to work every single day in these 22 different agencies, who have been working on their piece of the homeland security puzzle for a long, long time. The continuation of that professional work by these men and women, who wake up every single day and go to work to keep our nation secure.

And like us, like everybody in Homeland Security, I know you have not been standing still and you have not been waiting for the calendar to change, either. You work with us every day, you work with your state and local organizations and, frankly, I don't think there's been enough attention paid to the progress that has been made and the leadership that has been provided at the state and the local level as we take a look back and flash back to September 12, 2001, and see where we are as a country today. Some of it's been driven by the federal government, but there's an enormous amount of leadership out there, and even greater action that has been done at the state and local level without any incentive from the federal government. Your organization has been at the heart of driving much of that change and those protective enhancements that have occurred since 9/11.

Every day, this country does more to achieve the goals of homeland security, prevent terrorism, reduce our vulnerability to attack, and prepare to save lives and recover from future attack. Consider recent progress. The Transportation Security Administration met extraordinary congressional deadlines on passenger and baggage screening, and nearly 50,000 highly trained screeners are now posted at commercial airports. We've begun to restructure our border enforcement and immigration services, working daily and diligently with her friends in Canada and Mexico on new 21st century smart border agreements. We've created new plans to protect our critical physical and cyber infrastructure, dams and power plants, computer networks and communications systems. We've accelerated deployment of the nation's first early warning network of sensors to detect a bio attack, began smallpox vaccinations for those on the potential front lines of terror. We've laid groundwork for a terrorist threat integration center. The Customs Department has begun to deploy men and women offshore to check those commercial ships and that cargo, particularly those containers in foreign ports rather than waiting to inspect them when they arrive in this country. The list goes on and on of the initiatives that have been taken at the local and state and federal level.

As the President has noted, law enforcement and intelligence are working together as never before to assemble and analyze threat information. And I might add, that's between every level of government, federal, state and local, and I suspect it is going to get nothing but better and better in the months and years ahead.

The Department of Homeland Security has gone from an idea on paper to a reality, in large part because a few organizations in this town supported it, and we thank you for your support. You said it would help you in your day-to-day efforts, and I thank you for making a difference.

As you may know, the Department has an entire directorate focused on emergency preparedness and response that is led by the very able and very capable men and women of the Federal Emergency Management Agency. It will be the nation's incident manager, all-hazard incident manager. (Laughter and applause.) I don't want the tattoo, I don't need -- (laughter).

The nation's incident manager, providing funding and command and control support in crisis. This unit will consolidate five or more separate federal response plans into one genuinely all-hazard approach, and we look forward to working with this organization as we integrate those five plans. This new unit in this new department will give you one direct line of authority from the President through the Secretary of Homeland Security on down to the local level. The Department will provide one face, one voice, and one point of contact in an emergency. This is what emergency managers have asked for, and this is what we are doing.

It was very revealing to me, and I suspect some of you were probably well aware of it, but when the explosion occurred in Staten Island a couple of days ago and our incident management team in our coordination center was notified, within a very short period of time in our headquarters, we knew what was going on that the local level, the state level. We engaged immediately in conversations with the Coast Guard, the EPA, Health and Human Services. When you bring all these forces to bear, you get not only a good, clear picture to the extent that you can of what is happening and what occurred, but also I think you have a much greater understanding of the kind of response that is being generated, and what may be needed in terms of the follow-on effort. And that is precisely what we intend to do in this new directorate.

In addition, we will standardize the training of first responders to counter the new and deadly terrorist threats we face. These measures will help us plan efficiently for a crisis and respond more effectively in the event that one crisis -- more than one crisis occurs. In this new age, the connection between emergency management and public health has never been more important. We know what the terrorists can do and so we must train and equip ourselves to meet every threat, including a bio terrorist threat. Therefore, the President has directed billions of dollars to public health systems across this country to prepare for one, improve facilities, enhance communications, treatment of patients, new disease surveillance capabilities are all part of this enhance national effort. Now this, the Emergency Preparedness and Response Unit, will assist by directing several important assets to this kind of -- in the event that this kind of incident would occur. Among them, the strategic national stockpile and the national disaster medical system, formerly at HHS, becomes part of the Department of Homeland Security. Our great friends at HHS are going to manage the stockpile, make sure it has the requisite vaccines and -- vaccines and diagnostics and the like, and they will keep it updated, but it will be available to us and incumbent on us to get it distributed in response to a crisis if one occurs.

The Nuclear Incident Response Team, formerly of the Department of Energy, moves into this new Emergency Preparedness and Response Unit, along with the domestic emergency support teams from the Department of Justice and the National Domestic Preparedness Office, formerly of the FBI.

Now, our goal will be, and working with Michael I'm sure it will be done, our goal is to merge these programs and agencies, to integrate their capabilities, so that the men and women who so ably perform their task can perform their jobs even better. And one of the challenges of the new department, 22 different agencies, 175,000 strong, is to take these professional people who bring certain skills, but add value and enhance our preparedness and enhance our abilities and enhance our capacities by integrating them more effectively than they have been done before. They've been stovepiped before across the board. We think there are enormous capacities, stronger capacities we can build because Congress has given us the flexibility to merge and to integrate some of these units. The one they said you cannot merge and you cannot integrate, however, was the Federal Emergency Management Agency, and we're glad of that.

We know we will face some challenges along the way, clearly. The homeland security structure that had built up over time was -- over time was stovepiped, and we think there is a better way to integrate people, technology and funding. And sometimes the stovepiping makes coordination pretty difficult. You deal with it on a day-to-day basis. I asked your leadership a few minutes ago if you have the same challenge at the local level as we do it the national level, trying to bring these different groups together to set priorities. I was told that you don't have any problem whatsoever in that regard. (Laughter.) We're the only ones that apparently have the challenge.

But we face in many ways many of the same challenges, trying to break down traditional ways of looking at things in the post-9/11 environment, and getting people on board to help set emergency management priorities. I'm absolutely confident that we'll get it done and are doing it; it's just going to take some time, I think, to change some thinking.

Remember, emergency preparedness and response was divided between several agencies including FEMA, HHS, Justice, Treasury, and the Energy Department. Border protection was divided between Transportation, Justice, Agriculture Department, among others. Protection of our critical infrastructure, 85 percent of which is in private sector hands, was Commerce and the FBI, the Department of Energy, the Department of Defense, among others.

The President recognized that we need to reunite these disparate elements behind one primary mission and under one chain of command. And, starting on March 1st, that's exactly what we plan on doing.

There are going to be some other challenges. Whether federal, state and local -- whenever federal, state and local managers work together, there may be differences in procedures or points of view -- I didn't know that. (Laughter.) But it says it right here, so it must be true. (Laughter.) Of course there are. Everybody brings a different perspective.

Everybody brings a different perspective, depending on where you're working, the community you're working, the issues you've been dealing with. And our job is to try to work with you and others to resolve those differences as quickly as possible, to set those priorities and then act upon them. And I think the new federal structure will help us do that.

We will have a much more robust, much larger office of state and local coordination, and I don't mean a huge bureaucracy. We're not into building a huge bureaucracy in the nation's capital. If we're going to build assets and build structure, it's not going to be in Washington; it's going to be around the rest of the country, I assure you of that. But we will have an office of state and local coordination separate and distinct from the four directorates. There is some overlap. And this, these group of men and women in our shop will be working with you and others as we build the capacity around this country, set priorities, and hopefully work together on matters -- funding matters before the Hill, so we can speak with one voice.

In addition, our Homeland Security Command Center will track the status of homeland security across the nation at all times. We want to maintain constant communication with our states and territories and other stakeholders, and we look forward to getting your input as we build and enhance this capacity. Our all-hazards approach to a crisis is designed to multiply this force -- our force of strength.

What else can we do? What else do we need? We need an educated and where public. As we announced the other day in the Ready Campaign, and I won't belabor the issue, but terrorism forces us to make a choice. We can be afraid, or we can be ready. Americans aren't afraid of anybody or anything, so it's pretty clear we're just going to be ready.

And I just need to thank all those organizations that helped us launch that campaign, beginning with the Red Cross and the Sloan Foundation that helped fund it, and the Yellow Pages and the Postal Service, and I've probably already forgotten a couple and I'll get the letter saying you forgot to mention our name. But the fact of the matter is we're a great partnership, great collaboration. Salvation Army was included.

For additional analytical, business and investment opportunities information,
please contact Global Investment & Business Center, USA
at (202) 546-2103. Fax: (202) 546-3275. E-mail: rusric@erols.com

Because people asked us, what do we need to do in order to get ready? And we said, basically, have a communication plan, have emergency supply kit, stay informed. And then go about the business of being America, and let the professionals -- and you're among those professionals -- who go to work on a day-to-day basis worrying about terrorist threats and how we can prepare for it and how we can respond -- left the professionals. You as an individual citizen, you as a family member, you as a spouse, these are the things we would like you to do.

I know there was a lot of public discussion, a lot of political cartoons -- I've seen a couple -- of people using some duct tape. (Laughter.) And I believe humor communicates, is a good way to communicate a message. And we certainly never told anyone to use it. But the notion that people can be empowered with information and people want to act, and all we're saying is, be smart, have a communication plan, keep informed, put these supplies away and then go about your business and let the Department of Homeland Security, let the emergency management professionals in this country, let the Coast Guard, let the CIA, let the FBI, the military, Border Patrol and everybody, let them worry about the day-to-day elements of homeland security.

And I think this year-long public information campaign to mobilize citizens will help us be a much better prepared country in the future. We know that by individuals, by protecting themselves, help protect their community as well. By helping people avoid panic and confusion in a crisis, we help our first responders do their jobs better, saving lives in the process. That's why our message will be delivered by emergency managers and firefighters and EMT and other people Americans know and other people Americans trust.

We have a fairly ambitious agenda at the Department of Homeland Security, and we have budgeted the resources we believe to accomplish it. The President's budget reflects his continuing commitment to our priorities into the mission. The agencies that make up the Department would receive $36.2 billion for fiscal year 2004, a 7.4 percent increase over the previous fiscal year. It's the largest of any Cabinet department. For the past two years, nearly 60,000 new people have been added to protect the homeland.

The President's original proposal, going into the 2003 budget, was intended to let state and local governments decide what their needs were, statewide strategic planning, purchasing of equipment, training and exercises, mutual aid pacts, and then apply for the funding to meet those priorities. Unfortunately, Congress didn't provide the flexibility that the President -- frankly, I had hoped that we would receive. I must tell you, as a former governor, working with my local colleagues in public service, be they elected officials or the emergency management professionals and first responders, I'm not always -- I've never been convinced, particularly in a situation like this, that the folks in Washington can set the priorities as well as the folks back home. It's just a certain point of view that I have, and we regret that we didn't quite get the flexibility that we wanted. We got some, for a little over $1 billion, and that's fine. We wish we could've had it for others as well.

Nevertheless, Congress has made its decision, the money is coming in and much of it is flowing into the new Department. Our job is to get it out the door as quickly and effectively as possible, and I assure you we are working on doing just that. I just hope that we can work together, send a unified voice to Congress in the 2004 budget that, while we appreciate that earmarking historically is a congressional prerogative, more flexibility with regard to state and local planning and priorities is something that we think we need to build a national capacity to prepare for and respond to a terrorist event.

The issues we spoke about a year ago, mutual aid, information sharing, emergency credentialing, interoperability, security clearances, secure video teleconferencing our just as important today. You should know that I continue to promote, and we are going to finally see some action with regard to providing secure phones, faxes and videoconferencing in your emergency operations centers around the country. We've got the money for the equipment and we've got the money to do some background checks and getting security clearances. That's something -- that's an initiative we will be working with you on this year. We've also put in place means by which we are going to give your governors secure telephone links.

So we've begun developing this network in sharing -- and the capacity to share sensitive information. We will look to you to help us see that he gets done as quickly as possible. Obviously, you know, we do have to have some security clearances for some of these folks to receive threat and intelligence information, but we're going to try to promote and push that out as quickly as possible.

Last week when we announced the Ready Campaign, ready.gov, we tried to remind Americans and actually remind those who would challenge us that Americans do not submit to fear, that we will be prepared. We also tried to remind your fellow citizens around the country that the hard work, the professional work that goes on on a day-to-day basis includes organizations such as yours. We developed a pretty good partnership when I had the opportunity to serve the President as an Assistant to the President for Homeland Security, and I look forward to building on the partnership now as Secretary of the new Department for Homeland Security, and am grateful that you give me the opportunity to share with you these thoughts at this meeting, and would be happy to respond to some questions before I leave. Thank you very much. (Applause.)

Q: Mr. Secretary, I'd like to ask the first question. Our profession, our members and our association have had a long history and legacy of providing multidisciplined coordination and collaboration across the all phases if not beyond of emergency management, as well as coordination among multilevels of government. We stand by committed to support you in your strategy and your division in your department. What would you like NEMA to do for you?

SECRETARY RIDGE: Well, I don't get that offer too often. (Laughter.) But now that you've asked -- (laughter) -- well, I've got a couple ideas in mind, and I must tell you I was in Cincinnati announcing this campaign. But afterwards, we spent about an hour with some of the local officials, elected and others, and the county's emergency management director, and we started just talking about the real world practical problems of sitting down with these many, many interests involving security of the community, homeland security, and saying, one, how do we get -- how do we work together to get folks to accept the notion that they will be funding for these programs, multiyear funding, that we can't have it all in one year? And then how do we set priorities?

And I think between now and the 2004 budget, because we know there will be billions more in the 2004 budget, it would be good to work with you, maybe put up a little working group together to help set those priorities. Another facet, another characteristic of this department that I would like to be able to accomplish in the first year is a one-stop shop, so you don't have to go to FEMA for a couple of grants or to ODP, because FEMA is in the new Department, the Office of Domestic Preparedness is in the new Department. Maybe we could sit down together with a couple of other groups to determine the best way to secure the information as quickly as possible so in one venue, one place in the new department, we can get all our applications in, set priorities and get the dollars out the door.

We will never have as much money as everybody thinks they need, but once we get an appropriation, we need to get it out there as quickly as possible. And it's not just about spending the money, it's about spending it on the right things. And so I think, right off the top of my head, working on the one-stop shop concept, maybe taking a look at the applications to see if we can refine the process, one of these days I hope it's paperless, you know, that would be nice. And also to sit down and talk about priority setting nationally, because at the end of the day, we've said before and we believe it, the homeland is secure when the hometown is secure. So we start not from the top down but from the bottom up, setting priorities. So those would be two very helpful contributions to our process over the next several months.

Q: We very much appreciate the rapidity, for example, which you talked about on secured telecommunication. We actually had our secure video communication equipment several days before we got the documentation. But I think --

SECRETARY RIDGE: I didn't know we were that good. (Laughter.)

Q: I think the comments you just made were good segue into the problems that we're having with that, that deal with prioritization and characterization. The documents when they arrived require us to essentially construct a facility to house that, that is going to cost us a couple hundred thousand dollars. It not only required it, it was very strongly requiring it. And there is a provision for 50 percent federal match. The $100,000 that is implicitly the local match constitutes one-third of the total amount of money I get from the state, and all that right now is used for matching funds on salary and benefits for other funds we've got. We simply don't have the capability to do that. And it's an illustration of similar situations with the emergency operations center.

Now, secure telecommunications are very important to us for working with our partners --

SECRETARY RIDGE: Sure are.

For additional analytical, business and investment opportunities information, please contact Global Investment & Business Center, USA at (202) 546-2103. Fax: (202) 546-3275. E-mail: rusric@erols.com

Q: -- but it's not something my state legislators are going to understand, trying to come up with $100,000, when they are trying to avoid laying off 10,000 or 20,000 state employees. And I think there needs to be flexibility, particularly in those aspects of this program that are clearly primarily a federal requirement rather than a local requirement, to get rid of the match requirements, because you will find that a lot of states -- and we've been talking about that the last two days -- simply aren't going to be able to come up with it. We don't have the resources.

SECRETARY RIDGE: Okay. Well, let me say this. First of all, and I'm going to say this respectfully to you, this is something that I think we absolutely need in terms of a national infrastructure, the ability to communicate with governors and the Emergency Operations Center on a secure basis from time to time. I hope I never have to call, never have to call you. But in the event we do and it's secure, then I will be comfortable in our means of getting that out to you.

But that is also something that the states and folks have sought us and lobbied hard for us to deliver for you. And we understand that you are under very, very difficult budget situations, and so are we, in this country. I will certainly go back and take a look at that grant. But I do think on some of these, there is a shared public safety responsibility to incur some of these costs, and I do know, as a governor whose first two years were during very difficult budget times, I know the strain that you are under now, and we will just go back and take a look at that match requirement. But we have to -- I understand that the prevailing economic conditions make it very difficult. But I would say to the state legislators candidly, you've got to set priorities too, and everybody, everybody -- not just this organization and your dealing with the locals, but state legislators and governors and presidents and Congress have to set priorities.

And I would like to think that if an emergency management operation needed $50,000 or $100,000, that the state legislature could figure out a way to find it. But I understand what you've said and, hopefully, you could deliver my message to your legislature and blame it on me. (Laughter.)

But I know where you're coming from, and we need to be mindful of also sending down mandates that we don't pay for. We understand that. But this was almost a shared request and a shared opportunity. But we will look at those requirements and see if we can provide you some help.

Q: Mr. Secretary, many of us are familiar with the FEMA structure regionally in support of the states. What is your vision of a DHS regional support?

SECRETARY RIDGE: Well, we've made no final decisions yet, but the notion of getting -- of reconstituting much of this new department outside of Washington is at the heart of what we're doing.

We've got regional structures everywhere from two for the Animal and Plant Health Inspection Service to, I think, up to 33 for Customs, so we've got variations in number and size. So as we take a look at putting these 22 departments and agencies together, we look at the regions and we want to come up with a model that gets these resources and people out around the country. So we are looking at a regional model. We haven't made any final decision on it. But obviously we've got to rationalize anything from 22 to 33. But you will hear a little bit more about this in the months ahead.

Q: (Off mic.)

SECRETARY RIDGE: One of the additional responsibilities in the new Department is the whole question of immigration policy. I guess I need to better understand specifically the concerns that you have, whether it is a matter of personnel being assigned there, whether it is -- we know that the Coast Guard and the DEA and other agencies are aware that sometimes the islands are used to for transit points for contraband, drugs, people and the like. So if we had a little more information about your concern, I'd be happy to try to address it with you. But the chain of islands that we often associate publicly as wonderful places to vacation, wonderful places to take your family, wonderful places to go and visit, we also know that they do offer some challenges with regard to drugs contraband and illegals. So we are quite aware of that and much of that comes into the new Department as of March 1.

Q: (Off mic.)

SECRETARY RIDGE: Well, one of the challenges we have in the country is we've got 95,000 miles of open water, navigable water security, for which the Coast Guard is responsible. I really believe that there are some opportunities to use some technology that DOD has employed in the past on the battlefield, the eyes to take a look at the vast stretches of ocean, vast stretches of unpopulated border area and the like, that may be -- that need to be part of future border protection.

So I assure you that this Department views those wonderful islands as not only a place to visit, but some unique challenges, particularly as a stepping off point and transition point into the country.

I assure you that your governors in the Territories are very much that the heart of the funding formula, the secure communications link and the like, as well.

Q: Mr. Secretary, I've got to questions to request, and they won't cost you any money. (Laughter.)

The first one is, with Joe Allbaugh's leadership and now with you and Mike Brown, we again request your assistance in asking President Bush to declare a national week of hurricane preparedness. He is the first President of the United States to recognize hurricanes as a significant natural hazard. And we again will request your assistance this year in asking President Bush to proclaim a week of national hurricane preparedness during the month of May in conjunction with the National Weather Service, National Hurricane Center.

The second request, Mr. Secretary, is in dealing with a lot of different issues of which your agency is now taking a major role in communications, warning and spectrum. One of the issues that keeps coming up in looking at the national warning ability to basically warn the public of hazards, direct them to take action, has been the lack of leadership when we're dealing with the FCC, when we're dealing with the private sector. Your agency, your role, we're merely requesting that we see you as that leader, to help us when we're dealing with all of those issues now coming to your agency of how we warn our nation, how we make sure we are interoperable in our radio systems, and how we make sure that we have the spectrum for the public safety agencies to accomplish that task. And realizing that some of that his congressional and is regulated through the FCC, we really look to you, sir, as that leader to help us achieve those goals through your agencies and through the transferred agencies to accomplish that. So those are our requests, Mr. Secretary.

SECRETARY RIDGE: Thank you very much. And we will -- Mike and I, we will take on both challenges. All right. I appreciate that.

It's an interesting opportunity we have, although it's very difficult in a national government that is federal in nature, because as a former governor, I appreciated receiving certain things from the federal government, certain things I didn't appreciate. And so it is that balance that we walk. But I am aware of presently several initiatives that are being undertaken by different groups of states with regard to different aspects of homeland security. One of them is communication, involving several states, another group of states worrying about -- one is information sharing really with regard to law enforcement, threat and intelligence information. Another group of states are working on the bio terrorism threats and integrating disease surveillance networks and the like. So I think one of the opportunities we have and one of the things we need to stay informed of, your organization to work with us and us to work with you, is where we learn that the states, as the state-to-state level, are working some of these initiatives, we need to make sure -- and I suspect that you will be involved. But when you learn of something, if you are participating in a regional effort to get things done, we need to -- hopefully, we will be aware of it, but we need to be pulled into that equation to have our representative there as well.

The interoperability, and it's not just of communications, it's of equipment that goes out to our first responders, there is a long laundry list of interoperability concerns that we all have. And again that could very well be as we set the priorities for the following months, as we sit down with your organization and a few others, what are the interoperability priorities. I think number one is communication. But from there on in, there is a fairly lengthy list and we could work with you to try to set some of those priorities. All right.

SELECTED PERSS RELEASES

BCIS TAKES FIRST STEP TO OFFER ONLINE FILING

For Immediate Release
Office of the Press Secretary
April 25, 2003

For the first time in history, applicants for immigration benefits will soon be able to file two key immigration applications using the Internet. The Bureau of Citizenship and

Immigration Services (BCIS) announced today that beginning May 29 it plans to offer electronic filing (e-filing) as an option for two of the most commonly submitted immigration forms - the application used to renew or replace a "green card" (Form I-90) and the application for Employment Authorization (Form I-765).

For those who file electronically, BCIS confirms the identity of the customer early in the application process. BCIS also electronically collects a photograph, signature, and fingerprint for the individual. These biometrics are stored and can be used later for verification of the person's identity. Customers whose applications are approved receive high quality immigration documents with special security features produced from BCIS' centralized card production facility.

"The introduction of e-filing represents an important stride in our effort to deliver immigration services in a more efficient and customer-friendly way while meeting our national security objectives," said Tom Ridge, the Secretary of the Department of Homeland Security. "These two forms are the first of many immigration applications we plan to make available for online filing in the near future."

Customers who e-file do not have to submit photographs at the time they file their applications. They will schedule an appointment to visit an Application Support Center (ASC) at a convenient time for the electronic collection of a photograph, signature, and fingerprint. After filing electronically, customers will schedule their appointment by calling the National Customer Service Center at (800) 375-5283.

The Employment Authorization and "green card" replacement applications were selected as the first forms for e-filing because they account for approximately 30 percent of the applications received annually by the BCIS. Additionally, these forms are relatively easy to complete and require very little supporting documentation because these individuals already have records on file with BCIS. Electronic filing for other immigration applications will be phased in over the next several years.

BCIS customers who have e-filed or who have an application pending at one of BCIS' Service Centers can check the status of their application on line by visiting www.bcis.gov. The website also provides information and forms online for users to download free of charge. Electronic filing is a key facet of BCIS' Immigration Service Modernization program, a 10-year effort to transform the delivery of immigration services. The initiative focuses on improvements in a wide range of areas, including customer service, employee development, technology and processes, and management infrastructure.

U.S.-MEXICO BORDER PARTNERSHIP JOINT STATEMENT ON PROGRESS ACHIEVED

Otay Mesa, California
April 23, 2003

When President George W. Bush and President Vicente Fox met in Monterrey, Mexico on March 22, 2002, they endorsed a Border Partnership accord that was signed by

Santiago Creel, Secretary of Governance, and Colin Powell, Secretary of State. This accord was accompanied by a 22-point plan that outlined specific actions that would be taken to create a smart border for the 21st century, one that embraces technology and enhanced bilateral cooperation to ensure the secure flow of people and goods and the development of a secure and sufficient infrastructure necessary to facilitate the growing trade between Mexico and the United States, to promote legitimate travel across the border, and to protect against crime and terrorism.

Respecting the sovereignty of each party and in light of the principle of mutual responsibility, various agencies and departments in our two countries have worked hard - in conjunction with state and local governments and private-sector stakeholders - to achieve the aims of this plan. We are pleased with the tremendous progress achieved over the past year. Yet, we are just at the initial steps; there is more to be done. We must work to reduce bottlenecks and crossing delays for the legitimate flow of people and goods; we must work to strengthen our countries' national security; we must continue to work together to ensure prosperity for our countries.

Secure Infrastructure

In order to coordinate the infrastructure development plans, while improving the use of existing systems, Mexico and the United States have agreed to harmonize our planning systems and to better communicate between border-control agencies at ports of entry. Both governments are also examining modeling techniques and procedures to ensure that our border infrastructure is able to meet the demands placed on it by border communities and commerce.

The Border Partnership also calls upon Mexico and the United States to examine trans-border infrastructure and communication and transportation networks and their associated vulnerabilities in order to identify critical trans-border infrastructure protection deficiencies, and to take measures to remedy them. To seek to accomplish this, we have formed a bilateral steering committee and developed an infrastructure protection framework. We have also established sector-focused working groups in the areas of energy, telecommunications, transportation, dams, public health, and agriculture. These groups are tasked with identifying critical infrastructures with trans-border implications; developing protection priorities; and taking compatible steps to eliminate or mitigate vulnerabilities each country has in its own territory.

Secure Flow of People

Since signing the Border Partnership, Mexico and the United States have made significant progress in strengthening border security measures in both our countries. Through cooperative efforts and based on sound risk management principles, we are working to ensure safe, orderly and secure travel for legitimate border crossers. These bilateral actions will be further enhanced by the recent merging of the U.S. agencies responsible for the border into the new Department of Homeland Security, the formation of which provides the Mexican government with one point of contact for border security matters.

To encourage and promote low-risk travel, both pedestrian and vehicular, through congested ports of entry, the United States plans to expand, by using state-of-the-art technology, the Secure Electronic Network for Travelers Rapid Inspection (SENTRI). In conjunction with this expansion, the United States extended in February the enrollment period from one year to two years. The United States also plans to reduce the waiting period for issuance of the SENTRI card to 2 months or less by June. Further, plans are underway to establish the first dedicated pedestrian lane at the San Ysidro port of entry.

The United States and Mexico plan to accelerate their border safety collaboration to safeguard migrants by placing additional personnel and life-saving equipment along the border, placing special attention to the "high-risk" Arizona - Sonora corridor. Training of immigration officials and law enforcement authorities from both countries in life-saving techniques is underway. Equipment and additional resources necessary to support these efforts are in place as both governments focus together on protecting lives and preventing deaths. The authorities of both countries plan to continue to work jointly to arrest and prosecute smugglers who place migrants at risk.

Secure Flow of Goods

Based on a longstanding relationship of cooperation and mutual assistance, U.S. Customs and Border Protection (CBP) and the General Customs Administration of Mexico (GCAM) have begun the implementation of those action items designed to guarantee the secure and efficient flow of trade between our nations.

For purposes of developing and implementing initiatives identified in the U.S./Mexico Border Partnership Plan, CBP and GCAM have created three special working groups: the Border Working Group, the Enforcement Working Group, and the Technology & Customs Procedures Working Group. These groups have been meeting quarterly and are in constant communication. A Coordinating Committee leads and monitors all activities.

These groups have been working on a broad range of initiatives, namely:

(1)   harmonizing and extending the hours of service, in coordination with our trade communities, at the ports of entry located at our common border;

(2)   working to implement the Advanced Passenger Information System in Mexico that will collect and share data pertaining to air passengers arriving into and departing from Mexico and the United States;

(3)   deploying gamma ray machines at our railroad crossings;

(4)   expanding programs and partnerships with the private sector, such as the Business Anti-Smuggling Coalition (BASC), the Customs - Trade Partnership Against Terrorism (C-TPAT) and Mexico's Compliant Importer/Exporter Program (110 of the 300 largest traders, that account for 66 percent of our bilateral trade, have already been certified by this program);

(5)   exchanging core data on every transaction occurring through our common border in an electronic environment;

(6)   testing and implementing cutting edge technology such as electronic seals;

(7)   conducting joint investigations concerning fraudulent trade, which have led to significant seizures of illegally transshipped or undervalued goods;

(8)   developing systems to monitor in-transit shipments through our territories; and,

(9)   seizing illegal cash transported by air passengers.

CBP and GCAM are also currently working to develop hi-tech dedicated lanes, which will be made available only to those large companies willing to go the extra mile in securing their shipments. These dedicated lanes will expedite and facilitate the border crossing process, thus reducing the cost of doing business. We intend to open the first dedicated lane in El Paso/Juárez during 2003. The project will be evaluated to insure that it is both secure and efficient. Once we reach an acceptable level of confidence, we plan to replicate dedicated lanes throughout the U.S. - Mexico border.

Next Steps

Our two governments are committed to building an efficient border that simultaneously facilitates legitimate travel, goods, and services on which our economies depend while assuring the security of our two nations. Both sides recognize that many challenges lie ahead. Nonetheless, we are confident that the Border Partnership accord is the vehicle to attain the spirit of cooperation of our two presidents. We will continue our joint work to increase security, minimize delays at ports of entry and build a border that keeps pace with our growing partnership.

HOMELAND SECURITY AND DOE DELIVER REFURBISHED RADIOLOGICAL DETECTION EQUIPMENT

April 22, 2003

Equipment Will Be Used to Enhance the Domestic Preparedness Capabilities of Local Emergency Responders

The Department of Homeland Security and the Department of Energy have formally transferred a shipment of refurbished radiological detection equipment to the Los Angeles Fire Department Hazardous Waste Unit, the Los Angeles Port Authority and the San Francisco Health Department. The equipment, with a replacement value of approximately $60,000, is being provided to these emergency responder agencies under a DHS/DOE pilot project called the Homeland Defense Equipment Reuse (HDER) Program.

"The HDER Program is an excellent example of Federal agencies working together to address a critical homeland security issue," said Homeland Security Secretary Tom Ridge.

Los Angeles and San Francisco are the sixth and seventh cities that have received radiological detection equipment through the HDER partnership. Other cities that have received the equipment include Washington, D.C., Philadelphia, New York, Boston and Detroit.

The goal of the HDER Program is to provide surplus radiological detection instrumentation and other homeland security related equipment to state and local emergency first responder agencies nationwide to enhance their domestic preparedness capabilities. The agreement is part of the Administration's broader effort to enhance the equipment and training available to our nation's emergency responders.

A variety of equipment to measure the presence of radiation is being made available through the HDER Program. The equipment, which comes from Energy Department sites across the nation, is evaluated and refurbished by radiation equipment specialists at DOE's Office of Assets Utilization, National Center of Excellence for Materials Recycling in Oak Ridge, Tenn.

The Department of Homeland Security's Office for Domestic Preparedness (ODP) works with established contacts in each state to identify appropriate users in their local emergency responder communities, and the Department of Energy delivers the equipment to these jurisdictions at no cost.

Training on the use of the equipment is available to the emergency responders through ODP's Domestic Preparedness Equipment Technical Assistance Program (DPETAP). If requested, DPETAP will provide detailed technical information and hands-on equipment operation and maintenance training. Local support for the equipment, including calibration, maintenance and follow-on refresher training, is also be available through a partnership with the Health Physics Society, a 6,000 member national organization of radiation safety professionals.

To date, the HDER program has redeployed over 1,500 radiological detection instruments valued over $700,000 to first responder communities throughout major metropolitan areas of the United States.

DEPARTMENT OF HOMELAND SECURITY FY '03 SUPPLEMENTAL FUNDING FACT SHEET

April 16, 2003

Today, the President has signed the FY '03 Supplemental Bill authorizing an additional $6.71 billion for the Department of Homeland Security to support Departmental functions and domestic counterterrorism operations that have been activated as a part of Operation Liberty Shield at the start of the war in Iraq. The Department was allocated $4.31 billion to offset the costs of Operation Liberty Shield and an additional $2.4 billion was made available to the airline industry to help with costs associated with enhancing the capabilities of the airline industry to combat terrorism. As we make progress in establishing the appropriate mechanisms to fund homeland security needs around the country, we welcome Congress' cooperation in ensuring the Department has the necessary flexibility to direct funds so that we can further this important mission.

U.S. Coast Guard - $628 million

- Up to $628 million has been made available to the U.S. Coast Guard to support military activities in connections with operations in and around Iraq and the global war on terrorism, specifically, Operation Liberty Shield.
- Since the start of the war, the U.S. Coast Guard has increased patrols at major U.S. ports and waterways, increased escorts of ferries and cruise ships, and been involved with the arrival and departure of every high interest vessel within and around American ports.

Counterterrorism Fund - $150 million

- $150 million has been made available to the Department of Homeland Security to support expanded responsibilities of the Department to prevent, counter, investigate and respond to acts of terrorism.

Bureau of Customs and Border Protection - $333 million

- $333 million has been made available to BCBP to further enhance the security of our nation's borders and maritime ports of entry. Of this amount, $35 million is designated for the Container Security Initiative and $90 million has been designated for portal radiation detection and monitoring technology.

Bureau of Immigration and Customs Enforcement - $170 million

- $170 million has been made available for additional personnel at our country's borders and maritime ports of entry, to enhance the ability of BICE to develop the Entry-Exit system across our borders and for other necessary expenses related to Operation Liberty Shield.

Transportation Security Administration - $665 million

- $665 million has been made available to the TSA for modification of commercial airports for security enhancements, additional port security grants and for passenger screening, hiring, training and related costs.
- $20 million of those funds are designated for trucking industry grants to fund the nation-wide trucking security and safety initiative.
- $30 million will be used for Operation Safe Commerce to further enhance Maritime and Land Security.

Airline Support - $2.4 billion

- $2.4 billion is being provided under Title IV of the bill for costs affiliated with the enhancement of security of airliners and the ability of the airline companies to protect and combat terrorism.
- $100 million will be available to compensate airline companies for the costs associated with the strengthening of flight deck doors as required by the Aviation and Transportation Security Act.
- The remaining amount shall be distributed to U.S. airline companies proportional to the share each carrier has paid or collected in passenger security fees and air carrier security fees.

Office for Domestic Preparedness - $2.23 billion

- $2.23 billion will be provided to be used for state domestic preparedness plans.
- $1.3 billion is provided through a formula based grant program for state domestic preparedness efforts. Through the ODP grant program, 80 percent of the grant funding will be designated for localities, and 20 percent designated for the states to help assist first responders.
- $200 million is provided for critical infrastructure formula-based grants   for the states to protect their critical sites.
- $700 million is provided in grants for high-threat urban areas to be designated by the Secretary of Homeland Security.
- $30 million is provided for direct technical assistance to the States to further enhance their abilities to combat terrorism.

Emergency Preparedness and Response - $99.75 million

- $99.75 million is provided including; $45 million for operating expenses, and $54.75 million for Emergency Management Planning and Assistance account for interoperable communications.

In addition:

- $3 million was provided to the Bureau of Citizenship and Immigration Services,
- $30 million was provided to the U.S. Secret Service, and
- $2 million was provided for the Federal Law Enforcement Training Center to provide assistance with costs related to Operation Liberty Shield.

Securing the Homeland: Protecting Our States and Cities

April 8, 2003

Today the Department of Homeland Security, through the Office of Domestic Preparedness, announced that approximately $100 million dollars from the FY '03 Funding will be dedicated to large urban areas within the United States. The money, dispersed under the Urban Area Security Initiative, will help enhance the local governments' ability to prepare for and respond to threats or incidents of terrorism. The funds announced today are in addition to the $566 million that the Office for Domestic Preparedness announced last month from the FY'03 Funding for first responder needs such as equipment, training, planning and exercises.

The cities were chosen by applying a formula based upon a combination of factors including population density, critical infrastructure and threat/vulnerability assessment. The cities have all previously received funding from the Office for Domestic Preparedness in the form of grants for First Responders and will also potentially receive funds from the FY '03 Supplemental Budget Request currently pending in Congress.

New York City, New York

An additional $24.76 million from the FY '03 Budget is being made available to the City of New York to protect the city's critical sites as part of the Urban Area Security Initiative. This money has been designated to the New York Urban Area to further enhance the local government's ability to prepare for and respond to threats or potential incidents of terrorism. This is in addition to the $26 million previously made available to the State of New York in the form of an ODP grant to be used for equipment, training, exercise and planning for the city's first responder groups.

Washington, D.C. -- National Capital Region

An additional $18.08 million is being made available to the National Capital Region as part of the Urban Area Security Initiative. $4.91 million has previously been made available to Washington, D.C. from the Office for Domestic Preparedness within the Department of Homeland Security in the form of grants for First Responders.

Los Angeles, California

An additional $12.42 million is being made available to the City of Los Angeles as part of the Urban Area Security Initiative. $45 million has previously been made available to California from the Office for Domestic Preparedness within the Department of Homeland Security in the form of grants for First Responders.

Seattle, Washington

An additional $11.20 million is being made available to the City of Seattle as part of the Urban Area Security Initiative. $11.3 million has previously been made available to Washington from the Office for Domestic Preparedness within the Department of Homeland Security in the form of grants for First Responders.

Chicago, Illinois

An additional $10.89 million is being made available to the City of Chicago as part of the Urban Area Security Initiative. $18.8 million has previously been made available to Illinois from the Office for Domestic Preparedness within the Department of Homeland Security in the form of grants for First Responders

San Francisco, California

An additional $10.74 million is being made available to the City of San Francisco as part of the Urban Area Security Initiative. $45 million has previously been made available to California from the Office for Domestic Preparedness in the Department of Homeland Security in the form of grants for First Responders

Houston, Texas

An additional $8.63 million is being made available to the City of Houston as part of the Urban Area Security Initiative. $29.5 million has previously been made available to Texas from the Office for Domestic Preparedness within the Department of Homeland Security in the form of grants for First Responders

Future Funding...

- President Bush has requested an additional $2 billion in funds from the FY'03 Supplemental Budget request recently sent to Congress to help the states and localities confront threats to the United States and the American people. This funding request includes $2 billion to further support enhancements to state and local terrorism preparedness efforts as well as coordinated prevention and security enhancement for first responders.
- In FY'03, DHS/FEMA will provide $165 million in grants to the states in the form of Emergency Management Performance grants. These grants, expected to be announced soon, can be used by states for development, maintenance and improvement of state and local emergency management capabilities.
- In FY'03, DHS/FEMA will also provide $750 million in grants directly to fire departments around the country for equipment, training and education under the Assistance to Firefighters Grant program. This $750 million -- the largest amount in grants ever for firefighters -- is twice as much as FEMA distributed to firefighters in FY'02, when $334 million was distributed through more than 5000 grants nationwide.
- The President has requested $3.5 billion to be used for ODP grants dedicated to meeting state and local needs in his FY'04 budget request.

JOINT PRESS CONFERENCE WITH SECRETARY TOM RIDGE AND BRITISH HOME SECRETARY BLUNKETT

U.S. Department of Homeland Security
Office of the Press Secretary
For Immediate Release
April 1, 2003

U.S. Department of Homeland Security
Briefing Room

SECRETARY RIDGE: Good morning, all. It's good to be with you this morning. Sorry for the brief delay.

I'm certainly honored to welcome the Home Secretary from the United Kingdom, David Blunkett. We're grateful that he took time today to spend time with us. The Secretary and I have just finished another productive meeting, building on the series of meetings we had when I visited the U.K. several months ago, where we discussed strengthening the partnership between our two countries in fighting the war on terror. We shared ideas that will benefit both of our countries in the area of homeland security, and we explored additional areas of cooperation, specifically the sharing of best practices, joint training exercises, the security of cyber and physical infrastructure, border and transportation security, research and development, and science and technology.

The United Kingdom has extensive experience in battling the challenge of terrorism at home. This relationship will benefit the strong homeland security partnership that our countries have developed since the attacks on our country on September 11th. The United Kingdom has been a critically important ally in bringing our attackers to justice, and we look forward to continuing to work with them to battle terrorism at home and abroad.

The Secretary and I have discussed a couple of different ways and issues that we need -- we believe it is in our mutual interest as friends and allies to work together on, and I've asked -- actually asked the Secretary to elaborate on some of these initiatives in his opening remarks to you. So, again, it's my great pleasure to introduce the right honorable Secretary David Blunkett. David.

SECRETARY BLUNKETT: Thank you for being with us. I'd just like to underline immediately the unprecedented level of cooperation that we now have, which has been built up over the last 18 months, and has been enhanced by the development under Tom Ridge of the Homeland Security Department here, and the work that we've been doing on what we call resilience civil contingencies and counteracting internal terror and the threat to our population in the United Kingdom. And that is why I'm so very pleased indeed this morning, not only to reaffirm our cooperation, not only to build on the steps that have already been taken, but to go a stage further. We are announcing today that we will establish a joint working group, a contact group, which will involve officials from the Homeland Security Department and our own department in developing the work collaboratively so that, instead of just sharing best practice, they're actually working on that best practice, learning from each other and being able to develop the very similar approaches which are necessary to protect our population.

All of us know that we've never faced a threat like the one that has developed since the 11th of September 2001, and that the way in which the United Kingdom and the United States are working together ensures not only that we face that threat in a better shape and in a way that allows us to understand that best practice, but also that it actually means that, because we are partners, including with the conflict in Iraq, we need to be more vigilant and we need to be more aware than others across the world believe -- and I think they're often wrong -- believe is necessary for them.

So we are intent on developing joint exercises which will be built on the domestic exercises that you're undertaking in terms of counter terror and in terms of protection of the public, and the exercises that we're engaged in, in the United Kingdom, so that we

For additional analytical, business and investment opportunities information,
please contact Global Investment & Business Center, USA
at (202) 546-2103. Fax: (202) 546-3275. E-mail: rusric@erols.com

can look at what might formulate the necessary steps to protect us from simultaneous attacks, from joint attacks, and we're going to look at firstly desktop and then physical exercises in enhancing our capability and our protection.

We're also, as Tom Ridge has described, enhancing our work on border protection and surveillance, on biometrics and identification, on visa and passport controls, which will be sufficiently co-terminus, to make it possible not to interrupt unnecessarily business and commerce, but which will provide the security that you want and you need in terms of the future.

The pooling of research and training, the development of joint facilities that help us, for instance, with the danger of chemical, biological, radiological and nuclear imports, and the danger that people are transferring the capability across the world, we need to work together on those. And, of course, on cyber and electronic attack, which would disrupt our commerce.

We're also collaborating closely on the development of new assessment techniques. You have the new TTAC (phonetic) facility. We have developed still further our joint terrorism and assessment center so that we can better pull together the information we have from the lessons we've learned in terms of dealing with terror from Ireland that Tom Ridge described.

All of this means that we are literally shoulder to shoulder. We explored whether I should say "hip to hip," but we decided "shoulder to shoulder" was probably a better description -- (laughter) -- in terms of the joint threat that faces us, and the joint working that we'll see off that threat for the future.

Thank you very much indeed.

SECRETARY RIDGE: Thank you, David.

Ladies and gentlemen?

Q: Secretary Ridge, do you think that the chance of a simultaneous attack against Great Britain and the United States has been increased because of these two countries taking the lead in the war with Iraq? I mean, is that why you're doing this particular --

SECRETARY RIDGE: Oh, no, I think we have to prepared for -- and we are prepared domestically and we plan and work on the possibility of simultaneous attacks. But I think that it makes eminent good sense for two allies that are working together to develop best practices, two allies and friends working together on the science and technology of detection and protection, two friends and allies to engage in some responsible thinking with the possibility that we might have to endure simultaneous attacks and how we can be mutually supportive of each other in that process.

There's no -- there's nothing in the contemporary threat information that we have that suggests such attacks are imminent, but we know -- both our intelligence communities know full well that the United States and the United Kingdom are potentially subject to

For additional analytical, business and investment opportunities information,
please contact Global Investment & Business Center, USA
at (202) 546-2103. Fax: (202) 546-3275. E-mail: rusric@erols.com

attack. And if they would occur simultaneously, we want to be in a position to reinforce and to assist each other.

SECRETARY BLUNKETT: Yes, that is exactly the meaning I had. The thinking we're engaging in from today is, of course, by its very nature, for the future rather than for the weeks and immediate months ahead. So we're preparing for a very different world. And some of those attacks would not necessarily -- in fact, it's almost certain would not replicate what we've seen so far. So that's why I mentioned, for instance, cyber and electronic attack, which could disable the commerce of the future. All of these things we need to be aware of, and we need to ensure that those who are thinking of using those techniques are aware that we are literally on the ball, ahead of them, rather than waiting for something to happen and then chasing that eventuality once it's occurred.

Q: Secretary Blunkett, I was wondering, you say you've had so much success with the IRA. But the IRA and al Qaeda are very different organizations. How has your experience with the IRA helped you deal with al Qaeda?

SECRETARY BLUNKETT: Well, up to the Good Friday Agreement, which was brokered by our Prime Minister and was helped, it has to be said, by the U.S. administration, we had 30 years of conflict, not just in Ireland, but on the mainland of Britain. Of course, they are different in the sense that we had an identifiable opponent who, in the end, we could sit down with and find a way forward. That isn't true of al Qaeda and the network that exists across the world, the loose network.

Nevertheless, the techniques of intelligence and surveillance and the security techniques have to be and are developed from that experience. And we are able to share that with you, just as the experience that you've had internationally between the CIA and our intelligence service and GCHQ have been shared for many years. And we need to enhance and build on that. And we are learning all the time.

One of the things, I just want to make the point, Tom, is that the techniques that are used now by international terrorists and the organized groups behind them funding, facilitating those groups are using the best of technology, the most up-to-date methodology and government across the world, our government, your government, has to be ahead of that. And that is a major challenge, not just in terms of getting the right facilities in place, but actually being ahead in those rapid reaction techniques, which it's easy for groups working as cells to undertake, and it's more difficult for government.

Q: Mr. Blunkett, several years ago, right after the embassy bombings, the British government, at the American government's request, arrested three guys, Fawaz and a couple of other characters, on charges of being co-conspirators in the 1998 embassy bombings. I went to a hearing at the House of Lords in your -- in the Parliament building more than a year ago, at which the House of Lords ultimately dismissed their appeals against extradition. And yet those guys have still not been extradited.

Moreover, I think there's another guy named Rasheed Ramda, who the French have been trying to extradite in connection with the Paris subway bombings since 1996 and he still hasn't been extradited. I saw that in the material out of the Justice Department that you're changing your extradition laws. But, as I understand it, a lot of this power is up to you as Home Secretary. You have the power of the signature to extradite these people. Why hasn't more been done to get these people, you know, before the courts?

SECRETARY BLUNKETT: Forgive me if I don't get into the French Ramda case while I'm in the United States. I'm dealing with that with the French, as we all are.

The situation is this, that our outdated extradition procedures, both bilaterally with the United States and across the globe, are being completely reviewed and revised. I have legislation in front of Parliament at the moment that cuts out all the major delays, all the prevarication and the additional judicial blockages that are currently available to those trying to avoid extradition, even when I've certificated, as I have, those who should be transferred to the U.S.

I signed yesterday with John Ashcroft a new extradition -- updated extradition agreement, which will facilitate that, and will make it possible to immediately take steps when someone is identified and the proper evidence has been transferred, to take those steps to extradite, rather than the prolonged procedures we have at the moment. But I am, as part of the legislation, removing the layer on layer of judicial blockage.

Regrettably in our system, even the words of the House of Lords do not conclude the final blockage that exists through the judiciary, through appeals, in terms of the exact process for transfer. All of that will be dealt with in the new extradition legislation. So I plead guilty to the historic and arcane procedures that we've been operating and I put a plea of mitigation in terms of sorting them out.

Q: Secretary Ridge, we've now been at orange alert for a matter of weeks and the war appears that it's going to go on for some time now. Is there any reason to expect that we would not be at orange alert for the duration of the war? And how is the country going to maintain that? You're obviously seeing many, many complaints. Do you consider those complaints from states and cities legitimate? And what on earth can be done about it if this level has to be maintained for a long time?

SECRETARY RIDGE: I think it's pretty clear that, in anticipation of military activity in Iraq, at the President's direction, we added an enhanced layer of protection around the country called Liberty Shield. And with the collaboration of governors, major city mayors, the first responder and first preventer communities, we know that we do have an additional level of protection around this country, which we will sustain as long as the -- the threat and the -- our military activities in Iraq require us to sustain it.

It is in anticipation of absorbing some of those costs and helping defray some of those costs that the President has requested substantial dollars from the Congress in the supplemental, as you know, for the first responder community, for governors and for mayors, there's a request for $2 billion. And we applaud the commitment of both chambers and both parties of getting these dollars appropriated between now and the Easter recess. We want to work with them every step of the way in order to achieve that goal, so that we can ease some of that financial burden that we've asked them to sustain

For additional analytical, business and investment opportunities information,
please contact Global Investment & Business Center, USA
at (202) 546-2103. Fax: (202) 546-3275. E-mail: rusric@erols.com

with these dollars. As soon as we get them, it's our job to get them out and distribute them as quickly as possible. We're prepared to do that.

By the way, we also have the $1 billion plus that is in the pipeline now to get out to help our governors and our mayors absorb some of the costs of the added level of protection that they've given this country for the past 18 months.

Q: Democrats in the Congress have made it clear that they will not augment the money in the supplemental for Homeland Security because of the tremendous cost being incurred by the governors and by the mayors. Can you oppose this?

SECRETARY RIDGE: I've tried to explain to my colleagues in public service on either side of the aisle and in both chambers that if you take the dollars that are still available from the 2002 supplemental, you add it to the dollars that Congress appropriated in the 2003 budget, you add it to the dollars that we hope we receive in the supplemental, you add it to the $3.5 -- nearly $4 billion to combat terrorism in the 2004 budget, assuming they can complete their activity by October 1st, there will be $8- to $9 billion available to our states and local communities. And I think that's an enormous investment and we want to make absolutely certain that every single dollar is expended on what we need to not only help absorb some of the costs of Liberty Shield, but also to build a broader national capacity to prevent a terrorist attack, reduce our vulnerability or respond to one if it occurs.

Again, the figure that I hear fairly frequently is in the $8- to $9 billion range. But, in fact, if they honor our request for the supplemental and honor the request for the 2004 budget and conclude that process in a timely basis, that's precisely the amount that will be available to these states and local communities. And then we have to be concerned not just about inputs and dollars but how well they're expended and outcomes. And I think with the infusion of that dramatic amount of dollars, we have to be equally concerned that they are spent appropriately.

Q: Sir, have you taken steps to improve the computerized information sharing about watch lists and databases of terrorism information that your respective intelligence communities may maintain and operate?

SECRETARY RIDGE: Yes. One of the first priorities we have within the new Department is to consolidate the watch list information that is generated from different agencies within the federal government to ensure that it is available to all of the agencies. As you well know, we have several departments and units that develop their own watch lists. Our first priority, our first IT priority is to consolidate these watch lists so that the people at the borders, people at the airports and the respective agencies have access to that broader list of names, the aggregate of those names. And we are moving rapidly to a point where we'll be able to tell you that it's done. We're not quite there yet, but we will be there shortly.

Q: Mr. Blunkett, you introduced new asylum laws today that allow you to revoke citizenship for people you say abuse the privilege. Would you say -- would you like to see those -- the Abu Hamza subjected to those laws?

And, Secretary Ridge, are these laws something that you would like or intend to introduce in the United States?

SECRETARY BLUNKETT: Firstly, could I -- could I say that the laws are designed to ensure that, where people have had dual citizenship or where they have the opportunity of an alternative citizenship and they've abused the taking of nationality within the United Kingdom, we believe we have the right to withdraw that, and therefore to be able to expel that individual from the country. If I named any individual here in Washington, never mind back in London, I would immediately allow their lawyers a field day in terms of what decisions I'd already ratified. I don't intend to allow them -- anyone -- the pleasure of doing that. So you'll forgive me for not responding to a particular individual in a particular set of circumstances.

SECRETARY RIDGE: Thank you all.

Q: Secretary Ridge, did you intend on following those examples as well? Secretary Ridge? The second part of the question of whether or not the United States, if you intended on similar laws here in the United States to revoke citizenship if someone is found to be connected to a terrorist organization, or sort of blanket laws revoking citizenship?

SECRETARY RIDGE: I think it's clear that in the post 9/11 world, that at some point in time that may be a matter that we consider in this country as well. But I would tell you, at this time, that is not something that is presently under consideration. But let's not suggest that some time down the road it might not be.

We have matters dealing with immigration and asylum that we're dealing with on a regular basis. Whether or not that comes to the fore and we deal with it, remains to be seen. Under the circumstances, as the Secretary has described, it's entirely possible. We certainly haven't undertaken that review presently.

SUPPLEMENTS

STATE HOMELAND SECURITY CONTACTS

Alabama
James Walker
Homeland Security Director
Alabama Office of Homeland Security
401 Adams Ave. - Suite 560
Montgomery, AL 36103-5690
334-353-0242
Fax: 334-353-0606

Alaska
COL Craig Campbell
Adjutant General
PO Box 5800
Ft. Richardson, AK 99505-0800
907-428-6003
www.gov.state.ak.us/omb/Homeland1.pdf

Arizona
Chuck Blanchard
Director of Homeland Security
1700 West Washington Street, 3rd Floor
Phoenix, AZ 85007

Arkansas
Bud Harper
Director, Emergency Management
PO Box 758
Conway, AR 72033
501-730-9750
www.adem.state.ar.us

California
George Vinson
Special Advisor on State Security
State Capitol, 1st Floor
Sacramento, CA 95814
916-324-8908

Colorado
Sue Mencer
Executive Director, CO Dept of Public Safety
700 Kipling Street
Denver, CO 80215
303-273-1770

For additional analytical, business and investment opportunities information,
please contact Global Investment & Business Center, USA
at (202) 546-2103. Fax: (202) 546-3275. E-mail: rusric@erols.com

Connecticut
Vincent DeRosa
Deputy Commissioner, Division of Protective Services
55 West Main St., Suite 500
Waterbury, CT 06702
203-805-6600
www.state.ct.us/dps/PS/index.htm
DPS.Feedback@po.state.ct.us

Delaware
Phil Cabaud
Homeland Security Director
Office of the Governor
Tatnall Building – 2nd Floor
William Penn Street
Dover, DE 19901
302-744-4242

District of Columbia
Margret Nedelkoff Kellems
Deputy Mayor for Public Safety and Justice
202-727-4036
http://washingtondc.gov

Florida
Tim Moore
Commissioner, Florida Dept. of Law Enforcement
PO Box 1489
Tallahassee, FL 32302-1489
850-410-7233
www.fdle.state.fl.us

Georgia
Bill Hitchens
Director of Homeland Security
PO Box 1456
Atlanta, GA 30371
404-624-7030
www.gahomelandsecurity.com/

Hawaii
BG Robert Lee
Adjutant General
3949 Diamond Head Rd.
Honolulu, HI 96816-4495
808-733-4246
www.scd.state.hi.us

For additional analytical, business and investment opportunities information,
please contact Global Investment & Business Center, USA
at (202) 546-2103. Fax: (202) 546-3275. E-mail: rusric@erols.com

Idaho
MG Jack Kane
Adjutant General
4040 West Guard Street
Boise, ID 83705-5004
208-422-5242
www.state.id.us/government/executive.html

Illinois
Carl Hawkinson
Homeland Security Advisor
207 State House
Springfield, IL 62706
217-524-1486

Indiana
Clifford Ong
Director, Indiana Counter-Terrorism and Security Council
100 North Senate Avenue
Indianappolis, IN 46204
317-232-8303
www.in.gov/c-tasc

Iowa
Ellen Gordon
Administrator, Emergency Management
Hoover State Office Bldg
1305 E. Walnut
Des Moines, IA 50319
515-281-3231
www.iowahomelandsecurity.org

Kansas
MG Gregory Gardner
Adjutant General
2800 SW Topeka
Topeka, KS, 66611-1287
785-274-1121/1109

Kentucky
BG D. Allen Youngman
Adjutant General
100 Minuetman Parkway
Frankfurt, KY 40601-6168
502-607-1257
http://homeland.state.ky.us

For additional analytical, business and investment opportunities information,
please contact Global Investment & Business Center, USA
at (202) 546-2103. Fax: (202) 546-3275. E-mail: rusric@erols.com

Louisiana
MG Bennett C. Landreneau
Adjutant General and Director
Louisiana Office of Emergency Preparedness
7667 Independence Blvd.
Baton Rouge, LA 70806
225-925-7333

Maine
MG Joseph Tinkham, II
Adjutant General
Homeland Security
1 State House Station
Augusta, ME 04333-0001
Normal Working Hours: 207-626-4440

Maryland
Thomas J. Lockwood
Homeland Security Director
State House, 100 State Circle
Annapolis, MD 21401
410-974-3901
www.mema.state.md.us

Massachusetts
Richard Swensen
Office of Commonwealth Security
Executive Office of Public Safety
1 Ashburton Place, Rm. 2133
Boston, Ma 02108
617-727-3600x556

Michigan
COL Tadarial Sturdivant
Director of State Police
Contact: Capt. John Ort
713 South Harrison Rd
E. Lansing, MI 48823
517-336-6198
www.msp.state.mi.us

Minnesota
Rich Stanek
Commissioner of Public Safety and Homeland Security Director
DPS, North Central Life Tower
445 Minnesota St., St. 1000
St. Paul, MN 55101
dps.state.mn.us/homelandsecurity/index.htm

For additional analytical, business and investment opportunities information,
please contact Global Investment & Business Center, USA
at (202) 546-2103. Fax: (202) 546-3275. E-mail: rusric@erols.com

Mississippi
Robert Latham
Executive Director, Mississippi Emergency Management Agency
PO Box 4501
Jackson, MS 39296-4501
601-960-9999
www.homelandsecurity.ms.gov

Missouri
Col. Tim Daniel
Special Adviser for Homeland Security
PO Box 809
Jefferson City, MO 65102
573-522-3007
www.homelandsecurity.state.mo.us

Montana
Jim Greene
Administrator, Disaster and Emergency Services
Department of Military Affairs – HAFRC
Montana Disaster and Emergency Services
1900 Williams Street
PO Box 4789
Helena, MT 59604-4789
406-841-3911
www.discoveringmontana.com/css/default.asp

Nebraska
Lieutenant Governor Dave Heineman
PO Box 94848
Lincoln, NE 68509-4848
402-471-2256
dave.heineman@email.state.ne.us

Nevada
Jerry Bussell
Homeland Security Director
2525 S. Carson St
Carson City, NV 89710
775-687-7320

New Hampshire
Donald Bliss
Director, Emergency Management and State Fire Marshal
10 Hazen Drive
Concord, NH 03305
603-271-3294

For additional analytical, business and investment opportunities information,
please contact Global Investment & Business Center, USA
at (202) 546-2103. Fax: (202) 546-3275. E-mail: rusric@erols.com

New Jersey
Sidney Caspersen, Director
N.J. Office of Counter-Terrorism
P.O. Box 091
Trenton, NJ 08625
609-341-3434

New Mexico
R.L. Stockard
Homeland Security Director
New Mexico Office of Public Safety
P.O. Box 1628
Santa Fe, NM 87507-1628
505-827-3370

New York
John Scanlon
Director, Office of Public Security
Executive Chamber
633 3rd Ave, 38th Floor
NYC, NY 10017
212-867-7060
info@security.state.ny.us

North Carolina
Bryan Beatty
Secretary, Dept of Crime Control and Public Safety
4701 Mail Service Center
Raleigh, NC 27699
919-733-2126
www.ncgov.com/asp/subpages/safety_security

North Dakota
Doug Friez
Homeland Security Coordinator/Emergency Management Director
Fraine Barracks Ln, Bldg 35
Fraine Barracks
Bismark, ND 58504
701-328-8100
www.state.nd.us/dem/homesec.html

Ohio
Kenneth L. Morckel
Director of Public Safety
1970 W. Broad St.
Columbus, OH 43223-1102
614-466-4344
www.state.oh.us/odps/sos/ohshome.htm

Oklahoma
Bob Ricks
Secretary of Safety and Security
State Capitol Bldg, Room 212
Oklahoma City, OK 73105
405-425-2001

Oregon
Ronald C. Ruecker
Superintendent of Oregon State Police
400 Public Service Bldg
Salem, OR 97310
503-378-3725

Pennsylvania
Keith Martin
Director, Pennsylvania Office of Homeland Security
2605 Interstate Drive
Harrisburg, PA 17110
717-651-2715
www.homelandsecurity.state.pa.us

Puerto Rico
Annabelle Rodriguez
Attorney General
La Fortaleza
PO Box 9020082
San Juan, PR 00902-0082
787-721-7700

Rhode Island
MG Reginald Centracchio
Adjutant General
222 State House
Providence, RI 02903
401-275-4102

South Carolina
Robert M. Stewart
Chief, S.C. Law Enforcement Division (SLED)
PO Box 21398
Columbia, SC 29221-1398
803-737-9000

South Dakota
Deb Bowman
Chief of Homeland Security
500 East Capitol Avenue

For additional analytical, business and investment opportunities information,
please contact Global Investment & Business Center, USA
at (202) 546-2103. Fax: (202) 546-3275. E-mail: rusric@erols.com

Pierre, SD 57501
1-866-homland

Tennessee
MG (Ret.) Jerry Humble
215 Eighth Avenue, North
Nashville, TN 37203
615-532-7825

Texas
Jay Kimbrough
Deputy Attorney General for Criminal Justice
PO Box 12428
Austin, TX 78711
512-936-1882

Utah
Scott Behunin
Division Director, Comprehensive Emergency Management
210 State Capitol
Salt Lake City, UT 84114
801-538-3400
www.cem.utah.gov

Vermont
Kerry Sleeper
Commissioner, VT State Police
103 South Main Street
Waterbury, VT 05671-2101
802-244-8775

Virginia
Assistant to the Governor for Commonwealth Preparedness
John Hager
202 N. 9th Street, 5th Floor
Richmond, VA 23219
804-225-3826
http://www.commonwealthpreparedness.state.va.us

Washington
MG Timothy J. Lowenberg
Adjutant General and Director
State Military Department
Washington Military Dept., Bldg 1
Camp Murray, WA 98430-5000
253-512-8201

West Virginia
Joe Martin
Secretary, Dept. of Military Affairs and Public Safety
State Capitol Complex, Bldg 6, Rm B-122
Charleston, WV 25305
304-558-2930

Wisconsin
Ed Gleason
Administrator, Emergency Management
PO Box 7865
Madison, WI 53707-7865
608-242-3210
www.wisconsin.gov/state/core/domestic_prep.html

Wyoming
MG Ed Boenisch
Adjutant General
TAG Office - 5500 Bishop Blvd.
Cheyenne, WY 82009-3320
307-772-5234

Guam
Frank Blas
Homeland Security Advisor
PO Box 2950
Hagatna, GU 96932
671-475-9600 / 9602

Northern Mariana Islands
Jerry Crisostomo
Special Advisor for Homeland Security
Caller Box 10007
Saipan, MP 96950
670-664-2280

Virgin Islands
MG Cleave A. McBean
Adjutant General
21-22 Kongens Gade
St. Thomas, VI 00802
340-712-7711

American Samoa
Leiataua Birdsall V. Ala'ilima
Special Assistant to the Governor
Office of Territory Emergency Mgmt
American Somoa Government

For additional analytical, business and investment opportunities information,
please contact Global Investment & Business Center, USA
at (202) 546-2103. Fax: (202) 546-3275. E-mail: rusric@erols.com

Pago, Pago, AS 96799
011-684-633-4116

MAJOR DISASTER DECLARATIONS

Date	State	Incident	FEMA Disaster Number
04/25	Florida	Tornado	1460 Counties
04/24	Mississippi	Severe Storms, Tornadoes and Flooding	1459 Counties
03/27	Virginia	Severe Winter Storm, Flooding and Mudslide	1458 Counties
03/27	North Carolina	Ice Storm	1457 Counties
03/20	Tennessee	Severe Storms and Flooding	1456 Counties
03/14	West Virginia	Severe Winter Storms	1455 Counties
03/14	Kentucky	Severe Winter Storms	1454 Counties
03/14	Ohio	Severe Winter Storm	1453 Counties
02/04	Oklahoma	Severe Ice Storm	1452 Counties
01/08	South Carolina	Severe Ice Storm	1451 Counties
01/06	Arkansas	Severe Ice Storm	1450 Counties
01/06	Federated States of Micronesia	Typhoon Pongsona	1449 Counties

[Back to Top]

EMERGENCY DECLARATIONS

Date	State	Incident	Designation
04/09	Colorado	Snowstorm	FEMA-3185-EM | Counties
03/27	New York	Snowstorm	FEMA-3184-EM | Counties
03/27	Rhode Island	Snowstorm	FEMA-3182-EM | Counties
03/20	Delaware	Snowstorm	FEMA-3183-EM | Counties
03/20	New Jersey	Snowstorm	FEMA-3181-EM | Counties

For additional analytical, business and investment opportunities information,
please contact Global Investment & Business Center, USA
at (202) 546-2103. Fax: (202) 546-3275. E-mail: rusric@erols.com

03/14	Pennsylvania	Snowstorm	FEMA-3180-EM | Counties
03/14	Maryland	Snowstorm	FEMA-3179-EM | Counties
03/14	District of Columbia	Snowstorm	FEMA-3178-EM | Counties
03/11	New Hampshire	Snowstorm	FEMA-3177-EM | Counties
03/11	Connecticut	Snowstorm	FEMA-3176-EM | Counties
03/11	Massachusetts	Snowstorm	FEMA-3175-EM | Counties
03/11	Maine	Snowstorms	FEMA-3174-EM | Counties
02/26	New York	Snowstorm	FEMA-3173-EM | Counties
02/01	Louisiana	Loss of the Space Shuttle Columbia	FEMA-3172-EM | Counties
02/01	Texas	Loss of the Space Shuttle Columbia	FEMA-3171-EM | Counties

PERMITTED AND PROHIBITED ITEMS

Prohibited items are weapons, explosives, incendiaries, and include items that are seemingly harmless but may be used as weapons—the so-called "dual use" items. You may not bring these items to security checkpoints without authorization.

If you bring a prohibited item to the checkpoint, you may be criminally and/or civilly prosecuted or, at the least, asked to rid yourself of the item. A screener and/or Law Enforcement Officer will make this determination, depending on what the item is and the circumstances. This is because bringing a prohibited item to a security checkpoint—even accidentally—is illegal.

Your prohibited item may be detained for use in an investigation and, if necessary, as evidence in your criminal and/or civil prosecution. If permitted by the screener or Law Enforcement Officer, you may be allowed to: consult with the airlines for possible assistance in placing the prohibited item in checked baggage; withdraw with the item from the screening checkpoint at that time; make other arrangements for the item, such as taking it to your car; or, voluntarily abandon the item. Items that are voluntarily abandoned cannot be recovered and will not be returned to you.

For additional analytical, business and investment opportunities information, please contact Global Investment & Business Center, USA at (202) 546-2103. Fax: (202) 546-3275. E-mail: rusric@erols.com

The following chart outlines items that are permitted and items that are prohibited in your carry-on or checked baggage. You should note that some items are allowed in your checked baggage, but not your carry-on. Also pay careful attention to the "Notes" included at the bottom of each section – they contain important information about restrictions.

The prohibited and permitted items chart is not intended to be all-inclusive and is updated as necessary. To ensure everyone's security, the screener may determine that an item not on the prohibited items chart is prohibited. In addition, the screener may also determine that an item on the permitted chart is dangerous and therefore may not be brought through the security checkpoint.

The chart applies to flights originating within the United States. Please check with your airline or travel agent for restrictions at destinations outside of the United States.

For updates and for more information, visit our website at www.TSATravelTips.us or call our Consumer Response Center toll-free at 1-866-289-9673 or email TellTSA@tsa.dot.gov.

Can I take it?	Carry-on	Checked
Personal Items		
Cigar Cutters	Yes	Yes
Corkscrews	Yes	Yes
Cuticle Cutters	Yes	Yes
Eyeglass Repair Tools (including screwdrivers)	Yes	Yes
Eyelash Curlers	Yes	Yes
Knitting and Crochet Needles	Yes	Yes
Knives, round-bladed butter or plastic	Yes	Yes
Nail Clippers	Yes	Yes
Nail Files	Yes	Yes
Personal care or toiletries with aerosols, in limited quantities (such as hairsprays, deodorants)	Yes	Yes
Safety Razors (including disposable razors)	Yes	Yes
Scissors-plastic or metal with blunt tips	Yes	Yes
Scissors-metal with pointed tips	No	Yes
Toy Transformer Robots	Yes	Yes
Toy Weapons (if not realistic replicas)	Yes	Yes
Tweezers	Yes	Yes
Umbrellas (allowed in carry-on baggage once they have been inspected to ensure that prohibited items are not concealed)	Yes	Yes
Walking Canes (allowed in carry-on baggage once they have been inspected to ensure that prohibited items are not concealed)	Yes	Yes

Note Some personal care items containing aerosol are regulated as hazardous materials. The FAA regulates hazardous materials. This information is summarized at http://cas.faa.gov/these.html		
Medication and Special Needs Devices		
Braille Note-Taker, Slate and Stylus, Augmentation Devices	Yes	Yes
Diabetes-Related Supplies/Equipment, (once inspected to ensure prohibited items are not concealed) including: insulin and insulin loaded dispensing products; vials or box of individual vials; jet injectors; pens; infusers; and preloaded syringes; and an unlimited number of unused syringes, when accompanied by insulin; lancets; blood glucose meters; blood glucose meter test strips; insulin pumps; and insulin pump supplies. Insulin in any form or dispenser must be properly marked with a professionally printed label identifying the medication or manufacturer's name or pharmaceutical label.	Yes	Yes
Nitroglycerine pills or spray for medical use (if properly marked with a professionally printed label identifying the medication or manufacturer's name or pharmaceutical label)	Yes	Yes
Prosthetic Device Tools and Appliances, including drill, allen wrenches, pullsleeves used to put on or remove prosthetic devices, if carried by the individual with the prosthetic device or his or her companion	Yes	Yes
Can I take it?	Carry-on	Checked
Electronic Devices		
Camcorders	Yes	Yes
Camera Equipment . The checked baggage screening equipment will damage undeveloped film in camera equipment. We recommend that you either put undeveloped film and cameras containing undeveloped film in your carry-on baggage or take undeveloped film with you to the checkpoint and ask the screener to conduct a hand-inspection.	Yes	Yes
Laptop Computers	Yes	Yes
Mobile Phones	Yes	Yes
Pagers	Yes	Yes

Personal Data Assistants (PDA's)	Yes	Yes
Note Check with your airline or travel agent for restrictions on the use of these and other electronic items during your flight.		
Sharp Objects		
Box Cutters	No	Yes
Ice Axes/Ice Picks	No	Yes
Knives (any length and type except round-bladed, butter, and plastic cutlery)	No	Yes
Meat Cleavers	No	Yes
Razor-Type Blades, such as box cutters, utility knives, razor blades not in a cartridge, but excluding safety razors	No	Yes
Sabers	No	Yes
Scissors – metal with pointed tips Scissors with plastic or metal blunt tips are permitted in your carry-on.	No	Yes
Swords	No	Yes

Note Any sharp objects in checked baggage should be sheathed or securely wrapped to prevent injury to baggage handlers and inspectors.		
Sporting Goods		
Baseball Bats	No	Yes
Bows and Arrows	No	Yes
Cricket Bats	No	Yes
Golf Clubs	No	Yes
Hockey Sticks	No	Yes
Lacrosse Sticks	No	Yes
Pool Cues	No	Yes
Ski Poles	No	Yes
Spear Guns	No	Yes
Note Any sharp objects in checked baggage should be sheathed or securely wrapped to prevent injury to baggage handlers and security screeners.		

Can I take it?	Carry-on	Checked
Guns and Firearms		
Ammunition Check with your airline or travel agent to see if	No	Yes

For additional analytical, business and investment opportunities information, please contact Global Investment & Business Center, USA at (202) 546-2103. Fax: (202) 546-3275. E-mail: rusric@erols.com

ammunition is permitted in checked baggage on the airline you are flying. If ammunition is permitted, it must be declared to the airline at check-in. Small arms ammunitions for personal use must be securely packed in fiber, wood or metal boxes, or other packaging specifically designed to carry small amounts of ammunition. Ask about limitations or fees, if any, that apply.		
BB guns	No	Yes
Compressed Air Guns	No	Yes
Firearms	No	Yes
Flare Guns	No	No
Gun Lighters	No	No
Gun Powder	No	No
Parts of Guns and Firearms	No	Yes
Pellet Guns	No	Yes
Realistic Replicas of Firearms	No	Yes
Starter Pistols	No	Yes
Note Check with your airline or travel agent to see if firearms are permitted in checked baggage on the airline you are flying. Ask about limitations or fees, if any, that apply. Firearms carried as checked baggage MUST be unloaded, packed in a locked hard-sided gun case, and declared to the airline at check-in. Only you, the passenger, may have the key or combination.		

Tools		
Axes and Hatchets	**No**	Yes
Cattle Prods	No	Yes
Crowbars	No	Yes
Hammers	No	Yes
Drills (including cordless portable power drills)	No	Yes
Saws (including cordless portable power saws)	No	Yes
Screwdrivers (except those in eyeglass repair kits)	No	Yes
Tools (including but not limited to wrenches and pliers)	No	Yes
Wrenches and Pliers	No	Yes
Note Any sharp objects in checked baggage should be sheathed or securely wrapped to prevent injury to baggage handlers and security screeners.		

Martial Arts/Self Defense Items		
Billy Clubs	No	Yes
Black Jacks	No	Yes
Brass Knuckles	No	Yes

Kubatons	No	Yes
Mace/Pepper Spray One 118 ml or 4 Fl. oz. container of mace or pepper spray is permitted in checked baggage provided it is equipped with a safety mechanism to prevent accidental discharge. For more information on these and other hazardous materials, visit http://cas.faa.gov/these.html .	No	Yes
Martial Arts Weapons	No	Yes
Night Sticks	No	Yes
Nunchakus	No	Yes

Can I take it?	Carry-on	Checked
Martial Arts/Self Defense Items		
Stun Guns/Shocking Devices	No	Yes
Throwing Stars	No	Yes
Note Any sharp objects in checked baggage should be sheathed or securely wrapped to prevent injury to baggage handlers and security screeners.		
Explosive Materials		
Blasting caps	No	No
Dynamite	No	No
Fireworks	No	No
Flares in any form	No	No
Hand Grenades	No	No
Plastic Explosives	No	No
Flammable Items		
Aerosol (any except for personal care or toiletries in limited quantities)	No	No
Fuels (including cooking fuels and any flammable liquid fuel)	No	No
Gasoline	No	No
Gas Torches	No	No
Lighter Fluid	No	No
Strike-anywhere Matches	No	No
Turpentine and paint thinner	No	No
Note There are other hazardous materials that are regulated by the FAA. This information is summarized at http://cas.faa.gov/these.html		
Disabling Chemicals and Other Dangerous Items		
Chlorine for pools and spas	No	No

Compressed Gas Cylinders (including fire extinguishers)	No	No
Liquid Bleach	No	No
Spillable Batteries (except those in wheelchairs)	No	No
Spray Paint	No	No
Tear Gas	No	No

Note There are other hazardous materials that are regulated by the FAA. This information is summarized at http://cas.faa.gov/these.html

SMALLPOX FREQUENTLY ASKED QUESTIONS

Smallpox Response Teams

Why vaccinate health care workers and first responders?

We're asking these groups to volunteer to serve on smallpox response teams to help our country respond in the event of an attack. By vaccinating groups of health care workers and emergency responders, we will make sure that smallpox response teams are available who can vaccinate others and provide critical services in the days following an attack. This approach will make us better able to protect the American people in an emergency, which is our highest priority.

What will the smallpox response teams do?

Members of the Smallpox Response Teams will include people who will administer the smallpox vaccine in the event of an emergency and will be the first to investigate and evaluate initial suspected case(s) of smallpox and initiate measures to control the outbreak.

HHS and CDC will continue to advise and assist states in development of these teams.

How will the government decide who should serve on a smallpox response team?

State officials -- in consultation with CDC and local health departments -- are working to identify health care workers and first responders who could serve on response teams following a smallpox release. Participation on these teams and in the vaccination program is purely voluntary.

How many first responders and health care workers will be vaccinated?

We have asked states to identify workers who might serve on smallpox response teams to vaccinate others and provide critical services in the days following an attack. We are working with states to determine the exact number of individuals who will fall in these categories. To protect the American people, the important thing is to ensure that we have health care workers and first responders ready to serve as smallpox response teams. However, we expect that some of the people identified by the states will not be eligible for vaccination because of a medical condition, and others may choose not to be vaccinated.

It has been reported that we will be vaccinating up to 10 million health care workers and first responders. However, we do not expect that the numbers of first responders and health care workers vaccinated in this part of the program to be that high.

Are we less prepared to protect the American people if we don't get participation from millions of public health and health care workers or first responders?

Whatever the number of people who choose to participate and get vaccinated, we will be much more prepared to protect the American people than we are today.

Also, the very fact that states, hospitals and communities will have vaccination plans -- for emergency responders and for mass-vaccinating the general public -- makes us better prepared to protect Americans in an emergency.

These efforts will increase deterrence.

Will you administer tests to ensure that health care workers and first responders receiving the vaccine are not pregnant or HIV positive?

Every person volunteering to receive the vaccine will be asked detailed questions regarding their medical history and physical health and will be educated to the risks and possible side effects of the vaccine. If there is any indication that a person has a contraindication for the vaccine, the individual will be referred to the local public health department or another health care provider for testing.

How can a person protect against the risk of inadvertent transmission of the vaccine to another person?

Anyone receiving the vaccine will be instructed on several readily available steps to prevent the accidental transmission of the vaccine to another person. For example, the vaccinated person should use breathable bandages, wear a long-sleeve shirt, and use good hand hygiene.

How will the government monitor and report side effects?

The CDC is enlisting an outside group that will constitute an external data monitoring and safety review board. This external review board will review, in real time, vaccine adverse event reports and data, interpret findings, and provide guidance and advice for strengthening the overall safety of the program if needed.

How does this decision differ from the vaccination program in Israel? The vaccination program in the U.K.?

Israel is vaccinating health care workers and military personnel who were previously vaccinated. In the U.K., a small group of roughly 1000 people are being vaccinated.

Is it true that those who were vaccinated previously have a lower risk of adverse reaction?

Those who were vaccinated previously may have a lower risk of adverse reactions. It is appropriate for individuals, in deciding whether to be vaccinated, to consider whether they were vaccinated previously.

How will vaccine adverse events be handled? What protocols will be followed for actual or claimed serious adverse events?

Prospective vaccinees will be educated about the contraindications to smallpox vaccination in order to minimize serious adverse reactions to the vaccine. A good system to monitor and treat adverse events will be an integral part of this policy, and will be done in close collaboration between the CDC, states, and public health agencies and hospitals. The states will maintain records of people vaccinated and will work with hospitals to set up systems to diagnose, manage, and treat people who experience adverse reactions from the vaccine. This will include rapid access to the primary treatment for most serious adverse events, Vaccinia Immune Globulin (VIG).

It is expected that most of the side effects caused by smallpox vaccinations will not require special treatment or therapy. There are two treatments that may help people who have certain serious reactions to the smallpox vaccine. These are: Vaccinia Immune Globulin (VIG) and Cidofovir. Patients receiving these drugs would need to stay in the hospital for observation and possible additional treatment, as the VIG and Cidofovir may cause a number of side effects as well. CDC will review summary reports of adverse events and will investigate all individual reports of serious events.

General Public

What is the current threat assessment? Who are likely countries to obtain and use the virus?

Terrorists or governments hostile to the United States may have, or could obtain, some of the variola virus that causes smallpox disease. If so, these adversaries could use it as a biological weapon. This potential along with an appreciation for the potentially devastating consequences of a smallpox attack, suggests that we should take prudent steps to prepare our critical responders to protect the American public should an attack occur. People exposed to variola virus, or those at risk of being exposed, can be protected by vaccinia (smallpox) vaccine. The United States is taking precautions to deal with this possibility.

If a person wants to sign up to receive the vaccine as soon as possible, what should they do?

The federal government is not recommending that members of the general public be vaccinated at this point. Our government has no information that a biological attack is imminent, and there are significant side effects and risks associated with the vaccine. HHS is in the process of establishing an orderly process to make unlicensed vaccine available to those adult members of the general public without medical contraindications who insist on being vaccinated either in 2003, with an unlicensed vaccine, or in 2004, with a licensed vaccine. (A member of the general public may also be eligible to volunteer for an on-going clinical trial for next generation vaccines).

How long will it take before HHS begins administering vaccines to the general public under the new program?

Again, we do not recommend at this point that the general public be vaccinated. However, we expect to be able to make the unlicensed vaccine available to those who insist on being vaccinated sometime this spring. The immediate task for state and federal government will remain the implementation of our program to vaccinate our emergency responders. This is necessary to best protect Americans in the event of a release.

Of course, in the event of an actual attack, we will immediately make vaccine available to those at risk from disease.

Who will administer the vaccines?

State health departments, with guidance from CDC, will set up vaccination clinics and determine who will be staffing clinics and administering smallpox vaccine. The number of vaccination sites will be determined in the state plans, and depends in large part on the demand for the vaccines. CDC is assisting states with planning, technical assistance and education.

If you aren't recommending that the general public be vaccinated, why are you setting up this special program to allow them to get the vaccine?

We understand that some Americans will want to be vaccinated despite the risks. The President decided that the best course was to provide Americans with as much information as we can, help them weigh the risks, then let them decide for themselves.

Will you administer tests to ensure that members of the general public receiving the vaccine are not pregnant or HIV positive?

Every person volunteering to receive the vaccine will be asked detailed questions regarding their medical history and physical health. They will be educated to the risks and possible side effects of the vaccine. If there is any indication that a person has a contraindication for the vaccine, the individual will be referred to the local public health department or another health care provider for testing.

How will the government monitor and report side effects?

The CDC will enlist an outside group to constitute an external data monitoring and safety review board. This external review board will review vaccine adverse event reports and data, interpret findings, and provide guidance and advice for strengthening the overall safety of the program.

Military Personnel

Why are we vaccinating servicemembers?

We are concerned that terrorists or governments hostile to the United States may have, or could obtain, some of the variola virus that causes smallpox disease. If so, these adversaries could use it as a biological weapon. People exposed to variola virus, or those at risk of being exposed, can be protected by vaccinia (smallpox) vaccine.

Who in DoD is going to get the smallpox vaccine?

As part of this plan, the decision at this time is to vaccinate certain emergency response and medical personnel and other designated personnel that constitute critical mission capabilities, to include those essential to the accomplishment of U.S. Central Command's missions. The Department may expand the program at a later date.

The decision will be implemented using a portion of the existing licensed supplies of smallpox vaccine.

Will servicemembers still be deployable if they have not received the smallpox vaccine?

Yes, if they are in one of the groups that should not receive the smallpox vaccine they will still be deployable. In the event of an actual smallpox attack their vaccination status will be reevaluated.

When are the smallpox vaccinations going to start?

Smallpox vaccinations of DOD personnel will begin as soon as the vaccine is in place and medical training and troop education have been accomplished.

Has the Department of Defense vaccinated people against smallpox before?

Yes, the Department conducted major vaccination programs during WWI and WWII and servicemembers were routinely vaccinated from the 1940s until 1984. In 1984, routine military vaccinations were limited to recruits entering basic training. Between 1984 and

1990, recruit vaccinations were intermittent. In 1990, the Department of Defense discontinued vaccination of recruits.

How does the threat of a smallpox attack on US forces compare with that of an anthrax attack?

They are both known threats. Many factors go into such determinations including intelligence information, known capabilities and other variables. While we cannot quantify the threat of either one being used as a bioweapon, we know the consequences of their use could be great. Vaccination is a wise, logical step to ensure preparedness for the U.S.

Will the people receiving anthrax vaccinations be the same ones receiving the smallpox vaccinations?

Generally speaking, forces currently designated to receive anthrax vaccine also will receive smallpox vaccine. Additional forces will be vaccinated against smallpox given that smallpox, unlike anthrax, is contagious and can be prevented only with vaccine. The Secretary of Defense may decide in the future to expand the scope of both the anthrax and smallpox vaccination programs.

How does the smallpox vaccination interact with other drugs and vaccinations?

The smallpox vaccine should not be given to people taking medications that suppress their immune system. Smallpox vaccines should be spaced by one month from chickenpox vaccination. Other combinations of vaccines (e.g. smallpox and influenza or smallpox and anthrax) can be given.

Why is the Department of Defense administering the smallpox vaccine?

We cannot quantify the threat that smallpox would be used as a bioweapon, but we do know that the consequences of its use could be great. Military missions must go on even if a smallpox outbreak occurs. It may not be feasible to vaccinate military forces soon after exposure if they are deployed to remote locations and/or engaged in military operations. Some military personnel will not be able to postpone vital missions if smallpox is used as a weapon. Vaccination is a wise course for preparedness and may serve as a deterrent.

What should a person do if they don't get a blister?

If someone does not get the expected vaccination site reaction, they need to be revaccinated. If someone has a question or concern about the smallpox vaccination site they should contact their primary-care manager, medical department representative or their healthcare provider.

What should a person do if they have any adverse reactions?

If a person suspects an adverse reaction from the smallpox vaccine he or she should seek care from their primary-care manager, medical department representative, or go to their healthcare provider as soon as possible.

They should request that their healthcare provider file a Vaccine Adverse Event Reporting System (VAERS) form. If they don't believe their reaction is serious enough to visit a medical treatment facility, but they still wish to report it, they can contact VAERS themselves at 1.800.822.7967 or file a report at the following Web site: www.vaers.org.

What if somebody has already been vaccinated?

Immunity from smallpox vaccination decreases with the passage of time. Past experience indicates that the first dose of the vaccine offers protection from smallpox for three to five years, with decreasing immunity thereafter. If a person is vaccinated again later, immunity lasts longer. A report from Europe suggests that people vaccinated 10 or 20 or more years ago have enough immunity to lessen their chance of death if infected. However, these people need another dose of smallpox vaccine to restore their immunity.

State Department and Overseas Issues

Has the Department decided to vaccinate its personnel against smallpox or anthrax?

The Department plans to offer, on a voluntary basis, vaccination against anthrax and smallpox to personnel at certain posts.

While it is impossible to quantify the threat that such bio-weapons could be used, we know that the consequences of such use could be very grave. In that context, the Department believes offering the vaccine is a wise step.

What if someone cannot take the vaccine? Is the Department planning to evacuate those persons?

Pre-exposure administration of the vaccines is considered the most effective means to protect against these two health risks. However, we understand that there will be a number of people who cannot, or opt not to, receive the vaccines. We will be prepared to offer the vaccines or other appropriate treatment in the event of actual exposure.

Does Iraq have smallpox? Do you believe that Iraq may use a smallpox weapon if attacked by the United States?

It is possible, but not confirmed, that Iraq possesses the virus that causes smallpox. By protecting ourselves to respond to any smallpox attack, including through pre-exposure and post-exposure vaccination plans, we also help deter such attacks.

What is the Department planning to do for private American citizens in that region?

For additional analytical, business and investment opportunities information,
please contact Global Investment & Business Center, USA
at (202) 546-2103. Fax: (202) 546-3275. E-mail: rusric@erols.com

We provide extensive information to the American public about travel, security, health, and other conditions abroad to assist private Americans in making individual decisions about their own security and risks. We are following the same approach in this instance.

Has the Department told American citizens to leave the Middle East because of these biological threats? Have any warden messages been prepared for a possible attack?

The Department of State has issued a Worldwide Caution Public Announcement and a Middle East and North Africa Update that alerts American citizens to the continuing threat of terrorist actions that may target private Americans. The Department of State works with posts to disseminate threat information through its warden network when specific information is available. At present, there is no specific information to indicate that there is a likelihood of use of anthrax or smallpox as a weapon in the immediate future. Also, a Chemical-Biological Agent Fact Sheet, which includes information on anthrax and smallpox, is available on the Consular Affairs website at: http://travel.state.gov.

Are we planning to assist any other country in obtaining supplies of vaccines?

The United States recognizes that a smallpox attack in any nation is a potential threat to all nations. The United States, therefore, will work with like-minded nations and the World Health Organization (WHO) to facilitate and coordinate nations' access to existing global smallpox vaccine supplies and to increase the global supply through new production.

Will smallpox vaccine be provided to other countries for their civilian populations?

The United States will work with like-minded nations and the WHO to facilitate and coordinate nations' access to existing global smallpox vaccine supplies and to increase the global supply though new production.

Will the United States assist nations in the event of an actual smallpox or anthrax attack?

Recognizing the global threat posed by a bio-weapon attack, the U.S. Government stands prepared to lend all feasible assistance in the event of an actual anthrax or smallpox attack against a country.

Smallpox Disease

What is smallpox and what should I know about it?

Smallpox is a very serious disease; it is contagious and sometimes fatal. Smallpox is caused by the variola virus, which spreads from contact with infected persons.

- Smallpox can cause: A severe rash covering the whole body that can leave permanent scars
- High fever
- Severe headache or body aches
- Death (in about 30 percent of infected people)
- Blindness in some survivors

Natural cases of smallpox have been eradicated from the Earth. The last natural case of smallpox was recorded in 1977. In 1980, the disease was declared eradicated following worldwide vaccination programs.

However, in the aftermath of the events of September and October, 2001, the U.S. government is taking precautions to be ready to deal with a bioterrorist attack using smallpox as a weapon. As a result of these efforts:

1) There is a detailed nationwide smallpox response plan designed to quickly vaccinate people and contain a smallpox outbreak, and

2) There is enough smallpox vaccine to vaccinate everyone who would need it in the event of an emergency.

For more information, please visit the CDC Website at www.cdc.gov.

What are the symptoms of smallpox?

The symptoms of smallpox begin with high fever, head and body aches, and sometimes vomiting. A rash follows that spreads and progresses to raised bumps and pus-filled blisters that crust, scab, and fall off after about three weeks, leaving a pitted scar.

If someone comes in contact with smallpox, how long does it take to show symptoms?

After exposure, it takes between 7 and 17 days for symptoms of smallpox to appear (average incubation time is 12 to 14 days). During this time, the infected person feels fine and is not contagious.

Is smallpox fatal?

About 70 percent of patients infected with smallpox recover. Many smallpox survivors have permanent scars over large areas of their body, especially their face. Some are left blind.

Is smallpox contagious? How is smallpox spread?

Yes, smallpox is contagious. Smallpox normally spreads from contact with infected persons. Generally, direct and fairly prolonged face-to-face contact is required to spread smallpox from one person to another. People infected with smallpox exhale small droplets that carry the virus to the nose or mouth of close contacts. The greatest risk comes from prolonged close contact exposure (within seven feet) to an infected person. The longer somebody is in close contact with an infected person, the greater the chance of transmission. Indirect contact is less likely to transmit the virus, but infection still can occur via fine-particle aerosols or inanimate objects carrying the virus. For example, contaminated clothing or bed linen could spread the virus. Smallpox is not known to be transmitted by insects or animals.

People are most infectious during the first week of the rash, but a person with smallpox is sometimes contagious with the onset of fever (prodome phase). The infected person is contagious until the last smallpox scab falls off.

Is smallpox contagious before the smallpox symptoms show?

A person with smallpox is sometimes contagious with onset of fever (prodome phase), but the person becomes most contagious with the onset of rash. The infected person is contagious until the last smallpox scab falls off.

Is there any treatment for smallpox?

Smallpox can be prevented through the use of the smallpox vaccine. There is no proven treatment for smallpox, but research to evaluate new antiviral agents is ongoing. Early results from laboratory studies suggests that the drug cidofovir may fight against the smallpox virus. Currently, studies with animals are being done to better understand the drug's ability to treat smallpox disease. . The use of cidofovir to treat smallpox or smallpox vaccine reactions requires the use of an Investigational New Drug protocol and should be evaluated and monitored by medical experts, for example at the NIH and CDC. Patients with smallpox can benefit from supportive therapy such as intravenous fluids, medicine to control fever or pain and antibiotics for any secondary bacterial infections that may occur.

Smallpox Vaccine

What is the smallpox vaccine, and is it still required?

The smallpox vaccine is the best way to prevent smallpox. The vaccine is made from a virus called vaccinia, which is another "pox"-type virus related to smallpox. The vaccine helps the body develop immunity to smallpox. The vaccine does not contain the smallpox virus and cannot spread smallpox. It was successfully used to eradicate smallpox from the human population.

Getting smallpox vaccine before exposure will protect about 95 percent of people from getting smallpox. Vaccination within three days of exposure will prevent or significantly lessen the severity of smallpox in the vast majority of people. Vaccination four to seven days after exposure likely offers some protection from disease or may modify the severity of disease. Solid protection lasts for three to five years after vaccination. Partial protection lasts longer, but people need to be revaccinated if too much time has passed.

Routine vaccination of the American public against smallpox stopped in 1972 after the disease was eradicated in the United States. Until recently, the U.S. government provided the smallpox vaccine only to a few hundred scientists and medical professionals who work with smallpox and similar viruses in a research setting. After the events of September and October 2001, however, the U.S. government took further actions to improve its level of preparedness against terrorism. For smallpox, this included updating a response plan and ordering enough smallpox vaccine to immunize the American public in the event of a smallpox outbreak. The plans are in place, and there is sufficient vaccine available to immunize everyone who might need it in the event of an emergency.

How is the vaccine given?

The smallpox vaccine is not given with a hypodermic needle. It is not a "shot," like many vaccinations. The vaccine is given using a bifurcated (two-pronged) needle that is dipped into the vaccine solution. When removed, the needle retains a droplet of the vaccine. The needle is then used to quickly prick the skin several times for a few seconds. The pricking is not deep, but it will cause a sore spot and one or two drops of blood to form. The vaccine usually is given in the upper arm.

If the vaccination is successful, a red and itchy bump develops at the vaccination site in three or four days. In the first week after vaccination, the bump becomes a large blister, fills with pus, and begins to drain. During week two, the blister begins to dry up and a scab forms. The scab falls off in the third week, leaving a small scar. People who are being vaccinated for the first time may have a stronger "take" (a successful reaction) than those who are being revaccinated.

Why aren't people still routinely vaccinated for smallpox?

The last case of smallpox in the United States was in 1949. The last naturally occurring case in the world was in Somalia in 1977. After the disease was eliminated from the world, routine vaccination against smallpox among the general public was stopped because it was no longer necessary for prevention, and because of the risk of adverse events from the vaccine.

If someone receives that vaccine now or before an attack, will they need to be revaccinated if there is an attack?

In a post-attack emergency, to ensure everyone is protected as rapidly as possible, all exposed persons will be vaccinated regardless of smallpox vaccine history.

If someone is exposed to smallpox, is it too late to get a vaccination?

Vaccination within 3 days of exposure will completely prevent or significantly modify smallpox in the vast majority of persons. Vaccination 4 to 7 days after exposure likely offers some protection from disease or may modify the severity of disease.

How long does a smallpox vaccination last?

Past experience indicates that the first dose of the vaccine offers protection from smallpox for 3 to 5 years, with decreasing immunity thereafter. If a person is vaccinated again later, immunity lasts longer. A report from Europe suggests that people vaccinated 10 or 20 or more years ago have enough immunity to lessen their chance of death if infected. However, these people need another dose of smallpox vaccine to restore their immunity.

Are diluted doses of smallpox vaccine as effective?

Recent tests have indicated that diluted smallpox vaccine is just as effective in providing immunity as full-strength vaccine.

What is the smallpox vaccine made of?

The vaccine is made from a virus called vaccinia, a virus related to smallpox but that does not cause smallpox. The smallpox vaccine helps the body develop immunity to smallpox. It does not contain the smallpox virus and cannot spread smallpox.

Is it possible for people to get smallpox from the vaccination?

No. The smallpox vaccine does not contain smallpox virus and cannot spread or cause smallpox.

Is it possible for someone to get vaccinia, the virus in the vaccine, from someone who has been vaccinated?

The smallpox vaccine does contain another virus called vaccinia, which is "live" in the vaccine. Because the virus is live, it can spread to other parts of the body or to other people from the vaccine site. This can be prevented through proper care of the vaccination site (e.g. hand washing and careful disposal of used bandages).

What are the symptoms of the vaccine virus (vaccinia)?

In the unlikely event that the vaccinia virus is spread, symptoms may include rash, fever, and head and body aches.

How is the vaccine virus (vaccinia) spread?

The vaccine virus (Vaccinia) is spread by touching a vaccination site before it has healed or by touching bandages or clothing that have become contaminated with live virus from the vaccination site. Vaccinia is not spread through airborne contagion. Proper handling of the vaccine site includes these three key points:

1. Don't touch your vaccination site or materials that touched it.

For additional analytical, business and investment opportunities information, please contact Global Investment & Business Center, USA at (202) 546-2103. Fax: (202) 546-3275. E-mail: rusric@erols.com

2. If you touch either the site or materials in contact with the site by accident, clean your hands right away.

3. Don't let others touch your vaccination site or materials that touched it.

Vaccine Safety

How safe is the smallpox vaccine?

The smallpox vaccine is the best protection you can get if you are exposed to the smallpox virus. Most people experience normal, usually mild, reactions, such as sore arm, fever, headache, body ache, and fatigue. These symptoms may peak eight to 12 days after vaccination.

In the past, about 1,000 people for every 1,000,000 (1 million) vaccinated people experienced reactions that were serious, but not life-threatening. Most involved spread of virus elsewhere on the body.

In the past, between 14 and 52 people out of 1,000,000 vaccinated for the first time experienced potentially life-threatening reactions. These reactions included serious skin reactions and inflammation of the brain (encephalitis). From past experience, one or two people in 1 million who receive smallpox vaccine may die as a result.

Serious side effects generally are rarer after revaccination, compared to first vaccinations.

Careful screening of potential vaccine recipients is essential to ensure that those at increased risk do not receive the vaccine.

People most likely to have side effects are people who have, or even once had, skin conditions, (especially eczema or atopic dermatitis) and people with weakened immune systems, such as those who have received a transplant, are HIV positive, or are receiving treatment for cancer. Anyone who falls within these categories, or lives with someone, who falls into one of these categories, should NOT get the smallpox vaccine unless they are exposed, or at risk of exposure, to the disease. In addition, anyone who falls within the following categories should not get the smallpox vaccine unless they are exposed or at risk of exposure: pregnant women, breastfeeding mothers, anyone who is allergic to the vaccine or any of its components, and anyone under the age of 18.

So your estimate is that at least one person per million will die as a result of this vaccine?

This is a statistical estimate based on prior experience with the vaccine. However, we will work hard to prevent even these rare events from happening. Severe reactions can be minimized by screening people for bars to vaccination before vaccinating them and closely monitoring individuals for severe reactions with prompt treatment as necessary.

Is there any way to treat bad reactions to the vaccine?

Two treatments may help people who have certain serious reactions to the smallpox vaccine. These are Vaccinia Immune Globulin (VIG) and Cidofovir. We will have more than 2,700 treatment doses of VIG (enough for predicted reactions with more than 27 million people) at the end of December, and 3,500 doses of Cidofovir (enough for prediction reactions with 15 million people).

Has FDA approved the use of 15 pricks to vaccinate both primary vaccinees and revacinees? If not, will this approval have come before DoD begins to vaccinate troops?If it does not, will DoD be giving 15 pricks to 1st time vaccinees under IND? (The current package insert states 3 pricks for primary vaccinees and 15 pricks for revaccinees).

CDC and others are currently in the process of submitting data to the FDA to support changing the recommendation of 3 needle sticks for primary vaccinations to 15 needle sticks for both primary and revaccination. It is important to note that during the smallpox eradication period, the World Health Organization (WHO) program utilized 15 needle sticks universally to avoid confusion and to help decrease the number of vaccine take failures from flaws in vaccine administration techniques. However, until the FDA approves a package insert change, vaccinators should follow the instructions found on the vaccine package insert on the number of needle sticks to administer for primary vaccines and revaccinees.

What should I expect at the vaccination site?

If the vaccination is successful, a red and itchy bump develops at the vaccination site in three or four days. In the first week after vaccination, the bump becomes a large blister, fills with pus, and begins to drain. During week two, the blister begins to dry up and a scab forms. The scab falls off in the third week, leaving a small scar. People who are being vaccinated for the first time may have a stronger "take" (a successful reaction) than those who are being revaccinated. Most people experience normal, usually mild, reactions, such as sore arm, fever, headache, body ache, and fatigue. These symptoms may peak eight to 12 days after vaccination. The vaccine virus (vaccinia) is present on the skin at the vaccination site until the scab falls off. One must take care not to touch it so that the vaccine virus (vaccinia) is not spread elsewhere, especially to the eyes, nose, mouth, genitalia or rectum.

Are there any side effects of the vaccine?

Yes, side effects can result from smallpox vaccination. Mild reactions include swelling and tender lymph nodes that can last two to four weeks after the blister heals. Up to 20 percent of people develop headache, fatigue, muscle aches, pain, or chills after smallpox vaccination, usually about eight to 12 days later. Some individuals may have rashes that last two to four days. These side effects are usually temporary and self-limiting, meaning they go away on their own or with minimal medical treatment, for example aspirin and rest.

In the past, about 1,000 people for every 1,000,000 (1 million) vaccinated people experienced reactions that were serious, but not life-threatening. Most involved spread of virus elsewhere on the body.

In the past, between 14 and 52 people out of 1,000,000 vaccinated for the first time experienced potentially life-threatening reactions. These reactions included serious skin reactions and inflammation of the brain (encephalitis). From past experience, one or two people in 1 million who receive smallpox vaccine may die as a result.

Serious side effects generally are rarer after revaccination, compared to first vaccinations.

Medical experts believe that with careful screening, monitoring and early intervention the number of serious adverse reactions can be minimized.

H. R. 5005

One Hundred Seventh Congress
of the
United States of America

AT THE SECOND SESSION

Begun and held at the City of Washington on Wednesday,
the twenty-third day of January, two thousand and two

An Act

To establish the Department of Homeland Security, and for other purposes.

Be it enacted by the Senate and House of Representatives of
the United States of America in Congress assembled,

SECTION 1. SHORT TITLE; TABLE OF CONTENTS.

(a) SHORT TITLE.—This Act may be cited as the "Homeland Security Act of 2002".

(b) TABLE OF CONTENTS.—The table of contents for this Act is as follows:

Sec. 1. Short title; table of contents.
Sec. 2. Definitions.
Sec. 3. Construction; severability.
Sec. 4. Effective date.

TITLE I—DEPARTMENT OF HOMELAND SECURITY

Sec. 101. Executive department; mission.
Sec. 102. Secretary; functions.
Sec. 103. Other officers.

TITLE II—INFORMATION ANALYSIS AND INFRASTRUCTURE PROTECTION

Subtitle A—Directorate for Information Analysis and Infrastructure Protection;
Access to Information

Sec. 201. Directorate for Information Analysis and Infrastructure Protection.
Sec. 202. Access to information.

Subtitle B—Critical Infrastructure Information

Sec. 211. Short title.
Sec. 212. Definitions.
Sec. 213. Designation of critical infrastructure protection program.
Sec. 214. Protection of voluntarily shared critical infrastructure information.
Sec. 215. No private right of action.

Subtitle C—Information Security

Sec. 221. Procedures for sharing information.
Sec. 222. Privacy Officer.
Sec. 223. Enhancement of non-Federal cybersecurity.
Sec. 224. Net guard.
Sec. 225. Cyber Security Enhancement Act of 2002.

Subtitle D—Office of Science and Technology

Sec. 231. Establishment of office; Director.
Sec. 232. Mission of office; duties.
Sec. 233. Definition of law enforcement technology.
Sec. 234. Abolishment of Office of Science and Technology of National Institute of
Justice; transfer of functions.
Sec. 235. National Law Enforcement and Corrections Technology Centers.
Sec. 236. Coordination with other entities within Department of Justice.
Sec. 237. Amendments relating to National Institute of Justice.

TITLE III—SCIENCE AND TECHNOLOGY IN SUPPORT OF HOMELAND
SECURITY

Sec. 301. Under Secretary for Science and Technology.

Sec. 302. Responsibilities and authorities of the Under Secretary for Science and Technology.
Sec. 303. Functions transferred.
Sec. 304. Conduct of certain public health-related activities.
Sec. 305. Federally funded research and development centers.
Sec. 306. Miscellaneous provisions.
Sec. 307. Homeland Security Advanced Research Projects Agency.
Sec. 308. Conduct of research, development, demonstration, testing and evaluation.
Sec. 309. Utilization of Department of Energy national laboratories and sites in support of homeland security activities.
Sec. 310. Transfer of Plum Island Animal Disease Center, Department of Agriculture.
Sec. 311. Homeland Security Science and Technology Advisory Committee.
Sec. 312. Homeland Security Institute.
Sec. 313. Technology clearinghouse to encourage and support innovative solutions to enhance homeland security.

TITLE IV—DIRECTORATE OF BORDER AND TRANSPORTATION SECURITY

Subtitle A—Under Secretary for Border and Transportation Security

Sec. 401. Under Secretary for Border and Transportation Security.
Sec. 402. Responsibilities.
Sec. 403. Functions transferred.

Subtitle B—United States Customs Service

Sec. 411. Establishment; Commissioner of Customs.
Sec. 412. Retention of customs revenue functions by Secretary of the Treasury.
Sec. 413. Preservation of customs funds.
Sec. 414. Separate budget request for customs.
Sec. 415. Definition.
Sec. 416. GAO report to Congress.
Sec. 417. Allocation of resources by the Secretary.
Sec. 418. Reports to Congress.
Sec. 419. Customs user fees.

Subtitle C—Miscellaneous Provisions

Sec. 421. Transfer of certain agricultural inspection functions of the Department of Agriculture.
Sec. 422. Functions of Administrator of General Services.
Sec. 423. Functions of Transportation Security Administration.
Sec. 424. Preservation of Transportation Security Administration as a distinct entity.
Sec. 425. Explosive detection systems.
Sec. 426. Transportation security.
Sec. 427. Coordination of information and information technology.
Sec. 428. Visa issuance.
Sec. 429. Information on visa denials required to be entered into electronic data system.
Sec. 430. Office for Domestic Preparedness.

Subtitle D—Immigration Enforcement Functions

Sec. 441. Transfer of functions to Under Secretary for Border and Transportation Security.
Sec. 442. Establishment of Bureau of Border Security.
Sec. 443. Professional responsibility and quality review.
Sec. 444. Employee discipline.
Sec. 445. Report on improving enforcement functions.
Sec. 446. Sense of Congress regarding construction of fencing near San Diego, California.

Subtitle E—Citizenship and Immigration Services

Sec. 451. Establishment of Bureau of Citizenship and Immigration Services.
Sec. 452. Citizenship and Immigration Services Ombudsman.
Sec. 453. Professional responsibility and quality review.
Sec. 454. Employee discipline.
Sec. 455. Effective date.
Sec. 456. Transition.
Sec. 457. Funding for citizenship and immigration services.
Sec. 458. Backlog elimination.
Sec. 459. Report on improving immigration services.
Sec. 460. Report on responding to fluctuating needs.

Sec. 461. Application of Internet-based technologies.
Sec. 462. Children's affairs.

Subtitle F—General Immigration Provisions

Sec. 471. Abolishment of INS.
Sec. 472. Voluntary separation incentive payments.
Sec. 473. Authority to conduct a demonstration project relating to disciplinary action.
Sec. 474. Sense of Congress.
Sec. 475. Director of Shared Services.
Sec. 476. Separation of funding.
Sec. 477. Reports and implementation plans.
Sec. 478. Immigration functions.

TITLE V—EMERGENCY PREPAREDNESS AND RESPONSE

Sec. 501. Under Secretary for Emergency Preparedness and Response.
Sec. 502. Responsibilities.
Sec. 503. Functions transferred.
Sec. 504. Nuclear incident response.
Sec. 505. Conduct of certain public health-related activities.
Sec. 506. Definition.
Sec. 507. Role of Federal Emergency Management Agency.
Sec. 508. Use of national private sector networks in emergency response.
Sec. 509. Use of commercially available technology, goods, and services.

TITLE VI—TREATMENT OF CHARITABLE TRUSTS FOR MEMBERS OF THE ARMED FORCES OF THE UNITED STATES AND OTHER GOVERNMENTAL ORGANIZATIONS

Sec. 601. Treatment of charitable trusts for members of the Armed Forces of the United States and other governmental organizations.

TITLE VII—MANAGEMENT

Sec. 701. Under Secretary for Management.
Sec. 702. Chief Financial Officer.
Sec. 703. Chief Information Officer.
Sec. 704. Chief Human Capital Officer.
Sec. 705. Establishment of Officer for Civil Rights and Civil Liberties.
Sec. 706. Consolidation and co-location of offices.

TITLE VIII—COORDINATION WITH NON-FEDERAL ENTITIES; INSPECTOR GENERAL; UNITED STATES SECRET SERVICE; COAST GUARD; GENERAL PROVISIONS

Subtitle A—Coordination with Non-Federal Entities

Sec. 801. Office for State and Local Government Coordination.

Subtitle B—Inspector General

Sec. 811. Authority of the Secretary.
Sec. 812. Law enforcement powers of Inspector General agents.

Subtitle C—United States Secret Service

Sec. 821. Functions transferred.

Subtitle D—Acquisitions

Sec. 831. Research and development projects.
Sec. 832. Personal services.
Sec. 833. Special streamlined acquisition authority.
Sec. 834. Unsolicited proposals.
Sec. 835. Prohibition on contracts with corporate expatriates.

Subtitle E—Human Resources Management

Sec. 841. Establishment of Human Resources Management System.
Sec. 842. Labor-management relations.

Subtitle F—Federal Emergency Procurement Flexibility

Sec. 851. Definition.
Sec. 852. Procurements for defense against or recovery from terrorism or nuclear, biological, chemical, or radiological attack.

Sec. 853. Increased simplified acquisition threshold for procurements in support of humanitarian or peacekeeping operations or contingency operations.
Sec. 854. Increased micro-purchase threshold for certain procurements.
Sec. 855. Application of certain commercial items authorities to certain procurements.
Sec. 856. Use of streamlined procedures.
Sec. 857. Review and report by Comptroller General.
Sec. 858. Identification of new entrants into the Federal marketplace.

Subtitle G—Support Anti-terrorism by Fostering Effective Technologies Act of 2002

Sec. 861. Short title.
Sec. 862. Administration.
Sec. 863. Litigation management.
Sec. 864. Risk management.
Sec. 865. Definitions.

Subtitle H—Miscellaneous Provisions

Sec. 871. Advisory committees.
Sec. 872. Reorganization.
Sec. 873. Use of appropriated funds.
Sec. 874. Future Year Homeland Security Program.
Sec. 875. Miscellaneous authorities.
Sec. 876. Military activities.
Sec. 877. Regulatory authority and preemption.
Sec. 878. Counternarcotics officer.
Sec. 879. Office of International Affairs.
Sec. 880. Prohibition of the Terrorism Information and Prevention System.
Sec. 881. Review of pay and benefit plans.
Sec. 882. Office for National Capital Region Coordination.
Sec. 883. Requirement to comply with laws protecting equal employment opportunity and providing whistleblower protections.
Sec. 884. Federal Law Enforcement Training Center.
Sec. 885. Joint Interagency Task Force.
Sec. 886. Sense of Congress reaffirming the continued importance and applicability of the Posse Comitatus Act.
Sec. 887. Coordination with the Department of Health and Human Services under the Public Health Service Act.
Sec. 888. Preserving Coast Guard mission performance.
Sec. 889. Homeland security funding analysis in President's budget.
Sec. 890. Air Transportation Safety and System Stabilization Act.

Subtitle I—Information Sharing

Sec. 891. Short title; findings; and sense of Congress.
Sec. 892. Facilitating homeland security information sharing procedures.
Sec. 893. Report.
Sec. 894. Authorization of appropriations.
Sec. 895. Authority to share grand jury information.
Sec. 896. Authority to share electronic, wire, and oral interception information.
Sec. 897. Foreign intelligence information.
Sec. 898. Information acquired from an electronic surveillance.
Sec. 899. Information acquired from a physical search.

TITLE IX—NATIONAL HOMELAND SECURITY COUNCIL

Sec. 901. National Homeland Security Council.
Sec. 902. Function.
Sec. 903. Membership.
Sec. 904. Other functions and activities.
Sec. 905. Staff composition.
Sec. 906. Relation to the National Security Council.

TITLE X—INFORMATION SECURITY

Sec. 1001. Information security.
Sec. 1002. Management of information technology.
Sec. 1003. National Institute of Standards and Technology.
Sec. 1004. Information Security and Privacy Advisory Board.
Sec. 1005. Technical and conforming amendments.
Sec. 1006. Construction.

TITLE XI—DEPARTMENT OF JUSTICE DIVISIONS

Subtitle A—Executive Office for Immigration Review

Sec. 1101. Legal status of EOIR.

Sec. 1102. Authorities of the Attorney General.
Sec. 1103. Statutory construction.

Subtitle B—Transfer of the Bureau of Alcohol, Tobacco and Firearms to the
Department of Justice

Sec. 1111. Bureau of Alcohol, Tobacco, Firearms, and Explosives.
Sec. 1112. Technical and conforming amendments.
Sec. 1113. Powers of agents of the Bureau of Alcohol, Tobacco, Firearms, and Explosives.
Sec. 1114. Explosives training and research facility.
Sec. 1115. Personnel management demonstration project.

Subtitle C—Explosives

Sec. 1121. Short title.
Sec. 1122. Permits for purchasers of explosives.
Sec. 1123. Persons prohibited from receiving or possessing explosive materials.
Sec. 1124. Requirement to provide samples of explosive materials and ammonium nitrate.
Sec. 1125. Destruction of property of institutions receiving Federal financial assistance.
Sec. 1126. Relief from disabilities.
Sec. 1127. Theft reporting requirement.
Sec. 1128. Authorization of appropriations.

TITLE XII—AIRLINE WAR RISK INSURANCE LEGISLATION

Sec. 1201. Air carrier liability for third party claims arising out of acts of terrorism.
Sec. 1202. Extension of insurance policies.
Sec. 1203. Correction of reference.
Sec. 1204. Report.

TITLE XIII—FEDERAL WORKFORCE IMPROVEMENT

Subtitle A—Chief Human Capital Officers

Sec. 1301. Short title.
Sec. 1302. Agency Chief Human Capital Officers.
Sec. 1303. Chief Human Capital Officers Council.
Sec. 1304. Strategic human capital management.
Sec. 1305. Effective date.

Subtitle B—Reforms Relating to Federal Human Capital Management

Sec. 1311. Inclusion of agency human capital strategic planning in performance plans and programs performance reports.
Sec. 1312. Reform of the competitive service hiring process.
Sec. 1313. Permanent extension, revision, and expansion of authorities for use of voluntary separation incentive pay and voluntary early retirement.
Sec. 1314. Student volunteer transit subsidy.

Subtitle C—Reforms Relating to the Senior Executive Service

Sec. 1321. Repeal of recertification requirements of senior executives.
Sec. 1322. Adjustment of limitation on total annual compensation.

Subtitle D—Academic Training

Sec. 1331. Academic training.
Sec. 1332. Modifications to National Security Education Program.

TITLE XIV—ARMING PILOTS AGAINST TERRORISM

Sec. 1401. Short title.
Sec. 1402. Federal Flight Deck Officer Program.
Sec. 1403. Crew training.
Sec. 1404. Commercial airline security study.
Sec. 1405. Authority to arm flight deck crew with less-than-lethal weapons.
Sec. 1406. Technical amendments.

TITLE XV—TRANSITION

Subtitle A—Reorganization Plan

Sec. 1501. Definitions.
Sec. 1502. Reorganization plan.
Sec. 1503. Review of congressional committee structures.

Subtitle B—Transitional Provisions

Sec. 1511. Transitional authorities.

Sec. 1512. Savings provisions.
Sec. 1513. Terminations.
Sec. 1514. National identification system not authorized.
Sec. 1515. Continuity of Inspector General oversight.
Sec. 1516. Incidental transfers.
Sec. 1517. Reference.

TITLE XVI—CORRECTIONS TO EXISTING LAW RELATING TO AIRLINE
TRANSPORTATION SECURITY

Sec. 1601. Retention of security sensitive information authority at Department of
Transportation.
Sec. 1602. Increase in civil penalties.
Sec. 1603. Allowing United States citizens and United States nationals as screen-
ers.

TITLE XVII—CONFORMING AND TECHNICAL AMENDMENTS

Sec. 1701. Inspector General Act of 1978.
Sec. 1702. Executive Schedule.
Sec. 1703. United States Secret Service.
Sec. 1704. Coast Guard.
Sec. 1705. Strategic national stockpile and smallpox vaccine development.
Sec. 1706. Transfer of certain security and law enforcement functions and authori-
ties.
Sec. 1707. Transportation security regulations.
Sec. 1708. National Bio-Weapons Defense Analysis Center.
Sec. 1709. Collaboration with the Secretary of Homeland Security.
Sec. 1710. Railroad safety to include railroad security.
Sec. 1711. Hazmat safety to include hazmat security.
Sec. 1712. Office of Science and Technology Policy.
Sec. 1713. National Oceanographic Partnership Program.
Sec. 1714. Clarification of definition of manufacturer.
Sec. 1715. Clarification of definition of vaccine-related injury or death.
Sec. 1716. Clarification of definition of vaccine.
Sec. 1717. Effective date.

SEC. 2. DEFINITIONS.

In this Act, the following definitions apply:

(1) Each of the terms "American homeland" and "homeland" means the United States.

(2) The term "appropriate congressional committee" means any committee of the House of Representatives or the Senate having legislative or oversight jurisdiction under the Rules of the House of Representatives or the Senate, respectively, over the matter concerned.

(3) The term "assets" includes contracts, facilities, property, records, unobligated or unexpended balances of appropriations, and other funds or resources (other than personnel).

(4) The term "critical infrastructure" has the meaning given that term in section 1016(e) of Public Law 107–56 (42 U.S.C. 5195c(e)).

(5) The term "Department" means the Department of Homeland Security.

(6) The term "emergency response providers" includes Federal, State, and local emergency public safety, law enforcement, emergency response, emergency medical (including hospital emergency facilities), and related personnel, agencies, and authorities.

(7) The term "executive agency" means an executive agency and a military department, as defined, respectively, in sections 105 and 102 of title 5, United States Code.

(8) The term "functions" includes authorities, powers, rights, privileges, immunities, programs, projects, activities, duties, and responsibilities.

(9) The term "key resources" means publicly or privately controlled resources essential to the minimal operations of the economy and government.

(10) The term "local government" means—

(A) a county, municipality, city, town, township, local public authority, school district, special district, intrastate district, council of governments (regardless of whether the council of governments is incorporated as a nonprofit corporation under State law), regional or interstate government entity, or agency or instrumentality of a local government;

(B) an Indian tribe or authorized tribal organization, or in Alaska a Native village or Alaska Regional Native Corporation; and

(C) a rural community, unincorporated town or village, or other public entity.

(11) The term "major disaster" has the meaning given in section 102(2) of the Robert T. Stafford Disaster Relief and Emergency Assistance Act (42 U.S.C. 5122).

(12) The term "personnel" means officers and employees.

(13) The term "Secretary" means the Secretary of Homeland Security.

(14) The term "State" means any State of the United States, the District of Columbia, the Commonwealth of Puerto Rico, the Virgin Islands, Guam, American Samoa, the Commonwealth of the Northern Mariana Islands, and any possession of the United States.

(15) The term "terrorism" means any activity that—

(A) involves an act that—

(i) is dangerous to human life or potentially destructive of critical infrastructure or key resources; and

(ii) is a violation of the criminal laws of the United States or of any State or other subdivision of the United States; and

(B) appears to be intended—

(i) to intimidate or coerce a civilian population;

(ii) to influence the policy of a government by intimidation or coercion; or

(iii) to affect the conduct of a government by mass destruction, assassination, or kidnapping.

(16)(A) The term "United States", when used in a geographic sense, means any State of the United States, the District of Columbia, the Commonwealth of Puerto Rico, the Virgin Islands, Guam, American Samoa, the Commonwealth of the Northern Mariana Islands, any possession of the United States, and any waters within the jurisdiction of the United States.

(B) Nothing in this paragraph or any other provision of this Act shall be construed to modify the definition of "United States" for the purposes of the Immigration and Nationality Act or any other immigration or nationality law.

SEC. 3. CONSTRUCTION; SEVERABILITY.

Any provision of this Act held to be invalid or unenforceable by its terms, or as applied to any person or circumstance, shall be construed so as to give it the maximum effect permitted by law, unless such holding shall be one of utter invalidity or unenforceability, in which event such provision shall be deemed severable from this Act and shall not affect the remainder thereof, or the application of such provision to other persons not similarly situated or to other, dissimilar circumstances.

SEC. 4. EFFECTIVE DATE.

This Act shall take effect 60 days after the date of enactment.

TITLE I—DEPARTMENT OF HOMELAND SECURITY

SEC. 101. EXECUTIVE DEPARTMENT; MISSION.

(a) ESTABLISHMENT.—There is established a Department of Homeland Security, as an executive department of the United States within the meaning of title 5, United States Code.

(b) MISSION.—

(1) IN GENERAL.—The primary mission of the Department is to—

(A) prevent terrorist attacks within the United States;

(B) reduce the vulnerability of the United States to terrorism;

(C) minimize the damage, and assist in the recovery, from terrorist attacks that do occur within the United States;

(D) carry out all functions of entities transferred to the Department, including by acting as a focal point regarding natural and manmade crises and emergency planning;

(E) ensure that the functions of the agencies and subdivisions within the Department that are not related directly to securing the homeland are not diminished or neglected except by a specific explicit Act of Congress;

(F) ensure that the overall economic security of the United States is not diminished by efforts, activities, and programs aimed at securing the homeland; and

(G) monitor connections between illegal drug trafficking and terrorism, coordinate efforts to sever such connections, and otherwise contribute to efforts to interdict illegal drug trafficking.

(2) RESPONSIBILITY FOR INVESTIGATING AND PROSECUTING TERRORISM.—Except as specifically provided by law with respect to entities transferred to the Department under this Act, primary responsibility for investigating and prosecuting acts of terrorism shall be vested not in the Department, but rather in Federal, State, and local law enforcement agencies with jurisdiction over the acts in question.

SEC. 102. SECRETARY; FUNCTIONS.

(a) SECRETARY.—

(1) IN GENERAL.—There is a Secretary of Homeland Security, appointed by the President, by and with the advice and consent of the Senate.

(2) HEAD OF DEPARTMENT.—The Secretary is the head of the Department and shall have direction, authority, and control over it.

(3) FUNCTIONS VESTED IN SECRETARY.—All functions of all officers, employees, and organizational units of the Department are vested in the Secretary.

(b) FUNCTIONS.—The Secretary—

(1) except as otherwise provided by this Act, may delegate any of the Secretary's functions to any officer, employee, or organizational unit of the Department;

(2) shall have the authority to make contracts, grants, and cooperative agreements, and to enter into agreements with other executive agencies, as may be necessary and proper to carry out the Secretary's responsibilities under this Act or otherwise provided by law; and

(3) shall take reasonable steps to ensure that information systems and databases of the Department are compatible with each other and with appropriate databases of other Departments.

(c) COORDINATION WITH NON-FEDERAL ENTITIES.—With respect to homeland security, the Secretary shall coordinate through the Office of State and Local Coordination (established under section 801) (including the provision of training and equipment) with State and local government personnel, agencies, and authorities, with the private sector, and with other entities, including by—

(1) coordinating with State and local government personnel, agencies, and authorities, and with the private sector, to ensure adequate planning, equipment, training, and exercise activities;

(2) coordinating and, as appropriate, consolidating, the Federal Government's communications and systems of communications relating to homeland security with State and local government personnel, agencies, and authorities, the private sector, other entities, and the public; and

(3) distributing or, as appropriate, coordinating the distribution of, warnings and information to State and local government personnel, agencies, and authorities and to the public.

(d) MEETINGS OF NATIONAL SECURITY COUNCIL.—The Secretary may, subject to the direction of the President, attend and participate in meetings of the National Security Council.

(e) ISSUANCE OF REGULATIONS.—The issuance of regulations by the Secretary shall be governed by the provisions of chapter 5 of title 5, United States Code, except as specifically provided in this Act, in laws granting regulatory authorities that are transferred by this Act, and in laws enacted after the date of enactment of this Act.

(f) SPECIAL ASSISTANT TO THE SECRETARY.—The Secretary shall appoint a Special Assistant to the Secretary who shall be responsible for—

(1) creating and fostering strategic communications with the private sector to enhance the primary mission of the Department to protect the American homeland;

(2) advising the Secretary on the impact of the Department's policies, regulations, processes, and actions on the private sector;

(3) interfacing with other relevant Federal agencies with homeland security missions to assess the impact of these agencies' actions on the private sector;

(4) creating and managing private sector advisory councils composed of representatives of industries and associations designated by the Secretary to—

(A) advise the Secretary on private sector products, applications, and solutions as they relate to homeland security challenges; and

(B) advise the Secretary on homeland security policies, regulations, processes, and actions that affect the participating industries and associations;

(5) working with Federal laboratories, federally funded research and development centers, other federally funded organizations, academia, and the private sector to develop innovative approaches to address homeland security challenges to produce and deploy the best available technologies for homeland security missions;

(6) promoting existing public-private partnerships and developing new public-private partnerships to provide for collaboration and mutual support to address homeland security challenges; and

(7) assisting in the development and promotion of private sector best practices to secure critical infrastructure.

(g) STANDARDS POLICY.—All standards activities of the Department shall be conducted in accordance with section 12(d) of the National Technology Transfer Advancement Act of 1995 (15 U.S.C. 272 note) and Office of Management and Budget Circular A–119.

SEC. 103. OTHER OFFICERS.

(a) DEPUTY SECRETARY; UNDER SECRETARIES.—There are the following officers, appointed by the President, by and with the advice and consent of the Senate:

(1) A Deputy Secretary of Homeland Security, who shall be the Secretary's first assistant for purposes of subchapter III of chapter 33 of title 5, United States Code.

(2) An Under Secretary for Information Analysis and Infrastructure Protection.

(3) An Under Secretary for Science and Technology.

(4) An Under Secretary for Border and Transportation Security.

(5) An Under Secretary for Emergency Preparedness and Response.

(6) A Director of the Bureau of Citizenship and Immigration Services.

(7) An Under Secretary for Management.

(8) Not more than 12 Assistant Secretaries.

(9) A General Counsel, who shall be the chief legal officer of the Department.

(b) INSPECTOR GENERAL.—There is an Inspector General, who shall be appointed as provided in section 3(a) of the Inspector General Act of 1978.

(c) COMMANDANT OF THE COAST GUARD.—To assist the Secretary in the performance of the Secretary's functions, there is a Commandant of the Coast Guard, who shall be appointed as provided in section 44 of title 14, United States Code, and who shall report directly to the Secretary. In addition to such duties as may be provided in this Act and as assigned to the Commandant by the Secretary, the duties of the Commandant shall include those required by section 2 of title 14, United States Code.

(d) OTHER OFFICERS.—To assist the Secretary in the performance of the Secretary's functions, there are the following officers, appointed by the President:

(1) A Director of the Secret Service.

(2) A Chief Information Officer.

(3) A Chief Human Capital Officer.

(4) A Chief Financial Officer.

(5) An Officer for Civil Rights and Civil Liberties.

(e) PERFORMANCE OF SPECIFIC FUNCTIONS.—Subject to the provisions of this Act, every officer of the Department shall perform the functions specified by law for the official's office or prescribed by the Secretary.

TITLE II—INFORMATION ANALYSIS AND INFRASTRUCTURE PROTECTION

Subtitle A—Directorate for Information Analysis and Infrastructure Protection; Access to Information

SEC. 201. DIRECTORATE FOR INFORMATION ANALYSIS AND INFRASTRUCTURE PROTECTION.

(a) UNDER SECRETARY OF HOMELAND SECURITY FOR INFORMATION ANALYSIS AND INFRASTRUCTURE PROTECTION.—

(1) IN GENERAL.—There shall be in the Department a Directorate for Information Analysis and Infrastructure Protection headed by an Under Secretary for Information Analysis and Infrastructure Protection, who shall be appointed by the President, by and with the advice and consent of the Senate.

(2) RESPONSIBILITIES.—The Under Secretary shall assist the Secretary in discharging the responsibilities assigned by the Secretary.

(b) ASSISTANT SECRETARY FOR INFORMATION ANALYSIS; ASSISTANT SECRETARY FOR INFRASTRUCTURE PROTECTION.—

(1) ASSISTANT SECRETARY FOR INFORMATION ANALYSIS.— There shall be in the Department an Assistant Secretary for Information Analysis, who shall be appointed by the President.

(2) ASSISTANT SECRETARY FOR INFRASTRUCTURE PROTECTION.—There shall be in the Department an Assistant Secretary for Infrastructure Protection, who shall be appointed by the President.

(3) RESPONSIBILITIES.—The Assistant Secretary for Information Analysis and the Assistant Secretary for Infrastructure Protection shall assist the Under Secretary for Information Analysis and Infrastructure Protection in discharging the responsibilities of the Under Secretary under this section.

(c) DISCHARGE OF INFORMATION ANALYSIS AND INFRASTRUCTURE PROTECTION.—The Secretary shall ensure that the responsibilities of the Department regarding information analysis and infrastructure protection are carried out through the Under Secretary for Information Analysis and Infrastructure Protection.

(d) RESPONSIBILITIES OF UNDER SECRETARY.—Subject to the direction and control of the Secretary, the responsibilities of the

Under Secretary for Information Analysis and Infrastructure Protection shall be as follows:

(1) To access, receive, and analyze law enforcement information, intelligence information, and other information from agencies of the Federal Government, State and local government agencies (including law enforcement agencies), and private sector entities, and to integrate such information in order to—

(A) identify and assess the nature and scope of terrorist threats to the homeland;

(B) detect and identify threats of terrorism against the United States; and

(C) understand such threats in light of actual and potential vulnerabilities of the homeland.

(2) To carry out comprehensive assessments of the vulnerabilities of the key resources and critical infrastructure of the United States, including the performance of risk assessments to determine the risks posed by particular types of terrorist attacks within the United States (including an assessment of the probability of success of such attacks and the feasibility and potential efficacy of various countermeasures to such attacks).

(3) To integrate relevant information, analyses, and vulnerability assessments (whether such information, analyses, or assessments are provided or produced by the Department or others) in order to identify priorities for protective and support measures by the Department, other agencies of the Federal Government, State and local government agencies and authorities, the private sector, and other entities.

(4) To ensure, pursuant to section 202, the timely and efficient access by the Department to all information necessary to discharge the responsibilities under this section, including obtaining such information from other agencies of the Federal Government.

(5) To develop a comprehensive national plan for securing the key resources and critical infrastructure of the United States, including power production, generation, and distribution systems, information technology and telecommunications systems (including satellites), electronic financial and property record storage and transmission systems, emergency preparedness communications systems, and the physical and technological assets that support such systems.

(6) To recommend measures necessary to protect the key resources and critical infrastructure of the United States in coordination with other agencies of the Federal Government and in cooperation with State and local government agencies and authorities, the private sector, and other entities.

(7) To administer the Homeland Security Advisory System, including—

(A) exercising primary responsibility for public advisories related to threats to homeland security; and

(B) in coordination with other agencies of the Federal Government, providing specific warning information, and advice about appropriate protective measures and countermeasures, to State and local government agencies and authorities, the private sector, other entities, and the public.

(8) To review, analyze, and make recommendations for improvements in the policies and procedures governing the sharing of law enforcement information, intelligence information, intelligence-related information, and other information relating to homeland security within the Federal Government and between the Federal Government and State and local government agencies and authorities.

(9) To disseminate, as appropriate, information analyzed by the Department within the Department, to other agencies of the Federal Government with responsibilities relating to homeland security, and to agencies of State and local governments and private sector entities with such responsibilities in order to assist in the deterrence, prevention, preemption of, or response to, terrorist attacks against the United States.

(10) To consult with the Director of Central Intelligence and other appropriate intelligence, law enforcement, or other elements of the Federal Government to establish collection priorities and strategies for information, including law enforcement-related information, relating to threats of terrorism against the United States through such means as the representation of the Department in discussions regarding requirements and priorities in the collection of such information.

(11) To consult with State and local governments and private sector entities to ensure appropriate exchanges of information, including law enforcement-related information, relating to threats of terrorism against the United States.

(12) To ensure that—

(A) any material received pursuant to this Act is protected from unauthorized disclosure and handled and used only for the performance of official duties; and

(B) any intelligence information under this Act is shared, retained, and disseminated consistent with the authority of the Director of Central Intelligence to protect intelligence sources and methods under the National Security Act of 1947 (50 U.S.C. 401 et seq.) and related procedures and, as appropriate, similar authorities of the Attorney General concerning sensitive law enforcement information.

(13) To request additional information from other agencies of the Federal Government, State and local government agencies, and the private sector relating to threats of terrorism in the United States, or relating to other areas of responsibility assigned by the Secretary, including the entry into cooperative agreements through the Secretary to obtain such information.

(14) To establish and utilize, in conjunction with the chief information officer of the Department, a secure communications and information technology infrastructure, including datamining and other advanced analytical tools, in order to access, receive, and analyze data and information in furtherance of the responsibilities under this section, and to disseminate information acquired and analyzed by the Department, as appropriate.

(15) To ensure, in conjunction with the chief information officer of the Department, that any information databases and analytical tools developed or utilized by the Department—

(A) are compatible with one another and with relevant information databases of other agencies of the Federal Government; and

(B) treat information in such databases in a manner that complies with applicable Federal law on privacy.

(16) To coordinate training and other support to the elements and personnel of the Department, other agencies of the Federal Government, and State and local governments that provide information to the Department, or are consumers of information provided by the Department, in order to facilitate the identification and sharing of information revealed in their ordinary duties and the optimal utilization of information received from the Department.

(17) To coordinate with elements of the intelligence community and with Federal, State, and local law enforcement agencies, and the private sector, as appropriate.

(18) To provide intelligence and information analysis and support to other elements of the Department.

(19) To perform such other duties relating to such responsibilities as the Secretary may provide.

(e) STAFF.—

(1) IN GENERAL.—The Secretary shall provide the Directorate with a staff of analysts having appropriate expertise and experience to assist the Directorate in discharging responsibilities under this section.

(2) PRIVATE SECTOR ANALYSTS.—Analysts under this subsection may include analysts from the private sector.

(3) SECURITY CLEARANCES.—Analysts under this subsection shall possess security clearances appropriate for their work under this section.

(f) DETAIL OF PERSONNEL.—

(1) IN GENERAL.—In order to assist the Directorate in discharging responsibilities under this section, personnel of the agencies referred to in paragraph (2) may be detailed to the Department for the performance of analytic functions and related duties.

(2) COVERED AGENCIES.—The agencies referred to in this paragraph are as follows:

(A) The Department of State.

(B) The Central Intelligence Agency.

(C) The Federal Bureau of Investigation.

(D) The National Security Agency.

(E) The National Imagery and Mapping Agency.

(F) The Defense Intelligence Agency.

(G) Any other agency of the Federal Government that the President considers appropriate.

(3) COOPERATIVE AGREEMENTS.—The Secretary and the head of the agency concerned may enter into cooperative agreements for the purpose of detailing personnel under this subsection.

(4) BASIS.—The detail of personnel under this subsection may be on a reimbursable or non-reimbursable basis.

(g) FUNCTIONS TRANSFERRED.—In accordance with title XV, there shall be transferred to the Secretary, for assignment to the Under Secretary for Information Analysis and Infrastructure Protection under this section, the functions, personnel, assets, and liabilities of the following:

(1) The National Infrastructure Protection Center of the Federal Bureau of Investigation (other than the Computer Investigations and Operations Section), including the functions of the Attorney General relating thereto.

(2) The National Communications System of the Department of Defense, including the functions of the Secretary of Defense relating thereto.

(3) The Critical Infrastructure Assurance Office of the Department of Commerce, including the functions of the Secretary of Commerce relating thereto.

(4) The National Infrastructure Simulation and Analysis Center of the Department of Energy and the energy security and assurance program and activities of the Department, including the functions of the Secretary of Energy relating thereto.

(5) The Federal Computer Incident Response Center of the General Services Administration, including the functions of the Administrator of General Services relating thereto.

(h) INCLUSION OF CERTAIN ELEMENTS OF THE DEPARTMENT AS ELEMENTS OF THE INTELLIGENCE COMMUNITY.—Section 3(4) of the National Security Act of 1947 (50 U.S.C. 401(a)) is amended—

(1) by striking "and" at the end of subparagraph (I);

(2) by redesignating subparagraph (J) as subparagraph (K); and

(3) by inserting after subparagraph (I) the following new subparagraph:

"(J) the elements of the Department of Homeland Security concerned with the analyses of foreign intelligence information; and".

SEC. 202. ACCESS TO INFORMATION.

(a) IN GENERAL.—

(1) THREAT AND VULNERABILITY INFORMATION.—Except as otherwise directed by the President, the Secretary shall have such access as the Secretary considers necessary to all information, including reports, assessments, analyses, and unevaluated intelligence relating to threats of terrorism against the United States and to other areas of responsibility assigned by the Secretary, and to all information concerning infrastructure or other vulnerabilities of the United States to terrorism, whether or not such information has been analyzed, that may be collected, possessed, or prepared by any agency of the Federal Government.

(2) OTHER INFORMATION.—The Secretary shall also have access to other information relating to matters under the responsibility of the Secretary that may be collected, possessed, or prepared by an agency of the Federal Government as the President may further provide.

(b) MANNER OF ACCESS.—Except as otherwise directed by the President, with respect to information to which the Secretary has access pursuant to this section—

(1) the Secretary may obtain such material upon request, and may enter into cooperative arrangements with other executive agencies to provide such material or provide Department officials with access to it on a regular or routine basis, including requests or arrangements involving broad categories of material, access to electronic databases, or both; and

(2) regardless of whether the Secretary has made any request or entered into any cooperative arrangement pursuant to paragraph (1), all agencies of the Federal Government shall promptly provide to the Secretary—

(A) all reports (including information reports containing intelligence which has not been fully evaluated), assessments, and analytical information relating to threats of terrorism against the United States and to other areas of responsibility assigned by the Secretary;

(B) all information concerning the vulnerability of the infrastructure of the United States, or other vulnerabilities of the United States, to terrorism, whether or not such information has been analyzed;

(C) all other information relating to significant and credible threats of terrorism against the United States, whether or not such information has been analyzed; and

(D) such other information or material as the President may direct.

(c) TREATMENT UNDER CERTAIN LAWS.—The Secretary shall be deemed to be a Federal law enforcement, intelligence, protective, national defense, immigration, or national security official, and shall be provided with all information from law enforcement agencies that is required to be given to the Director of Central Intelligence, under any provision of the following:

(1) The USA PATRIOT Act of 2001 (Public Law 107–56).

(2) Section 2517(6) of title 18, United States Code.

(3) Rule 6(e)(3)(C) of the Federal Rules of Criminal Procedure.

(d) ACCESS TO INTELLIGENCE AND OTHER INFORMATION.—

(1) ACCESS BY ELEMENTS OF FEDERAL GOVERNMENT.—Nothing in this title shall preclude any element of the intelligence community (as that term is defined in section 3(4) of the National Security Act of 1947 (50 U.S.C. 401a(4)), or any other element of the Federal Government with responsibility for analyzing terrorist threat information, from receiving any intelligence or other information relating to terrorism.

(2) SHARING OF INFORMATION.—The Secretary, in consultation with the Director of Central Intelligence, shall work to ensure that intelligence or other information relating to terrorism to which the Department has access is appropriately shared with the elements of the Federal Government referred to in paragraph (1), as well as with State and local governments, as appropriate.

Subtitle B—Critical Infrastructure Information

SEC. 211. SHORT TITLE.

This subtitle may be cited as the "Critical Infrastructure Information Act of 2002".

SEC. 212. DEFINITIONS.

In this subtitle:

(1) AGENCY.—The term "agency" has the meaning given it in section 551 of title 5, United States Code.

(2) COVERED FEDERAL AGENCY.—The term "covered Federal agency" means the Department of Homeland Security.

(3) CRITICAL INFRASTRUCTURE INFORMATION.—The term "critical infrastructure information" means information not customarily in the public domain and related to the security of critical infrastructure or protected systems—

(A) actual, potential, or threatened interference with, attack on, compromise of, or incapacitation of critical infrastructure or protected systems by either physical or computer-based attack or other similar conduct (including the misuse of or unauthorized access to all types of communications and data transmission systems) that violates Federal, State, or local law, harms interstate commerce of the United States, or threatens public health or safety;

(B) the ability of any critical infrastructure or protected system to resist such interference, compromise, or incapacitation, including any planned or past assessment, projection, or estimate of the vulnerability of critical infrastructure or a protected system, including security testing, risk evaluation thereto, risk management planning, or risk audit; or

(C) any planned or past operational problem or solution regarding critical infrastructure or protected systems, including repair, recovery, reconstruction, insurance, or continuity, to the extent it is related to such interference, compromise, or incapacitation.

(4) CRITICAL INFRASTRUCTURE PROTECTION PROGRAM.—The term "critical infrastructure protection program" means any component or bureau of a covered Federal agency that has been designated by the President or any agency head to receive critical infrastructure information.

(5) INFORMATION SHARING AND ANALYSIS ORGANIZATION.— The term "Information Sharing and Analysis Organization" means any formal or informal entity or collaboration created or employed by public or private sector organizations, for purposes of—

(A) gathering and analyzing critical infrastructure information in order to better understand security problems and interdependencies related to critical infrastructure and protected systems, so as to ensure the availability, integrity, and reliability thereof;

(B) communicating or disclosing critical infrastructure information to help prevent, detect, mitigate, or recover from the effects of a interference, compromise, or a incapacitation problem related to critical infrastructure or protected systems; and

(C) voluntarily disseminating critical infrastructure information to its members, State, local, and Federal Governments, or any other entities that may be of assistance in carrying out the purposes specified in subparagraphs (A) and (B).

(6) PROTECTED SYSTEM.—The term "protected system"—

(A) means any service, physical or computer-based system, process, or procedure that directly or indirectly affects the viability of a facility of critical infrastructure; and

(B) includes any physical or computer-based system, including a computer, computer system, computer or communications network, or any component hardware or element thereof, software program, processing instructions, or information or data in transmission or storage therein, irrespective of the medium of transmission or storage.

(7) VOLUNTARY.—

(A) IN GENERAL.—The term "voluntary", in the case of any submittal of critical infrastructure information to a covered Federal agency, means the submittal thereof in the absence of such agency's exercise of legal authority to compel access to or submission of such information and may be accomplished by a single entity or an Information Sharing and Analysis Organization on behalf of itself or its members.

(B) EXCLUSIONS.—The term "voluntary"—

(i) in the case of any action brought under the securities laws as is defined in section 3(a)(47) of the Securities Exchange Act of 1934 (15 U.S.C. 78c(a)(47))—

(I) does not include information or statements contained in any documents or materials filed with the Securities and Exchange Commission, or with Federal banking regulators, pursuant to section 12(i) of the Securities Exchange Act of 1934 (15 U.S.C. 78l(I)); and

(II) with respect to the submittal of critical infrastructure information, does not include any disclosure or writing that when made accompanied the solicitation of an offer or a sale of securities; and

(ii) does not include information or statements submitted or relied upon as a basis for making licensing or permitting determinations, or during regulatory proceedings.

SEC. 213. DESIGNATION OF CRITICAL INFRASTRUCTURE PROTECTION PROGRAM.

A critical infrastructure protection program may be designated as such by one of the following:

(1) The President.

(2) The Secretary of Homeland Security.

SEC. 214. PROTECTION OF VOLUNTARILY SHARED CRITICAL INFRA- STRUCTURE INFORMATION.

(a) PROTECTION.—

(1) IN GENERAL.—Notwithstanding any other provision of law, critical infrastructure information (including the identity of the submitting person or entity) that is voluntarily submitted to a covered Federal agency for use by that agency regarding the security of critical infrastructure and protected systems, analysis, warning, interdependency study, recovery, reconstitution, or other informational purpose, when accompanied by an express statement specified in paragraph (2)—

(A) shall be exempt from disclosure under section 552 of title 5, United States Code (commonly referred to as the Freedom of Information Act);

(B) shall not be subject to any agency rules or judicial doctrine regarding ex parte communications with a decision making official;

(C) shall not, without the written consent of the person or entity submitting such information, be used directly by such agency, any other Federal, State, or local authority, or any third party, in any civil action arising under Federal or State law if such information is submitted in good faith;

(D) shall not, without the written consent of the person or entity submitting such information, be used or disclosed by any officer or employee of the United States for purposes other than the purposes of this subtitle, except—

(i) in furtherance of an investigation or the prosecution of a criminal act; or

(ii) when disclosure of the information would be—

(I) to either House of Congress, or to the extent of matter within its jurisdiction, any committee or subcommittee thereof, any joint committee thereof or subcommittee of any such joint committee; or

(II) to the Comptroller General, or any authorized representative of the Comptroller General, in the course of the performance of the duties of the General Accounting Office.

(E) shall not, if provided to a State or local government or government agency—

(i) be made available pursuant to any State or local law requiring disclosure of information or records;

(ii) otherwise be disclosed or distributed to any party by said State or local government or government agency without the written consent of the person or entity submitting such information; or

(iii) be used other than for the purpose of protecting critical infrastructure or protected systems, or in furtherance of an investigation or the prosecution of a criminal act; and

(F) does not constitute a waiver of any applicable privilege or protection provided under law, such as trade secret protection.

(2) EXPRESS STATEMENT.—For purposes of paragraph (1), the term "express statement", with respect to information or records, means—

(A) in the case of written information or records, a written marking on the information or records substantially similar to the following: "This information is voluntarily submitted to the Federal Government in expectation of protection from disclosure as provided by the provisions of the Critical Infrastructure Information Act of 2002."; or

(B) in the case of oral information, a similar written statement submitted within a reasonable period following the oral communication.

(b) LIMITATION.—No communication of critical infrastructure information to a covered Federal agency made pursuant to this subtitle shall be considered to be an action subject to the requirements of the Federal Advisory Committee Act (5 U.S.C. App. 2).

(c) INDEPENDENTLY OBTAINED INFORMATION.—Nothing in this section shall be construed to limit or otherwise affect the ability of a State, local, or Federal Government entity, agency, or authority, or any third party, under applicable law, to obtain critical infrastructure information in a manner not covered by subsection (a), including any information lawfully and properly disclosed generally or broadly to the public and to use such information in any manner permitted by law.

(d) TREATMENT OF VOLUNTARY SUBMITTAL OF INFORMATION.— The voluntary submittal to the Government of information or records that are protected from disclosure by this subtitle shall not be construed to constitute compliance with any requirement to submit such information to a Federal agency under any other provision of law.

(e) PROCEDURES.—

(1) IN GENERAL.—The Secretary of the Department of Homeland Security shall, in consultation with appropriate representatives of the National Security Council and the Office of Science and Technology Policy, establish uniform procedures for the receipt, care, and storage by Federal agencies of critical infrastructure information that is voluntarily submitted to the Government. The procedures shall be established not later than 90 days after the date of the enactment of this subtitle.

(2) ELEMENTS.—The procedures established under paragraph (1) shall include mechanisms regarding—

(A) the acknowledgement of receipt by Federal agencies of critical infrastructure information that is voluntarily submitted to the Government;

(B) the maintenance of the identification of such information as voluntarily submitted to the Government for purposes of and subject to the provisions of this subtitle;

(C) the care and storage of such information; and

(D) the protection and maintenance of the confidentiality of such information so as to permit the sharing of such information within the Federal Government and with State and local governments, and the issuance of notices and warnings related to the protection of critical infrastructure and protected systems, in such manner as to protect from public disclosure the identity of the submitting person or entity, or information that is proprietary, business sensitive, relates specifically to the submitting person or entity, and is otherwise not appropriately in the public domain.

(f) PENALTIES.—Whoever, being an officer or employee of the United States or of any department or agency thereof, knowingly publishes, divulges, discloses, or makes known in any manner or to any extent not authorized by law, any critical infrastructure information protected from disclosure by this subtitle coming to him in the course of this employment or official duties or by reason of any examination or investigation made by, or return, report, or record made to or filed with, such department or agency or officer or employee thereof, shall be fined under title 18 of the United States Code, imprisoned not more than 1 year, or both, and shall be removed from office or employment.

(g) AUTHORITY TO ISSUE WARNINGS.—The Federal Government may provide advisories, alerts, and warnings to relevant companies, targeted sectors, other governmental entities, or the general public regarding potential threats to critical infrastructure as appropriate. In issuing a warning, the Federal Government shall take appropriate actions to protect from disclosure—

(1) the source of any voluntarily submitted critical infrastructure information that forms the basis for the warning; or

(2) information that is proprietary, business sensitive, relates specifically to the submitting person or entity, or is otherwise not appropriately in the public domain.

(h) AUTHORITY TO DELEGATE.—The President may delegate authority to a critical infrastructure protection program, designated under section 213, to enter into a voluntary agreement to promote critical infrastructure security, including with any Information Sharing and Analysis Organization, or a plan of action as otherwise defined in section 708 of the Defense Production Act of 1950 (50 U.S.C. App. 2158).

SEC. 215. NO PRIVATE RIGHT OF ACTION.

Nothing in this subtitle may be construed to create a private right of action for enforcement of any provision of this Act.

Subtitle C—Information Security

SEC. 221. PROCEDURES FOR SHARING INFORMATION.

The Secretary shall establish procedures on the use of information shared under this title that—

(1) limit the redissemination of such information to ensure that it is not used for an unauthorized purpose;

(2) ensure the security and confidentiality of such information;

(3) protect the constitutional and statutory rights of any individuals who are subjects of such information; and

(4) provide data integrity through the timely removal and destruction of obsolete or erroneous names and information.

SEC. 222. PRIVACY OFFICER.

The Secretary shall appoint a senior official in the Department to assume primary responsibility for privacy policy, including—

(1) assuring that the use of technologies sustain, and do not erode, privacy protections relating to the use, collection, and disclosure of personal information;

(2) assuring that personal information contained in Privacy Act systems of records is handled in full compliance with fair information practices as set out in the Privacy Act of 1974;

(3) evaluating legislative and regulatory proposals involving collection, use, and disclosure of personal information by the Federal Government;

(4) conducting a privacy impact assessment of proposed rules of the Department or that of the Department on the privacy of personal information, including the type of personal information collected and the number of people affected; and

(5) preparing a report to Congress on an annual basis on activities of the Department that affect privacy, including complaints of privacy violations, implementation of the Privacy Act of 1974, internal controls, and other matters.

SEC. 223. ENHANCEMENT OF NON-FEDERAL CYBERSECURITY.

In carrying out the responsibilities under section 201, the Under Secretary for Information Analysis and Infrastructure Protection shall—

(1) as appropriate, provide to State and local government entities, and upon request to private entities that own or operate critical information systems—

(A) analysis and warnings related to threats to, and vulnerabilities of, critical information systems; and

(B) in coordination with the Under Secretary for Emergency Preparedness and Response, crisis management support in response to threats to, or attacks on, critical information systems; and

(2) as appropriate, provide technical assistance, upon request, to the private sector and other government entities, in coordination with the Under Secretary for Emergency Preparedness and Response, with respect to emergency recovery plans to respond to major failures of critical information systems.

SEC. 224. NET GUARD.

The Under Secretary for Information Analysis and Infrastructure Protection may establish a national technology guard, to be known as "NET Guard", comprised of local teams of volunteers with expertise in relevant areas of science and technology, to assist local communities to respond and recover from attacks on information systems and communications networks.

SEC. 225. CYBER SECURITY ENHANCEMENT ACT OF 2002.

(a) SHORT TITLE.—This section may be cited as the "Cyber Security Enhancement Act of 2002".

(b) AMENDMENT OF SENTENCING GUIDELINES RELATING TO CERTAIN COMPUTER CRIMES.—

(1) DIRECTIVE TO THE UNITED STATES SENTENCING COMMISSION.—Pursuant to its authority under section 994(p) of title 28, United States Code, and in accordance with this subsection, the United States Sentencing Commission shall review and, if appropriate, amend its guidelines and its policy statements applicable to persons convicted of an offense under section 1030 of title 18, United States Code.

(2) REQUIREMENTS.—In carrying out this subsection, the Sentencing Commission shall—

(A) ensure that the sentencing guidelines and policy statements reflect the serious nature of the offenses described in paragraph (1), the growing incidence of such offenses, and the need for an effective deterrent and appropriate punishment to prevent such offenses;

(B) consider the following factors and the extent to which the guidelines may or may not account for them—

(i) the potential and actual loss resulting from the offense;

(ii) the level of sophistication and planning involved in the offense;

(iii) whether the offense was committed for purposes of commercial advantage or private financial benefit;

(iv) whether the defendant acted with malicious intent to cause harm in committing the offense;

(v) the extent to which the offense violated the privacy rights of individuals harmed;

(vi) whether the offense involved a computer used by the government in furtherance of national defense, national security, or the administration of justice;

(vii) whether the violation was intended to or had the effect of significantly interfering with or disrupting a critical infrastructure; and

(viii) whether the violation was intended to or had the effect of creating a threat to public health or safety, or injury to any person;

(C) assure reasonable consistency with other relevant directives and with other sentencing guidelines;

(D) account for any additional aggravating or mitigating circumstances that might justify exceptions to the generally applicable sentencing ranges;

(E) make any necessary conforming changes to the sentencing guidelines; and

(F) assure that the guidelines adequately meet the purposes of sentencing as set forth in section 3553(a)(2) of title 18, United States Code.

(c) STUDY AND REPORT ON COMPUTER CRIMES.—Not later than May 1, 2003, the United States Sentencing Commission shall submit a brief report to Congress that explains any actions taken by the Sentencing Commission in response to this section and includes any recommendations the Commission may have regarding statutory penalties for offenses under section 1030 of title 18, United States Code.

(d) EMERGENCY DISCLOSURE EXCEPTION.—

(1) IN GENERAL.—Section 2702(b) of title 18, United States Code, is amended—

(A) in paragraph (5), by striking "or" at the end;

(B) in paragraph (6)(A), by inserting "or" at the end;

(C) by striking paragraph (6)(C); and

(D) by adding at the end the following:

"(7) to a Federal, State, or local governmental entity, if the provider, in good faith, believes that an emergency involving danger of death or serious physical injury to any person requires disclosure without delay of communications relating to the emergency.".

(2) REPORTING OF DISCLOSURES.—A government entity that receives a disclosure under section 2702(b) of title 18, United States Code, shall file, not later than 90 days after such disclosure, a report to the Attorney General stating the paragraph of that section under which the disclosure was made, the date of the disclosure, the entity to which the disclosure was made, the number of customers or subscribers to whom the information disclosed pertained, and the number of communications, if any, that were disclosed. The Attorney General shall publish all such reports into a single report to be submitted to Congress 1 year after the date of enactment of this Act.

(e) GOOD FAITH EXCEPTION.—Section 2520(d)(3) of title 18, United States Code, is amended by inserting "or 2511(2)(i)" after "2511(3)".

(f) INTERNET ADVERTISING OF ILLEGAL DEVICES.—Section 2512(1)(c) of title 18, United States Code, is amended—

(1) by inserting "or disseminates by electronic means" after "or other publication"; and

(2) by inserting "knowing the content of the advertisement and" before "knowing or having reason to know".

(g) STRENGTHENING PENALTIES.—Section 1030(c) of title 18, United States Code, is amended—

(1) by striking "and" at the end of paragraph (3);

(2) in each of subparagraphs (A) and (C) of paragraph (4), by inserting "except as provided in paragraph (5)," before "a fine under this title";

(3) in paragraph (4)(C), by striking the period at the end and inserting "; and"; and

(4) by adding at the end the following:

"(5)(A) if the offender knowingly or recklessly causes or attempts to cause serious bodily injury from conduct in violation of subsection (a)(5)(A)(i), a fine under this title or imprisonment for not more than 20 years, or both; and

"(B) if the offender knowingly or recklessly causes or attempts to cause death from conduct in violation of subsection (a)(5)(A)(i), a fine under this title or imprisonment for any term of years or for life, or both.".

(h) PROVIDER ASSISTANCE.—

(1) SECTION 2703.—Section 2703(e) of title 18, United States Code, is amended by inserting ", statutory authorization" after "subpoena".

(2) SECTION 2511.—Section 2511(2)(a)(ii) of title 18, United States Code, is amended by inserting ", statutory authorization," after "court order" the last place it appears.

(i) EMERGENCIES.—Section 3125(a)(1) of title 18, United States Code, is amended—

(1) in subparagraph (A), by striking "or" at the end;

(2) in subparagraph (B), by striking the comma at the end and inserting a semicolon; and

(3) by adding at the end the following:

"(C) an immediate threat to a national security interest; or

"(D) an ongoing attack on a protected computer (as defined in section 1030) that constitutes a crime punishable by a term of imprisonment greater than one year;".

(j) PROTECTING PRIVACY.—

(1) SECTION 2511.—Section 2511(4) of title 18, United States Code, is amended—

(A) by striking paragraph (b); and

(B) by redesignating paragraph (c) as paragraph (b).

(2) SECTION 2701.—Section 2701(b) of title 18, United States Code, is amended—

(A) in paragraph (1), by inserting ", or in furtherance of any criminal or tortious act in violation of the Constitution or laws of the United States or any State" after "commercial gain";

(B) in paragraph (1)(A), by striking "one year" and inserting "5 years";

(C) in paragraph (1)(B), by striking "two years" and inserting "10 years"; and

(D) by striking paragraph (2) and inserting the following:

"(2) in any other case—

"(A) a fine under this title or imprisonment for not more than 1 year or both, in the case of a first offense under this paragraph; and

"(B) a fine under this title or imprisonment for not more than 5 years, or both, in the case of an offense under this subparagraph that occurs after a conviction of another offense under this section.".

Subtitle D—Office of Science and Technology

SEC. 231. ESTABLISHMENT OF OFFICE; DIRECTOR.

(a) ESTABLISHMENT.—

(1) IN GENERAL.—There is hereby established within the Department of Justice an Office of Science and Technology (hereinafter in this title referred to as the "Office").

(2) AUTHORITY.—The Office shall be under the general authority of the Assistant Attorney General, Office of Justice Programs, and shall be established within the National Institute of Justice.

(b) DIRECTOR.—The Office shall be headed by a Director, who shall be an individual appointed based on approval by the Office of Personnel Management of the executive qualifications of the individual.

SEC. 232. MISSION OF OFFICE; DUTIES.

(a) MISSION.—The mission of the Office shall be—

(1) to serve as the national focal point for work on law enforcement technology; and

(2) to carry out programs that, through the provision of equipment, training, and technical assistance, improve the safety and effectiveness of law enforcement technology and improve access to such technology by Federal, State, and local law enforcement agencies.

(b) DUTIES.—In carrying out its mission, the Office shall have the following duties:

(1) To provide recommendations and advice to the Attorney General.

(2) To establish and maintain advisory groups (which shall be exempt from the provisions of the Federal Advisory Committee Act (5 U.S.C. App.)) to assess the law enforcement technology needs of Federal, State, and local law enforcement agencies.

(3) To establish and maintain performance standards in accordance with the National Technology Transfer and Advancement Act of 1995 (Public Law 104–113) for, and test and evaluate law enforcement technologies that may be used by, Federal, State, and local law enforcement agencies.

(4) To establish and maintain a program to certify, validate, and mark or otherwise recognize law enforcement technology products that conform to standards established and maintained by the Office in accordance with the National Technology Transfer and Advancement Act of 1995 (Public Law 104–113).

The program may, at the discretion of the Office, allow for supplier's declaration of conformity with such standards.

(5) To work with other entities within the Department of Justice, other Federal agencies, and the executive office of the President to establish a coordinated Federal approach on issues related to law enforcement technology.

(6) To carry out research, development, testing, evaluation, and cost-benefit analyses in fields that would improve the safety, effectiveness, and efficiency of law enforcement technologies used by Federal, State, and local law enforcement agencies, including, but not limited to—

(A) weapons capable of preventing use by unauthorized persons, including personalized guns;

(B) protective apparel;

(C) bullet-resistant and explosion-resistant glass;

(D) monitoring systems and alarm systems capable of providing precise location information;

(E) wire and wireless interoperable communication technologies;

(F) tools and techniques that facilitate investigative and forensic work, including computer forensics;

(G) equipment for particular use in counterterrorism, including devices and technologies to disable terrorist devices;

(H) guides to assist State and local law enforcement agencies;

(I) DNA identification technologies; and

(J) tools and techniques that facilitate investigations of computer crime.

(7) To administer a program of research, development, testing, and demonstration to improve the interoperability of voice and data public safety communications.

(8) To serve on the Technical Support Working Group of the Department of Defense, and on other relevant interagency panels, as requested.

(9) To develop, and disseminate to State and local law enforcement agencies, technical assistance and training materials for law enforcement personnel, including prosecutors.

(10) To operate the regional National Law Enforcement and Corrections Technology Centers and, to the extent necessary, establish additional centers through a competitive process.

(11) To administer a program of acquisition, research, development, and dissemination of advanced investigative analysis and forensic tools to assist State and local law enforcement agencies in combating cybercrime.

(12) To support research fellowships in support of its mission.

(13) To serve as a clearinghouse for information on law enforcement technologies.

(14) To represent the United States and State and local law enforcement agencies, as requested, in international activities concerning law enforcement technology.

(15) To enter into contracts and cooperative agreements and provide grants, which may require in-kind or cash matches from the recipient, as necessary to carry out its mission.

(16) To carry out other duties assigned by the Attorney General to accomplish the mission of the Office.

(c) COMPETITION REQUIRED.—Except as otherwise expressly provided by law, all research and development carried out by or through the Office shall be carried out on a competitive basis.

(d) INFORMATION FROM FEDERAL AGENCIES.—Federal agencies shall, upon request from the Office and in accordance with Federal law, provide the Office with any data, reports, or other information requested, unless compliance with such request is otherwise prohibited by law.

(e) PUBLICATIONS.—Decisions concerning publications issued by the Office shall rest solely with the Director of the Office.

(f) TRANSFER OF FUNDS.—The Office may transfer funds to other Federal agencies or provide funding to non-Federal entities through grants, cooperative agreements, or contracts to carry out its duties under this section.

(g) ANNUAL REPORT.—The Director of the Office shall include with the budget justification materials submitted to Congress in support of the Department of Justice budget for each fiscal year (as submitted with the budget of the President under section 1105(a) of title 31, United States Code) a report on the activities of the Office. Each such report shall include the following:

(1) For the period of 5 fiscal years beginning with the fiscal year for which the budget is submitted—

(A) the Director's assessment of the needs of Federal, State, and local law enforcement agencies for assistance with respect to law enforcement technology and other matters consistent with the mission of the Office; and

(B) a strategic plan for meeting such needs of such law enforcement agencies.

(2) For the fiscal year preceding the fiscal year for which such budget is submitted, a description of the activities carried out by the Office and an evaluation of the extent to which those activities successfully meet the needs assessed under paragraph (1)(A) in previous reports.

SEC. 233. DEFINITION OF LAW ENFORCEMENT TECHNOLOGY.

For the purposes of this title, the term "law enforcement technology" includes investigative and forensic technologies, corrections technologies, and technologies that support the judicial process.

SEC. 234. ABOLISHMENT OF OFFICE OF SCIENCE AND TECHNOLOGY OF NATIONAL INSTITUTE OF JUSTICE; TRANSFER OF FUNCTIONS.

(a) AUTHORITY TO TRANSFER FUNCTIONS.—The Attorney General may transfer to the Office any other program or activity of the Department of Justice that the Attorney General, in consultation with the Committee on the Judiciary of the Senate and the Committee on the Judiciary of the House of Representatives, determines to be consistent with the mission of the Office.

(b) TRANSFER OF PERSONNEL AND ASSETS.—With respect to any function, power, or duty, or any program or activity, that is established in the Office, those employees and assets of the element of the Department of Justice from which the transfer is made that the Attorney General determines are needed to perform that function, power, or duty, or for that program or activity, as the case may be, shall be transferred to the Office.

(c) REPORT ON IMPLEMENTATION.—Not later than 1 year after the date of the enactment of this Act, the Attorney General shall submit to the Committee on the Judiciary of the Senate and the Committee on the Judiciary of the House of Representatives a report on the implementation of this title. The report shall—

(1) provide an accounting of the amounts and sources of funding available to the Office to carry out its mission under existing authorizations and appropriations, and set forth the future funding needs of the Office; and

(2) include such other information and recommendations as the Attorney General considers appropriate.

SEC. 235. NATIONAL LAW ENFORCEMENT AND CORRECTIONS TECHNOLOGY CENTERS.

(a) IN GENERAL.—The Director of the Office shall operate and support National Law Enforcement and Corrections Technology Centers (hereinafter in this section referred to as "Centers") and, to the extent necessary, establish new centers through a merit-based, competitive process.

(b) PURPOSE OF CENTERS.—The purpose of the Centers shall be to—

(1) support research and development of law enforcement technology;

(2) support the transfer and implementation of technology;

(3) assist in the development and dissemination of guidelines and technological standards; and

(4) provide technology assistance, information, and support for law enforcement, corrections, and criminal justice purposes.

(c) ANNUAL MEETING.—Each year, the Director shall convene a meeting of the Centers in order to foster collaboration and communication between Center participants.

(d) REPORT.—Not later than 12 months after the date of the enactment of this Act, the Director shall transmit to the Congress a report assessing the effectiveness of the existing system of Centers and identify the number of Centers necessary to meet the technology needs of Federal, State, and local law enforcement in the United States.

SEC. 236. COORDINATION WITH OTHER ENTITIES WITHIN DEPARTMENT OF JUSTICE.

Section 102 of the Omnibus Crime Control and Safe Streets Act of 1968 (42 U.S.C. 3712) is amended in subsection (a)(5) by inserting "coordinate and" before "provide".

SEC. 237. AMENDMENTS RELATING TO NATIONAL INSTITUTE OF JUSTICE.

Section 202(c) of the Omnibus Crime Control and Safe Streets Act of 1968 (42 U.S.C. 3722(c)) is amended—

(1) in paragraph (3) by inserting ", including cost effectiveness where practical," before "of projects"; and

(2) by striking "and" after the semicolon at the end of paragraph (8), striking the period at the end of paragraph (9) and inserting "; and", and by adding at the end the following:

"(10) research and development of tools and technologies relating to prevention, detection, investigation, and prosecution of crime; and

"(11) support research, development, testing, training, and evaluation of tools and technology for Federal, State, and local law enforcement agencies.".

TITLE III—SCIENCE AND TECHNOLOGY IN SUPPORT OF HOMELAND SECURITY

SEC. 301. UNDER SECRETARY FOR SCIENCE AND TECHNOLOGY.

There shall be in the Department a Directorate of Science and Technology headed by an Under Secretary for Science and Technology.

SEC. 302. RESPONSIBILITIES AND AUTHORITIES OF THE UNDER SECRETARY FOR SCIENCE AND TECHNOLOGY.

The Secretary, acting through the Under Secretary for Science and Technology, shall have the responsibility for—

(1) advising the Secretary regarding research and development efforts and priorities in support of the Department's missions;

(2) developing, in consultation with other appropriate executive agencies, a national policy and strategic plan for, identifying priorities, goals, objectives and policies for, and coordinating the Federal Government's civilian efforts to identify and develop countermeasures to chemical, biological, radiological, nuclear, and other emerging terrorist threats, including the development of comprehensive, research-based definable goals for such efforts and development of annual measurable objectives and specific targets to accomplish and evaluate the goals for such efforts;

(3) supporting the Under Secretary for Information Analysis and Infrastructure Protection, by assessing and testing homeland security vulnerabilities and possible threats;

(4) conducting basic and applied research, development, demonstration, testing, and evaluation activities that are relevant to any or all elements of the Department, through both intramural and extramural programs, except that such responsibility does not extend to human health-related research and development activities;

(5) establishing priorities for, directing, funding, and conducting national research, development, test and evaluation, and procurement of technology and systems for—

(A) preventing the importation of chemical, biological, radiological, nuclear, and related weapons and material; and

(B) detecting, preventing, protecting against, and responding to terrorist attacks;

(6) establishing a system for transferring homeland security developments or technologies to Federal, State, local government, and private sector entities;

(7) entering into work agreements, joint sponsorships, contracts, or any other agreements with the Department of Energy regarding the use of the national laboratories or sites and support of the science and technology base at those facilities;

(8) collaborating with the Secretary of Agriculture and the Attorney General as provided in section 212 of the Agricultural Bioterrorism Protection Act of 2002 (7 U.S.C. 8401), as amended by section 1709(b);

(9) collaborating with the Secretary of Health and Human Services and the Attorney General in determining any new biological agents and toxins that shall be listed as "select agents" in Appendix A of part 72 of title 42, Code of Federal Regulations, pursuant to section 351A of the Public Health Service Act (42 U.S.C. 262a);

(10) supporting United States leadership in science and technology;

(11) establishing and administering the primary research and development activities of the Department, including the long-term research and development needs and capabilities for all elements of the Department;

(12) coordinating and integrating all research, development, demonstration, testing, and evaluation activities of the Department;

(13) coordinating with other appropriate executive agencies in developing and carrying out the science and technology agenda of the Department to reduce duplication and identify unmet needs; and

(14) developing and overseeing the administration of guidelines for merit review of research and development projects throughout the Department, and for the dissemination of research conducted or sponsored by the Department.

SEC. 303. FUNCTIONS TRANSFERRED.

In accordance with title XV, there shall be transferred to the Secretary the functions, personnel, assets, and liabilities of the following entities:

(1) The following programs and activities of the Department of Energy, including the functions of the Secretary of Energy relating thereto (but not including programs and activities relating to the strategic nuclear defense posture of the United States):

(A) The chemical and biological national security and supporting programs and activities of the nonproliferation and verification research and development program.

(B) The nuclear smuggling programs and activities within the proliferation detection program of the nonproliferation and verification research and development program. The programs and activities described in this subparagraph may be designated by the President either for transfer to the Department or for joint operation by the Secretary and the Secretary of Energy.

(C) The nuclear assessment program and activities of the assessment, detection, and cooperation program of the international materials protection and cooperation program.

(D) Such life sciences activities of the biological and environmental research program related to microbial pathogens as may be designated by the President for transfer to the Department.

(E) The Environmental Measurements Laboratory.

(F) The advanced scientific computing research program and activities at Lawrence Livermore National Laboratory.

(2) The National Bio-Weapons Defense Analysis Center of the Department of Defense, including the functions of the Secretary of Defense related thereto.

SEC. 304. CONDUCT OF CERTAIN PUBLIC HEALTH-RELATED ACTIVITIES.

(a) IN GENERAL.—With respect to civilian human health-related research and development activities relating to countermeasures for chemical, biological, radiological, and nuclear and other emerging terrorist threats carried out by the Department of Health and Human Services (including the Public Health Service), the Secretary of Health and Human Services shall set priorities, goals, objectives, and policies and develop a coordinated strategy for such activities in collaboration with the Secretary of Homeland Security to ensure consistency with the national policy and strategic plan developed pursuant to section 302(2).

(b) EVALUATION OF PROGRESS.—In carrying out subsection (a), the Secretary of Health and Human Services shall collaborate with the Secretary in developing specific benchmarks and outcome measurements for evaluating progress toward achieving the priorities and goals described in such subsection.

(c) ADMINISTRATION OF COUNTERMEASURES AGAINST SMALLPOX.—Section 224 of the Public Health Service Act (42 U.S.C. 233) is amended by adding the following:

"(p) ADMINISTRATION OF SMALLPOX COUNTERMEASURES BY HEALTH PROFESSIONALS.—

"(1) IN GENERAL.—For purposes of this section, and subject to other provisions of this subsection, a covered person shall be deemed to be an employee of the Public Health Service with respect to liability arising out of administration of a covered countermeasure against smallpox to an individual during the effective period of a declaration by the Secretary under paragraph (2)(A).

"(2) DECLARATION BY SECRETARY CONCERNING COUNTERMEASURE AGAINST SMALLPOX.—

"(A) AUTHORITY TO ISSUE DECLARATION.—

"(i) IN GENERAL.—The Secretary may issue a declaration, pursuant to this paragraph, concluding that an actual or potential bioterrorist incident or other actual or potential public health emergency makes advisable the administration of a covered countermeasure to a category or categories of individuals.

"(ii) COVERED COUNTERMEASURE.—The Secretary shall specify in such declaration the substance or substances that shall be considered covered countermeasures (as defined in paragraph (8)(A)) for purposes of administration to individuals during the effective period of the declaration.

"(iii) EFFECTIVE PERIOD.—The Secretary shall specify in such declaration the beginning and ending dates of the effective period of the declaration, and may subsequently amend such declaration to shorten or extend such effective period, provided that the new closing date is after the date when the declaration is amended.

"(iv) PUBLICATION.—The Secretary shall promptly publish each such declaration and amendment in the Federal Register.

"(B) LIABILITY OF UNITED STATES ONLY FOR ADMINISTRATIONS WITHIN SCOPE OF DECLARATION.—Except as provided in paragraph (5)(B)(ii), the United States shall be liable under this subsection with respect to a claim arising out of the administration of a covered countermeasure to an individual only if—

"(i) the countermeasure was administered by a qualified person, for a purpose stated in paragraph (7)(A)(i), and during the effective period of a declaration by the Secretary under subparagraph (A) with respect to such countermeasure; and

"(ii)(I) the individual was within a category of individuals covered by the declaration; or

"(II) the qualified person administering the countermeasure had reasonable grounds to believe that such individual was within such category.

"(C) PRESUMPTION OF ADMINISTRATION WITHIN SCOPE OF DECLARATION IN CASE OF ACCIDENTAL VACCINIA INOCULATION.—

"(i) IN GENERAL.—If vaccinia vaccine is a covered countermeasure specified in a declaration under subparagraph (A), and an individual to whom the vaccinia vaccine is not administered contracts vaccinia, then, under the circumstances specified in clause (ii), the individual—

"(I) shall be rebuttably presumed to have contracted vaccinia from an individual to whom such vaccine was administered as provided by clauses (i) and (ii) of subparagraph (B); and

"(II) shall (unless such presumption is rebutted) be deemed for purposes of this subsection to be an individual to whom a covered countermeasure was administered by a qualified person in accordance with the terms of such declaration and as described by subparagraph (B).

"(ii) CIRCUMSTANCES IN WHICH PRESUMPTION APPLIES.—The presumption and deeming stated in clause (i) shall apply if—

"(I) the individual contracts vaccinia during the effective period of a declaration under subparagraph (A) or by the date 30 days after the close of such period; or

"(II) the individual resides or has resided with an individual to whom such vaccine was administered as provided by clauses (i) and (ii) of subparagraph (B) and contracts vaccinia after such date.

"(3) EXCLUSIVITY OF REMEDY.—The remedy provided by subsection (a) shall be exclusive of any other civil action or proceeding for any claim or suit this subsection encompasses.

"(4) CERTIFICATION OF ACTION BY ATTORNEY GENERAL.—Subsection (c) applies to actions under this subsection, subject to the following provisions:

"(A) NATURE OF CERTIFICATION.—The certification by the Attorney General that is the basis for deeming an action or proceeding to be against the United States, and for removing an action or proceeding from a State court, is a certification that the action or proceeding is against a covered person and is based upon a claim alleging personal injury or death arising out of the administration of a covered countermeasure.

"(B) CERTIFICATION OF ATTORNEY GENERAL CONCLUSIVE.—The certification of the Attorney General of the facts specified in subparagraph (A) shall conclusively establish such facts for purposes of jurisdiction pursuant to this subsection.

"(5) DEFENDANT TO COOPERATE WITH UNITED STATES.—

"(A) IN GENERAL.—A covered person shall cooperate with the United States in the processing and defense of a claim or action under this subsection based upon alleged acts or omissions of such person.

"(B) CONSEQUENCES OF FAILURE TO COOPERATE.—Upon the motion of the United States or any other party and upon finding that such person has failed to so cooperate—

"(i) the court shall substitute such person as the party defendant in place of the United States and, upon motion, shall remand any such suit to the court in which it was instituted if it appears that the court lacks subject matter jurisdiction;

"(ii) the United States shall not be liable based on the acts or omissions of such person; and

"(iii) the Attorney General shall not be obligated to defend such action.

"(6) RECOURSE AGAINST COVERED PERSON IN CASE OF GROSS MISCONDUCT OR CONTRACT VIOLATION.—

"(A) IN GENERAL.—Should payment be made by the United States to any claimant bringing a claim under this subsection, either by way of administrative determination, settlement, or court judgment, the United States shall have, notwithstanding any provision of State law, the right to recover for that portion of the damages so awarded or paid, as well as interest and any costs of litigation, resulting from the failure of any covered person to carry out any obligation or responsibility assumed by such person under a contract with the United States or from any grossly negligent, reckless, or illegal conduct or willful misconduct on the part of such person.

"(B) VENUE.—The United States may maintain an action under this paragraph against such person in the district court of the United States in which such person resides or has its principal place of business.

"(7) DEFINITIONS.—As used in this subsection, terms have the following meanings:

"(A) COVERED COUNTERMEASURE.—The term 'covered countermeasure' or 'covered countermeasure against smallpox', means a substance that is—

"(i)(I) used to prevent or treat smallpox (including the vaccinia or another vaccine); or

"(II) vaccinia immune globulin used to control or treat the adverse effects of vaccinia inoculation; and "(ii) specified in a declaration under paragraph (2).

"(B) COVERED PERSON.—The term 'covered person', when used with respect to the administration of a covered countermeasure, includes any person who is—

"(i) a manufacturer or distributor of such countermeasure;

"(ii) a health care entity under whose auspices such countermeasure was administered;

"(iii) a qualified person who administered such countermeasure; or

"(iv) an official, agent, or employee of a person described in clause (i), (ii), or (iii).

"(C) QUALIFIED PERSON.—The term 'qualified person', when used with respect to the administration of a covered countermeasure, means a licensed health professional or other individual who is authorized to administer such countermeasure under the law of the State in which the countermeasure was administered.".

SEC. 305. FEDERALLY FUNDED RESEARCH AND DEVELOPMENT CENTERS.

The Secretary, acting through the Under Secretary for Science and Technology, shall have the authority to establish or contract with 1 or more federally funded research and development centers to provide independent analysis of homeland security issues, or to carry out other responsibilities under this Act, including coordinating and integrating both the extramural and intramural programs described in section 308.

SEC. 306. MISCELLANEOUS PROVISIONS.

(a) CLASSIFICATION.—To the greatest extent practicable, research conducted or supported by the Department shall be unclassified.

(b) CONSTRUCTION.—Nothing in this title shall be construed to preclude any Under Secretary of the Department from carrying out research, development, demonstration, or deployment activities, as long as such activities are coordinated through the Under Secretary for Science and Technology.

(c) REGULATIONS.—The Secretary, acting through the Under Secretary for Science and Technology, may issue necessary regulations with respect to research, development, demonstration, testing, and evaluation activities of the Department, including the conducting, funding, and reviewing of such activities.

(d) NOTIFICATION OF PRESIDENTIAL LIFE SCIENCES DESIGNATIONS.—Not later than 60 days before effecting any transfer of Department of Energy life sciences activities pursuant to section 303(1)(D) of this Act, the President shall notify the appropriate congressional committees of the proposed transfer and shall include the reasons for the transfer and a description of the effect of the transfer on the activities of the Department of Energy.

SEC. 307. HOMELAND SECURITY ADVANCED RESEARCH PROJECTS AGENCY.

(a) DEFINITIONS.—In this section:

(1) FUND.—The term "Fund" means the Acceleration Fund for Research and Development of Homeland Security Technologies established in subsection (c).

(2) HOMELAND SECURITY RESEARCH.—The term "homeland security research" means research relevant to the detection of, prevention of, protection against, response to, attribution of, and recovery from homeland security threats, particularly acts of terrorism.

(3) HSARPA.—The term "HSARPA" means the Homeland Security Advanced Research Projects Agency established in subsection (b).

(4) UNDER SECRETARY.—The term "Under Secretary" means the Under Secretary for Science and Technology.

(b) HOMELAND SECURITY ADVANCED RESEARCH PROJECTS AGENCY.—

(1) ESTABLISHMENT.—There is established the Homeland Security Advanced Research Projects Agency.

(2) DIRECTOR.—HSARPA shall be headed by a Director, who shall be appointed by the Secretary. The Director shall report to the Under Secretary.

(3) RESPONSIBILITIES.—The Director shall administer the Fund to award competitive, merit-reviewed grants, cooperative agreements or contracts to public or private entities, including businesses, federally funded research and development centers, and universities. The Director shall administer the Fund to—

(A) support basic and applied homeland security research to promote revolutionary changes in technologies that would promote homeland security;

(B) advance the development, testing and evaluation, and deployment of critical homeland security technologies; and

(C) accelerate the prototyping and deployment of technologies that would address homeland security vulnerabilities.

(4) TARGETED COMPETITIONS.—The Director may solicit proposals to address specific vulnerabilities identified by the Director.

(5) COORDINATION.—The Director shall ensure that the activities of HSARPA are coordinated with those of other relevant research agencies, and may run projects jointly with other agencies.

(6) PERSONNEL.—In hiring personnel for HSARPA, the Secretary shall have the hiring and management authorities described in section 1101 of the Strom Thurmond National Defense Authorization Act for Fiscal Year 1999 (5 U.S.C. 3104 note; Public Law 105–261). The term of appointments for employees under subsection (c)(1) of that section may not exceed 5 years before the granting of any extension under subsection (c)(2) of that section.

(7) DEMONSTRATIONS.—The Director, periodically, shall hold homeland security technology demonstrations to improve contact among technology developers, vendors and acquisition personnel.

(c) FUND.—

(1) ESTABLISHMENT.—There is established the Acceleration Fund for Research and Development of Homeland Security Technologies, which shall be administered by the Director of HSARPA.

(2) AUTHORIZATION OF APPROPRIATIONS.—There are authorized to be appropriated $500,000,000 to the Fund for fiscal year 2003 and such sums as may be necessary thereafter.

(3) COAST GUARD.—Of the funds authorized to be appropriated under paragraph (2), not less than 10 percent of such funds for each fiscal year through fiscal year 2005 shall be authorized only for the Under Secretary, through joint agreement with the Commandant of the Coast Guard, to carry out research and development of improved ports, waterways and coastal security surveillance and perimeter protection capabilities for the purpose of minimizing the possibility that Coast Guard cutters, aircraft, helicopters, and personnel will be diverted from non-homeland security missions to the ports, waterways and coastal security mission.

SEC. 308. CONDUCT OF RESEARCH, DEVELOPMENT, DEMONSTRATION, TESTING AND EVALUATION.

(a) IN GENERAL.—The Secretary, acting through the Under Secretary for Science and Technology, shall carry out the responsibilities under section 302(4) through both extramural and intramural programs.

(b) EXTRAMURAL PROGRAMS.—

(1) IN GENERAL.—The Secretary, acting through the Under Secretary for Science and Technology, shall operate extramural research, development, demonstration, testing, and evaluation programs so as to—

(A) ensure that colleges, universities, private research institutes, and companies (and consortia thereof) from as many areas of the United States as practicable participate;

(B) ensure that the research funded is of high quality, as determined through merit review processes developed under section 302(14); and

(C) distribute funds through grants, cooperative agreements, and contracts.

(2) UNIVERSITY-BASED CENTERS FOR HOMELAND SECURITY.—

(A) ESTABLISHMENT.—The Secretary, acting through the Under Secretary for Science and Technology, shall establish within 1 year of the date of enactment of this Act a university-based center or centers for homeland security. The purpose of this center or centers shall be to establish a coordinated, university-based system to enhance the Nation's homeland security.

(B) CRITERIA FOR SELECTION.—In selecting colleges or universities as centers for homeland security, the Secretary shall consider the following criteria:

(i) Demonstrated expertise in the training of first responders.

(ii) Demonstrated expertise in responding to incidents involving weapons of mass destruction and biological warfare.

(iii) Demonstrated expertise in emergency medical services.

(iv) Demonstrated expertise in chemical, biological, radiological, and nuclear countermeasures.

(v) Strong affiliations with animal and plant diagnostic laboratories.

(vi) Demonstrated expertise in food safety.

(vii) Affiliation with Department of Agriculture laboratories or training centers.

(viii) Demonstrated expertise in water and wastewater operations.

(ix) Demonstrated expertise in port and waterway security.

(x) Demonstrated expertise in multi-modal transportation.

(xi) Nationally recognized programs in information security.

(xii) Nationally recognized programs in engineering.

(xiii) Demonstrated expertise in educational outreach and technical assistance.

(xiv) Demonstrated expertise in border transportation and security.

(xv) Demonstrated expertise in interdisciplinary public policy research and communication outreach regarding science, technology, and public policy.

(C) DISCRETION OF SECRETARY.—The Secretary shall have the discretion to establish such centers and to consider additional criteria as necessary to meet the evolving needs of homeland security and shall report to Congress concerning the implementation of this paragraph as necessary.

(D) AUTHORIZATION OF APPROPRIATIONS.—There are authorized to be appropriated such sums as may be necessary to carry out this paragraph.

(c) INTRAMURAL PROGRAMS.—

(1) CONSULTATION.—In carrying out the duties under section 302, the Secretary, acting through the Under Secretary for Science and Technology, may draw upon the expertise of any laboratory of the Federal Government, whether operated by a contractor or the Government.

(2) LABORATORIES.—The Secretary, acting through the Under Secretary for Science and Technology, may establish a headquarters laboratory for the Department at any laboratory or site and may establish additional laboratory units at other laboratories or sites.

(3) CRITERIA FOR HEADQUARTERS LABORATORY.—If the Secretary chooses to establish a headquarters laboratory pursuant to paragraph (2), then the Secretary shall do the following:

(A) Establish criteria for the selection of the headquarters laboratory in consultation with the National Academy of Sciences, appropriate Federal agencies, and other experts.

(B) Publish the criteria in the Federal Register.

(C) Evaluate all appropriate laboratories or sites against the criteria.

(D) Select a laboratory or site on the basis of the criteria.

(E) Report to the appropriate congressional committees on which laboratory was selected, how the selected laboratory meets the published criteria, and what duties the headquarters laboratory shall perform.

(4) LIMITATION ON OPERATION OF LABORATORIES.—No laboratory shall begin operating as the headquarters laboratory

of the Department until at least 30 days after the transmittal of the report required by paragraph (3)(E).

SEC. 309. UTILIZATION OF DEPARTMENT OF ENERGY NATIONAL LABORATORIES AND SITES IN SUPPORT OF HOMELAND SECURITY ACTIVITIES.

(a) AUTHORITY TO UTILIZE NATIONAL LABORATORIES AND SITES.—

(1) IN GENERAL.—In carrying out the missions of the Department, the Secretary may utilize the Department of Energy national laboratories and sites through any 1 or more of the following methods, as the Secretary considers appropriate:

(A) A joint sponsorship arrangement referred to in subsection (b).

(B) A direct contract between the Department and the applicable Department of Energy laboratory or site, subject to subsection (c).

(C) Any "work for others" basis made available by that laboratory or site.

(D) Any other method provided by law.

(2) ACCEPTANCE AND PERFORMANCE BY LABS AND SITES.— Notwithstanding any other law governing the administration, mission, use, or operations of any of the Department of Energy national laboratories and sites, such laboratories and sites are authorized to accept and perform work for the Secretary, consistent with resources provided, and perform such work on an equal basis to other missions at the laboratory and not on a noninterference basis with other missions of such laboratory or site.

(b) JOINT SPONSORSHIP ARRANGEMENTS.—

(1) LABORATORIES.—The Department may be a joint sponsor, under a multiple agency sponsorship arrangement with the Department of Energy, of 1 or more Department of Energy national laboratories in the performance of work.

(2) SITES.—The Department may be a joint sponsor of a Department of Energy site in the performance of work as if such site were a federally funded research and development center and the work were performed under a multiple agency sponsorship arrangement with the Department.

(3) PRIMARY SPONSOR.—The Department of Energy shall be the primary sponsor under a multiple agency sponsorship arrangement referred to in paragraph (1) or (2).

(4) LEAD AGENT.—The Secretary of Energy shall act as the lead agent in coordinating the formation and performance of a joint sponsorship arrangement under this subsection between the Department and a Department of Energy national laboratory or site.

(5) FEDERAL ACQUISITION REGULATION.—Any work performed by a Department of Energy national laboratory or site under a joint sponsorship arrangement under this subsection shall comply with the policy on the use of federally funded research and development centers under the Federal Acquisition Regulations.

(6) FUNDING.—The Department shall provide funds for work at the Department of Energy national laboratories or

sites, as the case may be, under a joint sponsorship arrangement under this subsection under the same terms and conditions as apply to the primary sponsor of such national laboratory under section 303(b)(1)(C) of the Federal Property and Administrative Services Act of 1949 (41 U.S.C. 253(b)(1)(C)) or of such site to the extent such section applies to such site as a federally funded research and development center by reason of this subsection.

(c) SEPARATE CONTRACTING.—To the extent that programs or activities transferred by this Act from the Department of Energy to the Department of Homeland Security are being carried out through direct contracts with the operator of a national laboratory or site of the Department of Energy, the Secretary of Homeland Security and the Secretary of Energy shall ensure that direct contracts for such programs and activities between the Department of Homeland Security and such operator are separate from the direct contracts of the Department of Energy with such operator.

(d) AUTHORITY WITH RESPECT TO COOPERATIVE RESEARCH AND DEVELOPMENT AGREEMENTS AND LICENSING AGREEMENTS.—In connection with any utilization of the Department of Energy national laboratories and sites under this section, the Secretary may permit the director of any such national laboratory or site to enter into cooperative research and development agreements or to negotiate licensing agreements with any person, any agency or instrumentality, of the United States, any unit of State or local government, and any other entity under the authority granted by section 12 of the Stevenson-Wydler Technology Innovation Act of 1980 (15 U.S.C. 3710a). Technology may be transferred to a non-Federal party to such an agreement consistent with the provisions of sections 11 and 12 of that Act (15 U.S.C. 3710, 3710a).

(e) REIMBURSEMENT OF COSTS.—In the case of an activity carried out by the operator of a Department of Energy national laboratory or site in connection with any utilization of such laboratory or site under this section, the Department of Homeland Security shall reimburse the Department of Energy for costs of such activity through a method under which the Secretary of Energy waives any requirement for the Department of Homeland Security to pay administrative charges or personnel costs of the Department of Energy or its contractors in excess of the amount that the Secretary of Energy pays for an activity carried out by such contractor and paid for by the Department of Energy.

(f) LABORATORY DIRECTED RESEARCH AND DEVELOPMENT BY THE DEPARTMENT OF ENERGY.—No funds authorized to be appropriated or otherwise made available to the Department in any fiscal year may be obligated or expended for laboratory directed research and development activities carried out by the Department of Energy unless such activities support the missions of the Department of Homeland Security.

(g) OFFICE FOR NATIONAL LABORATORIES.—There is established within the Directorate of Science and Technology an Office for National Laboratories, which shall be responsible for the coordination and utilization of the Department of Energy national laboratories and sites under this section in a manner to create a networked laboratory system for the purpose of supporting the missions of the Department.

(h) DEPARTMENT OF ENERGY COORDINATION ON HOMELAND SECURITY RELATED RESEARCH.—The Secretary of Energy shall ensure that any research, development, test, and evaluation activities conducted within the Department of Energy that are directly or indirectly related to homeland security are fully coordinated with the Secretary to minimize duplication of effort and maximize the effective application of Federal budget resources.

SEC. 310. TRANSFER OF PLUM ISLAND ANIMAL DISEASE CENTER, DEPARTMENT OF AGRICULTURE.

(a) IN GENERAL.—In accordance with title XV, the Secretary of Agriculture shall transfer to the Secretary of Homeland Security the Plum Island Animal Disease Center of the Department of Agriculture, including the assets and liabilities of the Center.

(b) CONTINUED DEPARTMENT OF AGRICULTURE ACCESS.—On completion of the transfer of the Plum Island Animal Disease Center under subsection (a), the Secretary of Homeland Security and the Secretary of Agriculture shall enter into an agreement to ensure that the Department of Agriculture is able to carry out research, diagnostic, and other activities of the Department of Agriculture at the Center.

(c) DIRECTION OF ACTIVITIES.—The Secretary of Agriculture shall continue to direct the research, diagnostic, and other activities of the Department of Agriculture at the Center described in subsection (b).

(d) NOTIFICATION.—

(1) IN GENERAL.—At least 180 days before any change in the biosafety level at the Plum Island Animal Disease Center, the President shall notify Congress of the change and describe the reasons for the change.

(2) LIMITATION.—No change described in paragraph (1) may be made earlier than 180 days after the completion of the transition period (as defined in section 1501).

SEC. 311. HOMELAND SECURITY SCIENCE AND TECHNOLOGY ADVISORY COMMITTEE.

(a) ESTABLISHMENT.—There is established within the Department a Homeland Security Science and Technology Advisory Committee (in this section referred to as the "Advisory Committee"). The Advisory Committee shall make recommendations with respect to the activities of the Under Secretary for Science and Technology, including identifying research areas of potential importance to the security of the Nation.

(b) MEMBERSHIP.—

(1) APPOINTMENT.—The Advisory Committee shall consist of 20 members appointed by the Under Secretary for Science and Technology, which shall include emergency first-responders or representatives of organizations or associations of emergency first-responders. The Advisory Committee shall also include representatives of citizen groups, including economically disadvantaged communities. The individuals appointed as members of the Advisory Committee—

(A) shall be eminent in fields such as emergency response, research, engineering, new product development, business, and management consulting;

(B) shall be selected solely on the basis of established records of distinguished service;

(C) shall not be employees of the Federal Government; and

(D) shall be so selected as to provide representation of a cross-section of the research, development, demonstration, and deployment activities supported by the Under Secretary for Science and Technology.

(2) NATIONAL RESEARCH COUNCIL.—The Under Secretary for Science and Technology may enter into an arrangement for the National Research Council to select members of the Advisory Committee, but only if the panel used by the National Research Council reflects the representation described in paragraph (1).

(c) TERMS OF OFFICE.—

(1) IN GENERAL.—Except as otherwise provided in this subsection, the term of office of each member of the Advisory Committee shall be 3 years.

(2) ORIGINAL APPOINTMENTS.—The original members of the Advisory Committee shall be appointed to three classes of three members each. One class shall have a term of 1 year, 1 a term of 2 years, and the other a term of 3 years.

(3) VACANCIES.—A member appointed to fill a vacancy occurring before the expiration of the term for which the member's predecessor was appointed shall be appointed for the remainder of such term.

(d) ELIGIBILITY.—A person who has completed two consecutive full terms of service on the Advisory Committee shall thereafter be ineligible for appointment during the 1-year period following the expiration of the second such term.

(e) MEETINGS.—The Advisory Committee shall meet at least quarterly at the call of the Chair or whenever one-third of the members so request in writing. Each member shall be given appropriate notice of the call of each meeting, whenever possible not less than 15 days before the meeting.

(f) QUORUM.—A majority of the members of the Advisory Committee not having a conflict of interest in the matter being considered by the Advisory Committee shall constitute a quorum.

(g) CONFLICT OF INTEREST RULES.—The Advisory Committee shall establish rules for determining when 1 of its members has a conflict of interest in a matter being considered by the Advisory Committee.

(h) REPORTS.—

(1) ANNUAL REPORT.—The Advisory Committee shall render an annual report to the Under Secretary for Science and Technology for transmittal to Congress on or before January 31 of each year. Such report shall describe the activities and recommendations of the Advisory Committee during the previous year.

(2) ADDITIONAL REPORTS.—The Advisory Committee may render to the Under Secretary for transmittal to Congress such additional reports on specific policy matters as it considers appropriate.

(i) FEDERAL ADVISORY COMMITTEE ACT EXEMPTION.—Section 14 of the Federal Advisory Committee Act shall not apply to the Advisory Committee.

(j) TERMINATION.—The Department of Homeland Security Science and Technology Advisory Committee shall terminate 3 years after the effective date of this Act.

SEC. 312. HOMELAND SECURITY INSTITUTE.

(a) ESTABLISHMENT.—The Secretary shall establish a federally funded research and development center to be known as the "Homeland Security Institute" (in this section referred to as the "Institute").

(b) ADMINISTRATION.—The Institute shall be administered as a separate entity by the Secretary.

(c) DUTIES.—The duties of the Institute shall be determined by the Secretary, and may include the following:

(1) Systems analysis, risk analysis, and simulation and modeling to determine the vulnerabilities of the Nation's critical infrastructures and the effectiveness of the systems deployed to reduce those vulnerabilities.

(2) Economic and policy analysis to assess the distributed costs and benefits of alternative approaches to enhancing security.

(3) Evaluation of the effectiveness of measures deployed to enhance the security of institutions, facilities, and infrastructure that may be terrorist targets.

(4) Identification of instances when common standards and protocols could improve the interoperability and effective utilization of tools developed for field operators and first responders.

(5) Assistance for Federal agencies and departments in establishing testbeds to evaluate the effectiveness of technologies under development and to assess the appropriateness of such technologies for deployment.

(6) Design of metrics and use of those metrics to evaluate the effectiveness of homeland security programs throughout the Federal Government, including all national laboratories.

(7) Design of and support for the conduct of homeland security-related exercises and simulations.

(8) Creation of strategic technology development plans to reduce vulnerabilities in the Nation's critical infrastructure and key resources.

(d) CONSULTATION ON INSTITUTE ACTIVITIES.—In carrying out the duties described in subsection (c), the Institute shall consult widely with representatives from private industry, institutions of higher education, nonprofit institutions, other Government agencies, and federally funded research and development centers.

(e) USE OF CENTERS.—The Institute shall utilize the capabilities of the National Infrastructure Simulation and Analysis Center.

(f) ANNUAL REPORTS.—The Institute shall transmit to the Secretary and Congress an annual report on the activities of the Institute under this section.

(g) TERMINATION.—The Homeland Security Institute shall terminate 3 years after the effective date of this Act.

SEC. 313. TECHNOLOGY CLEARINGHOUSE TO ENCOURAGE AND SUPPORT INNOVATIVE SOLUTIONS TO ENHANCE HOMELAND SECURITY.

(a) ESTABLISHMENT OF PROGRAM.—The Secretary, acting through the Under Secretary for Science and Technology, shall establish and promote a program to encourage technological innovation in facilitating the mission of the Department (as described in section 101).

(b) ELEMENTS OF PROGRAM.—The program described in subsection (a) shall include the following components:

(1) The establishment of a centralized Federal clearinghouse for information relating to technologies that would further the mission of the Department for dissemination, as appropriate, to Federal, State, and local government and private sector entities for additional review, purchase, or use.

(2) The issuance of announcements seeking unique and innovative technologies to advance the mission of the Department.

(3) The establishment of a technical assistance team to assist in screening, as appropriate, proposals submitted to the Secretary (except as provided in subsection (c)(2)) to assess the feasibility, scientific and technical merits, and estimated cost of such proposals, as appropriate.

(4) The provision of guidance, recommendations, and technical assistance, as appropriate, to assist Federal, State, and local government and private sector efforts to evaluate and implement the use of technologies described in paragraph (1) or (2).

(5) The provision of information for persons seeking guidance on how to pursue proposals to develop or deploy technologies that would enhance homeland security, including information relating to Federal funding, regulation, or acquisition.

(c) MISCELLANEOUS PROVISIONS.—

(1) IN GENERAL.—Nothing in this section shall be construed as authorizing the Secretary or the technical assistance team established under subsection (b)(3) to set standards for technology to be used by the Department, any other executive agency, any State or local government entity, or any private sector entity.

(2) CERTAIN PROPOSALS.—The technical assistance team established under subsection (b)(3) shall not consider or evaluate proposals submitted in response to a solicitation for offers for a pending procurement or for a specific agency requirement.

(3) COORDINATION.—In carrying out this section, the Secretary shall coordinate with the Technical Support Working Group (organized under the April 1982 National Security Decision Directive Numbered 30).

TITLE IV—DIRECTORATE OF BORDER AND TRANSPORTATION SECURITY

Subtitle A—Under Secretary for Border and Transportation Security

SEC. 401. UNDER SECRETARY FOR BORDER AND TRANSPORTATION SECURITY.

There shall be in the Department a Directorate of Border and Transportation Security headed by an Under Secretary for Border and Transportation Security.

SEC. 402. RESPONSIBILITIES.

The Secretary, acting through the Under Secretary for Border and Transportation Security, shall be responsible for the following:

(1) Preventing the entry of terrorists and the instruments of terrorism into the United States.

(2) Securing the borders, territorial waters, ports, terminals, waterways, and air, land, and sea transportation systems of the United States, including managing and coordinating those functions transferred to the Department at ports of entry.

(3) Carrying out the immigration enforcement functions vested by statute in, or performed by, the Commissioner of Immigration and Naturalization (or any officer, employee, or component of the Immigration and Naturalization Service) immediately before the date on which the transfer of functions specified under section 441 takes effect.

(4) Establishing and administering rules, in accordance with section 428, governing the granting of visas or other forms of permission, including parole, to enter the United States to individuals who are not a citizen or an alien lawfully admitted for permanent residence in the United States.

(5) Establishing national immigration enforcement policies and priorities.

(6) Except as provided in subtitle C, administering the customs laws of the United States.

(7) Conducting the inspection and related administrative functions of the Department of Agriculture transferred to the Secretary of Homeland Security under section 421.

(8) In carrying out the foregoing responsibilities, ensuring the speedy, orderly, and efficient flow of lawful traffic and commerce.

SEC. 403. FUNCTIONS TRANSFERRED.

In accordance with title XV (relating to transition provisions), there shall be transferred to the Secretary the functions, personnel, assets, and liabilities of—

(1) the United States Customs Service of the Department of the Treasury, including the functions of the Secretary of the Treasury relating thereto;

(2) the Transportation Security Administration of the Department of Transportation, including the functions of the Secretary of Transportation, and of the Under Secretary of Transportation for Security, relating thereto;

(3) the Federal Protective Service of the General Services Administration, including the functions of the Administrator of General Services relating thereto;

(4) the Federal Law Enforcement Training Center of the Department of the Treasury; and

(5) the Office for Domestic Preparedness of the Office of Justice Programs, including the functions of the Attorney General relating thereto.

Subtitle B—United States Customs Service

SEC. 411. ESTABLISHMENT; COMMISSIONER OF CUSTOMS.

(a) ESTABLISHMENT.—There is established in the Department the United States Customs Service, under the authority of the Under Secretary for Border and Transportation Security, which shall be vested with those functions including, but not limited to those set forth in section 415(7), and the personnel, assets, and liabilities attributable to those functions.

(b) COMMISSIONER OF CUSTOMS.—

(1) IN GENERAL.—There shall be at the head of the Customs Service a Commissioner of Customs, who shall be appointed by the President, by and with the advice and consent of the Senate.

(2) COMPENSATION.—Section 5314 of title 5, United States Code, is amended by striking

"Commissioner of Customs, Department of the Treasury" and inserting

"Commissioner of Customs, Department of Homeland Security.".

(3) CONTINUATION IN OFFICE.—The individual serving as the Commissioner of Customs on the day before the effective date of this Act may serve as the Commissioner of Customs on and after such effective date until a Commissioner of Customs is appointed under paragraph (1).

SEC. 412. RETENTION OF CUSTOMS REVENUE FUNCTIONS BY SECRETARY OF THE TREASURY.

(a) RETENTION OF CUSTOMS REVENUE FUNCTIONS BY SECRETARY OF THE TREASURY.—

(1) RETENTION OF AUTHORITY.—Notwithstanding section 403(a)(1), authority related to Customs revenue functions that was vested in the Secretary of the Treasury by law before the effective date of this Act under those provisions of law set forth in paragraph (2) shall not be transferred to the Secretary by reason of this Act, and on and after the effective date of this Act, the Secretary of the Treasury may delegate any such authority to the Secretary at the discretion of the Secretary of the Treasury. The Secretary of the Treasury shall consult with the Secretary regarding the exercise of any such authority not delegated to the Secretary.

(2) STATUTES.—The provisions of law referred to in paragraph (1) are the following: the Tariff Act of 1930; section 249 of the Revised Statutes of the United States (19 U.S.C. 3); section 2 of the Act of March 4, 1923 (19 U.S.C. 6); section 13031 of the Consolidated Omnibus Budget Reconciliation Act of 1985 (19 U.S.C. 58c); section 251 of the Revised Statutes of the United States (19 U.S.C. 66); section 1 of the Act of June 26, 1930 (19 U.S.C. 68); the Foreign Trade Zones Act (19 U.S.C. 81a et seq.); section 1 of the Act of March 2, 1911 (19 U.S.C. 198); the Trade Act of 1974; the Trade Agreements Act of 1979; the North American Free Trade Area Implementation Act; the Uruguay Round Agreements Act; the Caribbean Basin Economic Recovery Act; the Andean Trade Preference Act; the African Growth and Opportunity Act; and any other provision of law vesting customs revenue functions in the Secretary of the Treasury.

(b) MAINTENANCE OF CUSTOMS REVENUE FUNCTIONS.—

(1) MAINTENANCE OF FUNCTIONS.—Notwithstanding any other provision of this Act, the Secretary may not consolidate, discontinue, or diminish those functions described in paragraph (2) performed by the United States Customs Service (as established under section 411) on or after the effective date of this Act, reduce the staffing level, or reduce the resources

attributable to such functions, and the Secretary shall ensure that an appropriate management structure is implemented to carry out such functions.

(2) FUNCTIONS.—The functions referred to in paragraph (1) are those functions performed by the following personnel, and associated support staff, of the United States Customs Service on the day before the effective date of this Act: Import Specialists, Entry Specialists, Drawback Specialists, National Import Specialist, Fines and Penalties Specialists, attorneys of the Office of Regulations and Rulings, Customs Auditors, International Trade Specialists, Financial Systems Specialists.

(c) NEW PERSONNEL.—The Secretary of the Treasury is authorized to appoint up to 20 new personnel to work with personnel of the Department in performing customs revenue functions.

SEC. 413. PRESERVATION OF CUSTOMS FUNDS.

Notwithstanding any other provision of this Act, no funds available to the United States Customs Service or collected under paragraphs (1) through (8) of section 13031(a) of the Consolidated Omnibus Budget Reconciliation Act of 1985 may be transferred for use by any other agency or office in the Department.

SEC. 414. SEPARATE BUDGET REQUEST FOR CUSTOMS.

The President shall include in each budget transmitted to Congress under section 1105 of title 31, United States Code, a separate budget request for the United States Customs Service.

SEC. 415. DEFINITION.

In this subtitle, the term "customs revenue function" means the following:

(1) Assessing and collecting customs duties (including antidumping and countervailing duties and duties imposed under safeguard provisions), excise taxes, fees, and penalties due on imported merchandise, including classifying and valuing merchandise for purposes of such assessment.

(2) Processing and denial of entry of persons, baggage, cargo, and mail, with respect to the assessment and collection of import duties.

(3) Detecting and apprehending persons engaged in fraudulent practices designed to circumvent the customs laws of the United States.

(4) Enforcing section 337 of the Tariff Act of 1930 and provisions relating to import quotas and the marking of imported merchandise, and providing Customs Recordations for copyrights, patents, and trademarks.

(5) Collecting accurate import data for compilation of international trade statistics.

(6) Enforcing reciprocal trade agreements.

(7) Functions performed by the following personnel, and associated support staff, of the United States Customs Service on the day before the effective date of this Act: Import Specialists, Entry Specialists, Drawback Specialists, National Import Specialist, Fines and Penalties Specialists, attorneys of the Office of Regulations and Rulings, Customs Auditors, International Trade Specialists, Financial Systems Specialists.

(8) Functions performed by the following offices, with respect to any function described in any of paragraphs (1) through (7), and associated support staff, of the United States

Customs Service on the day before the effective date of this Act: the Office of Information and Technology, the Office of Laboratory Services, the Office of the Chief Counsel, the Office of Congressional Affairs, the Office of International Affairs, and the Office of Training and Development.

SEC. 416. GAO REPORT TO CONGRESS.

Not later than 3 months after the effective date of this Act, the Comptroller General of the United States shall submit to Congress a report that sets forth all trade functions performed by the executive branch, specifying each agency that performs each such function.

SEC. 417. ALLOCATION OF RESOURCES BY THE SECRETARY.

(a) IN GENERAL.—The Secretary shall ensure that adequate staffing is provided to assure that levels of customs revenue services provided on the day before the effective date of this Act shall continue to be provided.

(b) NOTIFICATION OF CONGRESS.—The Secretary shall notify the Committee on Ways and Means of the House of Representatives and the Committee on Finance of the Senate at least 90 days prior to taking any action which would—

(1) result in any significant reduction in customs revenue services, including hours of operation, provided at any office within the Department or any port of entry;

(2) eliminate or relocate any office of the Department which provides customs revenue services; or

(3) eliminate any port of entry.

(c) DEFINITION.—In this section, the term "customs revenue services" means those customs revenue functions described in paragraphs (1) through (6) and paragraph (8) of section 415.

SEC. 418. REPORTS TO CONGRESS.

(a) CONTINUING REPORTS.—The United States Customs Service shall, on and after the effective date of this Act, continue to submit to the Committee on Ways and Means of the House of Representatives and the Committee on Finance of the Senate any report required, on the day before such the effective date of this Act, to be so submitted under any provision of law.

(b) REPORT ON CONFORMING AMENDMENTS.—Not later than 60 days after the date of enactment of this Act, the Secretary of the Treasury shall submit a report to the Committee on Finance of the Senate and the Committee on Ways and Means of the House of Representatives of proposed conforming amendments to the statutes set forth under section 412(a)(2) in order to determine the appropriate allocation of legal authorities described under this subsection. The Secretary of the Treasury shall also identify those authorities vested in the Secretary of the Treasury that are exercised by the Commissioner of Customs on or before the effective date of this section.

SEC. 419. CUSTOMS USER FEES.

(a) IN GENERAL.—Section 13031(f) of the Consolidated Omnibus Budget Reconciliation Act of 1985 (19 U.S.C. 58c(f)) is amended—

(1) in paragraph (1), by striking subparagraph (B) and inserting the following:

"(B) amounts deposited into the Customs Commercial and Homeland Security Automation Account under paragraph (5).";

(2) in paragraph (4), by striking "(other than the excess fees determined by the Secretary under paragraph (5))"; and

(3) by striking paragraph (5) and inserting the following:

"(5)(A) There is created within the general fund of the Treasury a separate account that shall be known as the 'Customs Commercial and Homeland Security Automation Account'. In each of fiscal years 2003, 2004, and 2005 there shall be deposited into the Account from fees collected under subsection (a)(9)(A), $350,000,000.

"(B) There is authorized to be appropriated from the Account in fiscal years 2003 through 2005 such amounts as are available in that Account for the development, establishment, and implementation of the Automated Commercial Environment computer system for the processing of merchandise that is entered or released and for other purposes related to the functions of the Department of Homeland Security. Amounts appropriated pursuant to this subparagraph are authorized to remain available until expended.

"(C) In adjusting the fee imposed by subsection (a)(9)(A) for fiscal year 2006, the Secretary of the Treasury shall reduce the amount estimated to be collected in fiscal year 2006 by the amount by which total fees deposited to the Account during fiscal years 2003, 2004, and 2005 exceed total appropriations from that Account.".

(b) CONFORMING AMENDMENT.—Section 311(b) of the Customs Border Security Act of 2002 (Public Law 107–210) is amended by striking paragraph (2).

Subtitle C—Miscellaneous Provisions

SEC. 421. TRANSFER OF CERTAIN AGRICULTURAL INSPECTION FUNCTIONS OF THE DEPARTMENT OF AGRICULTURE.

(a) TRANSFER OF AGRICULTURAL IMPORT AND ENTRY INSPECTION FUNCTIONS.—There shall be transferred to the Secretary the functions of the Secretary of Agriculture relating to agricultural import and entry inspection activities under the laws specified in subsection (b).

(b) COVERED ANIMAL AND PLANT PROTECTION LAWS.—The laws referred to in subsection (a) are the following:

(1) The Act commonly known as the Virus-Serum-Toxin Act (the eighth paragraph under the heading "Bureau of Animal Industry" in the Act of March 4, 1913; 21 U.S.C. 151 et seq.).

(2) Section 1 of the Act of August 31, 1922 (commonly known as the Honeybee Act; 7 U.S.C. 281).

(3) Title III of the Federal Seed Act (7 U.S.C. 1581 et seq.).

(4) The Plant Protection Act (7 U.S.C. 7701 et seq.).

(5) The Animal Health Protection Act (subtitle E of title X of Public Law 107–171; 7 U.S.C. 8301 et seq.).

(6) The Lacey Act Amendments of 1981 (16 U.S.C. 3371 et seq.).

(7) Section 11 of the Endangered Species Act of 1973 (16 U.S.C. 1540).

(c) EXCLUSION OF QUARANTINE ACTIVITIES.—For purposes of this section, the term "functions" does not include any quarantine activities carried out under the laws specified in subsection (b).

(d) EFFECT OF TRANSFER.—

(1) COMPLIANCE WITH DEPARTMENT OF AGRICULTURE REGULATIONS.—The authority transferred pursuant to subsection (a) shall be exercised by the Secretary in accordance with the regulations, policies, and procedures issued by the Secretary of Agriculture regarding the administration of the laws specified in subsection (b).

(2) RULEMAKING COORDINATION.—The Secretary of Agriculture shall coordinate with the Secretary whenever the Secretary of Agriculture prescribes regulations, policies, or procedures for administering the functions transferred under subsection (a) under a law specified in subsection (b).

(3) EFFECTIVE ADMINISTRATION.—The Secretary, in consultation with the Secretary of Agriculture, may issue such directives and guidelines as are necessary to ensure the effective use of personnel of the Department of Homeland Security to carry out the functions transferred pursuant to subsection (a).

(e) TRANSFER AGREEMENT.—

(1) AGREEMENT REQUIRED; REVISION.—Before the end of the transition period, as defined in section 1501, the Secretary of Agriculture and the Secretary shall enter into an agreement to effectuate the transfer of functions required by subsection (a). The Secretary of Agriculture and the Secretary may jointly revise the agreement as necessary thereafter.

(2) REQUIRED TERMS.—The agreement required by this subsection shall specifically address the following:

(A) The supervision by the Secretary of Agriculture of the training of employees of the Secretary to carry out the functions transferred pursuant to subsection (a).

(B) The transfer of funds to the Secretary under subsection (f).

(3) COOPERATION AND RECIPROCITY.—The Secretary of Agriculture and the Secretary may include as part of the agreement the following:

(A) Authority for the Secretary to perform functions delegated to the Animal and Plant Health Inspection Service of the Department of Agriculture regarding the protection of domestic livestock and plants, but not transferred to the Secretary pursuant to subsection (a).

(B) Authority for the Secretary of Agriculture to use employees of the Department of Homeland Security to carry out authorities delegated to the Animal and Plant Health Inspection Service regarding the protection of domestic livestock and plants.

(f) PERIODIC TRANSFER OF FUNDS TO DEPARTMENT OF HOMELAND SECURITY.—

(1) TRANSFER OF FUNDS.—Out of funds collected by fees authorized under sections 2508 and 2509 of the Food, Agriculture, Conservation, and Trade Act of 1990 (21 U.S.C. 136, 136a), the Secretary of Agriculture shall transfer, from time to time in accordance with the agreement under subsection (e), to the Secretary funds for activities carried out by the Secretary for which such fees were collected.

(2) LIMITATION.—The proportion of fees collected pursuant to such sections that are transferred to the Secretary under this subsection may not exceed the proportion of the costs incurred by the Secretary to all costs incurred to carry out activities funded by such fees.

(g) TRANSFER OF DEPARTMENT OF AGRICULTURE EMPLOYEES.— Not later than the completion of the transition period defined under section 1501, the Secretary of Agriculture shall transfer to the Secretary not more than 3,200 full-time equivalent positions of the Department of Agriculture.

(h) PROTECTION OF INSPECTION ANIMALS.—Title V of the Agricultural Risk Protection Act of 2000 (7 U.S.C. 2279e, 2279f) is amended—

(1) in section 501(a)—

(A) by inserting "or the Department of Homeland Security" after "Department of Agriculture"; and

(B) by inserting "or the Secretary of Homeland Security" after "Secretary of Agriculture";

(2) by striking "Secretary" each place it appears (other than in sections 501(a) and 501(e)) and inserting "Secretary concerned"; and

(3) by adding at the end of section 501 the following new subsection:

"(e) SECRETARY CONCERNED DEFINED.—In this title, the term 'Secretary concerned' means—

"(1) the Secretary of Agriculture, with respect to an animal used for purposes of official inspections by the Department of Agriculture; and

"(2) the Secretary of Homeland Security, with respect to an animal used for purposes of official inspections by the Department of Homeland Security.".

SEC. 422. FUNCTIONS OF ADMINISTRATOR OF GENERAL SERVICES.

(a) OPERATION, MAINTENANCE, AND PROTECTION OF FEDERAL BUILDINGS AND GROUNDS.—Nothing in this Act may be construed to affect the functions or authorities of the Administrator of General Services with respect to the operation, maintenance, and protection of buildings and grounds owned or occupied by the Federal Government and under the jurisdiction, custody, or control of the Administrator. Except for the law enforcement and related security functions transferred under section 403(3), the Administrator shall retain all powers, functions, and authorities vested in the Administrator under chapter 10 of title 40, United States Code, and other provisions of law that are necessary for the operation, maintenance, and protection of such buildings and grounds.

(b) COLLECTION OF RENTS AND FEES; FEDERAL BUILDINGS FUND.—

(1) STATUTORY CONSTRUCTION.—Nothing in this Act may be construed—

(A) to direct the transfer of, or affect, the authority of the Administrator of General Services to collect rents and fees, including fees collected for protective services; or

(B) to authorize the Secretary or any other official in the Department to obligate amounts in the Federal Buildings Fund established by section 490(f) of title 40, United States Code.

(2) USE OF TRANSFERRED AMOUNTS.—Any amounts transferred by the Administrator of General Services to the Secretary out of rents and fees collected by the Administrator shall be used by the Secretary solely for the protection of buildings or grounds owned or occupied by the Federal Government.

SEC. 423. FUNCTIONS OF TRANSPORTATION SECURITY ADMINISTRATION.

(a) CONSULTATION WITH FEDERAL AVIATION ADMINISTRATION.— The Secretary and other officials in the Department shall consult with the Administrator of the Federal Aviation Administration before taking any action that might affect aviation safety, air carrier operations, aircraft airworthiness, or the use of airspace. The Secretary shall establish a liaison office within the Department for the purpose of consulting with the Administrator of the Federal Aviation Administration.

(b) REPORT TO CONGRESS.—Not later than 60 days after the date of enactment of this Act, the Secretary of Transportation shall transmit to Congress a report containing a plan for complying with the requirements of section 44901(d) of title 49, United States Code, as amended by section 425 of this Act.

(c) LIMITATIONS ON STATUTORY CONSTRUCTION.—

(1) GRANT OF AUTHORITY.—Nothing in this Act may be construed to vest in the Secretary or any other official in the Department any authority over transportation security that is not vested in the Under Secretary of Transportation for Security, or in the Secretary of Transportation under chapter 449 of title 49, United States Code, on the day before the date of enactment of this Act.

(2) OBLIGATION OF AIP FUNDS.—Nothing in this Act may be construed to authorize the Secretary or any other official in the Department to obligate amounts made available under section 48103 of title 49, United States Code.

SEC. 424. PRESERVATION OF TRANSPORTATION SECURITY ADMINISTRATION AS A DISTINCT ENTITY.

(a) IN GENERAL.—Notwithstanding any other provision of this Act, and subject to subsection (b), the Transportation Security Administration shall be maintained as a distinct entity within the Department under the Under Secretary for Border Transportation and Security.

(b) SUNSET.—Subsection (a) shall cease to apply 2 years after the date of enactment of this Act.

SEC. 425. EXPLOSIVE DETECTION SYSTEMS.

Section 44901(d) of title 49, United States Code, is amended by adding at the end the following:

"(2) DEADLINE.—

"(A) IN GENERAL.—If, in his discretion or at the request of an airport, the Under Secretary of Transportation for Security determines that the Transportation Security Administration is not able to deploy explosive detection systems required to be deployed under paragraph (1) at all airports where explosive detection systems are required by December 31, 2002, then with respect to each airport for which the Under Secretary makes that determination—

"(i) the Under Secretary shall submit to the Senate Committee on Commerce, Science, and Transportation and the House of Representatives Committee on Transportation and Infrastructure a detailed plan (which may be submitted in classified form) for the deployment of the number of explosive detection systems at that airport necessary to meet the requirements of paragraph (1) as soon as practicable at that airport but in no event later than December 31, 2003; and

"(ii) the Under Secretary shall take all necessary action to ensure that alternative means of screening all checked baggage is implemented until the requirements of paragraph (1) have been met.

"(B) CRITERIA FOR DETERMINATION.—In making a determination under subparagraph (A), the Under Secretary shall take into account—

"(i) the nature and extent of the required modifications to the airport's terminal buildings, and the technical, engineering, design and construction issues;

"(ii) the need to ensure that such installations and modifications are effective; and

"(iii) the feasibility and cost-effectiveness of deploying explosive detection systems in the baggage sorting area or other non-public area rather than the lobby of an airport terminal building.

"(C) RESPONSE.—The Under Secretary shall respond to the request of an airport under subparagraph (A) within 14 days of receiving the request. A denial of request shall create no right of appeal or judicial review.

"(D) AIRPORT EFFORT REQUIRED.—Each airport with respect to which the Under Secretary makes a determination under subparagraph (A) shall—

"(i) cooperate fully with the Transportation Security Administration with respect to screening checked baggage and changes to accommodate explosive detection systems; and

"(ii) make security projects a priority for the obligation or expenditure of funds made available under chapter 417 or 471 until explosive detection systems required to be deployed under paragraph (1) have been deployed at that airport.

"(3) REPORTS.—Until the Transportation Security Administration has met the requirements of paragraph (1), the Under Secretary shall submit a classified report every 30 days after the date of enactment of this Act to the Senate Committee on Commerce, Science, and Transportation and the House of Representatives Committee on Transportation and Infrastructure describing the progress made toward meeting such requirements at each airport.".

SEC. 426. TRANSPORTATION SECURITY.

(a) TRANSPORTATION SECURITY OVERSIGHT BOARD.—

(1) ESTABLISHMENT.—Section 115(a) of title 49, United States Code, is amended by striking "Department of Transportation" and inserting "Department of Homeland Security".

(2) MEMBERSHIP.—Section 115(b)(1) of title 49, United States Code, is amended—

(A) by striking subparagraph (G);

(B) by redesignating subparagraphs (A) through (F) as subparagraphs (B) through (G), respectively; and

(C) by inserting before subparagraph (B) (as so redesignated) the following:

"(A) The Secretary of Homeland Security, or the Secretary's designee.".

(3) CHAIRPERSON.—Section 115(b)(2) of title 49, United States Code, is amended by striking "Secretary of Transportation" and inserting "Secretary of Homeland Security".

(b) APPROVAL OF AIP GRANT APPLICATIONS FOR SECURITY ACTIVITIES.—Section 47106 of title 49, United States Code, is amended by adding at the end the following:

"(g) CONSULTATION WITH SECRETARY OF HOMELAND SECURITY.—The Secretary shall consult with the Secretary of Homeland Security before approving an application under this subchapter for an airport development project grant for activities described in section 47102(3)(B)(ii) only as they relate to security equipment or section 47102(3)(B)(x) only as they relate to installation of bulk explosive detection system.".

SEC. 427. COORDINATION OF INFORMATION AND INFORMATION TECHNOLOGY.

(a) DEFINITION OF AFFECTED AGENCY.—In this section, the term "affected agency" means—

(1) the Department;

(2) the Department of Agriculture;

(3) the Department of Health and Human Services; and

(4) any other department or agency determined to be appropriate by the Secretary.

(b) COORDINATION.—The Secretary, in coordination with the Secretary of Agriculture, the Secretary of Health and Human Services, and the head of each other department or agency determined to be appropriate by the Secretary, shall ensure that appropriate information (as determined by the Secretary) concerning inspections of articles that are imported or entered into the United States, and are inspected or regulated by 1 or more affected agencies, is timely and efficiently exchanged between the affected agencies.

(c) REPORT AND PLAN.—Not later than 18 months after the date of enactment of this Act, the Secretary, in consultation with the Secretary of Agriculture, the Secretary of Health and Human Services, and the head of each other department or agency determined to be appropriate by the Secretary, shall submit to Congress—

(1) a report on the progress made in implementing this section; and

(2) a plan to complete implementation of this section.

SEC. 428. VISA ISSUANCE.

(a) DEFINITION.—In this subsection, the term "consular office" has the meaning given that term under section 101(a)(9) of the Immigration and Nationality Act (8 U.S.C. 1101(a)(9)).

(b) IN GENERAL.—Notwithstanding section 104(a) of the Immigration and Nationality Act (8 U.S.C. 1104(a)) or any other provision of law, and except as provided in subsection (c) of this section, the Secretary—

(1) shall be vested exclusively with all authorities to issue regulations with respect to, administer, and enforce the provisions of such Act, and of all other immigration and nationality

laws, relating to the functions of consular officers of the United States in connection with the granting or refusal of visas, and shall have the authority to refuse visas in accordance with law and to develop programs of homeland security training for consular officers (in addition to consular training provided by the Secretary of State), which authorities shall be exercised through the Secretary of State, except that the Secretary shall not have authority to alter or reverse the decision of a consular officer to refuse a visa to an alien; and

(2) shall have authority to confer or impose upon any officer or employee of the United States, with the consent of the head of the executive agency under whose jurisdiction such officer or employee is serving, any of the functions specified in paragraph (1).

(c) AUTHORITY OF THE SECRETARY OF STATE.—

(1) IN GENERAL.—Notwithstanding subsection (b), the Secretary of State may direct a consular officer to refuse a visa to an alien if the Secretary of State deems such refusal necessary or advisable in the foreign policy or security interests of the United States.

(2) CONSTRUCTION REGARDING AUTHORITY.—Nothing in this section, consistent with the Secretary of Homeland Security's authority to refuse visas in accordance with law, shall be construed as affecting the authorities of the Secretary of State under the following provisions of law:

(A) Section 101(a)(15)(A) of the Immigration and Nationality Act (8 U.S.C. 1101(a)(15)(A)).

(B) Section 204(d)(2) of the Immigration and Nationality Act (8 U.S.C. 1154) (as it will take effect upon the entry into force of the Convention on Protection of Children and Cooperation in Respect to Inter-Country adoption).

(C) Section 212(a)(3)(B)(i)(IV)(bb) of the Immigration and Nationality Act (8 U.S.C. 1182(a)(3)(B)(i)(IV)(bb)).

(D) Section 212(a)(3)(B)(i)(VI) of the Immigration and Nationality Act (8 U.S.C. 1182(a)(3)(B)(i)(VI)).

(E) Section 212(a)(3)(B)(vi)(II) of the Immigration and Nationality Act (8 U.S.C. 1182(a)(3)(B)(vi)(II)).

(F) Section 212(a)(3)(C) of the Immigration and Nationality Act (8 U.S.C. 1182(a)(3)(C)).

(G) Section 212(a)(10)(C) of the Immigration and Nationality Act (8 U.S.C. 1182(a)(10)(C)).

(H) Section 212(f) of the Immigration and Nationality Act (8 U.S.C. 1182(f)).

(I) Section 219(a) of the Immigration and Nationality Act (8 U.S.C. 1189(a)).

(J) Section 237(a)(4)(C) of the Immigration and Nationality Act (8 U.S.C. 1227(a)(4)(C)).

(K) Section 401 of the Cuban Liberty and Democratic Solidarity (LIBERTAD) Act of 1996 (22 U.S.C. 6034; Public Law 104–114).

(L) Section 613 of the Departments of Commerce, Justice, and State, the Judiciary and Related Agencies Appropriations Act, 1999 (as contained in section 101(b) of division A of Public Law 105–277) (Omnibus Consolidated and Emergency Supplemental Appropriations Act, 1999); 112 Stat. 2681; H.R. 4328 (originally H.R. 4276) as amended by section 617 of Public Law 106–553.

(M) Section 103(f) of the Chemical Weapon Convention Implementation Act of 1998 (112 Stat. 2681–865).

(N) Section 801 of H.R. 3427, the Admiral James W. Nance and Meg Donovan Foreign Relations Authorization Act, Fiscal Years 2000 and 2001, as enacted by reference in Public Law 106–113.

(O) Section 568 of the Foreign Operations, Export Financing, and Related Programs Appropriations Act, 2002 (Public Law 107–115).

(P) Section 51 of the State Department Basic Authorities Act of 1956 (22 U.S.C. 2723).

(d) CONSULAR OFFICERS AND CHIEFS OF MISSIONS.—

(1) IN GENERAL.—Nothing in this section may be construed to alter or affect—

(A) the employment status of consular officers as employees of the Department of State; or

(B) the authority of a chief of mission under section 207 of the Foreign Service Act of 1980 (22 U.S.C. 3927).

(2) CONSTRUCTION REGARDING DELEGATION OF AUTHORITY.—Nothing in this section shall be construed to affect any delegation of authority to the Secretary of State by the President pursuant to any proclamation issued under section 212(f) of the Immigration and Nationality Act (8 U.S.C. 1182(f)), consistent with the Secretary of Homeland Security's authority to refuse visas in accordance with law.

(e) ASSIGNMENT OF HOMELAND SECURITY EMPLOYEES TO DIPLOMATIC AND CONSULAR POSTS.—

(1) IN GENERAL.—The Secretary is authorized to assign employees of the Department to each diplomatic and consular post at which visas are issued, unless the Secretary determines that such an assignment at a particular post would not promote homeland security.

(2) FUNCTIONS.—Employees assigned under paragraph (1) shall perform the following functions:

(A) Provide expert advice and training to consular officers regarding specific security threats relating to the adjudication of individual visa applications or classes of applications.

(B) Review any such applications, either on the initiative of the employee of the Department or upon request by a consular officer or other person charged with adjudicating such applications.

(C) Conduct investigations with respect to consular matters under the jurisdiction of the Secretary.

(3) EVALUATION OF CONSULAR OFFICERS.—The Secretary of State shall evaluate, in consultation with the Secretary, as deemed appropriate by the Secretary, the performance of consular officers with respect to the processing and adjudication of applications for visas in accordance with performance standards developed by the Secretary for these procedures.

(4) REPORT.—The Secretary shall, on an annual basis, submit a report to Congress that describes the basis for each determination under paragraph (1) that the assignment of an employee of the Department at a particular diplomatic post would not promote homeland security.

(5) PERMANENT ASSIGNMENT; PARTICIPATION IN TERRORIST LOOKOUT COMMITTEE.—When appropriate, employees of the

Department assigned to perform functions described in paragraph (2) may be assigned permanently to overseas diplomatic or consular posts with country-specific or regional responsibility. If the Secretary so directs, any such employee, when present at an overseas post, shall participate in the terrorist lookout committee established under section 304 of the Enhanced Border Security and Visa Entry Reform Act of 2002 (8 U.S.C. 1733).

(6) TRAINING AND HIRING.—

(A) IN GENERAL.—The Secretary shall ensure, to the extent possible, that any employees of the Department assigned to perform functions under paragraph (2) and, as appropriate, consular officers, shall be provided the necessary training to enable them to carry out such functions, including training in foreign languages, interview techniques, and fraud detection techniques, in conditions in the particular country where each employee is assigned, and in other appropriate areas of study.

(B) USE OF CENTER.—The Secretary is authorized to use the National Foreign Affairs Training Center, on a reimbursable basis, to obtain the training described in subparagraph (A).

(7) REPORT.—Not later than 1 year after the date of enactment of this Act, the Secretary and the Secretary of State shall submit to Congress—

(A) a report on the implementation of this subsection; and

(B) any legislative proposals necessary to further the objectives of this subsection.

(8) EFFECTIVE DATE.—This subsection shall take effect on the earlier of—

(A) the date on which the President publishes notice in the Federal Register that the President has submitted a report to Congress setting forth a memorandum of understanding between the Secretary and the Secretary of State governing the implementation of this section; or

(B) the date occurring 1 year after the date of enactment of this Act.

(f) NO CREATION OF PRIVATE RIGHT OF ACTION.—Nothing in this section shall be construed to create or authorize a private right of action to challenge a decision of a consular officer or other United States official or employee to grant or deny a visa.

(g) STUDY REGARDING USE OF FOREIGN NATIONALS.—

(1) IN GENERAL.—The Secretary of Homeland Security shall conduct a study of the role of foreign nationals in the granting or refusal of visas and other documents authorizing entry of aliens into the United States. The study shall address the following:

(A) The proper role, if any, of foreign nationals in the process of rendering decisions on such grants and refusals.

(B) Any security concerns involving the employment of foreign nationals.

(C) Whether there are cost-effective alternatives to the use of foreign nationals.

(2) REPORT.—Not later than 1 year after the date of the enactment of this Act, the Secretary shall submit a report

containing the findings of the study conducted under paragraph (1) to the Committee on the Judiciary, the Committee on International Relations, and the Committee on Government Reform of the House of Representatives, and the Committee on the Judiciary, the Committee on Foreign Relations, and the Committee on Government Affairs of the Senate.

(h) REPORT.—Not later than 120 days after the date of the enactment of this Act, the Director of the Office of Science and Technology Policy shall submit to Congress a report on how the provisions of this section will affect procedures for the issuance of student visas.

(i) VISA ISSUANCE PROGRAM FOR SAUDI ARABIA.—Notwithstanding any other provision of law, after the date of the enactment of this Act all third party screening programs in Saudi Arabia shall be terminated. On-site personnel of the Department of Homeland Security shall review all visa applications prior to adjudication.

SEC. 429. INFORMATION ON VISA DENIALS REQUIRED TO BE ENTERED INTO ELECTRONIC DATA SYSTEM.

(a) IN GENERAL.—Whenever a consular officer of the United States denies a visa to an applicant, the consular officer shall enter the fact and the basis of the denial and the name of the applicant into the interoperable electronic data system implemented under section 202(a) of the Enhanced Border Security and Visa Entry Reform Act of 2002 (8 U.S.C. 1722(a)).

(b) PROHIBITION.—In the case of any alien with respect to whom a visa has been denied under subsection (a)—

(1) no subsequent visa may be issued to the alien unless the consular officer considering the alien's visa application has reviewed the information concerning the alien placed in the interoperable electronic data system, has indicated on the alien's application that the information has been reviewed, and has stated for the record why the visa is being issued or a waiver of visa ineligibility recommended in spite of that information; and

(2) the alien may not be admitted to the United States without a visa issued in accordance with the procedures described in paragraph (1).

SEC. 430. OFFICE FOR DOMESTIC PREPAREDNESS.

(a) IN GENERAL.—The Office for Domestic Preparedness shall be within the Directorate of Border and Transportation Security.

(b) DIRECTOR.—There shall be a Director of the Office for Domestic Preparedness, who shall be appointed by the President, by and with the advice and consent of the Senate. The Director of the Office for Domestic Preparedness shall report directly to the Under Secretary for Border and Transportation Security.

(c) RESPONSIBILITIES.—The Office for Domestic Preparedness shall have the primary responsibility within the executive branch of Government for the preparedness of the United States for acts of terrorism, including—

(1) coordinating preparedness efforts at the Federal level, and working with all State, local, tribal, parish, and private sector emergency response providers on all matters pertaining to combating terrorism, including training, exercises, and equipment support;

(2) coordinating or, as appropriate, consolidating communications and systems of communications relating to homeland security at all levels of government;

(3) directing and supervising terrorism preparedness grant programs of the Federal Government (other than those programs administered by the Department of Health and Human Services) for all emergency response providers;

(4) incorporating the Strategy priorities into planning guidance on an agency level for the preparedness efforts of the Office for Domestic Preparedness;

(5) providing agency-specific training for agents and analysts within the Department, other agencies, and State and local agencies and international entities;

(6) as the lead executive branch agency for preparedness of the United States for acts of terrorism, cooperating closely with the Federal Emergency Management Agency, which shall have the primary responsibility within the executive branch to prepare for and mitigate the effects of nonterrorist-related disasters in the United States;

(7) assisting and supporting the Secretary, in coordination with other Directorates and entities outside the Department, in conducting appropriate risk analysis and risk management activities of State, local, and tribal governments consistent with the mission and functions of the Directorate; and

(8) those elements of the Office of National Preparedness of the Federal Emergency Management Agency which relate to terrorism, which shall be consolidated within the Department in the Office for Domestic Preparedness established under this section.

(d) FISCAL YEARS 2003 and 2004.—During fiscal year 2003 and fiscal year 2004, the Director of the Office for Domestic Preparedness established under this section shall manage and carry out those functions of the Office for Domestic Preparedness of the Department of Justice (transferred under this section) before September 11, 2001, under the same terms, conditions, policies, and authorities, and with the required level of personnel, assets, and budget before September 11, 2001.

Subtitle D—Immigration Enforcement Functions

SEC. 441. TRANSFER OF FUNCTIONS TO UNDER SECRETARY FOR BORDER AND TRANSPORTATION SECURITY.

In accordance with title XV (relating to transition provisions), there shall be transferred from the Commissioner of Immigration and Naturalization to the Under Secretary for Border and Transportation Security all functions performed under the following programs, and all personnel, assets, and liabilities pertaining to such programs, immediately before such transfer occurs:

(1) The Border Patrol program.

(2) The detention and removal program.

(3) The intelligence program.

(4) The investigations program.

(5) The inspections program.

SEC. 442. ESTABLISHMENT OF BUREAU OF BORDER SECURITY.

(a) ESTABLISHMENT OF BUREAU.—

(1) IN GENERAL.—There shall be in the Department of Homeland Security a bureau to be known as the "Bureau of Border Security".

(2) ASSISTANT SECRETARY.—The head of the Bureau of Border Security shall be the Assistant Secretary of the Bureau of Border Security, who—

(A) shall report directly to the Under Secretary for Border and Transportation Security; and

(B) shall have a minimum of 5 years professional experience in law enforcement, and a minimum of 5 years of management experience.

(3) FUNCTIONS.—The Assistant Secretary of the Bureau of Border Security—

(A) shall establish the policies for performing such functions as are—

(i) transferred to the Under Secretary for Border and Transportation Security by section 441 and delegated to the Assistant Secretary by the Under Secretary for Border and Transportation Security; or

(ii) otherwise vested in the Assistant Secretary by law;

(B) shall oversee the administration of such policies; and

(C) shall advise the Under Secretary for Border and Transportation Security with respect to any policy or operation of the Bureau of Border Security that may affect the Bureau of Citizenship and Immigration Services established under subtitle E, including potentially conflicting policies or operations.

(4) PROGRAM TO COLLECT INFORMATION RELATING TO FOREIGN STUDENTS.—The Assistant Secretary of the Bureau of Border Security shall be responsible for administering the program to collect information relating to nonimmigrant foreign students and other exchange program participants described in section 641 of the Illegal Immigration Reform and Immigrant Responsibility Act of 1996 (8 U.S.C. 1372), including the Student and Exchange Visitor Information System established under that section, and shall use such information to carry out the enforcement functions of the Bureau.

(5) MANAGERIAL ROTATION PROGRAM.—

(A) IN GENERAL.—Not later than 1 year after the date on which the transfer of functions specified under section 441 takes effect, the Assistant Secretary of the Bureau of Border Security shall design and implement a managerial rotation program under which employees of such bureau holding positions involving supervisory or managerial responsibility and classified, in accordance with chapter 51 of title 5, United States Code, as a GS–14 or above, shall—

(i) gain some experience in all the major functions performed by such bureau; and

(ii) work in at least one local office of such bureau.

(B) REPORT.—Not later than 2 years after the date on which the transfer of functions specified under section

441 takes effect, the Secretary shall submit a report to the Congress on the implementation of such program.

(b) CHIEF OF POLICY AND STRATEGY.—

(1) IN GENERAL.—There shall be a position of Chief of Policy and Strategy for the Bureau of Border Security.

(2) FUNCTIONS.—In consultation with Bureau of Border Security personnel in local offices, the Chief of Policy and Strategy shall be responsible for—

(A) making policy recommendations and performing policy research and analysis on immigration enforcement issues; and

(B) coordinating immigration policy issues with the Chief of Policy and Strategy for the Bureau of Citizenship and Immigration Services (established under subtitle E), as appropriate.

(c) LEGAL ADVISOR.—There shall be a principal legal advisor to the Assistant Secretary of the Bureau of Border Security. The legal advisor shall provide specialized legal advice to the Assistant Secretary of the Bureau of Border Security and shall represent the bureau in all exclusion, deportation, and removal proceedings before the Executive Office for Immigration Review.

SEC. 443. PROFESSIONAL RESPONSIBILITY AND QUALITY REVIEW.

The Under Secretary for Border and Transportation Security shall be responsible for—

(1) conducting investigations of noncriminal allegations of misconduct, corruption, and fraud involving any employee of the Bureau of Border Security that are not subject to investigation by the Inspector General for the Department;

(2) inspecting the operations of the Bureau of Border Security and providing assessments of the quality of the operations of such bureau as a whole and each of its components; and

(3) providing an analysis of the management of the Bureau of Border Security.

SEC. 444. EMPLOYEE DISCIPLINE.

The Under Secretary for Border and Transportation Security may, notwithstanding any other provision of law, impose disciplinary action, including termination of employment, pursuant to policies and procedures applicable to employees of the Federal Bureau of Investigation, on any employee of the Bureau of Border Security who willfully deceives the Congress or agency leadership on any matter.

SEC. 445. REPORT ON IMPROVING ENFORCEMENT FUNCTIONS.

(a) IN GENERAL.—The Secretary, not later than 1 year after being sworn into office, shall submit to the Committees on Appropriations and the Judiciary of the House of Representatives and of the Senate a report with a plan detailing how the Bureau of Border Security, after the transfer of functions specified under section 441 takes effect, will enforce comprehensively, effectively, and fairly all the enforcement provisions of the Immigration and Nationality Act (8 U.S.C. 1101 et seq.) relating to such functions.

(b) CONSULTATION.—In carrying out subsection (a), the Secretary of Homeland Security shall consult with the Attorney General, the Secretary of State, the Director of the Federal Bureau of Investigation, the Secretary of the Treasury, the Secretary of Labor, the Commissioner of Social Security, the Director of the

Executive Office for Immigration Review, and the heads of State and local law enforcement agencies to determine how to most effectively conduct enforcement operations.

SEC. 446. SENSE OF CONGRESS REGARDING CONSTRUCTION OF FENCING NEAR SAN DIEGO, CALIFORNIA.

It is the sense of the Congress that completing the 14-mile border fence project required to be carried out under section 102(b) of the Illegal Immigration Reform and Immigrant Responsibility Act of 1996 (8 U.S.C. 1103 note) should be a priority for the Secretary.

Subtitle E—Citizenship and Immigration Services

SEC. 451. ESTABLISHMENT OF BUREAU OF CITIZENSHIP AND IMMIGRATION SERVICES.

(a) ESTABLISHMENT OF BUREAU.—

(1) IN GENERAL.—There shall be in the Department a bureau to be known as the "Bureau of Citizenship and Immigration Services".

(2) DIRECTOR.—The head of the Bureau of Citizenship and Immigration Services shall be the Director of the Bureau of Citizenship and Immigration Services, who—

(A) shall report directly to the Deputy Secretary;

(B) shall have a minimum of 5 years of management experience; and

(C) shall be paid at the same level as the Assistant Secretary of the Bureau of Border Security.

(3) FUNCTIONS.—The Director of the Bureau of Citizenship and Immigration Services—

(A) shall establish the policies for performing such functions as are transferred to the Director by this section or this Act or otherwise vested in the Director by law;

(B) shall oversee the administration of such policies;

(C) shall advise the Deputy Secretary with respect to any policy or operation of the Bureau of Citizenship and Immigration Services that may affect the Bureau of Border Security of the Department, including potentially conflicting policies or operations;

(D) shall establish national immigration services policies and priorities;

(E) shall meet regularly with the Ombudsman described in section 452 to correct serious service problems identified by the Ombudsman; and

(F) shall establish procedures requiring a formal response to any recommendations submitted in the Ombudsman's annual report to Congress within 3 months after its submission to Congress.

(4) MANAGERIAL ROTATION PROGRAM.—

(A) IN GENERAL.—Not later than 1 year after the effective date specified in section 455, the Director of the Bureau of Citizenship and Immigration Services shall design and implement a managerial rotation program under which employees of such bureau holding positions involving supervisory or managerial responsibility and classified, in accordance with chapter 51 of title 5, United States Code, as a GS–14 or above, shall—

(i) gain some experience in all the major functions performed by such bureau; and

(ii) work in at least one field office and one service center of such bureau.

(B) REPORT.—Not later than 2 years after the effective date specified in section 455, the Secretary shall submit a report to Congress on the implementation of such program.

(5) PILOT INITIATIVES FOR BACKLOG ELIMINATION.—The Director of the Bureau of Citizenship and Immigration Services is authorized to implement innovative pilot initiatives to eliminate any remaining backlog in the processing of immigration benefit applications, and to prevent any backlog in the processing of such applications from recurring, in accordance with section 204(a) of the Immigration Services and Infrastructure Improvements Act of 2000 (8 U.S.C. 1573(a)). Such initiatives may include measures such as increasing personnel, transferring personnel to focus on areas with the largest potential for backlog, and streamlining paperwork.

(b) TRANSFER OF FUNCTIONS FROM COMMISSIONER.—In accordance with title XV (relating to transition provisions), there are transferred from the Commissioner of Immigration and Naturalization to the Director of the Bureau of Citizenship and Immigration Services the following functions, and all personnel, infrastructure, and funding provided to the Commissioner in support of such functions immediately before the effective date specified in section 455:

(1) Adjudications of immigrant visa petitions.

(2) Adjudications of naturalization petitions.

(3) Adjudications of asylum and refugee applications.

(4) Adjudications performed at service centers.

(5) All other adjudications performed by the Immigration and Naturalization Service immediately before the effective date specified in section 455.

(c) CHIEF OF POLICY AND STRATEGY.—

(1) IN GENERAL.—There shall be a position of Chief of Policy and Strategy for the Bureau of Citizenship and Immigration Services.

(2) FUNCTIONS.—In consultation with Bureau of Citizenship and Immigration Services personnel in field offices, the Chief of Policy and Strategy shall be responsible for—

(A) making policy recommendations and performing policy research and analysis on immigration services issues; and

(B) coordinating immigration policy issues with the Chief of Policy and Strategy for the Bureau of Border Security of the Department.

(d) LEGAL ADVISOR.—

(1) IN GENERAL.—There shall be a principal legal advisor to the Director of the Bureau of Citizenship and Immigration Services.

(2) FUNCTIONS.—The legal advisor shall be responsible for—

(A) providing specialized legal advice, opinions, determinations, regulations, and any other assistance to the Director of the Bureau of Citizenship and Immigration Services with respect to legal matters affecting the Bureau of Citizenship and Immigration Services; and

(B) representing the Bureau of Citizenship and Immigration Services in visa petition appeal proceedings before the Executive Office for Immigration Review.

(e) BUDGET OFFICER.—

(1) IN GENERAL.—There shall be a Budget Officer for the Bureau of Citizenship and Immigration Services.

(2) FUNCTIONS.—

(A) IN GENERAL.—The Budget Officer shall be responsible for—

(i) formulating and executing the budget of the Bureau of Citizenship and Immigration Services;

(ii) financial management of the Bureau of Citizenship and Immigration Services; and

(iii) collecting all payments, fines, and other debts for the Bureau of Citizenship and Immigration Services.

(f) CHIEF OF OFFICE OF CITIZENSHIP.—

(1) IN GENERAL.—There shall be a position of Chief of the Office of Citizenship for the Bureau of Citizenship and Immigration Services.

(2) FUNCTIONS.—The Chief of the Office of Citizenship for the Bureau of Citizenship and Immigration Services shall be responsible for promoting instruction and training on citizenship responsibilities for aliens interested in becoming naturalized citizens of the United States, including the development of educational materials.

SEC. 452. CITIZENSHIP AND IMMIGRATION SERVICES OMBUDSMAN.

(a) IN GENERAL.—Within the Department, there shall be a position of Citizenship and Immigration Services Ombudsman (in this section referred to as the "Ombudsman"). The Ombudsman shall report directly to the Deputy Secretary. The Ombudsman shall have a background in customer service as well as immigration law.

(b) FUNCTIONS.—It shall be the function of the Ombudsman—

(1) to assist individuals and employers in resolving problems with the Bureau of Citizenship and Immigration Services;

(2) to identify areas in which individuals and employers have problems in dealing with the Bureau of Citizenship and Immigration Services; and

(3) to the extent possible, to propose changes in the administrative practices of the Bureau of Citizenship and Immigration Services to mitigate problems identified under paragraph (2).

(c) ANNUAL REPORTS.—

(1) OBJECTIVES.—Not later than June 30 of each calendar year, the Ombudsman shall report to the Committee on the Judiciary of the House of Representatives and the Senate on the objectives of the Office of the Ombudsman for the fiscal year beginning in such calendar year. Any such report shall contain full and substantive analysis, in addition to statistical information, and—

(A) shall identify the recommendations the Office of the Ombudsman has made on improving services and responsiveness of the Bureau of Citizenship and Immigration Services;

(B) shall contain a summary of the most pervasive and serious problems encountered by individuals and employers, including a description of the nature of such problems;

(C) shall contain an inventory of the items described in subparagraphs (A) and (B) for which action has been taken and the result of such action;

(D) shall contain an inventory of the items described in subparagraphs (A) and (B) for which action remains to be completed and the period during which each item has remained on such inventory;

(E) shall contain an inventory of the items described in subparagraphs (A) and (B) for which no action has been taken, the period during which each item has remained on such inventory, the reasons for the inaction, and shall identify any official of the Bureau of Citizenship and Immigration Services who is responsible for such inaction;

(F) shall contain recommendations for such administrative action as may be appropriate to resolve problems encountered by individuals and employers, including problems created by excessive backlogs in the adjudication and processing of immigration benefit petitions and applications; and

(G) shall include such other information as the Ombudsman may deem advisable.

(2) REPORT TO BE SUBMITTED DIRECTLY.—Each report required under this subsection shall be provided directly to the committees described in paragraph (1) without any prior comment or amendment from the Secretary, Deputy Secretary, Director of the Bureau of Citizenship and Immigration Services, or any other officer or employee of the Department or the Office of Management and Budget.

(d) OTHER RESPONSIBILITIES.—The Ombudsman—

(1) shall monitor the coverage and geographic allocation of local offices of the Ombudsman;

(2) shall develop guidance to be distributed to all officers and employees of the Bureau of Citizenship and Immigration Services outlining the criteria for referral of inquiries to local offices of the Ombudsman;

(3) shall ensure that the local telephone number for each local office of the Ombudsman is published and available to individuals and employers served by the office; and

(4) shall meet regularly with the Director of the Bureau of Citizenship and Immigration Services to identify serious service problems and to present recommendations for such administrative action as may be appropriate to resolve problems encountered by individuals and employers.

(e) PERSONNEL ACTIONS.—

(1) IN GENERAL.—The Ombudsman shall have the responsibility and authority—

(A) to appoint local ombudsmen and make available at least 1 such ombudsman for each State; and

(B) to evaluate and take personnel actions (including dismissal) with respect to any employee of any local office of the Ombudsman.

(2) CONSULTATION.—The Ombudsman may consult with the appropriate supervisory personnel of the Bureau of Citizenship and Immigration Services in carrying out the Ombudsman's responsibilities under this subsection.

(f) RESPONSIBILITIES OF BUREAU OF CITIZENSHIP AND IMMIGRATION SERVICES.—The Director of the Bureau of Citizenship and Immigration Services shall establish procedures requiring a formal response to all recommendations submitted to such director by the Ombudsman within 3 months after submission to such director.

(g) OPERATION OF LOCAL OFFICES.—

(1) IN GENERAL.—Each local ombudsman—

(A) shall report to the Ombudsman or the delegate thereof;

(B) may consult with the appropriate supervisory personnel of the Bureau of Citizenship and Immigration Services regarding the daily operation of the local office of such ombudsman;

(C) shall, at the initial meeting with any individual or employer seeking the assistance of such local office, notify such individual or employer that the local offices of the Ombudsman operate independently of any other component of the Department and report directly to Congress through the Ombudsman; and

(D) at the local ombudsman's discretion, may determine not to disclose to the Bureau of Citizenship and Immigration Services contact with, or information provided by, such individual or employer.

(2) MAINTENANCE OF INDEPENDENT COMMUNICATIONS.— Each local office of the Ombudsman shall maintain a phone, facsimile, and other means of electronic communication access, and a post office address, that is separate from those maintained by the Bureau of Citizenship and Immigration Services, or any component of the Bureau of Citizenship and Immigration Services.

SEC. 453. PROFESSIONAL RESPONSIBILITY AND QUALITY REVIEW.

(a) IN GENERAL.—The Director of the Bureau of Citizenship and Immigration Services shall be responsible for—

(1) conducting investigations of noncriminal allegations of misconduct, corruption, and fraud involving any employee of the Bureau of Citizenship and Immigration Services that are not subject to investigation by the Inspector General for the Department;

(2) inspecting the operations of the Bureau of Citizenship and Immigration Services and providing assessments of the quality of the operations of such bureau as a whole and each of its components; and

(3) providing an analysis of the management of the Bureau of Citizenship and Immigration Services.

(b) SPECIAL CONSIDERATIONS.—In providing assessments in accordance with subsection (a)(2) with respect to a decision of the Bureau of Citizenship and Immigration Services, or any of its components, consideration shall be given to—

(1) the accuracy of the findings of fact and conclusions of law used in rendering the decision;

(2) any fraud or misrepresentation associated with the decision; and

(3) the efficiency with which the decision was rendered.

SEC. 454. EMPLOYEE DISCIPLINE.

The Director of the Bureau of Citizenship and Immigration Services may, notwithstanding any other provision of law, impose disciplinary action, including termination of employment, pursuant to policies and procedures applicable to employees of the Federal Bureau of Investigation, on any employee of the Bureau of Citizenship and Immigration Services who willfully deceives Congress or agency leadership on any matter.

SEC. 455. EFFECTIVE DATE.

Notwithstanding section 4, sections 451 through 456, and the amendments made by such sections, shall take effect on the date on which the transfer of functions specified under section 441 takes effect.

SEC. 456. TRANSITION.

(a) REFERENCES.—With respect to any function transferred by this subtitle to, and exercised on or after the effective date specified in section 455 by, the Director of the Bureau of Citizenship and Immigration Services, any reference in any other Federal law, Executive order, rule, regulation, or delegation of authority, or any document of or pertaining to a component of government from which such function is transferred—

(1) to the head of such component is deemed to refer to the Director of the Bureau of Citizenship and Immigration Services; or

(2) to such component is deemed to refer to the Bureau of Citizenship and Immigration Services.

(b) OTHER TRANSITION ISSUES.—

(1) EXERCISE OF AUTHORITIES.—Except as otherwise provided by law, a Federal official to whom a function is transferred by this subtitle may, for purposes of performing the function, exercise all authorities under any other provision of law that were available with respect to the performance of that function to the official responsible for the performance of the function immediately before the effective date specified in section 455.

(2) TRANSFER AND ALLOCATION OF APPROPRIATIONS AND PERSONNEL.—The personnel of the Department of Justice employed in connection with the functions transferred by this subtitle (and functions that the Secretary determines are properly related to the functions of the Bureau of Citizenship and Immigration Services), and the assets, liabilities, contracts, property, records, and unexpended balance of appropriations, authorizations, allocations, and other funds employed, held, used, arising from, available to, or to be made available to, the Immigration and Naturalization Service in connection with the functions transferred by this subtitle, subject to section 202 of the Budget and Accounting Procedures Act of 1950, shall be transferred to the Director of the Bureau of Citizenship and Immigration Services for allocation to the appropriate component of the Department. Unexpended funds transferred

pursuant to this paragraph shall be used only for the purposes for which the funds were originally authorized and appropriated. The Secretary shall have the right to adjust or realign transfers of funds and personnel effected pursuant to this subtitle for a period of 2 years after the effective date specified in section 455.

SEC. 457. FUNDING FOR CITIZENSHIP AND IMMIGRATION SERVICES.

Section 286(m) of the Immigration and Nationality Act (8 U.S.C. 1356(m)) is amended by striking "services, including the costs of similar services provided without charge to asylum applicants or other immigrants." and inserting "services.".

SEC. 458. BACKLOG ELIMINATION.

Section 204(a)(1) of the Immigration Services and Infrastructure Improvements Act of 2000 (8 U.S.C. 1573(a)(1)) is amended by striking "not later than one year after the date of enactment of this Act;" and inserting "1 year after the date of the enactment of the Homeland Security Act of 2002;".

SEC. 459. REPORT ON IMPROVING IMMIGRATION SERVICES.

(a) IN GENERAL.—The Secretary, not later than 1 year after the effective date of this Act, shall submit to the Committees on the Judiciary and Appropriations of the House of Representatives and of the Senate a report with a plan detailing how the Bureau of Citizenship and Immigration Services, after the transfer of functions specified in this subtitle takes effect, will complete efficiently, fairly, and within a reasonable time, the adjudications described in paragraphs (1) through (5) of section 451(b).

(b) CONTENTS.—For each type of adjudication to be undertaken by the Director of the Bureau of Citizenship and Immigration Services, the report shall include the following:

(1) Any potential savings of resources that may be implemented without affecting the quality of the adjudication.

(2) The goal for processing time with respect to the application.

(3) Any statutory modifications with respect to the adjudication that the Secretary considers advisable.

(c) CONSULTATION.—In carrying out subsection (a), the Secretary shall consult with the Secretary of State, the Secretary of Labor, the Assistant Secretary of the Bureau of Border Security of the Department, and the Director of the Executive Office for Immigration Review to determine how to streamline and improve the process for applying for and making adjudications described in section 451(b) and related processes.

SEC. 460. REPORT ON RESPONDING TO FLUCTUATING NEEDS.

Not later than 30 days after the date of the enactment of this Act, the Attorney General shall submit to Congress a report on changes in law, including changes in authorizations of appropriations and in appropriations, that are needed to permit the Immigration and Naturalization Service, and, after the transfer of functions specified in this subtitle takes effect, the Bureau of Citizenship and Immigration Services of the Department, to ensure a prompt and timely response to emergent, unforeseen, or impending changes in the number of applications for immigration benefits, and otherwise to ensure the accommodation of changing immigration service needs.

SEC. 461. APPLICATION OF INTERNET-BASED TECHNOLOGIES.

(a) ESTABLISHMENT OF TRACKING SYSTEM.—The Secretary, not later than 1 year after the effective date of this Act, in consultation with the Technology Advisory Committee established under subsection (c), shall establish an Internet-based system, that will permit a person, employer, immigrant, or nonimmigrant who has filings with the Secretary for any benefit under the Immigration and Nationality Act (8 U.S.C. 1101 et seq.), access to online information about the processing status of the filing involved.

(b) FEASIBILITY STUDY FOR ONLINE FILING AND IMPROVED PROCESSING.—

(1) ONLINE FILING.—The Secretary, in consultation with the Technology Advisory Committee established under subsection (c), shall conduct a feasibility study on the online filing of the filings described in subsection (a). The study shall include a review of computerization and technology of the Immigration and Naturalization Service relating to the immigration services and processing of filings related to immigrant services. The study shall also include an estimate of the timeframe and cost and shall consider other factors in implementing such a filing system, including the feasibility of fee payment online.

(2) REPORT.—A report on the study under this subsection shall be submitted to the Committees on the Judiciary of the House of Representatives and the Senate not later than 1 year after the effective date of this Act.

(c) TECHNOLOGY ADVISORY COMMITTEE.—

(1) ESTABLISHMENT.—The Secretary shall establish, not later than 60 days after the effective date of this Act, an advisory committee (in this section referred to as the "Technology Advisory Committee") to assist the Secretary in—

(A) establishing the tracking system under subsection (a); and

(B) conducting the study under subsection (b).

The Technology Advisory Committee shall be established after consultation with the Committees on the Judiciary of the House of Representatives and the Senate.

(2) COMPOSITION.—The Technology Advisory Committee shall be composed of representatives from high technology companies capable of establishing and implementing the system in an expeditious manner, and representatives of persons who may use the tracking system described in subsection (a) and the online filing system described in subsection (b)(1).

SEC. 462. CHILDREN'S AFFAIRS.

(a) TRANSFER OF FUNCTIONS.—There are transferred to the Director of the Office of Refugee Resettlement of the Department of Health and Human Services functions under the immigration laws of the United States with respect to the care of unaccompanied alien children that were vested by statute in, or performed by, the Commissioner of Immigration and Naturalization (or any officer, employee, or component of the Immigration and Naturalization Service) immediately before the effective date specified in subsection (d).

(b) FUNCTIONS.—

(1) IN GENERAL.—Pursuant to the transfer made by subsection (a), the Director of the Office of Refugee Resettlement shall be responsible for—

(A) coordinating and implementing the care and placement of unaccompanied alien children who are in Federal custody by reason of their immigration status, including developing a plan to be submitted to Congress on how to ensure that qualified and independent legal counsel is timely appointed to represent the interests of each such child, consistent with the law regarding appointment of counsel that is in effect on the date of the enactment of this Act;

(B) ensuring that the interests of the child are considered in decisions and actions relating to the care and custody of an unaccompanied alien child;

(C) making placement determinations for all unaccompanied alien children who are in Federal custody by reason of their immigration status;

(D) implementing the placement determinations;

(E) implementing policies with respect to the care and placement of unaccompanied alien children;

(F) identifying a sufficient number of qualified individuals, entities, and facilities to house unaccompanied alien children;

(G) overseeing the infrastructure and personnel of facilities in which unaccompanied alien children reside;

(H) reuniting unaccompanied alien children with a parent abroad in appropriate cases;

(I) compiling, updating, and publishing at least annually a state-by-state list of professionals or other entities qualified to provide guardian and attorney representation services for unaccompanied alien children;

(J) maintaining statistical information and other data on unaccompanied alien children for whose care and placement the Director is responsible, which shall include—

(i) biographical information, such as a child's name, gender, date of birth, country of birth, and country of habitual residence;

(ii) the date on which the child came into Federal custody by reason of his or her immigration status;

(iii) information relating to the child's placement, removal, or release from each facility in which the child has resided;

(iv) in any case in which the child is placed in detention or released, an explanation relating to the detention or release; and

(v) the disposition of any actions in which the child is the subject;

(K) collecting and compiling statistical information from the Department of Justice, the Department of Homeland Security, and the Department of State on each department's actions relating to unaccompanied alien children; and

(L) conducting investigations and inspections of facilities and other entities in which unaccompanied alien children reside.

(2) COORDINATION WITH OTHER ENTITIES; NO RELEASE ON OWN RECOGNIZANCE.—In making determinations described in paragraph (1)(C), the Director of the Office of Refugee Resettlement—

(A) shall consult with appropriate juvenile justice professionals, the Director of the Bureau of Citizenship and Immigration Services, and the Assistant Secretary of the Bureau of Border Security to ensure that such determinations ensure that unaccompanied alien children described in such subparagraph—

(i) are likely to appear for all hearings or proceedings in which they are involved;

(ii) are protected from smugglers, traffickers, or others who might seek to victimize or otherwise engage them in criminal, harmful, or exploitive activity; and

(iii) are placed in a setting in which they are not likely to pose a danger to themselves or others; and

(B) shall not release such children upon their own recognizance.

(3) DUTIES WITH RESPECT TO FOSTER CARE.—In carrying out the duties described in paragraph (1)(G), the Director of the Office of Refugee Resettlement is encouraged to use the refugee children foster care system established pursuant to section 412(d) of the Immigration and Nationality Act (8 U.S.C. 1522(d)) for the placement of unaccompanied alien children.

(c) RULE OF CONSTRUCTION.—Nothing in this section may be construed to transfer the responsibility for adjudicating benefit determinations under the Immigration and Nationality Act (8 U.S.C. 1101 et seq.) from the authority of any official of the Department of Justice, the Department of Homeland Security, or the Department of State.

(d) EFFECTIVE DATE.—Notwithstanding section 4, this section shall take effect on the date on which the transfer of functions specified under section 441 takes effect.

(e) REFERENCES.—With respect to any function transferred by this section, any reference in any other Federal law, Executive order, rule, regulation, or delegation of authority, or any document of or pertaining to a component of government from which such function is transferred—

(1) to the head of such component is deemed to refer to the Director of the Office of Refugee Resettlement; or

(2) to such component is deemed to refer to the Office of Refugee Resettlement of the Department of Health and Human Services.

(f) OTHER TRANSITION ISSUES.—

(1) EXERCISE OF AUTHORITIES.—Except as otherwise provided by law, a Federal official to whom a function is transferred by this section may, for purposes of performing the function, exercise all authorities under any other provision of law that were available with respect to the performance of that function to the official responsible for the performance of the function immediately before the effective date specified in subsection (d).

(2) SAVINGS PROVISIONS.—Subsections (a), (b), and (c) of section 1512 shall apply to a transfer of functions under this section in the same manner as such provisions apply to a transfer of functions under this Act to the Department of Homeland Security.

(3) TRANSFER AND ALLOCATION OF APPROPRIATIONS AND PERSONNEL.—The personnel of the Department of Justice employed

in connection with the functions transferred by this section, and the assets, liabilities, contracts, property, records, and unexpended balance of appropriations, authorizations, allocations, and other funds employed, held, used, arising from, available to, or to be made available to, the Immigration and Naturalization Service in connection with the functions transferred by this section, subject to section 202 of the Budget and Accounting Procedures Act of 1950, shall be transferred to the Director of the Office of Refugee Resettlement for allocation to the appropriate component of the Department of Health and Human Services. Unexpended funds transferred pursuant to this paragraph shall be used only for the purposes for which the funds were originally authorized and appropriated.

(g) DEFINITIONS.—As used in this section—

(1) the term "placement" means the placement of an unaccompanied alien child in either a detention facility or an alternative to such a facility; and

(2) the term "unaccompanied alien child" means a child who—

(A) has no lawful immigration status in the United States;

(B) has not attained 18 years of age; and

(C) with respect to whom—

(i) there is no parent or legal guardian in the United States; or

(ii) no parent or legal guardian in the United States is available to provide care and physical custody.

Subtitle F—General Immigration Provisions

SEC. 471. ABOLISHMENT OF INS.

(a) IN GENERAL.—Upon completion of all transfers from the Immigration and Naturalization Service as provided for by this Act, the Immigration and Naturalization Service of the Department of Justice is abolished.

(b) PROHIBITION.—The authority provided by section 1502 may be used to reorganize functions or organizational units within the Bureau of Border Security or the Bureau of Citizenship and Immigration Services, but may not be used to recombine the two bureaus into a single agency or otherwise to combine, join, or consolidate functions or organizational units of the two bureaus with each other.

SEC. 472. VOLUNTARY SEPARATION INCENTIVE PAYMENTS.

(a) DEFINITIONS.—For purposes of this section—

(1) the term "employee" means an employee (as defined by section 2105 of title 5, United States Code) who—

(A) has completed at least 3 years of current continuous service with 1 or more covered entities; and

(B) is serving under an appointment without time limitation,

but does not include any person under subparagraphs (A)–(G) of section 663(a)(2) of Public Law 104–208 (5 U.S.C. 5597 note);

(2) the term "covered entity" means—

(A) the Immigration and Naturalization Service;

(B) the Bureau of Border Security of the Department of Homeland Security; and

(C) the Bureau of Citizenship and Immigration Services of the Department of Homeland Security; and

(3) the term "transfer date" means the date on which the transfer of functions specified under section 441 takes effect.

(b) STRATEGIC RESTRUCTURING PLAN.—Before the Attorney General or the Secretary obligates any resources for voluntary separation incentive payments under this section, such official shall submit to the appropriate committees of Congress a strategic restructuring plan, which shall include—

(1) an organizational chart depicting the covered entities after their restructuring pursuant to this Act;

(2) a summary description of how the authority under this section will be used to help carry out that restructuring; and

(3) the information specified in section 663(b)(2) of Public Law 104–208 (5 U.S.C. 5597 note).

As used in the preceding sentence, the "appropriate committees of Congress" are the Committees on Appropriations, Government Reform, and the Judiciary of the House of Representatives, and the Committees on Appropriations, Governmental Affairs, and the Judiciary of the Senate.

(c) AUTHORITY.—The Attorney General and the Secretary may, to the extent necessary to help carry out their respective strategic restructuring plan described in subsection (b), make voluntary separation incentive payments to employees. Any such payment—

(1) shall be paid to the employee, in a lump sum, after the employee has separated from service;

(2) shall be paid from appropriations or funds available for the payment of basic pay of the employee;

(3) shall be equal to the lesser of—

(A) the amount the employee would be entitled to receive under section 5595(c) of title 5, United States Code; or

(B) an amount not to exceed $25,000, as determined by the Attorney General or the Secretary;

(4) may not be made except in the case of any qualifying employee who voluntarily separates (whether by retirement or resignation) before the end of—

(A) the 3-month period beginning on the date on which such payment is offered or made available to such employee; or

(B) the 3-year period beginning on the date of the enactment of this Act,

whichever occurs first;

(5) shall not be a basis for payment, and shall not be included in the computation, of any other type of Government benefit; and

(6) shall not be taken into account in determining the amount of any severance pay to which the employee may be entitled under section 5595 of title 5, United States Code, based on any other separation.

(d) ADDITIONAL AGENCY CONTRIBUTIONS TO THE RETIREMENT FUND.—

(1) IN GENERAL.—In addition to any payments which it is otherwise required to make, the Department of Justice and the Department of Homeland Security shall, for each fiscal year with respect to which it makes any voluntary separation incentive payments under this section, remit to the Office of Personnel Management for deposit in the Treasury of the United States to the credit of the Civil Service Retirement and Disability Fund the amount required under paragraph (2).

(2) AMOUNT REQUIRED.—The amount required under this paragraph shall, for any fiscal year, be the amount under subparagraph (A) or (B), whichever is greater.

(A) FIRST METHOD.—The amount under this subparagraph shall, for any fiscal year, be equal to the minimum amount necessary to offset the additional costs to the retirement systems under title 5, United States Code (payable out of the Civil Service Retirement and Disability Fund) resulting from the voluntary separation of the employees described in paragraph (3), as determined under regulations of the Office of Personnel Management.

(B) SECOND METHOD.—The amount under this subparagraph shall, for any fiscal year, be equal to 45 percent of the sum total of the final basic pay of the employees described in paragraph (3).

(3) COMPUTATIONS TO BE BASED ON SEPARATIONS OCCURRING IN THE FISCAL YEAR INVOLVED.—The employees described in this paragraph are those employees who receive a voluntary separation incentive payment under this section based on their separating from service during the fiscal year with respect to which the payment under this subsection relates.

(4) FINAL BASIC PAY DEFINED.—In this subsection, the term "final basic pay" means, with respect to an employee, the total amount of basic pay which would be payable for a year of service by such employee, computed using the employee's final rate of basic pay, and, if last serving on other than a full-time basis, with appropriate adjustment therefor.

(e) EFFECT OF SUBSEQUENT EMPLOYMENT WITH THE GOVERNMENT.—An individual who receives a voluntary separation incentive payment under this section and who, within 5 years after the date of the separation on which the payment is based, accepts any compensated employment with the Government or works for any agency of the Government through a personal services contract, shall be required to pay, prior to the individual's first day of employment, the entire amount of the incentive payment. Such payment shall be made to the covered entity from which the individual separated or, if made on or after the transfer date, to the Deputy Secretary or the Under Secretary for Border and Transportation Security (for transfer to the appropriate component of the Department of Homeland Security, if necessary).

(f) EFFECT ON EMPLOYMENT LEVELS.—

(1) INTENDED EFFECT.—Voluntary separations under this section are not intended to necessarily reduce the total number of full-time equivalent positions in any covered entity.

(2) USE OF VOLUNTARY SEPARATIONS.—A covered entity may redeploy or use the full-time equivalent positions vacated by

voluntary separations under this section to make other positions available to more critical locations or more critical occupations.

SEC. 473. AUTHORITY TO CONDUCT A DEMONSTRATION PROJECT RELATING TO DISCIPLINARY ACTION.

(a) IN GENERAL.—The Attorney General and the Secretary may each, during a period ending not later than 5 years after the date of the enactment of this Act, conduct a demonstration project for the purpose of determining whether one or more changes in the policies or procedures relating to methods for disciplining employees would result in improved personnel management.

(b) SCOPE.—A demonstration project under this section—

(1) may not cover any employees apart from those employed in or under a covered entity; and

(2) shall not be limited by any provision of chapter 43, 75, or 77 of title 5, United States Code.

(c) PROCEDURES.—Under the demonstration project—

(1) the use of alternative means of dispute resolution (as defined in section 571 of title 5, United States Code) shall be encouraged, whenever appropriate; and

(2) each covered entity under the jurisdiction of the official conducting the project shall be required to provide for the expeditious, fair, and independent review of any action to which section 4303 or subchapter II of chapter 75 of such title 5 would otherwise apply (except an action described in section 7512(5) of such title 5).

(d) ACTIONS INVOLVING DISCRIMINATION.—Notwithstanding any other provision of this section, if, in the case of any matter described in section 7702(a)(1)(B) of title 5, United States Code, there is no judicially reviewable action under the demonstration project within 120 days after the filing of an appeal or other formal request for review (referred to in subsection (c)(2)), an employee shall be entitled to file a civil action to the same extent and in the same manner as provided in section 7702(e)(1) of such title 5 (in the matter following subparagraph (C) thereof).

(e) CERTAIN EMPLOYEES.—Employees shall not be included within any project under this section if such employees are—

(1) neither managers nor supervisors; and

(2) within a unit with respect to which a labor organization is accorded exclusive recognition under chapter 71 of title 5, United States Code.

Notwithstanding the preceding sentence, an aggrieved employee within a unit (referred to in paragraph (2)) may elect to participate in a complaint procedure developed under the demonstration project in lieu of any negotiated grievance procedure and any statutory procedure (as such term is used in section 7121 of such title 5).

(f) REPORTS.—The General Accounting Office shall prepare and submit to the Committees on Government Reform and the Judiciary of the House of Representatives and the Committees on Governmental Affairs and the Judiciary of the Senate periodic reports on any demonstration project conducted under this section, such reports to be submitted after the second and fourth years of its operation. Upon request, the Attorney General or the Secretary shall furnish such information as the General Accounting Office may require to carry out this subsection.

(g) DEFINITION.—In this section, the term "covered entity" has the meaning given such term in section 472(a)(2).

SEC. 474. SENSE OF CONGRESS.

It is the sense of Congress that—

(1) the missions of the Bureau of Border Security and the Bureau of Citizenship and Immigration Services are equally important and, accordingly, they each should be adequately funded; and

(2) the functions transferred under this subtitle should not, after such transfers take effect, operate at levels below those in effect prior to the enactment of this Act.

SEC. 475. DIRECTOR OF SHARED SERVICES.

(a) IN GENERAL.—Within the Office of Deputy Secretary, there shall be a Director of Shared Services.

(b) FUNCTIONS.—The Director of Shared Services shall be responsible for the coordination of resources for the Bureau of Border Security and the Bureau of Citizenship and Immigration Services, including—

(1) information resources management, including computer databases and information technology;

(2) records and file management; and

(3) forms management.

SEC. 476. SEPARATION OF FUNDING.

(a) IN GENERAL.—There shall be established separate accounts in the Treasury of the United States for appropriated funds and other deposits available for the Bureau of Citizenship and Immigration Services and the Bureau of Border Security.

(b) SEPARATE BUDGETS.—To ensure that the Bureau of Citizenship and Immigration Services and the Bureau of Border Security are funded to the extent necessary to fully carry out their respective functions, the Director of the Office of Management and Budget shall separate the budget requests for each such entity.

(c) FEES.—Fees imposed for a particular service, application, or benefit shall be deposited into the account established under subsection (a) that is for the bureau with jurisdiction over the function to which the fee relates.

(d) FEES NOT TRANSFERABLE.—No fee may be transferred between the Bureau of Citizenship and Immigration Services and the Bureau of Border Security for purposes not authorized by section 286 of the Immigration and Nationality Act (8 U.S.C. 1356).

SEC. 477. REPORTS AND IMPLEMENTATION PLANS.

(a) DIVISION OF FUNDS.—The Secretary, not later than 120 days after the effective date of this Act, shall submit to the Committees on Appropriations and the Judiciary of the House of Representatives and of the Senate a report on the proposed division and transfer of funds, including unexpended funds, appropriations, and fees, between the Bureau of Citizenship and Immigration Services and the Bureau of Border Security.

(b) DIVISION OF PERSONNEL.—The Secretary, not later than 120 days after the effective date of this Act, shall submit to the Committees on Appropriations and the Judiciary of the House of Representatives and of the Senate a report on the proposed division of personnel between the Bureau of Citizenship and Immigration Services and the Bureau of Border Security.

(c) IMPLEMENTATION PLAN.—

(1) IN GENERAL.—The Secretary, not later than 120 days after the effective date of this Act, and every 6 months thereafter until the termination of fiscal year 2005, shall submit to the Committees on Appropriations and the Judiciary of the House of Representatives and of the Senate an implementation plan to carry out this Act.

(2) CONTENTS.—The implementation plan should include details concerning the separation of the Bureau of Citizenship and Immigration Services and the Bureau of Border Security, including the following:

(A) Organizational structure, including the field structure.

(B) Chain of command.

(C) Procedures for interaction among such bureaus.

(D) Fraud detection and investigation.

(E) The processing and handling of removal proceedings, including expedited removal and applications for relief from removal.

(F) Recommendations for conforming amendments to the Immigration and Nationality Act (8 U.S.C. 1101 et seq.).

(G) Establishment of a transition team.

(H) Methods to phase in the costs of separating the administrative support systems of the Immigration and Naturalization Service in order to provide for separate administrative support systems for the Bureau of Citizenship and Immigration Services and the Bureau of Border Security.

(d) COMPTROLLER GENERAL STUDIES AND REPORTS.—

(1) STATUS REPORTS ON TRANSITION.—Not later than 18 months after the date on which the transfer of functions specified under section 441 takes effect, and every 6 months thereafter, until full implementation of this subtitle has been completed, the Comptroller General of the United States shall submit to the Committees on Appropriations and on the Judiciary of the House of Representatives and the Senate a report containing the following:

(A) A determination of whether the transfers of functions made by subtitles D and E have been completed, and if a transfer of functions has not taken place, identifying the reasons why the transfer has not taken place.

(B) If the transfers of functions made by subtitles D and E have been completed, an identification of any issues that have arisen due to the completed transfers.

(C) An identification of any issues that may arise due to any future transfer of functions.

(2) REPORT ON MANAGEMENT.—Not later than 4 years after the date on which the transfer of functions specified under section 441 takes effect, the Comptroller General of the United States shall submit to the Committees on Appropriations and on the Judiciary of the House of Representatives and the Senate a report, following a study, containing the following:

(A) Determinations of whether the transfer of functions from the Immigration and Naturalization Service to the Bureau of Citizenship and Immigration Services and the

Bureau of Border Security have improved, with respect to each function transferred, the following:

(i) Operations.

(ii) Management, including accountability and communication.

(iii) Financial administration.

(iv) Recordkeeping, including information management and technology.

(B) A statement of the reasons for the determinations under subparagraph (A).

(C) Any recommendations for further improvements to the Bureau of Citizenship and Immigration Services and the Bureau of Border Security.

(3) REPORT ON FEES.—Not later than 1 year after the date of the enactment of this Act, the Comptroller General of the United States shall submit to the Committees on the Judiciary of the House of Representatives and of the Senate a report examining whether the Bureau of Citizenship and Immigration Services is likely to derive sufficient funds from fees to carry out its functions in the absence of appropriated funds.

SEC. 478. IMMIGRATION FUNCTIONS.

(a) ANNUAL REPORT.—

(1) IN GENERAL.—One year after the date of the enactment of this Act, and each year thereafter, the Secretary shall submit a report to the President, to the Committees on the Judiciary and Government Reform of the House of Representatives, and to the Committees on the Judiciary and Government Affairs of the Senate, on the impact the transfers made by this subtitle has had on immigration functions.

(2) MATTER INCLUDED.—The report shall address the following with respect to the period covered by the report:

(A) The aggregate number of all immigration applications and petitions received, and processed, by the Department.

(B) Region-by-region statistics on the aggregate number of immigration applications and petitions filed by an alien (or filed on behalf of an alien) and denied, disaggregated by category of denial and application or petition type.

(C) The quantity of backlogged immigration applications and petitions that have been processed, the aggregate number awaiting processing, and a detailed plan for eliminating the backlog.

(D) The average processing period for immigration applications and petitions, disaggregated by application or petition type.

(E) The number and types of immigration-related grievances filed with any official of the Department of Justice, and if those grievances were resolved.

(F) Plans to address grievances and improve immigration services.

(G) Whether immigration-related fees were used consistent with legal requirements regarding such use.

(H) Whether immigration-related questions conveyed by customers to the Department (whether conveyed in person, by telephone, or by means of the Internet) were answered effectively and efficiently.

(b) SENSE OF CONGRESS REGARDING IMMIGRATION SERVICES.— It is the sense of Congress that—

(1) the quality and efficiency of immigration services rendered by the Federal Government should be improved after the transfers made by this subtitle take effect; and

(2) the Secretary should undertake efforts to guarantee that concerns regarding the quality and efficiency of immigration services are addressed after such effective date.

TITLE V—EMERGENCY PREPAREDNESS AND RESPONSE

SEC. 501. UNDER SECRETARY FOR EMERGENCY PREPAREDNESS AND RESPONSE.

There shall be in the Department a Directorate of Emergency Preparedness and Response headed by an Under Secretary for Emergency Preparedness and Response.

SEC. 502. RESPONSIBILITIES.

The Secretary, acting through the Under Secretary for Emergency Preparedness and Response, shall include—

(1) helping to ensure the effectiveness of emergency response providers to terrorist attacks, major disasters, and other emergencies;

(2) with respect to the Nuclear Incident Response Team (regardless of whether it is operating as an organizational unit of the Department pursuant to this title)—

(A) establishing standards and certifying when those standards have been met;

(B) conducting joint and other exercises and training and evaluating performance; and

(C) providing funds to the Department of Energy and the Environmental Protection Agency, as appropriate, for homeland security planning, exercises and training, and equipment;

(3) providing the Federal Government's response to terrorist attacks and major disasters, including—

(A) managing such response;

(B) directing the Domestic Emergency Support Team, the Strategic National Stockpile, the National Disaster Medical System, and (when operating as an organizational unit of the Department pursuant to this title) the Nuclear Incident Response Team;

(C) overseeing the Metropolitan Medical Response System; and

(D) coordinating other Federal response resources in the event of a terrorist attack or major disaster;

(4) aiding the recovery from terrorist attacks and major disasters;

(5) building a comprehensive national incident management system with Federal, State, and local government personnel,

agencies, and authorities, to respond to such attacks and disasters;

(6) consolidating existing Federal Government emergency response plans into a single, coordinated national response plan; and

(7) developing comprehensive programs for developing interoperative communications technology, and helping to ensure that emergency response providers acquire such technology.

SEC. 503. FUNCTIONS TRANSFERRED.

In accordance with title XV, there shall be transferred to the Secretary the functions, personnel, assets, and liabilities of the following entities:

(1) The Federal Emergency Management Agency, including the functions of the Director of the Federal Emergency Management Agency relating thereto.

(2) The Integrated Hazard Information System of the National Oceanic and Atmospheric Administration, which shall be renamed "FIRESAT".

(3) The National Domestic Preparedness Office of the Federal Bureau of Investigation, including the functions of the Attorney General relating thereto.

(4) The Domestic Emergency Support Teams of the Department of Justice, including the functions of the Attorney General relating thereto.

(5) The Office of Emergency Preparedness, the National Disaster Medical System, and the Metropolitan Medical Response System of the Department of Health and Human Services, including the functions of the Secretary of Health and Human Services and the Assistant Secretary for Public Health Emergency Preparedness relating thereto.

(6) The Strategic National Stockpile of the Department of Health and Human Services, including the functions of the Secretary of Health and Human Services relating thereto.

SEC. 504. NUCLEAR INCIDENT RESPONSE.

(a) IN GENERAL.—At the direction of the Secretary (in connection with an actual or threatened terrorist attack, major disaster, or other emergency in the United States), the Nuclear Incident Response Team shall operate as an organizational unit of the Department. While so operating, the Nuclear Incident Response Team shall be subject to the direction, authority, and control of the Secretary.

(b) RULE OF CONSTRUCTION.—Nothing in this title shall be construed to limit the ordinary responsibility of the Secretary of Energy and the Administrator of the Environmental Protection Agency for organizing, training, equipping, and utilizing their respective entities in the Nuclear Incident Response Team, or (subject to the provisions of this title) from exercising direction, authority, and control over them when they are not operating as a unit of the Department.

SEC. 505. CONDUCT OF CERTAIN PUBLIC HEALTH-RELATED ACTIVITIES.

(a) IN GENERAL.—With respect to all public health-related activities to improve State, local, and hospital preparedness and response to chemical, biological, radiological, and nuclear and other emerging terrorist threats carried out by the Department of Health and Human Services (including the Public Health Service), the Secretary of Health and Human Services shall set priorities and preparedness goals and further develop a coordinated strategy for such activities in collaboration with the Secretary.

(b) EVALUATION OF PROGRESS.—In carrying out subsection (a), the Secretary of Health and Human Services shall collaborate with the Secretary in developing specific benchmarks and outcome measurements for evaluating progress toward achieving the priorities and goals described in such subsection.

SEC. 506. DEFINITION.

In this title, the term "Nuclear Incident Response Team" means a resource that includes—

(1) those entities of the Department of Energy that perform nuclear or radiological emergency support functions (including accident response, search response, advisory, and technical operations functions), radiation exposure functions at the medical assistance facility known as the Radiation Emergency Assistance Center/Training Site (REAC/TS), radiological assistance functions, and related functions; and

(2) those entities of the Environmental Protection Agency that perform such support functions (including radiological emergency response functions) and related functions.

SEC. 507. ROLE OF FEDERAL EMERGENCY MANAGEMENT AGENCY.

(a) IN GENERAL.—The functions of the Federal Emergency Management Agency include the following:

(1) All functions and authorities prescribed by the Robert T. Stafford Disaster Relief and Emergency Assistance Act (42 U.S.C. 5121 et seq.).

(2) Carrying out its mission to reduce the loss of life and property and protect the Nation from all hazards by leading and supporting the Nation in a comprehensive, risk-based emergency management program—

(A) of mitigation, by taking sustained actions to reduce or eliminate long-term risk to people and property from hazards and their effects;

(B) of planning for building the emergency management profession to prepare effectively for, mitigate against, respond to, and recover from any hazard;

(C) of response, by conducting emergency operations to save lives and property through positioning emergency equipment and supplies, through evacuating potential victims, through providing food, water, shelter, and medical care to those in need, and through restoring critical public services;

(D) of recovery, by rebuilding communities so individuals, businesses, and governments can function on their own, return to normal life, and protect against future hazards; and

(E) of increased efficiencies, by coordinating efforts relating to mitigation, planning, response, and recovery.

(b) FEDERAL RESPONSE PLAN.—

(1) ROLE OF FEMA.—Notwithstanding any other provision of this Act, the Federal Emergency Management Agency shall

remain the lead agency for the Federal Response Plan established under Executive Order No. 12148 (44 Fed. Reg. 43239) and Executive Order No. 12656 (53 Fed. Reg. 47491).

(2) REVISION OF RESPONSE PLAN.—Not later than 60 days after the date of enactment of this Act, the Director of the Federal Emergency Management Agency shall revise the Federal Response Plan to reflect the establishment of and incorporate the Department.

SEC. 508. USE OF NATIONAL PRIVATE SECTOR NETWORKS IN EMERGENCY RESPONSE.

To the maximum extent practicable, the Secretary shall use national private sector networks and infrastructure for emergency response to chemical, biological, radiological, nuclear, or explosive disasters, and other major disasters.

SEC. 509. USE OF COMMERCIALLY AVAILABLE TECHNOLOGY, GOODS, AND SERVICES.

It is the sense of Congress that—

(1) the Secretary should, to the maximum extent possible, use off-the-shelf commercially developed technologies to ensure that the Department's information technology systems allow the Department to collect, manage, share, analyze, and disseminate information securely over multiple channels of communication; and

(2) in order to further the policy of the United States to avoid competing commercially with the private sector, the Secretary should rely on commercial sources to supply the goods and services needed by the Department.

TITLE VI—TREATMENT OF CHARITABLE TRUSTS FOR MEMBERS OF THE ARMED FORCES OF THE UNITED STATES AND OTHER GOVERNMENTAL ORGANIZATIONS

SEC. 601. TREATMENT OF CHARITABLE TRUSTS FOR MEMBERS OF THE ARMED FORCES OF THE UNITED STATES AND OTHER GOVERNMENTAL ORGANIZATIONS.

(a) FINDINGS.—Congress finds the following:

(1) Members of the Armed Forces of the United States defend the freedom and security of our Nation.

(2) Members of the Armed Forces of the United States have lost their lives while battling the evils of terrorism around the world.

(3) Personnel of the Central Intelligence Agency (CIA) charged with the responsibility of covert observation of terrorists around the world are often put in harm's way during their service to the United States.

(4) Personnel of the Central Intelligence Agency have also lost their lives while battling the evils of terrorism around the world.

(5) Employees of the Federal Bureau of Investigation (FBI) and other Federal agencies charged with domestic protection

of the United States put their lives at risk on a daily basis for the freedom and security of our Nation.

(6) United States military personnel, CIA personnel, FBI personnel, and other Federal agents in the service of the United States are patriots of the highest order.

(7) CIA officer Johnny Micheal Spann became the first American to give his life for his country in the War on Terrorism declared by President George W. Bush following the terrorist attacks of September 11, 2001.

(8) Johnny Micheal Spann left behind a wife and children who are very proud of the heroic actions of their patriot father.

(9) Surviving dependents of members of the Armed Forces of the United States who lose their lives as a result of terrorist attacks or military operations abroad receive a $6,000 death benefit, plus a small monthly benefit.

(10) The current system of compensating spouses and children of American patriots is inequitable and needs improvement.

(b) DESIGNATION OF JOHNNY MICHEAL SPANN PATRIOT TRUSTS.—Any charitable corporation, fund, foundation, or trust (or separate fund or account thereof) which otherwise meets all applicable requirements under law with respect to charitable entities and meets the requirements described in subsection (c) shall be eligible to characterize itself as a "Johnny Micheal Spann Patriot Trust".

(c) REQUIREMENTS FOR THE DESIGNATION OF JOHNNY MICHEAL SPANN PATRIOT TRUSTS.—The requirements described in this subsection are as follows:

(1) Not taking into account funds or donations reasonably necessary to establish a trust, at least 85 percent of all funds or donations (including any earnings on the investment of such funds or donations) received or collected by any Johnny Micheal Spann Patriot Trust must be distributed to (or, if placed in a private foundation, held in trust for) surviving spouses, children, or dependent parents, grandparents, or siblings of 1 or more of the following:

(A) members of the Armed Forces of the United States;

(B) personnel, including contractors, of elements of the intelligence community, as defined in section 3(4) of the National Security Act of 1947;

(C) employees of the Federal Bureau of Investigation; and

(D) officers, employees, or contract employees of the United States Government,

whose deaths occur in the line of duty and arise out of terrorist attacks, military operations, intelligence operations, or law enforcement operations or accidents connected with activities occurring after September 11, 2001, and related to domestic or foreign efforts to curb international terrorism, including the Authorization for Use of Military Force (Public Law 107–40; 115 Stat. 224).

(2) Other than funds or donations reasonably necessary to establish a trust, not more than 15 percent of all funds or donations (or 15 percent of annual earnings on funds invested in a private foundation) may be used for administrative purposes.

(3) No part of the net earnings of any Johnny Micheal Spann Patriot Trust may inure to the benefit of any individual based solely on the position of such individual as a shareholder, an officer or employee of such Trust.

(4) None of the activities of any Johnny Micheal Spann Patriot Trust shall be conducted in a manner inconsistent with any law that prohibits attempting to influence legislation.

(5) No Johnny Micheal Spann Patriot Trust may participate in or intervene in any political campaign on behalf of (or in opposition to) any candidate for public office, including by publication or distribution of statements.

(6) Each Johnny Micheal Spann Patriot Trust shall comply with the instructions and directions of the Director of Central Intelligence, the Attorney General, or the Secretary of Defense relating to the protection of intelligence sources and methods, sensitive law enforcement information, or other sensitive national security information, including methods for confidentially disbursing funds.

(7) Each Johnny Micheal Spann Patriot Trust that receives annual contributions totaling more than $1,000,000 must be audited annually by an independent certified public accounting firm. Such audits shall be filed with the Internal Revenue Service, and shall be open to public inspection, except that the conduct, filing, and availability of the audit shall be consistent with the protection of intelligence sources and methods, of sensitive law enforcement information, and of other sensitive national security information.

(8) Each Johnny Micheal Spann Patriot Trust shall make distributions to beneficiaries described in paragraph (1) at least once every calendar year, beginning not later than 12 months after the formation of such Trust, and all funds and donations received and earnings not placed in a private foundation dedicated to such beneficiaries must be distributed within 36 months after the end of the fiscal year in which such funds, donations, and earnings are received.

(9)(A) When determining the amount of a distribution to any beneficiary described in paragraph (1), a Johnny Micheal Spann Patriot Trust should take into account the amount of any collateral source compensation that the beneficiary has received or is entitled to receive as a result of the death of an individual described in paragraph (1).

(B) Collateral source compensation includes all compensation from collateral sources, including life insurance, pension funds, death benefit programs, and payments by Federal, State, or local governments related to the death of an individual described in paragraph (1).

(d) TREATMENT OF JOHNNY MICHEAL SPANN PATRIOT TRUSTS.— Each Johnny Micheal Spann Patriot Trust shall refrain from conducting the activities described in clauses (i) and (ii) of section 301(20)(A) of the Federal Election Campaign Act of 1971 so that a general solicitation of funds by an individual described in paragraph (1) of section 323(e) of such Act will be permissible if such solicitation meets the requirements of paragraph (4)(A) of such section.

(e) NOTIFICATION OF TRUST BENEFICIARIES.—Notwithstanding any other provision of law, and in a manner consistent with the protection of intelligence sources and methods and sensitive law enforcement information, and other sensitive national security information, the Secretary of Defense, the Director of the Federal Bureau of Investigation, or the Director of Central Intelligence, or their designees, as applicable, may forward information received from an executor, administrator, or other legal representative of the estate of a decedent described in subparagraph (A), (B), (C), or (D) of subsection (c)(1), to a Johnny Micheal Spann Patriot Trust on how to contact individuals eligible for a distribution under subsection (c)(1) for the purpose of providing assistance from such Trust: *Provided*, That, neither forwarding nor failing to forward any information under this subsection shall create any cause of action against any Federal department, agency, officer, agent, or employee.

(f) REGULATIONS.—Not later than 90 days after the date of enactment of this Act, the Secretary of Defense, in coordination with the Attorney General, the Director of the Federal Bureau of Investigation, and the Director of Central Intelligence, shall prescribe regulations to carry out this section.

TITLE VII—MANAGEMENT

SEC. 701. UNDER SECRETARY FOR MANAGEMENT.

(a) IN GENERAL.—The Secretary, acting through the Under Secretary for Management, shall be responsible for the management and administration of the Department, including the following:

(1) The budget, appropriations, expenditures of funds, accounting, and finance.

(2) Procurement.

(3) Human resources and personnel.

(4) Information technology and communications systems.

(5) Facilities, property, equipment, and other material resources.

(6) Security for personnel, information technology and communications systems, facilities, property, equipment, and other material resources.

(7) Identification and tracking of performance measures relating to the responsibilities of the Department.

(8) Grants and other assistance management programs.

(9) The transition and reorganization process, to ensure an efficient and orderly transfer of functions and personnel to the Department, including the development of a transition plan.

(10) The conduct of internal audits and management analyses of the programs and activities of the Department.

(11) Any other management duties that the Secretary may designate.

(b) IMMIGRATION.—

(1) IN GENERAL.—In addition to the responsibilities described in subsection (a), the Under Secretary for Management shall be responsible for the following:

(A) Maintenance of all immigration statistical information of the Bureau of Border Security and the Bureau of Citizenship and Immigration Services. Such statistical information shall include information and statistics of the type contained in the publication entitled "Statistical Year-book of the Immigration and Naturalization Service" prepared by the Immigration and Naturalization Service (as in effect immediately before the date on which the transfer of functions specified under section 441 takes effect), including region-by-region statistics on the aggregate number of applications and petitions filed by an alien (or filed on behalf of an alien) and denied by such bureau, and the reasons for such denials, disaggregated by category of denial and application or petition type.

(B) Establishment of standards of reliability and validity for immigration statistics collected by such bureaus.

(2) TRANSFER OF FUNCTIONS.—In accordance with title XV, there shall be transferred to the Under Secretary for Management all functions performed immediately before such transfer occurs by the Statistics Branch of the Office of Policy and Planning of the Immigration and Naturalization Service with respect to the following programs:

(A) The Border Patrol program.

(B) The detention and removal program.

(C) The intelligence program.

(D) The investigations program.

(E) The inspections program.

(F) Adjudication of immigrant visa petitions.

(G) Adjudication of naturalization petitions.

(H) Adjudication of asylum and refugee applications.

(I) Adjudications performed at service centers.

(J) All other adjudications performed by the Immigration and Naturalization Service.

SEC. 702. CHIEF FINANCIAL OFFICER.

The Chief Financial Officer shall report to the Secretary, or to another official of the Department, as the Secretary may direct.

SEC. 703. CHIEF INFORMATION OFFICER.

The Chief Information Officer shall report to the Secretary, or to another official of the Department, as the Secretary may direct.

SEC. 704. CHIEF HUMAN CAPITAL OFFICER.

The Chief Human Capital Officer shall report to the Secretary, or to another official of the Department, as the Secretary may direct and shall ensure that all employees of the Department are informed of their rights and remedies under chapters 12 and 23 of title 5, United States Code, by—

(1) participating in the 2302(c) Certification Program of the Office of Special Counsel;

(2) achieving certification from the Office of Special Counsel of the Department's compliance with section 2302(c) of title 5, United States Code; and

(3) informing Congress of such certification not later than 24 months after the date of enactment of this Act.

SEC. 705. ESTABLISHMENT OF OFFICER FOR CIVIL RIGHTS AND CIVIL LIBERTIES.

(a) IN GENERAL.—The Secretary shall appoint in the Department an Officer for Civil Rights and Civil Liberties, who shall—

(1) review and assess information alleging abuses of civil rights, civil liberties, and racial and ethnic profiling by employees and officials of the Department; and

(2) make public through the Internet, radio, television, or newspaper advertisements information on the responsibilities and functions of, and how to contact, the Officer.

(b) REPORT.—The Secretary shall submit to the President of the Senate, the Speaker of the House of Representatives, and the appropriate committees and subcommittees of Congress on an annual basis a report on the implementation of this section, including the use of funds appropriated to carry out this section, and detailing any allegations of abuses described under subsection (a)(1) and any actions taken by the Department in response to such allegations.

SEC. 706. CONSOLIDATION AND CO-LOCATION OF OFFICES.

Not later than 1 year after the date of the enactment of this Act, the Secretary shall develop and submit to Congress a plan for consolidating and co-locating—

(1) any regional offices or field offices of agencies that are transferred to the Department under this Act, if such officers are located in the same municipality; and

(2) portions of regional and field offices of other Federal agencies, to the extent such offices perform functions that are transferred to the Secretary under this Act.

TITLE VIII—COORDINATION WITH NON-FEDERAL ENTITIES; INSPECTOR GENERAL; UNITED STATES SECRET SERVICE; COAST GUARD; GENERAL PROVISIONS

Subtitle A—Coordination with Non-Federal Entities

SEC. 801. OFFICE FOR STATE AND LOCAL GOVERNMENT COORDINATION.

(a) ESTABLISHMENT.—There is established within the Office of the Secretary the Office for State and Local Government Coordination, to oversee and coordinate departmental programs for and relationships with State and local governments.

(b) RESPONSIBILITIES.—The Office established under subsection (a) shall—

(1) coordinate the activities of the Department relating to State and local government;

(2) assess, and advocate for, the resources needed by State and local government to implement the national strategy for combating terrorism;

(3) provide State and local government with regular information, research, and technical support to assist local efforts at securing the homeland; and

(4) develop a process for receiving meaningful input from State and local government to assist the development of the

national strategy for combating terrorism and other homeland security activities.

Subtitle B—Inspector General

SEC. 811. AUTHORITY OF THE SECRETARY.

(a) IN GENERAL.—Notwithstanding the last two sentences of section 3(a) of the Inspector General Act of 1978, the Inspector General shall be under the authority, direction, and control of the Secretary with respect to audits or investigations, or the issuance of subpoenas, that require access to sensitive information concerning—

(1) intelligence, counterintelligence, or counterterrorism matters;

(2) ongoing criminal investigations or proceedings;

(3) undercover operations;

(4) the identity of confidential sources, including protected witnesses;

(5) other matters the disclosure of which would, in the Secretary's judgment, constitute a serious threat to the protection of any person or property authorized protection by section 3056 of title 18, United States Code, section 202 of title 3 of such Code, or any provision of the Presidential Protection Assistance Act of 1976; or

(6) other matters the disclosure of which would, in the Secretary's judgment, constitute a serious threat to national security.

(b) PROHIBITION OF CERTAIN INVESTIGATIONS.—With respect to the information described in subsection (a), the Secretary may prohibit the Inspector General from carrying out or completing any audit or investigation, or from issuing any subpoena, after such Inspector General has decided to initiate, carry out, or complete such audit or investigation or to issue such subpoena, if the Secretary determines that such prohibition is necessary to prevent the disclosure of any information described in subsection (a), to preserve the national security, or to prevent a significant impairment to the interests of the United States.

(c) NOTIFICATION REQUIRED.—If the Secretary exercises any power under subsection (a) or (b), the Secretary shall notify the Inspector General of the Department in writing stating the reasons for such exercise. Within 30 days after receipt of any such notice, the Inspector General shall transmit a copy of such notice and a written response thereto that includes—

(1) a statement as to whether the Inspector General agrees or disagrees with such exercise; and

(2) the reasons for any disagreement, to the President of the Senate and the Speaker of the House of Representatives and to appropriate committees and subcommittees of Congress.

(d) ACCESS TO INFORMATION BY CONGRESS.—The exercise of authority by the Secretary described in subsection (b) should not be construed as limiting the right of Congress or any committee of Congress to access any information it seeks.

(e) OVERSIGHT RESPONSIBILITY.—The Inspector General Act of 1978 (5 U.S.C. App.) is amended by inserting after section 8I the following:

"SPECIAL PROVISIONS CONCERNING THE DEPARTMENT OF HOMELAND SECURITY

"SEC. 8J. Notwithstanding any other provision of law, in carrying out the duties and responsibilities specified in this Act, the Inspector General of the Department of Homeland Security shall have oversight responsibility for the internal investigations performed by the Office of Internal Affairs of the United States Customs Service and the Office of Inspections of the United States Secret Service. The head of each such office shall promptly report to the Inspector General the significant activities being carried out by such office.".

SEC. 812. LAW ENFORCEMENT POWERS OF INSPECTOR GENERAL AGENTS.

(a) IN GENERAL.—Section 6 of the Inspector General Act of 1978 (5 U.S.C. App.) is amended by adding at the end the following:

"(e)(1) In addition to the authority otherwise provided by this Act, each Inspector General appointed under section 3, any Assistant Inspector General for Investigations under such an Inspector General, and any special agent supervised by such an Assistant Inspector General may be authorized by the Attorney General to—

"(A) carry a firearm while engaged in official duties as authorized under this Act or other statute, or as expressly authorized by the Attorney General;

"(B) make an arrest without a warrant while engaged in official duties as authorized under this Act or other statute, or as expressly authorized by the Attorney General, for any offense against the United States committed in the presence of such Inspector General, Assistant Inspector General, or agent, or for any felony cognizable under the laws of the United States if such Inspector General, Assistant Inspector General, or agent has reasonable grounds to believe that the person to be arrested has committed or is committing such felony; and

"(C) seek and execute warrants for arrest, search of a premises, or seizure of evidence issued under the authority of the United States upon probable cause to believe that a violation has been committed.

"(2) The Attorney General may authorize exercise of the powers under this subsection only upon an initial determination that—

"(A) the affected Office of Inspector General is significantly hampered in the performance of responsibilities established by this Act as a result of the lack of such powers;

"(B) available assistance from other law enforcement agencies is insufficient to meet the need for such powers; and

"(C) adequate internal safeguards and management procedures exist to ensure proper exercise of such powers.

"(3) The Inspector General offices of the Department of Commerce, Department of Education, Department of Energy, Department of Health and Human Services, Department of Homeland Security, Department of Housing and Urban Development, Department of the Interior, Department of Justice, Department of Labor, Department of State, Department of Transportation, Department of the Treasury, Department of Veterans Affairs, Agency for International Development, Environmental Protection Agency, Federal Deposit Insurance Corporation, Federal Emergency Management Agency, General Services Administration, National Aeronautics and

Space Administration, Nuclear Regulatory Commission, Office of Personnel Management, Railroad Retirement Board, Small Business Administration, Social Security Administration, and the Tennessee Valley Authority are exempt from the requirement of paragraph (2) of an initial determination of eligibility by the Attorney General.

"(4) The Attorney General shall promulgate, and revise as appropriate, guidelines which shall govern the exercise of the law enforcement powers established under paragraph (1).

"(5)(A) Powers authorized for an Office of Inspector General under paragraph (1) may be rescinded or suspended upon a determination by the Attorney General that any of the requirements under paragraph (2) is no longer satisfied or that the exercise of authorized powers by that Office of Inspector General has not complied with the guidelines promulgated by the Attorney General under paragraph (4).

"(B) Powers authorized to be exercised by any individual under paragraph (1) may be rescinded or suspended with respect to that individual upon a determination by the Attorney General that such individual has not complied with guidelines promulgated by the Attorney General under paragraph (4).

"(6) A determination by the Attorney General under paragraph (2) or (5) shall not be reviewable in or by any court.

"(7) To ensure the proper exercise of the law enforcement powers authorized by this subsection, the Offices of Inspector General described under paragraph (3) shall, not later than 180 days after the date of enactment of this subsection, collectively enter into a memorandum of understanding to establish an external review process for ensuring that adequate internal safeguards and management procedures continue to exist within each Office and within any Office that later receives an authorization under paragraph (2). The review process shall be established in consultation with the Attorney General, who shall be provided with a copy of the memorandum of understanding that establishes the review process. Under the review process, the exercise of the law enforcement powers by each Office of Inspector General shall be reviewed periodically by another Office of Inspector General or by a committee of Inspectors General. The results of each review shall be communicated in writing to the applicable Inspector General and to the Attorney General.

"(8) No provision of this subsection shall limit the exercise of law enforcement powers established under any other statutory authority, including United States Marshals Service special deputation.".

(b) PROMULGATION OF INITIAL GUIDELINES.—

(1) DEFINITION.—In this subsection, the term "memoranda of understanding" means the agreements between the Department of Justice and the Inspector General offices described under section 6(e)(3) of the Inspector General Act of 1978 (5 U.S.C. App.) (as added by subsection (a) of this section) that—

(A) are in effect on the date of enactment of this Act; and

(B) authorize such offices to exercise authority that is the same or similar to the authority under section 6(e)(1) of such Act.

(2) IN GENERAL.—Not later than 180 days after the date of enactment of this Act, the Attorney General shall promulgate

guidelines under section 6(e)(4) of the Inspector General Act of 1978 (5 U.S.C. App.) (as added by subsection (a) of this section) applicable to the Inspector General offices described under section 6(e)(3) of that Act.

(3) MINIMUM REQUIREMENTS.—The guidelines promulgated under this subsection shall include, at a minimum, the operational and training requirements in the memoranda of understanding.

(4) NO LAPSE OF AUTHORITY.—The memoranda of understanding in effect on the date of enactment of this Act shall remain in effect until the guidelines promulgated under this subsection take effect.

(c) EFFECTIVE DATES.—

(1) IN GENERAL.—Subsection (a) shall take effect 180 days after the date of enactment of this Act.

(2) INITIAL GUIDELINES.—Subsection (b) shall take effect on the date of enactment of this Act.

Subtitle C—United States Secret Service

SEC. 821. FUNCTIONS TRANSFERRED.

In accordance with title XV, there shall be transferred to the Secretary the functions, personnel, assets, and obligations of the United States Secret Service, which shall be maintained as a distinct entity within the Department, including the functions of the Secretary of the Treasury relating thereto.

Subtitle D—Acquisitions

SEC. 831. RESEARCH AND DEVELOPMENT PROJECTS.

(a) AUTHORITY.—During the 5-year period following the effective date of this Act, the Secretary may carry out a pilot program under which the Secretary may exercise the following authorities:

(1) IN GENERAL.—When the Secretary carries out basic, applied, and advanced research and development projects, including the expenditure of funds for such projects, the Secretary may exercise the same authority (subject to the same limitations and conditions) with respect to such research and projects as the Secretary of Defense may exercise under section 2371 of title 10, United States Code (except for subsections (b) and (f)), after making a determination that the use of a contract, grant, or cooperative agreement for such project is not feasible or appropriate. The annual report required under subsection (b) of this section, as applied to the Secretary by this paragraph, shall be submitted to the President of the Senate and the Speaker of the House of Representatives.

(2) PROTOTYPE PROJECTS.—The Secretary may, under the authority of paragraph (1), carry out prototype projects in accordance with the requirements and conditions provided for carrying out prototype projects under section 845 of the National Defense Authorization Act for Fiscal Year 1994 (Public Law 103–160). In applying the authorities of that section 845, subsection (c) of that section shall apply with respect to prototype projects under this paragraph, and the Secretary shall

perform the functions of the Secretary of Defense under subsection (d) thereof.

(b) REPORT.—Not later than 2 years after the effective date of this Act, and annually thereafter, the Comptroller General shall report to the Committee on Government Reform of the House of Representatives and the Committee on Governmental Affairs of the Senate on—

(1) whether use of the authorities described in subsection (a) attracts nontraditional Government contractors and results in the acquisition of needed technologies; and

(2) if such authorities were to be made permanent, whether additional safeguards are needed with respect to the use of such authorities.

(c) PROCUREMENT OF TEMPORARY AND INTERMITTENT SERVICES.—The Secretary may—

(1) procure the temporary or intermittent services of experts or consultants (or organizations thereof) in accordance with section 3109(b) of title 5, United States Code; and

(2) whenever necessary due to an urgent homeland security need, procure temporary (not to exceed 1 year) or intermittent personal services, including the services of experts or consultants (or organizations thereof), without regard to the pay limitations of such section 3109.

(d) DEFINITION OF NONTRADITIONAL GOVERNMENT CONTRACTOR.—In this section, the term "nontraditional Government contractor" has the same meaning as the term "nontraditional defense contractor" as defined in section 845(e) of the National Defense Authorization Act for Fiscal Year 1994 (Public Law 103–160; 10 U.S.C. 2371 note).

SEC. 832. PERSONAL SERVICES.

The Secretary—

(1) may procure the temporary or intermittent services of experts or consultants (or organizations thereof) in accordance with section 3109 of title 5, United States Code; and

(2) may, whenever necessary due to an urgent homeland security need, procure temporary (not to exceed 1 year) or intermittent personal services, including the services of experts or consultants (or organizations thereof), without regard to the pay limitations of such section 3109.

SEC. 833. SPECIAL STREAMLINED ACQUISITION AUTHORITY.

(a) AUTHORITY.—

(1) IN GENERAL.—The Secretary may use the authorities set forth in this section with respect to any procurement made during the period beginning on the effective date of this Act and ending September 30, 2007, if the Secretary determines in writing that the mission of the Department (as described in section 101) would be seriously impaired without the use of such authorities.

(2) DELEGATION.—The authority to make the determination described in paragraph (1) may not be delegated by the Secretary to an officer of the Department who is not appointed by the President with the advice and consent of the Senate.

(3) NOTIFICATION.—Not later than the date that is 7 days after the date of any determination under paragraph (1), the Secretary shall submit to the Committee on Government

Reform of the House of Representatives and the Committee on Governmental Affairs of the Senate—

(A) notification of such determination; and

(B) the justification for such determination.

(b) INCREASED MICRO-PURCHASE THRESHOLD FOR CERTAIN PROCUREMENTS.—

(1) IN GENERAL.—The Secretary may designate certain employees of the Department to make procurements described in subsection (a) for which in the administration of section 32 of the Office of Federal Procurement Policy Act (41 U.S.C. 428) the amount specified in subsections (c), (d), and (f) of such section 32 shall be deemed to be $7,500.

(2) NUMBER OF EMPLOYEES.—The number of employees designated under paragraph (1) shall be—

(A) fewer than the number of employees of the Department who are authorized to make purchases without obtaining competitive quotations, pursuant to section 32(c) of the Office of Federal Procurement Policy Act (41 U.S.C. 428(c));

(B) sufficient to ensure the geographic dispersal of the availability of the use of the procurement authority under such paragraph at locations reasonably considered to be potential terrorist targets; and

(C) sufficiently limited to allow for the careful monitoring of employees designated under such paragraph.

(3) REVIEW.—Procurements made under the authority of this subsection shall be subject to review by a designated supervisor on not less than a monthly basis. The supervisor responsible for the review shall be responsible for no more than 7 employees making procurements under this subsection.

(c) SIMPLIFIED ACQUISITION PROCEDURES.—

(1) IN GENERAL.—With respect to a procurement described in subsection (a), the Secretary may deem the simplified acquisition threshold referred to in section 4(11) of the Office of Federal Procurement Policy Act (41 U.S.C. 403(11)) to be—

(A) in the case of a contract to be awarded and performed, or purchase to be made, within the United States, $200,000; and

(B) in the case of a contract to be awarded and performed, or purchase to be made, outside of the United States, $300,000.

(2) CONFORMING AMENDMENTS.—Section 18(c)(1) of the Office of Federal Procurement Policy Act is amended—

(A) by striking "or" at the end of subparagraph (F);

(B) by striking the period at the end of subparagraph (G) and inserting "; or"; and

(C) by adding at the end the following:

"(H) the procurement is by the Secretary of Homeland Security pursuant to the special procedures provided in section 833(c) of the Homeland Security Act of 2002.".

(d) APPLICATION OF CERTAIN COMMERCIAL ITEMS AUTHORITIES.—

(1) IN GENERAL.—With respect to a procurement described in subsection (a), the Secretary may deem any item or service to be a commercial item for the purpose of Federal procurement laws.

(2) LIMITATION.—The $5,000,000 limitation provided in section 31(a)(2) of the Office of Federal Procurement Policy Act (41 U.S.C. 427(a)(2)) and section 303(g)(1)(B) of the Federal Property and Administrative Services Act of 1949 (41 U.S.C. 253(g)(1)(B)) shall be deemed to be $7,500,000 for purposes of property or services under the authority of this subsection.

(3) CERTAIN AUTHORITY.—Authority under a provision of law referred to in paragraph (2) that expires under section 4202(e) of the Clinger-Cohen Act of 1996 (divisions D and E of Public Law 104–106; 10 U.S.C. 2304 note) shall, notwithstanding such section, continue to apply for a procurement described in subsection (a).

(e) REPORT.—Not later than 180 days after the end of fiscal year 2005, the Comptroller General shall submit to the Committee on Governmental Affairs of the Senate and the Committee on Government Reform of the House of Representatives a report on the use of the authorities provided in this section. The report shall contain the following:

(1) An assessment of the extent to which property and services acquired using authorities provided under this section contributed to the capacity of the Federal workforce to facilitate the mission of the Department as described in section 101.

(2) An assessment of the extent to which prices for property and services acquired using authorities provided under this section reflected the best value.

(3) The number of employees designated by each executive agency under subsection (b)(1).

(4) An assessment of the extent to which the Department has implemented subsections (b)(2) and (b)(3) to monitor the use of procurement authority by employees designated under subsection (b)(1).

(5) Any recommendations of the Comptroller General for improving the effectiveness of the implementation of the provisions of this section.

SEC. 834. UNSOLICITED PROPOSALS.

(a) REGULATIONS REQUIRED.—Within 1 year of the date of enactment of this Act, the Federal Acquisition Regulation shall be revised to include regulations with regard to unsolicited proposals.

(b) CONTENT OF REGULATIONS.—The regulations prescribed under subsection (a) shall require that before initiating a comprehensive evaluation, an agency contact point shall consider, among other factors, that the proposal—

(1) is not submitted in response to a previously published agency requirement; and

(2) contains technical and cost information for evaluation and overall scientific, technical or socioeconomic merit, or cost-related or price-related factors.

SEC. 835. PROHIBITION ON CONTRACTS WITH CORPORATE EXPATRIATES.

(a) IN GENERAL.—The Secretary may not enter into any contract with a foreign incorporated entity which is treated as an inverted domestic corporation under subsection (b).

(b) INVERTED DOMESTIC CORPORATION.—For purposes of this section, a foreign incorporated entity shall be treated as an inverted domestic corporation if, pursuant to a plan (or a series of related transactions)—

(1) the entity completes after the date of enactment of this Act, the direct or indirect acquisition of substantially all of the properties held directly or indirectly by a domestic corporation or substantially all of the properties constituting a trade or business of a domestic partnership;

(2) after the acquisition at least 80 percent of the stock (by vote or value) of the entity is held—

(A) in the case of an acquisition with respect to a domestic corporation, by former shareholders of the domestic corporation by reason of holding stock in the domestic corporation; or

(B) in the case of an acquisition with respect to a domestic partnership, by former partners of the domestic partnership by reason of holding a capital or profits interest in the domestic partnership; and

(3) the expanded affiliated group which after the acquisition includes the entity does not have substantial business activities in the foreign country in which or under the law of which the entity is created or organized when compared to the total business activities of such expanded affiliated group.

(c) DEFINITIONS AND SPECIAL RULES.—

(1) RULES FOR APPLICATION OF SUBSECTION (b).—In applying subsection (b) for purposes of subsection (a), the following rules shall apply:

(A) CERTAIN STOCK DISREGARDED.—There shall not be taken into account in determining ownership for purposes of subsection (b)(2)—

(i) stock held by members of the expanded affiliated group which includes the foreign incorporated entity; or

(ii) stock of such entity which is sold in a public offering related to the acquisition described in subsection (b)(1).

(B) PLAN DEEMED IN CERTAIN CASES.—If a foreign incorporated entity acquires directly or indirectly substantially all of the properties of a domestic corporation or partnership during the 4-year period beginning on the date which is after the date of enactment of this Act and which is 2 years before the ownership requirements of subsection (b)(2) are met, such actions shall be treated as pursuant to a plan.

(C) CERTAIN TRANSFERS DISREGARDED.—The transfer of properties or liabilities (including by contribution or distribution) shall be disregarded if such transfers are part of a plan a principal purpose of which is to avoid the purposes of this section.

(D) SPECIAL RULE FOR RELATED PARTNERSHIPS.—For purposes of applying subsection (b) to the acquisition of a domestic partnership, except as provided in regulations, all domestic partnerships which are under common control (within the meaning of section 482 of the Internal Revenue Code of 1986) shall be treated as I partnership.

(E) TREATMENT OF CERTAIN RIGHTS.—The Secretary shall prescribe such regulations as may be necessary to—

(i) treat warrants, options, contracts to acquire stock, convertible debt instruments, and other similar interests as stock; and

(ii) treat stock as not stock.

(2) EXPANDED AFFILIATED GROUP.—The term "expanded affiliated group" means an affiliated group as defined in section 1504(a) of the Internal Revenue Code of 1986 (without regard to section 1504(b) of such Code), except that section 1504 of such Code shall be applied by substituting "more than 50 percent" for "at least 80 percent" each place it appears.

(3) FOREIGN INCORPORATED ENTITY.—The term "foreign incorporated entity" means any entity which is, or but for subsection (b) would be, treated as a foreign corporation for purposes of the Internal Revenue Code of 1986.

(4) OTHER DEFINITIONS.—The terms "person", "domestic", and "foreign" have the meanings given such terms by paragraphs (1), (4), and (5) of section 7701(a) of the Internal Revenue Code of 1986, respectively.

(d) WAIVERS.—The Secretary shall waive subsection (a) with respect to any specific contract if the Secretary determines that the waiver is required in the interest of homeland security, or to prevent the loss of any jobs in the United States or prevent the Government from incurring any additional costs that otherwise would not occur.

Subtitle E—Human Resources Management

SEC. 841. ESTABLISHMENT OF HUMAN RESOURCES MANAGEMENT SYSTEM.

(a) AUTHORITY.—

(1) SENSE OF CONGRESS.—It is the sense of Congress that—

(A) it is extremely important that employees of the Department be allowed to participate in a meaningful way in the creation of any human resources management system affecting them;

(B) such employees have the most direct knowledge of the demands of their jobs and have a direct interest in ensuring that their human resources management system is conducive to achieving optimal operational efficiencies;

(C) the 21st century human resources management system envisioned for the Department should be one that benefits from the input of its employees; and

(D) this collaborative effort will help secure our homeland.

(2) IN GENERAL.—Subpart I of part III of title 5, United States Code, is amended by adding at the end the following:

"CHAPTER 97—DEPARTMENT OF HOMELAND SECURITY

"Sec.

"9701. Establishment of human resources management system.

"§ 9701. Establishment of human resources management system

"(a) IN GENERAL.—Notwithstanding any other provision of this part, the Secretary of Homeland Security may, in regulations prescribed jointly with the Director of the Office of Personnel Management, establish, and from time to time adjust, a human resources management system for some or all of the organizational units of the Department of Homeland Security.

"(b) SYSTEM REQUIREMENTS.—Any system established under subsection (a) shall—

"(1) be flexible;

"(2) be contemporary;

"(3) not waive, modify, or otherwise affect—

"(A) the public employment principles of merit and fitness set forth in section 2301, including the principles of hiring based on merit, fair treatment without regard to political affiliation or other nonmerit considerations, equal pay for equal work, and protection of employees against reprisal for whistleblowing;

"(B) any provision of section 2302, relating to prohibited personnel practices;

"(C)(i) any provision of law referred to in section 2302(b)(1), (8), and (9); or

"(ii) any provision of law implementing any provision of law referred to in section 2302(b)(1), (8), and (9) by—

"(I) providing for equal employment opportunity through affirmative action; or

"(II) providing any right or remedy available to any employee or applicant for employment in the civil service;

"(D) any other provision of this part (as described in subsection (c)); or

"(E) any rule or regulation prescribed under any provision of law referred to in any of the preceding subparagraphs of this paragraph;

"(4) ensure that employees may organize, bargain collectively, and participate through labor organizations of their own choosing in decisions which affect them, subject to any exclusion from coverage or limitation on negotiability established by law; and

"(5) permit the use of a category rating system for evaluating applicants for positions in the competitive service.

"(c) OTHER NONWAIVABLE PROVISIONS.—The other provisions of this part as referred to in subsection (b)(3)(D), are (to the extent not otherwise specified in subparagraph (A), (B), (C), or (D) of subsection (b)(3))—

"(1) subparts A, B, E, G, and H of this part; and

"(2) chapters 41, 45, 47, 55, 57, 59, 72, 73, and 79, and this chapter.

"(d) LIMITATIONS RELATING TO PAY.—Nothing in this section shall constitute authority—

"(1) to modify the pay of any employee who serves in—

"(A) an Executive Schedule position under subchapter II of chapter 53 of title 5, United States Code; or

"(B) a position for which the rate of basic pay is fixed in statute by reference to a section or level under subchapter II of chapter 53 of such title 5;

"(2) to fix pay for any employee or position at an annual rate greater than the maximum amount of cash compensation allowable under section 5307 of such title 5 in a year; or

"(3) to exempt any employee from the application of such section 5307.

"(e) PROVISIONS TO ENSURE COLLABORATION WITH EMPLOYEE REPRESENTATIVES.—

"(1) IN GENERAL.—In order to ensure that the authority of this section is exercised in collaboration with, and in a manner that ensures the participation of employee representatives in the planning, development, and implementation of any human resources management system or adjustments to such system under this section, the Secretary of Homeland Security and the Director of the Office of Personnel Management shall provide for the following:

"(A) NOTICE OF PROPOSAL.—The Secretary and the Director shall, with respect to any proposed system or adjustment—

"(i) provide to each employee representative representing any employees who might be affected, a written description of the proposed system or adjustment (including the reasons why it is considered necessary);

"(ii) give each representative 30 calendar days (unless extraordinary circumstances require earlier action) to review and make recommendations with respect to the proposal; and

"(iii) give any recommendations received from any such representatives under clause (ii) full and fair consideration in deciding whether or how to proceed with the proposal.

"(B) PRE-IMPLEMENTATION CONGRESSIONAL NOTIFICATION, CONSULTATION, AND MEDIATION.—Following receipt of recommendations, if any, from employee representatives with respect to a proposal described in subparagraph (A), the Secretary and the Director shall accept such modifications to the proposal in response to the recommendations as they determine advisable and shall, with respect to any parts of the proposal as to which they have not accepted the recommendations—

"(i) notify Congress of those parts of the proposal, together with the recommendations of employee representatives;

"(ii) meet and confer for not less than 30 calendar days with any representatives who have made recommendations, in order to attempt to reach agreement on whether or how to proceed with those parts of the proposal; and

"(iii) at the Secretary's option, or if requested by a majority of the employee representatives who have made recommendations, use the services of the Federal Mediation and Conciliation Service during such meet and confer period to facilitate the process of attempting to reach agreement.

"(C) IMPLEMENTATION.—

"(i) Any part of the proposal as to which the representatives do not make a recommendation, or as to which their recommendations are accepted by the

Secretary and the Director, may be implemented immediately.

"(ii) With respect to any parts of the proposal as to which recommendations have been made but not accepted by the Secretary and the Director, at any time after 30 calendar days have elapsed since the initiation of the congressional notification, consultation, and mediation procedures set forth in subparagraph (B), if the Secretary determines, in the Secretary's sole and unreviewable discretion, that further consultation and mediation is unlikely to produce agreement, the Secretary may implement any or all of such parts, including any modifications made in response to the recommendations as the Secretary determines advisable.

"(iii) The Secretary shall promptly notify Congress of the implementation of any part of the proposal and shall furnish with such notice an explanation of the proposal, any changes made to the proposal as a result of recommendations from employee representatives, and of the reasons why implementation is appropriate under this subparagraph.

"(D) CONTINUING COLLABORATION.—If a proposal described in subparagraph (A) is implemented, the Secretary and the Director shall—

"(i) develop a method for each employee representative to participate in any further planning or development which might become necessary; and

"(ii) give each employee representative adequate access to information to make that participation productive.

"(2) PROCEDURES.—Any procedures necessary to carry out this subsection shall be established by the Secretary and the Director jointly as internal rules of departmental procedure which shall not be subject to review. Such procedures shall include measures to ensure—

"(A) in the case of employees within a unit with respect to which a labor organization is accorded exclusive recognition, representation by individuals designated or from among individuals nominated by such organization;

"(B) in the case of any employees who are not within such a unit, representation by any appropriate organization which represents a substantial percentage of those employees or, if none, in such other manner as may be appropriate, consistent with the purposes of the subsection;

"(C) the fair and expeditious handling of the consultation and mediation process described in subparagraph (B) of paragraph (1), including procedures by which, if the number of employee representatives providing recommendations exceeds 5, such representatives select a committee or other unified representative with which the Secretary and Director may meet and confer; and

"(D) the selection of representatives in a manner consistent with the relative number of employees represented by the organizations or other representatives involved.

"(f) PROVISIONS RELATING TO APPELLATE PROCEDURES.—

"(1) SENSE OF CONGRESS.—It is the sense of Congress that—

"(A) employees of the Department are entitled to fair treatment in any appeals that they bring in decisions relating to their employment; and

"(B) in prescribing regulations for any such appeals procedures, the Secretary and the Director of the Office of Personnel Management—

"(i) should ensure that employees of the Department are afforded the protections of due process; and

"(ii) toward that end, should be required to consult with the Merit Systems Protection Board before issuing any such regulations.

"(2) REQUIREMENTS.—Any regulations under this section which relate to any matters within the purview of chapter 77—

"(A) shall be issued only after consultation with the Merit Systems Protection Board;

"(B) shall ensure the availability of procedures which shall—

"(i) be consistent with requirements of due process; and

"(ii) provide, to the maximum extent practicable, for the expeditious handling of any matters involving the Department; and

"(C) shall modify procedures under chapter 77 only insofar as such modifications are designed to further the fair, efficient, and expeditious resolution of matters involving the employees of the Department.

"(g) PROVISIONS RELATING TO LABOR-MANAGEMENT RELATIONS.—Nothing in this section shall be construed as conferring authority on the Secretary of Homeland Security to modify any of the provisions of section 842 of the Homeland Security Act of 2002.

"(h) SUNSET PROVISION.—Effective 5 years after the conclusion of the transition period defined under section 1501 of the Homeland Security Act of 2002, all authority to issue regulations under this section (including regulations which would modify, supersede, or terminate any regulations previously issued under this section) shall cease to be available.".

(3) TECHNICAL AND CONFORMING AMENDMENT.—The table of chapters for part III of title 5, United States Code, is amended by adding at the end of the following:

"97. Department of Homeland Security .... **9701".**

(b) EFFECT ON PERSONNEL.—

(1) NONSEPARATION OR NONREDUCTION IN GRADE OR COMPENSATION OF FULL-TIME PERSONNEL AND PART-TIME PERSONNEL HOLDING PERMANENT POSITIONS.—Except as otherwise provided in this Act, the transfer under this Act of full-time personnel (except special Government employees) and part-time personnel holding permanent positions shall not cause any such employee to be separated or reduced in grade or compensation for 1 year after the date of transfer to the Department.

(2) POSITIONS COMPENSATED IN ACCORDANCE WITH EXECUTIVE SCHEDULE.—Any person who, on the day preceding such person's date of transfer pursuant to this Act, held a position compensated in accordance with the Executive Schedule prescribed in chapter 53 of title 5, United States Code, and who, without a break in service, is appointed in the Department

to a position having duties comparable to the duties performed immediately preceding such appointment shall continue to be compensated in such new position at not less than the rate provided for such position, for the duration of the service of such person in such new position.

(3) COORDINATION RULE.—Any exercise of authority under chapter 97 of title 5, United States Code (as amended by subsection (a)), including under any system established under such chapter, shall be in conformance with the requirements of this subsection.

SEC. 842. LABOR-MANAGEMENT RELATIONS.

(a) LIMITATION ON EXCLUSIONARY AUTHORITY.—

(1) IN GENERAL.—No agency or subdivision of an agency which is transferred to the Department pursuant to this Act shall be excluded from the coverage of chapter 71 of title 5, United States Code, as a result of any order issued under section 7103(b)(1) of such title 5 after June 18, 2002, unless—

(A) the mission and responsibilities of the agency (or subdivision) materially change; and

(B) a majority of the employees within such agency (or subdivision) have as their primary duty intelligence, counterintelligence, or investigative work directly related to terrorism investigation.

(2) EXCLUSIONS ALLOWABLE.—Nothing in paragraph (1) shall affect the effectiveness of any order to the extent that such order excludes any portion of an agency or subdivision of an agency as to which—

(A) recognition as an appropriate unit has never been conferred for purposes of chapter 71 of such title 5; or

(B) any such recognition has been revoked or otherwise terminated as a result of a determination under subsection (b)(1).

(b) PROVISIONS RELATING TO BARGAINING UNITS.—

(1) LIMITATION RELATING TO APPROPRIATE UNITS.—Each unit which is recognized as an appropriate unit for purposes of chapter 71 of title 5, United States Code, as of the day before the effective date of this Act (and any subdivision of any such unit) shall, if such unit (or subdivision) is transferred to the Department pursuant to this Act, continue to be so recognized for such purposes, unless—

(A) the mission and responsibilities of such unit (or subdivision) materially change; and

(B) a majority of the employees within such unit (or subdivision) have as their primary duty intelligence, counterintelligence, or investigative work directly related to terrorism investigation.

(2) LIMITATION RELATING TO POSITIONS OR EMPLOYEES.— No position or employee within a unit (or subdivision of a unit) as to which continued recognition is given in accordance with paragraph (1) shall be excluded from such unit (or subdivision), for purposes of chapter 71 of such title 5, unless the primary job duty of such position or employee—

(A) materially changes; and

(B) consists of intelligence, counterintelligence, or investigative work directly related to terrorism investigation.

In the case of any positions within a unit (or subdivision) which are first established on or after the effective date of this Act and any employees first appointed on or after such date, the preceding sentence shall be applied disregarding subparagraph (A).

(c) WAIVER.—If the President determines that the application of subsections (a), (b), and (d) would have a substantial adverse impact on the ability of the Department to protect homeland security, the President may waive the application of such subsections 10 days after the President has submitted to Congress a written explanation of the reasons for such determination.

(d) COORDINATION RULE.—No other provision of this Act or of any amendment made by this Act may be construed or applied in a manner so as to limit, supersede, or otherwise affect the provisions of this section, except to the extent that it does so by specific reference to this section.

(e) RULE OF CONSTRUCTION.—Nothing in section 9701(e) of title 5, United States Code, shall be considered to apply with respect to any agency or subdivision of any agency, which is excluded from the coverage of chapter 71 of title 5, United States Code, by virtue of an order issued in accordance with section 7103(b) of such title and the preceding provisions of this section (as applicable), or to any employees of any such agency or subdivision or to any individual or entity representing any such employees or any representatives thereof.

Subtitle F—Federal Emergency Procurement Flexibility

SEC. 851. DEFINITION.

In this subtitle, the term "executive agency" has the meaning given that term under section 4(1) of the Office of Federal Procurement Policy Act (41 U.S.C. 403(1)).

SEC. 852. PROCUREMENTS FOR DEFENSE AGAINST OR RECOVERY FROM TERRORISM OR NUCLEAR, BIOLOGICAL, CHEMICAL, OR RADIOLOGICAL ATTACK.

The authorities provided in this subtitle apply to any procurement of property or services by or for an executive agency that, as determined by the head of the executive agency, are to be used to facilitate defense against or recovery from terrorism or nuclear, biological, chemical, or radiological attack, but only if a solicitation of offers for the procurement is issued during the 1-year period beginning on the date of the enactment of this Act.

SEC. 853. INCREASED SIMPLIFIED ACQUISITION THRESHOLD FOR PROCUREMENTS IN SUPPORT OF HUMANITARIAN OR PEACEKEEPING OPERATIONS OR CONTINGENCY OPERATIONS.

(a) TEMPORARY THRESHOLD AMOUNTS.—For a procurement referred to in section 852 that is carried out in support of a humanitarian or peacekeeping operation or a contingency operation, the simplified acquisition threshold definitions shall be applied as if the amount determined under the exception provided for such an operation in those definitions were—

(1) in the case of a contract to be awarded and performed, or purchase to be made, inside the United States, $200,000; or

(2) in the case of a contract to be awarded and performed, or purchase to be made, outside the United States, $300,000.

(b) SIMPLIFIED ACQUISITION THRESHOLD DEFINITIONS.—In this section, the term "simplified acquisition threshold definitions" means the following:

(1) Section 4(11) of the Office of Federal Procurement Policy Act (41 U.S.C. 403(11)).

(2) Section 309(d) of the Federal Property and Administrative Services Act of 1949 (41 U.S.C. 259(d)).

(3) Section 2302(7) of title 10, United States Code.

(c) SMALL BUSINESS RESERVE.—For a procurement carried out pursuant to subsection (a), section 15(j) of the Small Business Act (15 U.S.C. 644(j)) shall be applied as if the maximum anticipated value identified therein is equal to the amounts referred to in subsection (a).

SEC. 854. INCREASED MICRO-PURCHASE THRESHOLD FOR CERTAIN PROCUREMENTS.

In the administration of section 32 of the Office of Federal Procurement Policy Act (41 U.S.C. 428) with respect to a procurement referred to in section 852, the amount specified in subsections (c), (d), and (f) of such section 32 shall be deemed to be $7,500.

SEC. 855. APPLICATION OF CERTAIN COMMERCIAL ITEMS AUTHORITIES TO CERTAIN PROCUREMENTS.

(a) AUTHORITY.—

(1) IN GENERAL.—The head of an executive agency may apply the provisions of law listed in paragraph (2) to a procurement referred to in section 852 without regard to whether the property or services are commercial items.

(2) COMMERCIAL ITEM LAWS.—The provisions of law referred to in paragraph (1) are as follows:

(A) Sections 31 and 34 of the Office of Federal Procurement Policy Act (41 U.S.C. 427, 430).

(B) Section 2304(g) of title 10, United States Code.

(C) Section 303(g) of the Federal Property and Administrative Services Act of 1949 (41 U.S.C. 253(g)).

(b) INAPPLICABILITY OF LIMITATION ON USE OF SIMPLIFIED ACQUISITION PROCEDURES.—

(1) IN GENERAL.—The $5,000,000 limitation provided in section 31(a)(2) of the Office of Federal Procurement Policy Act (41 U.S.C. 427(a)(2)), section 2304(g)(1)(B) of title 10, United States Code, and section 303(g)(1)(B) of the Federal Property and Administrative Services Act of 1949 (41 U.S.C. 253(g)(1)(B)) shall not apply to purchases of property or services to which any of the provisions of law referred to in subsection (a) are applied under the authority of this section.

(2) OMB GUIDANCE.—The Director of the Office of Management and Budget shall issue guidance and procedures for the use of simplified acquisition procedures for a purchase of property or services in excess of $5,000,000 under the authority of this section.

(c) CONTINUATION OF AUTHORITY FOR SIMPLIFIED PURCHASE PROCEDURES.—Authority under a provision of law referred to in subsection (a)(2) that expires under section 4202(e) of the Clinger-

Cohen Act of 1996 (divisions D and E of Public Law 104–106; 10 U.S.C. 2304 note) shall, notwithstanding such section, continue to apply for use by the head of an executive agency as provided in subsections (a) and (b).

SEC. 856. USE OF STREAMLINED PROCEDURES.

(a) REQUIRED USE.—The head of an executive agency shall, when appropriate, use streamlined acquisition authorities and procedures authorized by law for a procurement referred to in section 852, including authorities and procedures that are provided under the following provisions of law:

(1) FEDERAL PROPERTY AND ADMINISTRATIVE SERVICES ACT OF 1949.—In title III of the Federal Property and Administrative Services Act of 1949:

(A) Paragraphs (1), (2), (6), and (7) of subsection (c) of section 303 (41 U.S.C. 253), relating to use of procedures other than competitive procedures under certain circumstances (subject to subsection (e) of such section).

(B) Section 303J (41 U.S.C. 253j), relating to orders under task and delivery order contracts.

(2) TITLE 10, UNITED STATES CODE.—In chapter 137 of title 10, United States Code:

(A) Paragraphs (1), (2), (6), and (7) of subsection (c) of section 2304, relating to use of procedures other than competitive procedures under certain circumstances (subject to subsection (e) of such section).

(B) Section 2304c, relating to orders under task and delivery order contracts.

(3) OFFICE OF FEDERAL PROCUREMENT POLICY ACT.—Paragraphs (1)(B), (1)(D), and (2) of section 18(c) of the Office of Federal Procurement Policy Act (41 U.S.C. 416(c)), relating to inapplicability of a requirement for procurement notice.

(b) WAIVER OF CERTAIN SMALL BUSINESS THRESHOLD REQUIREMENTS.—Subclause (II) of section 8(a)(1)(D)(i) of the Small Business Act (15 U.S.C. 637(a)(1)(D)(i)) and clause (ii) of section 31(b)(2)(A) of such Act (15 U.S.C. 657a(b)(2)(A)) shall not apply in the use of streamlined acquisition authorities and procedures referred to in paragraphs (1)(A) and (2)(A) of subsection (a) for a procurement referred to in section 852.

SEC. 857. REVIEW AND REPORT BY COMPTROLLER GENERAL.

(a) REQUIREMENTS.—Not later than March 31, 2004, the Comptroller General shall—

(1) complete a review of the extent to which procurements of property and services have been made in accordance with this subtitle; and

(2) submit a report on the results of the review to the Committee on Governmental Affairs of the Senate and the Committee on Government Reform of the House of Representatives.

(b) CONTENT OF REPORT.—The report under subsection (a)(2) shall include the following matters:

(1) ASSESSMENT.—The Comptroller General's assessment of—

(A) the extent to which property and services procured in accordance with this title have contributed to the capacity of the workforce of Federal Government employees within each executive agency to carry out the mission of the executive agency; and

(B) the extent to which Federal Government employees have been trained on the use of technology.

(2) RECOMMENDATIONS.—Any recommendations of the Comptroller General resulting from the assessment described in paragraph (1).

(c) CONSULTATION.—In preparing for the review under subsection (a)(1), the Comptroller shall consult with the Committee on Governmental Affairs of the Senate and the Committee on Government Reform of the House of Representatives on the specific issues and topics to be reviewed. The extent of coverage needed in areas such as technology integration, employee training, and human capital management, as well as the data requirements of the study, shall be included as part of the consultation.

SEC. 858. IDENTIFICATION OF NEW ENTRANTS INTO THE FEDERAL MARKETPLACE.

The head of each executive agency shall conduct market research on an ongoing basis to identify effectively the capabilities, including the capabilities of small businesses and new entrants into Federal contracting, that are available in the marketplace for meeting the requirements of the executive agency in furtherance of defense against or recovery from terrorism or nuclear, biological, chemical, or radiological attack. The head of the executive agency shall, to the maximum extent practicable, take advantage of commercially available market research methods, including use of commercial databases, to carry out the research.

Subtitle G—Support Anti-terrorism by Fostering Effective Technologies Act of 2002

SEC. 861. SHORT TITLE.

This subtitle may be cited as the "Support Anti-terrorism by Fostering Effective Technologies Act of 2002" or the "SAFETY Act".

SEC. 862. ADMINISTRATION.

(a) IN GENERAL.—The Secretary shall be responsible for the administration of this subtitle.

(b) DESIGNATION OF QUALIFIED ANTI-TERRORISM TECHNOLOGIES.—The Secretary may designate anti-terrorism technologies that qualify for protection under the system of risk management set forth in this subtitle in accordance with criteria that shall include, but not be limited to, the following:

(1) Prior United States Government use or demonstrated substantial utility and effectiveness.

(2) Availability of the technology for immediate deployment in public and private settings.

(3) Existence of extraordinarily large or extraordinarily unquantifiable potential third party liability risk exposure to the Seller or other provider of such anti-terrorism technology.

(4) Substantial likelihood that such anti-terrorism technology will not be deployed unless protections under the system of risk management provided under this subtitle are extended.

(5) Magnitude of risk exposure to the public if such anti-terrorism technology is not deployed.

(6) Evaluation of all scientific studies that can be feasibly conducted in order to assess the capability of the technology to substantially reduce risks of harm.

(7) Anti-terrorism technology that would be effective in facilitating the defense against acts of terrorism, including technologies that prevent, defeat or respond to such acts.

(c) REGULATIONS.—The Secretary may issue such regulations, after notice and comment in accordance with section 553 of title 5, United States Code, as may be necessary to carry out this subtitle.

SEC. 863. LITIGATION MANAGEMENT.

(a) FEDERAL CAUSE OF ACTION.—

(1) IN GENERAL.—There shall exist a Federal cause of action for claims arising out of, relating to, or resulting from an act of terrorism when qualified anti-terrorism technologies have been deployed in defense against or response or recovery from such act and such claims result or may result in loss to the Seller. The substantive law for decision in any such action shall be derived from the law, including choice of law principles, of the State in which such acts of terrorism occurred, unless such law is inconsistent with or preempted by Federal law. Such Federal cause of action shall be brought only for claims for injuries that are proximately caused by sellers that provide qualified anti-terrorism technology to Federal and non-Federal government customers.

(2) JURISDICTION.—Such appropriate district court of the United States shall have original and exclusive jurisdiction over all actions for any claim for loss of property, personal injury, or death arising out of, relating to, or resulting from an act of terrorism when qualified anti-terrorism technologies have been deployed in defense against or response or recovery from such act and such claims result or may result in loss to the Seller.

(b) SPECIAL RULES.—In an action brought under this section for damages the following provisions apply:

(1) PUNITIVE DAMAGES.—No punitive damages intended to punish or deter, exemplary damages, or other damages not intended to compensate a plaintiff for actual losses may be awarded, nor shall any party be liable for interest prior to the judgment.

(2) NONECONOMIC DAMAGES.—

(A) IN GENERAL.—Noneconomic damages may be awarded against a defendant only in an amount directly proportional to the percentage of responsibility of such defendant for the harm to the plaintiff, and no plaintiff may recover noneconomic damages unless the plaintiff suffered physical harm.

(B) DEFINITION.—For purposes of subparagraph (A), the term "noneconomic damages" means damages for losses for physical and emotional pain, suffering, inconvenience, physical impairment, mental anguish, disfigurement, loss of enjoyment of life, loss of society and companionship, loss of consortium, hedonic damages, injury to reputation, and any other nonpecuniary losses.

(c) COLLATERAL SOURCES.—Any recovery by a plaintiff in an action under this section shall be reduced by the amount of collateral source compensation, if any, that the plaintiff has received or is entitled to receive as a result of such acts of terrorism that result or may result in loss to the Seller.

(d) GOVERNMENT CONTRACTOR DEFENSE.—

(1) IN GENERAL.—Should a product liability or other lawsuit be filed for claims arising out of, relating to, or resulting from an act of terrorism when qualified anti-terrorism technologies approved by the Secretary, as provided in paragraphs (2) and (3) of this subsection, have been deployed in defense against or response or recovery from such act and such claims result or may result in loss to the Seller, there shall be a rebuttable presumption that the government contractor defense applies in such lawsuit. This presumption shall only be overcome by evidence showing that the Seller acted fraudulently or with willful misconduct in submitting information to the Secretary during the course of the Secretary's consideration of such technology under this subsection. This presumption of the government contractor defense shall apply regardless of whether the claim against the Seller arises from a sale of the product to Federal Government or non-Federal Government customers.

(2) EXCLUSIVE RESPONSIBILITY.—The Secretary will be exclusively responsible for the review and approval of anti-terrorism technology for purposes of establishing a government contractor defense in any product liability lawsuit for claims arising out of, relating to, or resulting from an act of terrorism when qualified anti-terrorism technologies approved by the Secretary, as provided in this paragraph and paragraph (3), have been deployed in defense against or response or recovery from such act and such claims result or may result in loss to the Seller. Upon the Seller's submission to the Secretary for approval of anti-terrorism technology, the Secretary will conduct a comprehensive review of the design of such technology and determine whether it will perform as intended, conforms to the Seller's specifications, and is safe for use as intended. The Seller will conduct safety and hazard analyses on such technology and will supply the Secretary with all such information.

(3) CERTIFICATE.—For anti-terrorism technology reviewed and approved by the Secretary, the Secretary will issue a certificate of conformance to the Seller and place the anti-terrorism technology on an Approved Product List for Homeland Security.

(e) EXCLUSION.—Nothing in this section shall in any way limit the ability of any person to seek any form of recovery from any person, government, or other entity that—

(1) attempts to commit, knowingly participates in, aids and abets, or commits any act of terrorism, or any criminal act related to or resulting from such act of terrorism; or

(2) participates in a conspiracy to commit any such act of terrorism or any such criminal act.

SEC. 864. RISK MANAGEMENT.

(a) IN GENERAL.—

(1) LIABILITY INSURANCE REQUIRED.—Any person or entity that sells or otherwise provides a qualified anti-terrorism technology to Federal and non-Federal Government customers ("Seller") shall obtain liability insurance of such types and in such amounts as shall be required in accordance with this section and certified by the Secretary to satisfy otherwise compensable third-party claims arising out of, relating to, or resulting from an act of terrorism when qualified anti-terrorism technologies have been deployed in defense against or response or recovery from such act.

(2) MAXIMUM AMOUNT.—For the total claims related to 1 such act of terrorism, the Seller is not required to obtain liability insurance of more than the maximum amount of liability insurance reasonably available from private sources on the world market at prices and terms that will not unreasonably distort the sales price of Seller's anti-terrorism technologies.

(3) SCOPE OF COVERAGE.—Liability insurance obtained pursuant to this subsection shall, in addition to the Seller, protect the following, to the extent of their potential liability for involvement in the manufacture, qualification, sale, use, or operation of qualified anti-terrorism technologies deployed in defense against or response or recovery from an act of terrorism:

(A) Contractors, subcontractors, suppliers, vendors and customers of the Seller.

(B) Contractors, subcontractors, suppliers, and vendors of the customer.

(4) THIRD PARTY CLAIMS.—Such liability insurance under this section shall provide coverage against third party claims arising out of, relating to, or resulting from the sale or use of anti-terrorism technologies.

(b) RECIPROCAL WAIVER OF CLAIMS.—The Seller shall enter into a reciprocal waiver of claims with its contractors, subcontractors, suppliers, vendors and customers, and contractors and subcontractors of the customers, involved in the manufacture, sale, use or operation of qualified anti-terrorism technologies, under which each party to the waiver agrees to be responsible for losses, including business interruption losses, that it sustains, or for losses sustained by its own employees resulting from an activity resulting from an act of terrorism when qualified anti-terrorism technologies have been deployed in defense against or response or recovery from such act.

(c) EXTENT OF LIABILITY.—Notwithstanding any other provision of law, liability for all claims against a Seller arising out of, relating to, or resulting from an act of terrorism when qualified anti-terrorism technologies have been deployed in defense against or response or recovery from such act and such claims result or may result in loss to the Seller, whether for compensatory or punitive damages or for contribution or indemnity, shall not be in an amount greater than the limits of liability insurance coverage required to be maintained by the Seller under this section.

SEC. 865. DEFINITIONS.

For purposes of this subtitle, the following definitions apply:

(1) QUALIFIED ANTI-TERRORISM TECHNOLOGY.—For purposes of this subtitle, the term "qualified anti-terrorism technology"

means any product, equipment, service (including support services), device, or technology (including information technology) designed, developed, modified, or procured for the specific purpose of preventing, detecting, identifying, or deterring acts of terrorism or limiting the harm such acts might otherwise cause, that is designated as such by the Secretary.

(2) ACT OF TERRORISM.—(A) The term "act of terrorism" means any act that the Secretary determines meets the requirements under subparagraph (B), as such requirements are further defined and specified by the Secretary.

(B) REQUIREMENTS.—An act meets the requirements of this subparagraph if the act—

(i) is unlawful;

(ii) causes harm to a person, property, or entity, in the United States, or in the case of a domestic United States air carrier or a United States-flag vessel (or a vessel based principally in the United States on which United States income tax is paid and whose insurance coverage is subject to regulation in the United States), in or outside the United States; and

(iii) uses or attempts to use instrumentalities, weapons or other methods designed or intended to cause mass destruction, injury or other loss to citizens or institutions of the United States.

(3) INSURANCE CARRIER.—The term "insurance carrier" means any corporation, association, society, order, firm, company, mutual, partnership, individual aggregation of individuals, or any other legal entity that provides commercial property and casualty insurance. Such term includes any affiliates of a commercial insurance carrier.

(4) LIABILITY INSURANCE.—

(A) IN GENERAL.—The term "liability insurance" means insurance for legal liabilities incurred by the insured resulting from—

(i) loss of or damage to property of others;

(ii) ensuing loss of income or extra expense incurred because of loss of or damage to property of others;

(iii) bodily injury (including) to persons other than the insured or its employees; or

(iv) loss resulting from debt or default of another.

(5) LOSS.—The term "loss" means death, bodily injury, or loss of or damage to property, including business interruption loss.

(6) NON-FEDERAL GOVERNMENT CUSTOMERS.—The term "non-Federal Government customers" means any customer of a Seller that is not an agency or instrumentality of the United States Government with authority under Public Law 85–804 to provide for indemnification under certain circumstances for third-party claims against its contractors, including but not limited to State and local authorities and commercial entities.

Subtitle H—Miscellaneous Provisions

SEC. 871. ADVISORY COMMITTEES.

(a) IN GENERAL.—The Secretary may establish, appoint members of, and use the services of, advisory committees, as the Secretary may deem necessary. An advisory committee established under this section may be exempted by the Secretary from Public Law 92–463, but the Secretary shall publish notice in the Federal Register announcing the establishment of such a committee and identifying its purpose and membership. Notwithstanding the preceding sentence, members of an advisory committee that is exempted by the Secretary under the preceding sentence who are special Government employees (as that term is defined in section 202 of title 18, United States Code) shall be eligible for certifications under subsection (b)(3) of section 208 of title 18, United States Code, for official actions taken as a member of such advisory committee.

(b) TERMINATION.—Any advisory committee established by the Secretary shall terminate 2 years after the date of its establishment, unless the Secretary makes a written determination to extend the advisory committee to a specified date, which shall not be more than 2 years after the date on which such determination is made. The Secretary may make any number of subsequent extensions consistent with this subsection.

SEC. 872. REORGANIZATION.

(a) REORGANIZATION.—The Secretary may allocate or reallocate functions among the officers of the Department, and may establish, consolidate, alter, or discontinue organizational units within the Department, but only—

(1) pursuant to section 1502(b); or

(2) after the expiration of 60 days after providing notice of such action to the appropriate congressional committees, which shall include an explanation of the rationale for the action.

(b) LIMITATIONS.—

(1) IN GENERAL.—Authority under subsection (a)(1) does not extend to the abolition of any agency, entity, organizational unit, program, or function established or required to be maintained by this Act.

(2) ABOLITIONS.—Authority under subsection (a)(2) does not extend to the abolition of any agency, entity, organizational unit, program, or function established or required to be maintained by statute.

SEC. 873. USE OF APPROPRIATED FUNDS.

(a) DISPOSAL OF PROPERTY.—

(1) STRICT COMPLIANCE.—If specifically authorized to dispose of real property in this or any other Act, the Secretary shall exercise this authority in strict compliance with section 204 of the Federal Property and Administrative Services Act of 1949 (40 U.S.C. 485).

(2) DEPOSIT OF PROCEEDS.—The Secretary shall deposit the proceeds of any exercise of property disposal authority into the miscellaneous receipts of the Treasury in accordance with section 3302(b) of title 31, United States Code.

(b) GIFTS.—Gifts or donations of services or property of or for the Department may not be accepted, used, or disposed of unless specifically permitted in advance in an appropriations Act and only under the conditions and for the purposes specified in such appropriations Act.

(c) BUDGET REQUEST.—Under section 1105 of title 31, United States Code, the President shall submit to Congress a detailed budget request for the Department for fiscal year 2004, and for each subsequent fiscal year.

SEC. 874. FUTURE YEAR HOMELAND SECURITY PROGRAM.

(a) IN GENERAL.—Each budget request submitted to Congress for the Department under section 1105 of title 31, United States Code, shall, at or about the same time, be accompanied by a Future Years Homeland Security Program.

(b) CONTENTS.—The Future Years Homeland Security Program under subsection (a) shall be structured, and include the same type of information and level of detail, as the Future Years Defense Program submitted to Congress by the Department of Defense under section 221 of title 10, United States Code.

(c) EFFECTIVE DATE.—This section shall take effect with respect to the preparation and submission of the fiscal year 2005 budget request for the Department and for any subsequent fiscal year, except that the first Future Years Homeland Security Program shall be submitted not later than 90 days after the Department's fiscal year 2005 budget request is submitted to Congress.

SEC. 875. MISCELLANEOUS AUTHORITIES.

(a) SEAL.—The Department shall have a seal, whose design is subject to the approval of the President.

(b) PARTICIPATION OF MEMBERS OF THE ARMED FORCES.—With respect to the Department, the Secretary shall have the same authorities that the Secretary of Transportation has with respect to the Department of Transportation under section 324 of title 49, United States Code.

(c) REDELEGATION OF FUNCTIONS.—Unless otherwise provided in the delegation or by law, any function delegated under this Act may be redelegated to any subordinate.

SEC. 876. MILITARY ACTIVITIES.

Nothing in this Act shall confer upon the Secretary any authority to engage in warfighting, the military defense of the United States, or other military activities, nor shall anything in this Act limit the existing authority of the Department of Defense or the Armed Forces to engage in warfighting, the military defense of the United States, or other military activities.

SEC. 877. REGULATORY AUTHORITY AND PREEMPTION.

(a) REGULATORY AUTHORITY.—Except as otherwise provided in sections 306(c), 862(c), and 1706(b), this Act vests no new regulatory authority in the Secretary or any other Federal official, and transfers to the Secretary or another Federal official only such regulatory authority as exists on the date of enactment of this Act within any agency, program, or function transferred to the Department pursuant to this Act, or that on such date of enactment is exercised by another official of the executive branch with respect to such agency, program, or function. Any such transferred authority may not be exercised by an official from whom it is transferred upon transfer of such agency, program, or function to the Secretary or another Federal official pursuant to this Act. This Act may not be construed as altering or diminishing the regulatory authority of any other executive agency, except to the extent that this Act transfers such authority from the agency.

(b) PREEMPTION OF STATE OR LOCAL LAW.—Except as otherwise provided in this Act, this Act preempts no State or local law, except that any authority to preempt State or local law vested in any Federal agency or official transferred to the Department pursuant to this Act shall be transferred to the Department effective on the date of the transfer to the Department of that Federal agency or official.

SEC. 878. COUNTERNARCOTICS OFFICER.

The Secretary shall appoint a senior official in the Department to assume primary responsibility for coordinating policy and operations within the Department and between the Department and other Federal departments and agencies with respect to interdicting the entry of illegal drugs into the United States, and tracking and severing connections between illegal drug trafficking and terrorism. Such official shall—

(1) ensure the adequacy of resources within the Department for illicit drug interdiction; and

(2) serve as the United States Interdiction Coordinator for the Director of National Drug Control Policy.

SEC. 879. OFFICE OF INTERNATIONAL AFFAIRS.

(a) ESTABLISHMENT.—There is established within the Office of the Secretary an Office of International Affairs. The Office shall be headed by a Director, who shall be a senior official appointed by the Secretary.

(b) DUTIES OF THE DIRECTOR.—The Director shall have the following duties:

(1) To promote information and education exchange with nations friendly to the United States in order to promote sharing of best practices and technologies relating to homeland security. Such exchange shall include the following:

(A) Exchange of information on research and development on homeland security technologies.

(B) Joint training exercises of first responders.

(C) Exchange of expertise on terrorism prevention, response, and crisis management.

(2) To identify areas for homeland security information and training exchange where the United States has a demonstrated weakness and another friendly nation or nations have a demonstrated expertise.

(3) To plan and undertake international conferences, exchange programs, and training activities.

(4) To manage international activities within the Department in coordination with other Federal officials with responsibility for counter-terrorism matters.

SEC. 880. PROHIBITION OF THE TERRORISM INFORMATION AND PREVENTION SYSTEM.

Any and all activities of the Federal Government to implement the proposed component program of the Citizen Corps known as Operation TIPS (Terrorism Information and Prevention System) are hereby prohibited.

SEC. 881. REVIEW OF PAY AND BENEFIT PLANS.

Notwithstanding any other provision of this Act, the Secretary shall, in consultation with the Director of the Office of Personnel Management, review the pay and benefit plans of each agency whose functions are transferred under this Act to the Department and, within 90 days after the date of enactment, submit a plan to the President of the Senate and the Speaker of the House of Representatives and the appropriate committees and subcommittees of Congress, for ensuring, to the maximum extent practicable, the elimination of disparities in pay and benefits throughout the Department, especially among law enforcement personnel, that are inconsistent with merit system principles set forth in section 2301 of title 5, United States Code.

SEC. 882. OFFICE FOR NATIONAL CAPITAL REGION COORDINATION.

(a) ESTABLISHMENT.—

(1) IN GENERAL.—There is established within the Office of the Secretary the Office of National Capital Region Coordination, to oversee and coordinate Federal programs for and relationships with State, local, and regional authorities in the National Capital Region, as defined under section 2674(f)(2) of title 10, United States Code.

(2) DIRECTOR.—The Office established under paragraph (1) shall be headed by a Director, who shall be appointed by the Secretary.

(3) COOPERATION.—The Secretary shall cooperate with the Mayor of the District of Columbia, the Governors of Maryland and Virginia, and other State, local, and regional officers in the National Capital Region to integrate the District of Columbia, Maryland, and Virginia into the planning, coordination, and execution of the activities of the Federal Government for the enhancement of domestic preparedness against the consequences of terrorist attacks.

(b) RESPONSIBILITIES.—The Office established under subsection (a)(1) shall—

(1) coordinate the activities of the Department relating to the National Capital Region, including cooperation with the Office for State and Local Government Coordination;

(2) assess, and advocate for, the resources needed by State, local, and regional authorities in the National Capital Region to implement efforts to secure the homeland;

(3) provide State, local, and regional authorities in the National Capital Region with regular information, research, and technical support to assist the efforts of State, local, and regional authorities in the National Capital Region in securing the homeland;

(4) develop a process for receiving meaningful input from State, local, and regional authorities and the private sector in the National Capital Region to assist in the development of the homeland security plans and activities of the Federal Government;

(5) coordinate with Federal agencies in the National Capital Region on terrorism preparedness, to ensure adequate planning, information sharing, training, and execution of the Federal role in domestic preparedness activities;

(6) coordinate with Federal, State, local, and regional agencies, and the private sector in the National Capital Region

on terrorism preparedness to ensure adequate planning, information sharing, training, and execution of domestic preparedness activities among these agencies and entities; and

(7) serve as a liaison between the Federal Government and State, local, and regional authorities, and private sector entities in the National Capital Region to facilitate access to Federal grants and other programs.

(c) ANNUAL REPORT.—The Office established under subsection (a) shall submit an annual report to Congress that includes—

(1) the identification of the resources required to fully implement homeland security efforts in the National Capital Region;

(2) an assessment of the progress made by the National Capital Region in implementing homeland security efforts; and

(3) recommendations to Congress regarding the additional resources needed to fully implement homeland security efforts in the National Capital Region.

(d) LIMITATION.—Nothing contained in this section shall be construed as limiting the power of State and local governments.

SEC. 883. REQUIREMENT TO COMPLY WITH LAWS PROTECTING EQUAL EMPLOYMENT OPPORTUNITY AND PROVIDING WHISTLE-BLOWER PROTECTIONS.

Nothing in this Act shall be construed as exempting the Department from requirements applicable with respect to executive agencies—

(1) to provide equal employment protection for employees of the Department (including pursuant to the provisions in section 2302(b)(1) of title 5, United States Code, and the Notification and Federal Employee Antidiscrimination and Retaliation Act of 2002 (Public Law 107–174)); or

(2) to provide whistleblower protections for employees of the Department (including pursuant to the provisions in section 2302(b)(8) and (9) of such title and the Notification and Federal Employee Antidiscrimination and Retaliation Act of 2002).

SEC. 884. FEDERAL LAW ENFORCEMENT TRAINING CENTER.

(a) IN GENERAL.—The transfer of an authority or an agency under this Act to the Department of Homeland Security does not affect training agreements already entered into with the Federal Law Enforcement Training Center with respect to the training of personnel to carry out that authority or the duties of that transferred agency.

(b) CONTINUITY OF OPERATIONS.—All activities of the Federal Law Enforcement Training Center transferred to the Department of Homeland Security under this Act shall continue to be carried out at the locations such activities were carried out before such transfer.

SEC. 885. JOINT INTERAGENCY TASK FORCE.

(a) ESTABLISHMENT.—The Secretary may establish and operate a permanent Joint Interagency Homeland Security Task Force composed of representatives from military and civilian agencies of the United States Government for the purposes of anticipating terrorist threats against the United States and taking appropriate actions to prevent harm to the United States.

(b) STRUCTURE.—It is the sense of Congress that the Secretary should model the Joint Interagency Homeland Security Task Force on the approach taken by the Joint Interagency Task Forces for drug interdiction at Key West, Florida and Alameda, California, to the maximum extent feasible and appropriate.

SEC. 886. SENSE OF CONGRESS REAFFIRMING THE CONTINUED IMPORTANCE AND APPLICABILITY OF THE POSSE COMITATUS ACT.

(a) FINDINGS.—Congress finds the following:

(1) Section 1385 of title 18, United States Code (commonly known as the "Posse Comitatus Act"), prohibits the use of the Armed Forces as a posse comitatus to execute the laws except in cases and under circumstances expressly authorized by the Constitution or Act of Congress.

(2) Enacted in 1878, the Posse Comitatus Act was expressly intended to prevent United States Marshals, on their own initiative, from calling on the Army for assistance in enforcing Federal law.

(3) The Posse Comitatus Act has served the Nation well in limiting the use of the Armed Forces to enforce the law.

(4) Nevertheless, by its express terms, the Posse Comitatus Act is not a complete barrier to the use of the Armed Forces for a range of domestic purposes, including law enforcement functions, when the use of the Armed Forces is authorized by Act of Congress or the President determines that the use of the Armed Forces is required to fulfill the President's obligations under the Constitution to respond promptly in time of war, insurrection, or other serious emergency.

(5) Existing laws, including chapter 15 of title 10, United States Code (commonly known as the "Insurrection Act"), and the Robert T. Stafford Disaster Relief and Emergency Assistance Act (42 U.S.C. 5121 et seq.), grant the President broad powers that may be invoked in the event of domestic emergencies, including an attack against the Nation using weapons of mass destruction, and these laws specifically authorize the President to use the Armed Forces to help restore public order.

(b) SENSE OF CONGRESS.—Congress reaffirms the continued importance of section 1385 of title 18, United States Code, and it is the sense of Congress that nothing in this Act should be construed to alter the applicability of such section to any use of the Armed Forces as a posse comitatus to execute the laws.

SEC. 887. COORDINATION WITH THE DEPARTMENT OF HEALTH AND HUMAN SERVICES UNDER THE PUBLIC HEALTH SERVICE ACT.

(a) IN GENERAL.—The annual Federal response plan developed by the Department shall be consistent with section 319 of the Public Health Service Act (42 U.S.C. 247d).

(b) DISCLOSURES AMONG RELEVANT AGENCIES.—

(1) IN GENERAL.—Full disclosure among relevant agencies shall be made in accordance with this subsection.

(2) PUBLIC HEALTH EMERGENCY.—During the period in which the Secretary of Health and Human Services has declared the existence of a public health emergency under section 319(a) of the Public Health Service Act (42 U.S.C. 247d(a)), the Secretary of Health and Human Services shall keep relevant agencies, including the Department of Homeland Security, the Department of Justice, and the Federal Bureau of Investigation, fully and currently informed.

(3) POTENTIAL PUBLIC HEALTH EMERGENCY.—In cases involving, or potentially involving, a public health emergency, but in which no determination of an emergency by the Secretary of Health and Human Services under section 319(a) of the Public Health Service Act (42 U.S.C. 247d(a)), has been made, all relevant agencies, including the Department of Homeland Security, the Department of Justice, and the Federal Bureau of Investigation, shall keep the Secretary of Health and Human Services and the Director of the Centers for Disease Control and Prevention fully and currently informed.

SEC. 888. PRESERVING COAST GUARD MISSION PERFORMANCE.

(a) DEFINITIONS.—In this section:

(1) NON-HOMELAND SECURITY MISSIONS.—The term "non-homeland security missions" means the following missions of the Coast Guard:

(A) Marine safety.

(B) Search and rescue.

(C) Aids to navigation.

(D) Living marine resources (fisheries law enforcement).

(E) Marine environmental protection.

(F) Ice operations.

(2) HOMELAND SECURITY MISSIONS.—The term "homeland security missions" means the following missions of the Coast Guard:

(A) Ports, waterways and coastal security.

(B) Drug interdiction.

(C) Migrant interdiction.

(D) Defense readiness.

(E) Other law enforcement.

(b) TRANSFER.—There are transferred to the Department the authorities, functions, personnel, and assets of the Coast Guard, which shall be maintained as a distinct entity within the Department, including the authorities and functions of the Secretary of Transportation relating thereto.

(c) MAINTENANCE OF STATUS OF FUNCTIONS AND ASSETS.—Notwithstanding any other provision of this Act, the authorities, functions, and capabilities of the Coast Guard to perform its missions shall be maintained intact and without significant reduction after the transfer of the Coast Guard to the Department, except as specified in subsequent Acts.

(d) CERTAIN TRANSFERS PROHIBITED.—No mission, function, or asset (including for purposes of this subsection any ship, aircraft, or helicopter) of the Coast Guard may be diverted to the principal and continuing use of any other organization, unit, or entity of the Department, except for details or assignments that do not reduce the Coast Guard's capability to perform its missions.

(e) CHANGES TO MISSIONS.—

(1) PROHIBITION.—The Secretary may not substantially or significantly reduce the missions of the Coast Guard or the Coast Guard's capability to perform those missions, except as specified in subsequent Acts.

(2) WAIVER.—The Secretary may waive the restrictions under paragraph (1) for a period of not to exceed 90 days upon a declaration and certification by the Secretary to Congress that a clear, compelling, and immediate need exists for

such a waiver. A certification under this paragraph shall include a detailed justification for the declaration and certification, including the reasons and specific information that demonstrate that the Nation and the Coast Guard cannot respond effectively if the restrictions under paragraph (1) are not waived.

(f) ANNUAL REVIEW.—

(1) IN GENERAL.—The Inspector General of the Department shall conduct an annual review that shall assess thoroughly the performance by the Coast Guard of all missions of the Coast Guard (including non-homeland security missions and homeland security missions) with a particular emphasis on examining the non-homeland security missions.

(2) REPORT.—The report under this paragraph shall be submitted to—

(A) the Committee on Governmental Affairs of the Senate;

(B) the Committee on Government Reform of the House of Representatives;

(C) the Committees on Appropriations of the Senate and the House of Representatives;

(D) the Committee on Commerce, Science, and Transportation of the Senate; and

(E) the Committee on Transportation and Infrastructure of the House of Representatives.

(g) DIRECT REPORTING TO SECRETARY.—Upon the transfer of the Coast Guard to the Department, the Commandant shall report directly to the Secretary without being required to report through any other official of the Department.

(h) OPERATION AS A SERVICE IN THE NAVY.—None of the conditions and restrictions in this section shall apply when the Coast Guard operates as a service in the Navy under section 3 of title 14, United States Code.

(i) REPORT ON ACCELERATING THE INTEGRATED DEEPWATER SYSTEM.—Not later than 90 days after the date of enactment of this Act, the Secretary, in consultation with the Commandant of the Coast Guard, shall submit a report to the Committee on Commerce, Science, and Transportation of the Senate, the Committee on Transportation and Infrastructure of the House of Representatives, and the Committees on Appropriations of the Senate and the House of Representatives that—

(1) analyzes the feasibility of accelerating the rate of procurement in the Coast Guard's Integrated Deepwater System from 20 years to 10 years;

(2) includes an estimate of additional resources required;

(3) describes the resulting increased capabilities;

(4) outlines any increases in the Coast Guard's homeland security readiness;

(5) describes any increases in operational efficiencies; and

(6) provides a revised asset phase-in time line.

SEC. 889. HOMELAND SECURITY FUNDING ANALYSIS IN PRESIDENT'S BUDGET.

(a) IN GENERAL.—Section 1105(a) of title 31, United States Code, is amended by adding at the end the following:

"(33)(A)(i) a detailed, separate analysis, by budget function, by agency, and by initiative area (as determined by the administration) for the prior fiscal year, the current fiscal year, the fiscal years for which the budget is submitted, and the ensuing fiscal year identifying the amounts of gross and net appropriations or obligational authority and outlays that contribute to homeland security, with separate displays for mandatory and discretionary amounts, including—

"(I) summaries of the total amount of such appropriations or new obligational authority and outlays requested for homeland security;

"(II) an estimate of the current service levels of homeland security spending;

"(III) the most recent risk assessment and summary of homeland security needs in each initiative area (as determined by the administration); and

"(IV) an estimate of user fees collected by the Federal Government on behalf of homeland security activities;

"(ii) with respect to subclauses (I) through (IV) of clause (i), amounts shall be provided by account for each program, project and activity; and

"(iii) an estimate of expenditures for homeland security activities by State and local governments and the private sector for the prior fiscal year and the current fiscal year.

"(B) In this paragraph, consistent with the Office of Management and Budget's June 2002 'Annual Report to Congress on Combatting Terrorism', the term 'homeland security' refers to those activities that detect, deter, protect against, and respond to terrorist attacks occurring within the United States and its territories.

"(C) In implementing this paragraph, including determining what Federal activities or accounts constitute homeland security for purposes of budgetary classification, the Office of Management and Budget is directed to consult periodically, but at least annually, with the House and Senate Budget Committees, the House and Senate Appropriations Committees, and the Congressional Budget Office.".

(b) REPEAL OF DUPLICATIVE REPORTS.—The following sections are repealed:

(1) Section 1051 of Public Law 105–85.

(2) Section 1403 of Public Law 105–261.

(c) EFFECTIVE DATE.—This section and the amendment made by this section shall apply beginning with respect to the fiscal year 2005 budget submission.

SEC. 890. AIR TRANSPORTATION SAFETY AND SYSTEM STABILIZATION ACT.

The Air Transportation Safety and System Stabilization Act (49 U.S.C. 40101 note) is amended—

(1) in section 408 by striking the last sentence of subsection (c); and

(2) in section 402 by striking paragraph (1) and inserting the following:

"(1) AIR CARRIER.—The term 'air carrier' means a citizen of the United States undertaking by any means, directly or indirectly, to provide air transportation and includes employees and agents (including persons engaged in the business of providing air transportation security and their affiliates) of such citizen. For purposes of the preceding sentence, the term 'agent', as applied to persons engaged in the business of providing air transportation security, shall only include persons that have contracted directly with the Federal Aviation Administration on or after and commenced services no later than February 17, 2002, to provide such security, and had not been or are not debarred for any period within 6 months from that date.".

Subtitle I—Information Sharing

SEC. 891. SHORT TITLE; FINDINGS; AND SENSE OF CONGRESS.

(a) SHORT TITLE.—This subtitle may be cited as the "Homeland Security Information Sharing Act".

(b) FINDINGS.—Congress finds the following:

(1) The Federal Government is required by the Constitution to provide for the common defense, which includes terrorist attack.

(2) The Federal Government relies on State and local personnel to protect against terrorist attack.

(3) The Federal Government collects, creates, manages, and protects classified and sensitive but unclassified information to enhance homeland security.

(4) Some homeland security information is needed by the State and local personnel to prevent and prepare for terrorist attack.

(5) The needs of State and local personnel to have access to relevant homeland security information to combat terrorism must be reconciled with the need to preserve the protected status of such information and to protect the sources and methods used to acquire such information.

(6) Granting security clearances to certain State and local personnel is one way to facilitate the sharing of information regarding specific terrorist threats among Federal, State, and local levels of government.

(7) Methods exist to declassify, redact, or otherwise adapt classified information so it may be shared with State and local personnel without the need for granting additional security clearances.

(8) State and local personnel have capabilities and opportunities to gather information on suspicious activities and terrorist threats not possessed by Federal agencies.

(9) The Federal Government and State and local governments and agencies in other jurisdictions may benefit from such information.

(10) Federal, State, and local governments and intelligence, law enforcement, and other emergency preparation and response agencies must act in partnership to maximize the benefits of information gathering and analysis to prevent and respond to terrorist attacks.

(11) Information systems, including the National Law Enforcement Telecommunications System and the Terrorist Threat Warning System, have been established for rapid sharing of classified and sensitive but unclassified information among Federal, State, and local entities.

(12) Increased efforts to share homeland security information should avoid duplicating existing information systems.

(c) SENSE OF CONGRESS.—It is the sense of Congress that Federal, State, and local entities should share homeland security information to the maximum extent practicable, with special emphasis on hard-to-reach urban and rural communities.

SEC. 892. FACILITATING HOMELAND SECURITY INFORMATION SHARING PROCEDURES.

(a) PROCEDURES FOR DETERMINING EXTENT OF SHARING OF HOMELAND SECURITY INFORMATION.—

(1) The President shall prescribe and implement procedures under which relevant Federal agencies—

(A) share relevant and appropriate homeland security information with other Federal agencies, including the Department, and appropriate State and local personnel;

(B) identify and safeguard homeland security information that is sensitive but unclassified; and

(C) to the extent such information is in classified form, determine whether, how, and to what extent to remove classified information, as appropriate, and with which such personnel it may be shared after such information is removed.

(2) The President shall ensure that such procedures apply to all agencies of the Federal Government.

(3) Such procedures shall not change the substantive requirements for the classification and safeguarding of classified information.

(4) Such procedures shall not change the requirements and authorities to protect sources and methods.

(b) PROCEDURES FOR SHARING OF HOMELAND SECURITY INFORMATION.—

(1) Under procedures prescribed by the President, all appropriate agencies, including the intelligence community, shall, through information sharing systems, share homeland security information with Federal agencies and appropriate State and local personnel to the extent such information may be shared, as determined in accordance with subsection (a), together with assessments of the credibility of such information.

(2) Each information sharing system through which information is shared under paragraph (1) shall—

(A) have the capability to transmit unclassified or classified information, though the procedures and recipients for each capability may differ;

(B) have the capability to restrict delivery of information to specified subgroups by geographic location, type of organization, position of a recipient within an organization, or a recipient's need to know such information;

(C) be configured to allow the efficient and effective sharing of information; and

(D) be accessible to appropriate State and local personnel.

(3) The procedures prescribed under paragraph (1) shall establish conditions on the use of information shared under paragraph (1)—

(A) to limit the redissemination of such information to ensure that such information is not used for an unauthorized purpose;

(B) to ensure the security and confidentiality of such information;

(C) to protect the constitutional and statutory rights of any individuals who are subjects of such information; and

(D) to provide data integrity through the timely removal and destruction of obsolete or erroneous names and information.

(4) The procedures prescribed under paragraph (1) shall ensure, to the greatest extent practicable, that the information sharing system through which information is shared under such paragraph include existing information sharing systems, including, but not limited to, the National Law Enforcement Telecommunications System, the Regional Information Sharing System, and the Terrorist Threat Warning System of the Federal Bureau of Investigation.

(5) Each appropriate Federal agency, as determined by the President, shall have access to each information sharing system through which information is shared under paragraph (1), and shall therefore have access to all information, as appropriate, shared under such paragraph.

(6) The procedures prescribed under paragraph (1) shall ensure that appropriate State and local personnel are authorized to use such information sharing systems—

(A) to access information shared with such personnel; and

(B) to· share, with others who have access to such information sharing systems, the homeland security information of their own jurisdictions, which shall be marked appropriately as pertaining to potential terrorist activity.

(7) Under procedures prescribed jointly by the Director of Central Intelligence and the Attorney General, each appropriate Federal agency, as determined by the President, shall review and assess the information shared under paragraph (6) and integrate such information with existing intelligence.

(c) SHARING OF CLASSIFIED INFORMATION AND SENSITIVE BUT UNCLASSIFIED INFORMATION WITH STATE AND LOCAL PERSONNEL.—

(1) The President shall prescribe procedures under which Federal agencies may, to the extent the President considers necessary, share with appropriate State and local personnel homeland security information that remains classified or otherwise protected after the determinations prescribed under the procedures set forth in subsection (a).

(2) It is the sense of Congress that such procedures may include 1 or more of the following means:

(A) Carrying out security clearance investigations with respect to appropriate State and local personnel.

(B) With respect to information that is sensitive but unclassified, entering into nondisclosure agreements with appropriate State and local personnel.

(C) Increased use of information-sharing partnerships that include appropriate State and local personnel, such as the Joint Terrorism Task Forces of the Federal Bureau of Investigation, the Anti-Terrorism Task Forces of the Department of Justice, and regional Terrorism Early Warning Groups.

(d) RESPONSIBLE OFFICIALS.—For each affected Federal agency, the head of such agency shall designate an official to administer this Act with respect to such agency.

(e) FEDERAL CONTROL OF INFORMATION.—Under procedures prescribed under this section, information obtained by a State or local government from a Federal agency under this section shall remain under the control of the Federal agency, and a State or local law authorizing or requiring such a government to disclose information shall not apply to such information.

(f) DEFINITIONS.—As used in this section:

(1) The term "homeland security information" means any information possessed by a Federal, State, or local agency that—

(A) relates to the threat of terrorist activity;

(B) relates to the ability to prevent, interdict, or disrupt terrorist activity;

(C) would improve the identification or investigation of a suspected terrorist or terrorist organization; or

(D) would improve the response to a terrorist act.

(2) The term "intelligence community" has the meaning given such term in section 3(4) of the National Security Act of 1947 (50 U.S.C. 401a(4)).

(3) The term "State and local personnel" means any of the following persons involved in prevention, preparation, or response for terrorist attack:

(A) State Governors, mayors, and other locally elected officials.

(B) State and local law enforcement personnel and firefighters.

(C) Public health and medical professionals.

(D) Regional, State, and local emergency management agency personnel, including State adjutant generals.

(E) Other appropriate emergency response agency personnel.

(F) Employees of private-sector entities that affect critical infrastructure, cyber, economic, or public health security, as designated by the Federal Government in procedures developed pursuant to this section.

(4) The term "State" includes the District of Columbia and any commonwealth, territory, or possession of the United States.

(g) CONSTRUCTION.—Nothing in this Act shall be construed as authorizing any department, bureau, agency, officer, or employee of the Federal Government to request, receive, or transmit to any other Government entity or personnel, or transmit to any State or local entity or personnel otherwise authorized by this Act to receive homeland security information, any information collected by the Federal Government solely for statistical purposes in violation of any other provision of law relating to the confidentiality of such information.

SEC. 893. REPORT.

(a) REPORT REQUIRED.—Not later than 12 months after the date of the enactment of this Act, the President shall submit to the congressional committees specified in subsection (b) a report on the implementation of section 892. The report shall include any recommendations for additional measures or appropriation requests, beyond the requirements of section 892, to increase the effectiveness of sharing of information between and among Federal, State, and local entities.

(b) SPECIFIED CONGRESSIONAL COMMITTEES.—The congressional committees referred to in subsection (a) are the following committees:

(1) The Permanent Select Committee on Intelligence and the Committee on the Judiciary of the House of Representatives.

(2) The Select Committee on Intelligence and the Committee on the Judiciary of the Senate.

SEC. 894. AUTHORIZATION OF APPROPRIATIONS.

There are authorized to be appropriated such sums as may be necessary to carry out section 892.

SEC. 895. AUTHORITY TO SHARE GRAND JURY INFORMATION.

Rule 6(e) of the Federal Rules of Criminal Procedure is amended—

(1) in paragraph (2), by inserting ", or of guidelines jointly issued by the Attorney General and Director of Central Intelligence pursuant to Rule 6," after "Rule 6"; and

(2) in paragraph (3)—

(A) in subparagraph (A)(ii), by inserting "or of a foreign government" after "(including personnel of a state or subdivision of a state";

(B) in subparagraph (C)(i)—

(i) in subclause (I), by inserting before the semicolon the following: "or, upon a request by an attorney for the government, when sought by a foreign court or prosecutor for use in an official criminal investigation";

(ii) in subclause (IV)—

(I) by inserting "or foreign" after "may disclose a violation of State";

(II) by inserting "or of a foreign government" after "to an appropriate official of a State or subdivision of a State"; and

(III) by striking "or" at the end;

(iii) by striking the period at the end of subclause (V) and inserting "; or"; and

(iv) by adding at the end the following:

"(VI) when matters involve a threat of actual or potential attack or other grave hostile acts of a foreign power or an agent of a foreign power, domestic or international sabotage, domestic or international terrorism, or clandestine intelligence gathering activities by an intelligence service or network of a foreign power or by an agent of a foreign power, within the United States or elsewhere, to any appropriate federal, state, local, or foreign government official for the purpose of preventing or responding to such a threat."; and

(C) in subparagraph (C)(iii)—

(i) by striking "Federal";

(ii) by inserting "or clause (i)(VI)" after "clause (i)(V)"; and

(iii) by adding at the end the following: "Any state, local, or foreign official who receives information pursuant to clause (i)(VI) shall use that information only consistent with such guidelines as the Attorney General and Director of Central Intelligence shall jointly issue.".

SEC. 896. AUTHORITY TO SHARE ELECTRONIC, WIRE, AND ORAL INTERCEPTION INFORMATION.

Section 2517 of title 18, United States Code, is amended by adding at the end the following:

"(7) Any investigative or law enforcement officer, or other Federal official in carrying out official duties as such Federal official, who by any means authorized by this chapter, has obtained knowledge of the contents of any wire, oral, or electronic communication, or evidence derived therefrom, may disclose such contents or derivative evidence to a foreign investigative or law enforcement officer to the extent that such disclosure is appropriate to the proper performance of the official duties of the officer making or receiving the disclosure, and foreign investigative or law enforcement officers may use or disclose such contents or derivative evidence to the extent such use or disclosure is appropriate to the proper performance of their official duties.

"(8) Any investigative or law enforcement officer, or other Federal official in carrying out official duties as such Federal official, who by any means authorized by this chapter, has obtained knowledge of the contents of any wire, oral, or electronic communication, or evidence derived therefrom, may disclose such contents or derivative evidence to any appropriate Federal, State, local, or foreign government official to the extent that such contents or derivative evidence reveals a threat of actual or potential attack or other grave hostile acts of a foreign power or an agent of a foreign power, domestic or international sabotage, domestic or international terrorism, or clandestine intelligence gathering activities by an intelligence service or network of a foreign power or by an agent of a foreign power, within the United States or elsewhere, for the purpose of preventing or responding to such a threat. Any official who receives information pursuant to this provision may use that information only as necessary in the conduct of that person's official duties subject to any limitations on the unauthorized disclosure of such information, and any State, local, or foreign official who receives information pursuant to this provision may use that information only consistent with such guidelines as the Attorney General and Director of Central Intelligence shall jointly issue.".

SEC. 897. FOREIGN INTELLIGENCE INFORMATION.

(a) DISSEMINATION AUTHORIZED.—Section 203(d)(1) of the Uniting and Strengthening America by Providing Appropriate Tools Required to Intercept and Obstruct Terrorism (USA PATRIOT ACT) Act of 2001 (Public Law 107–56; 50 U.S.C. 403–5d) is amended by adding at the end the following: "Consistent with the responsibility of the Director of Central Intelligence to protect intelligence sources and methods, and the responsibility of the Attorney General to protect sensitive law enforcement information, it shall be lawful for information revealing a threat of actual or potential attack or other grave hostile acts of a foreign power or an agent of a foreign power, domestic or international sabotage, domestic or international terrorism, or clandestine intelligence gathering activities by an intelligence service or network of a foreign power or by an agent of a foreign power, within the United States or elsewhere, obtained as part of a criminal investigation to be disclosed to any appropriate Federal, State, local, or foreign government official for the purpose of preventing or responding to such a threat. Any official who receives information pursuant to this provision may use that information only as necessary in the conduct of that person's official duties subject to any limitations on the unauthorized disclosure of such information, and any State, local, or foreign official who receives information pursuant to this provision may use that information only consistent with such guidelines as the Attorney General and Director of Central Intelligence shall jointly issue.".

(b) CONFORMING AMENDMENTS.—Section 203(c) of that Act is amended—

(1) by striking "section 2517(6)" and inserting "paragraphs (6) and (8) of section 2517 of title 18, United States Code,"; and

(2) by inserting "and (VI)" after "Rule 6(e)(3)(C)(i)(V)".

SEC. 898. INFORMATION ACQUIRED FROM AN ELECTRONIC SURVEILLANCE.

Section 106(k)(1) of the Foreign Intelligence Surveillance Act of 1978 (50 U.S.C. 1806) is amended by inserting after "law enforcement officers" the following: "or law enforcement personnel of a State or political subdivision of a State (including the chief executive officer of that State or political subdivision who has the authority to appoint or direct the chief law enforcement officer of that State or political subdivision)".

SEC. 899. INFORMATION ACQUIRED FROM A PHYSICAL SEARCH.

Section 305(k)(1) of the Foreign Intelligence Surveillance Act of 1978 (50 U.S.C. 1825) is amended by inserting after "law enforcement officers" the following: "or law enforcement personnel of a State or political subdivision of a State (including the chief executive officer of that State or political subdivision who has the authority to appoint or direct the chief law enforcement officer of that State or political subdivision)".

TITLE IX—NATIONAL HOMELAND SECURITY COUNCIL

SEC. 901. NATIONAL HOMELAND SECURITY COUNCIL.

There is established within the Executive Office of the President a council to be known as the "Homeland Security Council" (in this title referred to as the "Council").

SEC. 902. FUNCTION.

The function of the Council shall be to advise the President on homeland security matters.

SEC. 903. MEMBERSHIP.

The members of the Council shall be the following:
(1) The President.

(2) The Vice President.
(3) The Secretary of Homeland Security.
(4) The Attorney General.
(5) The Secretary of Defense.
(6) Such other individuals as may be designated by the President.

SEC. 904. OTHER FUNCTIONS AND ACTIVITIES.

For the purpose of more effectively coordinating the policies and functions of the United States Government relating to homeland security, the Council shall—

(1) assess the objectives, commitments, and risks of the United States in the interest of homeland security and to make resulting recommendations to the President;

(2) oversee and review homeland security policies of the Federal Government and to make resulting recommendations to the President; and

(3) perform such other functions as the President may direct.

SEC. 905. STAFF COMPOSITION.

The Council shall have a staff, the head of which shall be a civilian Executive Secretary, who shall be appointed by the President. The President is authorized to fix the pay of the Executive Secretary at a rate not to exceed the rate of pay payable to the Executive Secretary of the National Security Council.

SEC. 906. RELATION TO THE NATIONAL SECURITY COUNCIL.

The President may convene joint meetings of the Homeland Security Council and the National Security Council with participation by members of either Council or as the President may otherwise direct.

TITLE X—INFORMATION SECURITY

SEC. 1001. INFORMATION SECURITY.

(a) SHORT TITLE.—This title may be cited as the "Federal Information Security Management Act of 2002".

(b) INFORMATION SECURITY.—

(1) IN GENERAL.—Subchapter II of chapter 35 of title 44, United States Code, is amended to read as follows:

"SUBCHAPTER II—INFORMATION SECURITY

"§ 3531. Purposes

"The purposes of this subchapter are to—

"(1) provide a comprehensive framework for ensuring the effectiveness of information security controls over information resources that support Federal operations and assets;

"(2) recognize the highly networked nature of the current Federal computing environment and provide effective governmentwide management and oversight of the related information security risks, including coordination of information security efforts throughout the civilian, national security, and law enforcement communities;

"(3) provide for development and maintenance of minimum controls required to protect Federal information and information systems;

"(4) provide a mechanism for improved oversight of Federal agency information security programs;

"(5) acknowledge that commercially developed information security products offer advanced, dynamic, robust, and effective information security solutions, reflecting market solutions for the protection of critical information infrastructures important to the national defense and economic security of the nation that are designed, built, and operated by the private sector; and

"(6) recognize that the selection of specific technical hardware and software information security solutions should be left to individual agencies from among commercially developed products.".

"§ 3532. Definitions

"(a) IN GENERAL.—Except as provided under subsection (b), the definitions under section 3502 shall apply to this subchapter.

"(b) ADDITIONAL DEFINITIONS.—As used in this subchapter—

"(1) the term 'information security' means protecting information and information systems from unauthorized access, use, disclosure, disruption, modification, or destruction in order to provide—

"(A) integrity, which means guarding against improper information modification or destruction, and includes ensuring information nonrepudiation and authenticity;

"(B) confidentiality, which means preserving authorized restrictions on access and disclosure, including means for protecting personal privacy and proprietary information;

"(C) availability, which means ensuring timely and reliable access to and use of information; and

"(D) authentication, which means utilizing digital credentials to assure the identity of users and validate their access;

"(2) the term 'national security system' means any information system (including any telecommunications system) used or operated by an agency or by a contractor of an agency, or other organization on behalf of an agency, the function, operation, or use of which—

"(A) involves intelligence activities;

"(B) involves cryptologic activities related to national security;

"(C) involves command and control of military forces;

"(D) involves equipment that is an integral part of a weapon or weapons system; or

"(E) is critical to the direct fulfillment of military or intelligence missions provided that this definition does not apply to a system that is used for routine administrative and business applications (including payroll, finance, logistics, and personnel management applications);

"(3) the term 'information technology' has the meaning given that term in section 11101 of title 40; and

"(4) the term 'information system' means any equipment or interconnected system or subsystems of equipment that is used in the automatic acquisition, storage, manipulation, management, movement, control, display, switching, interchange, transmission, or reception of data or information, and includes—

"(A) computers and computer networks;

"(B) ancillary equipment;

"(C) software, firmware, and related procedures;

"(D) services, including support services; and

"(E) related resources.

"§ 3533. Authority and functions of the Director

"(a) The Director shall oversee agency information security policies and practices, by—

"(1) promulgating information security standards under section 11331 of title 40;

"(2) overseeing the implementation of policies, principles, standards, and guidelines on information security;

"(3) requiring agencies, consistent with the standards promulgated under such section 11331 and the requirements of this subchapter, to identify and provide information security protections commensurate with the risk and magnitude of the harm resulting from the unauthorized access, use, disclosure, disruption, modification, or destruction of—

"(A) information collected or maintained by or on behalf of an agency; or

"(B) information systems used or operated by an agency or by a contractor of an agency or other organization on behalf of an agency;

"(4) coordinating the development of standards and guidelines under section 20 of the National Institute of Standards and Technology Act (15 U.S.C. 278g–3) with agencies and offices operating or exercising control of national security systems (including the National Security Agency) to assure, to the maximum extent feasible, that such standards and guidelines are complementary with standards and guidelines developed for national security systems;

"(5) overseeing agency compliance with the requirements of this subchapter, including through any authorized action under section 11303(b)(5) of title 40, to enforce accountability for compliance with such requirements;

"(6) reviewing at least annually, and approving or disapproving, agency information security programs required under section 3534(b);

"(7) coordinating information security policies and procedures with related information resources management policies and procedures; and

"(8) reporting to Congress no later than March 1 of each year on agency compliance with the requirements of this subchapter, including—

"(A) a summary of the findings of evaluations required by section 3535;

"(B) significant deficiencies in agency information security practices;

"(C) planned remedial action to address such deficiencies; and

"(D) a summary of, and the views of the Director on, the report prepared by the National Institute of Standards and Technology under section 20(d)(9) of the National

Institute of Standards and Technology Act (15 U.S.C. 278g–3).

"(b) Except for the authorities described in paragraphs (4) and (7) of subsection (a), the authorities of the Director under this section shall not apply to national security systems.

"§ 3534. Federal agency responsibilities

"(a) The head of each agency shall—

"(1) be responsible for—

"(A) providing information security protections commensurate with the risk and magnitude of the harm resulting from unauthorized access, use, disclosure, disruption, modification, or destruction of—

"(i) information collected or maintained by or on behalf of the agency; and

"(ii) information systems used or operated by an agency or by a contractor of an agency or other organization on behalf of an agency;

"(B) complying with the requirements of this subchapter and related policies, procedures, standards, and guidelines, including—

"(i) information security standards promulgated by the Director under section 11331 of title 40; and

"(ii) information security standards and guidelines for national security systems issued in accordance with law and as directed by the President; and

"(C) ensuring that information security management processes are integrated with agency strategic and operational planning processes;

"(2) ensure that senior agency officials provide information security for the information and information systems that support the operations and assets under their control, including through—

"(A) assessing the risk and magnitude of the harm that could result from the unauthorized access, use, disclosure, disruption, modification, or destruction of such information or information systems;

"(B) determining the levels of information security appropriate to protect such information and information systems in accordance with standards promulgated under section 11331 of title 40 for information security classifications and related requirements;

"(C) implementing policies and procedures to cost-effectively reduce risks to an acceptable level; and

"(D) periodically testing and evaluating information security controls and techniques to ensure that they are effectively implemented;

"(3) delegate to the agency Chief Information Officer established under section 3506 (or comparable official in an agency not covered by such section) the authority to ensure compliance with the requirements imposed on the agency under this subchapter, including—

"(A) designating a senior agency information security officer who shall—

"(i) carry out the Chief Information Officer's responsibilities under this section;

"(ii) possess professional qualifications, including training and experience, required to administer the functions described under this section;

"(iii) have information security duties as that official's primary duty; and

"(iv) head an office with the mission and resources to assist in ensuring agency compliance with this section;

"(B) developing and maintaining an agencywide information security program as required by subsection (b);

"(C) developing and maintaining information security policies, procedures, and control techniques to address all applicable requirements, including those issued under section 3533 of this title, and section 11331 of title 40;

"(D) training and overseeing personnel with significant responsibilities for information security with respect to such responsibilities; and

"(E) assisting senior agency officials concerning their responsibilities under paragraph (2);

"(4) ensure that the agency has trained personnel sufficient to assist the agency in complying with the requirements of this subchapter and related policies, procedures, standards, and guidelines; and

"(5) ensure that the agency Chief Information Officer, in coordination with other senior agency officials, reports annually to the agency head on the effectiveness of the agency information security program, including progress of remedial actions.

"(b) Each agency shall develop, document, and implement an agencywide information security program, approved by the Director under section 3533(a)(5), to provide information security for the information and information systems that support the operations and assets of the agency, including those provided or managed by another agency, contractor, or other source, that includes—

"(1) periodic assessments of the risk and magnitude of the harm that could result from the unauthorized access, use, disclosure, disruption, modification, or destruction of information and information systems that support the operations and assets of the agency;

"(2) policies and procedures that—

"(A) are based on the risk assessments required by paragraph (1);

"(B) cost-effectively reduce information security risks to an acceptable level;

"(C) ensure that information security is addressed throughout the life cycle of each agency information system; and

"(D) ensure compliance with—

"(i) the requirements of this subchapter;

"(ii) policies and procedures as may be prescribed by the Director, and information security standards promulgated under section 11331 of title 40;

"(iii) minimally acceptable system configuration requirements, as determined by the agency; and

"(iv) any other applicable requirements, including standards and guidelines for national security systems issued in accordance with law and as directed by the President;

"(3) subordinate plans for providing adequate information security for networks, facilities, and systems or groups of information systems, as appropriate;

"(4) security awareness training to inform personnel, including contractors and other users of information systems that support the operations and assets of the agency, of—

"(A) information security risks associated with their activities; and

"(B) their responsibilities in complying with agency policies and procedures designed to reduce these risks;

"(5) periodic testing and evaluation of the effectiveness of information security policies, procedures, and practices, to be performed with a frequency depending on risk, but no less than annually, of which such testing—

"(A) shall include testing of management, operational, and technical controls of every information system identified in the inventory required under section 3505(c); and

"(B) may include testing relied on in a evaluation under section 3535;

"(6) a process for planning, implementing, evaluating, and documenting remedial action to address any deficiencies in the information security policies, procedures, and practices of the agency;

"(7) procedures for detecting, reporting, and responding to security incidents, including—

"(A) mitigating risks associated with such incidents before substantial damage is done; and

"(B) notifying and consulting with, as appropriate—

"(i) law enforcement agencies and relevant Offices of Inspector General;

"(ii) an office designated by the President for any incident involving a national security system; and

"(iii) any other agency or office, in accordance with law or as directed by the President; and

"(8) plans and procedures to ensure continuity of operations for information systems that support the operations and assets of the agency.

"(c) Each agency shall—

"(1) report annually to the Director, the Committees on Government Reform and Science of the House of Representatives, the Committees on Governmental Affairs and Commerce, Science, and Transportation of the Senate, the appropriate authorization and appropriations committees of Congress, and the Comptroller General on the adequacy and effectiveness of information security policies, procedures, and practices, and compliance with the requirements of this subchapter, including compliance with each requirement of subsection (b);

"(2) address the adequacy and effectiveness of information security policies, procedures, and practices in plans and reports relating to—

"(A) annual agency budgets;

"(B) information resources management under subchapter 1 of this chapter;

"(C) information technology management under subtitle III of title 40;

"(D) program performance under sections 1105 and 1115 through 1119 of title 31, and sections 2801 and 2805 of title 39;

"(E) financial management under chapter 9 of title 31, and the Chief Financial Officers Act of 1990 (31 U.S.C. 501 note; Public Law 101–576) (and the amendments made by that Act);

"(F) financial management systems under the Federal Financial Management Improvement Act (31 U.S.C. 3512 note); and

"(G) internal accounting and administrative controls under section 3512 of title 31, United States Code, (known as the 'Federal Managers Financial Integrity Act'); and

"(3) report any significant deficiency in a policy, procedure, or practice identified under paragraph (1) or (2)—

"(A) as a material weakness in reporting under section 3512 of title 31; and

"(B) if relating to financial management systems, as an instance of a lack of substantial compliance under the Federal Financial Management Improvement Act (31 U.S.C. 3512 note).

"(d)(1) In addition to the requirements of subsection (c), each agency, in consultation with the Director, shall include as part of the performance plan required under section 1115 of title 31 a description of—

"(A) the time periods; and

"(B) the resources, including budget, staffing, and training, that are necessary to implement the program required under subsection (b).

"(2) The description under paragraph (1) shall be based on the risk assessments required under subsection (b)(2)(1).

"(e) Each agency shall provide the public with timely notice and opportunities for comment on proposed information security policies and procedures to the extent that such policies and procedures affect communication with the public.

"§ 3535. Annual independent evaluation

"(a)(1) Each year each agency shall have performed an independent evaluation of the information security program and practices of that agency to determine the effectiveness of such program and practices.

"(2) Each evaluation by an agency under this section shall include—

"(A) testing of the effectiveness of information security policies, procedures, and practices of a representative subset of the agency's information systems;

"(B) an assessment (made on the basis of the results of the testing) of compliance with—

"(i) the requirements of this subchapter; and

"(ii) related information security policies, procedures, standards, and guidelines; and

"(C) separate presentations, as appropriate, regarding information security relating to national security systems.

"(b) Subject to subsection (c)—

"(1) for each agency with an Inspector General appointed under the Inspector General Act of 1978, the annual evaluation required by this section shall be performed by the Inspector

General or by an independent external auditor, as determined by the Inspector General of the agency; and

"(2) for each agency to which paragraph (1) does not apply, the head of the agency shall engage an independent external auditor to perform the evaluation.

"(c) For each agency operating or exercising control of a national security system, that portion of the evaluation required by this section directly relating to a national security system shall be performed—

"(1) only by an entity designated by the agency head; and

"(2) in such a manner as to ensure appropriate protection for information associated with any information security vulnerability in such system commensurate with the risk and in accordance with all applicable laws.

"(d) The evaluation required by this section—

"(1) shall be performed in accordance with generally accepted government auditing standards; and

"(2) may be based in whole or in part on an audit, evaluation, or report relating to programs or practices of the applicable agency.

"(e) Each year, not later than such date established by the Director, the head of each agency shall submit to the Director the results of the evaluation required under this section.

"(f) Agencies and evaluators shall take appropriate steps to ensure the protection of information which, if disclosed, may adversely affect information security. Such protections shall be commensurate with the risk and comply with all applicable laws and regulations.

"(g)(1) The Director shall summarize the results of the evaluations conducted under this section in the report to Congress required under section 3533(a)(8).

"(2) The Director's report to Congress under this subsection shall summarize information regarding information security relating to national security systems in such a manner as to ensure appropriate protection for information associated with any information security vulnerability in such system commensurate with the risk and in accordance with all applicable laws.

"(3) Evaluations and any other descriptions of information systems under the authority and control of the Director of Central Intelligence or of National Foreign Intelligence Programs systems under the authority and control of the Secretary of Defense shall be made available to Congress only through the appropriate oversight committees of Congress, in accordance with applicable laws.

"(h) The Comptroller General shall periodically evaluate and report to Congress on—

"(1) the adequacy and effectiveness of agency information security policies and practices; and

"(2) implementation of the requirements of this subchapter.

"§ 3536. National security systems

"The head of each agency operating or exercising control of a national security system shall be responsible for ensuring that the agency—

"(1) provides information security protections commensurate with the risk and magnitude of the harm resulting from the unauthorized access, use, disclosure, disruption, modification, or destruction of the information contained in such system;

"(2) implements information security policies and practices as required by standards and guidelines for national security systems, issued in accordance with law and as directed by the President; and

"(3) complies with the requirements of this subchapter.

"§ 3537. Authorization of appropriations

"There are authorized to be appropriated to carry out the provisions of this subchapter such sums as may be necessary for each of fiscal years 2003 through 2007.

"§ 3538. Effect on existing law

"Nothing in this subchapter, section 11331 of title 40, or section 20 of the National Standards and Technology Act (15 U.S.C. 278g–3) may be construed as affecting the authority of the President, the Office of Management and Budget or the Director thereof, the National Institute of Standards and Technology, or the head of any agency, with respect to the authorized use or disclosure of information, including with regard to the protection of personal privacy under section 552a of title 5, the disclosure of information under section 552 of title 5, the management and disposition of records under chapters 29, 31, or 33 of title 44, the management of information resources under subchapter I of chapter 35 of this title, or the disclosure of information to Congress or the Comptroller General of the United States.".

(2) CLERICAL AMENDMENT.—The items in the table of sections at the beginning of such chapter 35 under the heading "SUBCHAPTER II" are amended to read as follows:

"3531. Purposes.
"3532. Definitions.
"3533. Authority and functions of the Director.
"3534. Federal agency responsibilities.
"3535. Annual independent evaluation.
"3536. National security systems.
"3537. Authorization of appropriations.
"3538. Effect on existing law.".

(c) INFORMATION SECURITY RESPONSIBILITIES OF CERTAIN AGENCIES.—

(1) NATIONAL SECURITY RESPONSIBILITIES.—(A) Nothing in this Act (including any amendment made by this Act) shall supersede any authority of the Secretary of Defense, the Director of Central Intelligence, or other agency head, as authorized by law and as directed by the President, with regard to the operation, control, or management of national security systems, as defined by section 3532(3) of title 44, United States Code.

(B) Section 2224 of title 10, United States Code, is amended—

(i) in subsection 2224(b), by striking "(b) OBJECTIVES AND MINIMUM REQUIREMENTS.—(1)" and inserting "(b) OBJECTIVES OF THE PROGRAM.—";

(ii) in subsection 2224(b), by striking "(2) the program shall at a minimum meet the requirements of section 3534 and 3535 of title 44, United States Code."; and

(iii) in subsection 2224(c), by inserting ", including through compliance with subtitle II of chapter 35 of title 44" after "infrastructure".

(2) ATOMIC ENERGY ACT OF 1954.—Nothing in this Act shall supersede any requirement made by or under the Atomic Energy Act of 1954 (42 U.S.C. 2011 et seq.). Restricted Data or Formerly Restricted Data shall be handled, protected, classified, downgraded, and declassified in conformity with the Atomic Energy Act of 1954 (42 U.S.C. 2011 et seq.).

SEC. 1002. MANAGEMENT OF INFORMATION TECHNOLOGY.

(a) IN GENERAL.—Section 11331 of title 40, United States Code, is amended to read as follows:

"§ 11331. Responsibilities for Federal information systems standards

"(a) DEFINITION.—In this section, the term 'information security' has the meaning given that term in section 3532(b)(1) of title 44.

"(b) REQUIREMENT TO PRESCRIBE STANDARDS.—

"(1) IN GENERAL.—

"(A) REQUIREMENT.—Except as provided under paragraph (2), the Director of the Office of Management and Budget shall, on the basis of proposed standards developed by the National Institute of Standards and Technology pursuant to paragraphs (2) and (3) of section 20(a) of the National Institute of Standards and Technology Act (15 U.S.C. 278g–3(a)) and in consultation with the Secretary of Homeland Security, promulgate information security standards pertaining to Federal information systems.

"(B) REQUIRED STANDARDS.—Standards promulgated under subparagraph (A) shall include—

"(i) standards that provide minimum information security requirements as determined under section 20(b) of the National Institute of Standards and Technology Act (15 U.S.C. 278g–3(b)); and

"(ii) such standards that are otherwise necessary to improve the efficiency of operation or security of Federal information systems.

"(C) REQUIRED STANDARDS BINDING.—Information security standards described under subparagraph (B) shall be compulsory and binding.

"(2) STANDARDS AND GUIDELINES FOR NATIONAL SECURITY SYSTEMS.—Standards and guidelines for national security systems, as defined under section 3532(3) of title 44, shall be developed, promulgated, enforced, and overseen as otherwise authorized by law and as directed by the President.

"(c) APPLICATION OF MORE STRINGENT STANDARDS.—The head of an agency may employ standards for the cost-effective information security for all operations and assets within or under the supervision of that agency that are more stringent than the standards promulgated by the Director under this section, if such standards—

"(1) contain, at a minimum, the provisions of those applicable standards made compulsory and binding by the Director; and

"(2) are otherwise consistent with policies and guidelines issued under section 3533 of title 44.

"(d) REQUIREMENTS REGARDING DECISIONS BY DIRECTOR.—

"(1) DEADLINE.—The decision regarding the promulgation of any standard by the Director under subsection (b) shall occur not later than 6 months after the submission of the proposed standard to the Director by the National Institute of Standards and Technology, as provided under section 20 of the National Institute of Standards and Technology Act (15 U.S.C. 278g–3).

"(2) NOTICE AND COMMENT.—A decision by the Director to significantly modify, or not promulgate, a proposed standard submitted to the Director by the National Institute of Standards and Technology, as provided under section 20 of the National Institute of Standards and Technology Act (15 U.S.C. 278g–3), shall be made after the public is given an opportunity to comment on the Director's proposed decision.".

(b) CLERICAL AMENDMENT.—The table of sections at the beginning of chapter 113 of title 40, United States Code, is amended by striking the item relating to section 11331 and inserting the following:

"11331. Responsibilities for Federal information systems standards.".

SEC. 1003. NATIONAL INSTITUTE OF STANDARDS AND TECHNOLOGY.

Section 20 of the National Institute of Standards and Technology Act (15 U.S.C. 278g–3), is amended by striking the text and inserting the following:

"(a) The Institute shall—

"(1) have the mission of developing standards, guidelines, and associated methods and techniques for information systems;

"(2) develop standards and guidelines, including minimum requirements, for information systems used or operated by an agency or by a contractor of an agency or other organization on behalf of an agency, other than national security systems (as defined in section 3532(b)(2) of title 44, United States Code);

"(3) develop standards and guidelines, including minimum requirements, for providing adequate information security for all agency operations and assets, but such standards and guidelines shall not apply to national security systems; and

"(4) carry out the responsibilities described in paragraph (3) through the Computer Security Division.

"(b) The standards and guidelines required by subsection (a) shall include, at a minimum—

"(1)(A) standards to be used by all agencies to categorize all information and information systems collected or maintained by or on behalf of each agency based on the objectives of providing appropriate levels of information security according to a range of risk levels;

"(B) guidelines recommending the types of information and information systems to be included in each such category; and

"(C) minimum information security requirements for information and information systems in each such category;

"(2) a definition of and guidelines concerning detection and handling of information security incidents; and

"(3) guidelines developed in coordination with the National Security Agency for identifying an information system as a national security system consistent with applicable requirements for national security systems, issued in accordance with law and as directed by the President.

"(c) In developing standards and guidelines required by subsections (a) and (b), the Institute shall—

"(1) consult with other agencies and offices (including, but not limited to, the Director of the Office of Management and Budget, the Departments of Defense and Energy, the National Security Agency, the General Accounting Office, and the Secretary of Homeland Security) to assure—

"(A) use of appropriate information security policies, procedures, and techniques, in order to improve information security and avoid unnecessary and costly duplication of effort; and

"(B) that such standards and guidelines are complementary with standards and guidelines employed for the protection of national security systems and information contained in such systems;

"(2) provide the public with an opportunity to comment on proposed standards and guidelines;

"(3) submit to the Director of the Office of Management and Budget for promulgation under section 11331 of title 40, United States Code—

"(A) standards, as required under subsection (b)(1)(A), no later than 12 months after the date of the enactment of this section; and

"(B) minimum information security requirements for each category, as required under subsection (b)(1)(C), no later than 36 months after the date of the enactment of this section;

"(4) issue guidelines as required under subsection (b)(1)(B), no later than 18 months after the date of the enactment of this Act;

"(5) ensure that such standards and guidelines do not require specific technological solutions or products, including any specific hardware or software security solutions;

"(6) ensure that such standards and guidelines provide for sufficient flexibility to permit alternative solutions to provide equivalent levels of protection for identified information security risks; and

"(7) use flexible, performance-based standards and guidelines that, to the greatest extent possible, permit the use of off-the-shelf commercially developed information security products.

"(d) The Institute shall—

"(1) submit standards developed pursuant to subsection (a), along with recommendations as to the extent to which these should be made compulsory and binding, to the Director of the Office of Management and Budget for promulgation under section 11331 of title 40, United States Code;

"(2) provide assistance to agencies regarding—

"(A) compliance with the standards and guidelines developed under subsection (a);

"(B) detecting and handling information security incidents; and

"(C) information security policies, procedures, and practices;

"(3) conduct research, as needed, to determine the nature and extent of information security vulnerabilities and techniques for providing cost-effective information security;

"(4) develop and periodically revise performance indicators and measures for agency information security policies and practices;

"(5) evaluate private sector information security policies and practices and commercially available information technologies to assess potential application by agencies to strengthen information security;

"(6) evaluate security policies and practices developed for national security systems to assess potential application by agencies to strengthen information security;

"(7) periodically assess the effectiveness of standards and guidelines developed under this section and undertake revisions as appropriate;

"(8) solicit and consider the recommendations of the Information Security and Privacy Advisory Board, established by section 21, regarding standards and guidelines developed under subsection (a) and submit such recommendations to the Director of the Office of Management and Budget with such standards submitted to the Director; and

"(9) prepare an annual public report on activities undertaken in the previous year, and planned for the coming year, to carry out responsibilities under this section.

"(e) As used in this section—

"(1) the term 'agency' has the same meaning as provided in section 3502(1) of title 44, United States Code;

"(2) the term 'information security' has the same meaning as provided in section 3532(1) of such title;

"(3) the term 'information system' has the same meaning as provided in section 3502(8) of such title;

"(4) the term 'information technology' has the same meaning as provided in section 11101 of title 40, United States Code; and

"(5) the term 'national security system' has the same meaning as provided in section 3532(b)(2) of such title.".

SEC. 1004. INFORMATION SECURITY AND PRIVACY ADVISORY BOARD.

Section 21 of the National Institute of Standards and Technology Act (15 U.S.C. 278g–4), is amended—

(1) in subsection (a), by striking "Computer System Security and Privacy Advisory Board" and inserting "Information Security and Privacy Advisory Board";

(2) in subsection (a)(1), by striking "computer or telecommunications" and inserting "information technology";

(3) in subsection (a)(2)—

(A) by striking "computer or telecommunications technology" and inserting "information technology"; and

(B) by striking "computer or telecommunications equipment" and inserting "information technology";

(4) in subsection (a)(3)—

(A) by striking "computer systems" and inserting "information system"; and

(B) by striking "computer systems security" and inserting "information security";

(5) in subsection (b)(1) by striking "computer systems security" and inserting "information security";

(6) in subsection (b) by striking paragraph (2) and inserting the following:

"(2) to advise the Institute and the Director of the Office of Management and Budget on information security and privacy issues pertaining to Federal Government information systems, including through review of proposed standards and guidelines developed under section 20; and";

(7) in subsection (b)(3) by inserting "annually" after "report";

(8) by inserting after subsection (e) the following new subsection:

"(f) The Board shall hold meetings at such locations and at such time and place as determined by a majority of the Board.";

(9) by redesignating subsections (f) and (g) as subsections (g) and (h), respectively; and

(10) by striking subsection (h), as redesignated by paragraph (9), and inserting the following:

"(h) As used in this section, the terms 'information system' and 'information technology' have the meanings given in section 20.".

SEC. 1005. TECHNICAL AND CONFORMING AMENDMENTS.

(a) FEDERAL COMPUTER SYSTEM SECURITY TRAINING AND PLAN.—

(1) REPEAL.—Section 11332 of title 40, United States Code, is repealed.

(2) CLERICAL AMENDMENT.—The table of sections at the beginning of chapter 113 of title 40, United States Code, as amended by striking the item relating to section 11332.

(b) FLOYD D. SPENCE NATIONAL DEFENSE AUTHORIZATION ACT FOR FISCAL YEAR 2001.—The Floyd D. Spence National Defense Authorization Act for Fiscal Year 2001 (Public Law 106–398) is amended by striking subtitle G of title X (44 U.S.C. 3531 note).

(c) PAPERWORK REDUCTION ACT.—(1) Section 3504(g) of title 44, United States Code, is amended—

(A) by adding "and" at the end of paragraph (1);

(B) in paragraph (2)—

(i) by striking "sections 11331 and 11332(b) and (c) of title 40" and inserting "section 11331 of title 40 and subchapter II of this title"; and

(ii) by striking the semicolon and inserting a period; and

(C) by striking paragraph (3).

(2) Section 3505 of such title is amended by adding at the end the following:

"(c) INVENTORY OF INFORMATION SYSTEMS.—(1) The head of each agency shall develop and maintain an inventory of the information systems (including national security systems) operated by or under the control of such agency;

"(2) The identification of information systems in an inventory under this subsection shall include an identification of the interfaces between each such system and all other systems or networks, including those not operated by or under the control of the agency;

"(3) Such inventory shall be—

"(A) updated at least annually;

"(B) made available to the Comptroller General; and

"(C) used to support information resources management, including—

"(i) preparation and maintenance of the inventory of information resources under section 3506(b)(4);

"(ii) information technology planning, budgeting, acquisition, and management under section 3506(h), subtitle III of title 40, and related laws and guidance;

"(iii) monitoring, testing, and evaluation of information security controls under subchapter II;

"(iv) preparation of the index of major information systems required under section 552(g) of title 5, United States Code; and

"(v) preparation of information system inventories required for records management under chapters 21, 29, 31, and 33.

"(4) The Director shall issue guidance for and oversee the implementation of the requirements of this subsection.".

(3) Section 3506(g) of such title is amended—

(A) by adding "and" at the end of paragraph (1);

(B) in paragraph (2)—

(i) by striking "section 11332 of title 40" and inserting "subchapter II of this chapter"; and

(ii) by striking "; and" and inserting a period; and

(C) by striking paragraph (3).

SEC. 1006. CONSTRUCTION.

Nothing in this Act, or the amendments made by this Act, affects the authority of the National Institute of Standards and Technology or the Department of Commerce relating to the development and promulgation of standards or guidelines under paragraphs (1) and (2) of section 20(a) of the National Institute of Standards and Technology Act (15 U.S.C. 278g–3(a)).

TITLE XI—DEPARTMENT OF JUSTICE DIVISIONS

Subtitle A—Executive Office for Immigration Review

SEC. 1101. LEGAL STATUS OF EOIR.

(a) EXISTENCE OF EOIR.—There is in the Department of Justice the Executive Office for Immigration Review, which shall be subject to the direction and regulation of the Attorney General under section 103(g) of the Immigration and Nationality Act, as added by section 1102.

SEC. 1102. AUTHORITIES OF THE ATTORNEY GENERAL.

Section 103 of the Immigration and Nationality Act (8 U.S.C. 1103) as amended by this Act, is further amended by—

(1) amending the heading to read as follows:

"POWERS AND DUTIES OF THE SECRETARY, THE UNDER SECRETARY, AND THE ATTORNEY GENERAL";

(2) in subsection (a)—

(A) by inserting "Attorney General," after "President,"; and

(B) by redesignating paragraphs (8), (9), (8) (as added by section 372 of Public Law 104–208), and (9) (as added by section 372 of Public Law 104–208) as paragraphs (8), (9), (10), and (11), respectively; and

(3) by adding at the end the following new subsection:

"(g) ATTORNEY GENERAL.—

"(1) IN GENERAL.—The Attorney General shall have such authorities and functions under this Act and all other laws relating to the immigration and naturalization of aliens as were exercised by the Executive Office for Immigration Review, or by the Attorney General with respect to the Executive Office for Immigration Review, on the day before the effective date of the Immigration Reform, Accountability and Security Enhancement Act of 2002.

"(2) POWERS.—The Attorney General shall establish such regulations, prescribe such forms of bond, reports, entries, and other papers, issue such instructions, review such administrative determinations in immigration proceedings, delegate such authority, and perform such other acts as the Attorney General determines to be necessary for carrying out this section.".

SEC. 1103. STATUTORY CONSTRUCTION.

Nothing in this Act, any amendment made by this Act, or in section 103 of the Immigration and Nationality Act, as amended by section 1102, shall be construed to limit judicial deference to regulations, adjudications, interpretations, orders, decisions, judgments, or any other actions of the Secretary of Homeland Security or the Attorney General.

Subtitle B—Transfer of the Bureau of Alcohol, Tobacco and Firearms to the Department of Justice

SEC. 1111. BUREAU OF ALCOHOL, TOBACCO, FIREARMS, AND EXPLOSIVES.

(a) ESTABLISHMENT.—

(1) IN GENERAL.—There is established within the Department of Justice under the general authority of the Attorney General the Bureau of Alcohol, Tobacco, Firearms, and Explosives (in this section referred to as the "Bureau").

(2) DIRECTOR.—There shall be at the head of the Bureau a Director, Bureau of Alcohol, Tobacco, Firearms, and Explosives (in this subtitle referred to as the "Director"). The Director shall be appointed by the Attorney General and shall perform such functions as the Attorney General shall direct. The Director shall receive compensation at the rate prescribed by law under section 5314 of title V, United States Code, for positions at level III of the Executive Schedule.

(3) COORDINATION.—The Attorney General, acting through the Director and such other officials of the Department of Justice as the Attorney General may designate, shall provide for the coordination of all firearms, explosives, tobacco enforcement, and arson enforcement functions vested in the Attorney General so as to assure maximum cooperation between and among any officer, employee, or agency of the Department

of Justice involved in the performance of these and related functions.

(4) PERFORMANCE OF TRANSFERRED FUNCTIONS.—The Attorney General may make such provisions as the Attorney General determines appropriate to authorize the performance by any officer, employee, or agency of the Department of Justice of any function transferred to the Attorney General under this section.

(b) RESPONSIBILITIES.—Subject to the direction of the Attorney General, the Bureau shall be responsible for investigating—

(1) criminal and regulatory violations of the Federal firearms, explosives, arson, alcohol, and tobacco smuggling laws;

(2) the functions transferred by subsection (c); and

(3) any other function related to the investigation of violent crime or domestic terrorism that is delegated to the Bureau by the Attorney General.

(c) TRANSFER OF AUTHORITIES, FUNCTIONS, PERSONNEL, AND ASSETS TO THE DEPARTMENT OF JUSTICE.—

(1) IN GENERAL.—Subject to paragraph (2), but notwithstanding any other provision of law, there are transferred to the Department of Justice the authorities, functions, personnel, and assets of the Bureau of Alcohol, Tobacco and Firearms, which shall be maintained as a distinct entity within the Department of Justice, including the related functions of the Secretary of the Treasury.

(2) ADMINISTRATION AND REVENUE COLLECTION FUNCTIONS.—There shall be retained within the Department of the Treasury the authorities, functions, personnel, and assets of the Bureau of Alcohol, Tobacco and Firearms relating to the administration and enforcement of chapters 51 and 52 of the Internal Revenue Code of 1986, sections 4181 and 4182 of the Internal Revenue Code of 1986, and title 27, United States Code.

(3) BUILDING PROSPECTUS.—Prospectus PDC-98W10, giving the General Services Administration the authority for site acquisition, design, and construction of a new headquarters building for the Bureau of Alcohol, Tobacco and Firearms, is transferred, and deemed to apply, to the Bureau of Alcohol, Tobacco, Firearms, and Explosives established in the Department of Justice under subsection (a).

(d) TAX AND TRADE BUREAU.—

(1) ESTABLISHMENT.—There is established within the Department of the Treasury the Tax and Trade Bureau.

(2) ADMINISTRATOR.—The Tax and Trade Bureau shall be headed by an Administrator, who shall perform such duties as assigned by the Under Secretary for Enforcement of the Department of the Treasury. The Administrator shall occupy a career-reserved position within the Senior Executive Service.

(3) RESPONSIBILITIES.—The authorities, functions, personnel, and assets of the Bureau of Alcohol, Tobacco and Firearms that are not transferred to the Department of Justice under this section shall be retained and administered by the Tax and Trade Bureau.

SEC. 1112. TECHNICAL AND CONFORMING AMENDMENTS.

(a) The Inspector General Act of 1978 (5 U.S.C. App.) is amended—

H. R. 5005—142

(1) in section 8D(b)(1) by striking "Bureau of Alcohol, Tobacco and Firearms" and inserting "Tax and Trade Bureau"; and

(2) in section 9(a)(1)(L)(i), by striking "Bureau of Alcohol, Tobacco, and Firearms" and inserting "Tax and Trade Bureau".

(b) Section 1109(c)(2)(A)(i) of the Consolidated Omnibus Budget Reconciliation Act of 1985 (7 U.S.C. 1445–3(c)(2)(A)(i)) is amended by striking "(on ATF Form 3068) by manufacturers of tobacco products to the Bureau of Alcohol, Tobacco and Firearms" and inserting "by manufacturers of tobacco products to the Tax and Trade Bureau".

(c) Section 2(4)(J) of the Enhanced Border Security and Visa Entry Reform Act of 2002 (Public Law 107–173; 8 U.S.C.A. 1701(4)(J)) is amended by striking "Bureau of Alcohol, Tobacco, and Firearms" and inserting "Bureau of Alcohol, Tobacco, Firearms, and Explosives, Department of Justice".

(d) Section 3(1)(E) of the Firefighters' Safety Study Act (15 U.S.C. 2223b(1)(E)) is amended by striking "the Bureau of Alcohol, Tobacco, and Firearms," and inserting "the Bureau of Alcohol, Tobacco, Firearms, and Explosives, Department of Justice,".

(e) Chapter 40 of title 18, United States Code, is amended—

(1) by striking section 841(k) and inserting the following:

"(k) 'Attorney General' means the Attorney General of the United States.";

(2) in section 846(a), by striking "the Attorney General and the Federal Bureau of Investigation, together with the Secretary" and inserting "the Federal Bureau of Investigation, together with the Bureau of Alcohol, Tobacco, Firearms, and Explosives"; and

(3) by striking "Secretary" each place it appears and inserting "Attorney General".

(f) Chapter 44 of title 18, United States Code, is amended—

(1) in section 921(a)(4)(B), by striking "Secretary" and inserting "Attorney General";

(2) in section 921(a)(4), by striking "Secretary of the Treasury" and inserting "Attorney General";

(3) in section 921(a), by striking paragraph (18) and inserting the following:

"(18) The term 'Attorney General' means the Attorney General of the United States";

(4) in section 922(p)(5)(A), by striking "after consultation with the Secretary" and inserting "after consultation with the Attorney General";

(5) in section 923(l), by striking "Secretary of the Treasury" and inserting "Attorney General"; and

(6) by striking "Secretary" each place it appears, except before "of the Army" in section 921(a)(4) and before "of Defense" in section 922(p)(5)(A), and inserting the term "Attorney General".

(g) Section 1261(a) of title 18, United States Code, is amended to read as follows:

"(a) The Attorney General—

"(1) shall enforce the provisions of this chapter; and

"(2) has the authority to issue regulations to carry out the provisions of this chapter.".

(h) Section 1952(c) of title 18, United States Code, is amended by striking "Secretary of the Treasury" and inserting "Attorney General".

(i) Chapter 114 of title 18, United States Code, is amended—

(1) by striking section 2341(5), and inserting the following:

"(5) the term 'Attorney General' means the Attorney General of the United States"; and

(2) by striking "Secretary" each place it appears and inserting "Attorney General".

(j) Section 6103(i)(8)(A)(i) of the Internal Revenue Code of 1986 (relating to confidentiality and disclosure of returns and return information) is amended by striking "or the Bureau of Alcohol, Tobacco and Firearms" and inserting ", the Bureau of Alcohol, Tobacco, Firearms, and Explosives, Department of Justice, or the Tax and Trade Bureau, Department of the Treasury,".

(k) Section 7801(a) of the Internal Revenue Code of 1986 (relating to the authority of the Department of the Treasury) is amended—

(1) by striking "SECRETARY.—Except" and inserting "SECRETARY.—

"(1) IN GENERAL.—Except"; and

(2) by adding at the end the following:

"(2) ADMINISTRATION AND ENFORCEMENT OF CERTAIN PROVISIONS BY ATTORNEY GENERAL.—

"(A) IN GENERAL.—The administration and enforcement of the following provisions of this title shall be performed by or under the supervision of the Attorney General; and the term 'Secretary' or 'Secretary of the Treasury' shall, when applied to those provisions, mean the Attorney General; and the term 'internal revenue officer' shall, when applied to those provisions, mean any officer of the Bureau of Alcohol, Tobacco, Firearms, and Explosives so designated by the Attorney General:

"(i) Chapter 53.

"(ii) Chapters 61 through 80, to the extent such chapters relate to the enforcement and administration of the provisions referred to in clause (i).

"(B) USE OF EXISTING RULINGS AND INTERPRETATIONS.— Nothing in this Act alters or repeals the rulings and interpretations of the Bureau of Alcohol, Tobacco, and Firearms in effect on the effective date of the Homeland Security Act of 2002, which concern the provisions of this title referred to in subparagraph (A). The Attorney General shall consult with the Secretary to achieve uniformity and consistency in administering provisions under chapter 53 of title 26, United States Code.".

(l) Section 2006(2) of title 28, United States Code, is amended by inserting ", the Director, Bureau of Alcohol, Tobacco, Firearms, and Explosives, Department of Justice," after "the Secretary of the Treasury".

(m) Section 713 of title 31, United States Code, is amended—

(1) by striking the section heading and inserting the following:

"§ 713. Audit of Internal Revenue Service, Tax and Trade Bureau, and Bureau of Alcohol, Tobacco, Firearms, and Explosives";

(2) in subsection (a), by striking "Bureau of Alcohol, Tobacco, and Firearms," and inserting "Tax and Trade Bureau, Department of the Treasury, and the Bureau of Alcohol, Tobacco, Firearms, and Explosives, Department of Justice"; and

(3) in subsection (b)—

(A) in paragraph (1)(B), by striking "or the Bureau" and inserting "or either Bureau";

(B) in paragraph (2)—

(i) by striking "or the Bureau" and inserting "or either Bureau"; and

(ii) by striking "and the Director of the Bureau" and inserting "the Tax and Trade Bureau, Department of the Treasury, and the Director of the Bureau of Alcohol, Tobacco, Firearms, and Explosives, Department of Justice"; and

(C) in paragraph (3), by striking "or the Bureau" and inserting "or either Bureau".

(n) Section 9703 of title 31, United States Code, is amended—

(1) in subsection (a)(2)(B)—

(A) in clause (iii)(III), by inserting "and" after the semicolon;

(B) in clause (iv), by striking "; and" and inserting a period; and

(C) by striking clause (v);

(2) by striking subsection (o);

(3) by redesignating existing subsection (p) as subsection (o); and

(4) in subsection (o)(1), as redesignated by paragraph (3), by striking "Bureau of Alcohol, Tobacco and Firearms" and inserting "Tax and Trade Bureau".

(o) Section 609N(2)(L) of the Justice Assistance Act of 1984 (42 U.S.C. 10502(2)(L)) is amended by striking "Bureau of Alcohol, Tobacco, and Firearms" and inserting "Bureau of Alcohol, Tobacco, Firearms, and Explosives, Department of Justice".

(p) Section 32401(a) of the Violent Crime Control and Law Enforcement Act of 1994 (42 U.S.C. 13921(a)) is amended—

(1) by striking "Secretary of the Treasury" each place it appears and inserting "Attorney General"; and

(2) in subparagraph (3)(B), by striking "Bureau of Alcohol, Tobacco and Firearms" and inserting "Bureau of Alcohol, Tobacco, Firearms, and Explosives, Department of Justice".

(q) Section 80303 of title 49, United States Code, is amended—

(1) by inserting "or, when the violation of this chapter involves contraband described in paragraph (2) or (5) of section 80302(a), the Attorney General" after "section 80304 of this title."; and

(2) by inserting ", the Attorney General," after "by the Secretary".

(r) Section 80304 of title 49, United States Code, is amended—

(1) in subsection (a), by striking "(b) and (c)" and inserting "(b), (c), and (d)";

(2) by redesignating subsection (d) as subsection (e); and

(3) by inserting after subsection (c), the following:

"(d) ATTORNEY GENERAL.—The Attorney General, or officers, employees, or agents of the Bureau of Alcohol, Tobacco, Firearms, and Explosives, Department of Justice designated by the Attorney General, shall carry out the laws referred to in section 80306(b) of this title to the extent that the violation of this chapter involves contraband described in section 80302 (a)(2) or (a)(5).".

(s) Section 103 of the Gun Control Act of 1968 (Public Law 90–618; 82 Stat. 1226) is amended by striking "Secretary of the Treasury" and inserting "Attorney General".

SEC. 1113. POWERS OF AGENTS OF THE BUREAU OF ALCOHOL, TOBACCO, FIREARMS, AND EXPLOSIVES.

Chapter 203 of title 18, United States Code, is amended by adding the following:

"§ 3051. Powers of Special Agents of Bureau of Alcohol, Tobacco, Firearms, and Explosives

"(a) Special agents of the Bureau of Alcohol, Tobacco, Firearms, and Explosives, as well as any other investigator or officer charged by the Attorney General with the duty of enforcing any of the criminal, seizure, or forfeiture provisions of the laws of the United States, may carry firearms, serve warrants and subpoenas issued under the authority of the United States and make arrests without warrant for any offense against the United States committed in their presence, or for any felony cognizable under the laws of the United States if they have reasonable grounds to believe that the person to be arrested has committed or is committing such felony.

"(b) Any special agent of the Bureau of Alcohol, Tobacco, Firearms, and Explosives may, in respect to the performance of his or her duties, make seizures of property subject to forfeiture to the United States.

"(c)(1) Except as provided in paragraphs (2) and (3), and except to the extent that such provisions conflict with the provisions of section 983 of title 18, United States Code, insofar as section 983 applies, the provisions of the Customs laws relating to—

"(A) the seizure, summary and judicial forfeiture, and condemnation of property;

"(B) the disposition of such property;

"(C) the remission or mitigation of such forfeiture; and

"(D) the compromise of claims,

shall apply to seizures and forfeitures incurred, or alleged to have been incurred, under any applicable provision of law enforced or administered by the Bureau of Alcohol, Tobacco, Firearms, and Explosives.

"(2) For purposes of paragraph (1), duties that are imposed upon a customs officer or any other person with respect to the seizure and forfeiture of property under the customs laws of the United States shall be performed with respect to seizures and forfeitures of property under this section by such officers, agents, or any other person as may be authorized or designated for that purpose by the Attorney General.

"(3) Notwithstanding any other provision of law, the disposition of firearms forfeited by reason of a violation of any law of the United States shall be governed by the provisions of section 5872(b) of the Internal Revenue Code of 1986.".

SEC. 1114. EXPLOSIVES TRAINING AND RESEARCH FACILITY.

(a) ESTABLISHMENT.—There is established within the Bureau an Explosives Training and Research Facility at Fort AP Hill, Fredericksburg, Virginia.

(b) PURPOSE.—The facility established under subsection (a) shall be utilized to train Federal, State, and local law enforcement officers to—

(1) investigate bombings and explosions;

(2) properly handle, utilize, and dispose of explosive materials and devices;

(3) train canines on explosive detection; and

(4) conduct research on explosives.

(c) AUTHORIZATION OF APPROPRIATIONS.—

(1) IN GENERAL.—There are authorized to be appropriated such sums as may be necessary to establish and maintain the facility established under subsection (a).

(2) AVAILABILITY OF FUNDS.—Any amounts appropriated pursuant to paragraph (1) shall remain available until expended.

SEC. 1115. PERSONNEL MANAGEMENT DEMONSTRATION PROJECT.

Notwithstanding any other provision of law, the Personnel Management Demonstration Project established under section 102 of title I of division C of the Omnibus Consolidated and Emergency Supplemental Appropriations Act for Fiscal Year 1999 (Public Law 105–277; 122 Stat. 2681–585) shall be transferred to the Attorney General of the United States for continued use by the Bureau of Alcohol, Tobacco, Firearms, and Explosives, Department of Justice, and the Secretary of the Treasury for continued use by the Tax and Trade Bureau.

Subtitle C—Explosives

SEC. 1121. SHORT TITLE.

This subtitle may be referred to as the "Safe Explosives Act".

SEC. 1122. PERMITS FOR PURCHASERS OF EXPLOSIVES.

(a) DEFINITIONS.—Section 841 of title 18, United States Code, is amended—

(1) by striking subsection (j) and inserting the following:

"(j) 'Permittee' means any user of explosives for a lawful purpose, who has obtained either a user permit or a limited permit under the provisions of this chapter."; and

(2) by adding at the end the following:

"(r) 'Alien' means any person who is not a citizen or national of the United States.

"(s) 'Responsible person' means an individual who has the power to direct the management and policies of the applicant pertaining to explosive materials.".

(b) PERMITS FOR PURCHASE OF EXPLOSIVES.—Section 842 of title 18, United States Code, is amended—

(1) in subsection (a)(2), by striking "and" at the end;

(2) by striking subsection (a)(3) and inserting the following:

"(3) other than a licensee or permittee knowingly—

"(A) to transport, ship, cause to be transported, or receive any explosive materials; or

"(B) to distribute explosive materials to any person other than a licensee or permittee; or

"(4) who is a holder of a limited permit—

"(A) to transport, ship, cause to be transported, or receive in interstate or foreign commerce any explosive materials; or

"(B) to receive explosive materials from a licensee or permittee, whose premises are located outside the State of residence of the limited permit holder, or on more than 6 separate occasions, during the period of the permit, to receive explosive materials from 1 or more licensees or permittees whose premises are located within the State of residence of the limited permit holder."; and

(3) by striking subsection (b) and inserting the following:
"(b) It shall be unlawful for any licensee or permittee to knowingly distribute any explosive materials to any person other than—

"(1) a licensee;

"(2) a holder of a user permit; or

"(3) a holder of a limited permit who is a resident of the State where distribution is made and in which the premises of the transferor are located.".

(c) LICENSES AND USER PERMITS.—Section 843(a) of title 18, United States Code, is amended—

(1) in the first sentence—

(A) by inserting "or limited permit" after "user permit"; and

(B) by inserting before the period at the end the following: ", including the names of and appropriate identifying information regarding all employees who will be authorized by the applicant to possess explosive materials, as well as fingerprints and a photograph of each responsible person";

(2) in the second sentence, by striking "$200 for each" and inserting "$50 for a limited permit and $200 for any other"; and

(3) by striking the third sentence and inserting "Each license or user permit shall be valid for not longer than 3 years from the date of issuance and each limited permit shall be valid for not longer than 1 year from the date of issuance. Each license or permit shall be renewable upon the same conditions and subject to the same restrictions as the original license or permit, and upon payment of a renewal fee not to exceed one-half of the original fee.".

(d) CRITERIA FOR APPROVING LICENSES AND PERMITS.—Section 843(b) of title 18, United States Code, is amended—

(1) by striking paragraph (1) and inserting the following:
"(1) the applicant (or, if the applicant is a corporation, partnership, or association, each responsible person with respect to the applicant) is not a person described in section 842(i);";

(2) in paragraph (4)—

(A) by inserting "(A) the Secretary verifies by inspection or, if the application is for an original limited permit or the first or second renewal of such a permit, by such other means as the Secretary determines appropriate, that" before "the applicant"; and

(B) by adding at the end the following:

"(B) subparagraph (A) shall not apply to an applicant for the renewal of a limited permit if the Secretary has verified, by inspection within the preceding 3 years, the matters described in subparagraph (A) with respect to the applicant; and";

(3) in paragraph (5), by striking the period at the end and inserting a semicolon; and

(4) by adding at the end the following:

"(6) none of the employees of the applicant who will be authorized by the applicant to possess explosive materials is any person described in section 842(i); and

"(7) in the case of a limited permit, the applicant has certified in writing that the applicant will not receive explosive materials on more than 6 separate occasions during the 12-month period for which the limited permit is valid.".

(e) APPLICATION APPROVAL.—Section 843(c) of title 18, United States Code, is amended by striking "forty-five days" and inserting "90 days for licenses and permits,".

(f) INSPECTION AUTHORITY.—Section 843(f) of title 18, United States Code, is amended—

(1) in the first sentence—

(A) by striking "permittees" and inserting "holders of user permits"; and

(B) by inserting "licensees and permittees" before "shall submit";

(2) in the second sentence, by striking "permittee" the first time it appears and inserting "holder of a user permit"; and

(3) by adding at the end the following: "The Secretary may inspect the places of storage for explosive materials of an applicant for a limited permit or, at the time of renewal of such permit, a holder of a limited permit, only as provided in subsection (b)(4).

(g) POSTING OF PERMITS.—Section 843(g) of title 18, United States Code, is amended by inserting "user" before "permits".

(h) BACKGROUND CHECKS; CLEARANCES.—Section 843 of title 18, United States Code, is amended by adding at the end the following:

"(h)(1) If the Secretary receives, from an employer, the name and other identifying information of a responsible person or an employee who will be authorized by the employer to possess explosive materials in the course of employment with the employer, the Secretary shall determine whether the responsible person or employee is one of the persons described in any paragraph of section 842(i). In making the determination, the Secretary may take into account a letter or document issued under paragraph (2).

"(2)(A) If the Secretary determines that the responsible person or the employee is not one of the persons described in any paragraph of section 842(i), the Secretary shall notify the employer in writing or electronically of the determination and issue, to the responsible person or employee, a letter of clearance, which confirms the determination.

"(B) If the Secretary determines that the responsible person or employee is one of the persons described in any paragraph of section 842(i), the Secretary shall notify the employer in writing or electronically of the determination and issue to the responsible person or the employee, as the case may be, a document that—

"(i) confirms the determination;

"(ii) explains the grounds for the determination;

"(iii) provides information on how the disability may be relieved; and

"(iv) explains how the determination may be appealed.".

(i) EFFECTIVE DATE.—

(1) IN GENERAL.—The amendments made by this section shall take effect 180 days after the date of enactment of this Act.

(2) EXCEPTION.—Notwithstanding any provision of this Act, a license or permit issued under section 843 of title 18, United States Code, before the date of enactment of this Act, shall remain valid until that license or permit is revoked under section 843(d) or expires, or until a timely application for renewal is acted upon.

SEC. 1123. PERSONS PROHIBITED FROM RECEIVING OR POSSESSING EXPLOSIVE MATERIALS.

(a) DISTRIBUTION OF EXPLOSIVES.—Section 842(d) of title 18, United States Code, is amended—

(1) in paragraph (5), by striking "or" at the end;

(2) in paragraph (6), by striking the period at the end and inserting "or who has been committed to a mental institution;"; and

(3) by adding at the end the following:

"(7) is an alien, other than an alien who—

"(A) is lawfully admitted for permanent residence (as defined in section 101 (a)(20) of the Immigration and Nationality Act); or

"(B) is in lawful nonimmigrant status, is a refugee admitted under section 207 of the Immigration and Nationality Act (8 U.S.C. 1157), or is in asylum status under section 208 of the Immigration and Nationality Act (8 U.S.C. 1158), and—

"(i) is a foreign law enforcement officer of a friendly foreign government, as determined by the Secretary in consultation with the Secretary of State, entering the United States on official law enforcement business, and the shipping, transporting, possession, or receipt of explosive materials is in furtherance of this official law enforcement business;

"(ii) is a person having the power to direct or cause the direction of the management and policies of a corporation, partnership, or association licensed pursuant to section 843(a), and the shipping, transporting, possession, or receipt of explosive materials is in furtherance of such power;

"(iii) is a member of a North Atlantic Treaty Organization (NATO) or other friendly foreign military force, as determined by the Secretary in consultation with the Secretary of Defense, (whether or not admitted in a nonimmigrant status) who is present in the United States under military orders for training or other military purpose authorized by the United States, and the shipping, transporting, possession, or receipt of explosive materials is in furtherance of the military purpose; or

"(iv) is lawfully present in the United States in cooperation with the Director of Central Intelligence, and the shipment, transportation, receipt, or possession of the explosive materials is in furtherance of such cooperation;

"(8) has been discharged from the armed forces under dishonorable conditions;

"(9) having been a citizen of the United States, has renounced the citizenship of that person.".

(b) POSSESSION OF EXPLOSIVE MATERIALS.—Section 842(i) of title 18, United States Code, is amended—

(1) in paragraph (3), by striking "or" at the end; and

(2) by inserting after paragraph (4) the following:

"(5) who is an alien, other than an alien who—

"(A) is lawfully admitted for permanent residence (as that term is defined in section 101(a)(20) of the Immigration and Nationality Act); or

"(B) is in lawful nonimmigrant status, is a refugee admitted under section 207 of the Immigration and Nationality Act (8 U.S.C. 1157), or is in asylum status under section 208 of the Immigration and Nationality Act (8 U.S.C. 1158), and—

"(i) is a foreign law enforcement officer of a friendly foreign government, as determined by the Secretary in consultation with the Secretary of State, entering the United States on official law enforcement business, and the shipping, transporting, possession, or receipt of explosive materials is in furtherance of this official law enforcement business;

"(ii) is a person having the power to direct or cause the direction of the management and policies of a corporation, partnership, or association licensed pursuant to section 843(a), and the shipping, transporting, possession, or receipt of explosive materials is in furtherance of such power;

"(iii) is a member of a North Atlantic Treaty Organization (NATO) or other friendly foreign military force, as determined by the Secretary in consultation with the Secretary of Defense, (whether or not admitted in a nonimmigrant status) who is present in the United States under military orders for training or other military purpose authorized by the United States, and the shipping, transporting, possession, or receipt of explosive materials is in furtherance of the military purpose; or

"(iv) is lawfully present in the United States in cooperation with the Director of Central Intelligence, and the shipment, transportation, receipt, or possession of the explosive materials is in furtherance of such cooperation;

"(6) who has been discharged from the armed forces under dishonorable conditions;

"(7) who, having been a citizen of the United States, has renounced the citizenship of that person"; and

(3) by inserting "or affecting" before "interstate" each place that term appears.

SEC. 1124. REQUIREMENT TO PROVIDE SAMPLES OF EXPLOSIVE MATERIALS AND AMMONIUM NITRATE.

Section 843 of title 18, United States Code, as amended by this Act, is amended by adding at the end the following:

"(i) FURNISHING OF SAMPLES.—

"(1) IN GENERAL.—Licensed manufacturers and licensed importers and persons who manufacture or import explosive materials or ammonium nitrate shall, when required by letter issued by the Secretary, furnish—

"(A) samples of such explosive materials or ammonium nitrate;

"(B) information on chemical composition of those products; and

"(C) any other information that the Secretary determines is relevant to the identification of the explosive materials or to identification of the ammonium nitrate.

"(2) REIMBURSEMENT.—The Secretary shall, by regulation, authorize reimbursement of the fair market value of samples furnished pursuant to this subsection, as well as the reasonable costs of shipment.".

SEC. 1125. DESTRUCTION OF PROPERTY OF INSTITUTIONS RECEIVING FEDERAL FINANCIAL ASSISTANCE.

Section 844(f)(1) of title 18, United States Code, is amended by inserting before the word "shall" the following: "or any institution or organization receiving Federal financial assistance,".

SEC. 1126. RELIEF FROM DISABILITIES.

Section 845(b) of title 18, United States Code, is amended to read as follows:

"(b)(1) A person who is prohibited from shipping, transporting, receiving, or possessing any explosive under section 842(i) may apply to the Secretary for relief from such prohibition.

"(2) The Secretary may grant the relief requested under paragraph (1) if the Secretary determines that the circumstances regarding the applicability of section 842(i), and the applicant's record and reputation, are such that the applicant will not be likely to act in a manner dangerous to public safety and that the granting of such relief is not contrary to the public interest.

"(3) A licensee or permittee who applies for relief, under this subsection, from the disabilities incurred under this chapter as a result of an indictment for or conviction of a crime punishable by imprisonment for a term exceeding 1 year shall not be barred by such disability from further operations under the license or permit pending final action on an application for relief filed pursuant to this section.".

SEC. 1127. THEFT REPORTING REQUIREMENT.

Section 844 of title 18, United States Code, is amended by adding at the end the following:

"(p) THEFT REPORTING REQUIREMENT.—

"(1) IN GENERAL.—A holder of a license or permit who knows that explosive materials have been stolen from that licensee or permittee, shall report the theft to the Secretary not later than 24 hours after the discovery of the theft.

"(2) PENALTY.—A holder of a license or permit who does not report a theft in accordance with paragraph (1), shall be fined not more than $10,000, imprisoned not more than 5 years, or both.".

SEC. 1128. AUTHORIZATION OF APPROPRIATIONS.

There is authorized to be appropriated such sums as necessary to carry out this subtitle and the amendments made by this subtitle.

TITLE XII—AIRLINE WAR RISK INSURANCE LEGISLATION

SEC. 1201. AIR CARRIER LIABILITY FOR THIRD PARTY CLAIMS ARISING OUT OF ACTS OF TERRORISM.

Section 44303 of title 49, United States Code, is amended—
(1) by inserting "(a) IN GENERAL.—" before "The Secretary of Transportation";
(2) by moving the text of paragraph (2) of section 201(b) of the Air Transportation Safety and System Stabilization Act (115 Stat. 235) to the end and redesignating such paragraph as subsection (b);
(3) in subsection (b) (as so redesignated)—
(A) by striking the subsection heading and inserting "AIR CARRIER LIABILITY FOR THIRD PARTY CLAIMS ARISING OUT OF ACTS OF TERRORISM.—";
(B) in the first sentence by striking "the 180-day period following the date of enactment of this Act, the Secretary of Transportation" and inserting "the period beginning on September 22, 2001, and ending on December 31, 2003, the Secretary"; and
(C) in the last sentence by striking "this paragraph" and inserting "this subsection".

SEC. 1202. EXTENSION OF INSURANCE POLICIES.

Section 44302 of title 49, United States Code, is amended by adding at the end the following:
"(f) EXTENSION OF POLICIES.—
"(1) IN GENERAL.—The Secretary shall extend through August 31, 2003, and may extend through December 31, 2003, the termination date of any insurance policy that the Department of Transportation issued to an air carrier under subsection (a) and that is in effect on the date of enactment of this subsection on no less favorable terms to the air carrier than existed on June 19, 2002; except that the Secretary shall amend the insurance policy, subject to such terms and conditions as the Secretary may prescribe, to add coverage for losses or injuries to aircraft hulls, passengers, and crew at the limits carried by air carriers for such losses and injuries as of such date of enactment and at an additional premium comparable to the premium charged for third-party casualty coverage under such policy.
"(2) SPECIAL RULES.—Notwithstanding paragraph (1)—
"(A) in no event shall the total premium paid by the air carrier for the policy, as amended, be more than twice

the premium that the air carrier was paying to the Department of Transportation for its third party policy as of June 19, 2002; and

"(B) the coverage in such policy shall begin with the first dollar of any covered loss that is incurred.".

SEC. 1203. CORRECTION OF REFERENCE.

Effective November 19, 2001, section 147 of the Aviation and Transportation Security Act (Public Law 107–71) is amended by striking "(b)" and inserting "(c)".

SEC. 1204. REPORT.

Not later than 90 days after the date of enactment of this Act, the Secretary shall transmit to the Committee on Commerce, Science, and Transportation of the Senate and the Committee on Transportation and Infrastructure of the House of Representatives a report that—

(A) evaluates the availability and cost of commercial war risk insurance for air carriers and other aviation entities for passengers and third parties;

(B) analyzes the economic effect upon air carriers and other aviation entities of available commercial war risk insurance; and

(C) describes the manner in which the Department could provide an alternative means of providing aviation war risk reinsurance covering passengers, crew, and third parties through use of a risk-retention group or by other means.

TITLE XIII—FEDERAL WORKFORCE IMPROVEMENT

Subtitle A—Chief Human Capital Officers

SEC. 1301. SHORT TITLE.

This title may be cited as the "Chief Human Capital Officers Act of 2002".

SEC. 1302. AGENCY CHIEF HUMAN CAPITAL OFFICERS.

(a) IN GENERAL.—Part II of title 5, United States Code, is amended by inserting after chapter 13 the following:

"CHAPTER 14—AGENCY CHIEF HUMAN CAPITAL OFFICERS

"Sec.
"1401. Establishment of agency Chief Human Capital Officers.
"1402. Authority and functions of agency Chief Human Capital Officers.

"§ 1401. Establishment of agency Chief Human Capital Officers

"The head of each agency referred to under paragraphs (1) and (2) of section 901(b) of title 31 shall appoint or designate a Chief Human Capital Officer, who shall—

"(1) advise and assist the head of the agency and other agency officials in carrying out the agency's responsibilities for selecting, developing, training, and managing a high-quality, productive workforce in accordance with merit system principles;

"(2) implement the rules and regulations of the President and the Office of Personnel Management and the laws governing the civil service within the agency; and

"(3) carry out such functions as the primary duty of the Chief Human Capital Officer.

"§ 1402. Authority and functions of agency Chief Human Capital Officers

"(a) The functions of each Chief Human Capital Officer shall include—

"(1) setting the workforce development strategy of the agency;

"(2) assessing workforce characteristics and future needs based on the agency's mission and strategic plan;

"(3) aligning the agency's human resources policies and programs with organization mission, strategic goals, and performance outcomes;

"(4) developing and advocating a culture of continuous learning to attract and retain employees with superior abilities;

"(5) identifying best practices and benchmarking studies, and

"(6) applying methods for measuring intellectual capital and identifying links of that capital to organizational performance and growth.

"(b) In addition to the authority otherwise provided by this section, each agency Chief Human Capital Officer—

"(1) shall have access to all records, reports, audits, reviews, documents, papers, recommendations, or other material that—

"(A) are the property of the agency or are available to the agency; and

"(B) relate to programs and operations with respect to which that agency Chief Human Capital Officer has responsibilities under this chapter; and

"(2) may request such information or assistance as may be necessary for carrying out the duties and responsibilities provided by this chapter from any Federal, State, or local governmental entity.".

(b) TECHNICAL AND CONFORMING AMENDMENT.—The table of chapters for chapters for part II of title 5, United States Code, is amended by inserting after the item relating to chapter 13 the following:

"14. Agency Chief Human Capital Officers .... 1401".

SEC. 1303. CHIEF HUMAN CAPITAL OFFICERS COUNCIL.

(a) ESTABLISHMENT.—There is established a Chief Human Capital Officers Council, consisting of—

(1) the Director of the Office of Personnel Management, who shall act as chairperson of the Council;

(2) the Deputy Director for Management of the Office of Management and Budget, who shall act as vice chairperson of the Council; and

(3) the Chief Human Capital Officers of Executive departments and any other members who are designated by the Director of the Office of Personnel Management.

(b) FUNCTIONS.—The Chief Human Capital Officers Council shall meet periodically to advise and coordinate the activities of the agencies of its members on such matters as modernization of human resources systems, improved quality of human resources information, and legislation affecting human resources operations and organizations.

(c) EMPLOYEE LABOR ORGANIZATIONS AT MEETINGS.—The Chief Human Capital Officers Council shall ensure that representatives of Federal employee labor organizations are present at a minimum of 1 meeting of the Council each year. Such representatives shall not be members of the Council.

(d) ANNUAL REPORT.—Each year the Chief Human Capital Officers Council shall submit a report to Congress on the activities of the Council.

SEC. 1304. STRATEGIC HUMAN CAPITAL MANAGEMENT.

Section 1103 of title 5, United States Code, is amended by adding at the end the following:

"(c)(1) The Office of Personnel Management shall design a set of systems, including appropriate metrics, for assessing the management of human capital by Federal agencies.

"(2) The systems referred to under paragraph (1) shall be defined in regulations of the Office of Personnel Management and include standards for—

"(A)(i) aligning human capital strategies of agencies with the missions, goals, and organizational objectives of those agencies; and

"(ii) integrating those strategies into the budget and strategic plans of those agencies;

"(B) closing skill gaps in mission critical occupations;

"(C) ensuring continuity of effective leadership through implementation of recruitment, development, and succession plans;

"(D) sustaining a culture that cultivates and develops a high performing workforce;

"(E) developing and implementing a knowledge management strategy supported by appropriate investment in training and technology; and

"(F) holding managers and human resources officers accountable for efficient and effective human resources management in support of agency missions in accordance with merit system principles.".

SEC. 1305. EFFECTIVE DATE.

This subtitle shall take effect 180 days after the date of enactment of this Act.

Subtitle B—Reforms Relating to Federal Human Capital Management

SEC. 1311. INCLUSION OF AGENCY HUMAN CAPITAL STRATEGIC PLANNING IN PERFORMANCE PLANS AND PROGRAMS PERFORMANCE REPORTS.

(a) PERFORMANCE PLANS.—Section 1115 of title 31, United States Code, is amended—

(1) in subsection (a), by striking paragraph (3) and inserting the following:

"(3) provide a description of how the performance goals and objectives are to be achieved, including the operation processes, training, skills and technology, and the human, capital, information, and other resources and strategies required to meet those performance goals and objectives.";

(2) by redesignating subsection (f) as subsection (g); and

(3) by inserting after subsection (e) the following:

"(f) With respect to each agency with a Chief Human Capital Officer, the Chief Human Capital Officer shall prepare that portion of the annual performance plan described under subsection (a)(3).".

(b) PROGRAM PERFORMANCE REPORTS.—Section 1116(d) of title 31, United States Code, is amended—

(1) in paragraph (4), by striking "and" after the semicolon;

(2) by redesignating paragraph (5) as paragraph (6); and

(3) by inserting after paragraph (4) the following:

"(5) include a review of the performance goals and evaluation of the performance plan relative to the agency's strategic human capital management; and".

SEC. 1312. REFORM OF THE COMPETITIVE SERVICE HIRING PROCESS.

(a) IN GENERAL.—Chapter 33 of title 5, United States Code, is amended—

(1) in section 3304(a)—

(A) in paragraph (1), by striking "and" after the semicolon;

(B) in paragraph (2), by striking the period and inserting "; and"; and

(C) by adding at the end of the following:

"(3) authority for agencies to appoint, without regard to the provision of sections 3309 through 3318, candidates directly to positions for which—

"(A) public notice has been given; and

"(B) the Office of Personnel Management has determined that there exists a severe shortage of candidates or there is a critical hiring need.

The Office shall prescribe, by regulation, criteria for identifying such positions and may delegate authority to make determinations under such criteria."; and

(2) by inserting after section 3318 the following:

"§ 3319. Alternative ranking and selection procedures

"(a) The Office, in exercising its authority under section 3304, or an agency to which the Office has delegated examining authority under section 1104(a)(2), may establish category rating systems for evaluating applicants for positions in the competitive service, under 2 or more quality categories based on merit consistent with regulations prescribed by the Office of Personnel Management, rather than assigned individual numerical ratings.

"(b) Within each quality category established under subsection (a), preference-eligibles shall be listed ahead of individuals who are not preference eligibles. For other than scientific and professional positions at GS–9 of the General Schedule (equivalent or higher), qualified preference-eligibles who have a compensable service-connected disability of 10 percent or more shall be listed in the highest quality category.

"(c)(1) An appointing official may select any applicant in the highest quality category or, if fewer than 3 candidates have been assigned to the highest quality category, in a merged category consisting of the highest and the second highest quality categories.

"(2) Notwithstanding paragraph (1), the appointing official may not pass over a preference-eligible in the same category from which selection is made, unless the requirements of section 3317(b) or 3318(b), as applicable, are satisfied.

"(d) Each agency that establishes a category rating system under this section shall submit in each of the 3 years following that establishment, a report to Congress on that system including information on—

"(1) the number of employees hired under that system;

"(2) the impact that system has had on the hiring of veterans and minorities, including those who are American Indian or Alaska Natives, Asian, Black or African American, and native Hawaiian or other Pacific Islanders; and

"(3) the way in which managers were trained in the administration of that system.

"(e) The Office of Personnel Management may prescribe such regulations as it considers necessary to carry out the provisions of this section.".

(b) TECHNICAL AND CONFORMING AMENDMENT.—The table of sections for chapter 33 of title 5, United States Code, is amended by striking the item relating to section 3319 and inserting the following:

"3319. Alternative ranking and selection procedures.".

SEC. 1313. PERMANENT EXTENSION, REVISION, AND EXPANSION OF AUTHORITIES FOR USE OF VOLUNTARY SEPARATION INCENTIVE PAY AND VOLUNTARY EARLY RETIREMENT.

(a) VOLUNTARY SEPARATION INCENTIVE PAYMENTS.—

(1) IN GENERAL.—

(A) AMENDMENT TO TITLE 5, UNITED STATES CODE.—Chapter 35 of title 5, United States Code, is amended by inserting after subchapter I the following:

"SUBCHAPTER II—VOLUNTARY SEPARATION INCENTIVE PAYMENTS

"§ 3521. Definitions

"In this subchapter, the term—

"(1) 'agency' means an Executive agency as defined under section 105; and

"(2) 'employee'—

"(A) means an employee as defined under section 2105 employed by an agency and an individual employed by a county committee established under section 8(b)(5) of the Soil Conservation and Domestic Allotment Act (16 U.S.C. 590h(b)(5)) who—

"(i) is serving under an appointment without time limitation; and

"(ii) has been currently employed for a continuous period of at least 3 years; and

"(B) shall not include—

"(i) a reemployed annuitant under subchapter III of chapter 83 or 84 or another retirement system for employees of the Government;

"(ii) an employee having a disability on the basis of which such employee is or would be eligible for disability retirement under subchapter III of chapter 83 or 84 or another retirement system for employees of the Government;

"(iii) an employee who is in receipt of a decision notice of involuntary separation for misconduct or unacceptable performance;

"(iv) an employee who has previously received any voluntary separation incentive payment from the Federal Government under this subchapter or any other authority;

"(v) an employee covered by statutory reemployment rights who is on transfer employment with another organization; or

"(vi) any employee who—

"(I) during the 36-month period preceding the date of separation of that employee, performed service for which a student loan repayment benefit was or is to be paid under section 5379;

"(II) during the 24-month period preceding the date of separation of that employee, performed service for which a recruitment or relocation bonus was or is to be paid under section 5753; or

"(III) during the 12-month period preceding the date of separation of that employee, performed service for which a retention bonus was or is to be paid under section 5754.

"§ 3522. Agency plans; approval

"(a) Before obligating any resources for voluntary separation incentive payments, the head of each agency shall submit to the Office of Personnel Management a plan outlining the intended use of such incentive payments and a proposed organizational chart for the agency once such incentive payments have been completed.

"(b) The plan of an agency under subsection (a) shall include—

"(1) the specific positions and functions to be reduced or eliminated;

"(2) a description of which categories of employees will be offered incentives;

"(3) the time period during which incentives may be paid;

"(4) the number and amounts of voluntary separation incentive payments to be offered; and

"(5) a description of how the agency will operate without the eliminated positions and functions.

"(c) The Director of the Office of Personnel Management shall review each agency's plan an may make any appropriate modifications in the plan, in consultation with the Director of the Office of Management and Budget. A plan under this section may not be implemented without the approval of the Directive of the Office of Personnel Management.

"§ 3523. Authority to provide voluntary separation incentive payments

"(a) A voluntary separation incentive payment under this subchapter may be paid to an employee only as provided in the plan of an agency established under section 3522.

"(b) A voluntary incentive payment—

"(1) shall be offered to agency employees on the basis of—

"(A) 1 or more organizational units;

"(B) 1 or more occupational series or levels;

"(C) 1 or more geographical locations;

"(D) skills, knowledge, or other factors related to a position;

"(E) specific periods of time during which eligible employees may elect a voluntary incentive payment; or

"(F) any appropriate combination of such factors;

"(2) shall be paid in a lump sum after the employee's separation;

"(3) shall be equal to the lesser of—

"(A) an amount equal to the amount the employee would be entitled to receive under section 5595(c) if the employee were entitled to payment under such section (without adjustment for any previous payment made); or

"(B) an amount determined by the agency head, not to exceed $25,000;

"(4) may be made only in the case of an employee who voluntarily separates (whether by retirement or resignation) under this subchapter;

"(5) shall not be a basis for payment, and shall not be included in the computation, of any other type of Government benefit;

"(6) shall not be taken into account in determining the amount of any severance pay to which the employee may be entitled under section 5595, based on another other separation; and

"(7) shall be paid from appropriations or funds available for the payment of the basic pay of the employee.

"§ 3524. Effect of subsequent employment with the Government

"(a) The term 'employment'—

"(1) in subsection (b) includes employment under a personal services contract (or other direct contract) with the United States Government (other than an entity in the legislative branch); and

"(2) in subsection (c) does not include employment under such a contract.

"(b) An individual who has received a voluntary separation incentive payment under this subchapter and accepts any employment for compensation with the Government of the United States with 5 years after the date of the separation on which the payment is based shall be required to pay, before the individual's first day of employment, the entire amount of the incentive payment to the agency that paid the incentive payment.

"(c)(1) If the employment under this section is with an agency, other than the General Accounting Office, the United States Postal Service, or the Postal Rate Commission, the Director of the Office of Personnel Management may, at the request of the head of the agency, may waive the repayment if—

"(A) the individual involved possesses unique abilities and is the only qualified applicant available for the position; or

"(B) in case of an emergency involving a direct threat to life or property, the individual—

"(i) has skills directly related to resolving the emergency; and

"(ii) will serve on a temporary basis only so long as that individual's services are made necessary by the emergency.

"(2) If the employment under this section is with an entity in the legislative branch, the head of the entity or the appointing official may waive the repayment if the individual involved possesses unique abilities and is the only qualified applicant available for the position.

"(3) If the employment under this section is with the judicial branch, the Director of the Administrative Office of the United States Courts may waive the repayment if the individual involved possesses unique abilities and is the only qualified applicant available for the position.

"§ 3525. Regulations

"The Office of Personnel Management may prescribe regulations to carry out this subchapter.".

(B) TECHNICAL AND CONFORMING AMENDMENTS.—Chapter 35 of title 5, United States Code, is amended—

(i) by striking the chapter heading and inserting the following:

"CHAPTER 35—RETENTION PREFERENCE, VOLUNTARY SEPARATION INCENTIVE PAYMENTS, RESTORATION, AND REEMPLOYMENT";

and

(ii) in the table of sections by inserting after the item relating to section 3504 the following:

"SUBCHAPTER II—VOLUNTARY SEPARATION INCENTIVE PAYMENTS

"3521. Definitions.
"3522. Agency plans; approval.
"3523. Authority to provide voluntary separation incentive payments.
"3524. Effect of subsequent employment with the Government.
"3525. Regulations.".

(2) ADMINISTRATIVE OFFICE OF THE UNITED STATES COURTS.—The Director of the Administrative Office of the United States Courts may, by regulation, establish a program substantially similar to the program established under paragraph (1) for individuals serving in the judicial branch.

(3) CONTINUATION OF OTHER AUTHORITY.—Any agency exercising any voluntary separation incentive authority in effect on the effective date of this subsection may continue to offer voluntary separation incentives consistent with that authority until that authority expires.

(4) EFFECTIVE DATE.—This subsection shall take effect 60 days after the date of enactment of this Act.

(b) FEDERAL EMPLOYEE VOLUNTARY EARLY RETIREMENT.—

(1) CIVIL SERVICE RETIREMENT SYSTEM.—Section 8336(d)(2) of title 5, United States Code, is amended to read as follows:

"(2)(A) has been employed continuously, by the agency in which the employee is serving, for at least the 31-day period ending on the date on which such agency requests the determination referred to in subparagraph (D);

"(B) is serving under an appointment that is not time limited;

"(C) has not been duly notified that such employee is to be involuntarily separated for misconduct or unacceptable performance;

"(D) is separated from the service voluntarily during a period in which, as determined by the office of Personnel Management (upon request of the agency) under regulations prescribed by the Office—

"(i) such agency (or, if applicable, the component in which the employee is serving) is undergoing substantial delayering, substantial reorganization, substantial reductions in force, substantial transfer of function, or other substantial workforce restructuring (or shaping);

"(ii) a significant percentage of employees servicing in such agency (or component) are likely to be separated or subject to an immediate reduction in the rate of basic pay (without regard to subchapter VI of chapter 53, or comparable provisions); or

"(iii) identified as being in positions which are becoming surplus or excess to the agency's future ability to carry out its mission effectively; and

"(E) as determined by the agency under regulations prescribed by the Office, is within the scope of the offer of voluntary early retirement, which may be made on the basis of—

"(i) 1 or more organizational units;

"(ii) 1 or more occupational series or levels;

"(iii) 1 or more geographical locations;

"(iv) specific periods;

"(v) skills, knowledge, or other factors related to a position; or

"(vi) any appropriate combination of such factors;".

(2) FEDERAL EMPLOYEES' RETIREMENT SYSTEM.—Section 8414(b)(1) of title 5, United States Code, is amended by striking subparagraph (B) and inserting the following:

"(B)(i) has been employed continuously, by the agency in which the employee is serving, for at least the 31-day period ending on the date on which such agency requests the determination referred to in clause (iv);

"(ii) is serving under an appointment that is not time limited;

"(iii) has not been duly notified that such employee is to be involuntarily separated for misconduct or unacceptable performance;

"(iv) is separate from the service voluntarily during a period in which, as determined by the Office of Personnel Management (upon request of the agency) under regulations prescribed by the Office—

"(I) such agency (or, if applicable, the component in which the employee is serving) is undergoing substantial delayering, substantial reorganization, substantial reductions in force, substantial transfer of function, or other substantial workforce restructuring (or shaping);

"(II) a significant percentage of employees serving in such agency (or component) are likely to be separated or subject to an immediate reduction in the rate of basic pay (without regard to subchapter VI of chapter 53, or comparable provisions); or

"(III) identified as being in positions which are becoming surplus or excess to the agency's future ability to carry out its mission effectively; and

"(v) as determined by the agency under regulations prescribed by the Office, is within the scope of the offer of voluntary early retirement, which may be made on the basis of—

"(I) 1 or more organizational units;

"(II) 1 or more occupational series or levels;

"(III) 1 or more geographical locations;

"(IV) specific periods;

"(V) skills, knowledge, or other factors related to a position; or

"(VI) any appropriate combination of such factors.".

(3) GENERAL ACCOUNTING OFFICE AUTHORITY.—The amendments made by this subsection shall not be construed to affect the authority under section 1 of Public Law 106–303 (5 U.S.C. 8336 note; 114 State. 1063).

(4) TECHNICAL AND CONFORMING AMENDMENTS.—Section 7001 of the 1998 Supplemental Appropriations and Rescissions Act (Public Law 105–174; 112 Stat. 91) is repealed.

(5) REGULATIONS.—The Office of Personnel Management may prescribe regulations to carry out this subsection.

(c) SENSE OF CONGRESS.—It is the sense of Congress that the implementation of this section is intended to reshape the Federal workforce and not downsize the Federal workforce.

SEC. 1314. STUDENT VOLUNTEER TRANSIT SUBSIDY.

(a) IN GENERAL.—Section 7905(a)(1) of title 5, United States Code, is amended by striking "and a member of a uniformed service" and inserting ", a member of a uniformed service, and a student who provides voluntary services under section 3111".

(b) TECHNICAL AND CONFORMING AMENDMENT.—Section 3111(c)(1) of title 5, United States Code, is amended by striking "chapter 81 of this title" and inserting "section 7905 (relating to commuting by means other than single-occupancy motor vehicles), chapter 81".

Subtitle C—Reforms Relating to the Senior Executive Service

SEC. 1321. REPEAL OF RECERTIFICATION REQUIREMENTS OF SENIOR EXECUTIVES.

(a) IN GENERAL.—Title 5, United States Code, is amended—

(1) in chapter 33—

(A) in section 3393(g) by striking "3393a";

(B) by repealing section 3393a; and

(C) in the table of sections by striking the item relating to section 3393a;

(2) in chapter 35—

    (A) in section 3592(a)—

        (i) in paragraph (1), by inserting "or" at the end;

        (ii) in paragraph (2), by striking "or" at the end;

        (iii) by striking paragraph (3); and

        (iv) by striking the last sentence;

    (B) in section 3593(a), by striking paragraph (2) and inserting the following:

"(2) the appointee left the Senior Executive Service for reasons other than misconduct, neglect of duty, malfeasance, or less than fully successful executive performance as determined under subchapter II of chapter 43."; and

    (C) in section 3594(b)—

        (i) in paragraph (1), by inserting "or" at the end;

        (ii) in paragraph (2), by striking "or" at the end; and

        (iii) by striking paragraph (3);

(3) in section 7701(c)(1)(A), by striking "or removal from the Senior Executive Service for failure to be recertified under section 3393a";

(4) in chapter 83—

    (A) in section 8336(h)(1), by striking "for failure to be recertified as a senior executive under section 3393a or"; and

    (B) in section 8339(h), in the first sentence, by striking ", except that such reduction shall not apply in the case of an employee retiring under section 8336(h) for failure to be recertified as a senior executive"; and

(5) in chapter 84—

    (A) in section 8414(a)(1), by striking "for failure to be recertified as a senior executive under section 3393a or"; and

    (B) in section 8421(a)(2), by striking ", except that an individual entitled to an annuity under section 8414(a) for failure to be recertified as a senior executive shall be entitled to an annuity supplement without regard to such applicable retirement age".

(b) SAVINGS PROVISION.—Notwithstanding the amendments made by subsection (a)(2)(A), an appeal under the final sentence of section 3592(a) of title 5, United States Code, that is pending on the day before the effective date of this section—

(1) shall not abate by reason of the enactment of the amendments made by subsection (a)(2)(A); and

(2) shall continue as if such amendments had not been enacted.

(c) APPLICATION.—The amendment made by subsection (a)(2)(B) shall not apply with respect to an individual who, before the effective date of this section, leaves the Senior Executive Service for failure to be recertified as a senior executive under section 3393a of title 5, United States Code.

SEC. 1322. ADJUSTMENT OF LIMITATION ON TOTAL ANNUAL COMPENSATION.

(a) IN GENERAL.—Section 5307 of title 5, United States Code, is amended by adding at the end the following:

"(d)(1) Notwithstanding any other provision of this section, subsection (a)(1) shall be applied by substituting 'the total annual compensation payable to the Vice President under section 104 of title 3' for 'the annual rate of basic pay payable for level I of the Executive Schedule' in the case of any employee who—

"(A) is paid under section 5376 or 5383 of this title or section 332(f), 603, or 604 of title 28; and

"(B) holds a position in or under an agency which is described in paragraph (2).

"(2) An agency described in this paragraph is any agency which, for purposes of the calendar year involved, has been certified under this subsection as having a performance appraisal system which (as designed and applied) makes meaningful distinctions based on relative performance.

"(3)(A) The Office of Personnel Management and the Office of Management and Budget jointly shall promulgate such regulations as may be necessary to carry out this subsection, including the criteria and procedures in accordance with which any determinations under this subsection shall be made.

"(B) An agency's certification under this subsection shall be for a period of 2 calendar years, except that such certification may be terminated at any time, for purposes of either or both of those years, upon a finding that the actions of such agency have not remained in conformance with applicable requirements.

"(C) Any certification or decertification under this subsection shall be made by the Office of Personnel Management, with the concurrence of the Office of Management and Budget.

"(4) Notwithstanding any provision of paragraph (3), any regulations, certifications, or other measures necessary to carry out this subsection with respect to employees within the judicial branch shall be the responsibility of the Director of the Administrative Office of the United States Courts. However, the regulations under this paragraph shall be consistent with those promulgated under paragraph (3).".

(b) CONFORMING AMENDMENTS.—(1) Section 5307(a) of title 5, United States Code, is amended by inserting "or as otherwise provided under subsection (d)," after "under law,".

(2) Section 5307(c) of such title is amended by striking "this section," and inserting "this section (subject to subsection (d)),".

Subtitle D—Academic Training

SEC. 1331. ACADEMIC TRAINING.

(a) ACADEMIC DEGREE TRAINING.—Section 4107 of title 5, United States Code, is amended to read as follows:

"§ 4107. Academic degree training

"(a) Subject to subsection (b), an agency may select and assign an employee to academic degree training and may pay or reimburse the costs of academic degree training from appropriated or other available funds if such training—

"(1) contributes significantly to—

"(A) meeting an identified agency training need;

"(B) resolving an identified agency staffing problem; or

"(C) accomplishing goals in the strategic plan of the agency;

"(2) is part of a planned, systemic, and coordinated agency employee development program linked to accomplishing the strategic goals of the agency; and

"(3) is accredited and is provided by a college or university that is accredited by a nationally recognized body.

"(b) In exercising authority under subsection (a), an agency shall—

"(1) consistent with the merit system principles set forth in paragraphs (2) and (7) of section 2301(b), take into consideration the need to—

"(A) maintain a balanced workforce in which women, members of racial and ethnic minority groups, and persons with disabilities are appropriately represented in Government service; and

"(B) provide employees effective education and training to improve organizational and individual performance;

"(2) assure that the training is not for the sole purpose of providing an employee an opportunity to obtain an academic degree or qualify for appointment to a particular position for which the academic degree is a basic requirement;

"(3) assure that no authority under this subsection is exercised on behalf of any employee occupying or seeking to qualify for—

"(A) a noncareer appointment in the senior Executive Service; or

"(B) appointment to any position that is excepted from the competitive service because of its confidential policy-determining, policy-making or policy-advocating character; and

"(4) to the greatest extent practicable, facilitate the use of online degree training.".

(b) TECHNICAL AND CONFORMING AMENDMENT.—The table of sections for chapter 41 of title 5, United States Code, is amended by striking the item relating to section 4107 and inserting the following:

"4107. Academic degree training.".

SEC. 1332. MODIFICATIONS TO NATIONAL SECURITY EDUCATION PROGRAM.

(a) FINDINGS AND POLICIES.—

(1) FINDINGS.—Congress finds that—

(A) the United States Government actively encourages and financially supports the training, education, and development of many United States citizens;

(B) as a condition of some of those supports, many of those citizens have an obligation to seek either compensated or uncompensated employment in the Federal sector; and

(C) it is in the United States national interest to maximize the return to the Nation of funds invested in the development of such citizens by seeking to employ them in the Federal sector.

(2) POLICY.—It shall be the policy of the United States Government to—

(A) establish procedures for ensuring that United States citizens who have incurred service obligations as the result of receiving financial support for education and training from the United States Government and have applied for Federal positions are considered in all recruitment and hiring initiatives of Federal departments, bureaus, agencies, and offices; and

(B) advertise and open all Federal positions to United States citizens who have incurred service obligations with the United States Government as the result of receiving financial support for education and training from the United States Government.

(b) FULFILLMENT OF SERVICE REQUIREMENT IF NATIONAL SECURITY POSITIONS ARE UNAVAILABLE.—Section 802(b)(2) of the David L. Boren National Security Education Act of 1991 (50 U.S.C. 1902) is amended—

(1) in subparagraph (A), by striking clause (ii) and inserting the following:

"(ii) if the recipient demonstrates to the Secretary (in accordance with such regulations) that no national security position in an agency or office of the Federal Government having national security responsibilities is available, work in other offices or agencies of the Federal Government or in the field of higher education in a discipline relating to the foreign country, foreign language, area study, or international field of study for which the scholarship was awarded, for a period specified by the Secretary, which period shall be determined in accordance with clause (i); or"; and

(2) in subparagraph (B), by striking clause (ii) and inserting the following:

"(ii) if the recipient demonstrates to the Secretary (in accordance with such regulations) that no national security position is available upon the completion of the degree, work in other offices or agencies of the Federal Government or in the field of higher education in a discipline relating to foreign country, foreign language, area study, or international field of study for which the fellowship was awarded, for a period specified by the Secretary, which period shall be determined in accordance with clause (i); and".

TITLE XIV—ARMING PILOTS AGAINST TERRORISM

SEC. 1401. SHORT TITLE.

This title may be cited as the "Arming Pilots Against Terrorism Act".

SEC. 1402. FEDERAL FLIGHT DECK OFFICER PROGRAM.

(a) IN GENERAL.—Subchapter I of chapter 449 of title 49, United States Code, is amended by adding at the end the following:

"§ 44921. Federal flight deck officer program

"(a) ESTABLISHMENT.—The Under Secretary of Transportation for Security shall establish a program to deputize volunteer pilots of air carriers providing passenger air transportation or intrastate passenger air transportation as Federal law enforcement officers to defend the flight decks of aircraft of such air carriers against acts of criminal violence or air piracy. Such officers shall be known as 'Federal flight deck officers'.

"(b) PROCEDURAL REQUIREMENTS.—

"(1) IN GENERAL.—Not later than 3 months after the date of enactment of this section, the Under Secretary shall establish procedural requirements to carry out the program under this section.

"(2) COMMENCEMENT OF PROGRAM.—Beginning 3 months after the date of enactment of this section, the Under Secretary shall begin the process of training and deputizing pilots who are qualified to be Federal flight deck officers as Federal flight deck officers under the program.

"(3) ISSUES TO BE ADDRESSED.—The procedural requirements established under paragraph (1) shall address the following issues:

"(A) The type of firearm to be used by a Federal flight deck officer.

"(B) The type of ammunition to be used by a Federal flight deck officer.

"(C) The standards and training needed to qualify and requalify as a Federal flight deck officer.

"(D) The placement of the firearm of a Federal flight deck officer on board the aircraft to ensure both its security and its ease of retrieval in an emergency.

"(E) An analysis of the risk of catastrophic failure of an aircraft as a result of the discharge (including an accidental discharge) of a firearm to be used in the program into the avionics, electrical systems, or other sensitive areas of the aircraft.

"(F) The division of responsibility between pilots in the event of an act of criminal violence or air piracy if only 1 pilot is a Federal flight deck officer and if both pilots are Federal flight deck officers.

"(G) Procedures for ensuring that the firearm of a Federal flight deck officer does not leave the cockpit if there is a disturbance in the passenger cabin of the aircraft or if the pilot leaves the cockpit for personal reasons.

"(H) Interaction between a Federal flight deck officer and a Federal air marshal on board the aircraft.

"(I) The process for selection of pilots to participate in the program based on their fitness to participate in the program, including whether an additional background check should be required beyond that required by section 44936(a)(1).

"(J) Storage and transportation of firearms between flights, including international flights, to ensure the security of the firearms, focusing particularly on whether such security would be enhanced by requiring storage of the firearm at the airport when the pilot leaves the airport to remain overnight away from the pilot's base airport.

"(K) Methods for ensuring that security personnel will be able to identify whether a pilot is authorized to carry a firearm under the program.

"(L) Methods for ensuring that pilots (including Federal flight deck officers) will be able to identify whether a passenger is a law enforcement officer who is authorized to carry a firearm aboard the aircraft.

"(M) Any other issues that the Under Secretary considers necessary.

"(N) The Under Secretary's decisions regarding the methods for implementing each of the foregoing procedural requirements shall be subject to review only for abuse of discretion.

"(4) PREFERENCE.—In selecting pilots to participate in the program, the Under Secretary shall give preference to pilots who are former military or law enforcement personnel.

"(5) CLASSIFIED INFORMATION.—Notwithstanding section 552 of title 5 but subject to section 40119 of this title, information developed under paragraph (3)(E) shall not be disclosed.

"(6) NOTICE TO CONGRESS.—The Under Secretary shall provide notice to the Committee on Transportation and Infrastructure of the House of Representatives and the Committee on Commerce, Science, and Transportation of the Senate after completing the analysis required by paragraph (3)(E).

"(7) MINIMIZATION OF RISK.—If the Under Secretary determines as a result of the analysis under paragraph (3)(E) that there is a significant risk of the catastrophic failure of an aircraft as a result of the discharge of a firearm, the Under Secretary shall take such actions as may be necessary to minimize that risk.

"(c) TRAINING, SUPERVISION, AND EQUIPMENT.—

"(1) IN GENERAL.—The Under Secretary shall only be obligated to provide the training, supervision, and equipment necessary for a pilot to be a Federal flight deck officer under this section at no expense to the pilot or the air carrier employing the pilot.

"(2) TRAINING.—

"(A) IN GENERAL.—The Under Secretary shall base the requirements for the training of Federal flight deck officers under subsection (b) on the training standards applicable to Federal air marshals; except that the Under Secretary shall take into account the differing roles and responsibilities of Federal flight deck officers and Federal air marshals.

"(B) ELEMENTS.—The training of a Federal flight deck officer shall include, at a minimum, the following elements:

"(i) Training to ensure that the officer achieves the level of proficiency with a firearm required under subparagraph (C)(i).

"(ii) Training to ensure that the officer maintains exclusive control over the officer's firearm at all times, including training in defensive maneuvers.

"(iii) Training to assist the officer in determining when it is appropriate to use the officer's firearm and when it is appropriate to use less than lethal force.

"(C) TRAINING IN USE OF FIREARMS.—

"(i) STANDARD.—In order to be deputized as a Federal flight deck officer, a pilot must achieve a level of proficiency with a firearm that is required by the Under Secretary. Such level shall be comparable to the level of proficiency required of Federal air marshals.

"(ii) CONDUCT OF TRAINING.—The training of a Federal flight deck officer in the use of a firearm may be conducted by the Under Secretary or by a firearms training facility approved by the Under Secretary.

"(iii) REQUALIFICATION.—The Under Secretary shall require a Federal flight deck officer to requalify to carry a firearm under the program. Such requalification shall occur at an interval required by the Under Secretary.

"(d) DEPUTIZATION.—

"(1) IN GENERAL.—The Under Secretary may deputize, as a Federal flight deck officer under this section, a pilot who submits to the Under Secretary a request to be such an officer and whom the Under Secretary determines is qualified to be such an officer.

"(2) QUALIFICATION.—A pilot is qualified to be a Federal flight deck officer under this section if—

"(A) the pilot is employed by an air carrier;

"(B) the Under Secretary determines (in the Under Secretary's discretion) that the pilot meets the standards established by the Under Secretary for being such an officer; and

"(C) the Under Secretary determines that the pilot has completed the training required by the Under Secretary.

"(3) DEPUTIZATION BY OTHER FEDERAL AGENCIES.—The Under Secretary may request another Federal agency to deputize, as Federal flight deck officers under this section, those pilots that the Under Secretary determines are qualified to be such officers.

"(4) REVOCATION.—The Under Secretary may, (in the Under Secretary's discretion) revoke the deputization of a pilot as a Federal flight deck officer if the Under Secretary finds that the pilot is no longer qualified to be such an officer.

"(e) COMPENSATION.—Pilots participating in the program under this section shall not be eligible for compensation from the Federal Government for services provided as a Federal flight deck officer. The Federal Government and air carriers shall not be obligated to compensate a pilot for participating in the program or for the pilot's training or qualification and requalification to carry firearms under the program.

"(f) AUTHORITY TO CARRY FIREARMS.—

"(1) IN GENERAL.—The Under Secretary shall authorize a Federal flight deck officer to carry a firearm while engaged in providing air transportation or intrastate air transportation. Notwithstanding subsection (c)(1), the officer may purchase a firearm and carry that firearm aboard an aircraft of which the officer is the pilot in accordance with this section if the firearm is of a type that may be used under the program.

"(2) PREEMPTION.—Notwithstanding any other provision of Federal or State law, a Federal flight deck officer, whenever necessary to participate in the program, may carry a firearm in any State and from 1 State to another State.

"(3) CARRYING FIREARMS OUTSIDE UNITED STATES.—In consultation with the Secretary of State, the Under Secretary may take such action as may be necessary to ensure that a Federal flight deck officer may carry a firearm in a foreign country whenever necessary to participate in the program.

"(g) AUTHORITY TO USE FORCE.—Notwithstanding section 44903(d), the Under Secretary shall prescribe the standards and circumstances under which a Federal flight deck officer may use, while the program under this section is in effect, force (including lethal force) against an individual in the defense of the flight deck of an aircraft in air transportation or intrastate air transportation.

"(h) LIMITATION ON LIABILITY.—

"(1) LIABILITY OF AIR CARRIERS.—An air carrier shall not be liable for damages in any action brought in a Federal or State court arising out of a Federal flight deck officer's use of or failure to use a firearm.

"(2) LIABILITY OF FEDERAL FLIGHT DECK OFFICERS.—A Federal flight deck officer shall not be liable for damages in any action brought in a Federal or State court arising out of the acts or omissions of the officer in defending the flight deck of an aircraft against acts of criminal violence or air piracy unless the officer is guilty of gross negligence or willful misconduct.

"(3) LIABILITY OF FEDERAL GOVERNMENT.—For purposes of an action against the United States with respect to an act or omission of a Federal flight deck officer in defending the flight deck of an aircraft, the officer shall be treated as an employee of the Federal Government under chapter 171 of title 28, relating to tort claims procedure.

"(i) PROCEDURES FOLLOWING ACCIDENTAL DISCHARGES.—If an accidental discharge of a firearm under the pilot program results in the injury or death of a passenger or crew member on an aircraft, the Under Secretary—

"(1) shall revoke the deputization of the Federal flight deck officer responsible for that firearm if the Under Secretary determines that the discharge was attributable to the negligence of the officer; and

"(2) if the Under Secretary determines that a shortcoming in standards, training, or procedures was responsible for the accidental discharge, the Under Secretary may temporarily suspend the program until the shortcoming is corrected.

"(j) LIMITATION ON AUTHORITY OF AIR CARRIERS.—No air carrier shall prohibit or threaten any retaliatory action against a pilot employed by the air carrier from becoming a Federal flight deck officer under this section. No air carrier shall—

"(1) prohibit a Federal flight deck officer from piloting an aircraft operated by the air carrier; or

"(2) terminate the employment of a Federal flight deck officer, solely on the basis of his or her volunteering for or participating in the program under this section.

"(k) APPLICABILITY.—

"(1) EXEMPTION.—This section shall not apply to air carriers operating under part 135 of title 14, Code of Federal Regulations, and to pilots employed by such carriers to the extent that such carriers and pilots are covered by section 135.119 of such title or any successor to such section.

"(2) PILOT DEFINED.—The term 'pilot' means an individual who has final authority and responsibility for the operation and safety of the flight or, if more than 1 pilot is required for the operation of the aircraft or by the regulations under

which the flight is being conducted, the individual designated
as second in command.".

(b) CONFORMING AMENDMENTS.—

(1) CHAPTER ANALYSIS.—The analysis for such chapter is
amended by inserting after the item relating to section 44920
the following:

"44921. Federal flight deck officer program.".

(2) FLIGHT DECK SECURITY.—Section 128 of the Aviation
and Transportation Security Act (Public Law 107–71) is
repealed.

(c) FEDERAL AIR MARSHAL PROGRAM.—

(1) SENSE OF CONGRESS.—It is the sense of Congress that
the Federal air marshal program is critical to aviation security.

(2) LIMITATION ON STATUTORY CONSTRUCTION.—Nothing in
this Act, including any amendment made by this Act, shall
be construed as preventing the Under Secretary of Transportation for Security from implementing and training Federal
air marshals.

SEC. 1403. CREW TRAINING.

(a) IN GENERAL.—Section 44918(e) of title 49, United States
Code, is amended—

(1) by striking "The Administrator" and inserting the following:

"(1) IN GENERAL.—The Under Secretary";

(2) by adding at the end the following:

"(2) ADDITIONAL REQUIREMENTS.—In updating the training
guidance, the Under Secretary, in consultation with the
Administrator, shall issue a rule to—

"(A) require both classroom and effective hands-on
situational training in the following elements of self
defense:

"(i) recognizing suspicious activities and determining the seriousness of an occurrence;

"(ii) deterring a passenger who might present a
problem;

"(iii) crew communication and coordination;

"(iv) the proper commands to give to passengers
and attackers;

"(v) methods to subdue and restrain an attacker;

"(vi) use of available items aboard the aircraft
for self-defense;

"(vii) appropriate and effective responses to defend
oneself, including the use of force against an attacker;

"(viii) use of protective devices assigned to crew
members (to the extent such devices are approved by
the Administrator or Under Secretary);

"(ix) the psychology of terrorists to cope with their
behavior and passenger responses to that behavior;
and

"(x) how to respond to aircraft maneuvers that
may be authorized to defend against an act of criminal
violence or air piracy;

"(B) require training in the proper conduct of a cabin
search, including the duty time required to conduct the
search;

"(C) establish the required number of hours of training and the qualifications for the training instructors;

"(D) establish the intervals, number of hours, and elements of recurrent training;

"(E) ensure that air carriers provide the initial training required by this paragraph within 24 months of the date of enactment of this subparagraph; and

"(F) ensure that no person is required to participate in any hands-on training activity that that person believes will have an adverse impact on his or her health or safety.

"(3) RESPONSIBILITY OF UNDER SECRETARY.—(A) CONSULTATION.—In developing the rule under paragraph (2), the Under Secretary shall consult with law enforcement personnel and security experts who have expertise in self-defense training, terrorism experts, and representatives of air carriers, the provider of self-defense training for Federal air marshals, flight attendants, labor organizations representing flight attendants, and educational institutions offering law enforcement training programs.

"(B) DESIGNATION OF OFFICIAL.—The Under Secretary shall designate an official in the Transportation Security Administration to be responsible for overseeing the implementation of the training program under this subsection.

"(C) NECESSARY RESOURCES AND KNOWLEDGE.—The Under Secretary shall ensure that employees of the Administration responsible for monitoring the training program have the necessary resources and knowledge."; and

(3) by aligning the remainder of the text of paragraph (1) (as designated by paragraph (1) of this section) with paragraphs (2) and (3) (as added by paragraph (2) of this section).

(b) ENHANCE SECURITY MEASURES.—Section 109(a) of the Aviation and Transportation Security Act (49 U.S.C. 114 note; 115 Stat. 613–614) is amended by adding at the end the following:

"(9) Require that air carriers provide flight attendants with a discreet, hands-free, wireless method of communicating with the pilots.".

(c) BENEFITS AND RISKS OF PROVIDING FLIGHT ATTENDANTS WITH NONLETHAL WEAPONS.—

(1) STUDY.—The Under Secretary of Transportation for Security shall conduct a study to evaluate the benefits and risks of providing flight attendants with nonlethal weapons to aide in combating air piracy and criminal violence on commercial airlines.

(2) REPORT.—Not later than 6 months after the date of enactment of this Act, the Under Secretary shall transmit to Congress a report on the results of the study.

SEC. 1404. COMMERCIAL AIRLINE SECURITY STUDY.

(a) STUDY.—The Secretary of Transportation shall conduct a study of the following:

(1) The number of armed Federal law enforcement officers (other than Federal air marshals), who travel on commercial airliners annually and the frequency of their travel.

(2) The cost and resources necessary to provide such officers with supplemental training in aircraft anti-terrorism training that is comparable to the training that Federal air marshals are provided.

(3) The cost of establishing a program at a Federal law enforcement training center for the purpose of providing new Federal law enforcement recruits with standardized training comparable to the training that Federal air marshals are provided.

(4) The feasibility of implementing a certification program designed for the purpose of ensuring Federal law enforcement officers have completed the training described in paragraph (2) and track their travel over a 6-month period.

(5) The feasibility of staggering the flights of such officers to ensure the maximum amount of flights have a certified trained Federal officer on board.

(b) REPORT.—Not later than 6 months after the date of enactment of this Act, the Secretary shall transmit to Congress a report on the results of the study. The report may be submitted in classified and redacted form.

SEC. 1405. AUTHORITY TO ARM FLIGHT DECK CREW WITH LESS-THAN-LETHAL WEAPONS.

(a) IN GENERAL.—Section 44903(i) of title 49, United States Code (as redesignated by section 6 of this Act) is amended by adding at the end the following:

"(3) REQUEST OF AIR CARRIERS TO USE LESS-THAN-LETHAL WEAPONS.—If, after the date of enactment of this paragraph, the Under Secretary receives a request from an air carrier for authorization to allow pilots of the air carrier to carry less-than-lethal weapons, the Under Secretary shall respond to that request within 90 days.".

(b) CONFORMING AMENDMENTS.—Such section is further amended—

(1) in paragraph (1) by striking "Secretary" the first and third places it appears and inserting "Under Secretary"; and

(2) in paragraph (2) by striking "Secretary" each place it appears and inserting "Under Secretary".

SEC. 1406. TECHNICAL AMENDMENTS.

Section 44903 of title 49, United States Code, is amended—

(1) by redesignating subsection (i) (relating to short-term assessment and deployment of emerging security technologies and procedures) as subsection (j);

(2) by redesignating the second subsection (h) (relating to authority to arm flight deck crew with less-than-lethal weapons) as subsection (i); and

(3) by redesignating the third subsection (h) (relating to limitation on liability for acts to thwart criminal violence for aircraft piracy) as subsection (k).

TITLE XV—TRANSITION

Subtitle A—Reorganization Plan

SEC. 1501. DEFINITIONS.

For purposes of this title:

(1) The term "agency" includes any entity, organizational unit, program, or function.

(2) The term "transition period" means the 12-month period beginning on the effective date of this Act.

SEC. 1502. REORGANIZATION PLAN.

(a) SUBMISSION OF PLAN.—Not later than 60 days after the date of the enactment of this Act, the President shall transmit to the appropriate congressional committees a reorganization plan regarding the following:

(1) The transfer of agencies, personnel, assets, and obligations to the Department pursuant to this Act.

(2) Any consolidation, reorganization, or streamlining of agencies transferred to the Department pursuant to this Act.

(b) PLAN ELEMENTS.—The plan transmitted under subsection (a) shall contain, consistent with this Act, such elements as the President deems appropriate, including the following:

(1) Identification of any functions of agencies transferred to the Department pursuant to this Act that will not be transferred to the Department under the plan.

(2) Specification of the steps to be taken by the Secretary to organize the Department, including the delegation or assignment of functions transferred to the Department among officers of the Department in order to permit the Department to carry out the functions transferred under the plan.

(3) Specification of the funds available to each agency that will be transferred to the Department as a result of transfers under the plan.

(4) Specification of the proposed allocations within the Department of unexpended funds transferred in connection with transfers under the plan.

(5) Specification of any proposed disposition of property, facilities, contracts, records, and other assets and obligations of agencies transferred under the plan.

(6) Specification of the proposed allocations within the Department of the functions of the agencies and subdivisions that are not related directly to securing the homeland.

(c) MODIFICATION OF PLAN.—The President may, on the basis of consultations with the appropriate congressional committees, modify or revise any part of the plan until that part of the plan becomes effective in accordance with subsection (d).

(d) EFFECTIVE DATE.—

(1) IN GENERAL.—The reorganization plan described in this section, including any modifications or revisions of the plan under subsection (d), shall become effective for an agency on the earlier of—

(A) the date specified in the plan (or the plan as modified pursuant to subsection (d)), except that such date may not be earlier than 90 days after the date the President has transmitted the reorganization plan to the appropriate congressional committees pursuant to subsection (a); or

(B) the end of the transition period.

(2) STATUTORY CONSTRUCTION.—Nothing in this subsection may be construed to require the transfer of functions, personnel, records, balances of appropriations, or other assets of an agency on a single date.

(3) SUPERSEDES EXISTING LAW.—Paragraph (1) shall apply notwithstanding section 905(b) of title 5, United States Code.

SEC. 1503. REVIEW OF CONGRESSIONAL COMMITTEE STRUCTURES.

It is the sense of Congress that each House of Congress should review its committee structure in light of the reorganization of responsibilities within the executive branch by the establishment of the Department.

Subtitle B—Transitional Provisions

SEC. 1511. TRANSITIONAL AUTHORITIES.

(a) PROVISION OF ASSISTANCE BY OFFICIALS.—Until the transfer of an agency to the Department, any official having authority over or functions relating to the agency immediately before the effective date of this Act shall provide to the Secretary such assistance, including the use of personnel and assets, as the Secretary may request in preparing for the transfer and integration of the agency into the Department.

(b) SERVICES AND PERSONNEL.—During the transition period, upon the request of the Secretary, the head of any executive agency may, on a reimbursable basis, provide services or detail personnel to assist with the transition.

(c) ACTING OFFICIALS.—(1) During the transition period, pending the advice and consent of the Senate to the appointment of an officer required by this Act to be appointed by and with such advice and consent, the President may designate any officer whose appointment was required to be made by and with such advice and consent and who was such an officer immediately before the effective date of this Act (and who continues in office) or immediately before such designation, to act in such office until the same is filled as provided in this Act. While so acting, such officers shall receive compensation at the higher of—

(A) the rates provided by this Act for the respective offices in which they act; or

(B) the rates provided for the offices held at the time of designation.

(2) Nothing in this Act shall be understood to require the advice and consent of the Senate to the appointment by the President to a position in the Department of any officer whose agency is transferred to the Department pursuant to this Act and whose duties following such transfer are germane to those performed before such transfer.

(d) TRANSFER OF PERSONNEL, ASSETS, OBLIGATIONS, AND FUNCTIONS.—Upon the transfer of an agency to the Department—

(1) the personnel, assets, and obligations held by or available in connection with the agency shall be transferred to the Secretary for appropriate allocation, subject to the approval of the Director of the Office of Management and Budget and in accordance with the provisions of section 1531(a)(2) of title 31, United States Code; and

(2) the Secretary shall have all functions relating to the agency that any other official could by law exercise in relation to the agency immediately before such transfer, and shall have in addition all functions vested in the Secretary by this Act or other law.

(e) PROHIBITION ON USE OF TRANSPORTATION TRUST FUNDS.—

(1) IN GENERAL.—Notwithstanding any other provision of this Act, no funds derived from the Highway Trust Fund,

Airport and Airway Trust Fund, Inland Waterway Trust Fund, or Harbor Maintenance Trust Fund, may be transferred to, made available to, or obligated by the Secretary or any other official in the Department.

(2) LIMITATION.—This subsection shall not apply to security-related funds provided to the Federal Aviation Administration for fiscal years preceding fiscal year 2003 for (A) operations, (B) facilities and equipment, or (C) research, engineering, and development.

SEC. 1512. SAVINGS PROVISIONS.

(a) COMPLETED ADMINISTRATIVE ACTIONS.—(1) Completed administrative actions of an agency shall not be affected by the enactment of this Act or the transfer of such agency to the Department, but shall continue in effect according to their terms until amended, modified, superseded, terminated, set aside, or revoked in accordance with law by an officer of the United States or a court of competent jurisdiction, or by operation of law.

(2) For purposes of paragraph (1), the term "completed administrative action" includes orders, determinations, rules, regulations, personnel actions, permits, agreements, grants, contracts, certificates, licenses, registrations, and privileges.

(b) PENDING PROCEEDINGS.—Subject to the authority of the Secretary under this Act—

(1) pending proceedings in an agency, including notices of proposed rulemaking, and applications for licenses, permits, certificates, grants, and financial assistance, shall continue notwithstanding the enactment of this Act or the transfer of the agency to the Department, unless discontinued or modified under the same terms and conditions and to the same extent that such discontinuance could have occurred if such enactment or transfer had not occurred; and

(2) orders issued in such proceedings, and appeals therefrom, and payments made pursuant to such orders, shall issue in the same manner and on the same terms as if this Act had not been enacted or the agency had not been transferred, and any such orders shall continue in effect until amended, modified, superseded, terminated, set aside, or revoked by an officer of the United States or a court of competent jurisdiction, or by operation of law.

(c) PENDING CIVIL ACTIONS.—Subject to the authority of the Secretary under this Act, pending civil actions shall continue notwithstanding the enactment of this Act or the transfer of an agency to the Department, and in such civil actions, proceedings shall be had, appeals taken, and judgments rendered and enforced in the same manner and with the same effect as if such enactment or transfer had not occurred.

(d) REFERENCES.—References relating to an agency that is transferred to the Department in statutes, Executive orders, rules, regulations, directives, or delegations of authority that precede such transfer or the effective date of this Act shall be deemed to refer, as appropriate, to the Department, to its officers, employees, or agents, or to its corresponding organizational units or functions. Statutory reporting requirements that applied in relation to such an agency immediately before the effective date of this Act shall continue to apply following such transfer if they refer to the agency by name.

(e) EMPLOYMENT PROVISIONS.—(1) Notwithstanding the generality of the foregoing (including subsections (a) and (d)), in and for the Department the Secretary may, in regulations prescribed jointly with the Director of the Office of Personnel Management, adopt the rules, procedures, terms, and conditions, established by statute, rule, or regulation before the effective date of this Act, relating to employment in any agency transferred to the Department pursuant to this Act; and

(2) except as otherwise provided in this Act, or under authority granted by this Act, the transfer pursuant to this Act of personnel shall not alter the terms and conditions of employment, including compensation, of any employee so transferred.

(f) STATUTORY REPORTING REQUIREMENTS.—Any statutory reporting requirement that applied to an agency, transferred to the Department under this Act, immediately before the effective date of this Act shall continue to apply following that transfer if the statutory requirement refers to the agency by name.

SEC. 1513. TERMINATIONS.

Except as otherwise provided in this Act, whenever all the functions vested by law in any agency have been transferred pursuant to this Act, each position and office the incumbent of which was authorized to receive compensation at the rates prescribed for an office or position at level II, III, IV, or V, of the Executive Schedule, shall terminate.

SEC. 1514. NATIONAL IDENTIFICATION SYSTEM NOT AUTHORIZED.

Nothing in this Act shall be construed to authorize the development of a national identification system or card.

SEC. 1515. CONTINUITY OF INSPECTOR GENERAL OVERSIGHT.

Notwithstanding the transfer of an agency to the Department pursuant to this Act, the Inspector General that exercised oversight of such agency prior to such transfer shall continue to exercise oversight of such agency during the period of time, if any, between the transfer of such agency to the Department pursuant to this Act and the appointment of the Inspector General of the Department of Homeland Security in accordance with section 103(b).

SEC. 1516. INCIDENTAL TRANSFERS.

The Director of the Office of Management and Budget, in consultation with the Secretary, is authorized and directed to make such additional incidental dispositions of personnel, assets, and liabilities held, used, arising from, available, or to be made available, in connection with the functions transferred by this Act, as the Director may determine necessary to accomplish the purposes of this Act.

SEC. 1517. REFERENCE.

With respect to any function transferred by or under this Act (including under a reorganization plan that becomes effective under section 1502) and exercised on or after the effective date of this Act, reference in any other Federal law to any department, commission, or agency or any officer or office the functions of which are so transferred shall be deemed to refer to the Secretary, other official, or component of the Department to which such function is so transferred.

TITLE XVI—CORRECTIONS TO EXISTING LAW RELATING TO AIRLINE TRANSPORTATION SECURITY

SEC. 1601. RETENTION OF SECURITY SENSITIVE INFORMATION AUTHORITY AT DEPARTMENT OF TRANSPORTATION.

(a) Section 40119 of title 49, United States Code, is amended—

(1) in subsection (a)—

(A) by inserting "and the Administrator of the Federal Aviation Administration each" after "for Security"; and

(B) by striking "criminal violence and aircraft piracy" and inserting "criminal violence, aircraft piracy, and terrorism and to ensure security"; and

(2) in subsection (b)(1)—

(A) by striking ", the Under Secretary" and inserting "and the establishment of a Department of Homeland Security, the Secretary of Transportation";

(B) by striking "carrying out" and all that follows through "if the Under Secretary" and inserting "ensuring security under this title if the Secretary of Transportation"; and

(C) in subparagraph (C) by striking "the safety of passengers in transportation" and inserting "transportation safety".

(b) Section 114 of title 49, United States Code, is amended by adding at the end the following:

"(s) NONDISCLOSURE OF SECURITY ACTIVITIES.—

"(1) IN GENERAL.—Notwithstanding section 552 of title 5, the Under Secretary shall prescribe regulations prohibiting the disclosure of information obtained or developed in carrying out security under authority of the Aviation and Transportation Security Act (Public Law 107–71) or under chapter 449 of this title if the Under Secretary decides that disclosing the information would—

"(A) be an unwarranted invasion of personal privacy;

"(B) reveal a trade secret or privileged or confidential commercial or financial information; or

"(C) be detrimental to the security of transportation.

"(2) AVAILABILITY OF INFORMATION TO CONGRESS.—Paragraph (1) does not authorize information to be withheld from a committee of Congress authorized to have the information.

"(3) LIMITATION ON TRANSFERABILITY OF DUTIES.—Except as otherwise provided by law, the Under Secretary may not transfer a duty or power under this subsection to another department, agency, or instrumentality of the United States.".

SEC. 1602. INCREASE IN CIVIL PENALTIES.

Section 46301(a) of title 49, United States Code, is amended by adding at the end the following:

"(8) AVIATION SECURITY VIOLATIONS.—Notwithstanding paragraphs (1) and (2) of this subsection, the maximum civil penalty for violating chapter 449 or another requirement under this title administered by the Under Secretary of Transportation for Security shall be $10,000; except that the maximum civil penalty shall be $25,000 in the case of a person operating an aircraft for the transportation of passengers or property for compensation (except an individual serving as an airman).".

SEC. 1603. ALLOWING UNITED STATES CITIZENS AND UNITED STATES NATIONALS AS SCREENERS.

Section 44935(e)(2)(A)(ii) of title 49, United States Code, is amended by striking "citizen of the United States" and inserting "citizen of the United States or a national of the United States, as defined in section 1101(a)(22) of the Immigration and Nationality Act (8 U.S.C. 1101(a)(22))".

TITLE XVII—CONFORMING AND TECHNICAL AMENDMENTS

SEC. 1701. INSPECTOR GENERAL ACT OF 1978.

Section 11 of the Inspector General Act of 1978 (Public Law 95–452) is amended—

(1) by inserting "Homeland Security," after "Transportation," each place it appears; and

(2) by striking "; and" each place it appears in paragraph (1) and inserting ";".

SEC. 1702. EXECUTIVE SCHEDULE.

(a) IN GENERAL.—Title 5, United States Code, is amended—

(1) in section 5312, by inserting "Secretary of Homeland Security." as a new item after "Affairs.";

(2) in section 5313, by inserting "Deputy Secretary of Homeland Security." as a new item after "Affairs.";

(3) in section 5314, by inserting "Under Secretaries, Department of Homeland Security.", "Director of the Bureau of Citizenship and Immigration Services." as new items after "Affairs." the third place it appears;

(4) in section 5315, by inserting "Assistant Secretaries, Department of Homeland Security.", "General Counsel, Department of Homeland Security.", "Officer for Civil Rights and Civil Liberties, Department of Homeland Security.", "Chief Financial Officer, Department of Homeland Security.", "Chief Information Officer, Department of Homeland Security.", and "Inspector General, Department of Homeland Security." as new items after "Affairs." the first place it appears; and

(5) in section 5315, by striking "Commissioner of Immigration and Naturalization, Department of Justice.".

(b) SPECIAL EFFECTIVE DATE.—Notwithstanding section 4, the amendment made by subsection (a)(5) shall take effect on the date on which the transfer of functions specified under section 441 takes effect.

SEC. 1703. UNITED STATES SECRET SERVICE.

(a) IN GENERAL.—(1) The United States Code is amended in section 202 of title 3, and in section 3056 of title 18, by striking "of the Treasury", each place it appears and inserting "of Homeland Security".

(2) Section 208 of title 3, United States Code, is amended by striking "of Treasury" each place it appears and inserting "of Homeland Security".

(b) EFFECTIVE DATE.—The amendments made by this section shall take effect on the date of transfer of the United States Secret Service to the Department.

SEC. 1704. COAST GUARD.

(a) TITLE 14, UNITED STATES CODE.—Title 14, United States Code, is amended in sections 1, 3, 53, 95, 145, 516, 666, 669, 673, 673a (as redesignated by subsection (e)(1)), 674, 687, and 688 by striking "of Transportation" each place it appears and inserting "of Homeland Security".

(b) TITLE 10, UNITED STATES CODE.—(1) Title 10, United States Code, is amended in sections 101(9), 130b(a), 130b(c)(4), 130c(h)(1), 379, 513(d), 575(b)(2), 580(e)(6), 580a(e), 651(a), 671(c)(2), 708(a), 716(a), 717, 806(d)(2), 815(e), 888, 946(c)(1), 973(d), 978(d), 983(b)(1), 985(a), 1033(b)(1), 1033(d), 1034, 1037(c), 1044d(f), 1058(c), 1059(a), 1059(k)(1), 1073(a), 1074(c)(1), 1089(g)(2), 1090, 1091(a), 1124, 1143, 1143a(h), 1144, 1145(e), 1148, 1149, 1150(c), 1152(a), 1152(d)(1), 1153, 1175, 1212(a), 1408(h)(2), 1408(h)(8), 1463(a)(2), 1482a(b), 1510, 1552(a)(1), 1565(f), 1588(f)(4), 1589, 2002(a), 2302(1), 2306b(b), 2323(j)(2), 2376(2), 2396(b)(1), 2410a(a), 2572(a), 2575(a), 2578, 2601(b)(4), 2634(e), 2635(a), 2734(g), 2734a, 2775, 2830(b)(2), 2835, 2836, 4745(a), 5013a(a), 7361(b), 10143(b)(2), 10146(a), 10147(a), 10149(b), 10150, 10202(b), 10203(d), 10205(b), 10301(b), 12103(b), 12103(d), 12304, 12311(c), 12522(c), 12527(a)(2), 12731(b), 12731a(e), 16131(a), 16136(a), 16301(g), and 18501 by striking "of Transportation" each place it appears and inserting "of Homeland Security".

(2) Section 801(1) of such title is amended by striking "the General Counsel of the Department of Transportation" and inserting "an official designated to serve as Judge Advocate General of the Coast Guard by the Secretary of Homeland Security".

(3) Section 983(d)(2)(B) of such title is amended by striking "Department of Transportation" and inserting "Department of Homeland Security".

(4) Section 2665(b) of such title is amended by striking "Department of Transportation" and inserting "Department in which the Coast Guard is operating".

(5) Section 7045 of such title is amended—

(A) in subsections (a)(1) and (b), by striking "Secretaries of the Army, Air Force, and Transportation" both places it appears and inserting "Secretary of the Army, the Secretary of the Air Force, and the Secretary of Homeland Security"; and

(B) in subsection (b), by striking "Department of Transportation" and inserting "Department of Homeland Security".

(6) Section 7361(b) of such title is amended in the subsection heading by striking "TRANSPORTATION" and inserting "HOMELAND SECURITY".

(7) Section 12522(c) of such title is amended in the subsection heading by striking "TRANSPORTATION" and inserting "HOMELAND SECURITY".

(c) TITLE 37, UNITED STATES CODE.—Title 37, United States Code, is amended in sections 101(5), 204(i)(4), 301a(a)(3), 306(d), 307(c), 308(a)(1), 308(d)(2), 308(f), 308b(e), 308c(c), 308d(a), 308e(f), 308g(g), 308h(f), 308i(e), 309(d), 316(d), 323(b), 323(g)(1), 325(i), 402(d), 402a(g)(1), 403(f)(3), 403(l)(1), 403b(i)(5), 406(b)(1), 417(a), 417(b), 418(a), 703, 1001(c), 1006(f), 1007(a), and 1011(d) by striking "of Transportation" each place it appears and inserting "of Homeland Security".

(d) TITLE 38, UNITED STATES CODE.—Title 38, United States Code, is amended in sections 101(25)(d), 1560(a), 3002(5), 3011(a)(1)(A)(ii)(I), 3011(a)(1)(A)(ii)(II), 3011(a)(1)(B)(ii)(III), 3011(a)(1)(C)(iii)(II)(cc), 3012(b)(1)(A)(v), 3012(b)(1)(B)(ii)(V), 3018(b)(3)(B)(iv), 3018A(a)(3), 3018B(a)(1)(C), 3018B(a)(2)(C), 3018C(a)(5), 3020(m), 3035(b)(2), 3035(c), 3035(d), 3035(e), 3680A(g), and 6105(c) by striking "of Transportation" each place it appears and inserting "of Homeland Security".

(e) OTHER DEFENSE-RELATED LAWS.—(1) Section 363 of Public Law 104–193 (110 Stat. 2247) is amended—

(A) in subsection (a)(1) (10 U.S.C. 113 note), by striking "of Transportation" and inserting "of Homeland Security"; and

(B) in subsection (b)(1) (10 U.S.C. 704 note), by striking "of Transportation" and inserting "of Homeland Security".

(2) Section 721(1) of Public Law 104–201 (10 U.S.C. 1073 note) is amended by striking "of Transportation" and inserting "of Homeland Security".

(3) Section 4463(a) of Public Law 102–484 (10 U.S.C. 1143a note) is amended by striking "after consultation with the Secretary of Transportation".

(4) Section 4466(h) of Public Law 102–484 (10 U.S.C. 1143 note) is amended by striking "of Transportation" and inserting "of Homeland Security".

(5) Section 542(d) of Public Law 103–337 (10 U.S.C. 1293 note) is amended by striking "of Transportation" and inserting "of Homeland Security".

(6) Section 740 of Public Law 106–181 (10 U.S.C. 2576 note) is amended in subsections (b)(2), (c), and (d)(1) by striking "of Transportation" each place it appears and inserting "of Homeland Security".

(7) Section 1407(b)(2) of the Defense Dependents' Education Act of 1978 (20 U.S.C. 926(b)) is amended by striking "of Transportation" both places it appears and inserting "of Homeland Security".

(8) Section 2301(5)(D) of the Elementary and Secondary Education Act of 1965 (20 U.S.C. 6671(5)(D)) is amended by striking "of Transportation" and inserting "of Homeland Security".

(9) Section 2307(a) of the Elementary and Secondary Education Act of 1965 (20 U.S.C. 6677(a)) is amended by striking "of Transportation" and inserting "of Homeland Security".

(10) Section 1034(a) of Public Law 105–85 (21 U.S.C. 1505a(a)) is amended by striking "of Transportation" and inserting "of Homeland Security".

(11) The Military Selective Service Act is amended—

(A) in section 4(a) (50 U.S.C. App. 454(a)), by striking "of Transportation" in the fourth paragraph and inserting "of Homeland Security";

(B) in section 4(b) (50 U.S.C. App. 454(b)), by striking "of Transportation" both places it appears and inserting "of Homeland Security";

(C) in section 6(d)(1) (50 U.S.C. App. 456(d)(1)), by striking "of Transportation" both places it appears and inserting "of Homeland Security";

(D) in section 9(c) (50 U.S.C. App. 459(c)), by striking "Secretaries of Army, Navy, Air Force, or Transportation" and inserting "Secretary of a military department, and the Secretary of Homeland Security with respect to the Coast Guard,"; and

(E) in section 15(e) (50 U.S.C. App. 465(e)), by striking "of Transportation" both places it appears and inserting "of Homeland Security".

(f) TECHNICAL CORRECTION.—(1) Title 14, United States Code, is amended by redesignating section 673 (as added by section 309 of Public Law 104–324) as section 673a.

(2) The table of sections at the beginning of chapter 17 of such title is amended by redesignating the item relating to such section as section 673a.

(g) EFFECTIVE DATE.—The amendments made by this section (other than subsection (f)) shall take effect on the date of transfer of the Coast Guard to the Department.

SEC. 1705. STRATEGIC NATIONAL STOCKPILE AND SMALLPOX VACCINE DEVELOPMENT.

(a) IN GENERAL.—Section 121 of the Public Health Security and Bioterrorism Preparedness and Response Act of 2002 (Public Law 107–188; 42 U.S.C. 300hh–12) is amended—

(1) in subsection (a)(1)—

(A) by striking "Secretary of Health and Human Services" and inserting "Secretary of Homeland Security";

(B) by inserting "the Secretary of Health and Human Services and" between "in coordination with" and "the Secretary of Veterans Affairs"; and

(C) by inserting "of Health and Human Services" after "as are determined by the Secretary"; and

(2) in subsections (a)(2) and (b), by inserting "of Health and Human Services" after "Secretary" each place it appears.

(b) EFFECTIVE DATE.—The amendments made by this section shall take effect on the date of transfer of the Strategic National Stockpile of the Department of Health and Human Services to the Department.

SEC. 1706. TRANSFER OF CERTAIN SECURITY AND LAW ENFORCEMENT FUNCTIONS AND AUTHORITIES.

(a) AMENDMENT TO TITLE 40.—Section 581 of title 40, United States Code, is amended—

(1) by striking subsection (a); and

(2) in subsection (b)—

(A) by inserting "and" after the semicolon at the end of paragraph (1);

(B) by striking "; and" at the end of paragraph (2) and inserting a period; and

(C) by striking paragraph (3).

(b) LAW ENFORCEMENT AUTHORITY.—

(1) IN GENERAL.—Section 1315 of title 40, United States Code, is amended to read as follows:

"§ 1315. Law enforcement authority of Secretary of Homeland Security for protection of public property

"(a) IN GENERAL.—To the extent provided for by transfers made pursuant to the Homeland Security Act of 2002, the Secretary of Homeland Security (in this section referred to as the 'Secretary') shall protect the buildings, grounds, and property that are owned, occupied, or secured by the Federal Government (including any agency, instrumentality, or wholly owned or mixed-ownership corporation thereof) and the persons on the property.

"(b) OFFICERS AND AGENTS.—

"(1) DESIGNATION.—The Secretary may designate employees of the Department of Homeland Security, including employees transferred to the Department from the Office of the Federal Protective Service of the General Services Administration pursuant to the Homeland Security Act of 2002, as officers and agents for duty in connection with the protection of property owned or occupied by the Federal Government and persons on the property, including duty in areas outside the property to the extent necessary to protect the property and persons on the property.

"(2) POWERS.—While engaged in the performance of official duties, an officer or agent designated under this subsection may—

"(A) enforce Federal laws and regulations for the protection of persons and property;

"(B) carry firearms;

"(C) make arrests without a warrant for any offense against the United States committed in the presence of the officer or agent or for any felony cognizable under the laws of the United States if the officer or agent has reasonable grounds to believe that the person to be arrested has committed or is committing a felony;

"(D) serve warrants and subpoenas issued under the authority of the United States;

"(E) conduct investigations, on and off the property in question, of offenses that may have been committed against property owned or occupied by the Federal Government or persons on the property; and

"(F) carry out such other activities for the promotion of homeland security as the Secretary may prescribe.

"(c) REGULATIONS.—

"(1) IN GENERAL.—The Secretary, in consultation with the Administrator of General Services, may prescribe regulations necessary for the protection and administration of property owned or occupied by the Federal Government and persons on the property. The regulations may include reasonable penalties, within the limits prescribed in paragraph (2), for violations of the regulations. The regulations shall be posted and remain posted in a conspicuous place on the property.

"(2) PENALTIES.—A person violating a regulation prescribed under this subsection shall be fined under title 18, United States Code, imprisoned for not more than 30 days, or both.

"(d) DETAILS.—

"(1) REQUESTS OF AGENCIES.—On the request of the head of a Federal agency having charge or control of property owned or occupied by the Federal Government, the Secretary may detail officers and agents designated under this section for the protection of the property and persons on the property.

"(2) APPLICABILITY OF REGULATIONS.—The Secretary may—

"(A) extend to property referred to in paragraph (1) the applicability of regulations prescribed under this section and enforce the regulations as provided in this section; or

"(B) utilize the authority and regulations of the requesting agency if agreed to in writing by the agencies.

"(3) FACILITIES AND SERVICES OF OTHER AGENCIES.—When the Secretary determines it to be economical and in the public interest, the Secretary may utilize the facilities and services of Federal, State, and local law enforcement agencies, with the consent of the agencies.

"(e) AUTHORITY OUTSIDE FEDERAL PROPERTY.—For the protection of property owned or occupied by the Federal Government and persons on the property, the Secretary may enter into agreements with Federal agencies and with State and local governments to obtain authority for officers and agents designated under this section to enforce Federal laws and State and local laws concurrently with other Federal law enforcement officers and with State and local law enforcement officers.

"(f) SECRETARY AND ATTORNEY GENERAL APPROVAL.—The powers granted to officers and agents designated under this section shall be exercised in accordance with guidelines approved by the Secretary and the Attorney General.

"(g) LIMITATION ON STATUTORY CONSTRUCTION.—Nothing in this section shall be construed to—

"(1) preclude or limit the authority of any Federal law enforcement agency; or

"(2) restrict the authority of the Administrator of General Services to promulgate regulations affecting property under the Administrator's custody and control.".

(2) DELEGATION OF AUTHORITY.—The Secretary may delegate authority for the protection of specific buildings to another Federal agency where, in the Secretary's discretion, the Secretary determines it necessary for the protection of that building.

(3) CLERICAL AMENDMENT.—The table of sections at the beginning of chapter 13 of title 40, United States Code, is amended by striking the item relating to section 1315 and inserting the following:

"1315. Law enforcement authority of Secretary of Homeland Security for protection of public property.".

SEC. 1707. TRANSPORTATION SECURITY REGULATIONS.

Title 49, United States Code, is amended—

(1) in section 114(l)(2)(B), by inserting "for a period not to exceed 90 days" after "effective"; and

(2) in section 114(l)(2)(B), by inserting "ratified or" after "unless".

SEC. 1708. NATIONAL BIO-WEAPONS DEFENSE ANALYSIS CENTER.

There is established in the Department of Defense a National Bio-Weapons Defense Analysis Center, whose mission is to develop countermeasures to potential attacks by terrorists using weapons of mass destruction.

SEC. 1709. COLLABORATION WITH THE SECRETARY OF HOMELAND SECURITY.

(a) DEPARTMENT OF HEALTH AND HUMAN SERVICES.—The second sentence of section 351A(e)(1) of the Public Health Service Act (42 U.S.C. 262A(e)(1)) is amended by striking "consultation with" and inserting "collaboration with the Secretary of Homeland Security and".

(b) DEPARTMENT OF AGRICULTURE.—The second sentence of section 212(e)(1) of the Agricultural Bioterrorism Protection Act of 2002 (7 U.S.C. 8401) is amended by striking "consultation with" and inserting "collaboration with the Secretary of Homeland Security and".

SEC. 1710. RAILROAD SAFETY TO INCLUDE RAILROAD SECURITY.

(a) INVESTIGATION AND SURVEILLANCE ACTIVITIES.—Section 20105 of title 49, United States Code, is amended—

(1) by striking "Secretary of Transportation" in the first sentence of subsection (a) and inserting "Secretary concerned";

(2) by striking "Secretary" each place it appears (except the first sentence of subsection (a)) and inserting "Secretary concerned";

(3) by striking "Secretary's duties under chapters 203–213 of this title" in subsection (d) and inserting "duties under chapters 203–213 of this title (in the case of the Secretary of Transportation) and duties under section 114 of this title (in the case of the Secretary of Homeland Security)";

(4) by striking "chapter." in subsection (f) and inserting "chapter (in the case of the Secretary of Transportation) and duties under section 114 of this title (in the case of the Secretary of Homeland Security)."; and

(5) by adding at the end the following new subsection:
"(g) DEFINITIONS.—In this section—

"(1) the term 'safety' includes security; and

"(2) the term 'Secretary concerned' means—

"(A) the Secretary of Transportation, with respect to railroad safety matters concerning such Secretary under laws administered by that Secretary; and

"(B) the Secretary of Homeland Security, with respect to railroad safety matters concerning such Secretary under laws administered by that Secretary.".

(b) REGULATIONS AND ORDERS.—Section 20103(a) of such title is amended by inserting after "1970." the following: "When prescribing a security regulation or issuing a security order that affects the safety of railroad operations, the Secretary of Homeland Security shall consult with the Secretary.".

(c) NATIONAL UNIFORMITY OF REGULATION.—Section 20106 of such title is amended—

(1) by inserting "and laws, regulations, and orders related to railroad security" after "safety" in the first sentence;

(2) by inserting "or security" after "safety" each place it appears after the first sentence; and

(3) by striking "Transportation" in the second sentence and inserting "Transportation (with respect to railroad safety matters), or the Secretary of Homeland Security (with respect to railroad security matters),".

SEC. 1711. HAZMAT SAFETY TO INCLUDE HAZMAT SECURITY.

(a) GENERAL REGULATORY AUTHORITY.—Section 5103 of title 49, United States Code, is amended—

(1) by striking "transportation" the first place it appears in subsection (b)(1) and inserting "transportation, including security,";

(2) by striking "aspects" in subsection (b)(1)(B) and inserting "aspects, including security,"; and

(3) by adding at the end the following:

"(C) CONSULTATION.—When prescribing a security regulation or issuing a security order that affects the safety of the transportation of hazardous material, the Secretary of Homeland Security shall consult with the Secretary.".

(b) PREEMPTION.—Section 5125 of that title is amended—

(1) by striking "chapter or a regulation prescribed under this chapter" in subsection (a)(1) and inserting "chapter, a regulation prescribed under this chapter, or a hazardous materials transportation security regulation or directive issued by the Secretary of Homeland Security";

(2) by striking "chapter or a regulation prescribed under this chapter." in subsection (a)(2) and inserting "chapter, a regulation prescribed under this chapter, or a hazardous materials transportation security regulation or directive issued by the Secretary of Homeland Security."; and

(3) by striking "chapter or a regulation prescribed under this chapter," in subsection (b)(1) and inserting "chapter, a regulation prescribed under this chapter, or a hazardous materials transportation security regulation or directive issued by the Secretary of Homeland Security,".

SEC. 1712. OFFICE OF SCIENCE AND TECHNOLOGY POLICY.

The National Science and Technology Policy, Organization, and Priorities Act of 1976 is amended—

(1) in section 204(b)(1) (42 U.S.C. 6613(b)(1)), by inserting "homeland security," after "national security,"; and

(2) in section 208(a)(1) (42 U.S.C. 6617(a)(1)), by inserting "the Office of Homeland Security," after "National Security Council,".

SEC. 1713. NATIONAL OCEANOGRAPHIC PARTNERSHIP PROGRAM.

Section 7902(b) of title 10, United States Code, is amended by adding at the end the following new paragraphs:

"(13) The Under Secretary for Science and Technology of the Department of Homeland Security.

"(14) Other Federal officials the Council considers appropriate.".

SEC. 1714. CLARIFICATION OF DEFINITION OF MANUFACTURER.

Section 2133(3) of the Public Health Service Act (42 U.S.C. 300aa–33(3)) is amended—

(1) in the first sentence, by striking "under its label any vaccine set forth in the Vaccine Injury Table" and inserting "any vaccine set forth in the Vaccine Injury table, including any component or ingredient of any such vaccine"; and

(2) in the second sentence, by inserting "including any component or ingredient of any such vaccine" before the period.

SEC. 1715. CLARIFICATION OF DEFINITION OF VACCINE-RELATED INJURY OR DEATH.

Section 2133(5) of the Public Health Service Act (42 U.S.C. 300aa–33(5)) is amended by adding at the end the following: "For purposes of the preceding sentence, an adulterant or contaminant shall not include any component or ingredient listed in a vaccine's product license application or product label.".

SEC. 1716. CLARIFICATION OF DEFINITION OF VACCINE.

Section 2133 of the Public Health Service Act (42 U.S.C. 300aa–33) is amended by adding at the end the following:

"(7) The term 'vaccine' means any preparation or suspension, including but not limited to a preparation or suspension containing an attenuated or inactive microorganism or subunit thereof or toxin, developed or administered to produce or enhance the body's immune response to a disease or diseases and includes all components and ingredients listed in the vaccines's product license application and product label.".

SEC. 1717. EFFECTIVE DATE.

The amendments made by sections 1714, 1715, and 1716 shall apply to all actions or proceedings pending on or after the date of enactment of this Act, unless a court of competent jurisdiction has entered judgment (regardless of whether the time for appeal has expired) in such action or proceeding disposing of the entire action or proceeding.

Speaker of the House of Representatives.

Vice President of the United States and
President of the Senate.

GLOBAL BUSINESS, RESEARCH AND POLITICAL LIBRARIES

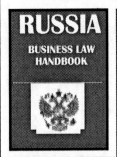

RUSSIA BUSINESS LAW HANDBOOK

SOUTH AFRICA INVESTMENT & BUSINESS GUIDE

JAPAN BUSINESS & INVESTMENT OPPORTUNITIES YEARBOOK

BAHAMAS OFFSHORE INVESTMENT & BUSINESS GUIDE

LIBYA A "SPY" GUIDE"

CHINA FOREIGN POLICY & GOVERNMENT GUIDE

RUSSIA A COUNTRY STUDY

INDIA BUSINESS INTELLIGENCE REPORT

US-ISRAEL POLITICAL & ECONOMIC COOPERATION HANDBOOK

ARMENIA EXPORT-IMPORT & BUSINESS DIRECTORY

Guides, reports and handbooks are available for the following countries:

Albania
Algeria
Andorra
Angola
Antigua and
Barbuda
Argentina
Armenia
Australia
Austria
Azerbaijan
Bahamas
Bahrain
Bangladesh
Barbados
Belarus
Belgium
Belize
Benin
Bhutan
Bolivia
Bosnia &
Herzegovina
Botswana
Brazil
Brunei
Bulgaria
Burkina Faso
Burundi
Cambodia
Cameroon
Canada
Cape Verde

Central African
Republic
Chad
Chile
China
Colombia
Comoros
Congo,
Democratic
Republic
Costa Rica
Côte d'Ivoire
Croatia
Cuba
Cyprus
Czech Republic
Denmark
Djibouti
Dominica
Dominican
Republic
Ecuador
Egypt
El Salvador
Equatorial
Guinea
Eritrea
Estonia
Ethiopia
Faroe Islands
Fiji
Finland
France

Gabon
Gambia
Georgia
Germany
Ghana
Greece
Grenada
Guatemala
Guinea
Guinea-Bissau
Guyana
Haiti
Honduras
Hungary
Iceland
India
Indonesia
Iran
Ireland
Israel
Italy
Jamaica
Japan
Jordan
Kazakhstan
Kenya
Kiribati
Korea, North
Korea, South
Kuwait
Kyrgyzstan
Laos
Latvia

Lebanon
Lesotho
Liberia
Libya
Liechtenstein
Lithuania
Luxembourg
Macedonia
Madagascar
Malawi
Malaysia
Maldives
Mali
Malta
Marshall
Islands
Mauritania
Mauritius
Mexico
Micronesia
Moldova
Monaco
Mongolia
Morocco
Mozambique
Myanmar
(Burma)
Namibia
Nauru
Nepal
Netherlands
New Zealand
Nicaragua

Niger
Nigeria
Norway
Oman
Pakistan
Palau
Panama
Papua New
Guinea
Paraguay
Peru
Philippines
Poland
Portugal
Qatar
Romania
Russia
Rwanda
Saint Kitts &
Nevis
Saint Lucia
Saint Vincent
& Grenadines
San Marino
San Tome
and Principe
Saudi Arabia
Senegal
Seychelles
Sierra Leone
Singapore
Slovakia
Slovenia

Solomon
Islands
Somalia
South Africa
Spain
Sri Lanka
Sudan
Suriname
Swaziland
Sweden
Switzerland
Syria
Taiwan
Tajikistan
Tanzania
Thailand
Togo
Tonga
Trinidad &
Tobago
Tunisia
Turkey
Turkmenistan
Tuvalu
Uganda
Ukraine
United Arab
Emirates
United
Kingdom
United States
Uruguay
Uzbekistan

GLOBAL BUSINESS & INVESTMENT LIBRARY

PRICE $129.95

Ultimate directories for export-import, investment, government and

 GLOBAL LAW FIRMS DIRECTORY ISBN 0739767089

GLOBAL BUSINESS CONTACTS DIRECTORY ISBN 073976702X

 GLOBAL CHAMBERS OF WORLD ISBN 0739767054

 GLOBAL CHAMBERS OF COMMERCE USA ISBN 0739767046

 GLOBAL SLAVIC LIBRARIES DIRECTORY ISBN 0739767100

 GLOBAL BUSINESS AND INDUSTRIAL DIRECTORIES PUBLISHERS DIRECTORY ISBN 0739767003

AFRICA UNIVERSITY LIBRARIES ISBN 073900936

 UNITED KINGDOM UNIVERSITY DIRECTORY ISBN 0739700928

 GLOBAL OFFSHORE INVESTMENT & BUSINESS ISBN 0739767097

 GLOBAL BUSINESS ASSOCIATIONS DIRECTORY ISBN 0739767011

 GLOBAL TAX GUIDE EUROPE ISBN 0739767119

 GLOBAL INVESTMENT FUNDS DIRECTORY ISBN 0739767070

 GLOBAL US ECONOMIC ISBN 0739767143

 GLOBAL WORLD TRADE ISBN 073976716X

 WORLD TRADE ORGANIZATION ISBN 0739707426

 KOREA UNIFICATION HANDBOOK ISBN 0739700936

 GLOBAL OFFSHORE INVESTMENT & BUSINESS ISBN 0739767097

 GLOBAL OFFSHORE BUSINESS CONTACTS ISBN 0739739336

 GLOBAL TAX GUIDE ASIA ISBN 0739767127

 GLOBAL OFFSHORE BUSINESS LAW HANDBOOK ISBN 0739739344

 GLOBAL OFFSHORE TAX HANDBOOK ISBN 0739739352

 GLOBAL TRANSPORTATION BUSINESS CONTACTS ISBN 073970091X

 UNITED STATES TV BROADCASTIN ISBN 0739707442

 PORTUGAL TELECOM INDUSTRY INVESTMENT & BUSINESS GUIDE ISBN 0739707434

US REGIONAL INVESTMENT & BUSINESS LIBRARY-2000

Investment and Business are available for the following states and cities

 ALASKA INVESTMENT & BUSINESS GUIDE

Price: $99.95 each

1. Alabama
2. Alaska
3. Arizona
4. Arkansas
5. Atlanta
6. Boston
7. California
8. Chicago
9. Colorado
10. Connecticut
11. Dallas
12. District of Columbia
13. Florida
15. Hawaii
16. Idaho
17. Illinois
18. Indiana
19. Iowa
20. Kansas
21. Kentucky
22. Los Angeles
23. Louisiana
24. Maine
25. Marylamd
26. Massachusetts
27. Miami
28. Michigan
29. Minnesota
30. Mississippi
31. Missouri
32. Montana
33. Nebraska
34. Nevada
35. New Hampshire
36. New Jersey
38. New York City
39. New York
40. North Carolina
41. North Dakota
42. Ohio
43. Oklahoma
44. Oregon
45. Pennsylvania
46. Philadelphia
47. Rhode Island
48. San Francisco
49. South Carolina
50. South Dakota
51. Tennessee
52. Texas
53. Utah
54. Vermont
55. Virginia
56. Washington
56. West Virginia
57. Wisconsin
58. Wyoming

 GLOBAL ECONOMIC, FINANCIAL DEVELOPMENT ORGANIZATIONS ISBN 0739767062

Intl economic development agencies and investment funds in over 100 countries

GLOBAL CENTRAL BANK ISBN 0739767038

Central banks in about 100 countries

GLOBAL INTERNATIONAL HUMANITARIAN ORGANIZATIONS DIRECTORY ISBN 0739767186

International organizations worldwide

WORLD EXPORT-IMPORT & BUSINESS LIBRARY

Ultimate directories for conducting export-import operations in the country. Largest exporters and

Directories are available for the following countries

 RUSSIAN Export-Import BUSINESS DIRECTORY

Armenia	Israel	Switzerland
Austria	Italy	Tajikistan
Azerbaijan	Kazakhstan	Turkmenistan
Belarus	Kyrgyzstan	Ukraine
Belgium	Latvia	UK
Czech Rep	Liechtenstein	USA
Denmark	Lithuania	Uzbekistan
Estonia	Luxemburg	
France	Moldova	
Georgia	Netherlands	
Germany	Pakistan	
Greece	Portugal	
Ireland	Russia	
	Spain	

Price: $99.95 each

US FEDERAL GOVERNMENT LIBRARY-2003

ULTIMATE INFORMATION ON US FEDERAL GOVERNMENT
AGENCUES

The ultimate handbook with detailed information on US Federal Government Agencies and more

Price: $99.95 each

Title *	ISBN
1. Overseas Private Investment Corporation (OPIC) Handbook	0739731835
2. The White House Handbook	0739731815
3. U.S. House Committee on Agriculture	0739727370
4. U.S. House Committee on Appropriations	0739727389
5. U.S. House Committee on Armed Services	0739727397
6. U.S. House Committee on Education and the Workforce	0739727710
7. U.S. House Committee on Energy and Commerce	0739727435
8. U.S. House Committee on Financial Services	0739727745
9. U.S. House Committee on Government Reform	0739727443
10. U.S. House Committee on House Administration	0739727788
11. U.S. House Committee on International Relations	0739727451
12. U.S. House Committee on Resources	0739727486
13. U.S. House Committee on Rules	073972780X
14. U.S. House Committee on Science	0739727494
15. U.S. House Committee on Small Business	0739727729
16. U.S. House Committee on Standards of Official Conduct	0739727737
17. U.S. House Committee on the Budget	0739727419
18. U.S. House Committee on the Judiciary	073972746X
19. U.S. House Committee on Transportation and Infrastructure	0739727453
20. U.S. House Committee on Veterans Affairs	0739727761
21. U.S. House Committee on Ways and Means	073972777X
22. U.S. House Joint Committee on Printing	0739727699
23. U.S. House Joint Committee on Taxation	0739727362
24. U.S. House Joint Economic Committee	0739727354
25. U.S. House Permanent Select Committee on Intelligence	0739727796
26. U.S. Senate Agriculture, Nutrition, And Forestry Committee	0739727818
27. U.S. Senate Appropriations Committee	0739727826
28. U.S. Senate Armed Services Committee	0739727834
29. U.S. Senate Banking, Housing, And Urban Affairs	0739727842
30. U.S. Senate Budget Committee	0739727850
31. U.S. Senate Commerce, Science, And Transportation	0739727869
32. U.S. Senate Committee On Indian Affairs	0739727990
33. U.S. Senate Energy And Natural Resources Committee	0739727877
34. U.S. Senate Environment And Public Works Committee	0739727885
35. U.S. Senate Finance Committee	0739727893

To order and for additional analytical and marketing information, please contacrt
International Business Publications, USA at:
P.O. Box 15343, Washington, DC 20003, USA. Phone: (202) 546-2103. Fax: (202) 546-3275.
E-mail: rusric@erols.com

Title *	ISBN
36. U.S. Senate Foreign Relations Committee	0739727907
37. U.S. Senate Governmental Affairs Committee	0739727915
38. U.S. Senate Health, Education, Labor And Pensions Committee	0739727931
39. U.S. Senate Joint Committee On Taxation	0739728644
40. U.S. Senate Joint Economic Committee	0739728636
41. U.S. Senate Judiciary Committee	0739727923
42. U.S. Senate Rules And Administration Committee	073972794X
43. U.S. Senate Select Committee On Ethics	0739727982
44. U.S. Senate Select Committee On Intelligence	0739727974
45. U.S. Senate Small Business Committee	0739727958
46. U.S. Senate Special Committee On Aging	0739728628
47. U.S. Senate Veterans' Affairs Committee	0739727966
48. US African Development Fund Handbook	073973184X
49. US AGENCY FOR INTERNATIONAL DEVELOPMENT BUSINESS OPPORTUNITIES HANDBOOK	0739731866
50. US Agency for International Development Handbook	0739731874
51. US Arms Control and Disarmament Agency Handbook	0739739832
52. US CENTRAL INTELLIGENCE AGENCY (CIA) HANDBOOK	0739732757
53. US Civil Rights Policy Handbook	073976201X
54. US Commodity Futures Trading Commission Handbook	0739762028
55. US Congressional Budget Office Handbook	0739762036
56. US Defense Intelligence Agency Handbook	0739711709
57. US Department of Agriculture Business Opportunities Handbook	0739762044
58. US Department of Agriculture Handbook	0739762052
59. US Department of Commerce Handbook	0739762079
60. US Department of Defense Handbook	0739762087
61. US Department of Energy Business Opportunities Handbook	0739762095
62. US Department of Energy Handbook	0739762109
63. US Department of Health and Human Services Handbook	0739762117
64. US Department of Housing and Urban Services Handbook	0739762125
65. US Department of Interior Handbook	0739762133
66. US Department of Justice Handbook	0739762141
67. US Department of Labor Handbook	073976215X
68. US Department of State Handbook	0739762168
69. US Department of the Air Force Handbook	0739762060
70. US Department of the Army Handbook	0739762176
71. US Department of the Navy Handbook	0739762184
72. US Department of the Treasury Handbook	0739762192
73. US Department of Transport Handbook	0739762206
74. US Department of Veteran Affairs Handbook	0739762214
75. US Environmental Protection Agency Handbook	0739762222
76. US Export-Import Bank Handbook	0739762230

To order and for additional analytical and marketing information, please contacrt
International Business Publications, USA at:
P.O. Box 15343, Washington, DC 20003, USA. Phone: (202) 546-2103. Fax: (202) 546-3275.
E-mail: rusric@erols.com

Title *	ISBN
77. US FBI ACADEMY HANDBOOK	0739731858
78. US Federal Bureau of Investigation (FBI) Business Opportunities Handbook	0739762370
79. US Federal Bureau of Investigation (FBI) Handbook	073976246X
80. US Federal Communication Commission Handbook	0739733494
81. US Federal Election Commission Handbook	0739762400
82. US Federal Energy Sector Regulations Handbook	0739762419
83. US Federal Executive Government Handbook	0739731823
84. US Federal Maritime Commission Handbook	0739762427
85. US Federal Mine Safety and Health Commission Handbook	0739762435
86. US Federal Reserve System Handbook	0739762532
87. US Federal Trade Commission Handbook	0739762451
88. US Food and Drug Administration Handbook	0739762397
89. US Food Assistance to Russia Handbook	0739762478
90. US Information Agency Handbook	0739762486
91. US Intelligence Policy Handbook	0739762494
92. US Internal Revenue Service Handbook	0739762508
93. US Libraries and Information Science National Commission Handbook	0739762516
94. US National Academy of Science and Research Policy Handbook	0739762524
95. US National Aeronautics and Space Administration Handbook	0739762249
96. US National Drug Control Policy Handbook	0739762389
97. US National Institute of Health Handbook	0739762443
98. US National Science Foundation Handbook	0739762362
99. US National Security Policy Handbook	0739762354
100. US Navy Seals Handbook	0739762540
101. US Office of Management and Budget Handbook	0739762346
102. US Office of Personnel Management Handbook	0739762338
103. US Peace Corp Handbook	073976232X
104. US Postal Service Handbook	0739762311
105. US Science and Technology Policy Handbook	0739762303
106. US Securities and Exchange Commission Handbook	073976229X
107. US Small Business Administration Handbook	0739762281
108. US Special Combat Fources Handbook	0739762001
109. US Submarine Force Hnadbook	0739764136
110. US Trade and Development Agency Handbook	0739762273
111. US Trade Representative Office Handbook	0739762265
112. WORLD BANK BUSINESS OPPORTUNITES HANDBOOK	0739762257

To order and for additional analytical and marketing information, please contacrt
International Business Publications, USA at:
P.O. Box 15343, Washington, DC 20003, USA. Phone: (202) 546-2103. Fax: (202) 546-3275.
E-mail: rusric@erols.com

.

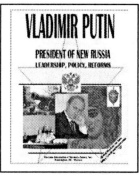

VLADIMIR PUTIN

PRESIDENT OF NEW RUSSIA
LEADERSHIP, POLICY, REFORMS

NEW WORLD POLITICAL LEADERS LIBRARY-2003
ULTIMATE INFORMATION ON LOLITICAL AND BUSINESS
LEADERS OF FOREING COUNTRIES

The ultimate handbook with detailed information on foreign leaders, including biographic data, position on domestic and international issues, economic policy and more

Price: $89.95 each

TITLE	ISBN
1. Albania President Rexhep Meidani Handbook	07397-2762-8
2. Armenia President Robert Kocharian Handbook	07397-1180-6
3. Austria President Dr. Thomas Klestil Handbook	07397-05997
4. Azerbaijan President Heydar Aliyev Handbook	07397-1072-9
5. Bangladesh Prime Minister Khaleda Zia Handbook	07397-1181-4
6. Belarus President Alexander LUKASHENKO Handbook	07397-1073-7
7. Brunei Sultan Haji Hassanal Bolkiah Mu'izzaddin Waddaulah Handbook	07397-1190-3
8. Canada Prime Minister Joseph Jacques Jean Chrétien Handbook	07397-09488
9. China President Jiang Zemin Handbook	07397-09976
10. Cuba President Fidel Castro Handbook	07397-1183-0
11. Egypt President Hosny Mubarak Handbook	07397-1185-7
12. France President Jacques Chirac Handbook	07397-1188-1
13. Germany President Johannes Rau Handbook	07397-09968
14. Guyana President BHARRAT JAGDEO Handbook	0739764152
15. Iran President Hojjatoleslam Seyed Mohammad Khatami Handbook	07397-1178-4
16. Iraq President Saddam Hussein Handbook	07397-1179-2
17. Israel Prime Minister Ariel Sharon Handbook	07397-1192-X
18. Japan Prime Minister Junichiro Koizumi Handbook	07397-1194-6
19. Korea North General Secretary Kim Jong II Handbook	07397-1197-0
20. Korea South President Kim Dae-jung Handbook	07397-1198-9
21. Libya President Muammar Muhammad Abd as-Salam al-Gaddafi Handbook	07397-1175-X
22. Norway Queen Sonja Handbook	07397-2699-4
23. Pakistan President Pervez Musharraf Handbook	07397-2735-4
24. Palestine President Yasser Arafat Handbook	07397-2766-0
25. Philippines President Gloria Macapagal Arroyo Handbook	07397-2737-0
26. Poland President Aleksander Kwasniewski Handbook	07397-2738-9
27. Russia President Vladimir Putin Handbook	07397-0999-2
28. Saudi Arabia King Fahd bin Abdul Aziz Handbook	07397-2740-0
29. Syria President Bashar Hafez Al-Assad Handbook	07397-2744-3
30. Taiwan President Chen Shui-bian Handbook	07397-64160
31. Thailand King Bhumibol Adulyadej Handbook	07397-2747-8
32. United Arab Emirates Ruler Sheikh Zayed bin Sultan Al Nahyan Handbook	07397-2736-2
33. United States President George W. Bush Handbook	07397-0998-4
34. Uzbekistan President Islam Karimov Handbook	07397-2764-4
35. Yugoslavia President Vojislav Koštunica Handbook	07397-0995X

**To order and for additional analytical and marketing information, please contacrt
International Business Publications, USA at:
P.O. Box 15343, Washington, DC 20003, USA.
Phone: (202) 546-2103. Fax: (202) 546-3275. E-mail: IBPUSA@comcast.net**

US GOVERNMENT LIBRARY-2002

TITLE *	ISBN
Overseas Private Investment Corporation (OPIC) Handbook	0739731835
THE FBI ACADEMY HANDBOOK	0739731858
The White House Handbook	0739731815
US African Development Fund Handbook	073973184X
US AGENCY FOR INTERNATIONAL DEVELOPMENT BUSINESS OPPORTUNITIES HANDBOOK	0739731866
US Agency for International Development Handbook	0739731874
US Arms Control and Disarmament Agency Handbook	0739739832
US CENTRAL INTELLIGENCE AGENCY (CIA) HANDBOOK	0739732757
US Civil Rights Policy Handbook	073976201X
US Commodity Futures Trading Commission Handbook	0739762028
US Congressional Budget Office Handbook	0739762036
US Defense Intelligence Agency Handbook	0739711709
US Department of Agriculture Business Opportunities Handbook	0739762044
US Department of Agriculture Handbook	0739762052
US Department of Air Force Handbook	0739762060
US Department of Commerce Handbook	0739762079
US Department of Defense Handbook	0739762087
US Department of Energy Business Opportunities Handbook	0739762095
US Department of Energy Handbook	0739762109
US Department of Health and Human Services Handbook	0739762117
US Department of Housing and Urban Services Handbook	0739762125
US Department of Interior Handbook	0739762133
US Department of Justice Handbook	0739762141
US Department of Labor Handbook	073976215X
US Department of State Handbook	0739762168
US Department of the Army Handbook	0739762176
US Department of the Navy Handbook	0739762184
US Department of the Treasury Handbook	0739762192
US Department of Transport Handbook	0739762206
US Department of Veteran Affairs Handbook	0739762214
US Environmental Protection Agency Handbook	0739762222

To order and for additional analytical and marketing information, please contacrt
International Business Publications, USA at:
P.O. Box 15343, Washington, DC 20003, USA. Phone: (202) 546-2103. Fax: (202) 546-3275.
E-mail: rusric@erols.com
World Business Catalog on Line: http://world.mirhouse.com

TITLE *	ISBN
US Export-Import Bank Handbook	0739762230
US Federal Bureau of Investigation (FBI) Business Opportunities Handbook	0739762370
US Federal Bureau of Investigation (FBI) Handbook	073976246X
US Federal Communication Commission Handbook	0739733494
US Federal Election Commission Handbook	0739762400
US Federal Energy Sector Regulations Handbook	0739762419
US Federal Executive Government Handbook	0739731823
US Federal Maritime Commission Handbook	0739762427
US Federal Mine Safety and Health Commission Handbook	0739762435
US Federal Reserve System Handbook	0739762532
US Federal Trade Commission Handbook	0739762451
US Food and Drug Administration Handbook	0739762397
US Food Assistance to Russia Handbook	0739762478
US Information Agency Handbook	0739762486
US Intelligence Policy Handbook	0739762494
US Internal Revenue Service Handbook	0739762508
US Libraries and Information Science National Commission Handbook	0739762516
US National Academy of Science and Research Policy Handbook	0739762524
US National Aeronautics and Space Administration Handbook	0739762249
US National Drug Control Policy Handbook	0739762389
US National Institute of Health Handbook	0739762443
US National Science Foundation Handbook	0739762362
US National Security Policy Handbook	0739762354
US Navy Seals Handbook	0739762540
US Office of Management and Budget Handbook	0739762346
US Office of Personnel Management Handbook	0739762338
US Peace Corp Handbook	073976232X
US Postal Service Handbook	0739762311
US Science and Technology Policy Handbook	0739762303
US Securities and Exchange Commission Handbook	073976229X
US Small Business Administration Handbook	0739762281
US Special Operation Forces Handbook	0739762001
US Trade and Development Agency Handbook	0739762273
US Trade Representative Office Handbook	0739762265
WORLD BANK BUSINESS OPPORTUNITES HANDBOOK	0739762257
US Homeland Security Handbook	073976277X
US Air Force Academy Handbook	0739762753
US Pacific Air Force Handbook	0739762788

To order and for additional analytical and marketing information, please contacrt
International Business Publications, USA at:
P.O. Box 15343, Washington, DC 20003, USA. Phone: (202) 546-2103. Fax: (202) 546-3275.
E-mail: rusric@erols.com
World Business Catalog on Line: http://world.mirhouse.com

Printed in the United States
1409500001B/45